WINNIE AND NELSON

. . .

Also by Jonny Steinberg

One Day in Bethlehem

A Man of Good Hope

Little Liberia

Sizwe's Test

Thin Blue

Notes from a Fractured Country

The Number

Midlands

WINNIE
and
NELSON

. . .

Portrait of a Marriage

Jonny Steinberg

WILLIAM
COLLINS

William Collins
An imprint of HarperCollins*Publishers*
1 London Bridge Street
London SE1 9GF

WilliamCollinsBooks.com

HarperCollins*Publishers*
Macken House,
39/40 Mayor Street Upper,
Dublin 1, D01 C9W8, Ireland

First published in Great Britain in 2023 by William Collins
First published in the US in 2023 by Alfred A. Knopf

1

A catalogue record for this book is available from the British Library

ISBN 978-0-00-835378-0 (Hardback)
ISBN 978-0-00-835379-7 (Trade paperback)

Printed and bound in the UK
using 100% renewable electricity at CPI Group (UK) Ltd

MIX
Paper | Supporting
responsible forestry
FSC
www.fsc.org   FSC™ C007454

This book is produced from independently certified FSC™ paper
to ensure responsible forest management.

For more information visit: www.harpercollins.co.uk/green

LOOMIS: Joe Turner let me loose and I felt all turned around inside. I just wanted to see your face to know that the world was still there. Make sure everything still in its place so I could reconnect myself together. I got there and you was gone, Martha.

—AUGUST WILSON, *Joe Turner's Come and Gone*

Contents

Introduction

The story they were to tell about their courtship – the story *both* of them were to tell, Nelson and Winnie alike, over and over again, told so often they appear to have forgotten that it was not entirely true – went like this.

It was a weekday afternoon in the summer of 1956–57. Nelson was giving his friend, the medical student Diliza Mji, a ride from Orlando West to central Johannesburg, when he saw, waiting at a bus stop outside Baragwanath Hospital, a beautiful girl, indeed, one so beautiful that he considered turning his car around and going back.

He does not describe her. In the thousands of pages of letters and memoirs Nelson wrote, there are almost no physical descriptions of women, only of men. One is left to imagine that he was struck by the huge mournful eyes, so out of place on her youthful face; by the high, sculptured cheeks; and, incongruous with the mournfulness, by a regal authority, quite formidable, even at a glance. She was very young, barely out of her teens, he might well have surmised, and indeed, on the day he clapped eyes on her, she was not yet twenty-one years old.[1]

Nelson, famously, drove a two-tone Oldsmobile, the paintwork pastel green, the hubcaps walled and brilliant white. Everyone in Orlando West knew the Oldsmobile, and everyone in Orlando West knew of the man behind the wheel. When he drove through his neighbourhood on a Saturday or a Sunday afternoon, a time when people were out on the streets, they gathered and waved and shouted his name.

And when he drove through central Johannesburg to his law firm, Mandela and Tambo, the heads of the drivers in the cars on Fox Street, almost all of them white, turned. For although most white people still did not know the name Nelson Mandela, or, if they had heard the name, could not put it to a face, the sight of a black man in so extravagant a vehicle signalled that something was up.

And Nelson himself was as much a spectacle as his car. Six feet two, with the body of an athlete, at thirty-eight years old still youthful and strong, he wore double-breasted suits, made bespoke by the most sought-after, and the most expensive, tailor in Johannesburg, Alfred Kahn, whose clients included many of the city's white mining magnates.[2]

And if the sight of him was arresting, the idea of him was no less so. It was not just that he was a lawyer, indeed, one of only sixty or so black lawyers in all of South Africa, placing him in the top echelons of the black elite; it was not just that he was famously theatrical in court, his aura of command a lesson to white judges and lawyers that he was their equal: five years earlier, he had become the poster child of the Defiance Campaign, a nationwide action of civil disobedience in which more than 8,000 people, among them the most esteemed black men and women in the land, went to prison for defying segregationist laws. Just then, in late 1956 and early 1957, he and 155 others were standing trial for treason, a trial covered faithfully in the black press day after day, month after month, and about which black South Africans were speaking incessantly at their kitchen tables.

And if Nelson's public performances were growing increasingly famous, his private exploits were becoming less and less private. Among Nelson's colleagues and friends it was no secret that he liked women and that they often liked him back. 'I can't help it if the ladies take note of me,' he told a biographer. 'I'm not going to protest.'[3] His marriage – to Evelyn Mase, with whom he had three children – was in ruins, and rumours about his love life were much discussed among his comrades, his legal colleagues and his friends.

And so if there was any man in South Africa, hitting forty and married, who might turn his car around because he had glimpsed waiting at a bus stop a magnificent woman almost half his age, it was Nelson Mandela.

·   ·

Although he could not have known it, he and the girl on the side of the road were bound to meet. For Nomzamo Winifred Madikizela resided at the Helping Hand Club for Native Girls at 76 Hans Street on the eastern side of town, and there she was becoming increasingly friendly with Adelaide Tshukudu, fiancée of Oliver Tambo, Nelson's partner in the law firm Mandela and Tambo.

One afternoon in early March 1957 it was pouring rain – as it often does in Johannesburg on summer afternoons – and hailing, to boot. Adelaide, who did not fancy the prospect of making her way from work at Johannesburg's General Hospital to Park Station in such weather, phoned Oliver to ask for a ride. Barely had she and Oliver left the hospital than they spotted Winnie and another woman, Florence Dube, making their way to the station on foot; they invited the two women into the car.

Adelaide announced that she was ravenously hungry, and so they stopped at a delicatessen on the side of the road. But as Oliver searched in vain for his wallet, it appeared that the four people in the car did not have a penny between them. And then, from the driver's seat, Oliver spotted the tall figure of Nelson in the delicatessen; he told Adelaide to get whatever she wanted and ask Nelson to pay. A few moments later, Adelaide emerged from the delicatessen with Nelson in tow. He peered through the car window, and there on the backseat was the woman he had glimpsed at the side of the road. Oliver introduced her as Winnie Madikizela from Bizana.

'Oh, so she's a relative,' Nelson said, for Oliver, too, was from Bizana.

'Don't you know Winnie?' Oliver replied. 'She is always dancing up and down the newspapers', for Winnie's beauty had caught the attention of Johannesburg's press and her photographs had appeared in two widely read publications.[4]

The next day, Nelson phoned Winnie in her office. Would she have lunch with him? he asked.

Years later, Winnie recalled being scared out of her wits. What did this famous man, held in such godlike regard, want with her? She was pretty, to be sure; she had been aware of that for a long time. But she was a nobody, desperately young and utterly unknown, her career hardly begun.

She swallowed her fear and told him that she might indeed be available for lunch, if they could find a suitable time.

And so they agreed that on the coming Sunday, March 10, she would be fetched from her hostel and taken to an Indian restaurant near Nelson's office.

Winnie spent the period between the phone call and the date with Nelson in a state of high anxiety, she recalled: What should she say in response to his questions, and what questions might she possibly ask him?

And, as she remembers it, the lunch itself did little to calm her, for she understood after just a few moments that she would have to share this man, even now, on their first date; no sooner had they sat down than a line of people formed at their table to talk to him. She looked on, silent and self-conscious. And just when the line evaporated and she and Nelson began to talk, a new ensemble would come to greet him. She felt she was an audience to a show in which she had no part.

And, to make matters worse, she had never eaten spicy Indian cuisine; her whole life she had lived on the institutional food of boarding schools and women's hostels and on the stodgy meals prepared in her father's rural home. Her tongue burned whenever she put her fork in her mouth; she had constantly to drink from her water glass, but with each sip the burning only grew worse.[5]

After lunch, things went on in the same vein. The short journey from the restaurant to his car took half an hour because so many people stopped him to talk, to consult, to ask advice. She had never before witnessed a human being who belonged so wholly to *everybody*, she recalled. She was 'stunned and fascinated'.

If they were to get any time alone together, they resolved, they would have to quite literally leave town, and so they drove into the countryside and went walking in an empty field. But, even here, alone, the inequality between them was palpable. Her sandal strap broke, and she had to walk barefoot over rocky ground. She was hobbling and tripping over, and to balance her, 'he held my hand just as my father would hold a little girl's hand', and when they got back to the car, he suddenly kissed her.[6]

He phoned a few days later; he wanted to see her again. But between his law practice and the endless Treason Trial, between his escalating work in the African National Congress (ANC) and his insistence that he exercise every weekday, without fail, he simply did not have time to see her. He would have to double up, to have her with him while he was doing something else.

And so their second date, she discovered, was to take place at his boxing gym at the Donaldson Orlando Community Centre, less than two miles from his home, a space that doubled on weekend evenings as a theatre and music venue. She was to watch him while he laid into a punching bag and skipped and did push-ups, this big, imposing man, the sweat pouring off him, his body sculpted and fit. This was not a shy man. Neither of them ever said when they first slept together, but on this, their second date, he was preening, without shame, showing his body to her, displaying its sheer impressiveness.

Neither Winnie nor Nelson recounts when exactly they decided to marry; it was sometime in 1957, in the months after they met. The point, though, is that Nelson did not *ask* her to marry him; he *informed* her that they were to marry, informed her in passing, as it were. As she recalls it, they were saying goodbye at the end of a date when he mentioned, casually, that the wife of the head of the South African Communist Party (SACP), a woman called Ray Harmel, was a seamstress in a factory and that Winnie should talk to her about making a wedding dress.

. .

Nelson and Winnie married in June 1958, fifteen months after they'd met, Nelson's divorce from Evelyn Mase finalized three months earlier. They exchanged their vows on the grounds of a Methodist mission near Winnie's ancestral home in Bizana, more than six hundred miles from Johannesburg, in a ceremony that was more a Madikizela than a Mandela affair. Winnie's father, Columbus, was a significant figure in the district, and it was expected that his daughter's wedding would be large and generous; hundreds of Bizana's citizens crammed the church pews.

The ceremony's only recognition of the bridegroom's political standing was the car in which the couple left the mission grounds; it was draped in the black, green and gold of the African National Congress, the organization that had dominated Nelson's life since the mid-1940s. Nelson himself barely managed to obtain permission to attend his own wedding. Serving a banning order, his movement heavily restricted, he was granted leave from Johannesburg for less than a week.

After the ceremony, the wedding party returned to Columbus's home, where a feast rolled on unabated for five days before Winnie and Nelson took their leave to return to Johannesburg.[7]

. .

They lived under the same roof such a short time. Less than two years passed before Nelson went to prison for five months, and then, shortly after his release, he disappeared underground. During this brief period – the only period in which friends and comrades observed them together until after Nelson's release from prison decades later – the story that Winnie and Nelson themselves came to tell, of the powerful public man and the gorgeous naïf, was repeated ad infinitum. Winnie was 'as shy as she was beautiful', one of Nelson's political associates recalled years later. 'It was hard to get to know her because she said so little.' And when Nelson and his peers gathered socially for Sunday lunch at the suburban home of a white comrade, Winnie wandered off alone with a pile of fashion magazines.[8]

Many of Nelson's male comrades teased him, with a nod and an understanding wink, for following the blind heat of his desire. One morning during a recess in the Treason Trial, while the accused were chatting outside, Moses Kotane, a comrade of Nelson's and a fellow co-accused, nodded his head at Winnie, who had been watching the trial from the gallery.

'Such an intimidating and seductive beauty does not go with a revolutionary!' he said to Nelson, bursting into laughter.[9]

Years later, Nelson's authorized biographer chided him for his choice of second wife. She provided an 'exotic contrast' to his political life, the biographer wrote, and in choosing excitement, he was sacrificing something else, something he might sorely miss in the troubled times ahead, for Winnie would not provide 'the kind of stable home base which many of his political friends took for granted', and which he would desperately need when imprisonment threw his affairs into disarray.[10]

· ·

This depiction – of the celebrated man besotted with a girl barely out of adolescence, and of a raw young woman swept off her feet by a powerful older man – is deceptive. The bare facts are without doubt true. Nelson *did* do a double take upon sighting a beautiful young woman on the side of the road. And they *were* introduced in a delicatessen one afternoon in early March; many years later, Adelaide Tambo remembered the moment vividly. And Nelson *did* invite Winnie to lunch, for his comrade Joe Matthews remembers picking her up at midday to take her to Nelson.

But the *sense* of what happened between them is what is deceptive.

Much later, in 1970, when Nelson was six years into his life sentence, he wrote Winnie a letter filled mainly with family matters.

'By the way,' he added, near the end of the letter, apropos of nothing at all, 'the other day I dreamt of you convulsing your entire body with a graceful Hawaiian dance at the BMSC [Bantu Men's Social Centre]. I stood at one end of the famous hall with arms outstretched ready to embrace you as you whirled towards me with the enchanting smile that I miss so desperately.'

He went on to try to interpret his dream:

> I cannot explain why the scene should have been located at the BMSC. To my recollection we have been there for a dance only once – on the night of Lindi's wedding reception. The other occasion was the concert we organised in 1957 when I was courting you, or you me. I am never certain whether I am free to remind you that you took the initiative in this regard. Anyway the dream was for me a glorious moment. If I must dream in my sleep, please Hawaii for me.[11]

And so we are informed, in passing, many years later, as we eavesdrop on a letter between husband and wife, that the story they tell, not just for public consumption, but for their own consumption – 'I am never certain whether I am free to remind you,' Nelson writes – is not true.

Another letter from that time, from Nelson to Winnie, gives an inkling of what actually happened between them. It is written in deep code, for Nelson is aware that the prison authorities and the security police will see it long before it reaches his wife.

He has been in prison for seven years. Winnie has sent him a photograph of herself; he has been staring at it endlessly and is beguiled. His thoughts, he tells her, have wandered 'to Hans St. where a friend used to jump into a blue van & unburden herself of all the solemn vows that are due from fiancée to her betrothed & immediately thereafter dash across to an Olds on the opposite end of the block with vows equally sweet and reassuring'.[12]

Seventy-Six Hans Street is the address of the Helping Hand Club for Native Girls, the women's hostel where Winnie lived when she and Nelson were courting. And the 'Olds', of course, is Nelson's Oldsmobile. Winnie was not only engaged to Nelson and another man at the same time; she would, in Nelson's account, literally dash between the cars of her respective fiancés as each waited for her outside.

Nelson remembers, too, 'the skill with which she manipulated her evening "studies" at Chancellor House [the building in which Nelson's law firm rented offices] & made it possible to receive and entertain old friends as soon as new ones proceeded to the boxing gym'.[13]

Again, Nelson is concealing the meaning of his story from prying eyes. But he is clearly reminding Winnie that when she spent her evenings in Nelson's offices, 'studying', she received another lover the moment he left for the gym.

They had been apart for seven years when Nelson wrote this letter. His infatuation heightened by the photograph Winnie had sent him – it 'depicts . . . the devastating beauty and charm which ten stormy years of married life have not chilled', he wrote – he remembered how audacious, how self-possessed, how positively scandalous she was, when they were courting.

The other fiancé, incidentally, who waited in Hans Street in the blue van and who visited Winnie in Nelson's office when Nelson was at the boxing gym, was a man called Barney Sampson. A little older than Winnie, he was stylish and good-looking; he also did not have a drop of political blood in his body. When Winnie told him that she was marrying Nelson, Sampson, heartbroken, tried to take his own life with an overdose of pills. Nelson rushed Winnie to the hospital to be at Sampson's side.[14]

And so the notion that Winnie was a young naïf when she married Nelson, a notion both of them did so much to encourage, is not entirely true. And, indeed, if we interpret the biographical facts of Winnie's early life correctly, the idea that she was witless and shy when she met Nelson becomes improbable.

As a child, Winnie was formed in a world quite unlike our own; the danger of reading her anachronistically is great. Winnie did not help much in this regard; aware of her audience's ignorance of her childhood milieu, she encouraged a great deal of misunderstanding. One of her white lecturers at the school for social work where Winnie studied described her as the equivalent of a 'dumb blonde', concerned with clothes and men and with little else.[15] It was hardly possible to get further from the truth.

If we read Winnie's childhood as it ought to be read, the notion that any man, no matter how powerful, might sweep her off her feet becomes highly dubious. When Winnie met Nelson, she was young and beautiful, but she was also an extremely serious young woman of whom a prestigious career was not just expected but demanded. She had indeed been groomed for the highest accomplishments possible for a black woman at that time.

Nor was she new to the advances of men much older and more powerful than herself. Her recollection that Nelson's phone call took her utterly by surprise – what could such a man want with me? – is disingenuous to say the least. By the time she met Nelson, she had been the object of at least half a dozen such advances, each of them persistent, each of them pursued, not just by influential men, but by *the most* influential men: lawyers, doctors, and senior members of various Xhosa-speaking royal families. And she had honed an arsenal of defensive weapons against these advances; she had mastered quickly, because she had had to, elegant ways of dodging them.

.   .

Why did Nelson and Winnie spin a story that wasn't quite right: a story told not just to the world but to themselves? Why might Nelson tell Winnie, thirteen years after they met, that he was 'never certain whether I am free to remind you' that it was *she* who courted *him*?

We need to think ourselves back into the sexual mores of those times. A married man, prominent, powerful, and almost forty years old going hard after a twenty-year-old beauty: such a scene might have seemed daring, perhaps even presumptuous. But the reverse was positively scandalous: a pretty girl, barely out of adolescence, pursuing a married man; pretty girls did not wear their sexual desire on their sleeves, not unless they were prepared to be branded as dishonourable.

Winnie and Nelson censored their tale, even when they told it to themselves, because at the time Winnie's role was barely tolerable. Nelson took the burden of the seduction onto his broad shoulders, for it sat more comfortably there.

.   .

There is another reason Winnie and Nelson told the story that they did: they had neither the words nor, indeed, the concepts to describe the partnership they were actually creating, so they told an inadequate story instead.

Nelson and Winnie met more than six years before the assassination of John F. Kennedy, and so they could not have known, because the world had yet to witness it, what it meant for every inch of a family's private life, every tear shed, every heartbreak suffered, every grin and every laugh, to have a double life, to be at once deeply personal and yet also to exemplify the collective life of millions.

The closest either of them had come to grasping this phenomenon was in their understanding of the life of Jesus, which they both had fully imbibed as children. By now, Nelson had grown resolutely sceptical of Christian doctrine, but he borrowed richly from it nonetheless. When he wrote to Winnie from prison, to counsel her that her every gesture was a lesson to her people, it was through the trial of Jesus that he told his tale.

By 1957, Nelson was on his way to becoming a man whose consciousness of his performance on the political stage had penetrated the depths of his being. As such, he was never alone with himself, for even in his most private meditations he was shoring up what he would need for his political life.

As for Winnie, among the most important aspects of her childhood is that the last two generations of her paternal family remade their world and everyone in it. The Madikizelas were not just notable; they were exemplary. Everything they said, everything they did, was emblematic of the new world they had made. And Winnie herself was a central figure in these exemplary performances. The idea that she stood before an audience of people who learned to live their own lives by watching her live hers was familiar to her.

And so, although I cannot prove it with incontrovertible evidence, it is deeply plausible that when Nelson and Winnie met, they shared an affinity; they both understood, dimly, the words for it not yet formed, the sheer force of their appearance as a couple.

And it was not long before the cameras of photojournalists and the pens of magazine writers were drawn to them and their marriage. This was the late 1950s; nearly two decades passed before the apartheid government permitted the introduction of television to South Africa; we are not talking of the saturated coverage of personal life with which we are familiar today. But the degree of media interest in their romance was unusual for the time. When they visited a jazz venue together, their picture appeared the following day in *The World*. Soon after, they were pictured together by a photographer from *Drum* magazine.

This degree and type of attention was not unusual for figures in the world of entertainment and sport: it was quite unusual for a political figure. Nelson grasped the significance of this; the spectacle of himself with Winnie was not 'an exotic contrast' to his political life; it was deeply political. If any man understood that the force of his politics resided not just in the content of what he said but in his appearance when he said it, it was Nelson. And if any woman understood that how and with whom she appeared constituted a route to public life, it was Winnie.

They did not yet have the experience to grasp the full implications of what they were getting into: they did not yet know its dangers. For it was not just their appearance that they were casting into the public sphere but their very lives. The idea that public life might swallow private life in its entirety, all of it, was foreign to them. They were throwing themselves into the maelstrom of history, and nobody in a maelstrom is in control of their journey.

. .

To appreciate the novelty of what was happening between Nelson and Winnie, it is necessary to step back from the Johannesburg milieu in which they met, and back, too, from the country in which they were both born. For they courted at an auspicious moment in world history, and their romance should be placed in its broadest context.

Across Africa, across the Asian subcontinent, through to the Dutch East Indies, British Malaya and French Indochina, the great European empires of the nineteenth and early twentieth centuries were surrendering their colonies when Winnie and Nelson met. Just four days before their first date, on March 6, 1957, a black man, Kwame Nkrumah, had been sworn in as prime minister of Ghana, the first of sub-Saharan Africa's postcolonial independent states. The remainder of Britain's, France's and Belgium's African colonies followed in a rapid cascade.

A decade earlier, in India and in Pakistan, indigenous South Asian men had come to power and for the first time since imperial conquest began to rule their lands. And five months after Nelson and Winnie met, in August 1957, the Federation of Malaya declared independence from Britain.

In short, not just across much of the African continent but through a huge swathe of the world, previously colonized men were either beginning or about to take office. And in all of these places a question was asked: what sorts of men were fit to exercise power? What should men who had been colonized do to prepare for public office?

The answers of course varied from place to place; we are talking, after all, about a broad ensemble of human beings. But one answer, and a surprisingly common one given the diversity of people involved, was that to command the public sphere, men must be patriarchs. The vast audiences that watched these men perform their public duties should clock the fact that they possessed a hinterland, glimpsed briefly on ceremonial occasions, in which there was a wife, or wives, and children and servants. That this hinterland was largely *private*, that its innards were sheltered from public view, was extremely important. Between their lives as statesmen and their lives as patriarchs a line was drawn; the drawing of this line was a *sine qua non* of the dignity required to exercise power.[16]

'It is held', wrote Jomo Kenyatta, the founding father of independent Kenya, 'that if a man can control and manage effectively the affairs of a large family, this is an excellent testimonial of his capacity to look after the interests of the tribe.'[17] Kenyatta was talking about the mores of the Gikuyu, into which he had been born and raised, but he might as well have been talking about much of the early postcolonial world.

The wives of anticolonial leaders were never entirely invisible; in fact, many of the men who liberated their people from imperialism spoke and wrote about the women they married. But the way they did so often only reinforced the public/private divide. This was true even of Mohandas Gandhi, more interested in the soul, and thus in the interior life of people, than any other anticolonial leader and liable at any moment to discourse at length on sexuality, male and female alike.

Since his parents died, Gandhi told an audience in 1929, his wife, Kasturba, had 'been my mother, friend, nurse, cook, bottle-washer and all these things'. And, he added, he and his wife had 'come to a reasonable understanding that I should have all the honours and she should have all the drudgery'. As his biographer points out, Gandhi was both mocking himself and being quite serious.[18]

Kasturba was in fact actively involved in many of Gandhi's political campaigns and was on more than one occasion jailed for her troubles. But they were very much *his* campaigns. Indeed, he understood her growing political involvement as a wife's act of submission to her husband. 'According to my earlier experience,' he wrote, 'she was very obstinate. In spite of all my pressure she would do as she wished. This led to short or long periods of estrangement between us. But as my public life expanded, my wife bloomed forth and deliberately lost herself in my work.'[19]

Gandhi's close colleague Jawaharlal Nehru, who became independent India's first prime minister and in whose career Nelson was to develop an intense interest, wrote movingly about his wife, Kamala, for she died young, leaving him bereft. When he was 'living like a person possessed, giving myself utterly to the cause I had espoused', he wrote more than a decade after Kamala's death, she was his 'haven ... What indeed could I have done if she had not been there to comfort me and give me my strength, and thus enable me to re-charge the exhausted battery of my mind and body?'[20]

This, indeed, was in many parts of the world the ideal figure of the freedom fighter's wife: a woman as impassioned by the struggle as her husband and who thus sympathized with his consuming commitment to public life; a woman who understood that giving him succour and keeping his house were *political* tasks because they gave him the space to do his work.

It was rare that a marriage became a truly *political* spectacle. There were exceptions, though. One was when a prominent leader wed a white woman; such a union overflowed with political meaning and demanded public management. Thus, when Léopold Senghor, the great intellectual of francophone decolonization and the first president of Senegal, married Colette Hubert, a Frenchwoman who had been his secretary, in 1957, he wrote poetry about her. And in his poems she became a stand-in for Europeans in general; he was *choosing* a relationship with a white woman, he wrote, because in loving her he could also find love for those who had invaded his land. His marriage thus became an exemplar of his capacity to forgive and of the collective forgiveness he wanted his people to offer their erstwhile colonizers.[21]

But what he presented, of course, was *his* capacity to forgive; Hubert herself played no part at all other than to be written about.

. . .

By the time he met Winnie in 1957, Nelson understood himself to be a major political figure in the making. His first marriage had broken down in part because his wife neither shared his political passion nor accepted the extent to which his work took him from home. And so there is little question that while he and Winnie courted, the marriage he imagined was one in which politics would be central.

But, when he cast an eye around the decolonizing world – and he certainly *did* cast an eye, for black South Africa's political leaders watched with obsessive interest as indigenous men took office in Asia and then in Africa – there was no model for the marriage he and Winnie were to make. Such a marriage had yet to be invented.

And, indeed, we can be certain that Nelson, as co-creator of his marriage to Winnie, had only the dimmest sense of what their union would become. For Nelson was in fact one of those who thought that the hinterland of a public man should be screened. When his first wife, Evelyn Mase, confided in one of Nelson's colleagues about their marital strife, he was beside himself with rage. Airing delicate household matters in public, no matter how small that public, was, for him, beyond the pale.

And yet Nelson also understood the potency of public performance like few others in his political milieu, and there is abundant evidence that he wanted the theatre he and Winnie made to be *seen*. He did so precisely because he knew that it emitted political meaning, that the appearance of a desirable black couple carried immense power.

Between these two competing ideas – that a public man has a private hinterland and that his marriage should be seen – was, I believe, a zone of cognitive dissonance. Nelson simply did not have the experience to grasp how incompatible these ideas might become. Bringing a marriage into the public sphere means bringing with it attendant matters of gender and, most especially, of sexuality, complicated matters to contend with in public to say the least. Nor did he know, despite his excitement at her audacity, what a powerful woman he was marrying, a woman who would not only demand a place in public life but also perform there as few other women ever had.

NELSON:
EARLY YEARS

. . .

Chapter 1

If the middle-aged Nelson Mandela understood his childhood via a single moment, a moment he believed shaped what was to come, it was the death of his father.

He was just eleven or twelve years old. And he was there, in the room; he was watching.

It was by chance, really. For Gadla Henry Mphakanyiswa Mandela was a polygamist married to four women and each had a home many miles from the next. Gadla circulated among them, spending a week with one wife, then a week with another. It so happened that on the evening of his death he was visiting Nelson's mother, his third wife, and thus died in Nelson's home.

He had been ill a long time, probably with tuberculosis. That evening, on a mat on the floor, Gadla lay down and coughed without pause. Two women were with him: Nelson's mother and his father's fourth wife.

The dying patriarch called for his tobacco and his pipe. But Nelson's mother demurred; permitting a man in his condition to smoke did not seem right to her.

Gadla did not like this at all. Through the course of the evening, he fought her stubbornly, repeating his demand over and over again.

Finally, she relented; she filled his pipe with fresh tobacco, lit it, and gave it to him. He lay there smoking for some time, his coughing stilled, until the pipe fell from his mouth and he was dead.[1]

In the days that followed, Nelson's world fell apart. Not long after the funeral, his mother took him on a journey by foot westward from Qunu, the village that had been his home since he was an infant. She delivered him to a place he had never visited and to a household whose members he had never met. He would not live with his mother again, not until he himself was married and invited her to move in with his

young family. And he would not have a home in Qunu until he built a
house there more than sixty years later.

During his long years in prison, he thought a great deal of that
journey with his mother; he recalled looking back over his shoulder
at Qunu and feeling not so much bereft as cut adrift.[2] And as he grew
older, his memory of that day changed, making him frailer and more
vulnerable; by the time he was in his late sixties, he remembered being
nine, instead of the eleven- or twelve-year-old boy he was.*

He looked back on Qunu with the most extraordinary nostalgia,
the river swollen, the fields verdant, the bees forever making the honey
a boy might steal.

.   .

He was born Rolihlahla Mandela – the name Nelson given to him
by his teacher on his first day of school – on July 18, 1918, in the Transkei
on South Africa's southeastern seaboard. It is a world of luminous green;
shelves of bright grassland lie scattered as far as the eye can see, as if the
pieces of the earth were set one atop the other, instead of side by side.

Most people in the Transkei at this time lived in huts made from
mud and grass; women and children wore ochre blankets rather than
trousers and skirts. Very few people could read or write. Those who
were literate and numerate were usually Christians; they wore Western-
style clothes; they attended church on Sundays; they were known as
amaqoboka: people who have turned.

They were one of many signs of roiling change. In Nelson's grandparents' time, the region that became known as the Eastern Cape was the
site of twelve independent, Xhosa-speaking kingdoms. Over the course
of the nineteenth century, the British conquered each in turn. Some of
these conquests were achieved without a shot fired; some handed over
their sovereignty at meetings in which decorum was observed. But in
other instances, conquest was devastating, involving mass hunger and
landlessness across large parts of the countryside.[3]

---

* It is hard to pinpoint when Nelson began to misremember his age when his
father died. When he secretly wrote his autobiography in prison in 1976, he still recalled
that he had been twelve. But in an authorized biography – *Higher Than Hope* by Fatima
Meer, published in 1988 – his father's death is brought forward by three years. And in
1992 he told the ghostwriter of his autobiography, *Long Walk to Freedom,* that he was nine
when his father died.

The aristocracies that once ruled these kingdoms were humbled, but they were not crushed. Famously, Britain governed its black subjects not directly, through British law, but indirectly, through the subdued kingdoms, the power of black aristocrats clipped by the white magistrates who watched over their work. The relations that evolved between these black aristocrats and their white conquerors became ever so opaque, a ceaseless relay of collaboration and deceit, proud black patriarchs on one side, on the other, proud whites.

And then there was the Church. The seaboard on which Nelson was born was the site of the densest Christian proselytizing activity in Africa.[4] And the missionaries were enormously influential. For one, they administered the only schools in the Transkei; aristocrats who wanted their children to read and write – and most *did* want their children to read and write, for these were the tools of the future – surrendered their progeny to Christian belief. And the missions, too, were the only sites of Western medicine and of modernizing technologies in agriculture. The priests were also in many instances diplomatic conduits to white power at home and to European influence abroad.

And so the relationships that evolved between black aristocrats and white clergy were of great consequence. Many clergymen lived much of their adult lives in the conquered kingdoms; in some instances, their allegiances to the black aristocracies grew deep. Some found the doctrine in which they had been schooled harshly tested by their exposure to black people's realms and returned home quite different men.[5]

The world of Nelson's childhood was changing in more ways still. When his father was born, most men in villages like Qunu lived their lives in the Transkei. By the time Nelson's father died, tens of thousands of the Transkei's men were spending their working lives more than eight hundred miles away, deep underground, in the Witwatersrand's gold mines. It was the most rapid and dramatic change that followed conquest, this propulsion of rural men into an industry that had begun to produce much of the world's gold. When Nelson himself left for Johannesburg as a young man, his first stop was a gold mine.

. .

Nelson was born into the aristocracy of one of the twelve conquered kingdoms, the Thembu; his father was both a royal and, for some years, a senior official. In 1916, two years before Nelson's birth, he was appointed jointly by the white magistrate and the Thembu paramount chief as headman of the village of Mveso, not far from Qunu, his primary responsibility to administer the allocation of land.

But to say that Nelson was an aristocrat is to risk the gravest misunderstanding. The Xhosa-speaking aristocracies were large and sprawling, and many in their ranks died in poverty; being an aristocrat was no guarantee of either prosperity or fame.

When Nelson's mother walked him westward shortly after his father's death, she was taking him to the very centre of Thembu influence, the Great Place of the regent to the Thembu throne, Jongintaba Dalindyebo, in the village of Mqhekezweni. But Qunu itself, the only place Nelson had known until then, was not resplendent at all. Nelson, his mother, and his three sisters lived in a homestead consisting of three beehive-shaped huts built from mud, cow dung and grass. There was no furniture in the room where his father died, only mats, and there was certainly no electricity. Nelson's mother worked the fields around the homestead, and the family ate what she grew – maize, pumpkins sorghum.

None of the children of Nelson's father's first two wives went to school; each lived and died illiterate.

Nelson's mother took him to Jongintaba's Great Place after his father died because the regent had agreed to take Nelson as his ward. Had he not done so, the Nelson Mandela the world came to know would not have existed; he would have had neither the schooling nor the networks of influence to make of himself a person whose name endures.

· ·

When he first glimpsed the Great Place, on the last stretch of his journey with his mother, he was awestruck.

'We came across a village,' he later recalled, 'at the centre of which was a large and gracious home that so far exceeded anything that I had ever seen that all I could do was marvel at it.' There were orchards of peach and apple trees, a vegetable garden, and flower beds. There was rich grassland on which large herds of cattle and sheep grazed.

As he stood there, wide-eyed, a large car approached, and everyone sitting around the house promptly rose, doffed their hats and shouted a salute.

'Out of the motorcar', Nelson remembered, 'stepped a short, thick-set man wearing a smart suit. I could see that he had the confidence and the bearing of a man who was used to the exercise of authority.'[6] It was the regent, Jongintaba, Nelson's new guardian.

·   ·

Several witnesses recalled the depth of Nelson's distress during the first months in his new home. The regent's older daughter described him as a shy and lonely boy, wandering around by himself in the new outfit her father had bought him.[7] And three of his playmates remembered that Nelson often wet his sleeping mat at night and surreptitiously swapped it with the mat of another; an innocent child woke in the morning to be accused of Nelson's crime.[8] Twelve years old is a late age to be wetting one's bed. His private world was insecure and secretive and full of cunning.

And why would it not be? Just a boy, he had been separated from his home, his village and his mother, his father recently dead. And the people and the things around him were not only unfamiliar but grandiose. He was out of his depth. Years later, he described his feelings after settling at the Great Place as those of an orphan.[9]

Shortly after he arrived, Nelson was dressed in clothes befitting his new station – crisp khaki shorts and a khaki shirt, according to one witness.[10] Imagining what he looked like in his unaccustomed attire, he saw more an ornament than a boy, 'a polished piece of bronze'.[11]

When Nelson first glimpsed the regent, he was struck at once by the comportment of a man accustomed to power. But it was not just the regent himself: all the people around him at the Great Place seemed quite otherworldly in their glamour and their grace. There was, for instance, the regent's son and heir, Justice Dalindyebo, who was four years older than Nelson. On the day Nelson met him, he was wearing a fine suit and a shirt that was tailored to fit him. And the body underneath the shirt, Nelson could not but notice, was fit and strong. And beyond the clothes and the body was something else, something he hadn't the language to describe but that is perhaps best named as charisma.[12]

'Justice', Nelson was to write, 'became my first hero after my father ... Tall, handsome and muscular, he was a fine sportsman [and] a natural performer who enchanted audiences with his singing and transfixed them with his ballroom dancing. He had a bevy of female admirers – but also a coterie of critics, who considered him a dandy and a playboy."[13]

It is important to mark this image: a shy and timid boy taking in an idol. Throughout his childhood and youth Nelson painted the most overblown portraits of the men he admired: they were not just fit; they were well built and tall. They were not just seductive; they positively trailed admirers. They were not just eloquent; their speeches dazzled. He was an audience to a pantheon of heroes.

Years later, when he himself was the one with charisma and broad shoulders and an audience, he understood himself as an impostor summoning the idols in his head.

Chapter 2

Nelson's memories of the regent and his world possess the spirit of a fairy tale: the splendour of the Great Place and its grounds, the physical strength of the young men who lived there, the esteem in which the regent was held. Even Nelson himself was sprinkled with magic: in his recent past lay the Edenic Qunu, forever unchanged.

Many of his recollections seem tailored to protect the integrity of this scene, his memories of white people in particular.

As an elderly man, he remembered living in a child's state of cognitive dissonance. On the one hand, he overheard the regent's counsellors tell the bitter story of conquest, of African heroes who went to battle with whites and lost. On the other hand, there were the white people in his life, the magistrates and senior police officers who visited the Great Place. They were lustrous figures, almost grander than human, but they were entirely benign. For when they came to the Great Place, it was to meet with the regent to the Thembu paramountcy, and they approached him with grace.

There is reason to distrust the spirit of Nelson's memories, for he almost certainly had grimmer encounters with whites. When he and his peers were in the fields herding sheep and cattle, white policemen often approached on horseback, dismounted and demanded to see the knobkerries the boys carried. A knobkerrie is a club made of dense wood with a large, heavy knob on one end. The officers would order each boy to put the big, round head in his mouth, and if it did not fit, if he could not wrap his jaws around the whole ball, he would be arrested for carrying a dangerous weapon.[1]

This story was told by three old men who had lived at the Great Place with Nelson. It was not, they insisted, an isolated event; it was an everyday ritual of racial violence, seared for always in their minds.

We cannot know whether Nelson forgot it, or whether he simply chose not to tell it; dwelling on bitter memories in public, he came to believe, was politically poisonous. But from the letters to intimates he wrote from prison, letters in which he ached for the land of his boyhood, it appears that such unpleasantness simply had no place in his remembered world.

Between his memories of childhood and his politics lay an intimate connection. He came to fear violent change, fear revolution; the world, to him, as it was, contained much to cherish, and woe betide those who did anything to tear it apart.

. .

In Nelson's sixteenth year, the regent decided that he was to embark upon two great rituals. The first was his circumcision, marking a Xhosa boy's transition to manhood. The second was his registration at an elite mission school, the start of a black boy's journey to a distinguished career.

It is inconceivable for a Xhosa boy to move into the world of men with his foreskin. And as important as the act of removing it is the ritual: a prolonged procedure, drawn out over as long as two months, which boys experience together and about which they are forbidden to speak.

It is private and secret, but for one moment: the circumcision itself. That is performed in front of a large and intensely interested crowd.

For several days before the ceremony, Nelson, Justice and twenty-four other initiates lived together in two grass huts on the banks of the Mbashe River, a few miles from the Great Place. Then, at dawn on the morning of the ceremony, they were led to the river to bathe. By midday, they stood in a row in a clearing where an audience had gathered to watch: the parents and relatives of the initiate boys, prominent members of the Thembu aristocracy, the regent himself.

Naked but for their blankets, they were ordered to sit on the ground and spread their legs. To the sound of pounding drums, a thin, elderly man moved his way down the line of boys. Working fast, he took the foreskin of each boy in his fingers, pulled it forward, and in a single motion lopped it off with his assegai, a thin, hard-tipped spear. Upon losing his foreskin, each boy was to shout out, '*Ndiyindoda!*' I am a man!

Nelson was some way down the line and so had to wait a while for his turn. He must have escaped in his mind, inhabiting some oblivion, for without warning the old man was kneeling before him. Nelson looked straight into his eyes. Although it was a cold day, the man's forehead was covered in sweat.

And then it was done, and it felt as if molten lead were flowing through his veins. He buried his head in his chest, forgetting all about the declaration he was meant to cry out. Suddenly he remembered, and he shouted, '*Ndiyindoda!*' But he felt that he had waited too long; the other boys had delivered it immediately; they had been brave and strong. Before this esteemed and watchful audience, he had, he felt, been caught out.[2]

We will never know whether anyone in the audience marked Nelson's hesitation. But his experience of this signal moment is so precisely expressive of his character. For one, the other boys were better than him; they had mastered pain as Nelson could not.

There was also, in what happened, the summation of a lesson, one he had no doubt begun to master from the day he was taken from Qunu. What is happening inside should be divorced from how one appears; one may be in the grip of the most unsettling thoughts and the most agonizing pain; none of that ought to show.

. .

Shortly after his initiation, the regent enrolled Nelson in Clarkebury Boarding Institute, the highest place of learning in Thembuland, where he began studying for his Standard Six, the equivalent of the American eighth grade. Until now, he had attended the local school at Mqhekezweni.

Between the Thembu royal house and Clarkebury was an intimate history. The mission had been founded in 1830 when a direct forebear of Nelson's, Ngubengcuka, was the Thembu king and had given the Methodist missionary William Shaw a piece of land.[3] The upper ranks of the Thembu aristocracy had sent their children to study there ever since. The regent himself had been a student at the school, and on the very day Nelson arrived, Justice, the regent's son left to continue his education at another famous establishment.

Through this century-long relationship between paramountcy and church, the Methodists watched the Thembu decline. Back in 1830, Ngubengcuka had granted Shaw ground because it was on Thembu territory and thus in his power to grant. A little more than half a century later, Thembuland was annexed by the British; the ground on which Clarkebury stood, on which the Thembu paramountcy's Great Place stood, *all* the ground that lay in what was once an independent kingdom, was now part of the Cape Colony. Nelson's own father had been dismissed from his position as a headman playing the impossible role the white authorities had given him to allocate its land.

This history of subjugation and decline marked Nelson's journey to Clarkebury in ways he did not know.

The regent personally took him to the school in his magnificent Ford V8, a chauffeur in the driver's seat, Nelson and the regent in the back: a grand man in a grand vehicle, taking his ward to the finest school.

This image is filled with pathos, for the regent had gone into debt to pay for the Ford, a debt he was unable to service. When Nelson had joined his household four years earlier, the regent was avoiding the Transkei's largest city, Umtata, because of writs and judgments against him. And the year after Nelson enrolled at Clarkebury, the regent went further into debt to pay for Nelson's and Justice's education. Indeed, Jongintaba's relationship with the magistrate of Umtata was a humiliating one; serially, he petitioned the white man for a larger allowance.[4]

Nelson had no idea. It was inconceivable to him that a man as powerful as the regent might be vulnerable and exposed. He himself was the frail one; the men who commanded his world were like steel.

. .

In the year Nelson began at Clarkebury, 1935, black schooling in South Africa was in terrible repair. Schools across the country were housed in Christian missions and run by clergymen. Although the provincial governments paid teachers' salaries, for the rest the mission schools had to fend for themselves. The vast majority had barely enough to provide a rudimentary education.[5]

In the Transkei, the situation was dire. In at least one large area, almost certainly reflecting the territory as a whole, one in seven children went to school. Among those who did, the vast majority attended institutions that went no further than Standard Four or Five, imparting to their students basic reading and writing in Xhosa and elementary arithmetic. The bulk of teachers were barely educated themselves; they instructed their charges via rote learning, not through reason or debate. And most schools had no more than one teacher and one classroom; all classes and all age-groups were taught at once.[6]

And so Clarkebury was not just in a different league from the schools around it; it might as well have been on another planet. Nelson was exposed to classes in which the teachers had university degrees; indeed, two of those teachers were black, one of them among the first black women to graduate from a South African university. Relative to other *black* South Africans, although certainly not to whites, Nelson was receiving an education of extraordinary privilege.

He found Clarkebury awfully intimidating at first. The Great Place might have seemed grand, but it was at least recognizably African; the two main houses aside, the built structures were made of mud and grass and shaped like beehives. But here he confronted for the first time a place that felt entirely Western. A compound of two dozen rectangular, mortar-and-brick buildings, it was a truly foreign place.

Soon he was to mortify himself. On his first day in school, he ascended a flight of wooden stairs clad in a brand-new pair of boots. Nelson had neither ascended stairs nor worn boots in his life, and the task unmoored him; before an audience of his peers, he clomped around like a newly shod horse.

Among the crowd watching him was a girl. Turning to her friends, she said in a voice loud enough for him to hear, 'I am not used to wearing shoes.'

He was wild with rage. It took all his self-restraint to stop himself from doing her physical violence. 'I almost manhandled her,' he recalled.[7]

It is a story so typical of Nelson's memories of childhood and youth; he is forever out of his depth, on the verge of humiliation, his dignity scarcely intact.

.   .

Clarkebury was a place of severe Wesleyan austerity. From their first waking moment long before dawn until lights out some sixteen hours later, the students' days were divided into fragments and to each fragment was assigned a task. It must have made for a bewildering contrast to life at the Great Place and, before that, at Qunu, where for hours on end children were left to themselves. The Wesleyans' great fear of sex must have been bewildering, too; but for their unavoidable co-presence in the classroom, the mingling of boys and girls was forbidden.

The governor of Clarkebury, the Reverend Cecil Harris, was himself an emblem of this ethic. He was more a field commander than a school head, Nelson later recalled. Everybody, even the white principals of Clarkebury's training and secondary schools, rose when he entered a room.[8]

But Nelson, it seems, took naturally to the discipline. As an astute biographer has suggested, the self-mastery forced upon him when his family disintegrated was perhaps reinforced by the austere rigors of boarding school.[9] In later years, he spoke fondly of Clarkebury and more fondly still of Harris. Working in the afternoons in the white man's garden, Nelson watched the reverend intently. More often than not, he noticed, Harris was lost in thought. This solitary meditation intrigued Nelson greatly. He doubted that what was happening in the reverend's head was as severe as his persona. Indeed, he remembered Harris as a gentle soul, not from his public performances, but from the expression on his face when he was unaware of being watched.[10]

He was at Clarkebury for just two years. In 1937, at the age of eighteen, he joined Justice at a much grander and more famous Methodist school, Healdtown. It was his first journey outside Thembuland, for Healdtown was a good two hundred miles from the regent's Great Place. It was also probably the first time he stepped on a train.

He would have arrived at the station in the town of Fort Beaufort in the early evening. No transport was provided for students from the station to Healdtown, a good ten miles away. A lorry greeted them to take their luggage; they themselves had to walk deep into the night.[11] Nelson would thus have seen little of the school on his arrival.

What he saw when he woke in the morning was arresting. Built on a hilltop, Healdtown was a series of interlocking ivy-clad buildings, a veritable replica of an Oxbridge college. Wandering through its innards, he found himself in tree-lined courtyards, their whitewashed walls thicker than any built structure he had seen.

More than a thousand African students registered there for study in the year Nelson arrived, and although Healdtown was situated in the

Xhosa heartland, youths from all over southern Africa were enrolled. For the first time, he was to break bread with black people whose first language was not Xhosa.

The pomp of Healdtown's rituals dwarfed what he had witnessed at Clarkebury. On Sunday mornings, the girls marched down a jacaranda-lined avenue to the rhythm of a brass band, their uniforms an impeccable ensemble of black and white. From the opposite end of the complex, the boys, too, marched, clad in suits and ties. They met in the central square, in sight, but never close enough to touch. The Union Jack was hoisted, and the students stood to attention and sang 'God Save the King'. Then the whole assembly marched to the church for morning service, girls filling the pews on the left, boys on the right.[12]

. .

Nowhere does Nelson tell us of the first book he read. Nor do any of his biographers. It might well have been John Bunyan's *Pilgrim's Progress,* which had been translated into Xhosa decades earlier and was a staple on mission school syllabuses.[13] What we do know is that during his final year at Healdtown he read the first volume of Lord Macaulay's *History of England,* for students were examined on it at the end of the year.

Here was a Thembu boy, his political consciousness barely formed, reading of an England superior in every conceivable way: it had built the fiercest navy and commanded the seas; it was home to the world's first factories and produced most of the manufactured goods humanity consumed; it had developed the common law, the most civilized means devised, Macaulay averred, for regulating human affairs.

Might Nelson have felt humbled and small? Probably. He was later to complain that the history syllabus at school was all about white people, Africans appearing as no more than 'savages and thieves'.[14] But reading is a complicated business, and a book can form a person in contradictory ways.

Taking in *The History of England* now, one can only be struck by the power it must have exercised over a boy like Nelson.

For countless generations, Macaulay writes, there was nothing about England that indicated greatness. Cut off from civilization, it was a place of magic and darkness and superstition. And when the world did finally come, it was as conquerors, the Romans first, then the Saxons, then the Danes. And the last of these conquests was brutal. 'The subjugation of a nation by a nation has seldom, even in Asia, been more complete.'[15]

Then came yet another, Norman, invasion, but in this instance the English fought back with the cunning of a conquered people. 'Some bold men ... betook themselves to the woods ... and there ... waged a predatory war against their oppressors ... Many Normans suddenly disappeared leaving no trace ... Death by torture was denounced against the murderers, and a strict search was made for them, but generally in vain; for the whole nation was in a conspiracy to conceal them.'[16]

In Macaulay's hands, England's greatness arises when conqueror and conquered make common cause. Four generations after the Norman invasion, a rift opened between the Norman throne on the continent and the Norman aristocrats who ruled England; estranged from their motherland, the oppressors began to identify with the land of the oppressed. 'The great grandsons of those who had fought under William and the great grandsons of those who had fought under Harold began to draw near to each other in friendship.' Hence begins the history of the English nation. In the absence of that Norman rift, Macaulay writes, the language of Milton would have remained a local language; Englishmen who had hungered for fame would have made their way to France.

It is extraordinary to contemplate how much of Nelson's career is foretold in these pages: the revolutionary concealed among his people; the leader of the conquered building a new nation alongside his erstwhile oppressor.

It is all there.

Chapter 3

While Nelson was completing his final year at Healdtown in 1938, the regent was preparing his future. From out of the blue he simply announced it: Nelson would go to the University of Fort Hare to study for a BA. The regent had made the application himself: it was done.

To be going to Fort Hare was a huge leap forward. Aside from a handful of lucky exceptions, it was the only university where black people could study in all of southern Africa. And in the year Nelson enrolled, there were no more than 150 students. To leave with a degree would be to join a very exclusive club.

Not even Justice, the regent's son, was going to Fort Hare; an indifferent student at Healdtown, he graduated with a Junior Certificate, itself an unusual achievement for a black youth at that time.

When he enrolled at the university, Nelson imagined that upon graduating, he might work in the Department of Native Affairs as an interpreter; with his handsome salary he could raise his family to a new standard; maybe Nosekeni, his mother, would live in 'a home as spacious and beautiful' as the Great Place.[1]

Nelson had yet to leave South Africa's southeastern seaboard and knew no other world. By the standards of *his* world, his sights were lofty; an interpreter mediated between the public and the very highest white officials; he was imagining coming as close to power as he might. Indeed, the regent had invested so much in Nelson's education precisely so that a man as worldly as an interpreter might act as counsel to the future king.

. .

Fort Hare was founded in 1916, twenty-three years before Nelson entered its gates. It stood on the site of an old British fort outside the town of Alice, the symbolism of its location almost too clunky to be true; it was quite literally built on the battlements from which the imperial military crossed the frontier. Two generations later, the fort had become a university; it gathered the grandchildren of the aristocrats the army had conquered to give them a British education.

But the reality of the place was more complicated than the symbolism of its location might suggest. It harboured an assortment of people with complex ideas. Among its teaching staff were two of the most distinguished black scholars on the continent, D. D. T. Jabavu and Z. K. Matthews. Trained by the pioneering anthropologist Bronisław Malinowski at the London School of Economics, Matthews was one of several Africans who used the tools of European ethnography to anti-colonial ends.[2] Nelson found himself in Matthews's classroom; Matthews taught Nelson social anthropology and native law. Sixteen years later, he and Nelson stood trial together for treason.

Fort Hare was just fifteen miles or so from Healdtown, and just a stone's throw away was another famous mission-run high school for blacks, Lovedale. The three institutions formed a trio in which white and black educators mixed. And the gap between what went on at the surface and underneath was telling. When a visiting speaker addressed a public meeting, for instance, white people sat at the front, while the black teachers employed at the three institutions sat with black students at the back. To question this display of racial hierarchy was beyond the pale; it was simply the way things were. But late at night, the black teachers of Healdtown, Lovedale, and Fort Hare assembled separately and talked, and on at least one of these nights they ridiculed their white colleagues until daybreak, heaping upon them the greatest scorn.[3]

By Nelson's telling, he was oblivious to these currents. When they washed up against him, he was left confused. World War II began when he was at Fort Hare, and each evening the warden of his boardinghouse briefed the students on the state of the war. When a peer of Nelson's, Nyathi Khongisa, suggested that it was best that Britain lose, for in a weakened state it might be dispossessed of its empire, Nelson was shocked to his core.[4]

· ·

Like the British institutions on which it was modelled, the university observed rigid hierarchies, and few were as fastidious as the one that decided where students slept. Freshers were thrown together in enormous dormitories. Seniors got their own rooms or, at worst, were paired. Each dormitory elected a house committee, but, incongruously, freshers were ineligible to stand for election, and so dormitories were represented by students who did not sleep in them.

In Nelson's first year, the freshers usurped this long-standing practice and chose their own committee. Nelson was one of those elected. The seniors objected, of course. One of them, an eloquent English speaker named Rex Tatane, asked out loud how the seniors could possibly accept being governed by a bumpkin like Mandela who could not even speak proper English. He switched accents, replacing his very proper elocution with an exaggerated version of Nelson's country tongue. The group of seniors surrounding him laughed scathingly.

Nelson and his comrades said nothing, but the following day they passed a resolution that the seniors would from now on sleep in the big dormitories. It was a humiliation too intolerable to contemplate. Rex Tatane, in something of a panic, appealed to the college warden, the Reverend A. J. Cook, and the two sides assembled in Cook's office. No sooner had the meeting begun than Tatane began to weep; to undress and lie down to sleep among boys his junior was to die a thousand deaths, he pleaded. Alarmed, Cook took mercy on him. He positively begged the freshers to change their minds. 'No, no, no, no, please,' Nelson later recalled him saying. 'This chap, you see, is going to break down completely.'

Nelson and his colleagues were unmoved. The harder Tatane wept, the deeper their resolve grew. They tossed Cook a wager. If he reversed their decision, they told him, they would resign. And they had strong student support, enough to ensure that nobody would stand in their place. Cook realized that he was defeated. 'I will back you,' he said, 'but I thought you could excuse this chap, you see, because he has broken down.'

It was Nelson's first foray into politics. He had shown that he understood intuitively the currencies in which it traded: dignity and humiliation. And why would he not? Ever since his move to the Great Place he had faced daily the prospect of embarrassment. He knew the labyrinths of dignity as only one constantly threatened with its loss might do. And he understood, too, that politics, in the end, boils down to the manner in which a person appears; to rob one's foe of the capacity to stage his own appearance is to defeat him.

Nelson remembered this incident into his old age. He would be appalled at himself. It was his first taste of authority and he had used it to exact revenge.[5]

. .

Justice was not at Fort Hare, but Nelson soon found a replacement for him, another young man who was astonishingly tall, astoundingly handsome, a supreme athlete and dancer, a winner with women. He was Nelson's nephew Kaiser Daliwonga Matanzima, although the designation 'nephew' is misleading, for Daliwonga was older than Nelson and very much his senior.

Years later, when they were political foes – for Daliwonga became apartheid's most famous black ally – the two men recalled how much they had excited each other. The university's students were housed according to religious denomination, and since Nelson and Daliwonga were both Methodists, they lived together. And they played football together, and they went into Alice together at night to dance. 'We were *always* together,' Daliwonga recalled as an old man. 'When someone saw me alone, they would say, "Where's Nelson?"'

And then, his thoughts and his feelings reeling back more than half a century, he chose the loveliest phrase to describe how things were between Nelson and him. 'We had warm hearts together,' he said.

They were also clearly *vain* together, strutting around and courting girls. 'The two of us were very handsome young men,' Daliwonga recalled, 'and all the women wanted us.'[6]

Whether this is true is impossible to say now. Men outnumbered women by fifteen to one among the Fort Hare student body, and pretty women did not have to chase anybody. 'Men were buzzing around me, trying their luck,' a woman who studied at Fort Hare in the late 1930s recalled. 'I hoofed and kicked them with a vengeance, and in the end only the most daring came anywhere near me.'[7]

It was with Daliwonga at his side that Nelson gathered the courage to flirt. One night, the two men, along with a few others, stole out of their boardinghouse to attend a ballroom dance in town, an excursion strictly disallowed. Nelson approached a beautiful young woman and requested a dance. On the dance floor, he asked her name. 'Mrs. Bokwe,' she replied. Nelson almost fled in alarm. He looked across the floor and saw Dr. Roseberry Bokwe, one of the most distinguished African scholars of the time, talking to Nelson's professor Z. K. Matthews. He apologized to Mrs. Bokwe and, under the glare of her husband and Professor Matthews, escorted her off the dance floor.[8]

Nelson tells the story for its levity, but it is in fact of critical importance. The extreme discretion with which people of his generation recount their sex lives renders their deepest sensibilities almost invisible. But there are traces, if one cares to find them.

In her memoir, for instance, Phyllis Ntantala, who was at Fort Hare just before Nelson, briefly recounts an argument with her boyfriend over whether she should wear makeup. 'Good wine needs no bush,' her boyfriend tells her, quoting Shakespeare's *As You Like It*.[9] In this brief comment lies a whole world: Shakespeare, makeup, good wine – what a heady and stylish mix.

Whence does this debate about whether a girl should wear makeup come? Most directly, from the pages of *The Bantu World*, the largest English-language newspaper for Africans in the country, which ran a series of debates during the 1930s, one that Fort Hare students would have read with interest, on whether makeup raised or lowered a young woman's status.

What *The Bantu World* was funnelling into Fort Hare was a black diasporic conversation stretching into West Africa and across the ocean into the Caribbean and North America, on what it was to be young and black and experimenting with the new. One of the most powerful ideas to emerge from this conversation, as the historian Lynn Thomas has pointed out, was that of 'the modern girl' – a young woman, 'often with some schooling, who had a panache for fashion and choosing [her] own lovers'.[10]

Nelson tells us next to nothing of his encounters with 'modern girls' at Fort Hare. But it is enough for us to know that there, at university, he was inducted into a canon, the origins of which lay not in his Thembu heritage but in global circuits of commerce and media. It was a canon of romantic love.

· ·

His adoration of Daliwonga changed Nelson's fate; the trouble started over the question of food.

Fort Hare student meals were notoriously bad. A visitor who spent an evening there in the late 1930s recorded that students were given a small loaf of bread, a tin of green jam and tea.'' In 1940, Nelson's second year, the students rebelled. They demanded that the Student Representative Council (SRC) be given greater power to address the quality of food. When the university governor, Alexander Kerr, rejected their demands, the students resolved to boycott SRC elections. When 25 students from a body of about 150 turned up to vote, Nelson discovered that he was among six elected to take up positions on the council.

The six met and resolved to resign on the grounds that the majority had not voted. Kerr accepted their resignations, but immediately announced that new elections were to be held the next day at suppertime, a cunning move because the entire student body would be present. But most of those assembled refused to vote; again, just twenty-five elected Nelson and his five colleagues.

The councillors met again to decide what to do, and this time there was disagreement among them. The other five argued that since the entire study body was present for the election, they should serve. Nelson was not so sure. He went to Daliwonga for advice.

Years later, Nelson told the novelist Nadine Gordimer that he was utterly enthralled with Daliwonga at the time and did whatever he said.[12]

Daliwonga told Nelson to stand his ground.

When Dr. Kerr heard that he had a recalcitrant councillor on his hands, he called Nelson in and gave him a choice: serve or be expelled. Nelson was terrified. He returned to Daliwonga and asked again what he should do. 'It's a matter of principle,' he recalled Daliwonga telling him. 'You must just tell them you are not going to serve.'

Nelson faced, on the one hand, the severity of Dr. Kerr, expulsion from Fort Hare, and the fury of the regent. On the other, he faced the disapproval of the peer he idealized, Daliwonga.

'I feared [Daliwonga] more than I feared Kerr,' Nelson recalled. 'I took it that [Daliwonga] knew *everything,* that he could never make a mistake . . . I went back and told the principal [that I was not going to serve], and the principal told me, then you don't come back.'[13]

· ·

When Nelson returned to the Great Place with the news of his expulsion, the regent was irate. What Nelson had done was unfathomable to him – to sacrifice his education over a dispute about food? He ordered his ward to return to Fort Hare in the new year and make amends.

It was early December 1940. The new academic year began in mid-January. Nelson had time to stew. While he waited, something else happened, something unheralded and life changing. Justice returned from Cape Town, where he had been living for the past year; no sooner had he settled in than the regent summoned the two young men to say that he had arranged for both of them to wed.

For Justice he had chosen the daughter of a well-regarded aristocratic family, for Nelson the daughter of a local clergyman.

In the milieu of Nelson's youth, one did not openly question one's elders. The two listened in silence and waited to be dismissed. Only once they were alone did they ask each other what on earth they would do.

What the regent had arranged was not out of the ordinary. One did not have to have royal blood flowing through one's veins to wind up in an arranged marriage. There are stories from those times of esteemed families arriving en masse at a home of good standing to search among its daughters for a bride.[14]

But, as Nelson pointed out later, the regent had sent him to school, and in doing so had delivered him to a world that harboured rival values. Among them was the idea that two young people wed because they had fallen in love.[15]

The sex lives of their offspring were foreign territory to the Thembu aristocrats of that time; talk of romance simply did not cross generational lines. So the regent could not have known that the bride he had chosen for Nelson was Justice's lover. The whole business was something of a farce.

Which of them came up with the idea is now irretrievable. Nelson and Justice waited for the regent's next excursion and in his absence took two of his cattle to market. With the proceeds in their hands, they offered a local trader a good sum of money to drive them to a distant train station. Their intention was to escape to Johannesburg, a place sufficiently large for a Thembu royal to get lost.

It turned out to be much more complicated than that. Preparing for the first time to travel some distance, Nelson ran into the bureaucratic net white South Africa had set for young black men like him. Africans over the age of sixteen had by law to carry a 'native pass'; it stated where one lived, whether one had paid one's poll tax and who was one's chief. To leave one's magisterial district, one needed a letter of authorization.

Nelson and Justice got off the train in Queenstown, over six hundred miles from their intended destination.* Their royal connections, they believed, would help them. They went to the regent's brother, Chief Mpondombini, who lived in Queenstown, told him that they were going to Johannesburg to deliver a message for the regent, and asked if he would take them to the white magistrate to get the requisite papers.

The chief was cheerfully compliant and took the two young men personally to the magistrate, who was equally warm; he made out travelling papers and stamped them.

As they turned to leave, the magistrate called them back. Just as a courtesy, he said, he ought to call the Umtata magistrate, under whose jurisdiction Justice and Nelson fell, to tell him what he was doing. He cranked his phone and began speaking to his colleague; to the young men's horror, it became apparent, as the conversation went on, that at that precise moment the regent himself was paying the Umtata magistrate a visit. His voice exploded into the receiver, denouncing his children as thieves and demanding their arrest.

At Fort Hare, Nelson had taken a course in legal studies and thus had a smattering of knowledge of the subject. Shrewdly, he pointed out to the magistrate that while he and Justice had lied, they had broken no law; they could not be arrested simply because the regent to the Thembu paramountcy had lost his temper. Thus began Nelson's legal career, his first case a success, for the magistrate told them to get out of his office and never return. As for Chief Mpondombini, he felt embarrassed and deceived and washed his hands of his young relatives.

Alone now on the streets of Queenstown, their plans discovered, their trouble deep, the young men racked their brains. Justice had a friend in Queenstown, a young man named Sidney Nxu, who worked in the office of a white attorney. They visited Nxu, who told them that

---

* They were in white South Africa now, where the law stipulated that they could not own land and could live only in areas set aside for blacks and where their presence was permitted at all only if they had work or were on an officially sanctioned visit. That these laws were often practiced in the breach throughout the epoch of white minority rule made them no less insidious. Indeed, their inconsistent application meant that millions of people did not know where they stood.

the attorney's mother was driving to Johannesburg; he would ask if she would give them a lift.

She would, it turned out, but for a staggering fee of £15, about £1000 adjusted to 2022 values. They accepted, not knowing what on earth they would do when they got to Johannesburg, for the cost of the journey cleaned them out.

A black man did not sit in the passenger seat of a car alongside a white woman, certainly not if she was twice his age. Nelson and Justice thus took their places in the back, Nelson behind the passenger seat, Justice behind the driver.

Justice was a regent's son. He felt no need for servility, not even before a white woman he had never met. And he was, as Nelson later recalled, 'exuberant, wild'.[16] That is precisely why Nelson had spent the previous decade enamored of him.

But it was too much for their driver: this forceful black youth, so scandalously without inhibition, going on merrily behind her back. She stopped the car and ordered the young men to swap places. The quiet one could sit behind her; the boisterous one she wanted to keep in view.

And so Nelson was introduced to the pungent racism of the city even before he got there. And the nature of his arrival reinforced the rude lessons he had learned in the car. The attorney's mother skirted the city centre and drove into a suburb more lavish than Nelson could ever have imagined; staring out the window, he saw row after row of mansions, every one of them a thousand times grander than the regent's Great Place.

The white woman drove through the entrance of one of these colossi and disappeared through the front door, leaving Nelson and Justice to the servants' quarters, where they slept on the floor.

The Transkei was eight hundred miles away. Among the hundreds of thousands of people they had left there was Nomzamo Winifred Zanyiwe Madikizela. She was four years old.

WINNIE:
EARLY YEARS

. . .

Chapter 4

On November 17, 1908, a steamer carrying two American missionaries left New York. The Reverend J. P. Brodhead and his wife, Anna, were embarking on their second voyage to Africa. Eight years earlier, they had set out for the first time, leaving their two small children with Anna's aged mother, to establish a Free Methodist presence in the British colony of Natal. By any reasonable measure, their work was a success; they learned the native language, Zulu, gathered a large and dedicated flock, established a school, and took back with them to Pennsylvania a young Zulu woman, Elizabeth Nombango Zelemu, to train as a teacher.[1]

Now they were returning, this time to start a new mission as far from the boundaries of established Christendom as they could get. Six years had passed since God had spoken to Anna directly, instructing that her and her husband's 'highest calling . . . meant going personally, more fully than ever before, to the "raw" heathen'.[2]

From Durban, the Brodheads took a train southward along the seaboard as far as Port Shepstone. There, they hired two mule transport wagons fitted with shock absorbers, one to carry their possessions, the other themselves, and travelled thus for ninety miles. Then they were forced to swap to ox wagons, these without shock absorbers, and for the last sixty-five miles of their passage were thrown about the inside of the wagon like wooden blocks.

Their discomfort only lifted their spirits; their purpose, after all, was to live among 'the multitudes . . . destitute of the Bible', and the remoteness of the territory confirmed that they had chosen well.[3]

Their new mission was in Mpondoland, the last of the twelve Xhosa-speaking kingdoms to be annexed by the British; when the Brodheads arrived, the ground on which they stood had been Cape Colony territory for less than fifteen years. The mission they established was called Critchlow, after the Pennsylvania oil baron and evan-

gelist J. M. Critchlow, who had acquired the land on behalf of the Free
Methodist Church.[4]

The Brodheads were right in thinking that they were in the depths
of 'heathen' country. For although the Wesleyans had established a mission in Mpondoland in 1828, and while in subsequent years the Anglicans and the Presbyterians had also established a considerable presence
in the territory,[5] the twenty-five-mile radius around Critchlow contained just one church and one white missionary, an Australian Baptist
named J. W. Joyce.[6]

Upon settling, the missionaries announced themselves to the chief
of the largest Mpondo clan in the area; his name was Langasike, son
of the legendary founder of the Ngutyana clan, Madikizela. The chief
received the missionaries cordially but with caution. When the meal he
shared with them was over, a minion brought out an American rocking
chair, not dissimilar to those the Brodheads were accustomed to seeing
on porches back home. The chief rocked sceptically in his chair as he
listened to his guests' account of their work, his wariness undisguised.[7]

.   .

What happened with the Brodheads over the next few years followed so typically the early history of countless Protestant missions
across Africa. Those at the apex of native authority kept a cautious
distance. The real enthusiasts, the ones with both the means and the
desire to experiment with novelty, were neither the most nor the least
powerful, but those on the edges of aristocratic society. For it is they
who were close enough to power to harbour grand ambitions, but sufficiently far to have to try out new and uncertain routes to greatness.[8]

And so it was that more than two decades before her birth, Winnie
Madikizela's paternal grandfather, Mazingi, and his brother, Marashule,
approached the Brodheads with the intent of converting to Free Meth-
odism and learning to read and write. The date on which they did so is
now lost forever, but it was most likely sometime in 1910.

In middle age, Winnie offered her various biographers a wildly fic-
titious account of Mazingi. He was a great chief with no fewer than
twenty-nine wives, she would say, and his landholdings stretched for
miles between his home in the village of Mbongweni all the way to
the coast at Port Shepstone. None of this is so. It is true that Mazingi
and Marashule were direct descendants of Madikizela, a famous states-

man and warrior. But Madikizela had dozens of children and hundreds of grandchildren, and Mazingi and Marashule were not in the line of succession.[9]

By the time they met the Brodheads, the brothers had been pursuing the prospect of conversion for years. Both had had long discussions with the Baptist Joyce about the Bible and its contents; they were put off when the Australian refused to teach them to read the holy text, advising them that his own reading of the Bible was authority enough. Next, they knocked on the door of the only other white man in the area, a carpenter and independent evangelist by the name of Miller. It so happened that Miller was the man from whom the Free Methodists were to buy the land that became the Critchlow mission. When the Brodheads arrived, Miller informed them immediately of the two Ngutyana princes with a hunger for the Bible.[10]

By the time Mazingi and Marashule met the Free Methodists, they were established men with families. Despite their age and status, they insisted on enrolling in the modest primary school the Brodheads were establishing. And so these two patriarchs took their places alongside children to study their letters. They even wore the same school uniform as their fellow students: a long, collared shirt that dangled around their knees.[11]

Perhaps they were simply too old to learn to read. Or perhaps the experience was too humbling. According to one oral record, they abandoned school in their third year of study,[12] according to another, much earlier.[13]

But they were hardly dissuaded. Their ambitions were not just for themselves but for the generations, and the measures they took next suggest that they were playing a long game indeed.

Both were married men with children; each had a wife unschooled in letters and in the Christian faith. They resolved to seek literate Christians as second wives. Marashule found a wife in the town of Mount Ayliff, seventy miles from his home in Mbongweni. Mazingi had to travel farther afield and came back with a woman named Mamphele.[14]

What the Brodheads said about the polygamous ways of these converts has gone unrecorded. But of all the indigenous practices to which the missionaries of that time objected, they considered polygamy among the gravest. It is doubtful that they easily tolerated what Mazingi and Marashule had done, leaving us to wonder what sort of modus vivendi the brothers and the Free Methodists worked out between them.

We *do* know that the respective first wives of the two men did not take kindly to the additions to their husbands' families. Winnie's grandmother Seyina bore hostility toward Christians for the rest of her days. At her husband's insistence, she eventually underwent conversion herself, but with bitterness.

The next step the two men took would have great consequence. The nearest school to their village, Mbongweni, was the one the Brodheads had established at Critchlow, some eight miles away. This was not close enough for the brothers. They wanted to establish schools in Mbongweni itself, for it appears that their ambition was to alter the trajectories not simply of their immediate families but of their entire world.

At this point, a rivalry grew between them, one their children would not only inherit but inflame. Mazingi went back to the Baptists and asked them to help him build a school in Mbongweni; Joyce had left by now, and it was his successor whom Mazingi approached. Marashule, for his part, went to the Brodheads and asked of them the same. For some time, it seemed that two schools might be built in the village, each brother presiding over his domain.

The Cape government put an early end to the story of the brothers' twin empires, for it made plain that it would fund the teachers' salaries of one school in Mbongweni, not two. And so Mazingi's Baptist school was built while Marashule's Free Methodist School was not.

That marks the end of the Brodheads' role in the Madikizela family's fate. They returned to America late in the second decade of the twentieth century, too soon ever to learn of the extraordinary history to which they had helped give birth.

. .

We cannot know why the brothers did what they did. In hindsight, we can only say that they chose extremely well, for the men of their times who threw everything at the education of their children built dynasties. To be among the small minority to receive a decent education in the first half of the twentieth century was to be spared the life of a migrant mine worker. But more than that, what these men were bringing to their descendants was authority and renown. In the decades after their conversion in 1910, the most influential men in any given village in the Transkei were the local school principal and the headman, the educator and the aristocrat.[15] Well-educated men would go on to play prominent roles in public affairs, men whose names would be remembered after their deaths.

Mazingi and Marashule might well have dreamed of all this. It is improbable, though, that they ever imagined their project's greatest prize would take form not in a famous man but in a woman.

. .

The brothers' project achieved extraordinary success in the shortest time. Each of their many children would enroll in the school Mazingi had built; some went on to complete their education at the Methodist mission at Mfundisweni, the most prestigious of Mpondoland's educational institutions. Many became white-collar professionals of one sort or another: schoolteachers, nurses, ministers of religion, agricultural officers. Winnie's father, Columbus, served as a school principal. So did her uncle Walter. He also enrolled to study for a BA at the University of South Africa.[16]

Walter was born in 1910, the very year his father and his uncle met the Brodheads. That the encounter produced a university student within a generation is a remarkable tale by anyone's measure.

And to hear the story from the tongue of a Madikizela is to witness its remarkableness made epic.

When Walter sat down with a historian in 1982, not long before his death, to talk about the role he had played in political events two decades earlier, he insisted on beginning the tale in the early nineteenth century. For the heft of his story took in the generations. And when this author sat down with Walter's son, Prince, in 2018, when he was in his early seventies, to talk about his cousin Winnie, he also insisted on beginning with the arresting tale of the Madikizelas through time.

It matters that we frame things thus, for we need to understand the milieu into which Winnie was born. It was a world of great ambition and rapid self-transformation. It was also a world of treachery. Between Columbus and Walter, two of the most successful of Mazingi's and Marashule's children, would grow the sharpest rivalry. It would find expression in politics, where they would become enemies. And it would find expression, too, in the quest to bring greatness to their children.

Chapter 5

Winnie Madikizela was born on September 26, 1936, twenty-six years after the first encounter between her forebears and the Brodheads. The second generation of Christian Madikizelas was in adulthood now and had announced its formidable presence to the world. Winnie's father, Columbus, was principal of a school at Dutyini, a village not far from Mbongweni. He had married a woman whose pedigree could not have been better suited to a man in his position. A second-generation Methodist, Gertrude Nomathamsanqa Mzaidume was, like her husband, a mission-educated schoolteacher.

Columbus and Gertrude bore all the trappings of their ascendance. The house they built when Winnie was a child was not just a home but a beacon visible across their world. It was large and rectangular and made of brick and mortar, not unlike the structures that so dazzled Nelson when he arrived at Dalindyebo's Great Place. Pride among its rooms was Columbus's study, filled with a growing collection of books.[1]

As a middle-aged woman, when her global fame was growing, Winnie regaled a series of biographers with outlandish tales about her childhood. The deeper meaning of the stories she told – that in the frenzy of its self-transformation her family harboured much pain – contains powerful and important truths. But she chose to people her public story with a series of fanciful characters.

She often, for instance, exaggerated to the point of absurdity her grandparents' aristocratic roots. That Mazingi was a chief with twenty-nine wives, for instance, became standard fare. More darkly, she also said of him that he ordered girls to be killed at birth.[2]

From her mother's Christian piety Winnie spun dramatic tales. Gertrude, she would say throughout her life, had straight hair and green eyes. Indeed, well into middle age, Winnie would pose in profile and ask her audience to look carefully at her nose. 'I am 25 percent white!' she exclaimed. 'It is from my mother's side.'[3]

And yet, although Gertrude was indeed light-skinned, the Mzai-dumes this author met chuckled at the idea that among their ancestors were whites. Winnie, they said with a laugh, what tales she told.

Of her paternal grandmother, Seyina, Winnie also painted a myth-ical figure. She was not just the first of Mazingi's twenty-nine wives, Winnie said, but his business manager, running his sizable trading stores on his behalf, and thus the real power behind his throne. Yet Seyina was in fact the first of Mazingi's two wives, her place in the family increasingly marginal after her husband converted to Christian-ity. Those whose memories reach back to the days when Seyina was alive do not recall her running a business; the first trading store anyone can remember a Madikizela managing was started by Columbus, when Seyina was old.

Armed with these boldly drawn figures, Winnie depicted a most spectacular clash. The protagonists were two powerful women, Sey-ina, representing tradition, and Gertrude Methodist piety. Seyina's home, Winnie often said, was sprawling and messy, and it brimmed with people and chatter, with *life*. It boasted not a single item of the dark furniture Winnie's parents so coveted. Instead, it was strewn with mats, the floors made of cow dung, as a traditional Mpondo home should be. And although Seyina occasionally gave her granddaughter chores, work with her was really just an extension of play.

Gertrude's spirit could not have been more different. Her Victorian home was so austere that a child could not possibly feel comfortable there. Nor did people outside the nuclear family feel free to drop by. As for work, in Gertrude's view no chore was worthwhile unless it was *hard*, and there were always chores, endlessly, from morning until night.

Alongside this cultural clash between Seyina and Gertrude, Win-nie told of a political battle. Seyina loathed Gertrude for her green eyes and her straight hair; in Seyina's view, these Caucasian features were of a piece with her puritan deathliness. Christianity was a white implant that had come in the guise of her daughter-in-law and was stealing her son before her very eyes.[4]

And yet this account, too, should be treated with caution, for Win-nie's surviving siblings do not remember Seyina as warm or earthy or politically combative. They recall a remote, somewhat detached woman who gave them little comfort after their mother died.[5]

What are we to make of Winnie's stories?

By the time she began talking to biographers, Winnie was famous and had given herself over to spectacle. And the spectacle she created was, aside from its many other functions, a screen. She had by now cuckolded her famous husband with several men, had been tortured in jail – itself a powerful motivation for sheltering her interior from a prying world – and had for some time been sheltering guerrillas in her home. Much of her life was conducted discreetly, despite, indeed, *because of,* the growing public attention she commanded.

That the presence of a biographer might offer an opportunity for candid exploration, to be relayed to an audience of countless readers, is laughable. Why on earth would Winnie have done that? The stories she told of her past speak of a will for privacy. My past is *mine,* she was perhaps saying; the stories I tell are a deflection.

But even embellished stories contain truths, and even tales spoken for public consumption reveal intimate struggles. And in the stories she told of her childhood, Winnie meted out upon her mother the most punishing revenge. The austere Victorian home, the endless chores, the absence of *life* – these stand out starkly.

Winnie was to insist, again and again, to every biographer who darkened her door, that her birth was a disappointment to her mother. She was Gertrude's fifth child, and while the first, Christopher, had been a boy, the second, third, and fourth – Vuyelwa, Nikiwe, and Nonalithi – had been girls. Yet another daughter was the last thing her mother wanted.[6]

We can never know whether this was so; Gertrude died in 1945, her voice long drowned out by that of her daughter. But from Winnie's anger we can learn a great deal.

By the time she died, Gertrude had given birth to eleven children, two of whom had died. The division of labour between her and her husband was stark. Columbus's public esteem was growing: as the school principal he was among Dutyini's most exemplary figures; and he was soon to take a place on the Bhunga, the Transkei's deliberative and advisory assembly, at which notables from across the territory assembled. Gertrude's burden was to give birth to and properly raise not just children but the next generation of *Madikizela* children, charged with no less than remaking their world. And the more the better, it seems, lest some of them fail.

Had she the time or the strength to devote attention to all individually? How likely is it that a mother of eleven will love every child she has spawned?

Winnie complained that she scarcely remembered a moment when she and her mother were alone. And on the rare occasion when it was just the two of them, Gertrude's attention was *still* trained upon somebody else – her God. Winnie accompanied her mother when she went to her 'secret place' to pray, and what Gertrude asked for, Winnie would recall, was another son.[7]

.   .

Winnie was nine when Gertrude died. What a business to lose a parent when one's feelings for her are as fraught as Winnie's appear to have been. Unsurprisingly, her recollections of her mother's death veer a great deal.

In one telling, the story begins three years earlier, in Dutyini, when Winnie was six. Vuyelwa, her oldest sister, returned home from school one day coughing blood. Over the following period – whether weeks or months we are not sure – she lay dying.

Of Vuyelwa's death Winnie painted a shorn, vivid scene. Columbus spreads a white sheet over her corpse. In the corner of the room, Gertrude, dressed only in a starched white petticoat, kneels before her God, begging him to keep her daughter alive.

There is scorn in this image. Gertrude is always praying. And her praying is destructive. Either she is giving her attention to her God instead of to her daughter, or she is exhorting a God to save a child who is already dead.

From the moment of Vuyelwa's death, Winnie recalled, her mother was never the same. 'I watched her wither away, sitting in dark corners and praying silently . . . [F]or me as a little girl, she was literally disappearing.

'She probably had too many children for her age,' Winnie concluded coolly. 'We were nine.'[8]

.   .

To another biographer, Winnie gave a much richer, and substantially different, account of her mother's death.

The two children Gertrude bore after Winnie, Lungile and

Msuthu, were boys, just as she had wanted. Then there were two more girls, Nobantu and Nonyaniso, and then another boy, Thanduxolo. In the second story of Gertrude's death, she is sick for months, not years; she falls gravely ill after giving birth to Thanduxolo and dies three months after he is born.

In this telling, Winnie drew close to Gertrude as she lay dying. She and her next older sister, Nonalithi, took turns going to school so that one of them was always nursing their mother. Winnie would sit at her bedside and hold her infant brother. Gertrude was wasting away, vomiting, her brow wet with fever, her eyes hollowed into her face. She would nonetheless raise her head and look Winnie in the eye.

It was now, at Gertrude's deathbed, that Winnie acquired a mother's full attention. Gertrude focused upon her with intensity and told her that she should make her life pure.

As their mother's death approached, Winnie and Nonalithi took fright and retreated to an outhouse. There they waited all night. Toward dawn, their older sister Nikiwe burst into the room, wailing and beating her chest. That is how they learned that their mother was dead.

Once dawn broke, the house filled with relatives. Reams of black cloth arrived; Gertrude's old sewing machine was taken out, and mourning dresses were hastily sewn. The children's heads were shaved, and they were put into black dresses. The outer walls of the house were painted black.[9]

There is much more tenderness in this account of Gertrude; there is shock and pain; there is a girl's incomprehension in the face of death.

. .

What happened with Winnie after her mother died is so very intricate, so filled with opposites. On the one hand, she finally acquired the intense attention of a parent. But this attention was anything but unconditional; what she had to do to get it and then keep it filled the following decade of her life.

Shortly before Gertrude's death, Columbus was appointed principal of the very school Mazingi had built. The family moved from Dutyini back to Mbongweni, the village of Columbus's birth.

To run the school in the Madikizela heartland, thus taking up his father's and his uncle's mantle, was a very big deal. It was here in Mbong-

weni that Columbus built his house with its Victorian furnishings, a
house that signalled the wider family's ascendance.

Winnie marked the move to Mbongweni as the birth of a powerful bond between her and her father. In middle age, she described
their coming together in a charged, mystical idiom. She chose a single image: she and her father alone together preparing his fields for
sowing.

> I led the oxen and Father drove the plough. We both hoed
> together. Even though the work was hard I never complained
> as I was too overcome by the specialness of this new relation-
> ship with [him]. We hardly spoke but his gentle presence gave
> me support. It was as if God walked with me.[10]

This is evocative language indeed. It is also unusually candid: such
a proud woman, so vigilant in guarding her inner world, offering an
account of such grateful surrender.

The way Winnie tells it, there is no narrative thread, no cause and
effect. She plucks a scene from nowhere, denuding it of its context. We
are left to stitch the thread ourselves and to surmise that Columbus
drew close to Winnie as a result of gratitude. For in the wake of Gertrude's death, the responsibilities she began to take on in his household
and in his wider public life in order to garner his attention and his
favour were nothing less than extraordinary.

When they were elderly women, Winnie's two younger sisters –
Nobantu and Nonyaniso – had only the vaguest memories of Gertrude; they remembered Winnie as their mother. Looking back upon
her childhood, Nonyaniso recalled seeing the world from her place
on Winnie's back. And she recalled, too, calling Winnie 'mama' until
Columbus informed her that her biological mother was in the grave-
yard behind the house.[11]

And then, of course, there was the youngest, Thanduxolo, just an
infant; he, too, was Winnie's charge. We can only imagine the complexity of her feelings as she tended him; it was his arrival in the world that
triggered Gertrude's illness and death.

Winnie played another role at the age of ten. From outlying villages,
children, many of them Madikizelas, would descend upon Mbongweni
to study at Columbus's school. And since there was nowhere else for

them to stay, they moved en masse into his home. He was to be not just their teacher but their parent in loco and their provider.

The grand house that Columbus had built, a house like none other in Mbongweni, was not just a nuclear family's home. It was a conduit through which any child in the area who wished to ascend had to travel. And those who made the journey came out the other side transformed. Educated, literate and Christian, they were also saved from migrant labour, saved from the depths of South Africa's gold mines, preserved for lives of pen and paper, if they took the chance Columbus had handed them.

Columbus's house and the people in it were thus in the profoundest sense exemplary; they lived on public display, their very demeanour an ongoing lesson in what it might mean to ascend.

After her mother's death, Winnie became the mistress of this home. It was she who arranged sleeping places for the incoming horde at the beginning of the academic year; she who ensured that there was food on everyone's plate, that by nine in the evening the boarders were in bed, that in the morning each had risen and prepared for school.

Winnie was famous for playing this role. Throughout Mbongweni and beyond, she was referred to not as Winnie but as *Mamomncinci* – little mother.[12]

One must imagine that Winnie performed these roles in a colossal effort to lodge herself in her father's thoughts. In her memories of her first decade, she was forever on the brink of disappearing: one child among eleven, barely noticed, barely registered as a being in this world. In the wake of her mother's death, she stood up to be seen, and with what energy she did so: the ceaselessness of her activity, the multiplicity of her roles, are something to behold.

It was all very effective, for if her memory is right, Columbus made of her a genuine companion.

They continued to farm his land together. She was by now considerably more than an extra pair of hands. He discussed with her in great detail the technical difficulties of growing maize. He handed her copies of *Farmer's Weekly*, South Africa's iconic trade magazine. From the problem of pests, to worms, to the timing of planting and harvesting, he drew her close, addressing her not as a daughter but as an adult.[13]

To see just how special the bond between father and daughter must have become, we must look, too, at the fates of Winnie's siblings.

In this sprawling family, a division of roles set in early and lasted forever. Nonyaniso and Nobantu, Winnie's younger sisters, became her children when she was ten and remained so through much of her life; neither went nearly as far as Winnie in school, and both depended upon their older sister a great deal until the day she died.

Nor did her brothers do nearly as well as their ambitious father must have wanted. The oldest, Christopher, became a schoolteacher, and, indeed, was appointed principal of the school at Mbongweni, thus continuing a venerable family tradition. But he remained a resolutely local figure; he never acquired a university education, never took the Madikizela name beyond a corner of the Transkei. As for Winnie's younger brother Lungile, his fate, we shall soon see, became a family tragedy.

Among Columbus's children, then, achievement was distributed with stark inequality; of the nine surviving children, the two most robust and powerful turned out to be girls. Winnie and her older sister Nikiwe went on to flourish in school, marry distinguished men and launch their own professional careers.

And, indeed, it seems that Columbus was early to mark Winnie's potential, not just as mother, as mistress of the house and as farmer, but as a highly educated professional in the making. We cannot ever know what he envisaged, when he married Gertrude, for his sons and his daughters. But as his children grew, he began investing as heavily in the education of girls as he did in boys.

When Gertrude died, Nikiwe was already a student at Mfundisweni, the finest mission school in Mpondoland. And when Winnie passed her Standard Six, some four years after her mother's death, she too went on to study at Mfundisweni.

It is extraordinary to think that at the age of thirteen she was taking on yet another role in the grand Madikizela project. Matriarch, mother, farm labourer – to these was now added sterling academic achiever. She had taken on board every conceivable responsibility available to a Madikizela child, both male and female.

Chapter 6

The annual Madikizela expedition to the school at Mfundisweni, undertaken at the beginning of the academic year, was legendary. Columbus and his cousin, Walter, who by now was principal at the school in the nearby village of Monti, would prepare half a dozen horses. They were harnessed to wagons loaded with the possessions of the Madikizela children who were to attend Mfundisweni that year. The children themselves, freed from their burdens, walked alongside wagons all the way to the school some thirty miles away.[1]

There were always a lot of children on that expedition, for Mfundisweni was filled with Madikizelas. In the year Winnie arrived, one of her classmates recalls, there were seven Madikizelas boarding in the girls' hostel and perhaps double that number in the boys' hostel.[2]

Upon entering the gates of Mfundisweni, one looked squarely upon a single-story, brick-and-mortar building, the residence of the Methodist minister who governed the mission. A succession of Englishmen ran it over the years – Raymond Parsley, Deryck Dugmore, Theodore Crabtree – missionaries far from home.[3]

In Winnie's time, the governor was Francis Perry. The sphere over which he presided was large and complex. Mfundisweni was a sprawling compound consisting of a school, a church, a series of dormitories for boys and another series for girls, a residential settlement for white teachers and another for black teachers.

The puritan severity of Mfundisweni rivaled that encountered by Nelson at Clarkebury and Healdtown. Girls in the junior forms rose at 3:00 a.m. to shower, for they were not allowed in the ablution facilities when the senior girls were there. And while there was electric light at Mfundisweni, there were no geysers, and so these 3:00 a.m. showers were cold. After washing themselves, the junior girls had to clean their dormitories and then sweep the areas outside. All of this labour was performed in strict silence.

Although the girls slept together in dormitories, and although they showered side by side in the mornings, they did not once see each other naked, not in all their time at Mfundisweni. A cubicle was built around each shower, and it was understood that there, and only there, the one place on the premises where a girl was unseen, could she disrobe.

And the attention paid to the attire that hid these bodies was equally severe. A girl's uniform consisted of a white collared shirt and a black pinafore. Her parents were instructed to buy five identical shirts, for there was no time for ironing during the week and it was not permitted for a girl to wear a shirt twice without ironing it. On Saturday mornings the girls washed their uniforms, and in the late afternoons, once their clothes had dried, they ironed their shirts and their pinafores, the irons, which they had to provide themselves, heated on a coal stove.

During the week, they went barefoot; the black lace-up shoes accompanying the school uniform were only to be worn on Sundays. It was unreasonable, the school authorities believed, to ask parents to purchase more than one pair, and the scuffs and bumps they would receive were they to be worn as a matter of course would leave them unfit for church.[4]

Despite the several biographies and the countless interviews, Winnie appears to have said next to nothing about her time at Mfundisweni. We are left with the fraying memories of some of those who remember her from those days, memories re-formed not simply by time but by her subsequent fame.

One of those who knew her – an octogenarian who remembers daily life at Mfundisweni with astonishing precision – recalls two things about Winnie, and both seem highly plausible. The first is that she was, before anything else, a *Madikizela*. There were so many of them, the old woman recalls, and they were so very proud of who they were. Whatever else distinguished them, the first thing one clocked was that they were members of that great family. And they looked out for one another. No Madikizela wanted to see another humbled.

The second thing she remembers about Winnie is that she was a Goody Two-Shoes. There were girls who railed against the school's puritan ways, girls who forever tested the limits of its tolerance, girls forever being punished.

Winnie was not among them. She worked very hard, did extremely well, and fell into the rhythms of the school's discipline without complaint.[5]

In his sermons from the pulpit on Sunday mornings, Francis Perry stressed to his congregants, again and again, that they were at an *elite* school. Their parents had sacrificed a great deal to get them there, he would say; they *owed* it to their families to succeed.

There is every sign that Winnie took this to heart. From her subsequent relationships as an adult – from the ways she loved and the ways she suffered – it is clear that Columbus's attention mattered to her a great deal. And her fear that his attention might drift elsewhere almost certainly preoccupied her. She worked very hard while at Mfundisweni, as much for her father as for herself.

The rewards were great indeed. At the end of her three years at Mfundisweni, Winnie not only received her Junior Certificate, as her older sister Nikiwe and older brother, Christopher, had done before her. It was decided that she should go further.

Upon acquiring their Junior Certificates, Nikiwe and Christopher trained as a nurse and as a teacher, respectively. These career paths were highly respectable. But they did not entail completing high school. They were *good* careers, to be sure, careers that would place them squarely in the ranks of the elite. But for a family that aimed as high as the Madikizelas, they were no more than good.

Winnie, though, and, after her, her younger brother Lungile were chosen to go on and complete their secondary schooling. Winnie would do so at Shawbury, another elite Methodist institution, this one farther afield. There could be only one reason to choose this path for a child; Columbus intended Winnie and Lungile to go on to studying beyond high school.

To aim this loftily for a son was one thing. To do so for a daughter was highly unusual. Few of the girls Winnie encountered at Mfundisweni were to go on to finish secondary school, let alone contemplate further study.

There is no record of what Columbus thought of Winnie during the time she studied at Mfundisweni. But his actions speak clearly. He must have thought the world of her.

· ·

Winnie arrived at Shawbury at the beginning of 1951 and left at the end of 1952. She has fictionalized her time there extravagantly, leaving her biographer feeling like a spoiler and a sleuth.

In middle age, Winnie spoke at length about the house mistress who ran the dormitory in which she lived at Shawbury, Mrs. Mtshali, a woman who took the severity of her Methodist creed to frightening extremes. In Winnie's account, Mrs. Mtshali lined the girls up, had them stripped naked by the prefects, and inspected them. If she found anything of which she did not approve – Winnie does not elaborate on what it was about a naked girl that might give Mrs. Mtshali offense – she made the girl lie flat on the floor, still stark naked, and beat her with a whip. More intense than the physical pain was the dishonour; the prospect of being treated thus before an audience was something Winnie did her utmost to avoid.[6]

Others who attended Shawbury at the time confirm that Mrs. Mtshali was notorious for her severity. And yet, when asked about the scene Winnie describes, those this author spoke to were puzzled. Such a ritual, they insist, would have been inconceivable. For public nakedness was a taboo, and to treat a girl thus was a bridge not even Mrs. Mtshali dared cross.[7]

What are we to make of the sadistic scene Winnie conjured? In the childhood she offered her biographers, there is no shortage of horrible women: her mother, who prays for a son in front of her daughter; a schoolmistress with a taste for whipping young flesh. Tensions that in all likelihood were expressed with some subtlety – a mother's longing for a son, a woman's enjoyment of the punishment she administered – become garish in the tales Winnie tells. The world is recast with the ferocity of the offense she has taken; her stories are, above all, a measure of the temperature in her inner world.

Winnie herself, it appears, exercised authority lightly. She was Shawbury's head prefect in 1952 and thus the student with the greatest responsibility for discipline. Mrs. Mtshali's regime gave her much opportunity to be cruel if she wished. Instead, she exercised restraint.

A girl who was a junior at Shawbury when Winnie was head prefect recounted vividly a particular incident. One of the school's strictest rules was the banishment of Xhosa from the premises. Whether in private conversation or in the classroom, students were to speak English, for this was the language, they were told, a young person must imbibe to succeed. This girl was deep in conversation with a friend, in Xhosa, when she looked up to find Winnie standing nearby. It was clear that she had been there for some time. Momentarily, she and Winnie made eye contact. And in that flash, Winnie communicated, without words, that she would not dream of meting out punishment, that such a role simply did not fit her.[8]

Thus stands the figure of the antiauthoritarian Winnie. Her relationship to power – as one who exercised it, as one who fought it – became her most mercurial quality.

. .

Winnie told another fiction about her time at Shawbury, this one puzzling and hard to interpret.

At Shawbury, Winnie recalled, she was confronted for the first time by the dilemma of whether to become involved in politics. Her teachers were members of the Non-European Unity Movement (NEUM), a far-left organization founded in Cape Town that had recruited with much success among Transkei teachers through their professional body, the Cape African Teachers' Association. Political talk was very much in the air.

Nineteen fifty-two was also the year in which the ANC and its allies launched its Defiance Campaign, a nationwide programme of civil disobedience led by the charismatic young Johannesburg lawyer Nelson Mandela. Winnie recalled news of the campaign circulating among the students and an ensuing debate about whether to boycott exams in support of the defiance. She faced a terrible choice, she recalled. When the school authorities heard of the boycott plans, they promised to expel everyone who participated in the action. For Winnie, the prospect of going home to Columbus having been expelled from school, or even with the news that she would have to repeat her final year, was unthinkable.[9]

And so a woman celebrated throughout the globe for her courage sat out the first political action that entered her world for fear of her father. While much of the class refused to sit their exams, she and the rest of the prefect body dutifully wrote theirs.

It is hard to know what to make of this story, for it is untrue. Oddly enough, in 1952, students at Mfundisweni, Winnie's old school, took militant protest action against the authorities. And at other elite mission schools in the Transkei that year, there were reports of NEUM's publication, *The Torch*, being distributed.[10] But there were no reports of trouble at Shawbury in 1952. Classes were not boycotted. The contemporaries of Winnie's whom this author interviewed have no memory of plans to take any action. And upon perusing the school's records, one of Winnie's biographers discovered that everybody in her year took their exams.[11]

There *had* been student action at Shawbury, but in 1950, the year before Winnie arrived. It was not a boycott of exams. In protest against poor food and inadequate accommodation, a group of girls decided to exercise silence at school gatherings; they did not sing hymns in church or say grace before meals. And when mealtime began, they refused to eat. It caused a scandal. A girl was expelled.[12]

One of those who participated in the action became a roommate of Winnie's in Johannesburg in 1955 and told Winnie what had happened. Winnie, she recalled, was entranced by the story; she gobbled it up and wanted to know more.[13] Little did her roommate know that she would take it away and put it in her own biography.

She modified the action, turning a silent protest into a boycott of exams. And although she placed herself in the story, it was as a coward, not a hero.

. .

Winnie told her biographers something else about her time at Shawbury, something far more believable. She was fourteen when she arrived, already tall and strikingly beautiful, and her beauty attracted attention.

Once, on a school outing, she and her companions were passing through a busy market town when a diminutive, middle-aged man approached her.

'Do you know what a pretty girl you are?' she recalled him asking. He put a ten-shilling note in her hand, saying that it was a down payment on bridewealth; Winnie would be his wife once she had 'grown fuller', he said.

It was the famous Khotso Sethuntsa; barely more than five feet high, he was among the most well-known personalities in the Transkei, with a palatial house, more than a dozen wives, and a fabled personal history.

Winnie told another story of being pursued by an older man.

One of her tasks as a prefect, she related to a biographer, was to fetch the keys for the bookshelves from the assistant principal. In passing her the keys, the older man would surreptitiously slip a love letter into her hand.

Winnie was beside herself. She approached her boyfriend for advice, a fellow student, their relationship chaste and consisting largely of an exchange of letters. He was out of his depth; the whole business embarrassed him and left him speechless.

'The assistant principal taught us three subjects,' Winnie recalled, 'and after those notes I could not learn from him. I could tell neither my father nor . . . Mrs. Mtshali,' her father because discussing such matters with him was inconceivable, Mrs. Mtshali because she would simply beat Winnie on the grounds that she had 'provoked the sin in the assistant principal's heart'.

Her schoolwork suffered. When Columbus saw her declining grades, he was furious. He had great plans for Winnie, he said, and now they might have to be abandoned.[14]

As Winnie came to remember it, her beauty was a source of great danger. She had no armour against lascivious men with authority. And the damage they could do to her cut deep.

When did this change? Whence did she gather the material to turn her beauty from a source of vulnerability into a wellspring of power?

This is among the most important questions to ask of the young Winnie Madikizela.

The evidence is scant. But there is a trace, slight but suggestive. It is contained in an offhand comment she made to a biographer in the late 1980s.

'Our teachers', she explained, while talking of her growing political awareness at Shawbury, 'were members of the Non-European Unity Movement and I was influenced by them. But I also read about the ANC in *Zonk!* magazine.'[15]

This memory cannot be right; from its inaugural issue in 1949 to the time Winnie came across it in 1952, the pages of *Zonk!* do not contain a single reference to the ANC; it was a steadfastly antipolitical publication, which, as one historian has put it, pretended 'that apartheid did not exist'.[16]

But that Winnie was reading *Zonk!* at Shawbury is of great interest. The magazine was founded by a white man, Ike Brookes, who, as an army lieutenant in World War II, recruited black soldiers to serve as entertainers for the troops. When the war ended, and his ensemble was facing unemployment back in South Africa, its members asked him to form a civilian performance group. The result was *Zonk!,* a stage show that toured the country with breathtaking success, playing to an estimated 1.5 million people before being turned into an iconic movie.[17]

From the stage show and film came the magazine *Zonk!* Its inaugural issue featured a full-page photograph of the black American actress Lena Horne.[18] Horne was famous among urban black South Africans. *Cabin in the Sky* (1943) and *Stormy Weather* (also 1943), two films in which she starred, were watched by township audiences over and over again throughout the 1940s.[19]

What one would give to know which issues of *Zonk!* Winnie saw. Perhaps it does not matter, for they all shared something vitally important: they pictured women. And these women were not just beautiful and groomed; what they were *doing* was being beautiful and groomed; they were choreographing themselves to be seen by a camera.

Perhaps Winnie saw the 1952 *Zonk!* with a shot of Eartha Kitt in a full-length ball gown that tightly followed the contours of her hips and her thighs, or the 1951 edition with a woman posing for a portraitist, one leg resting provocatively on a chair.

'I had to become a city girl, acquire glamour,' Winnie was to tell a reporter, 'before I could begin to be processed into a personality.'[20]

That transformation might well have begun, if only inchoately, at Shawbury in 1952.

. .

While Winnie was completing her final year at Shawbury, Columbus was making great plans for her and her younger brother. Although they were numbers five and six, Winnie and Lungile were the first of Columbus's children to walk through the doors of an institution of higher education. For Lungile, Columbus planned study at the University of Fort Hare, for Winnie, a three-year course at the Jan Hofmeyr School of Social Work in Johannesburg.

Why did he choose a university for the boy, a vocational school for the girl? From remarks Winnie made in a letter to Nelson years later, it seems that she was bitterly disappointed at Columbus's choice and perhaps even quarrelled with him. She was, it seems, chafing heavily against the idea that her gender sentenced her to a lesser education.

Columbus was not exceptional in this; the ambitions of the most illustrious black families at this time were highly gendered. The first

black woman to qualify as a doctor in South Africa did so just five years
before Winnie finished high school,[21] and it was not until 1967 that a
black woman was admitted as an attorney.[22] The rare exception aside,
teaching, nursing, and social work were the professions available to
elite black women in mid-century South Africa.

Given how gendered the world of work was, Columbus's ambitions
for Winnie were not inconsiderable. Social work was several rungs
above teaching and nursing, in pay, to be sure, but especially in status.
For one, it was very rare: before the Jan Hofmeyr School opened its
doors in 1941, there was no institution where a black person might train
as a social worker; as a new, modernizing profession, its practitioners
were highly regarded. And that it paid considerably better than teaching and nursing[23] explains why many black men chose it as a profession,
too; in the first decade of its existence, only a third of the Jan Hofmeyr
School's graduates were women.[24] The profession also boasted towering
female role models. The most illustrious black woman in South Africa
at that time, regarded with reverence in elite households – a woman
who had gone to America and come back with a university degree,
indeed, the first black South African woman to acquire a degree – was
a social worker, Charlotte Maxeke.[25]

The correspondence Columbus must have started with the founder
and principal of the Jan Hofmeyr School, the Reverend Ray Phillips, is
lost, but he surely went to great lengths to get his daughter admitted.
For the school was extremely reluctant to take prospective students
still in their teens.

'We have already refused several . . . applicants for admission . . .
on account of their youth,' Phillips wrote three years before admitting
Winnie to his institution. 'We cannot receive boys and girls of 16–18
years of age who have never been employed and whose experience of
life is very meagre.'[26]

Winnie was sixteen when Phillips gave her a place at Jan Hofmeyr;
she was among the approximately 10 percent of applicants admitted
each year. Columbus Madikizela must have pulled his weight to get his
daughter into the school, informing the principal, one imagines, that he
was not only himself a school principal, and thus a fellow educational
leader, but a distinguished member of the Transkei Bhunga.

And the price, too, was steep – £15 a year for fees and another £20
a year for board and lodging, a total of about £1,130 in today's values.
While Columbus forked out the money for six months of Winnie's

studies, he asked her to do her absolute utmost to try and win a scholarship to pay for the rest.[27]

.   .

When successful Madikizela men are questioned about the course
of their lives, it was noted earlier, they start in the nineteenth century;
their individual stories, they insist, should be placed in an epic journey
across time. Through his two most promising children, Columbus was
investing in the next stage of that journey.

Columbus wanted *his* children to cut the next portion of the trail.
Between him and his cousin Walter was a great rivalry. It was not visible
on the surface of life. Those on Walter's side of the family remember
Columbus as a garrulous man. But beneath the bonhomie was something quite different. Walter's son, Prince, recalls that his father did not
permit him to attend the school at which Columbus was principal, for
he was certain that in the fierceness of the family competition Columbus would hold back his son.

And Prince recalls something else, too. To be chosen as a leading
Madikizela child was to have the greatest burden placed on one's shoulders. It was not just that *everyone* knew you were going to university.
Everyone *watched*. Your progress was communal business. When you
came home for the holidays, your presence was noted. Wherever you
went, no matter to whose home or to which church, you were asked
how you were doing in class.[28]

The memory is as uncomfortable as it is pervasive, as vague as it is
important. But if one talks to them for long enough, everybody raises
it – Winnie's sisters, Winnie's cousins. Lungile did not last at Fort Hare.
He returned home ill, long before completing his degree. And his illness was not in his body but in his mind, and he did not ever recover.
He would be diagnosed with schizophrenia and interned at a psychiat-
ric hospital.[29]

Decades later, when this author asked one of Winnie's sisters about
the events that marked her childhood, she replied, unbidden, 'My
brother Lungile fell ill.'[30] It must have been a catastrophic episode in
the history of Columbus's family, the son marked out for greatness falling as he did. It has become a beacon, a moral lesson, and everyone
takes from it what they will. The scale of Columbus's ambitions had
driven his children insane, it was whispered among Walter's family.

An immediate consequence of Lungile's breakdown was that Winnie was left as the foremost of Columbus's children. It is improbable that he imagined this role for a daughter.

He did not live to see how far and wide she would take the family name. Nor did he see her defend it with her considerable might. 'I was not going ... [to] be known as Mandela's wife,' Winnie reflected toward the end of her life. 'They were going to know me as Zanyiwe Madikizela.'[31]

JOHANNESBURG

. . .

Chapter 7

On a weekday morning in the autumn of 1941, Nelson Mandela – twenty-two years old, just a few weeks in Johannesburg, and ill at ease – walked into the offices of a black estate agent. At his side was a relative, Garlick Mbekeni, who was helping Nelson find his feet.

A few days earlier, Mbekeni had asked Nelson what he wanted to do.

He wanted to become a lawyer, Nelson had replied, betraying, with those words, that despite his expulsion from Fort Hare, despite the regent's rage, despite the many tentacles the regent appeared to cast across this vast city, tentacles Nelson and Justice were at their wit's end to escape, his ambitions had not dimmed. For a twenty-two-year-old black man fresh to Johannesburg to declare that he wanted to become a lawyer was to declare that he wanted the world.

Mbekeni, himself a modest street hawker, suggested a path that must have seemed improbable. He would introduce Nelson not to an attorney, nor to a lecturer at the university, but to an estate agent. Walter Sisulu, Mbekeni said, knew all there was to know about Johannesburg and could connect anybody to anybody else.

What Mbekeni apparently did not tell Nelson was that in addition to being an estate agent and a supremely well-connected man, Walter Sisulu was steeped in politics; he was, indeed, several years hence, to abandon his estate agency, abandon any livelihood at all, in fact, to throw himself, heart and soul, into full-time political work.

When Nelson and Mbekeni walked into the outer office of Sisulu's suite, a young black woman looked up from her typewriter. While Nelson himself was to use tamer language when he recalled this moment later, it is clear that he felt a bolt of desire. What drew him was not her body or her face, nor the clothes she was wearing, but 'her pretty fingers dancing on the keyboard'. He had never seen a professional typist before; in the government and business offices he had visited in Umtata, he had observed white men bashing two fingers against their keyboards. That the business of typing could conjure black feminine elegance – a young woman using all ten fingers with such consummate speed – 'amazed' him. Before he had even met the estate agent, his introduction to Sisulu's world – one of thoroughgoing black modernity – had provoked the most urgent feelings.[1]

He might well have been equally surprised by the appearance of the man waiting for him in the inner office. Walter Sisulu was just six years older than Nelson. He was short and light-skinned, and while his clothes were certainly presentable – he wore a double-breasted suit – he seemed to dress simply for form's sake, without paying special care. But once he opened his mouth and began to talk, Nelson was more than impressed: he was intimidated. For in Sisulu's manner of speaking was a confidence, a versatility, as if the city outside his window, a *great* city that Nelson could not yet fathom, were at his command. And the outer office through which Nelson had just passed was full of waiting clients; Sisulu was a man people wanted to see, a man who was *busy*.

.   .

What did Sisulu see when he laid eyes on the young man from the Transkei?

Sisulu understood in a flash, he was to say later, that the man before him had a role to play in politics. 'He [struck] me more than any person I had met.' He was 'a godsend'.[2] Elsewhere Sisulu says that Nelson 'answered my hope, my aspiration . . . If he had not come back the next day, I would have gone looking for him.'[3]

Sisulu was responding to a powerful intuition, and the content of any intuition is difficult to express in words. But it is important to try.

One thing about Nelson, so obvious that there is a danger of dismissing it, was his height and his beauty. Had the young man who walked into Walter Sisulu's office looked like Walter Sisulu – short, stocky, a little awkward – it is unlikely that he would have excited the estate agent much. Instead, what confronted him was 'this young, strapping, budding attorney, with shoulders as wide as an air force carrier', as a perceptive observer of Nelson Mandela has put it.

But it is one thing being tall and good to look at. What one does with one's body and one's face is another. From the age of twelve, Nelson had lived in a world of aristocrats, a world that was never quite his; he had looked on with the anxiousness and the observational power that only an outsider has. His own aristocratic bearing was *made;* indeed, it was long and painful in the making.

Nelson, the same perceptive observer has noted, was *plus royaliste que le roi* – more kingly than the king.[4]

And the thing about the one more kingly than the king is that his aristocratic bearing is born from *neediness;* he requires recognition from others, and from this requirement comes charisma. Observing Nelson in his office, Sisulu clocked an amalgam of a great many things: his height and his looks, his royal pedigree, his studies at Fort Hare, his desire to become a lawyer. But what he stressed above all when he looked back on this moment was Nelson's *warmth.* He saw Nelson addressing a room, or indeed, a large crowd, and he saw everyone in that crowd loving Nelson.

There is an old Christian concept, its meaning obscured by subsequent uses. It is the concept of 'grace'. Grace is a bit like luck, but even more elusive and strange. It is the benevolence God chooses to bestow upon a person, unearned, without regard to merit.

Nelson was a recipient of a secularized form of grace. From the moment he got to Johannesburg, men older and wiser than he noticed him and picked him up; they bestowed benevolence upon him in heaps. Sisulu was the first, but others would follow. Nelson did not entirely earn this attention. It was simply a question of who he was – a combination of the biological inheritance that made him look as he did and the biography that made him behave as he did.

His first decade in Johannesburg was tough, as we shall soon see. He was to be exposed repeatedly to the cruelties of white supremacy – meted out upon him personally and upon the countless people with whom he brushed shoulders. These cruelties might have crushed him, as they did many, or they might have produced in him a politics of rage. That they produced the Nelson Mandela the world came to know is in part because of the excitement men like Walter Sisulu felt when they met him.

. .

Regarding their origins and their upbringing, Nelson Mandela and Walter Sisulu shared a great deal. The sharp differences in their respective trajectories are thus all the more interesting, each man launched into adult life by his unique responses to the same world.

Like Nelson, Sisulu was a Thembu from the Transkei, and although he was not a royal, he was raised in a home of relative privilege. The person ultimately responsible for his upbringing – not his biological father (Sisulu was in fact the illegitimate son of a white bureaucrat), but his father de facto – was the headman of the village in which Sisulu was raised, Qutubeni, the leader of his clan, and in charge of the affairs of the entire district of Engcobo. He was also an Anglican lay preacher. And so, from his earliest days, Sisulu was exposed to courtly Thembu politics, to missionary influence, and to good education.[5]

Some children are so willful and irreverent, so sceptical of the adult world, that it is hard to fathom from whence they come. So it was with Sisulu. In a childhood that was largely happy and filled with adult love, he was beaten, for the first time, for his inquiring mind. At home, there were prayers in the morning and prayers in the evening; at school there was endless Bible study. His head filled with biblical narrative, little Walter once piped up, no doubt aware that his question was cheeky, if God created the world, who created God?

'Because they couldn't answer this, they didn't like the question,' Sisulu recalled much later. He was taken aside and thrashed.[6]

From early Sisulu was undazzled by the grand edifice the adult world presented. And his scepticism was ubiquitous; it extended to those who offered him affirmation. At school, for instance, his white teacher took a shine to him. Suspecting that she liked him only because he was the lightest-skinned child in the class, he spurned her favour with contempt.[7]

It was his unwillingness to subordinate himself that caused a dramatic turn in his fate. He was fifteen or sixteen years old and in Standard Five, the equivalent to America's seventh grade. He was involved in a fight. A teacher witnessed the commotion and instructed that the names of those who were fighting be taken. Sisulu decided on the spot that he would not go back to school to be beaten. He does not elaborate on this teacher's character, but the prospect of being bent over and caned by a person he did not respect was clearly intolerable.

And so he upped and left, joining a group of young men heading to Johannesburg to work on the mines, young men who, unlike Sisulu, had little prospect of completing their schooling. He was choosing to go forth in the world barely educated, opting for a harsh, working-class life other boys in his position of relative privilege avoided like the plague.

The contrast between Sisulu and Nelson could not be starker. Nelson was in awe of the adult world and idealized it. He was, as a result, a *good* boy and was rewarded for his compliance by flourishing in elite schools and attending university. Sisulu walked around with hackles raised. He was untamable. And so he ended up on the mines.

. .

If Sisulu had been rebellious back in the Transkei, his exposure to the racism of Johannesburg made him positively ungovernable. Deemed too young to work underground, he got a job at a dairy that supplied the mines with milk. The work was punishing: seven days a week, he woke at 2:00 a.m. to prepare for the 6:00 a.m. milk drop, rest for a few hours, and then prepare for the milk drop that began at 4:00 p.m.

Within months, he had quarrelled with his white employer. Almost certainly unused to a young black teen who talked back to him, the dairy manager beat Sisulu with a sjambok – a long, stiff whip made from animal hide. Sisulu promptly went to the police station to lay a charge of assault. When the policeman on duty learned that the perpetrator was the complainant's white employer, he slapped Sisulu across the face, threw him in a cell and sent word to the dairy manager to fetch him. And so Sisulu walked out of his job and soon found another as a domestic worker for a senior mine official; within weeks, his new employer had accused him of eating the meat set aside for the dog, and Sisulu was fired.[8]

The first few years of his adult life went like this; he drifted from one white employer to another, but could stomach none.

He befriended intellectuals during the course of his wanderings and was introduced to books that would mark him: Booker T. Washington's *Up from Slavery*, for instance, and W. E. B. Du Bois's *Souls of Black Folk*. He read them as an autodidact does, painfully slowly and with scrupulous care. While he found Du Bois's politics more congenial, Washington's personal journey mesmerized him. And of all the elements in this astonishing tale, the one that impressed him most was of the young Washington, newly enrolled as a student at the Hampton Institute after an impossible odyssey, washing each evening his only set of clothes. For years, Sisulu's mother, Alice – who had been regaled with this story more often than she could count – referred to young men who always appeared in the same clothes as Booker T. Washington.[9] One of those young men was almost certainly Nelson Mandela.

Still a young man, barely in his mid-twenties, Sisulu began getting to know well Johannesburg's most influential black men. Such an unusual personality – this youngster of high Thembu pedigree with all the pride and dignity his upbringing bequeathed to him, and yet also little educated, his experience of adult life closer to that of an illiterate worker than a noble – he was *sui generis*, and he turned heads. Soon he was close to Selope Thema, editor of *The Bantu World*, the largest black-readership newspaper in the country; to A. B. Xuma, an American-trained medical doctor and ANC leader; and to Govan Mbeki, a militant communist who had recently visited Johannesburg from the Transkei. By 1940, aged twenty-seven, he was steeped in Johannesburg's politics and girding himself for a life of activism.

It was with his wits that Sisulu freed himself from subservience to white people. In 1939, he and four other black men opened an estate agency serving the property markets of the two areas of Johannesburg where black people could hold title deed, Sophiatown and Alexandra. The career he had found was highly attractive. For one, he was self-employed, a rare situation for a black man at that time; for another, his capacity to connect with anyone and everyone made him an effective businessman.

There was a Jewish legal firm in town, Witkin, Sidelsky and Eidelman, with a large black clientele. In addition to offering legal services, the firm had a side business; in partnership with a small-time money-lender, it sold credit to prospective black house buyers. Black people struggled to raise mortgages, and so the legal firm and its money-lending partner had a captive market. This is where Sisulu came in. He brought his credit-hungry clients to the firm and received a commission for each one who signed up for a loan.[10]

When Nelson Mandela walked into Walter Sisulu's office announcing that he wanted to be a lawyer, Sisulu heard him out, leaned back in his chair and looked Nelson over carefully. He knew just what to do, he said finally. He would talk to Lazar Sidelsky about taking Nelson on as a law clerk.[11]

Nelson was awed by Walter Sisulu, and in the time ahead his awe grew. Johannesburg, we shall soon see, had robbed him of his self-confidence. And Sisulu was one more reason to feel insecure. When he began at Fort Hare, Nelson was told that he had arrived at the pinnacle of black achievement; the certificate one received when graduating was a license to lead one's people. Now, here, in this illegible city, was a barely educated man 'who towered above me in almost everything'.[12] He walked out of Sisulu's office feeling that he did not begin to know what he did not know.

Chapter 8

When Nelson arrived in Johannesburg in 1941, the city was changing dramatically. World War II had been on the go for nineteen months, and the wartime economy's demand for labour had brought unprecedented numbers of people to the city. Until now, black South Africa had been a largely rural population; as late as 1936, only 17 percent of black people lived in a city for any part of the year. By 1946, the black urban population of Johannesburg was double what it had been in 1930.[1]

From this influx arose new forms of life, like the vast shack settlements born on the edges of the city and a massively expanded blue-collar workforce. Nelson took his place among the young activists aspiring to mobilize these new urban masses into a political movement. The increased numbers of urban blacks also triggered fear among whites – blacks began to outnumber them in urban South Africa for the first time in 1946 – leading to the surprise election in 1948 of the National Party with its doctrine of apartheid.

All of this lay ahead. In his first encounter with it, the city offered Nelson a cruel face. He had not arrived on the best terms; his only connections here were with Thembu people, and he was on the run from no one less than the regent to the Thembu throne. Wherever he went, news of his misdeeds followed. He worked for a short time as a night watchman at a mine before his trouble with the regent led to his being fired; then he moved in with a Thembu family that evicted him the moment it learned what he had done.

Eventually, Nelson was taken in as a tenant in the home of a Mr. and Mrs. Xhoma and their six children in Alexandra township. He rented a tin shack in their backyard; it had a dirt floor, no running water, no heating and no electricity.[2]

As for the world beyond the Xhoma property, Alexandra was a wild place. Packed to overflowing with recent arrivals to the city, it was, as

Nelson would discover to his horror, barely governed and very dangerous. And its most glaring, its most aggressive, its most unapologetically
visible residents were its adolescent boys and young men. There was
no escaping them – they were *always* on the street – for many neither
worked nor went to school.

When Nelson arrived in Johannesburg, urban South Africa was still
shockingly ill-equipped to host a large black population. The number
of black high schools across the Witwatersrand – the thirty-five-mile
reef of gold along which Africa's largest urban agglomeration had arisen
– could be counted on the fingers of one's hands. Shortly before Nelson settled there, it was estimated that of the ninety thousand school-
age black children on the Witwatersrand, eighteen thousand were in
school. The majority of the rest were on the streets.

There is a word in South Africa's urban lingua franca for the boys
who owned the streets: *tsotsis*. The term is derived from the Sesotho *ha
tsotsa* – to sharpen – and describes the shape of the trousers they wore.
When viewed from head to toe, they were inverted pyramids: a wide-
brimmed fedora worn with waistcoat, tie, and trousers that tapered into
ankles so narrow wearers were said to have to smear Vaseline on their
legs to get them off. The fashion arose when the film *Stormy Weather*
was screened in Johannesburg's black townships in the early 1940s and
spread through the city like a firestorm.

Indeed, American film saturated the *tsotsi* world. In *tsotsitaal* –
'tsotsi language', literally – the word for a gang was *resnj*, derived from
'ranch', describing a group of cowboys gathered around a cattle post.
If a boy's name was Humphrey, he would be called Bogart; if his name
was James, he would be Jesse James; if he was John, he would be called
Dillinger.

Young men interpreted the movies they saw to express their hostility to white South Africa; their heroes were the baddies – bank robbers,
rogue Indians who slaughtered white men, Hitlerian German soldiers.
One street gang was called Gestapo, another the Apaches, still another
Mau Mau.

Given that there were only a handful of cinemas accessible to
black people across Johannesburg, the influence of movies is astonishing. Boys who could afford to go to the cinema would enact what they
had witnessed on-screen to large audiences. The crowds of secondhand
movie watchers at times swelled into the hundreds.[3]

These were young men born and bred in the city, young men who refused point-blank to do the backbreaking manual work people from the countryside were coming to Johannesburg to perform; young men whose aspirations were sophisticated and thoroughly middle-class, but whose lack of education and distaste for blue-collar work confined them to the streets.[4]

In the eyes of such young men, Nelson was no prince; he was a lowly rural, his gentlemanly air a cause for scorn. And Nelson was terrified of them. He came quickly to understand that they were unpoliceable. The most notorious of the gangs, the Msomis and the Spoilers, ran protection rackets, casually taking money, in broad daylight, from respected businessmen two or three times their age.

Nelson himself was an easy target for their violence. There was a gang in his area of Alexandra called Thutha Ranch. *Thutha* means 'collect' or 'take away', and they were so called because when they pillaged your house, they left with everything. Late one night, in his shack in the Xhomas' backyard, Nelson was woken by voices outside. As he listened, he learned, to his horror, that two men were arguing over whether to break down his door. One voice was pleading for Nelson: 'No, man, this chap has no money, nothing, he's just a student.' But the other voice was insistent. Nelson listened intently, awaiting news of his fate.

The voice of reason finally won out; the aggressive one reluctantly conceded that there was probably little to steal. He was so angry he had lost the argument that he gave Nelson's door a furious kick. The bolt snapped and the door gaped open.[5]

.   .

He was dirt poor. When he started work as a clerk at Witkin, Sidelsky and Eidelman, he earned £2 a month, £125 in today's values. Just the bus fare between Alexandra and the centre of town stole more than half his wage; and then there was still rent to be paid to the Xhomas and food. On the days he had no money for the bus, he would walk the twelve miles to work in the morning and twelve miles back in the evening.[6]

Once, after work, on the bus back to Alexandra, Nelson sat down next to a well-dressed young man – the wide hat, the tapered pants – and the young man edged away, making sure that Nelson's worn-out jacket did not touch his clothes.

'It was painful, you know, it was painful,' Nelson recalled.[7] And although he is here freely acknowledging his hurt, retrospect is a great tamer of difficult feelings. 'The humiliation, the anonymity ... of Johannesburg was more of a shock probably than Mandela's ever been able to describe,' his authorized biographer once reflected.[8]

Chapter 9

Witkin, Sidelsky and Eidelman was not a large firm. Aside from the three partners, there were, on the day Nelson joined, two white secretaries, a white articled clerk, and a black man named Gaur Radebe. As she showed him around the office, one of the secretaries told Nelson proudly that at *this* firm there was no colour bar: Nelson and Radebe would drink tea with the rest of them. And then she explained, delicately, that she had bought two new cups specially for the black men and that they were to drink only from those cups. Finally, she asked that Nelson convey all of this to Radebe.

Nelson dutifully reported the information about the new cups to his black colleague, whom he did not know from Adam, a short, chunky man about a decade his senior. From the look that came over Radebe's face, Nelson understood that already, his working life not an hour old, there was to be trouble. 'I will show you what to do,' Radebe told him briskly. And he strode across the office, Nelson meekly in tow, took from the tray a white person's cup, made his tea, and drank it in full view. Nelson, beside himself with anguish, abandoned his tea and retreated to his office.[1]

These racial knife cuts were to become quotidian at Witkin, Sidelsky and Eidelman. They could strike at any moment, as quick as a flash. Once, Nelson was dictating a memo to a white secretary when a client walked in. Embarrassed to be seen taking instruction from a black man, she pushed some money into Nelson's hand and ordered him to go out and buy her a bottle of shampoo.

These experiences were wounding – he remembered them all until well into old age – but hovering above them was the benign and protective spirit of Walter Sisulu. For Gaur Radebe, the cheeky native who drank from the wrong cup, was a friend and a comrade of Walter's, and when Sisulu sent Nelson to work for Lazar Sidelsky, he was, unbeknown to Nelson, delivering him into Radebe's care.

Radebe was as extraordinary, indeed, as inexplicable a man, as Sisulu. Also an autodidact – he had just seven years of formal schooling – he was widely read and supremely eloquent, in English, to be sure, but also in an array of African languages. He was deeply involved in Johannesburg's politics and a member of the Communist Party of South Africa. Two years after Nelson met him, he mobilized the residents of Alexandra to boycott their buses and walk to work; he also co-founded a trade union among the Witwatersrand's mine workers, an initiative that would lead, in 1946, to one of the most famous strikes in the country's history.

Radebe also dabbled as a playwright. The year before he met Nelson, his play *The Rude Criminal* was performed at the Bantu Men's Social Centre, a venue for Johannesburg's black elite. The play opened with an actor dressed as a policeman bursting into the theatre and demanding of members of the audience their passbooks. Many audience members, who had no prior experience of a theatre that broke the invisible wall between performers and spectators, mistook it for a real raid and fled.[2]

It is hard to exaggerate the influence Radebe wielded over Nelson for the next two years. In his relations with whites, Radebe was more than self-assured; he was positively provocative. Once, when Nelson returned from yet another errand on behalf of Sidelsky, Radebe reminded his white boss that Nelson was a *royal*. 'You sit there like a Lord whilst my chief runs around doing errands for you,' he said. 'The situation should be reversed and one day it will, and we will dump all of you into the sea.'[3]

Radebe was also the first to begin instructing Nelson in the tools of analytical thought. Nelson went home in the evenings with books Radebe had suggested he read; lunch breaks became the occasion for impromptu tutorials. This autodidact, his formal schooling scant, made the Fort Hare boy his pupil.

'I had taken two courses in modern history at Fort Hare,' Nelson recalled, 'but . . . Gaur Radebe . . . learned not just the facts, he was able to get *behind* the facts and explain to you the causes for a particular viewpoint.'[4]

That it was a black man who introduced Nelson to critical thought is important. In years to come, Nelson met white and Indian communists, and their analytical prowess impressed him deeply. But it is doubtful that in 1941 and 1942 he had the psychological facility to learn from people who were not black, for their knowledge would have been poisoned by the racial hierarchy through which it was transmitted.

· ·

Until now, Nelson had been employed at the firm as a clerk. If he was to qualify as a lawyer, the firm would have to change his status to that of candidate attorney, for this practical apprenticeship was a compulsory component of one's training. Nelson had not even considered whether his boss, Lazar Sidelsky, would change his status thus until Gaur Radebe raised the matter in the most dramatic fashion.

'My boy,' Nelson recalled Radebe saying, 'as long as I am here these chaps will never article you. I am interested in you being articled because it means a great deal for the future of our struggle in this country – I am going to leave. I do not know what is going to happen to me.'[5]

Radebe was nominally employed at Witkin, Sidelsky and Eidelman as a messenger and an interpreter. But in reality he was the firm's conduit to its black clientele. He had surmised that his continued employment at the firm would make the second black man, Nelson, redundant. He gave up his job so that Nelson could stay.

It is a remarkable moment; were it not for the fact that Walter Sisulu confirmed its veracity, one might question Nelson's memory. Nelson had done no more than flirt with political activism by the beginning of 1943. That Radebe was surrendering his livelihood because Nelson's legal career meant 'a great deal for the future of our struggle' is cause to stop and think about all manner of things. The words 'grace' and 'luck' do not quite do justice to what was happening to Nelson. The seas were parting before him. These wise, gifted men had *chosen* him, and now they were moving heaven and earth to clear his way.

Chapter 10

Nelson did not last long in Alexandra. By the spring of 1942 he had moved in with Walter Sisulu and Sisulu's mother and sister. They lived in Orlando, a settlement ten miles southwest of the city centre created less than a decade earlier.

Like so much of the geography of black South Africa, the meanings Orlando emits are complex and contradictory. On the one hand, it offers the first traces of the nightmare to come. For Orlando was an Orwellian distortion of the idea of the 'garden city', a self-contained community, surrounded by greenbelts but close to work – the best of the countryside and the city rolled into one.[1]

In reality, Orlando was none of these things. 'It was like travelling back a century, across treacherous roads, to this desolate city,' a British journalist wrote upon visiting for the first time. 'I looked around at the rows of small box houses, like a giant chicken farm.'[2] And these rows of identical houses were really all there was: no tarred roads, no electricity, no waterborne sewerage. Out of sight, beyond the edge of the city, designed to be sealed off in a flash in case of rebellion, it was built *to be administered*.

And the houses themselves could barely be called modest. When the Sisulus arrived in 1934, they found a place without the basic innards of a home: no toilet, no working kitchen, indeed no floors, just the same dirt ground as in the tiny yard outside.[3]

And yet Orlando – and the locations that would grow around it, the composite becoming Soweto – was never reducible to the sterility of its conception. Its inhabitants were offered thirty-year leases and thus a place in the city. Upon this foundation a whole world developed. The matchbox houses would host the same families from one generation to the next; ordinary men thus became urban patriarchs, ordinary women presiders over urban families. Women and men of the professional classes – nurses, teachers, social workers, lawyers, doctors – made

homes there, and from the sameness of the houses the force of respectability glowed. Young couples who fell in love found in Orlando a structure to house their union and call their own.

On this 'giant chicken farm' the whole ensemble of black middle-
class modernity took form.

· ·

The Sisulu home was perhaps the most convivial Nelson ever knew.
Long after he had moved out, he kept coming back, at times every day,
to sit and talk and take in its spirit. His most important political friendships formed there. Aside from Walter, another young man, Oliver
Tambo, whom Nelson had known vaguely at Fort Hare, was always
at the Sisulus. He became Nelson's law partner and lifelong comrade.

But there was considerably more than politics in the Sisulu home.
Sisulu's mother, Alice, presided, and she adored Nelson and Tambo
alike. She and Tambo were both devout Anglicans; they went regularly
to church together, the two of them. As for Nelson, he was 'like a son of
the family', Sisulu recalled.[4]

The house was always full, for family from the Transkei were forever coming to stay, some for short visits, others for years; each night,
the furniture in the living room was pushed against the walls to make
space for people to sleep.[5] Among the long-term visitors were Sam
Mase, a nephew of Alice's, and his younger sister, Evelyn. By the time
Nelson arrived on the scene, Sam had married, and he and Evelyn had
moved to a house in Orlando East, but they visited often. Within days
of meeting each other at the Sisulu home, Nelson and Evelyn Mase
were 'going steady', as Evelyn would put it, and within months they
were married.

· ·

Long after it had all ended so badly, Nelson and Evelyn both
refused to speak of their courtship. There is an amusing scene in the
rushes of a documentary about Nelson from the early 1990s. The film-
makers have persuaded Evelyn to interview. She sits before the camera,
petite, groomed, and supremely proud. Her interviewer asks her to tell
of how she and Nelson met and fell in love. 'No,' she replies curtly, and
stares ahead, waiting for the next question.[6]

And Nelson, when asked by the ghostwriter of his autobiography to describe his courtship with Evelyn, similarly refused. 'It is sufficient to say that I met Evelyn in 1944, fell in love with her and we got married,' he declared. Clearly alarmed, the ghostwriter suggested diplomatically that the publisher would not be happy. 'Just tell them to phone me, you see,' Nelson replied, 'and I'll speak to them.'[7]

And yet Nelson and Evelyn's courtship speaks volumes. 'I think I loved him the first time I saw him,' Evelyn confessed some time before she stopped talking about the matter. The Sisulus' home was so warm, so generous, she recalled, and all sorts of young men flitted in and out. But once her eyes alighted on Nelson, the others dissolved from view.[8]

Everything suggests that their connection was urgent and erotically charged. Evelyn was more than four months pregnant on the day they married on October 5, 1944, which may account for why they wed so discreetly and so utterly without ceremony. They simply went to the Native Commissioner's Court in downtown Johannesburg, where a nameless bureaucrat married them.

We know so little about that day. Did Walter Sisulu come along to witness the marriage of his exciting new friend? Was Sam Mase there? In the same year, Sisulu married Albertina Thethiwe, a nurse who would become a leading figure in the struggle against apartheid; they threw a grand feast. Nelson was best man. He was outrageously handsome that day; wrapped in a pin-striped suit of thick, coarse cloth, an outsized arrangement of white flowers on his lapel, his presence eclipsed that of the poor groom. What he wore to his own wedding we do not know.

October 5 was an ordinary working Thursday. One might take the liberty to imagine Nelson and Evelyn boarding a train in Orlando that morning and heading into town. Perhaps Walter and Sam Mase took off work that morning to accompany them. Perhaps Alice Sisulu came, too. The little retinue would have walked the busy streets en route to the Native Commissioner's Court. Young, good-looking and well groomed, the bridal couple would have made enough of a spectacle to turn the head of the odd passerby.

They chose not to wed in community of property, a striking sign of the modernity of their union. Not that either had anything to hoard. Nelson was working as an articled clerk for a pittance, and Evelyn was in her final year of nursing school. Between them, they hadn't the funds to start a new home.

It is hard to exaggerate how much this story conveys. Nelson was an aristocrat. He came from a world in which marriage signified, above all, an alignment of lineages. To be sure, he was marrying the most eligible of girls: Evelyn was a beautiful young Thembu, a relative of Sisulu's, and a nurse; she oozed respectability. But the marriage upon which they embarked would have been foreign to Nelson just three or four years earlier. The bare bureaucrat's courtroom, the absence of his mother, Nosekeni, or the regent's wife, Noengland.

This wedding was unwitnessed by Nelson's family and unsanctified by tradition.

It was about the two of them. It was an act of romantic love.[9]

. .

At first, Nelson and Evelyn could not afford a place of their own; they occupied a room in Evelyn's sister's house on the grounds of City Deep Mine. Nelson went off to Witkin, Sidelsky and Eidelman in the mornings and to law classes at Wits University in the late afternoons. Evelyn found a low-paying job on the mine, earning just £7 a month. As a part-time articled law clerk, Nelson now earned £8 a month; had they not been living rent-free with family, it is uncertain how they would have made ends meet.[10]

On February 23, 1945, Evelyn gave birth to a son, Madiba Thembekile Mandela. 'Madiba' was Nelson's clan, and the naming thus signalled recognition of the addition of a new generation to a lineage. Nelson, in Evelyn's recollection, was over the moon. He had arranged for her to give birth at Bertrams Nursing Home, and he arrived there shortly after his son was born, bearing nighties for the mother and clothes for the boy. When Evelyn returned home, she found in their single room a cot Nelson had bought for their child.

Evelyn probably did not stay at home with Thembi for long; Nelson was earning little, and the couple relied heavily on what Evelyn brought home. She soon found a far better-paying job with the Johannesburg City Council; she would work as a nurse at the city's General Hospital, earning £14 a month, double what she had earned at the mine.[11]

Her salary freed them from their borrowed room in City Deep; shortly after she began her new job, they moved to a two-room house in Orlando East, and then, in early 1947, to a three-room house, 8115 Orlando West.

Nelson and Winnie were to make that address famous. Today, thousands of tourists visit each year; it is something of a shrine.

'The house was identical to hundreds of others built on postage-stamp sized plots on dirt roads,' Nelson writes in his autobiography. 'It had the same standard tin roof, the same cement floor, a narrow kitchen and a bucket toilet at the back ... The bedroom was so small that a double bed took up almost the entire floor space.' He went on to say something that has been quoted countless times: 'It was the opposite of grand but it was my first true home of my own and I was mightily proud. A man is not a man until he has a house of his own.'[12]

This is among the more unfortunate of Nelson's recollections. It was Evelyn who secured their residence at 8115 Orlando West because of her position as a city-council nurse. The house was clearly marked with a large sign: 'Nurse' in English, 'Mooki' in Sesotho, signalling that the woman who lived there provided a public service.[13] The lease was in Nelson's name only because of the patriarchal mores of the time.

Nelson had married a woman of extraordinary Christian industry. Evelyn was just two years old when her father died and twelve when her mother passed away. She spent the following five years living with an uncle. She thus knew, as Nelson did, what it was to lose one's world at a tender age; she understood the wherewithal required to regroup on unfamiliar ground. When she moved to Johannesburg in 1939 to join her brother, Sam, in the Sisulus' Orlando home, she was seventeen years old, her education very much incomplete. By the time Nelson met her five years later, she had obtained her Junior Certificate and had almost qualified as a nurse. She had come to the city with a painful past behind her, an uncertain future ahead; she had put her head down and worked.[14]

After he married her, Nelson became the primary beneficiary of her industry. She found him a house, bore his children, paid the lion's share of his rent, and, more often than not, paid for the groceries in his cupboard. She never forgot this; indeed, she would come to believe, with some justice, that she was among the few who remembered.

. . .

In 1948, tragedy struck the young family. Evelyn had given birth to a second child the previous year, a girl. They had called her Makaziwe. She was nine months old when she died. Nelson was to say that she had

been sickly from birth. Evelyn remembered that she contracted menin-
gitis without warning and quickly died.

More than two decades later, in a letter from prison, Nelson wrote
for the first time of her death.

'I managed to see her during the critical moments when she was
struggling desperately to hold within her body the last sparks of life
which were flickering away,' he wrote. 'I have never known whether I
was fortunate to witness that grievous scene. It haunted me for many
days thereafter and still provokes painful memories right up to the
present day.'[15]

There is no record of how Evelyn dealt with the death of her
daughter, nor of the consequences of the tragedy for her and Nelson's
marriage. Evelyn was to give birth two years later to a son, Makgatho.
The name the couple chose was significant. Sefako Mapogo Makgatho
was an early leader of the ANC legendary for the campaigns of civil
disobedience he led. In naming their son after him, the couple was
choosing a Pedi, rather than a Xhosa, name, which was highly unusual
and thus a bold statement of Nelson's growing commitment to African nationalism.[16] Indeed, one can only imagine that they named the
child thus at Nelson's insistence; it was very much an expression of *his*
preoccupations.

Four years later, in 1954, amid the death throes of their marriage,
Nelson and Evelyn were to have another daughter; this child they were
to call Makaziwe, the same name as the girl who had died. Might it be
that Evelyn got to choose this time? Was it that she still mourned her
daughter and hungrily took the newborn girl as a means to heal? It is
impossible to know.

. .

Back in the mid-1940s, when they moved from their borrowed room
at City Deep to Orlando, the advent of a place of their own brought
something else: family. The first to come and live with them was Nelson's sister Leabie, who enrolled at Orlando High School. The next
person to visit for an extended period was Nelson's mother, Nosekeni.
She came in 1949. She had not met Evelyn or her grandson, Thembi;
neither, it seems, had she seen Nelson in a very long time.

The reason for her visit was illness, ostensibly so, at any rate; she
had wanted to consult doctors in the city. But the moment she arrived,

Evelyn noted that she was not so much ill as 'weak and distraught'. Her problem, her daughter-in-law surmised, was that she had missed her son. Back in Nelson's presence, she recovered her health and thrived. She stayed a long while 'and filled our house with a gentle authority', Evelyn later recalled.[17]

Nosekeni had some mental adjusting to do, for her son had adopted new ways. When Makgatho was born, Nosekeni was astonished to learn that Nelson was not planning to slaughter a beast, a custom practiced since time immemorial announcing the infant's arrival to his ancestors. She tried to insist. But Nelson was equally stubborn, and it was he who prevailed. 'I have left those customary things,' Evelyn recalled him saying to his mother. 'I will not do them.'[18]

The greatest beneficiary of Nosekeni's presence, it appears, was her daughter-in-law; with another woman to share the burden of childcare, Evelyn was free to pursue her interests in public and professional life. It is not that Nelson refused to play a part. He took great pleasure in his children; nothing pleased him more than bathing the babies in the evenings;[19] and visitors to the house noted that he was a demonstrative father, forever holding and hugging his children.[20]

But Evelyn had done the lion's share of the work, and with Nosekeni in the house she had freer rein in the world outside. After her mother-in-law moved in, she became increasingly involved in the Nursing Union.

Moved especially by the yawning pay gap between white and black nurses, she 'threw my weight behind' the issue, as she would recall, attending several public meetings.[21] And, in 1952, with Nelson now earning a living as a lawyer and Nosekeni there to take care of the children, Evelyn went to Durban for an extended time; she had a long-held desire to study midwifery, and now she did so, enrolling in a course at King Edward VIII Hospital.[22]

There is no record of Nosekeni's feelings about her daughter-in-law. But it appears that she placed much store in Evelyn's presence in Nelson's life. When the marriage began falling apart, Nosekeni would do her utmost to keep it together, and once she understood that she had failed, she packed up, distraught, and returned to the Transkei. Indeed, the breakup would inflict wounds on many people and they would take forever to heal.

Chapter 11

Around the time he met Evelyn, Nelson threw himself at politics. He was asked countless times what drew him into a life of public commitment; he offered different answers at different times. The most candid is in the memoir he secretly wrote from prison. 'The process of deciding was not simple and straightforward,' he wrote. 'I often realised the full implications of what I had done, not before, but after, taking the first step.'[1]

In the mid-1940s, three rival trajectories lay before him. He might have returned to the Transkei to play the role in Thembu royal politics for which he had been groomed. As Walter Sisulu remembers it, this possibility lingered in Nelson's mind for years. There was no single moment when he *decided* against it; he simply understood, at some point, that he had ventured too deep into something else to contemplate a return.[2]

He might also have remained in Johannesburg, kept out of politics, and built his legal career. There was no shortage of people urging this course upon him. Foremost among them was his employer, Lazar Sidelsky, who warned him, prophetically, that if he did not shake off Gaur Radebe's influence, he would go to jail.[3] A lawyer's vocation was an enormously tempting prospect. In the mid-1940s, Nelson aspired to become more than an attorney; he wanted to become the first black advocate at the Johannesburg bar, the South African equivalent of a barrister. There is little doubt that the most illustrious career lay before him.

But he was drawn – neither consciously nor unconsciously, but in that strange zone in between ('I often realised the full implications not before . . . but after,' he said) – by the two men he had come to admire most, Gaur Radebe and Walter Sisulu. It is well to describe things exactly thus: that he was borne into politics by admiration; for this is often how it works, especially in a young man like Nelson, so practiced, by now, at emulating others, and so prone to idealizing what he esteemed.

They were deeply ensconced in his life by now, both of them. While Radebe still worked at the law firm, Nelson spent every weekday with him from morning until late afternoon, for the two men shared an office. And the Sisulus were his adopted family: he was a son there; he met his wife there; their home was his centre of gravity.

He had a front-row seat to the lives of two men who had given themselves over to politics. He could see right before him what was possible.

And, as odd as it may sound, he perhaps chose politics in part because of his desire to *live*. His marriage to Evelyn was extravagant in its boldness. There was little in his past quite like it, and so its future was unpredictable. Perhaps he entered politics in a similar spirit. It set him on a path equally without precedent. He might not know what his choice would bring, but he had brought it on himself: he had *acted*.

But it is of course not enough to say that he admired Sisulu and Radebe, nor that he wanted to act. For what did he admire them? And to what end did he wish to act? It is difficult to answer such questions about Nelson Mandela because he has been so assiduous in shrouding his anger. But he was extremely angry and we can get a glimpse of its intensity, especially when we turn to his experiences as a law student at Wits University.

· ·

Studying law at Wits in the mid-1940s was an intimate business. There were only thirty-five students in the entire law school when Nelson arrived and only one full-time professor, a recent immigrant from Germany named H. R. 'Bobby' Hahlo.[4] Nelson was not just the only African student in his class: he was the first African law student in the university's history. And Hahlo made no bones of his prejudices. No sooner had Nelson arrived than Hahlo encouraged him to leave and instead study by correspondence through the University of South Africa; the study of law, he told Nelson to his face, was not suitable for women or for black men.[5]

Nelson started at Wits in 1943 and finally left in 1949 without a degree. To his dying day, he insisted that he alone was responsible for his failure. And it is true that Evelyn's income, together with loans he had acquired, freed him to study full-time from 1947; his escalating involvement in politics during this period must account in part for his poor results. But a major contributing factor was the racism he was up against at Wits. It is not just that the rules and rhythms of the place were designed to make him feel alien; while black students could sit in the same lecture theatres as whites, they were not permitted to use the university swimming pool, nor to participate in any of its sporting codes, nor to attend formal social occasions like university dances.[6] More than that, the university showed little sensitivity to the conditions under which Nelson had to study, conditions that arose because he was black.

The law school had a fail-one-fail-all rule; candidates had to pass all of their courses for a particular year of study to get credits for any of them. Those who failed one or two courses could sit them again in a supplementary examination. But those who failed three would have to sit the entire year again.

Nelson wrote exams for his final year three times, in 1947, 1948, and 1949. At first, he failed all six subjects; on his second attempt, he failed four. Finally, in 1949, he passed three subjects – Law of Mortgage and Pledge, Conflict of Laws, and Civil Procedure; he had failed Jurisprudence, Delict, and Law of Evidence. He applied for permission to break the two-supplementary-exams rule and sit for the three courses he had failed. In his application he explained that he was deep in debt and was unable to pay the following year's fees; if the university did not allow him to sit the three supplementary exams, he would never get the degree. He also pointed out that he lived in Orlando, where there was no electricity and he was forced to study by the light of a paraffin lamp. Orlando, he added, was a long commute from Johannesburg: 'I . . . returned home after 8 p.m. tired and hungry and unfit to concentrate on my studies.'[7]

The university said no. Hahlo advised Nelson to abandon his law degree, thus giving up his aspiration to become an advocate, and instead sit the examination to qualify as an attorney, which is what Nelson did.

He was gutted. And he was bitter. Evelyn recalled him fuming about 'people at [Wits] University . . . blocking him from becoming an attorney'.[8] And a friend remembered Nelson wishing upon Hahlo that he would one day be forced to write by paraffin lamp in Orlando.[9]

He later expunged such feelings from his repertoire; those who harbour deep grievances can hardly reconcile.

.   .

As instructive as his relationship with the Wits authorities were his interactions with his fellow students. In 1943, the year Nelson began studying at Wits, a group of left-wing students, most of them white and Indian communists, formed an organization called the Federation of Progressive Students. Among them were people who would become lifelong comrades of Nelson's. There was the Greek immigrant George Bizos, who would become Nelson's lawyer and close friend; Harold Wolpe, who escaped from jail and fled into exile in 1963, saving himself from a life sentence; Ismail Meer, whose future wife, Fatima Meer, wrote a biography of Nelson; Joe Slovo and Ruth First, who, in very different ways from each other, became leading figures in exile, and whose marriage, Nelson and Winnie's aside, became the most spoken about in South Africa's liberation movement.

But all of this lay ahead. How these people seemed to Nelson when they were still strange to him speaks volumes. Decades later, during a conversation about other things, Nelson was asked about Ruth First. His talk suddenly became very animated, and in his excitement he bypassed hindsight and saw First as if he were just getting to know her all over again.

'She was not the type of white', he recalled, 'who was progressive when she was with you in a room, or away from the public. If she met you in one of the corridors of the university or in the street, Ruth will stand and talk to you, very comfortable, in a very relaxed manner.'[10]

That this is noteworthy enough to recall nearly half a century later tells us so much of what Nelson experienced. And it is even more illuminating to compare Nelson's recollections of First with First's memories of Nelson. He was 'good-looking, very proud, very dignified, very prickly, rather sensitive, perhaps even arrogant', she recalled shortly before she was assassinated by agents of the South African government. 'But, of course,' she added, 'he was exposed to all the humiliations.'[11]

One can imagine Nelson hiding behind his height, his grace and his looks, haughty and distant, even to Ruth First, the rare white person who put him at ease. Day in and day out for seven years he walked those corridors and sat in those classrooms; it must have been exhausting.

. .

In 1946, Nelson's fourth year at Wits, a young Jewish military veteran called Jules Browde enrolled as a law student. As Browde sat waiting for his first class to commence, Nelson walked in. 'He was a strapping man,' Browde would recall, 'very tall, handsome.' And while Nelson, the only black person in the room, searched for a seat, 'everybody was looking at him – some secretly, some not trying to hide it'.

Nelson spotted an empty chair next to Browde and made his way toward it. The moment he sat down, the student sitting on the other side of him, a thick, broad-shouldered man, made a great show of getting up and finding a place across the table.

Nobody said a word. The professor walked in and the class commenced.

Browde introduced himself to Nelson when the lecture was over. Neither mentioned what had happened in that moment before the class began. The two became friendly and had sporadic professional dealings with each other over the coming years.

Nearly half a century later, when Nelson was president of South Africa, he hosted a lunch to which Browde was invited. It was a large affair; several hundred people attended. At some point, Nelson scanned the crowd, caught Browde's eye, called him over and asked him to arrange a reunion of their law class.

'And, Jules,' Nelson added. 'Do you remember, when I came into the class . . . and sat down, the man next to me got up and went and sat on the other side of the table?'

Browde remembered the incident clearly. The man's name, he told Nelson, was Ballie de Klerk.

'Please see that you ask *him* to come,' Nelson said.

'Why?' Browde asked.

Because, Nelson replied, he wanted to remind De Klerk of what he had done those many decades ago. 'I don't mind whether he says he remembers or he doesn't remember. Because I want to take his hand,' and at this point he took *Browde's* hands, and he held them in his. 'And I want to say, "*I* remember. But I forgive you. Now let's see what we can do together for the good of this country."' [12]

Nelson never got to take the hand of Jan Adriaan Enslin 'Ballie' de Klerk, for De Klerk was dead.

Some might take this story as an example of Nelson's remarkable generosity. But its deepest meaning is surely more complex than that. Half a century later, Nelson had not only forgotten nothing; he felt compelled to *seek out* the one who had offended him and to rub his face in the memory.

Forgiveness seldom wears its deepest motivation on its sleeve. It is hardly a sign that the anger preceding it has vanished: rather, it has been reworked into another state. What remains is the very core of anger: the desire, no matter how gentle and civilized it has become, to avenge. There is one-upmanship in the offer to forgive, a soft triumph, a gentle torturing of the other into a position of compliance.[13]

Nelson remembered everything and his anger was still live. And he *knew* this. He knew this absolutely and he said it with clarity.

'Wits made me what I am today,' he told the audience at the reunion the late Ballie de Klerk did not attend. 'I am what I am both as a result of people who respected me and helped me, and those who did not respect me and treated me badly'.[14]

Chapter 12

When Nelson began studying at Wits, he was barely involved in politics. By the time he left, his political commitment was consuming. But while his activist career started in part *because of* his experiences at Wits, it did not start *at* Wits with its noxious racial atmosphere. It commenced instead in a place that could not have been more comfortable or salubrious, nor more exclusively black – the Sisulu home in Orlando, where a handful of young men, among them Oliver Tambo, Peter Mda, and Anton Lembede, came together to talk. Toward the end of 1943, one of these men, Lionel Majombozi, a medical student at Wits, proposed the formation of the ANC Youth League; it was founded the following year.[1]

All manner of aspects of the mid-1940s inspired the formation of the Youth League. One was World War II. The wartime economy had triggered massive migration to Johannesburg and had swelled the ranks of the city's working class. Trade unions were forming, thanks, in part, to men like Nelson's mentor, Gaur Radebe, and a future mentor, J. B. Marks, and the political allegiances of this nascent labour movement were up for grabs. Everyone on the left was interested in capturing them – the Soviet-supporting Communist Party of South Africa, several of whose members Nelson had encountered at Wits; the Trotskyists who had gathered in the Non-European Unity Movement, the very same movement that had successfully recruited many of Winnie's high school teachers in the Transkei.

'The Youth League formed to warn black workers against both the Trotskyists and the Stalinists,' the league's intellectual lodestar, Peter Mda, would reflect. 'We formed to tell them: your interests will never coincide with white workers.'[2]

But if the Youth League formed to capture the new urban masses, then to what end? The question cut deep; it cut all the way down, in fact, to what the struggle against white domination was for. Its leaders never answered this question with one voice; the signal documents they produced in the 1940s contained rival answers.

South African circumstances made the question difficult. In most European colonial possessions in Africa, the object of the nationalist struggle was to transfer sovereignty from the occupying power to the indigenous people; the point, in other words, was that the occupying power *leave*.[3] South Africa, though, was governed not by an imperialist power abroad but by a settled white population of almost two and a half million people. The question of who precisely belonged to the sovereign entity that would form at the end of white rule was thus more complicated.

From its inception in 1912, the ANC's answer to this question had been steeped in moderation. Its mission was to win rights for Africans within a multiracial polity. At first, this imagined polity was a deracialized British empire, later a national sovereign. But at bottom, black people would join whites in equal citizenship.

Ultimate political goals aside, there was the question of the ANC's style. Until now, the organization had been led by God-fearing Protestant men. Each of its first seven presidents was highly educated; three had university degrees acquired in the United States. Their travels abroad had been life-altering pilgrimages. They had returned with the conviction that they were exceptional people, their relation to their indigenous African heritages often complex and fraught.

Nobody exemplified this genre of African leadership more thoroughly than Dr. A. B. Xuma, president of the ANC from 1940 to 1949. A medical doctor who trained at Northwestern University – he also studied at Booker T. Washington's Tuskegee and at the University of Minnesota, earning his keep in the United States as a stable hand, a domestic worker, and much else besides – he had practiced medicine in Edinburgh and Budapest before returning to South Africa.

In his sartorial tastes, in his manner of speaking, in the music that played on his gramophone, he was less a Xhosa-speaking man from the Transkei than a member of a diasporic black elite. And he believed this membership to be a necessary qualification for a black leader. Those who have studied abroad, he wrote shortly after his return to South Africa, 'are well educated, civilised, and, above all, cultured ... They plead the cause of the Bantu with dignity and consideration.' Indeed, they were 'the safest bridge for race contact in the present state of race relations in South Africa.'[4]

His sense of himself as a civilized cosmopolitan went all the way down. When his Liberian wife died in childbirth, leaving him a single parent of small children, he asked a friend travelling to Wilberforce University in the United States to search for a suitable bride. Soon he was in correspondence with Madie Hall, daughter of a respectable North Carolina family. A couple of years later Xuma and Hall were married and living in Xuma's house in Sophiatown, Johannesburg.

'The moral of the story', the historian James Campbell has commented, 'rests in Xuma's conviction that only in America could he find a wife who shared his perspective and experience, not to mention his social status.'[5]

The young men who formed the Youth League in 1944 were certainly out to escape Xuma's stifling patriarchal spirit. 'We were . . . stuck under the heavy hand of Dr. Xuma,' Peter Mda would say years later. 'We just liked the idea of running our own show.'[6]

When they sent a delegation to his house in Sophiatown with their idea to form a Youth League, he was awfully threatened. He accepted it with great reluctance, chafing against the proposition that it would write its own constitution.

In 1949, five years after he had reluctantly agreed to its formation, the Youth Leaguers ousted Xuma from the presidency of the ANC. They did so brutally, persuading another genteel, middle-aged doctor, the witless James Moroka, to stand against him; they then flooded the floor of the 1949 ANC national conference with their delegates and voted Xuma out.

Xuma is remembered unkindly because the young men who ousted him triumphed and told his story. He was in fact a deeply consequential figure. When he took over as ANC president in 1940, he pulled the organization back from the brink of self-destruction. It was ramshackle, disorganized and broke. Xuma bureaucratized the party, built its branches, restored its finances, and introduced basic bookkeeping. In short, he saved it.[7]

But even while he mended the organization, new forms of politics were emerging; they were creative, confrontational and mass based, and they were not spearheaded by Xuma's ANC. In 1946, a mine workers' strike was brutally crushed; it was led by the Communist Party's J. B. Marks. Also in 1946, the Gandhian tradition reemerged in South Africa – it had indeed begun in South Africa in 1911[8] – as Indians organized a campaign of passive resistance against a new law restricting Asian property ownership.[9] Again, the ANC looked on as a spectator.

Something else happened after World War II, something fated to make the politics of men like Xuma look weak: in 1948, the party of Afrikaner nationalism won a surprise electoral victory. It brought with it to power two generations of resentment against what English speakers had done to Afrikaners, not only in the South African War that ended in 1902, but in all the years since, and it brought to power, too, a great fear of the amassing of black people in urban South Africa.

The ticket on which the National Party had campaigned was called 'apartheid', a term the wider world had not yet come to know. And, in truth, nobody knew at the time what it might mean, not even those who had devised it: it was an embryonic idea, its substance still vague.[10] But clear beyond doubt was that the liberal whites whom the likes of Xuma had been talking to for decades had been pushed from the mainstay of power; the sort of political business Xuma had always conducted was disintegrating.

The Youth League formed because its leaders did not want the ANC to be left behind. More to the point, they did not want *black* leaders to be left behind. The Natal Indian Congress, which had organized the campaign of passive resistance; the Communist Party of South Africa, many of whose officeholders were white: racial minorities, better educated and more confident, were taking the lead in the struggle against white rule. The Youth League wanted African leaders to lead African followers in mass action; they were acting against Xuma, but they were acting *for* their race.

They wanted to lead African followers, but to what end was less clear. They knew the actions they wished to take: strikes, boycotts, campaigns of civil disobedience. But for what purpose?

'Africa was, has been and still is the blackman's continent,' the Youth League's Basic Policy, written in 1948, read. 'Although conquered and subjugated ... the Africans ... will never give up their claim and title to Africa.'

The implications of this statement were far-reaching. For one, South Africa, with its large, settled white and Indian populations, disappeared into the folds of a greater entity, Africa, which belonged to its indigenous inhabitants, the 'blackman'. The implication was that white South Africans were, like the British, French, Belgian and Portuguese imperialists elsewhere on the continent, an occupying force without 'title' or 'claim'.

But the very same 'Basic Policy' says other things. 'Two conditions', it declares, are necessary for 'the achievement of true democracy', the 'removal of discriminatory laws and colour bars' and the admission of the African into 'full citizenship of the country so that he has direct representation in parliament on a democratic basis'.[11] This statement could have come from any previous ANC leader. It imagines South Africa as a pluralist democracy in which all have equal political and civil rights.

For now, the Youth Leaguers could manage the differences between them; they had a common agenda, after all, to bring mass-based campaigns to the ANC. But by the early 1950s, once they had had their way, installing strikes, boycotts and civil disobedience in the organization's programme of action, their differences crystallized into opposing factions, and the conflict between them turned nasty. And the central question that came to divide them – what exactly might it mean to maintain political and social friendships with whites and Indians? – brought to the surface a host of uncomfortable feelings.

. .

For a long while, it was not clear where Nelson stood on these fundamental questions.

While a student at Wits, he rose meteorically through the ranks of the ANC Youth League. He was elected national secretary in 1948 and president in 1950. In these capacities he presented himself as an uncompromising Africanist, implacably opposed to working with other races.

In early 1950, for instance, at a public meeting in Johannesburg, Nelson and a group of other Youth Leaguers physically pulled the Indian leader Yusuf Cachalia from the stage. Nelson, in the memory of one who witnessed the event, the white Communist Party activist Rusty Bernstein, was raw and 'very naïve'.

And yet the bullying, hectoring Nelson was just one of several faces he presented. Just a couple of months later, Bernstein encountered Nelson again. This time he talked to him, engaged with him, met him eye to eye. And he immediately revised his views. The Nelson he had seen pulling Cachalia off the platform had been replaced by a man of obvious subtlety and sophistication.[12]

At around the same time, Nelson hounded another man off a public stage, the Communist Party leader J. B. Marks. And yet even this man, the victim of Nelson's aggression, by no means understood Nelson's thuggishness to be the sum of him. Marks, Nelson was to recall, took Nelson's 'rabid nationalism, anti-communism' to be something of a facade. 'He just kept me close to him and visited me in my house and invited me to his house.'[13]

What exactly was going on with Nelson at this time? There is little doubt that for much of the 1940s, he came away from cross-racial encounters feeling belittled. 'We were dominated by the other groups,' Nelson later recalled, 'dominated by whites [and Indians] who had better opportunities, who spoke better English, who could read, who were more well-informed than us.'[14] At the Great Place, at Clarkebury, at Fort Hare, he had been thin-skinned and prickly, liable to take offense at the hint of a slight; he had been primed, for much of his life, to feel the indignity of condescension.

And yet, as Marks and Bernstein clearly understood, something else was going on with Nelson at the same time.

For one, Nelson had, by now, in fact spent a great deal of time with Indians and whites, many of them communists, and he had done so in settings that were sufficiently relaxed for ideas and feelings to have been shared. In particular, his friendships with his fellow law students Ismail Meer and J. N. Singh had transcended the racial awkwardness of their first encounters. They invited him into their homes, where he broke bread with their friends and families; sometimes, when it got too late for him to go home, he would stay overnight with Meer and talk into the early hours of the morning.[15]

He had also, by now, spent time with Michael Harmel and Moses Kotane, two senior members of the Communist Party, and he had been several times to the house of the newly married Ruth First and Joe Slovo. Such people had influenced him profoundly. Their genre of Marxism offered him his first full-scale exposure to the notion that society was an object to be analyzed. And he found this notion the most powerful he had ever come across. It upended a great deal of what he had thought before. He had been a Christian until now; Marxist thought was putting paid to that.

'Those of us who have been brought up in religious homes ... and modelled their lives on religious principles are grieved when scientific truth forces them to abandon established belief,' he wrote from prison.

'They feel as St. Peter did when thrice he denied Christ . . . As scientific knowledge increases and man masters the natural forces, supernatural beliefs will be correspondingly weakened.'[16]

Through the influence of his Marxist friends, Nelson had become a secular modernist, as so many of the twentieth century's reformists and revolutionaries were. But although he was influenced by Marxist thought, and although he almost certainly secretly joined the South African Communist Party for a brief time in 1960, he was not *possessed by* Marxism. He simply found its analytical acumen *useful*. In this he was not unlike many of the mid-century's anticolonial leaders, taking from the Marxist canon what was helpful while retaining a fundamental commitment to nationalism. In the early 1960s, Nelson would show how brittle his commitment to the Communist Party was, to the chagrin of many of his white and Indian comrades.

Indeed, Nelson's growing ease both with multiracial politics and with Marxist thought in the early 1950s was not a symptom of radicalization; it was more a sign of his growing status and prosperity.

In 1951, he qualified as an attorney. He must have known in the preceding year or two that it was likely to happen, notwithstanding his troubles at Wits. This change brought him illustriousness and fame. Newspapers ran stories of his appearances in court; his attendance at social functions was noted in the social pages of *The Bantu World*. He began to earn a good living as an independent professional, independent, that is, of white employers. He earned the money to buy a car, and thus was saved from the daily indignities Africans suffered on the streets.[17]

Nelson became as elevated, as esteemed – and as insulated from racism – as a black man of those times could be.

Many years later, he recalled with great pleasure the atmosphere at the house of Ruth First and Joe Slovo. They were 'very broad', he said. 'In those days when they were young Communists, and very radical, they had friends amongst the liberals and amongst prominent businessmen and [their] house was a crossroad of people of different political persuasions.'[18]

He *liked* this capacity to be at ease amid a plurality. It excited him greatly. What he admired most in First and Slovo were precisely the qualities he would come to prize in himself.

Chapter 13

It was Nelson's voracious ambition that tipped him over into a formal allegiance with multiracial politics. A rapid sequence of events at the end of 1951 makes this plain.

That December, the ANC held its annual conference in Bloemfontein. A proposal for a Defiance Campaign was tabled; it envisaged tens of thousands of Africans, Coloureds (mixed race), and Indians collectively breaking segregationist laws.

Nelson led the Youth League into the conference breathing Africanist fire; he endorsed the idea of defiance, he said, but Africans should defy alone. Lukewarm applause greeted his speech, and as the conference proceeded, he watched the tide turn against him. And so he did a volte-face; in his closing address, just forty-eight hours or so after his opening speech, he endorsed a multiracial Defiance Campaign with vigour. Nelson, as one scholar has put it, 'had to move forward or he would be left behind'.[1]

He was duly rewarded; in the opening months of 1952, as the ANC prepared to launch the Defiance Campaign, the organization's executive offered Nelson the role of volunteer in chief. Overnight he'd become the face of the most talked-about political campaign in recent history and thus the most visible political activist in the country. He accepted with alacrity.

Offering the job to Nelson was shrewd; with its president fronting a multiracial campaign, the Youth League's Africanism would likely wither.[2] Somebody with cunning had turned Nelson's vanity into a sharp political tool.

Who in the national executive put forward his name is not known. But the street-smart Walter Sisulu was by now the secretary-general of the ANC. His fingerprints are all over the decision.

On the last day of May 1952, three and a half weeks before the launch of the Defiance Campaign, a banquet was held in honour of Nelson's former teacher Z. K. Matthews, who was leaving for a visiting professorship in New York. Nelson, in his capacity as Youth League president, made a speech. He was wearing 'a magnificent brown suit', a person there that night recalled. Exuberant, his head no doubt swollen with the publicity he would enjoy when the Defiance Campaign began, he made a joke that did not go down well. Everyone in the room, Nelson quipped, knew of his ambition to become South Africa's first black president.

In the audience was the ANC's *sitting* president, James Moroka, as well as Matthews, who was the organization's vice president. These men were considerably senior to Nelson, in age, in rank and in gravitas. It was an inappropriate comment in the circumstances, and audible 'murmurs' about this 'little fellow' circled the room.[3]

. .

Less than a week before the launch of the Defiance Campaign in June 1952, Nelson drove to Durban, where he addressed a crowd of ten thousand. His role as volunteer in chief was off to a momentous start; he had never in his life addressed a crowd even a tenth of this size. There is no recording of his speech; nor is there a written description of his delivery. But the words he chose were very dramatic indeed. He told his listeners that they were inaugurating the most powerful action ever undertaken by the South African masses, that they were to make history.

He believed what he said. A contemporaneous note has him saying that the Defiance Campaign would overwhelm the government: either it would give in to the campaign's demands – and they were far-reaching indeed, including the dismantling of the key legislation that made apartheid possible, the Group Areas Act, the pass laws – or in the wake of the campaign the government would be voted out of office.[4]

It is no wonder that Nelson accepted the role of volunteer in chief. And it puts in perspective his tongue-in-cheek remark that he wished to be South Africa's first black president. He believed that he was to lead a campaign in which people would defy segregationist laws in their tens of thousands and that the government would fall.

In the end, the masses *watched* the Defiance Campaign, and while

they did so with awe and admiration, they did not participate themselves, certainly not in the numbers Nelson had imagined. During
its six-month duration, some eight and a half thousand people were
arrested for breaking segregationist laws. Nelson himself was among
the first of them to be jailed; he spent two winter nights in police cells
for defying a nighttime curfew.

The Defiance Campaign was, to be sure, a massive accomplishment. Among the thousands imprisoned were lawyers, doctors and
teachers; black South Africa watched on as the most respectable in its
ranks submitted themselves to prison. As Nelson was to observe much
later, one of the campaign's objectives was to dampen 'the fear of the
white man ... We wanted people to know that they can actually *challenge* injustice and go to jail and still come out.'[5] In the wake of the campaign, people flocked to join the ANC; its membership swelled from
fewer than 20,000 at the beginning of 1952 to almost 100,000 a year later.
The organization's prestige had never been this high.

And yet something happened four months into the campaign, the
memory of which Nelson and his comrades spent subsequent decades
suppressing. Amid the defiance, violence erupted. The first incident
occurred in the city of Port Elizabeth on the southeast seaboard on
October 18 when a railway policeman attempted to arrest two black
men for stealing a drum of paint. The men resisted and a hostile crowd
formed; in his panic, the policeman started shooting his pistol. Within
minutes, an angry multitude some two or three thousand strong had
assembled and during the course of the afternoon cut a path of destruction. By early evening, a lorry and a cinema had been set alight, and four
white men, who had found themselves in the crowd's path, were killed.
The police then descended in large numbers and fired live ammunition, killing seven and wounding twenty-three.

Two weeks later, rioting erupted at a workers' hostel on the outskirts of Johannesburg, and five days after that violence broke out in the
town of Kimberley in the Northern Cape.[6]

A day later, on November 9, the most disturbing incident of all
occurred. In the poverty-stricken township of Duncan Village on the
outskirts of East London, the police broke up a large, open-air meeting
the ANC Youth League had called. The crowd stoned the police, the
police shot into the crowd, and in the mayhem that followed, buildings throughout the township associated with whites – the Catholic
mission, administrative offices, a trading store – were burned to the

ground. How many people died that day is unknown: the official count was nine; unofficial police records show that as many as two hundred might have been killed, most of them by police bullets. It is extraordinary that the incident was for so long largely forgotten, for it is most likely the most lethal massacre of black civilians by white officials in South African history.

Not all those killed were black, however. Among the dead was an Irish nun and medical doctor, Sister Aidan Quinlan, who had established a clinic in Duncan Village three years earlier. She was on a customary Sunday drive when she heard of the disturbances and returned immediately to the township, probably to tend to the wounded. As she made her way to her clinic, a mob surrounded her car, turned it on its side, and set it alight. At what point in the attack she died is unclear, but she was dragged into the street, and chunks of flesh were hacked from her corpse. By the time the crowd was done with her, her arms had been removed from the elbows down and her legs were missing from her hips.[7]

White South Africa responded with revulsion and fear, and in the midst of the moral panic the government took a series of measures that ended the Defiance Campaign. In December, a statutory amendment was passed making deliberate lawbreaking punishable by flogging and by prison sentences of up to three years. In the wake of the new law, none but the bravest or the craziest would defy. And this was just one of a series of harsh measures the government took. Also in December, Nelson, along with fifty-one other ANC leaders, was banned from attending any meeting, from holding office in the ANC, from talking to more than one person at a time and from leaving Johannesburg without permission.[8] Barring two brief periods of remission, he would remain under a host of successive restrictions until he disappeared underground in 1961.

· ·

The manner in which the Defiance Campaign ended raised hard questions. The ANC dissociated itself from the violence; it blamed the killing of Sister Quinlan on agents provocateurs. Shamefully, it had little to say about the scores of black people who had died that day. In later years, Nelson and Walter Sisulu simply did not speak of the tragedy at

Duncan Village; when asked about it, they quickly dismissed it as having had nothing to do with the Defiance Campaign.[9]

But it had everything to do with the Defiance Campaign. The ANC Youth League had toppled the old guard in order to institute a programme of mass action. Now they had done so. And what they learned was that mobilizing ordinary people to end white minority rule was formidably difficult. On the one hand, the vast majority of black people were too afraid to participate in collective action; they might take inspiration as they watched, but no more. And those who did participate were not always amenable to control. Why members of the crowd in Duncan Village took slices off Sister Aidan Quinlan will never be definitively established. The most convincing investigation to date suggests that her flesh was to be used in an occult medicine for the purpose of borrowing her power.[10] Collective action, Nelson and his comrades learned, happens locally, in particular places, and is liable to be seized by local currents whose meanings are impenetrable to national organizers.[11]

Even more concerning to Nelson and his comrades was the ease with which the apartheid government finally ended the Defiance Campaign. It took a single incident, the killing of a white nun, to bring on unprecedented state repression. The moral resolve and coercive strength of the government went considerably deeper than Nelson had thought.

The campaign's greatest lesson, Nelson came to believe in its wake, was that peaceful action would never dislodge apartheid. In 1953, Walter Sisulu was smuggled out of South Africa to attend the World Festival of Youth and Students in Romania. While abroad, he was also to visit Israel, the U.K., the Soviet Union and China. On the eve of his departure, Nelson asked Sisulu to seek Chinese backing for violent revolution.

Sisulu's trip abroad was life changing. He took in Jerusalem, which, for a man steeped all his life in biblical narrative, was meaningful beyond words; he witnessed formal equality among black and white people on the streets of London; above all, he was exposed to the leadership of the Chinese Communist Party. He came away believing them to be among the most impressive people he had met. And what they said about the prospect of violent revolution was positively alarming. 'Revolution is a very serious affair,' they advised him. 'Don't play with it. Don't take chances unless you are really ready for it.' By the time he returned home, Sisulu felt the heaviest burden on his shoulders; turning to violence, he understood, might destroy the movement against apartheid, not just now, but for generations.[12]

Sisulu, Nelson, and others would inaugurate an armed struggle eight years later. Whether the decision was indeed their greatest strategic blunder, delaying freedom by decades, is impossible ever to know.

Chapter 14

At precisely the time Nelson was chosen to lead the Defiance Campaign, he began practicing as an attorney. He started in the spring of 1951 at a white law firm. Early the following winter, he and Oliver Tambo opened their own practice.

He was, finally, a professional, charging clients for his work, and the transformation in his household economy was dramatic. By the end of 1952, Evelyn was saving her entire salary each month; not long earlier, she had been the family's breadwinner. Nelson's income from his new law practice paid the bills, refurbished their home and filled the cupboards with groceries.[1] Indeed, he now insisted on doing the weekly food shopping himself, packing the trunk of his new Oldsmobile with his purchases; in 1951 he had acquired a driver's license, and shortly thereafter he had bought his enormous green car.

His life began to fill with minor extravagances. In addition to the weekly grocery shopping, he took to calling in the late afternoons at an upmarket European delicatessen in town, bringing home for dinner delicacies that in Orlando were considered exotic.[2]

And he began to appear at the downtown premises of Alfred Kahn, tailor of choice to some of Johannesburg's wealthiest white men.[3] In the late 1940s, Nelson had been known for his immaculate brown suit and a white silk scarf that he flung around his neck on winter evenings,[4] but they had been his *only* good clothes; now his wardrobe began to fill with Kahn's bespoke suits.

Within months, the law practice he started with Oliver Tambo was famous, for they immediately opened it to black Johannesburg, to *all* of black Johannesburg. Their clients included both the most auspicious men and women in the city and its lowliest attendants. The law they practiced ranged from high-profile divorces to assault, murder and the infraction of the city's ubiquitous pass laws. Their poorest clients paid what they could, if anything at all.

They worked extraordinarily hard. On Saturdays and Sundays, their offices in Chancellor House on Fox Street were packed with clients; people lined the corridors between the offices and stood in the stairwell outside. For it was only on weekends that clients could get to consult Mandela and Tambo face-to-face. During the week, they were inevitably out of the office, appearing in one of the magistrate's courts distributed across Greater Johannesburg, or farther afield, for their work often took them hundreds of miles from home.

And many of these prospective clients whispered quietly to the firm's clerks that they wanted to be represented by Nelson Mandela, if at all possible, rather than by Oliver Tambo. For while Tambo was quiet and demure, his teeth forever gnawing at a scholarly pipe, Nelson was outsized both in stature and in character.[5]

Indeed, the aura Nelson exuded in court was legendary. 'Everybody took notice of him,' his former clerk, Godfrey Pitje, recalled. 'The prosecutor, the magistrate, the interpreter, the police constable, not to mention the public gallery. All he needed to do was turn around and look up and there was almost a flare around him.' And his court style, Pitje described, 'was hard and harsh and blustery which made him very popular with the black public'.[6] *The Bantu World* took careful note of his court schedule; when he was due to appear before a magistrate, the newspaper would be sure to assign a journalist to record what he said.

When he performed in court, Nelson understood, he was representing black Johannesburg in its battle against those who exercised power. And what he did best – or, what the black audience in the public gallery enjoyed most, at any rate – was to make those who exercised power look foolish. Reading his cross-examinations today can be a little disappointing. It is not hard, after all, for an educated man, empowered by the inequality lodged in the very form of a cross-examination, to embarrass a low-level functionary. But the spectacle it created in the context of mid-twentieth-century South Africa was formidable: this tall, handsome black man, wrapped in the most elegant of suits, mesmerizing the gallery with his mastery of *words*, English words, the weapon par excellence of educated white South Africa.

And so, for instance, when Nelson represented twenty-one women arrested for a public protest in early 1955, he ran circles around the white police officer who had arrested them. He began his cross-examination by asking the officer whether he spoke Zulu, a question that surely provoked a quiet titter in the black gallery, presaging the mortification to come. The women had been arrested for protesting the implementation of the Bantu Education Act, a signal piece in the apartheid government's legislative armoury, enforcing racial segregation in schools.

'Do you know what Bantu Education is?' Nelson asked the police officer. As he fumbled his reply, one can imagine Nelson standing there, his face deadpan, his dignity swelling in increments as the white man displayed the depth of his ignorance of the political system his work defended.[7]

.   .

In the 1940s, the two white-dominated environments Nelson came to know well were the university and the law firm. Now a third had been added: the courts. He flourished there. And what he seemed to enjoy most was the law's formal qualities: its reduction of human intercourse to a set of rules. For one of the worldly phenomena the formal qualities of law dissolved was racism. When Nelson stood to perform, he was in the first instance not a black man but an officer of the court, and the magistrate, the prosecutor and the phalanx of court functionaries were bound by the rubric of their world to recognize him as such.

In no other institution had the very *logic* of the place forced white people to treat him as an equal. At Wits, Professor Hahlo could tell Nelson to his face that law was not a suitable subject of study for blacks and for women. At Witkin, Sidelsky and Eidelman, the unexpected appearance of a client could suddenly cause the secretary to pretend that he was a messenger. When he stood up in court, however, its rules demanded that he be treated as the representative of the accused, no more and no less. And when a magistrate breached the law's code, when he signalled that he was talking to Nelson as a black man rather than to an officer of the court, Nelson exploded.[8]

Law became more than a profession for Nelson. The values embedded in law had enormous significance, he came to see, not just for the freedom they gave him to act in the courtroom but for relationships between human beings in the world. There is little evidence that he had fully imbibed this in the early 1950s, but a decade later Nelson understood that racial domination and the rule of law were uneasy bedfellows. And he saw, too, that white South Africans *valued* the rule of law; drawing attention to the moments when they breached it was thus to expose a contradiction in their very beings. Indeed, that white people had internalized the rule of law, that they valued it, was a feature of South Africa that, by Nelson's lights, would make thinkable a peaceful transition from apartheid.[9]

. .

But being a lawyer meant other things to Nelson, too. And some of those other things were not about equality; on the contrary, they were about aristocracy.

Standing up in a white man's court on behalf of black people made men like Nelson godlike. And so it is unsurprising that in the pages of the black press the fact that Nelson was a lawyer and an aristocrat became linked. By 1955, *The Bantu World* had begun to refer to him habitually as 'a prominent Transvaal attorney and a member of the Thembu royal house', or, incorrectly, as 'the son of a Thembu chief'.

And that Nelson was tall made the connection all the more natural, for the Thembu royal family was *notoriously* tall; indeed, reporting on their height became de rigueur in *The Bantu World*. When Daliwonga Matanzima's younger brother, George, visited Johannesburg, the fact that he was in town, and that he stayed not just with anyone but with Nelson Mandela, was important enough to find a place in the newspaper's pages. 'Mr. Mandela and Mr. Matanzima both stand six feet high,' the report on the visit gushed.[10]

Nelson *enjoyed* this new status. More than enjoyed it, he wore it; it began to shape his demeanour and his relationship with others.

Among the most instructive testimonies about Nelson at this time is that of his law clerk, Godfrey Pitje. During an extended stay in Johannesburg, Z. K. Matthews and Albert Luthuli, two of the most eminent figures in the ANC, used the post office box of Mandela and Tambo to have mail forwarded from their respective homes. Once, they arrived at the office and informed Pitje that they had urgent mail; would he please hurry to the post office to get it. Pitje returned to find Nelson Mandela fuming; how dare he leave the office without permission, Nelson raged. Pitje apologized and put it down to an error of judgment. This was not enough for Nelson; he ordered Pitje to write the apology as an affidavit and sign it under oath.

In the wake of this incident, Pitje grew enormously wary of Nelson. He was a candidate attorney; his admission to the roll would depend upon a recommendation. Lying in Nelson's drawer was an affidavit, coerced from Pitje, that could be used against him should Nelson ever feel the whim.[11]

Neither was Nelson's aristocratic mien evident only in his role as a lawyer and a boss.

In the early 1950s, Nelson took up boxing; in no time, it became something of an obsession. Given how frantic his life had become, it is remarkable not just that he carved out the time for it – he spent ninety minutes in the boxing gym four evenings a week, and on most mornings began his day with a predawn run – but that he kept at it, religiously, seldom missing a day's training, for a decade. What did it mean to Nelson to box?

The outstanding feature of boxing in mid-century black South Africa was its wholesome and egalitarian dignity. Wholesome because it could be contrasted to the brash honour of a gangster, and the township gangs of those times loomed large in people's minds, their violence dominating the newspaper headlines every day. And egalitarian because the dignity it conferred was available to everyone.[12] Nelson understood this and he delighted in it. 'In the ring,' he remarked much later, 'rank, age, colour and wealth are irrelevant. When you are circling your opponent, probing his strengths and weaknesses, you are not thinking about his colour or social status.'[13]

And yet, even here, in an environment he entered with the express purpose of becoming one of the boys, he was unable to leave his aristocratic spirit at the door. 'He thought that boxing made him an ordinary man of the people,' his close friend and comrade from that time Joe Matthews said, 'but he always stuck out, no matter how hard he tried.' Indeed, 'the fellows he was with in the boxing fraternity never called him Nelson ... You never got a kind of intimacy with a man like [him].'

When his interviewer pressed Matthews on why exactly Nelson could never become ordinary, he reached for the two qualities everybody at that time seemed to clock about him: his height and his royal pedigree.

'He was too tall, for a start,' Matthews offered. 'And then the royal family people ... tend to be very strict, you know, and when they enter a room, they really stand out ... [T]he children who grew up in the royal household, perhaps through no fault of their own, everybody defers to them.'[14]

Nelson remained forever touchy about the preening, haughty persona he had presented in the 1950s. Four decades later, when he was sitting for a documentary film on his life, his interviewer joked that he had been something of a dandy back then. Nelson frowned and changed the subject. The moment the camera was turned off, he gave the interviewer a dressing-down. 'Your comment so incensed me,' one of those who was in the room recalls him saying, 'I was mindful to call off this film there and then.'[15]

Chapter 15

It is hard to conceive how Nelson found the time for all he was doing. While he worked his law practice at full throttle, so too did he work his political career.

In later years, Nelson, along with many others, would dress the political campaigns of the 1950s in romantic garb, obscuring just how fractious ANC politics was. The organization was deeply divided, and its conflicts were rancorous and personal.

When Nelson took up the offer to lead the Defiance Campaign, he made adversaries of those who believed that Africans should organize alone. The most formidable among them was Peter Mda, the undisputed intellectual heavyweight of the Youth League. When Nelson, Walter Sisulu and Oliver Tambo embraced multiracial politics, Mda and those who followed him were faced with a choice: leave the ANC or contest it from within. They chose the latter, staying in the organization for another six acrimonious years.

Mda's distaste for the role of whites and Indians in the struggle was visceral, their presence, he believed, comprehensively destructive. South Africa's racial order had handed them a battery of resources denied to Africans. 'They could get funds,' he recalled later. 'They had a powerful propaganda machine in the communist press.' Africans went into alliance with them in part for the embarrassment of riches they offered – offices, printing machines, money, and, more intangibly, an old and deep capacity to organize.

The price, Mda believed, was the obliteration of African politics. South Africa was colonized; its struggle was principally one of the indigenous masses against those who had occupied their land. And white and Indian leftists *were* occupiers, notwithstanding the radical veneer of their politics. They were frightened by the prospect of black people getting up to their own devices; they were instinctively suspicious of mass action unless they themselves commanded it. Africans who worked with them were involved in an act of surrender.

At a deeper level, Mda believed, it was not just for their resources that Africans made allies of other races. It was for their approval. Many middle-class Africans felt diminished by the colour of their skin. They hankered after the recognition other races might offer. And this handed the tiny minority of whites and Indians who participated in the struggle inordinate influence.

'Communists had a way of pumping a man up,' Mda said later, 'flattering him, making him feel as though he had ideas, making him feel like a messiah even greater than Marx. They achieved extraordinary results.' They also offered something primal and much harder to put into words. 'If you went along with them,' Mda added, 'you would get the opportunity of dancing with white girls, going to parties, even kissing white girls ... We ... couldn't offer any of these advantages.'[1]

Mda is referring to the famous multiracial parties held at the homes of white communists in the bourgeois suburbs of Johannesburg, the kinds of parties Ruth First and Joe Slovo hosted. There was music and dancing. Plenty of drink was on hand. Although the First-Slovo home had no swimming pool, the homes of other white communists did, and in the summer guests would disrobe, put on swimming trunks and convene around the pool.

In later years, many of those involved would be at pains to play down the transgressive excitement of these events. Nelson himself was positively coy. He did not go to parties much, he said, when asked about these gatherings; he preferred to stay at home and read.[2]

But however much he and others wished to dampen the meanings the parties emitted, they were undeniably explosive. The response of Nelson's law clerk, Godfrey Pitje, when he first attended one of these occasions makes for a powerful tale.

'You would find a young black man lying side by side with a young white girl sharing peanuts or whatever,' he recalled, 'and this was not the kind of scene or sight I was used to ... I don't know how to describe my feeling, it is a feeling of revulsion, what the hell is going on, what are blacks doing with whites here, what is the basic thing here, is there something behind this?'[3]

Mda's excoriating commentary on these parties was not levelled at Nelson in particular. The two men in fact remained friends, despite their differences. Indeed, at some point in the mid-1950s, all three of

Mda's children moved in with Nelson and Evelyn for several weeks while their parents were away.[4] But it remains to be asked whether Mda's criticisms hit their mark.

That Nelson reversed his publicly held views in order to lead the Defiance Campaign is not in dispute. And that he did so in service of his searing ambition is more than plausible. But whether he was surrendering his personality to those he considered his racial superiors is another matter. Most striking about Nelson at this time was his remarkable plasticity. He was a haughty Thembu aristocrat. He was a lawyer cloaked in dignity and fine thread. He was a revolutionary sending signals to foreign governments that he wanted arms. And he was making close friendships across the chasm of South Africa's racial divide.

In the decade since his arrival in Johannesburg, Nelson had developed an enormous range. And in each of the many spheres he moved, he was somebody else. In his capacity to embody the spirit of the world he happened to inhabit, whatever that world might be, lay the seeds of his later genius.

Mda nonetheless illuminated something important. In the late 1970s, an attentive scholar searched with great care for social distinctions between those in the ANC who turned to multiracialism in the 1950s and those who did not. At first, she found little to separate them: they were all lettered, mission-educated people. And then she stumbled upon something else. The Africanist leadership of the 1950s consisted overwhelmingly of schoolteachers. Among those who embraced multiracialism, in contrast, there was a preponderance of lawyers and doctors. Schoolteachers worked for the apartheid state and were thus, in a profound sense, chained to it. Lawyers and doctors had not only escaped the state as an employer: they had escaped all whites as employers. They enjoyed an autonomy so unusual in urban South Africa as to be remarkable.[5]

Mandela, Tambo, Sisulu: they had a license, a freedom to roam, both materially and in spirit, denied to all but a couple of hundred black South Africans. Their political and social capaciousness was surely an expression of this unusual freedom. It remains to ponder: Who would Nelson Mandela have become had a couple of guardian angels not paved the road to his legal career?

The four years that followed the Defiance Campaign witnessed many failed projects: to boycott government schools and establish an alternative education system; to mobilize residents of Sophiatown to resist their forced removal. But there were also successes, and between them they secured the ascendance of multiracial politics in the late 1950s.

The first was a choice of leader. In the wake of the Defiance Campaign, the ANC got rid of James Moroka, who had embarrassed himself during the campaign, and elected as its president Albert Luthuli, a devout Christian whose commitment to a multiracial South Africa was sophisticated, original and philosophically deep. As the 1950s waned, he became an exalted national figure. He went on to win the Nobel Peace Prize in 1960 and in his Nobel lecture painted a vivid portrait of a multiracial South Africa.[6] In many ways, the Nelson Mandela to emerge from prison in 1990 was a Luthuli-like figure, bearing the aura of a society not yet born.

Among the campaigns Luthuli shepherded was the writing of the Freedom Charter. The original idea was to assemble a Congress of the People, truly representative of all South Africans, to write a new constitution. As the campaign proceeded, its ambitions were scaled down. Volunteers spread out across the country gathering from ordinary people scraps of paper on which they had written how they understood freedom. As might be expected, some of the suggestions were eccentric; one man said that his definition of freedom was to have ten wives.

In the end, nearly three thousand delegates attended a gathering at Kliptown, outside Johannesburg, on June 25 and 26, 1955, where they adopted the Freedom Charter, a document written hurriedly in the preceding days. Nelson, who was banned, could only watch the gathering stealthily from the edges of the crowd. The charter's opening line – 'South Africa belongs to all who live in it, black and white' – raised the hackles of the ANC's Africanists, and they rallied immediately against it. For them, South Africa did not belong to all who lived in it; it belonged to the indigenous population.

Who knows how the battle between the Africanists and the 'Charterists' would have played out had the government not blundered? On December 5, 1956, Nelson and 155 others were arrested and charged with treason on the grounds that the aim of the Congress of the People had been to overthrow the state. The ensuing trial, which dragged on for four years, the Treason Trial, would become among the most famous in South African history.

On the one hand, it was a catastrophe for the accused. The hearing convened in Pretoria every day for months on end. Holding down a job while attending an interminable trial was well-nigh impossible. The black press was strewn with stories of the children of defendants going hungry, of aunts and uncles giving up work to become child carers, of careers shutting down.

Nelson himself paid a bitter price. For a whole epoch in his life, it dominated his days. He woke long before dawn each morning to travel to Pretoria, returning to Johannesburg as the sun went down. At night and on weekends, he tried to attend to his clients. It was, in the end, a futile battle; as the trial dragged on, his attorney's practice slowly eroded.

And yet, for all the personal suffering it caused, the trial was a gift for those in the ANC who championed multiracial politics, and it was a curse for the Africanists. Day after day, a display of distinguished South Africans of all colours, on trial for their principles, dominated the news. In households across the country, the grace of these leaders and the eloquence of their lawyers became quotidian fare. The state's case, in contrast, was often farcically poor.

On the eve of the mass arrests, the celebrated essayist Can Themba wrote, the Congress movement was in decline. Overnight, it had 'become famous and real ... [People say] they now know their Congresses are representative bodies of the people.'[7]

It was the last major error the government would make for a while. In the years to come, it would hone a methodical ruthlessness few in the Congress movement anticipated.

Chapter 16

As his law career flourished and his activism deepened, Nelson Mandela's marriage fell apart. It did so with drama and with pain, wounding many bystanders – his mother, his children, the Mases, the Sisulus.

The life Evelyn must have imagined when she married Nelson may seem conventional to us now; together they were to build a *professional* household, he a prospective lawyer, she a nurse. It is difficult to exaggerate the sense of distinction the idea exuded in Orlando in 1944.

'It was almost like their home had an aura around it,' a woman who grew up on their street in the late 1940s and early 1950s recalled. 'Many adults in the neighbourhood one got to know well because they were around, on the streets, visiting our home. Nelson and Evelyn: one did not see much of them; they left early and returned late. They were *working*.'[1]

From Evelyn's vantage point, Nelson tore this household down as they were building it. It is not just that he was consumed by his political commitments; it is that he chose these commitments over two of the fundamental roles he ought to have played in their home. The first was paterfamilias. Nelson supported the family financially when he began to earn a good living. And there are many witnesses to the affection he showed his children. But by the early 1950s his presence in their lives was sporadic. As an elderly man he would recall overhearing his five-year-old son, Thembi, ask Evelyn, 'Where does Daddy live now?'[2]

And politics stole Evelyn's husband in another way, too: as a monogamous romantic partner. For it is not just that Nelson had lovers; his affairs were with political activists, and for Evelyn this was painful beyond forbearance. Politics had taken *all* of her husband: the father of her children and the lover in her bed.

Talk about Nelson's affairs among Johannesburg's black elite assailed Evelyn's honour. Peter Mda's son, Zakes, recalls how his mother and her friends spoke of Nelson in the mid-1950s. Referring to him as Nel or Nelly, they giggled. 'Nelly' was 'a ladies' man', they said. Zakes, a prepubescent child, hadn't a clue what a ladies' man was, but given the excitement Mandela instilled in his mother and her friends, he aspired to be one, too.[3]

References to Nelson's reputation as a playboy entered formal politics, too. At an ill-tempered meeting of the Transvaal ANC in 1953, for instance, Nelson accused a group of Africanists of conspiring against him.

Among them was Ellen Molapo, a famously beautiful widow. In the face of Nelson's charge, she stood up to speak.

'How can I be against Mr. Mandela,' she asked, 'when he left his hat in my house?'

The conference broke down in thunderous laughter, leaving Nelson not just embarrassed but disarmed.[4]

Evelyn was tortured by Nelson's affairs. Once, in 1953, when Nelson was giving a female colleague a lift to work, Evelyn protested in the street in front of the car, eventually forcing Nelson's passenger to get out and find another way to town. She also threatened to take the matter of his love life to the National Executive Committee of the ANC, for she believed that he was besmirching both his marriage and his organization.[5]

In February 1955, the acrimony between them took the nastiest turn. In Nelson's account, a former police detective he knew, a man named Edward Majola, came to him with news that shocked him to his core. For some time now, Evelyn had accused Nelson of having an affair with the ANC Women's League leader, Lilian Ngoyi. Now Ngoyi was about to embark upon an overseas tour. She planned to leave the country without a passport, for she was a prominent activist and if the authorities caught wind of her trip, they would stop her.

Evelyn, Majola informed Nelson, had told him of Ngoyi's plan and urged him to report her to the police; had he done so, Ngoyi might well have gone to jail. Evelyn also gave Majola £6 to pay a diviner for a substance to sneak into Nelson's food that would rekindle his love for her.

When Nelson heard what Evelyn had done, he left the marital bed and set up makeshift sleeping quarters in the dining room. And he resolved not to eat food that she had prepared.[6]

The situation was ghastly; at war with each other, they shared their tiny house, day in and day out, their children an audience to their mutual rage. They were to live like this for more than a year, until March 1956, when Evelyn finally left; she moved first into the nurses' quarters at the hospital, then to her brother Sam's house in Orlando East, leaving the children, for now, to be cared for by Nelson's mother, who had come to Johannesburg to try to mend the marriage.

What happened between them during this unbearable period, Nelson sleeping in the dining room, Evelyn in their bed, is in dispute. When she filed for divorce, Evelyn claimed that Nelson had beaten her on several occasions. The most serious assault, she said, came in February 1956. He had tried to throw her out of the house. When she refused to leave, he hit her with his fists and throttled her until she choked. She ran to a neighbour, clad only in her nightdress.

Doggedly, she returned to the marital home and remained there another month, until Nelson finally threatened to kill her with an ax unless she left.[7]

In his replying claim, Nelson denied all the acts of violence Evelyn had described save for two. In July 1955, he said, she had taken money from his suit pocket, money that a client had paid him that day and belonged to his law firm. When he snatched it back from her, she attacked him with her fists; he hit her in the face and she fell to the floor.

Then there was the incident in February 1956 when Evelyn claimed that Nelson had tried to strangle her. During a quarrel, she had reached for a stove poker, he said, and made to attack him. He was carrying a baby in his arms – he must have been referring to Makaziwe, who was less than two years old. Holding the baby with one hand, he grabbed Evelyn by the throat with the other, dragged her away from the stove to the bedroom, put the baby down on the bed, then pushed Evelyn out of the house.

Evelyn laid a charge of assault with the police; to ward off his prospective prosecution, Nelson agreed to attend a family meeting at which he was fined £5.[8]

Committing this account to paper must have tormented Nelson. He conceded as much as he did, one must guess, because the February incident was too widely known to be denied; indeed, Nelson had admitted to assaulting Evelyn in a family forum when he agreed to pay the fine.

He never submitted the affidavit in which he made these admissions. He put it, unsigned, in an office drawer. It is dated October 4, 1956. Shortly afterward, Evelyn withdrew her divorce plea; the couple remained legally married another twenty months until Nelson divorced Evelyn in order to marry Winnie. On the day the police arrested Nelson for treason in early December 1956, they raided his offices on Fox Street and found the document among his papers. A handwritten note on the first page reads, 'Defence knows contents', in parentheses. The prosecutor in the Treason Trial must have discussed the document with Nelson's lawyers before filing it away. It lay unseen in South Africa's National Archives for more than half a century until a historian stumbled upon it around the time of Nelson's death.[9]

. .

For Nelson's family, his war with Evelyn was a catastrophe. 'It was as if the ground beneath us was breaking and we were falling,' Nelson's sister Leabie said of that time. Nelson's mother packed her bags and returned to the Transkei, unwilling to bear further witness to the destruction of her son's marriage.[10]

As for the three children, they witnessed at close quarters their parents at war. In the wake of the separation, the two older children, Thembi and Makgatho, lived sometimes with Evelyn, sometimes with Nelson, until Winnie moved in with Nelson in June 1958; after that, neither boy lived with his father again.

The boys took sides in their parents' feud, Makgatho his father's, Thembi his mother's.[11] The atmosphere in the Mandela home, it seems, did not create a space for neutrality. Thembi's fury with his father lasted until the end of his short life; as a young man, he refused to visit Nelson in prison.

Yet the relationship between son and father was thicker than simple estrangement. A peer of Thembi's, who attended high school with him in Swaziland in the early 1960s, recalls a young man who was very tall and obsessed with boxing. By then, Nelson's name had reached every corner of black South Africa; that he boxed was legendary; pictures of him sparring were famous. In taking to the ring, Thembi could not but step into his father's orbit, emulating him, fighting him.[12]

In 1992, when Nelson's ghostwriter asked him about the children from his first marriage, he spoke immediately of Thembi. He took the boy with him to the boxing gym on most days, relations between them fraught and laden, his son hating him, loving him, straining to better him. Sometimes, Nelson recalled, Thembi was assigned to lead a group exercise session. He would strut around, wearing his authority heavily, and he would pick on Nelson. 'Mr. Mandela,' he would bark. 'We have no time to waste!'[13]

.   .

In his autobiography, Nelson honed a compact tale about his marriage to Evelyn. They were young when they fell in love; neither knew yet who each would become. He evolved into a political being while she became a devout Jehovah's Witness. They grew incompatible as they matured.

That is surely true, as far as it goes, but there is so much more to be said.

Divorce proceedings do not bring out one's best colours. In response to Evelyn's contention that she had married a violent man, Nelson wrote that his wife was delusional: her jealousy had conjured phantom lovers; her rage had triggered irrational violence; and she was in the grip of primitive superstition, to boot. He was appealing to the prejudices the magistrate might hold about women's erratic emotions and about black people's spiritual worlds.

Evelyn was hardly deluded; she took the deepest offense to what she knew to be true. The best that can be said is that Evelyn and Nelson held incompatible values; she regarded monogamy as sacrosanct, while he, as one of his biographers has suggested, was surprised by her puritanical zeal.[14]

It should be said, though, that if Evelyn did indeed conspire to have Ngoyi arrested, the implications for Nelson were nightmarish. It is hard to imagine a marriage going more awry. From Nelson's perspective, their relationship was well and truly broken. That Evelyn persisted in trying to mend it into the late 1950s must have astounded him.

As for the violence, we have no basis on which to judge who between them was the more faithful witness to what happened in their home. What we can say is that the Nelson Mandela the world came to know, famous for subordinating his emotional life to his political goals, had yet to be forged. There was a wildness in his home and in his heart, a spiralling of events and of feelings out of his control.

.   .

Nelson started a young family twice, first with Evelyn, then with Winnie. On both occasions, he scarcely inhabited his own house. One is left to wonder whether this driven, talented man, who made searing art on the political stage, was prone to flee the grinding domesticity of his home. It is striking that in the early and mid-1950s he found erotic fulfilment in the thick of politics, with other activists, who shared with him his frenetic life, and also the encroaching danger.

There is in fact no direct evidence that Nelson and Lilian Ngoyi were lovers. But they almost certainly were. Nelson's authorized biographer states matter-of-factly that Ngoyi was one of Nelson's 'female companions'.[15] And the activist Helen Joseph, who worked closely with Ngoyi and grew close to Nelson, wonders in her memoir why they did not marry.[16] When Nelson and Ngoyi were among the 156 people tried for treason, travelling each day to Pretoria to attend their trial, it was understood among at least some of their fellow defendants that they were lovers but that talking about their relationship was indiscreet.[17] Nor were Nelson and Ngoyi overly concerned to conceal their relationship; they were a regular fixture at Blue Lagoon, the only night-time entertainment venue in central Johannesburg run and frequented by black people.[18]

Nelson and Ngoyi were from different worlds. While he was an aristocrat, she grew up in poverty, abandoning school at the age of eleven to support her family. When Nelson moved to Orlando West with Evelyn in 1945, Ngoyi was already a longtime resident there. But, unlike Nelson, she spent her first years in Orlando sharing a windowless shack with her parents and her daughter.

Ngoyi began her political career as a worker-militant. Employed as a machinist, she joined the Garment Workers' Union, was soon elected as a shop steward, and rose to the union's national executive. In 1952, when she was forty-one years old, she watched the Defiance Campaign unfold and decided at once that she must get involved. She joined the ANC, signed up as a campaign volunteer, and was duly arrested for standing in the whites-only line at a post office.

Her rise was meteoric. She became president of the ANC Women's League, was a founding member of the Federation of South African Women (FEDSAW), later becoming its president, and was the first woman to serve on the ANC's National Executive Committee. The greatest triumph of her political career came on August 9, 1956, when she and three others led twenty thousand women to the Union Buildings in Pretoria, the seat of executive power, to protest against the extension of South Africa's pass laws to women.

Ngoyi was neither an intellectual nor a strategic thinker; she would apologize all her life for her lack of education. Instead, she rose on account of her explosive public speaking. She was petite, pretty, and famously well groomed, and the combination of her femininity and her militant rhetoric turned heads; Johannesburg's black press dubbed her 'the stormy petrel'.[19] Her rabble-rousing got her into much trouble; during the Treason Trial, the prosecution cited her saying in a speech that apartheid's defenders would be 'taken alive and thrown into the fire'.[20] Her lawyers expended several hours of court time trying to explain her words away.

Nor was she slow to cut Nelson down for his sexism. On the eve of the famous women's march of 1956, she was to recall many years later, Nelson asked what might become of the nation's children were something to happen to their mothers. Children also had fathers, she shot back, and childcare was surely not beyond the capabilities of men.[21]

Ngoyi and Nelson have both taken to the grave what they felt for each other. One is left to imagine the charged field that must have existed between these two charismatic figures, both living such giddy, dangerous lives, their relationship carried on in a zone of ostensible secrecy.

They remained close after Nelson met Winnie and benignly interested in each other's lives. Ngoyi was among only a handful of Nelson's friends who travelled to the Transkei for his wedding. And upon Nelson and Winnie's return to Johannesburg it was to Ngoyi's house that they went to await sunset, the customary time for a newlywed couple to enter their marital home.[22]

Ngoyi and Nelson worked together in politics until the last moment of his aboveground career. She was at his side, on the speaker's platform in Pietermaritzburg, for his last public address before he disappeared underground in March 1961.

They met again just once, in 1973; after more than a decade of successive banning orders were finally lifted, Ngoyi was free, at last, to visit Nelson in prison. She travelled to Cape Town, took the ferry to Robben Island, and spent the better part of a day being funnelled through the prison's bureaucracy. Finally, moments after she had been led to a room filled with guards, Nelson appeared suddenly on the other side of a glass pane. She could see him only from the shoulders up.

'Ah! Lily, my dearest!' he exclaimed.

'I felt we should kiss each other,' she wrote to a comrade afterward, 'but there [was] the glass between us.'[23]

And then Nelson said the most generous thing. When he and his comrades were released – and they *would* be released, he said, freedom *would* come – Ngoyi should be the one to take them home.[24]

She never saw him again; she died in March 1980, aged sixty-eight, just shy of a decade before his release. The last eighteen years of her life had been harsh. Confined by her banning orders to her house in Soweto, she had struggled to earn a living. At times, the scramble to survive became desperate: briefly, she resorted to selling alcohol to make ends meet. In later years, she became a supplicant to Amnesty International, whose New York office sent her a modest monthly allowance. She felt the indignity of it deeply. 'You know if you have noticed birds,' she wrote to her benefactor in New York, 'the young ones open their mouths while their mothers are gone out seeking food. The same applies to me.'[25]

It is unlikely that Nelson ever spoke to anybody about his romantic relationship with Ngoyi. But speak about her he did. A close confidante of his in the early 1990s, who was also his head of staff, and spent a good sixteen hours a day at his side, reports that he talked of her frequently, with great admiration, almost in a stream of consciousness, for, on any given day, something would happen to remind him of her.[26]

At about that time, in the early 1990s, an interviewer, aware that Nelson and Ngoyi had probably been lovers, asked him carefully for his thoughts about her. While his answer casts her strictly as a comrade, it reveals more than first meets the eye.

'She . . . was a very powerful person,' he replied, 'but with humble educational qualifications and she was inclined to be a demagogue in her speeches . . . but nevertheless a person of great talent, fearless and who could organize. She also tended to be an individualist and not to value the importance of teamwork and organization. For example, she was national President [of the Women's League] but she refused . . . to give up her position . . . Just like Helen Joseph . . . [W]e tried very hard as the ANC to get both of them to surrender their provincial offices but they challenged us.'[27]

He could have been describing Winnie Mandela. Powerful, dem-
agogic, a maverick ungovernable to the point of unreason: Nelson
entered substantial relationships with formidable women with a taste
for the stage.

But there is an important difference between Ngoyi and Winnie.

It is impossible to say why Nelson and Ngoyi never married. It
might have been at her insistence, not his. Asked by a journalist in the
late 1950s why she remained single, she said that her children were
used to having her as a father and a mother.[28] Perhaps this answer was
entirely candid; perhaps she enjoyed the fact that her family had no
patriarch and prized her autonomy.

But it is hard to hold back the suspicion that for Nelson, Ngoyi was
not enough. It is not just that she was barely educated; she carried her
unworldliness heavily. She did not attend the parties at the First-Slovo
house; she was not comfortable there.[29] And when she went abroad in
1955, she asked the superintendent of a Berlin hospital if the staff were
so respectful to her because they thought she was educated.[30] One can
hardly imagine Winnie in a similar state of self-doubt.

'Lilian was not as emancipated as either Nelson or Winnie,' a comrade who knew all three of them commented decades later. 'Nelson and
Winnie didn't carry their burdens on their backs. They delighted in all
sorts of people. Lilian . . . did not have that confidence.'[31]

. .

There was another woman in Nelson's life in the early and mid-
1950s. Her name was Ruth Mompati. How one introduces her matters,
for to begin a tale of a lawyer who sleeps with his secretary is to risk
losing control over what it might mean.

Mompati was in her late twenties and newlywed. She and her husband had just settled in Johannesburg: they had moved into a home in
Orlando West just a stone's throw from Walter and Albertina Sisulu.

She had trained as a schoolteacher, but had given it up by the time
she met Nelson. When the apartheid government introduced its infamous Bantu Education Act in 1953, which created a separate and inferior education system for black students, she had put down her chalk
and refused to teach. She spent the days at home, listless and bored. In
the evenings, she attended ANC meetings where, among many others,

she met Nelson Mandela. He was a flirt: a 'Casanova' is the word she used many years later, ever so charming and unashamedly on the hunt.

It was Albertina Sisulu who suggested that she enroll in a typing course; she must do *something*, Albertina urged; if she stayed at home she would go insane. It happened that among Mompati's early friends in Johannesburg was a typist employed at Mandela and Tambo; when she left her employment, she recommended Ruth Mompati, who had just completed her course in shorthand, to replace her. Mompati was immensely proud to accept a job at Mandela and Tambo; she was a political woman, to her depths, and although the firm was not yet a year old, its reputation in black Johannesburg was soaring.

At about this time, her marriage took a ghastly turn. Her husband had found work in Durban and was away from home for weeks, sometimes months at a time. At some point she discovered – it is not clear precisely when – that he had started a second family in Durban.

There is a sadness about Mompati's relationship with Nelson. In exile circles in Lusaka, where she would spend many years of her life, it was widely known that her elder son, Mompati, was his; indeed, the boy was the spitting image of his biological father. Yet even close friends, with whom she shared intimacies, understood that discussion of her son's paternity was off-limits. And when a biographer of Nelson's wrote that Nelson and Mompati had been lovers, she was deeply pained and threatened to sue.

And yet Mompati did in fact talk about her relationship with Nelson, in awkward circumstances, several years before her death. She had resisted him for months, she said. He was so relentlessly flirtatious, so wonderfully at ease in her presence, so beguiling: she fell for him long before she became his lover. She refused him for so long in part for the embarrassment of it all: to be known as the girlfriend of this famously philandering man was diminishing. And she understood, she said, that the tragedy of her marriage had left her lonely and in need.

There is another reason she held Nelson off for so long. She imagined the sheer practicalities of an affair. They could not conduct their relationship in his house or in hers; they would have to drive out of the city, to a secluded place, and make love on a rug by the side of the car. She understood that for Nelson this was part of the allure; the spirit of it was in sympathy with his increasingly dangerous life. He had been banned ever since the closing days of the Defiance Campaign, after all, and the very act of driving beyond Johannesburg's city limits was forbidden to him.

For her, though, the prospect of conducting a relationship in this manner reminded her that she was a black woman in South Africa. 'We lived in such confined spaces,' she told her interviewer, 'with so little room for privacy. Sneaking off to be together on the side of the road,' she said, 'that is what black people were reduced to.'

And yet it was precisely there, outside the city limits, that her relationship with Nelson reached moments of transcendence. She painted for her interviewer an image of the two of them, sitting on the bonnet of Nelson's car, staring out over farmland. In such moments, she said, apartheid Johannesburg seemed to dissolve; they were imagining another world, and the value of what they thought and felt was beyond measure.

. .

Ruth Mompati worked at Mandela and Tambo until the firm closed its doors in 1961. By then, Tambo had gone into exile and Nelson was underground. Mompati was among those charged with settling the accounts, steering clients to other lawyers, easing the firm into extinction.

Sometime in 1962, in a secret rendezvous with Nelson and Walter Sisulu, the two men urged her to steal across South Africa's border to undergo military training in the Soviet Union. She resisted at first. Her older son, Mompati, was just six years old. Her younger boy was two. Mandela and Sisulu pressed her. She would be gone for three months, they assured her, and then she could come back to her children.

Leaving South Africa was a cloak-and-dagger affair. She was to stand at a specific point on Bree Street in downtown Johannesburg, wearing a distinctive skirt and carrying a distinctive bag; she was to get into a strange man's car that would take her to Botswana. Later, she recalled crying all the way to the border post, beside herself with guilt about her children.

In the end, the trip abroad lasted a year. In September 1963, almost twelve months since her departure, her military training now behind her, she found herself standing once more on Botswanan soil, in the capital, Gaborone, preparing to reenter South Africa. Oliver Tambo was there. What he told her was grievous beyond endurance. Before she left, she had been a member of an underground ANC cell. Now, Tambo told her, one of the members of that cell, a man named Bruno Mtolo, had been discovered to be a spy. Were she to return, Tambo said, it would be to certain arrest.

She simply did not believe what Tambo was saying. And she said so. He could not stop her, she told him; she was going home.

'I cannot allow you to do that,' she recalled him saying. 'They will catch you.' He quite literally restrained her as she battled to free herself from his grasp.

· ·

She did not lay eyes on her children for another ten years. When they finally joined her, the older boy was sixteen, the younger one twelve.

'You always think of them as being the age when you left,' she told an interviewer many years later. 'When I met the twelve-year-old after ten years it wasn't too bad; I could still cuddle him. He hadn't shot up as one would have expected. But my other boy was a tall sixteen-year-old. I didn't know him. I didn't know how to behave towards this boy. It broke my heart. And neither of them knew how to behave towards me.'[32]

Mompati threw herself at political work during her decades in exile, travelling the world as an ambassador for the ANC. She was the organization's chief representative in Britain and Ireland for several years and worked in East Berlin for some time. And for more than a decade, she ran the secretariat of the ANC's National Executive Committee in Lusaka. When the organization was unbanned, she was one of only three women on its executive body, earning her the moniker 'the most powerful woman in the ANC'.

There was always a sense, among those who knew her well, that under her tremendous work ethic lay sadness and pain. When she moved to Lusaka in 1976 and stayed as a lodger in the home of friends, her hosts seldom saw her. 'We never once shared a meal with her,' one of them remembered. 'She left in the morning before breakfast and returned late at night and went to bed.'[33]

She was among the first to return home when the ANC was unbanned in 1990, representing the organization in its first encounter with the apartheid government in Cape Town. In the group photographs taken that day, she cuts a striking figure. A pudgy black man on her left, a balding white man on her right, she is tall and erect and ever so alive.

Not long after her return, Nelson phoned her.

'How is the boy?' she recalled him asking. Noting that he chose not to call his son by his name, she realized in a flash how Mompati had settled in Nelson's mind. He was racked with remorse about the children he had sired in wedlock, but this child he had placed in another, much more distant category: biologically his, to be sure, but that was all.

Ruth Mompati lost both her children in quick succession in the early 1990s. Her younger son took his own life. The older, Mompati, died with little warning after suffering an aneurysm. She phoned Nelson hours after his death.

'The boy has passed away', are the words she remembered choosing.

There was a long silence. 'Is there anything you need?' Nelson finally asked.

She began to weep, she recalled, and put down the phone.[34]

Chapter 17

In January 1953, six months after the Defiance Campaign made Nelson Mandela famous, Winnie Madikizela arrived in Johannesburg. She was not yet seventeen.

Although a chaperone had accompanied her for most of the journey, he had left the train three stops earlier, and she walked onto the platform at Park Station alone.

She came to Johannesburg as millions before her had done: the eastern approach to the city, the blond grassland harder, blunter, more scorched than any landscape she would ever have seen; the arc of tall buildings ahead as the train made directly for downtown Johannesburg, dozens of them, all concrete and steel; the platform at Park Station, a vast, liquid crowd of strangers, people reduced to the thinnest existence and never to be seen again.

She stood there in her school uniform and her Sunday shoes, her trunk balanced on her head. She was not sure how to dress for Johannesburg, and her Shawbury clothes – a signal of studenthood recognizable everywhere, surely – seemed appropriate enough. It was by virtue of the uniform that the woman who had come to meet her – Mrs. Frieda Hough, wife of M. A. Hough, lecturer at the Jan Hofmeyr School of Social Work – recognized her charge.[1]

Mrs. Hough must have led Winnie up the long flight of stairs ascending from the station hall. How did they get the trunk up those stairs? Racial codes surrounding the performance of physical labour were awfully delicate. It is improbable that Mrs. Hough offered to carry it or even suggested that they share the burden. She might have brought with her a male domestic servant, his task to bear the trunk from the station hall, to lift it into the boot of the car, to carry it inside at journey's end. Or perhaps the trunk simply remained on Winnie's head: bearing her load above her, she arrived in Johannesburg the very sym-

bol of rural womanhood, a great irony, given what she would come to
mean to generations of cosmopolitan women.

Mrs. Hough drove Winnie eastward into Hillbrow, an inner-city
district of high-rise apartments and restaurants. Skirting the boundary
of Berea, they turned southward into Doornfontein and then eastward
into Jeppestown, the city's skyline now behind their backs, before arriving at 76 Hans Street, the Helping Hand Club for Native Girls, where
Winnie lived for the next four years.

They would have entered the main building, home to an assortment of single black working women – seamstresses, factory workers,
domestic servants – most of them by now gone to their places of work.
And then, in all likelihood, the superintendent, Mrs. Bruce, showed
Winnie to the two cottages at the back of the property that housed
eleven young women studying at the Jan Hofmeyr School of Social
Work. Mrs. Bruce no doubt reeled off the list of house rules, and if the
traces of her demeanour left in the minutes of monthly management
meetings are an indication, she *barked out* those rules. And there were
many rules, as we shall see, too many for Winnie to have absorbed, an
epic journey behind her, the prospect of a bewildering city ahead.[2]

. .

The days that followed tested Winnie severely.

Between the showers in the cottage's ablution facilities there were
no partitions or screens; it was customary, Winnie soon learned, for
women to stand naked together under the showerheads. She was deeply
shocked; in her years of schooling in the Transkei, living, sleeping, and
washing side by side with dozens of girls, she had never seen a school-
mate fully unclothed. Now she found that she simply could not disrobe
as if nobody else were in the room. She made a spectacle of herself,
attempting the impossible, to conceal her nakedness in a place where
one simply could not do so. Soon, she fathomed, a rumour was doing
the rounds: there was something the matter with the new girl from the
Transkei; she was hiding some sort of blemish.

With this bodily exposure came some awkward revelations. Winnie had never worn a brassiere and never used sanitary pads, and if
her recollections are right, she soon discovered that she was the only
woman in the cottages who did not. Via the shame of being different,

she was introduced, in one fell swoop, to a new relationship with the whole drama of bodily care before an audience of prying eyes.

And if nakedness was not easy, nor was being clothed. Winnie does not tell us what was in the trunk she brought with her from home, but it appears that none of her clothes were right. Before long, she was tearing pictures of women from the pages of magazines and posting them to her sister Nonalithi back home; her sister bought fabric from the local store in Bizana and went to a cousin who was a seamstress; she, in turn, imitated the dresses in the pictures. Nonalithi then sent the dresses up to Johannesburg by mail.

Dresses aside, being an urban girl was more expensive than her family had imagined – the pajamas she must wear at night, the bras and the sanitary pads she had so rudely discovered, the cosmetics. Her grandfather Mazingi had owned a large wattle forest, a useful source of income, for its bark was easy to strip and sell. Now Nonalithi took charge of the stripping and selling of the bark, raising £5 a month for her sister in this way.[3]

A conveyer belt was thus hastily improvised, stretching from Mbongweni to Johannesburg, bearing the material required for Winnie to make herself. For what she encountered during her first weeks and months in Johannesburg was the question not just of what to wear on one's skin but of who to become.

Nor was this easy to learn. As a student at the Jan Hofmeyr School of Social Work, Winnie was a career woman in the making and thus the epitome of respectability. And yet, by the very same token, she was a 'modern girl', in the parlance of the day, a girl who dressed fashionably and chose her lovers.[4]

Unmarried professional women were required to strike a delicate balance: toppling one way, into the invisibility of an asexual existence, was as fateful as toppling the other, into scandal.[5]

The first danger, an asexual invisibility, was never open to Winnie. She was stunningly beautiful. There is not a single person from those times this author has interviewed who did not remark, whether casually in passing, or, more commonly, with forceful exclamation, how striking Winnie was. That her sexuality would be front and centre was scarcely a decision of her making. It was the material with which she was presented and with which she worked.

In the memoir of one of Winnie's contemporaries at Jan Hofmeyr,

Ellen Kuzwayo, there is a scene as telling as it is brief. Kuzwayo was much older than most of the students in her cohort, and in her second marriage. Once a week, she and three other students, Winnie among them, walked from Hans Street to the trading centre at Wemmer, where they attended what Kuzwayo describes as 'modern cookery' classes; to sever ties with the stodgy staples of one's childhood and master a more cosmopolitan cuisine was a part of the modern girl's repertoire. It was a forty-five-minute journey by foot, presumably undertaken on Saturday mornings, when the streets of inner-city Johannesburg were crowded.

'As their senior in age,' Kuzwayo writes, 'I often performed the duty of chaperone when some wayward man tried to interfere with one of us... They all were very attractive women.'[6]

As she walked the city streets, men undressed Winnie with their eyes. And not just with their eyes. Johannesburg was unapologetically lascivious. The young men who so frightened Nelson, with their wide fedoras and their narrow pants, were without the slightest reserve, unafraid to shout out to a stranger precisely what it was about her buttocks or her breasts that they admired.[7]

. . .

In truth, every aspect of the Johannesburg world Winnie had entered – the institution in which she lived, the school in which she studied, the social clubs she was encouraged to join – was shaped by a preoccupation, to the point of obsession, with the sex lives of young black women. The Helping Hand Club for Native Girls, where Winnie lived, and the Jan Hofmeyr School of Social Work, where she studied, were founded by the same man, the American Board missionary the Reverend Ray Phillips. He was also the founder of the debating society Winnie signed up to, the Gamma Sigma Club, and a co-founder of the institution in which she attended many social functions, the Bantu Men's Social Centre. Phillips's wife, Dora, would have fetched Winnie from the station in January 1953, but for the fact that she was on a year-long sabbatical and had returned to the United States.[8]

Phillips was among a set of people – English speaking, Christian, liberal, and paternalistic – who dominated race relations in South Africa for a quarter of a century. The other prominent figure in that circle was J. D. Rheinallt Jones. Like Phillips, he founded a raft of institutions to manage relations between black and white, among them the

South African Institute of Race Relations, a think tank that flourishes to this day.

Dr. A. B. Xuma, for whom Nelson had recently caused such grief, sat on the boards of most of the institutions these men founded, including the Jan Hofmeyr School of Social Work. Nor was it just men like Xuma. In the 1920s, Jones had founded a nationwide network of joint councils in which members of the African elite met with white people of influence. There was a time when just about every black urban notable sat on a joint council, even Nelson's radical mentor, Gaur Radebe.

History has been as unkind to men like Phillips and Jones as it has been to black men like Xuma. A century after they began their work, their paternalism grates. 'I have seen a white man deal with a motor car,' Phillips cites approvingly the comments of a black man he encountered at a township meeting. 'He does not kick it. He looks at it carefully, methodically. He sees what's wrong. Then he fixes it. I ask', the man says, now addressing Phillips directly, 'that you treat us blacks like that motor car.'[9]

The Reverend Ray Phillips was nonetheless an extraordinary man whose influence over Winnie and her peers the condescension of hindsight threatens to obscure. His sheer energy was something to behold; the number of institutions he founded, raised money for, and managed was staggering.

For Phillips, South Africa's destiny would be shaped by how it managed the mass settlement of people in cities. The American Board Mission, to which he belonged, had begun its South African work in rural Natal and followed the members of its flock as they migrated to Johannesburg; its sense of its mission thus grew from witnessing at close quarters the drama of black urbanization in a white-ruled land. Seeing to the moral lives of one's congregants, it understood, was without meaning if one did not attend to the social calamities that engulfed their lives in the cities. It was thus Phillips's theological convictions that drew him to quantitative social science – he became an impressive gatherer of social data relating to housing, labour markets, informal trade, transport, schooling, delinquency, crime, leisure, drinking, marriage, sex work, the black market in abortion, and much else besides[10] – as well as to social work; he founded the Jan Hofmeyr School in 1940 because he felt that the absence of black social workers in urbanizing South Africa was a scandal.

What exercised Phillips above all was the manner in which young black women were settling in South Africa's cities. The greatest curse whites had cast upon black people, he believed, was to have shaped urban life in ways that made monogamous unions all but impossible.

At the heart of the problem, Phillips believed, was white South Africa's refusal to countenance the reality of permanent black settlement in the cities. White South Africa required the labour of young men in mining and industry, but regarded them as migrants, assuming that the families they formed would remain in the countryside. But in reality, urban labour markets were emptying the countryside of eligible bachelors; young women were following young men to the cities, for the alternative was 'an inglorious spinsterhood' in rural South Africa.

The result, for Phillips, was abhorrent. He wrote of 'young girls in the urban areas, unattached, attractive, flitting about from job to job as nursemaid and housegirl, living on premises of employers who care not at all what goes on in the girls' . . . outside room'. With unconcealed distaste he wrote of 'women to be obtained for the asking'.[11]

What to do? In the 1920s, Phillips advocated heavy restrictions on female migration to the cities.[12] But by the late 1930s, he was instead throwing his energy into a grand urban project: the corralling of single women into institutions that would preserve their virtue. Such institutions should be run by 'a resident matron' who 'supervises the grounds, protects women against unwelcome visitors, and organises activities of a social nature to occupy leisure-time hours'.[13]

The Helping Hand Club for Native Girls was precisely such an institution. The majority of its residents were working women in their twenties and thirties. At an earlier stage in its history, the institution itself had trained them in cookery, housework, laundry work and needlework as well as English, arithmetic and home nursing. This practical and moral training played a dual role: it was to render black women acceptable to the white housewives who might employ them; and it was preparation for the monogamous housewifery Phillips dearly hoped was in their own futures.

From the early 1940s, the Helping Hand also provided accommodation for female students at the newly established Jan Hofmeyr School. Housed separately in the cottages at the back of the property, they were set apart from the rest of the women in the hostel in other ways, too. For one, they were not destined to see the inside of a factory or to work in a white woman's kitchen; they were receiving an elite education and would thus take their place in a rarefied circle of black professionals.

And they were not just any professionals; they were *social workers* in the
making and thus occupied two positions that sat awkwardly together.
On the one hand, they were single black women whose chastity was
to be preserved; on the other, they were being trained to preserve the
chastity and, more broadly, the moral well-being of others.

During Winnie's time, every Jan Hofmeyr student housed at Helping Hand had to be home by 7:30 on weekday evenings unless Mrs.
Bruce had given express permission otherwise. Students were permitted no more than two visitors each weekend. And if these visitors were
men, they could not 'mill about' the entrance of the property; they were
required to briskly make their presence known to the authorities, to
sign the guest register, and to meet Helping Hand residents only in
public areas. By 9:00 p.m. they had to have cleared out.[14]

· ·

It is easy to mistake where Winnie stood in regard to Phillips's
project. She was young and beautiful and discovering the power of
her sexuality. In time to come, she made a mockery of Helping Hand's
attempts to keep her chaste. During her last months at the institution,
she spent her evenings with Nelson in his office ostensibly 'to study'.
And when Nelson went out, she invited her other lover, Barney Sampson, to share his office with her.

The street outside Helping Hand became her playground. With
Nelson's Oldsmobile parked at one end of Hans Street and Sampson's
blue van at the other, she flitted between her lovers under Mrs. Bruce's
nose.

But that is hardly the end of the story. Since the period after Gertrude's death, Winnie had been accustomed to inhabiting multiple
roles: to her younger siblings, she was the mother they had lost; to her
father, she was the prodigal son he did not have; she was also the work-
horse in his fields. Each of these roles required a matching subjectivity,
an interior fitted to the external role. In a large family where love was
spread thin, one carved out the spaces in which one was valued – if one
had wherewithal to do so, that is. And it did not matter that these roles
coupled strangely in one person; for the most commanding personalities, dissonance presents no limit to the power of self-creation.

As Winnie grew older, the antinomies inside her grew more numerous. The new roles did not displace the old; they lived together within

her, side by side. In relation to the Reverend Ray Phillips, she stood in two quite different places. On the one hand, she was a black woman who chose her lovers freely, both before and after she married. She was the great undoer of Phillips's project, a glorious rival to his vision of what a modern woman should be.

And yet she also became more Phillips than Phillips himself. This role was less apparent when she was young. But she imbibed it, and it nestled inside her. In time to come, she became a ferocious enforcer of conservative sexual mores among young black South Africans, even while she herself flouted sexual norms. She did this enforcing in the name of an ascendant African nationalism, Phillips in all probability long banished from her mind. He was there nonetheless, modified almost beyond recognition.

Chapter 18

It is hard to exaggerate the prestige of the Jan Hofmeyr School. The names of its alumni in just its first year, 1941, are a roll call of South Africa's black elite: Bokwe, Msimang, Makiwane[1] — these are among the names that have dominated public life since the mid-nineteenth century. Many of the school's former students spoke of it with awe. Writing decades after he studied there, the Zimbabwean liberation movement leader Joshua Nkomo described the work as 'very much more difficult than anything I had done before'.[2] Prospective students went to extraordinary lengths to be admitted. Ellen Kuzwayo 'literally lived on the doorstep' of the institution for two months in 1952, 'waiting to see the authorities'. Her husband, meanwhile, helped her 'to meet people who were influential and informed about the work of that school and who could give [her] an insight into what the authorities expected from the students'. Years later, she came to regard her registration as a student there 'as a remarkable achievement' that she 'guarded very jealously'.[3]

Perusing the school's syllabus decades later, scholars expressed distaste: so much attention to moral betterment — sports, crafts, basic musical instruction — so little to political analysis; posterity casts a wary eye on Phillips's old liberalism.[4] But his students saw things differently. They were taking in so much more than the syllabus, after all. 'Phillips addressed us as Mr. So-and-So and Miss So-and-So,' Brigalia Bam, who studied with Winnie, recalled. 'It was more than courtesy; it was respect, and it was highly impressive. He also insisted that we read the newspapers scrupulously. Every week, someone would have to stand up in front of the class and summarize the week's news. He was instilling a culture of discipline, of trained attentiveness to the world.'

Most striking were the models of female intellectual prowess the school displayed. Among the lecturers was the prominent anthropologist Ellen Hellmann. 'She wore to class the highest heels I had ever seen,' Bam recalled, 'and she would smoke a cigarette while she lectured. The combination of scholarship and style was something to behold.'[5]

The Hofmeyr School taught something else. Annually, each student interned for several months at an active institution: orphanages, feeding schemes, projects of postpartum care. So many of the school's students came from elite rural mission schools. For the first time in their lives, they were shown, with painful intimacy, the texture of urban poverty. Everyone remembers this – Winnie, Nkomo, Kuzwayo, Bam – as the most visceral lesson they learned.

In her first year, Winnie was assigned to work at a Salvation Army home for delinquent girls. The very idea of the place puzzled her. 'There was no such thing as a delinquent girl back home,' she recalled later. 'Some of us were more spirited than others, but none of us had problems with our parents or dared to live on their own.'[6]

If the idea was wholly foreign at first, she later imbibed it fully. In years to come, she turned her own home in Soweto into a makeshift institution for youths, ruled with an authoritarian hand.

Winnie's second assignment was back in the Transkei at the Ncora Rural Centre in Thembuland, home to Nelson's people. Her status since she had last lived in the Transkei had ascended; just a schoolgirl back then, she was now, as a trainee social worker, permitted to attend public meetings reserved for men. She thus witnessed Nelson's nephew Kaiser Daliwonga Matanzima, now chief of the Emigrant Thembu, address a crowded hall at his Great Place, Qamata. He was tall, lean and aloof, she observed; she found his arrogance distasteful.

She left Ncora in haste, she tells us, before her internship ended. The local chief was eyeing her as a wife for his son, a student at Fort Hare whom she had never met. The chief had in mind to *thwala* her, she reports, a word that has been translated into English as 'abduct'. 'His tribesmen . . . would ride over on their horses and await their chance to pounce on me and carry me away. I would then be locked up while the chief's son would be brought from college and the marriage would be forced on us.'[7]

She was embellishing wildly, as was her wont. *Thwala* seldom, if ever, worked this way when Winnie was young. More often than not, young couples orchestrated it themselves to force their parents to allow them to marry; a young man 'abducted' his bride and took her to his home, presenting their parents with a fait accompli. In rare cases, a young woman was indeed abducted against her will, but her father's consent was required for the marriage to go ahead; if he said no, she was released.[8] That a chief might kidnap a highly educated young woman and force his will upon her, her father, and his highly educated son was outlandish. Winnie so often played on her biographers' limited knowledge of her milieu, reminding herself, perhaps, that she, not they, commanded her story.

If she exaggerated the danger, the point she made was serious. From the Johannesburg youths who imagined out loud what was under her skirt to the Transkei nobles who eyed her for their sons, men believed that they had business with her. The record of how she fended them off is all too thin. Beyond her tale of literally escaping Ncora, beyond having Ellen Kuzwayo guard her and her friends as they walked the streets, we have little that is granular in her dealings with predatory men.

We have something about the men she *did* choose, for we know whom she took as her first steady lover. He was neither a chief's son, nor a lawyer, nor a doctor from the ranks of Johannesburg's elite. Her first long-term boyfriend, Barney Sampson, was a part-time office worker, seemingly without pedigree.

She chose him, it appears, for his striking beauty and his attention to style.

'He was as handsome as she was beautiful,' Brigalia Bam remembered. 'They made such a spectacle. People would stop and stare. It was like they were brother and sister, two great beauties standing side by side.'[9]

Winnie spoke at length to Fatima Meer about Sampson. He 'was fun and he knew all the fun places', Meer wrote. 'They were soon going out together, to dances and parties, the cinema, to other social events.'

He lived very modestly, in the backyard of a white suburban home, a place customarily reserved for live-in black servants; if he skimped on accommodation, Meer comments, it was because he 'appeared to spend most of his money on clothes'.[10]

Winnie, it seems, spent her first years in Johannesburg in ways that echoed Nelson's a decade earlier, distancing herself with some daring from the traditions in which she was schooled. In Nelson's case, it took the form of a hasty court wedding to a pregnant bride. Winnie, it seems from Meer's opaque description, found, through Barney Sampson, a way onto the fringes of Sophiatown's jazz culture.

We do not know what this world looked like through Winnie's eyes; she spoke only briefly and elliptically about this time – 'I had to become a city girl, acquire glamour,' she said later, 'before I could begin to be processed into a personality.'[11] But we can guess that she and Barney went to the Odin or the Harlem, Sophiatown's two cinemas, where Westerns would compete with reruns of *Stormy Weather* and *Cabin in the Sky*, featuring Lena Horne, and *King Solomon's Mines*, with Paul Robeson.

In the pages of the magazines Winnie read, in the talk around her, in the films she watched, and perhaps in the flesh, on the stage, she would have encountered Dolly Rathebe, black Johannesburg's first genuine celebrity. Winnie has left no record of her thoughts about Rathebe, but she was ubiquitous in the mid-1950s. As a young black woman new to the city, learning how to assemble her persona, Winnie would have found her attention drawn to this star: it could not have been otherwise.

A jazz singer and a film actress, Rathebe became instantly famous in 1949 when, aged twenty-one, she starred in the film *Jim Comes to Jo'burg*. Utterly novel, it depicted a modern black South African city for the first time.

From the moment she became a star, Rathebe's private life was talked and written about as much as her life on the stage. And quite where her public life ended and her personal life began was never clear: her very name, Dolly Rathebe, was borrowed from a high school friend.

Her love life was famously dangerous; at least two of Rathebe's lovers were notorious gangsters. 'Her . . . affairs . . . were like wisps of smoke,' the great Sophiatown writer and onetime lover of Rathebe, Can Themba, wrote, 'one moment thick and meaningful, next moment gone and forgotten.'[12]

More important than her accumulation of lovers was what Rathebe made of sexual desire, both her own and that of her admirers. A man who did not 'throw her into spasms and thrilling sensations' was soon discarded. And onstage, as a torch singer, hers was a 'voice that . . . flashed before [men's] tired, after-work imaginations dreams of torrid love and wanton abandon'.[13] Rathebe was no pretty cover girl, a passive object for men's contemplation.[14] She was a woman who *commanded* men by arousing their desire and dumped them when they could not arouse hers.

Coupled with this power was a refusal to submit to whites. That she might enter a factory to operate a machine or a suburban family's kitchen to cook and clean was unthinkable. She encountered white men as she did black men, she onstage, they in the audience, her performance dizzying them with desire. For in the mid-1950s, Dolly broke out of the townships and into white Johannesburg's nightclub scene.

What Winnie took from Rathebe might have been highly selective. Indeed, among the things she could have learned was how *not* to be.[15] Moving in a world of high respectability, Winnie did not scan Johannesburg's underworld for potential lovers. Nor did she want to be known as a woman who went through one man after another. The connection between the two women is far subtler than that, but no less powerful for it: in what Winnie did with Barney Sampson and with Nelson Mandela there is more than a hint of Dolly Rathebe.

Winnie's relationship with Sampson was a long one. We know from her roommates that they were going steady throughout 1955. She was still with Sampson when she met Nelson in March 1957. And she kept dating both men throughout the remainder of the year.[16] Indeed, she worked both relationships at full throttle, telling Nelson and Barney alike that she would marry them; she did so until the last moment, it seems, before finally breaking with Sampson, following which he attempted suicide.

In its melodrama, in the crazed obsession of its men, in the proximity of sexual desire to a woman's command, it is a story Can Themba might have written about Dolly Rathebe.

. .

When one scans the black Johannesburg press during Winnie's three-year career at the Jan Hofmeyr School – *Golden City Post, Drum, The Bantu World* – something striking comes to light.

Five photographs of Jan Hofmeyr students were published from the beginning of 1953, when Winnie arrived, to the end of 1955, when she graduated. The first is a group picture of the class of 1954. There are eleven men in the photograph and three women. Some of the men are in suits and ties, others in dress suits and bow ties. Those sitting in the front row reveal bright white socks above black brogue shoes. The women are in white full-length gowns that narrow at the waist before puffing out along the contours of a wide tulle. Each has an elaborate bouquet above her left breast. This is clearly a world that invests a great deal in ceremony and sartorial precision.[17]

The next photograph was taken at the Jan Hofmeyr School sum-mer ball held at the Bantu Men's Social Centre in December 1954. The photographer is elevated above the dance floor, and when the shutter clicks, everyone in frame is looking up at the camera. It is an image of consummate style. The men in their coats and ties, handkerchiefs in their pockets, some in white dinner jackets with tails. The women in angle-length ball gowns, cut low, with much embroidery and lacework about the chest. The caption accompanying the photograph tells us that the Merry Blackbirds are playing, a five-piece dance band that had been performing in Johannesburg venues for more than twenty years.[18]

The last three pictures taken during those years are solo por-traits and each is of Winnie Madikizela. The first is at that same ball in December 1954. She looks out, away from the camera; she seems to have been taken unawares. She is wearing round tortoise-shell glasses and a pearl in each ear; she looks very young and quietly composed. In the caption, she is misnamed: 'Miss Winnie Madikazi, a student at the Jan Hofmeyr School of Social Work.'[19]

The picture ran in *The Bantu World*, which was delivered free of charge to 76 Hans Street every day.[20] One wonders whether Winnie noted that the photographer had found *her* face, of all the faces at that ball, but had paid such careless attention to her name.

The next photograph of Winnie was taken at the Hofmeyr ball the following December. It is clearly late in the evening, dinner long since consumed. She stands majestically over piles of used dishes, her out-stretched arm pointing over them, as if they were her pawns. She is wearing a ring of pearls around her neck and a white dress, cut low and tight around the torso. Most striking about the picture is neither her youth nor her beauty but her aristocratic bearing. She does not look like a girl taken by surprise in the kitchen at a ball; she appears to have summoned the photographer and composed the shot herself, doing all but click the shutter.[21]

The final photograph of Winnie shows her receiving her diploma at her graduation ceremony. The distinguished educationalist Dr. P. A. W. Cook, technical adviser at the national Department of Bantu Education, has been sent off to the Jan Hofmeyr School to give a speech and hand the students their diplomas. He strikes an awkward pose, leaning over from a distance while passing Winnie the scroll, as if he were afraid to catch a germ. The caption accompanying the photograph explains his reluctance. The previous year, a Hofmeyr student refused to shake the hand of the government official who gave him his diploma, causing much embarrassment to the man concerned. Dr. Cook had clearly been warned not to put out his hand.[22]

On the day Oliver Tambo introduced Nelson to Winnie outside the delicatessen at the side of the road, Nelson had asked whether she was a relative. 'Don't you know Winnie?' Tambo had replied. 'She is always dancing up and down the newspapers.' It was to this series of portraits that he must have been referring. During the three years Winnie studied at the Jan Hofmeyr School, about 110 students were admitted there.[23] Of these, just one had a solo portrait published in a newspaper, not once, but three times. It was a measure of the power of her presence.

.   .

In her final year at the Jan Hofmeyr School, Winnie interned in the social work department at Baragwanath Hospital outside Soweto. Just over a decade old, it was a vast institution with one thousand five hundred beds, most of them occupied on any given day.[24] It employed just two social workers, both white. Not only were they stunningly overworked; the cultural distance between them and the people in their care made their task all the harder.

Then the young intern from the Jan Hofmeyr School arrived, and overnight the nature of the work changed. It was not just that Winnie took it upon herself to act as an interpreter for the Xhosa- and Zulu-speaking patients: she brought their case histories to life. Suddenly, the two white social workers found, their 'cases' became rounded human beings; the *detail* of the obstacles they faced lit up as it never had before. And Winnie's sense of what to do showed a wisdom that belied her age and a knowledge of black Johannesburg the white social workers simply did not possess.

Winnie was far too precious to let go. One of the social workers, Doris Goldberg, was due to retire at the end of 1955. The other, June Dwolatzky, lobbied among the hospital's administrators to offer Winnie the post that would become vacant. They, in turn, took the case to the public authorities. The bureaucratic obstacles they encountered were immense; the post had to be rewritten from scratch, for there was no precedent for it; a South African hospital had never employed a black social worker before. It all came together at the last moment, in October

1955. On the first Monday of January the following year, Winnie began work.[25]

She had been there just a few days when Columbus Madikizela visited. More than sixty years later, the image of him walking into her office was still emblazoned in Dwolatzky's mind. It was as if a patriarch had walked out of the pages of the Old Testament; clutching a staff, he was 'decked up to the nines, an *extremely* elegant man'. She had never encountered a rural aristocrat before, and he seemed so out of place in this urban hospital, its emergency room peppered with wounded gangsters, its ward beds filled with factory workers, vagrants and single mothers.

Columbus had come to give his stamp of approval to his daughter's new career. And as his visit proceeded, it dawned on Dwolatzky that she herself was the primary object of his scrutiny, for it appeared that he was placing Winnie in her care. The idea seemed totally preposterous to her; true, she was Winnie's boss, but she was not yet twenty-two years old.[26]

.   .

The conditions under which Winnie was forced to practice her profession would have made her skin crawl. Two social workers servicing a fifteen-hundred-bed hospital. 'Real social work we never really did,' Dwolatzky recalled. 'Beyond making sure that patients had a place to go after they were discharged, it was difficult to do very much.'

At times Winnie did considerably more. In early 1958, for instance, a Congolese national in her care, a man named Ismail Sali, found himself in a bizarre predicament. He had come to Johannesburg from the Belgian Congo in the employ of a white couple. When their stay in South Africa was over, they had simply abandoned him. Without work papers, he was twice arrested and sent into the countryside to perform farm labour. But when he tried to return home to the Belgian Congo, he was refused a rail travel permit. The authorities permitted him neither to remain in the city nor to leave.

In late January 1958 a story appeared in *Golden City Post* describing Sali's extraordinary predicament. It was Winnie's doing. She had not only worked her contacts in the press; she had urged the newspaper to approach the native commissioner to demand an explanation and to publish his embarrassed response.[27]

There is much in this story. Ismail Sali's problem was not his inca-
pacity to adjust to urban life, as Winnie's textbooks would have told her.
His grief was profoundly political; a black man, and a foreigner to boot,
he had been caught in the cogs of a hostile bureaucratic machine. Winnie's task, as she understood it, was to take on that machine with wile.

There are other signs of Winnie's growing political confidence
at that time. It is hard to pin down precisely when the incident happened, but it was almost certainly in 1956 or 1957. Neil Riekert, a general
practitioner in Bizana, the nearest town to Winnie's village, Mbongweni, came home from work one afternoon in a rage about Columbus
Madikizela's daughter.

In addition to his surgery in the town centre, Riekert set up satellite
surgeries in the villages around Bizana. Among the places he stopped
was Ndlovu, where Columbus Madikizela had built a new home. During Riekert's visits, he and Madikizela often talked together for hours.

Riekert's main surgery in Bizana had two consulting rooms, one
for whites and another for blacks. On a day in 1956 or 1957, Madikizela's
daughter, who was visiting from Johannesburg, took umbrage when
ushered into the consulting room for blacks. One can imagine that she
did so with theatre and with force, the assembled audience of patients
looking on aghast. Riekert appears to have kept his composure: he told
her that she was welcome to wait in the white consulting room if she was
prepared to pay the same fee that white patients did. He did not report
to his family how she responded, nor how the incident concluded, but
his son remembers that he was fuming.

'Mark my words,' he told his family. 'That girl is going to come to
a sticky end.'[28]

On display that day in Bizana was the later Winnie to a T: the
implacable stubbornness, the aristocratic defiance, the joy she took in
humbling authority. It is remarkable that it was all there, fully assembled, in her twentieth or twenty-first years.

. .

On an afternoon in the winter of 1957, June Dwolatzky recalled,
Nelson Mandela walked into the social welfare department at Baragwanath Hospital. She had never before encountered so imposing, so
intimidating a man, either black or white. It was not just that he was very
tall, nor that his suit and tie were immaculate; the air with which he

carried himself made him all but unapproachable. When he announced that he had come to see Winnie Madikizela, it was as if he were issuing an underling an instruction. Dwolatzky did not dare try to begin a conversation; his mien simply did not allow for it.

After Mandela had left, Dwolatzky resolved not to raise his visit with Winnie. She knew him as a famous lawyer married to a Baragwanath nurse. And she knew, too, that his marriage was in strife; he had come to the hospital sometime earlier to see his wife – marching down the corridor with regal bearing, as he had done just now – and it had been whispered that his visit was in connection with their impending divorce.

Now Dwolatzky remembered Columbus Madikizela's admonishment that he was leaving his daughter in her care. 'I had better keep out of this,' she remembered thinking. Mandela was a married man twice Winnie's age, and about the whole business, she felt, was a whiff of impropriety. She could not imagine that the Madikizela patriarch would be pleased. She wondered, too, whether Mandela's haughtiness had the same source as her unease; with his imposing display he was banishing any thought of indecorum.[29]

Chapter 19

Of the men courting her at that time, why did Winnie choose Nelson Mandela?

There is an obvious answer. 'If a woman was ambitious ... [when] Winnie and I were young,' a prominent figure of her generation told this author, 'she would have to get what she wanted through a man. We were all trained that way. You look for somebody powerful, not a weakling, not a quiet-spoken poet. You choose a man like Mandela.'[1]

Winnie's choice of a partner was, at least in part, an expression of her desire for a role of her own in public life.

But something less apparent might have attracted her, too: her father was dead against her marriage to Nelson Mandela.

Columbus Madikizela went to considerable lengths to pry his daughter from Nelson. He actively sought an alternative: a medical student in Cape Town was found; and he was an Mpondo of the highest pedigree, to boot. At Columbus's urging the young man wrote Winnie a string of letters, courting her, cajoling her. Winnie was unmoved.[2]

Some recall Columbus Madikizela in a state of rage. 'Why is she marrying that old man?' a cousin of Winnie's remembered his uncle asking. 'Especially one who will live the rest of his life running away from the police and sleeping in the bush.'[3]

'My father was worried about my age,' Winnie said in a later interview. 'He was worried that Nelson was so politically involved. The family elders felt that he was marrying me just as a maid to look after his children because he was going to spend the rest of his life in prison. And he had children from his first marriage.

'I totally disagreed,' she said. And then, unguardedly, she let slip a comment that betrayed her standard story of the courtship. 'We were madly in love,' she said.[4]

Her father's hostility to the marriage went far deeper than that. Columbus was on the brink of signing up to the apartheid project; he was about to join Kaiser Daliwonga Matanzima in establishing the Transkei as an ersatz independent state; he in fact became a member of Matanzima's inaugural cabinet. Winnie was marrying her father's enemy, and the implications were terribly grave. 'My father said to me that . . . by virtue of bringing such a man to him as a son-in-law I was in fact introducing the African National Congress to that part of the country,' Winnie remembered more than twenty years later.[5]

Why would her father's resistance have made Nelson all the more desirable? Recall that as one of eleven children, and as a girl, to boot, Winnie had felt her birth to have been of little value to her parents. She had spent much of her childhood in a quest to become consequential, a quest that required not just that she please her father but that she dazzle him. And she had. By the time she left school, she had her father's undivided attention.

But Columbus had favoured her as a patriarch does, calling all the shots. He had refused to send her to university, insisting that she become a social worker. Barely a week into her first job, he had arrived at Baragwanath, a grand man clutching a staff, to stamp his approval upon her work.

Now, as quick as a flash, she had turned the tables, besting him comprehensively.

One can only imagine the extent of Columbus's surprise: his beautiful, prodigal daughter turning like quicksilver.

There was a sharply agonistic quality to Winnie Madikizela; she understood, and traded in, power.

.   .

The wedding was a Madikizela affair. It is not just that it was held on Columbus's turf, nor that the pews were filled with Winnie's kin; even the minister who married them was a Madikizela. Nelson was by now a famous man. But while he brought a small retinue with him, the spirit of the celebration bore few traces of the life he had made.

He had invited all his closest comrades—Mick and Ray Harmel, Walter and Albertina Sisulu, Joe Slovo and Ruth First, as well as the entire national executive of the ANC. But the invitations were courtesies, for most of these people were banned and thus prohibited from leaving Johannesburg.[6] Nelson was permitted to absent himself from the city for just six days, and only because the wedding he was to attend was his own. He was a leader of a multiracial movement, his white and Indian comrades the source of controversy in the ANC, yet not a single non-African appears to have attended his wedding.*

The few in his circle who did make it tell a story. Among the modest party that travelled from Johannesburg were Ruth Mompati and Lilian Ngoyi. Whether Columbus suspected that the women with Nelson were his lovers we cannot know. It would certainly have confirmed his dim view of the marriage.

The contrast between this and Nelson's earlier wedding, to Evelyn, could not have been starker. These were not two young lovers stealing away to be married in a court. It was *Columbus's* wedding, its trappings those of a Christian notable displaying his status to his world.

The rituals began months before the wedding when two of Nelson's relatives – one of them his beloved boyhood friend Justice Mtirara – came to the Madikizela homestead to negotiate bridewealth. All the while, in Johannesburg, Ray Harmel was at work on Winnie's dress, a virginal-white satin gown, the sleeves worked with floral-patterned lace.

This ritualistic coupling – the African practice of bridewealth and the white-wedding tradition of Christians – was a standard feature of elite African marriages, both then and now. And it continued on the wedding day itself. In the wake of the church ceremony the guests assembled first at the Mbongweni homestead where Winnie had lived as a girl. There, Nelson presented head cloths to the elder Madikizela women; each danced and ululated as she approached him to receive her gift. Then the bride's retinue circled the family homestead, Nelson and his retinue forming a parallel chain. True to tradition, a group of Madikizela men kidnapped Nelson's best man, the lawyer Duma Nokwe, and demanded a ransom.

When the traditional ceremony was over, the party made its way to the town centre of Bizana – a long and difficult journey from Mbongweni, the road poor, the going slow – where Columbus had hired the

---

* There is a famous wedding photograph of Winnie and Nelson, the bridesmaids and friends. Among those in the photograph are Ray and Mick Harmel, their daughter, Barbara, and Toni Bernstein, the daughter of Rusty and Hilda Bernstein. But contrary to common understanding, the picture was taken at a dress fitting at Ray Harmel's house, and not at the wedding itself (Barbara Harmel, email to author, June 14, 2018). It is possible that Fatima Meer attended the wedding; in her biography of Nelson she describes it in some detail in what may be a firsthand account.

town hall. There, another reception commenced. The band played a wedding march, and the bride and groom led the gathering into the hall. A five-tier wedding cake awaited them, covered with white icing and two figurines, a bride and a groom.

In the speech he delivered that evening, Columbus was positively rude. Turning to the small retinue Nelson had brought with him, he offered his sharpest tongue. 'People who come from urban areas have a tendency to look down on those in rural communities,' Winnie later recalled her father saying. 'As if people have a choice to be born where they are born.'[7]

What he said next was so shocking that in Bizana his words remain famous to this day.

'He was not optimistic about the future,' Nelson once said, paraphrasing Columbus's speech. 'Such a marriage, in such difficult times, would be unremittingly tested. He told Winnie she was marrying a man already married to the struggle. He bade his daughter good luck, and ended his speech by saying: "If your man is a wizard, you must become a witch!"'[8]

Nelson recounts the speech in English, but it was delivered in Xhosa; the difference matters a great deal. 'Witch' is a translation of the word *umthakathi,* and it does not refer to a figure who resides in the safety of a fairy tale. Most citizens of the Transkei then, as today, would have understood that *abathakathi* were ordinary people, close family, even, their powers concealed by their apparent normality. They would use occult means to make all sorts of dark wishes come true, including death wishes.

As an educated Christian, Columbus spoke of *abathakathi* with transparent irony; it would have been clear to his audience that he did not literally mean what he said. But the word carried powerful connotations. In front of the assembled guests, he told his daughter that she was marrying a man who dabbled in the dark arts. He could not have made his distaste clearer. You have chosen him against my wishes, he was saying to Winnie, and so you will become a witch.[9]

Chapter 20

They lived together for such a short time. It is striking how differently they came to remember this period of their lives.

'[Thembi and I] would spend about 1½ hours in the gym,' Nelson wrote to his daughter Zindzi in the eighteenth year of his imprisonment, describing what he remembered to be a normal weekday evening.

> I was home about 9 pm. Tired & with hardly a drop of
> water in my body. Mum would give me a glass of fresh and
> cold orange juice, supper served with well-prepared sour
> milk. Mum was gloweth with good health & happiness those
> d[a]ys . . . For more than 2 yrs she and I literally lived on
> honey-moon. I quietly resisted any activity that kept me away
> from home after office hrs.[1]

Compare Nelson's memory with Winnie's.

'The only time we had a normal life', she told an interviewer in 2007, 'was just that week of our wedding. That week was to me a whole lifetime because it symbolised what life might have been.'[2]

At other times, she put it more cruelly. 'He was never really a father to his family, even before he went to jail,' she told Nelson's authorized biographer. 'I rarely sat down with him as a husband and the honest truth of god is that I didn't know him at all. We never lived together. We managed to get two children by him paying visits through the Treason Trial.'

'But he was very much in love with you,' the biographer protested.

'So was I,' Winnie replied. 'So was I.'[3]

Winnie is without doubt the more faithful witness. Nelson's weekdays began at 4:00 a.m. with a predawn run through the empty streets. He came home, bathed, ate, and then headed early to Pretoria for the Treason Trial. His evenings were consumed by ANC meetings and by the increasingly quixotic quest to maintain a law practice. More often than not, he returned home after midnight. And weekends were hardly quieter; the pause in the trial proceedings made precious time for political work.[4]

The scene of domestic bliss Nelson penned for his daughter two decades later is a fantasy. While he was in prison, many aspects of the past became fantastical in his mind, rendering his adjustment to the world when he was freed immeasurably painful.

As for Winnie, her memories of this time are so powerfully affecting. For a woman who self-consciously mythologized her past, there is a searing candour in the way she remembers *this*. Half a century after the fact, when her interviewer asked her to describe her wedding cake, she wept.[5] The idea that one week was a lifetime, for it embodied the promise of a life that failed, is excruciatingly sad. It expresses, more than anything else she said on the record, how besotted she was, and how excited.

It is remarkable to think of how much Winnie *did* in the brief time between her wedding and Nelson's imprisonment. She bore two daughters; the first, Zenani, was conceived less than a month after the wedding. She ran the household. And as his law practice crumbled under the weight of the Treason Trial and his ANC work, she became the family breadwinner.

If the responsibilities of mother, household manager, and breadwinner were not enough, Winnie also made a foray into public life. She soon became close to several older women in Nelson's political circles. Chief among them were Helen Joseph and Fatima Meer: both would remain staunch allies in the decades ahead. She also joined the ANC Women's League and became intimately involved in its political campaigns.

Then, four months after her wedding, at the end of the first trimester of her pregnancy, she was thrown in jail. She knew beforehand that it would happen; she had chosen to join a delegation to protest the extension of pass laws to women, and it was clear from the start that the delegation was going to be arrested. Nelson pleaded with her not to go. She was pregnant, he said, and might lose the child in prison. She might also lose her job, which the family could ill afford.[6] His protestations only cemented her decision. The division of labour Nelson envisaged – she bringing home a salary, managing the house, bearing and rearing the children, while he did politics – did not impress her. She worked at full throttle on both sides of the divide.

Jail was a grim experience. Upon arrival at the Fort, central Johannesburg's notorious prison, the women were lined up, stripped naked and ordered to spread their legs and squat, more a ritual of racial humiliation than a security procedure. And in the days and weeks ahead, as more and more protesting women were detained, the prison filled to the brim. The sanitary buckets overflowed, creating a permanent stench. There were insufficient showers for everyone to use, and inmates began to go unwashed. At night the women slept squashed together on the floor.

A few days into her imprisonment, Winnie began to bleed; for a few hours, she feared she was losing her child. Among the women with her was Albertina Sisulu, Walter's wife, by now a highly experienced nurse. She rushed to Winnie and attended to her until the bleeding stopped, the care she administered as much emotional as medical.[7] It was a rare moment of tenderness between two women whose subsequent feuds grew very bitter indeed.

. .

In Nelson's political circles, Winnie's youth and her beauty were a mask, at least to those paying insufficient attention. Many wrote her off as young and naive and spoke of her thus behind her back. There was a famous story about her behaviour over Sunday lunches at the houses of white comrades in the suburbs. While the others spoke politics, it was said, Winnie sat by herself paging through fashion magazines.

At least one person who attended such Sunday lunches, somebody who, thanks to her age and her state of mind, was more attentive, has a different story to tell.

Mick and Ray Harmel's daughter, Barbara, was sixteen years old when Nelson and Winnie wed. The prospect of her father's comrade and his new wife coming to Sunday lunch never failed to delight her. For one, she enjoyed the reaction their visits provoked in her hard-bitten communist mother. Nelson and Winnie seldom arrived on time, their extravagant green car pulling into the drive as late as three o'clock in the afternoon. And they were always groomed to the hilt, Nelson in a bespoke suit, Winnie in a stylish dress. 'Damn bloody bourgeois,' Barbara recalled Ray muttering under her breath.

These lunches at the Harmels, Winnie later recounted, were a cover for political work. Nelson and Mick did not even eat their meal with the others; barely had the visitors arrived when the two men went off alone.[8] Winnie, her choice for company Ray or Barbara, often followed the teenager to her bedroom.

What happened between them there was life changing for Barbara. She was a tortured girl, suffering bitterly from distracted parenting, her relation to Ray full of rage. Winnie, Barbara recalled six decades later, sized her up at once. She showed Barbara, as much through the aura of her presence as via words, that she understood the hatred she felt for her mother, understood how painful it was to have such feelings at all.

'She was so grown-up to me,' Barbara recalled. 'I did not consider her only six years older than me. She was kind, generous, loving. I was so hungry for that kind of parenting. I was her first little white child.'

Winnie understood what she meant to Barbara, it seems. At least twice a week, on a working afternoon, the phone rang in the Harmel household and it was Winnie. 'Are you still fighting with the tall girl?' Barbara recalled Winnie asking. 'Did you get your geography assignment in on time?' Her attentiveness to the minutiae of Barbara's life seemed not to falter. These were questions her parents simply never asked.

When Barbara Harmel shared her memories with this author, she was old and unwell and just four months from death.

'Did you ever meet Winnie?' she asked. 'Because you can't see from photographs how beautiful she was. At fifteen, sixteen, teenagers are obsessed with their appearance. Are you gorgeous, or do you look like the back of a bus? Everything turns on the answer. I fixated on her skin. It was the clearest, most beautiful skin. I was mesmerized by her.'[9]

Harmel was one of many vulnerable people to take to Winnie. This author has now interviewed half a dozen men and women who have recounted the same moment Harmel described: in a flash, Winnie seemed to see right inside them, witnessing anger, fear, sadness. And she was the most benign witness to these feelings; one *wanted* to share them with her.

It appears that Winnie herself required the intensity; she nurtured it with persistence and with vigour. There would be many equivalents to the twice-weekly phone calls to Barbara. She wanted not just to enter a person's internal world but to *occupy* it.

Born into a large brood, she knew all about what it took to wedge herself into another's thoughts. Indeed, perhaps the greatest talent she took into the world was the capacity not just to understand the person sitting next to her but to become what that person wanted. In Barbara Harmel's case, it was a parent; for others, we shall see, it was somebody to whom to confess; for others, still, a lover.

Her propensity to take this talent for intimacy everywhere, across the lines of race, class, and gender, was notable. Often, it was white men who noticed her power, for Winnie flirted across racial boundaries with an ease that struck them.

Ben Turok, for instance, who stood trial for treason alongside Nelson, recalls that for all that black and white activists socialized together, 'the racial differences were substantial'. There were many, he was to observe, 'who did not make the adjustment easily'.

Not so with Winnie; not even remotely. On the day they met, Turok told Winnie that upon finishing high school, he and a group of friends had backpacked their way through the Mpondoland, at one point passing close to her home. At every subsequent party, Winnie called Turok 'my Mpondo boyfriend' and asked him to dance. There was a self-command in her teasing, and a provocation in her flirting, that stayed with him for decades.[10]

Other white men were similarly struck. Leon Levy, who also stood trial for treason with Nelson, recalled regularly arranging to meet Winnie on a busy street in the inner city. At each of these encounters, Winnie flung her arms around him, her embrace extravagant and tactile. He would consciously stop himself from recoiling; a white man and a black woman embracing thus on a busy street was more than provocative; he feared that passersby would lynch them.

Levy recalled something else about Winnie. At a gathering in the suburbs, while he and Winnie were dancing, she put her lips to his ear: these parties were preparations for the state balls they would host one day, she whispered. It struck him that this young woman, barely in her twenties, had given much consideration to the prospect of exercising power.[11]

. .

Her life during her brief time with Nelson was considerably more constrained than she desired.

When she went to prison in 1958, she was fired from her job at Baragwanath, as Nelson had predicted. Still bitter that Columbus had prevented her from enrolling at university, she wanted to use the opportunity unemployment presented to study for a degree. It was not easy. As Nelson's law practice declined, so did the state of the family's finances. By rights, she ought to have been looking instead for another job. She applied unsuccessfully for a grant to cover the household expenses while she studied; university remained elusive, much to her discontent.

During her period of unemployment she gave birth to her first child. She was alone in the house on the evening she went into labour. Nelson returned home after midnight to find his wife in agony. He fetched Winnie's maternal aunt Phyllis Mzaidume, and the two took Winnie to Baragwanath Hospital, her former place of work. The labour, they were told, was going to last a long time. At daybreak Nelson left for Pretoria for the day's proceedings at the Treason Trial. He returned in the evening to find that his wife had given birth to a daughter. It was February 4, 1959.

Nelson and Evelyn had not followed convention when they named their children; they had chosen the names themselves, without family consultation. Now Nelson and Winnie allowed tradition to take over. The naming of the child was handed to a Thembu royal, Chief Jongin-taba Mdingi. He called the girl Zenani, which is a question: *What have you brought?*

Winnie has left no public record of her feelings toward her infant children. She said a great deal about what it meant to be a mother after Nelson went to prison, but nothing of these earliest days. Nelson's mother came immediately from the Transkei to help with the child. Winnie went out looking for a job. Five months after Zenani was born, she was in full-time employment once more, this time at the Johannesburg Child Welfare Society, a charity run by the very same circle of people who had founded the Jan Hofmeyr School and the Helping Hand.[12]

Looked at from afar, the household taking shape at 8115 Orlando West in the final months of 1959 was legible and familiar. Like many Soweto homes, it was filling with kin from the countryside. Aside from Nelson's mother, his sister Leabie had now lived there for years; having finished high school, she was training as a nurse. Madikizelas began coming too: by the time Zenani was born, Winnie's younger sisters, Nobantu and Nonyaniso, were spending considerable time at the Mandela residence. There was a household dog, a Rhodesian ridge-back called Gompo. Years later, Nobantu recalled Nelson forcing her to spend a night with Gompo in the yard as punishment for staying out too late.[13] And there was a trusty, full-time domestic worker, for the two principal residents, Nelson and Winnie, were professionals, the household's greatest distinction.

True, aspects of 8115 Orlando West were distinctive. The house had a former mistress who now resided less than a mile away. And three older Mandela children once lived there, but no more. They seldom visited. Their father, after all, was barely at home. As for his new wife, they regarded her with caution, if not with suspicion, for her presence in their lives had arisen from the trouble between their parents.

But all homes have their distinctive histories, after all.

Come the new decade, the household would resemble no other in its country's history. Its patriarch a legendary fugitive, its matriarch a symbol of strength, it assumed the character of a public myth. Its principal parties spent the following decades tending that myth, their every move a double move, one in private life, the other on a stage.

Chapter 21

The story in fact begins in November 1958, when Africanists in the ANC, chafing at its multiracial alliances, finally broke away. The split was dramatic, ugly, and very nearly violent.

It happened at the Transvaal ANC's annual two-day conference, by now a familiarly stormy affair. The organization's president, Albert Luthuli, opened proceedings with a barbed commentary on the Africanists, lamenting how tragic it was that there were black people who emulated the apartheid government's thinking on race. During his speech, 'a horde of Africanists', as a journalist put it, entered the hall and drowned out his speech by stamping their feet in unison against the floor.

By the next morning, the Africanists had mobilized scores of young men who stood outside the conference hall carrying sticks and clubs. The Charterists, in turn, surrounded the venue with a phalanx of guards. When the Africanist delegates approached the hall to take part in the day's proceedings, they were told that their credentials were not in order and were turned away. They gathered at a nearby house to deliberate. Finally, at around lunchtime, one of them made his way to the hall and asked to be admitted; he wished to hand over a letter announcing that the Africanists were leaving the ANC. The letter was forcibly taken from him, and he was chased from the hall.[1]

In April 1959, the dissenters launched a new organization, the Pan Africanist Congress (PAC). It elected as its founding president Robert Sobukwe, a thirty-four-year-old former schoolteacher and a lecturer at Wits University. He had been recruited into the ANC Youth League eleven years earlier, when he was a student at Fort Hare, by the man who would become Nelson's disgruntled law clerk, Godfrey Pitje.

And so, at the advent of the new decade, two rival organizations stood head-to-head. Under the leadership of its president, Albert Luthuli, the ANC envisaged a multiparty democracy for South Africa, one in which, as Luthuli liked to stress, a white person could become president, so long as an inclusive electorate had voted him into power.[2] The PAC, in contrast, envisaged the dissolution of colonial borders and the rise of a continent-wide, federal African state. Freedom, the PAC declared, resided in the return of the continent to its indigenous people.[3]

If the goals of the two organizations were different, so were their visions of change. The ANC imagined that campaigns of civil disobedience, boycotts and strikes would weaken the ruling minority's resolve. The white electorate would vote the National Party out of office and install a more liberal government in its place. This new government would concede to the idea of a democratic convention charged with writing a new constitution for a multiracial democracy.

The PAC, in contrast, believed that white rule would end only with the total collapse of the regime, either by insurrection or by the mass withdrawal of labour. The organization was imbued with a highly masculinist spirit. Its membership was younger than the ANC's and almost entirely male. And it openly courted a constituency from which the ANC had always shied away: the unemployed urban youth, until now organized largely through the great criminal gangs of mid-century South Africa. The culture the gangs inculcated was violent, menacing and openly hostile to whites, an insurrectionary resource if ever there was one, as far as some in the PAC were concerned.[4]

But for all their differences, the two organizations held something in common: they both misread the South African situation, and they did so for the same reason.

Four days before Nelson and Winnie's first date, on March 6, 1957, Kwame Nkrumah was sworn in as the prime minister of Ghana, the first British colony to acquire independence. The previous year, Morocco, Tunisia and Sudan acquired independence. Guinea would follow in 1958, Cameroon, Senegal, Togo, Mali, Madagascar and Congo in 1960. In Algeria, a country whose permanent white settlement made comparison to South Africa inevitable, a war for independence was raging.

Seduced by the excitement of these times, senior figures in both organizations imagined white rule to be dying. 'It is no mere rhetoric to say that apartheid is proving to be a Frankenstein,' Luthuli declared in December 1959. 'Industry and Commerce are beginning to squeal . . . White South Africa is vulnerable.'[5] And the father of Winnie's new-found young friend, Barbara, Michael Harmel, a leading theoretician of the South African Communist Party, wrote in the same year that apartheid was 'a freak, an anachronism which cannot have much longer to survive.'[6]

As for the PAC, it declared that it would take power in South Africa by 1963.

The year it chose was not arbitrary. In December 1958, four months before the PAC was launched, a meeting of great significance had convened in Accra, the capital of Nkrumah's newly independent Ghana. The All-African People's Conference brought together leaders of independent African states and national liberation movements from twenty-eight countries and colonies, an unprecedented display of Pan-African purpose. No part of Africa could consider itself free, the conference resolved, until every part of it had been liberated. The conference set 1963 as the year of continental liberation.

At the PAC's launch in April the following year, letters of support were read out from Nkrumah and from Sékou Touré, who was on the brink of becoming the first president of Guinea. This was a coup for the PAC, for it now boasted a direct link with the very heart of the Pan-African movement. In declaring that it would take power by 1963, it was signalling its intent that South Africa become part of a federal African state.

The PAC's programme to topple apartheid began on March 21, 1960, with a campaign against the country's pass laws. PAC leaders across South Africa would leave their passes at home that morning – illegal for black people, of course – and present themselves at their local police stations for arrest. Hundreds of thousands of people, perhaps even millions, would be inspired to follow: the prisons would fill up, immobilizing the criminal justice system; the economy would cease to function as workers failed to come to work. The government in its desperation would abolish the pass laws, and white rule would begin to fall apart.[7]

It was a hopelessly romantic illusion that nonetheless changed the course of history.

On the morning of March 21, a tiny minority of black South Africa heeded the PAC's call. In Orlando, where Sobukwe lived, just 120 or so people followed him to the local police station to present themselves for arrest. Elsewhere, the numbers were even smaller.

But in two pockets of the country, the black townships of Langa and Nyanga in Cape Town, and in the settlements of Sharpeville and Evaton, which buttressed the steelmaking town of Vereeniging on the banks of the Vaal River, the PAC had built a successful grassroots organization. Here people assembled in front of police stations in large numbers.

In Sharpeville, a massive crowd, by some estimates twenty-five thousand strong, had gathered by lunchtime. During the morning, attempts to disperse it by flying military aircraft low over the township had only attracted greater numbers. At about 1:30 p.m., a section of the wire fence surrounding the police station collapsed, an officer was pushed over, and the front ranks of the crowd surged forward. When somebody in the crowd fired two pistol shots into the air, somebody in the police ranks shouted 'shoot'. At least one officer took this as an instruction to open fire; 167 constables followed his lead, together discharging more than thousand rounds of ammunition into the crowd. By 2:00 p.m., sixty-nine corpses lay strewn in the vicinity of the police station, most of them with bullet wounds in their backs.[8]

.   .

In the days that followed, South Africa entered a period of crisis. International condemnation was immediate. Johannesburg's bourse crashed and capital flowed out of the country. Astonishingly, the resolve of the apartheid government appeared to waver; four days after the massacre, the commissioner of police announced that his officers would stop arresting pass law offenders.

The mood in the top echelons of the ANC was as fluid and unstable as the state of the country. Nelson and his colleagues' most immediate fear was that the PAC had stolen the initiative. He spent the night of March 21 locked in a meeting with Sisulu, Slovo and Duma Nokwe. Sitting around Slovo's dining room table, the group resolved that ANC leaders should publicly burn their passbooks, starting with the organization's president, Albert Luthuli. And they would appeal to the country to stay at home for a day of mourning.

The leaders, Nelson among them, duly set their passbooks alight in full view of the press. And, two days later, on March 28, the stay away the ANC called was widely observed. But by the end of the month, events in Cape Town, the other city where the anti-pass campaign had been successful, had only brightened the PAC's star. A general strike had brought the city to a standstill. And when the police invaded Langa township to break it, a crowd of thirty thousand marched into the city to protest. It was unprecedented: thousands upon thousands of black people descending on the country's legislative capital, an image previously conjured only by white fear. The day would live on in memory, in photographs, in poetry, and in some of the country's finest prose.[9]

History might have taken a different turn had the Cape Town police not been shrewder. The leader of the march, a youthful protégé of Sobukwe's called Philip Kgosana, was promised a meeting with the justice minister on condition that the marchers go home. Naively, he agreed. The crowd dispersed, and when Kgosana returned in the afternoon for the promised meeting, he was arrested and thrown in prison.

On March 31, a state of emergency was declared. Over the following twenty-four hours, police swooped on the homes of activists across the country, detaining almost two thousand people. Having received a tip-off about the impending mass arrests from a sympathetic black security policeman, Nelson conferred with close colleagues. It was decided that a handful of activists would disappear underground. In addition, a much-discussed plan for Oliver Tambo to leave the country and establish an ANC presence abroad was now set into motion. Tambo had broached the question with his wife, Adelaide, weeks earlier. The ANC's national executive had decided that she would go with him, he told her, because if he pined for his family, he would not be effective in his work. Adelaide had demurred. Now, in the turmoil following Sharpeville, he upped and left; she would join him in Tanzania's capital city, Dar es Salaam, from where the couple would move to London.[10] They did not return to their native land for three decades.

As for Nelson, it was decided that he, along with most of the ANC leadership, would submit to arrest. The police took him from his home on the night of March 31. Eight days later, parliament passed legislation banning the ANC and the PAC.

And then, on April 9, South Africa's prime minister Hendrik Verwoerd was shot in the face at point-blank range by a white man at an agricultural show in Johannesburg. As he lay stricken in the hospital, the prospect of significant reform appeared to swell. The man deputizing as prime minister, Paul Sauer, declared on April 19 that Sharpeville had closed a chapter in the country's history and that race relations would be reexamined. Afrikaner nationalism's flagship newspaper, *Die Burger,* declared in its editorials that week and the next that South Africa was becoming a pariah and had to change.

And yet Verwoerd not only survived but made an astonishing

recovery; by the end of May he was back at work. A blisteringly self-righteous man, hardly in need of the notion of providence to bolster his confidence, he declared that God had spared him that he might continue to lead; he suppressed dissent and doubled down.[11]

The state of emergency continued. The two thousand or so arrested in the wake of Sharpeville remained in jail. Many others were on the run. The journalist Benjamin Pogrund drove to Swaziland, the tiny, landlocked British protectorate a five-hour drive from Johannesburg. Edging down the main street of the capital, Mbabane, he saw on the sidewalk several activists he knew from home. They had all fled.[12] The Sharpeville explosion had scattered like shrapnel several layers of South Africa's activist leadership.

. .

Nelson was incarcerated for exactly five months at Pretoria Local Prison. During this time, as he and his comrades monitored as best they could the mood in the world outside, what dismayed them most was the growing stature of the PAC.

When Robert Sobukwe and his PAC comrades were arrested on March 21, 1960, they were quickly put on trial, and their performance in court inspired awe. Quite simply, they refused to defend themselves. They used the pulpit afforded them only to denounce the legitimacy of the court. And, under the slogan 'no bail, no defence, no fine', they submitted to whatever the judge had in store for them.

Behind this course of action lay a pointed criticism of the ANC. Its leaders might have defied apartheid laws, Sobukwe declared, but only once they had lined up a battery of lawyers to defend them. PAC leaders, in contrast, 'are not afraid of the consequences of our actions, and it is not our intention to plead for mercy'.[13]

The ANC fought apartheid comfortably, safely, even luxuriously, Sobukwe contended. He aimed to inspire black South Africans by suffering.

One after the other, the accused refused to plead: because they had had no hand in making the law, each said, they had no moral obligation to obey it.[14]

It was an immensely effective performance. To make of apartheid's courts a theatre for sacrifice was both new and ever so old, for Sobukwe's audience was nothing if not schooled in the Gospels and had thus watched Saint Peter, and indeed had watched Jesus, become a martyr in an enemy's court.

Nelson was taken aback by the effects of his rival's stance. 'Sobukwe was praised by the press and individuals inside and outside the country as a man of the future,' he wrote from prison sixteen years later. 'The "Voice" of Ghana hailed him as a Messiah arisen from amongst the people and who was carrying the cross of freedom to Mount Golgotha.'[15] Nelson's sarcasm, all those years later, betrays the residues of his original fear.

The power of the PAC's display was all the more galling for its growing inconsistencies. Once it became clear that they would face much stiffer sentences than they had anticipated – Sobukwe himself initially got three years – its leaders began to doubt the wisdom of what they had done. Before Sobukwe's trial was over, the defendants had split over whether to hire lawyers after all. And that was just the start. In the months to come, PAC leaders flouted every component of their slogan, 'no bail, no defence, no fine'.[16] Sobukwe himself appealed his sentence.

He had nonetheless put down a marker in the sand. He was in jail for his principles and would remain there a long time: the spectacle was proving formidable.

From his own prison cell, Nelson watched with escalating alarm. So much of what he did in the following two years was aimed to take back the initiative from Sobukwe and the PAC.

. .

Several people who brushed shoulders with Nelson during his confinement in 1960 noticed something new. One of them was Leon Levy. Among the two thousand people arrested when the emergency was declared, he was also held at Pretoria Local Prison. Although as a white man he was kept separately from the black prisoners, he at times had the opportunity to consult with his comrades over their Treason Trial defense. What he observed in the black section of the jail stayed with him forever.

He had never considered Nelson a potential leader of the ANC. The bespoke suits, the gaudy car, the incessant flirting with pretty women – Levy was among those who felt Nelson too frivolous to lead. But now, in the cells in Pretoria, he saw a side of Nelson he had not imagined existed.

'He was making sure that the hundreds of young people detained with him were reading books, were warmly dressed, that they had the facilities they needed,' Levy recalled. 'One after the other, he checked that they had contacted their parents. When things were not right, he was the one to complain to the station commander, not an easy man, but Nelson had the ability to stand up to him and get him to converse in a reasonable way. I understood for the first time that I was looking at an unusually talented leader.'[17]

Levy would not have known that at around this time Nelson was in fact *chosen* to lead. The decision was made not by any formal ANC structure but in secret by a small coterie of people around Walter Sisulu.

What the conspirators imagined him leading was not another pass-burning campaign or the defiance of racist laws. They imagined him leading an armed struggle.*

If Sobukwe's stature was growing because he had become a symbol of sacrifice, Nelson would better him as a symbol of *action:* dramatic, violent action.

---

* Sisulu was coy on this point. He told Nelson's biographer Anthony Sampson that Nelson was chosen at this time to be the ANC's leader in jail. But he could not have forecast in mid-1960 that Nelson would be sentenced to life in prison. It is almost certain that what Sisulu intended at this point was to turn the ANC to armed struggle and to have Nelson lead it. See Sisulu, interview by Sampson, Nov. 1995, ASP, Dep. 168.

Chapter 22

Nelson was released on the last afternoon of August. He got a lift to Johannesburg, caught a bus to Orlando, then made his way home by foot. From a block away, he spotted his wife in the garden. She ran into the street, barefoot, and embraced him before an audience of neighbours.[1] That night, they lay down in the same bed, in *their* bed, for the first time since March.

Winnie was four months pregnant. The child was almost certainly conceived when Nelson was let out of prison on the weekends to attend to his law practice at Chancellor House. Winnie would come to see him there, and Nelson's kindly police chaperone, a sergeant Kruger, would leave the couple alone together.

Though she had missed him, Nelson's absence had hardly left her by herself. His sister Leabie was living there, and his mother was a regular visitor. Two of Winnie's sisters, Nobantu and Nonyaniso, were residents of the Mandela home.

The house was tiny, the kitchen and living room jammed together, the modest bedrooms to the side. One imagines that Winnie enjoyed the crowdedness; for much of her life, she reveled in keeping a full house, the many people about her a requisite of her well-being.

She was the sole breadwinner now, her work at the Johannesburg Child Welfare Society keeping the family afloat. Nelson's law practice was a walking ghost, its demise a matter of time.

When Nelson returned, another task was added to Winnie's already formidable load. In addition to earning the family's income, raising its first child, and carrying its second, she catered for the political gatherings that would assemble at her house. Sometimes as many as a dozen men would appear without notice: that she would cook them a meal was taken for granted; that her work in the kitchen precluded her from participating in their discussions was assumed.[2]

Winnie was hardly alone in playing these many roles. Several blocks from Vilakazi Street, Albertina Sisulu's nursing career fed a family she was raising largely alone. The everyday challenges these women faced reached the level of satire. Sometime in the late 1950s, Albertina gave Walter a list of groceries and some money as he was leaving the house and asked him to buy food on his way home. He returned empty-handed that evening, confessing that he had used the money for ANC business.[3] As for Nelson, in matters of household economy he was clueless, Winnie recalled. Whatever he earned he spent. Winnie watched in alarm as the household coffers ebbed and swelled, depending on whether something he fancied had caught Nelson's eye.[4]

This is how the revolutionaries of mid-twentieth-century South Africa joined the struggle: in married couples, the baggage each union carried bursting at the seams, the distribution of burdens lopsided. They raised children as a matter of course, for they were traditional enough to embrace the sanctity of nuclear families. Yet the role of women in these marriages was hardly reduced to motherhood. The Winnies and Albertinas of the world were highly educated and expected to conduct professional careers; indeed, their vocational expertise put bread on the table. They were also expected to be as politically conscious as their husbands and to engage in activism, at least insofar as their other duties permitted. And in addition to being professionals, activists and breadwinners, they performed all the household duties expected of a traditional wife.

They carried the burdens of women past and of women to come, all in one life. In this, they were very much of the global mid-century, bearing the load of one of humanity's greatest transitions.

. .

Winnie went into labour several weeks early, on December 20, 1960, and was urgently admitted to the non-European wing of the Bridgman Memorial Hospital. While the birth itself was normal and the child healthy, the labour was extremely difficult; battered and weak, Winnie was taken from her newborn daughter and placed in an oxygen tent.[5]

Nelson was not in town, for he was attending to an emergency of his own. His younger son, Makgatho, had fallen ill at his boarding school in the Transkei; on hearing the news, Nelson had driven to him through the night, violating his banning order. Not satisfied that his son would receive adequate medical care, he drove him immediately to Johannesburg. He arrived home deliriously tired to be told that his wife was in labour; he rushed to the hospital to find a healthy girl and an ailing mother.

They named their daughter Zindziswa. As with Makgatho, the name had a nationalist pedigree; Zindziswa is what the famous Xhosa poet Samuel Mqhayi, whom Nelson had seen perform as a schoolboy, called *his* daughter.

But behind the naming there lay, too, a more complex story about Nelson and Winnie.

Why Mqhayi named his child Zindziswa is an edgy tale. Returning from a long journey, he discovered that his wife had just given birth, and he assumed that the infant was another man's. Enraged, he stormed his own house with an assegai, his intent to murder mother and child. But upon looking the little girl in the face, he saw only a reflection of himself. '*Uzindzile*,' he had said, his doubts allayed. 'You are well established.'[6]

It is Nelson who shared this story, and one must guess that in naming his daughter thus, he mocked his own fears. He had married a beautiful, flirtatious woman, and since the wedding he had been more away than at home.

Chapter 23

Between his release from prison and the birth of his daughter, Nelson's appearance began to change. The clean-shaven face gave way to a coarse beard; as he grew his hair, the middle parting at times disappeared.[1] Self-consciously, Nelson Mandela was transfiguring himself: the lawyer was giving way to another role.

In September, the National Executive Committee of the ANC met secretly and agreed to dissolve its formal structures: the Youth League, the Women's League, the elected provincial and branch executives. Nelson was tasked with bringing to life across the country a centralized structure of underground cells. The ANC was preparing for a new era, one in which it was banned.

In December, just four days before Zindzi was born, a meeting of African political notables resolved to call an 'All-In African Conference' for the end of the following March. It was envisaged that thousands would attend; a nationwide strike would follow, then rent and tax boycotts. These actions would culminate in a national convention tasked with drawing up a constitution for a democratic South Africa. Nelson was elected secretary of the committee that would make the preparations for the conference.[2]

On the face of it, the campaign appeared naive. '[It] showed just how intellectually unprepared the leadership of the Congress alliance was in 1961 to embark on a revolutionary struggle,' one historian has remarked.[3] It is likely, though, that at least some in the alliance understood that the campaign would be put down, forming the narrative foundation for a turn to armed struggle.[4]

At first, the ANC worked with members of the PAC and the Liberal Party on the conference preparations, but by March only the ANC remained. The Liberals backed away because of feared Communist Party influence. As for the PAC, it resolved to 'crush' the proposed conference on the grounds that its primary purpose was 'to build up Mandela as a hero in opposition to Sobukwe'.[5]

The PAC was surely correct. The All-In African Conference was scheduled to take place over the last weekend of March in Pieter-maritzburg. In mid-March, at a clandestine meeting of the ANC's national working committee, a series of decisions were made. The first was that Nelson would appear at the conference unannounced and give the keynote address. He had been banned for more than eight years and had not addressed a public gathering since 1952. His current banning order was about to lapse, and due to bureaucratic inattention a new one had yet to be imposed. He would simply appear at the conference, with great drama, from out of the blue.

That was just the first decision the meeting made about Nelson. There were more, and they were dramatic.

Nelson's speech was scheduled to be delivered on March 25. Four days later, the judge would finally hand down his verdict in the intermi-nable Treason Trial. It was expected that the accused would be acquit-ted. The moment the court proceedings ended, Nelson would vanish.

'I would go underground to travel about the country organising the proposed national convention,' he recalled later. 'It was decided that I would surface at certain events, hoping for a maximum of publicity, to show that the ANC was still fighting.'[6]

Robert Sobukwe remained in prison, martyr-like, unblemished. Nelson and his comrades wanted very much to present a counterim-age, and the opposite of a man sitting helplessly in jail is a man who *acts*. Like many black South Africans, they were casting around the decolo-nizing world: for ideas, for inspiration, and, indeed, for styles. And the Cuban Revolution was at this moment *the cause célèbre* across what was coming to be known as the Third World: a band of twelve men had raised a guerrilla army in eighteen months; just now, in January 1959, they had marched on Havana and taken power.

His beard, his growing hair: Nelson was looking a lot like Fidel Castro.

Throughout his adult life, Nelson had made of his appearance a drama. To be six feet two and *big*, he had understood for the longest time, was not just an accident of nature, but a resource to be used. Now, for the first time, it would be his *vocation* to appear, his full-time job, as it were. But much more than that, for even from a full-time job one takes time off. Nelson's entire life, literally every second of it, would be enlisted into a great theatre: that of a man who is almost always invisible, but for when he miraculously, without warning, *appears*.

. .

The All-In African Conference took place in a spirit of surreal optimism. It was nothing less than an assembly of all of South Africa, a triumphant report in *Drum* magazine declared. In the face of the banning of their organizations and the jailing of hundreds of their leaders, fourteen hundred people from across the country arrived.

'They came by train, by car, by foot, by bicycle. They came carrying bundles of food, which they shared out as if at a family picnic.' And when it turned out that there were more delegates than available rooms, people simply slept in the fields.[7]

Even the distant *New York Times* gushed, describing the event as 'the biggest political meeting of Africans ever held in South Africa'.[8]

Nelson's surprise appearance was as effective as intended.

'I was sitting next to a man who was busy taking notes while Mandela was speaking,' *Drum*'s reporter wrote. 'Suddenly the man turned to me and remarked, "This is like a State of the Nation address by an American President." '[9]

All the black newspapers carried photographs of Nelson delivering his speech, his appearance reflecting his state of transition: the lawyer's checked suit, the revolutionary's straggly beard. Most reports described him with reverence.

. .

Four days later, Nelson and his co-accused in the Treason Trial were finally acquitted after four gruelling years in court, years that had robbed them of their livelihoods, their professions, their domestic lives.

And then Nelson disappeared.

His and Winnie's memories of his parting are sharply at odds. In Nelson's recollection, he gave Winnie two weeks' warning, telling her that he would be going underground as early as mid-March.

'It was as if Winnie could read my thoughts,' he wrote, recalling the moment he shared the news with her. 'Seeing my face, she knew that I was about to embark on a life that neither of us wanted . . . She took this stoically, as if she had expected it all along.'[10]

How different Winnie's recollection is. In her account, there is no forewarning; there isn't even the barest discussion between husband and wife.

She was not at court on the last day of the Treason Trial, March 29. Nelson came home that evening among a party of ANC leaders, their mood ebullient. They did not enter the house; they stood outside in the street, laughing, celebrating, enjoying the victory.

One of them, a man named Joe Modise, walked into the house and asked Winnie to pack Nelson a bag. He would be gone just a few days, Modise explained.[11]

He returned twenty-nine years later, his homecoming broadcast throughout the world.

. .

Nelson hid initially in the home of two close comrades, Paul and Adelaide Joseph, in the inner-city neighbourhood of Fordsburg. From this base, he began to cultivate carefully chosen journalists. His first task was to organize, and win sympathetic press coverage for, a three-day national stay away planned for the end of May, the first in a series of actions to culminate in the national convention.

The entire Joseph family was enlisted into the operation. Adelaide drove her eleven-year-old niece to within a block of the offices of the *Rand Daily Mail,* South Africa's liberal daily. The child walked the final block and handed to the receptionist a note addressed to Benjamin Pogrund, one of the newspaper's political reporters, informing him of a time and a place to meet. It was usually late at night, on a street corner somewhere in Fordsburg. Pogrund arrived in his car to find the tall figure of Nelson Mandela in the shadows; his disguise, a pair of worker's overalls, was pitifully thin.[12]

With other newspapers, Nelson developed different relationships. In late April, a typed statement signed by Mandela was delivered, anonymously, to the offices of *Golden City Post.* The newspaper ran a story quoting the statement, but it also carried the caution that it could not verify the document's provenance. From then on, Nelson called the *Post*'s newsroom from a public phone. Of the newspaper's staff, just two reporters were sufficiently familiar with his voice to swear that it was him. The *Post* resolved that one of them would always be on hand in the event that Nelson rang.

It was extremely effective. The idea of this single man, orchestrating from hiding a vast action, seized black South Africa's imagination.

'The voice of Nelson Mandela once again came across to the *Post* by telephone,' *Golden City Post* reported on the eve of the three-day strike. 'I am so fit I could take on Floyd Patterson,' the newspaper cited Nelson saying.[13] In the absence of political representation, the black press had for some time been something of a proxy government.[14] Now a shadow leader was talking via the newspapers to the people, describing his health, his spirit, his state of mind.

In mid-May, *The World* ran a stunningly audacious front page. On the left-hand side was a small, head-and-shoulders photograph of the South African prime minister, Hendrik Verwoerd. Towering over him was Nelson Mandela, his photograph running halfway down the page. The accompanying story reported on a letter Nelson had written to Verwoerd, reminding him that if a national convention had not been called by May 31, the strike would go ahead.[15]

Within weeks of his going into hiding, the black press had dubbed Nelson the Black Pimpernel, an allusion to Baroness Orczy's 1905 novel, *The Scarlet Pimpernel*. Set in Paris during the Reign of Terror, the novel centres on an English gentleman who leads a double life. Ostensibly a harmless dandy, he is secretly a brilliant swordsman and escape artist who rescues condemned French aristocrats from the guillotine. At the scene of his exploits he leaves his signature: a scarlet pimpernel. A forebear of the superheroes Clark Kent and Peter Parker, he appears from nowhere to perform outlandish acts in defense of the meek.

Nelson was coming to incarnate one of the oldest fantasies of the weak: a slippery, perhaps even a magical, being, taking on an empire.

Chapter 24

When the proposed three-day stay away began, Nelson and the entire committee tasked with its execution were underground. Detached from the world, they were hardly well placed to assess its progress. Early on the morning of the first day of action, Walter Sisulu, who was in hiding with Nelson, drove with a comrade, Wolfie Kodesh, to a bus terminus and watched; people seemed to be going to work as normal. The two men made their way back to their place of hiding and clicked on the radio; the state broadcaster was reporting that the strike had failed. That evening, Nelson called off the action, unaware that it had in fact been highly successful in several parts of the country.[1]

What he and his comrades did next would evoke lasting controversy. Nelson was driven to the house of a sympathetic university professor in the northwestern suburbs of Johannesburg where a BBC television crew was waiting. He spoke on camera for twenty minutes, three of which would be broadcast in Britain the following day. It was his first television interview and his last for nearly three decades. Looking stiff and tired, against the backdrop of a bare brick wall, he said that the government's brutal response to the stay away had closed the chapter on non-violent protest.[2]

Whether Nelson and his comrades were predisposed to believe that the stay away had failed is hard to know. But it remains a great irony that on a day peaceful protest was successful, he declared it defeated and implied, without a mandate from his organization, that the time for violence had arrived.

A month later, at two marathon meetings at Stanger in Natal, Nelson, Walter Sisulu and others attempted to persuade the Congress movement to turn to armed struggle. The first was an ANC meeting chaired by the organization's president, Albert Luthuli. Luthuli was enormously reluctant. He was among the most thoughtful activists of his generation, his commitment to nonviolence, while not unconditional, was philosophically sophisticated and emotionally deep. After several hours of argument, a delicate compromise was reached, the precise terms of which were disputed for decades to come. A structure quite separate from the ANC, led by Mandela, would prepare a military campaign. Called Umkhonto we Sizwe (MK), 'Spear of the Nation', it would restrict itself to the sabotage of government installations and would avoid loss of life. For his part, Luthuli kept advocating for nonviolence, but undertook not to condemn the campaign once it was under way.[3]

At a second meeting, the ANC met with its Indian, Coloured and white allies. Again, the advocates for violence encountered dissent, and the meeting dragged on until dawn. The cornerstone of Nelson's argument was that the turn to violence was a fait accompli. He spoke at length about a rebellion under way in Winnie's home territory of Mpondoland and how its underground leaders were talking of armed struggle. Young white Liberal Party members were just now forming a group that would soon commit acts of sabotage. The Communist Party had been preparing for violent action since mid-1960. The Non-European Unity Movement, to which Winnie's high school teachers had belonged, was preparing its own underground sabotage campaign. The PAC would soon launch a wild armed campaign.

'Violence would begin whether we initiated it or not,' Nelson wrote later from prison. 'If we did not take the lead now, we would soon be latecomers and followers in a movement we did not control.'[4]

Some have said that the ANC was dragged into armed struggle by a Communist Party conspiracy.[5] The picture was more complex than that. It is true that in December 1960 the Communist Party made a formal decision to take up violence, and it appears that Nelson was at that meeting, probably as a party member.[6] But while fair-weather party members like Nelson argued for armed struggle, some stalwart communists pitted themselves against it. Indeed, among the most eloquent sceptics of violence at those two meetings in Natal was a senior party figure: Moses Kotane.

The argument Kotane and others put forward was simple: launching an armed struggle would not only drain energy and personnel from mass politics; it would give the apartheid state license to crush all opposition.[7] The bracing advice Walter Sisulu had received when he visited China eight years earlier was echoing in his ears.

We cannot know which way history would have turned had

Nelson and his allies lost the argument.[8] But we do know that their detractors' prognosis was right. In the wake of the turn to violence, the ANC was all but wiped off the face of South Africa, its leadership dispersed between prison and exile.[9] Marooned in the wasteland that remained were the wives of the struggle: Albertina Sisulu, Winnie Mandela and others. Barely in contact with those in exile and in prison, some attempted, each after her own fashion, to build an underground organization.

Nelson was party to what might have been one of the most fateful strategic errors in his country's history. Among the consequences were a life in prison and the evolution of a marriage too astonishing for anyone to have made up.

·   ·

He spent August and September holed up in a studio apartment in the Johannesburg suburbs with Wolfie Kodesh. A Thembu royal and a Jewish communist, they were a couple fit for comedy.

Before dawn on their first morning together, Kodesh woke to find Nelson in tracksuit and trainers on the brink of leaving for a run. He was horrified: a black man running through the empty streets of an all-white suburb seemed obviously foolish; he refused to give Nelson a front door key. Instead of arguing, Nelson simply began running on the spot. Kodesh stared in wonder for a while, then turned his back and tried to sleep. He woke an hour later to find Nelson frog jumping across the room.

From the following morning on, Kodesh woke with Nelson and joined him at exercise. It seemed the path of least resistance. At first, he lasted just fifteen minutes; by the time the two men parted, he was keeping up with Nelson for the full two hours.[10]

Nelson *enjoyed* his time underground. Some who visited him clandestinely in Kodesh's flat found themselves in the company of an ebullient, charming, flirtatious man. 'He was, quite simply, full of beans,' one of them recalled.[11]

Among the sources of his good spirits, it seems, was the experience of an unusual new source of danger. He was not just underground; he was notoriously so, the mysterious existence of the Black Pimpernel reported in the newspapers every day. And his efforts to conceal himself were lacklustre. He did not confine himself to Kodesh's flat; from

time to time he would drive to meetings in the most unconvincing disguise: a cap, blue overalls, a thick beard, a pair of rimless sunglasses
– he was meant to pass for a chauffeur. In truth, people recognized him
all the time; they recognized him and they kept his secret, and from
this he derived much pleasure.

One was a Zulu-speaking man Kodesh employed to clean his
apartment. He arrived each morning to what in South Africa in 1961
was the strangest scene: a black and a white man alone together in a
single room, the relation between them one of evident equality. This
man could only have suspected, Nelson commented years later, that
he was in the presence of the Black Pimpernel. And yet he remained
poker-faced, coming each day, cleaning, then leaving.[12]

Once, Kodesh walked into the servants' quarters on the roof of his
building to talk to his employee. The man's door was open, and Kodesh
knocked and poked his head inside. The room was empty, but lying on
the bed was a newspaper from which a headline blared: 'Black Pimpernel Still at Large'. Below it were four photographs of Nelson.

Kodesh rushed downstairs and told Nelson to pack a bag at once.
Nelson just smiled serenely. 'Don't worry, man,' Kodesh recalled him
saying. 'This fellow will never give me away. I know he won't.'[13]

He had many such encounters. Shortly after hiding with Kodesh,
he spent two weeks in northern Natal, in a small settlement of sugar-
cane workers. He posed as an agricultural officer, going through the
motions of asking those with whom he was staying to collect samples of
cane from the fields. It was the thinnest of covers, for Nelson's real work
plainly began at night. Cars came and went at all hours; Nelson himself
often stayed out until dawn and then slept through the day.

When time came for him to leave, and Nelson went to thank his
hosts, they began firing questions. 'What does Chief Luthuli want?'
they asked him. 'Why does he want us to strike? Why can Luthuli [not]
ask us to take up arms?'[14]

They had had the sense to keep up the facade until the moment
Nelson was leaving; only then did they lead him to understand that
they knew precisely who he was.[15]

These encounters were more than titillating. Through them, Nelson could feel his prowess. Black South Africa had assembled to watch
the pursuit of the Pimpernel. And they were on Nelson's side, rooting
for him, loving him, hoping against hope that their love would see him
through.

In October 1961, seven months into his clandestine life, Nelson moved to a twenty-eight-acre farm on the northern fringes of Johannesburg. The property was called Liliesleaf, the municipal district in which it fell Rivonia.

The South African Communist Party had bought the farm two months earlier under the nominal ownership of a man with no apparent political connections.[16] A team of labourers soon arrived and established a working farm. A young white family installed itself in the main house. It was a simple front behind which underground work could be conducted.

Nelson was the first to move in. He lived in a small room in the farm's outbuildings while a group of labourers, all of them black men from Alexandra township, renovated the main house. He was known to them as David Motsamayi – a name he borrowed from a former client – his cover that of a lowly servant. He cooked them breakfast in the mornings and served tea in the afternoons. They treated him with the disdain they felt fit for a man with no trade, forgetting his name, addressing him merely as 'boy'. Black people had never before looked upon Nelson as an inferior. A prince playing a pauper – the timelessness of the tale seized his imagination; he relished it, taking pleasure in their condescension.[17]

Soon he had company. Michael Harmel came to live there for some time. Raymond Mhlaba, a comrade from the Eastern Cape, stayed en route to China for military training. And then an entire family moved into the main house: Arthur Goldreich, a friend of Nelson's, the police still unaware of his political involvement, his wife, Hazel, and their children.

At Liliesleaf, Nelson saw a good deal more of Winnie and his children. It is not that they had had no contact while he was staying with Kodesh. Upon going underground, Nelson had arranged for a young man 'to be Winnie's infrastructure', as a comrade of his put it, 'to support her and the kids, and to connect her to Nelson'.[18] One of the tasks given to this young man was especially delicate: he was to ferry Winnie to Nelson in secret from time to time. En route from Orlando, they drove from one meeting point to another, each time changing cars. On other occasions, Kodesh took Nelson to a safe house where Winnie and the young man were waiting.[19]

His name was Brian Somana. He was twenty-six years old when Nelson tapped him to perform these tasks. A distant relative of Nelson's, he had an excellent cover for spending time at the Mandela house. And he was trusted; a journalist and photographer at *New Age*, the Congress-aligned newspaper, he had worked closely with several of Nelson's comrades. He had also earned his stripes, having been jailed several times, once for attempting to unionize construction workers during their lunch break.[20]

Now, with Nelson at Liliesleaf, Somana drove Winnie and the children to Rivonia.[21] They stayed for entire weekends, sometimes longer. With a farm for the children to wander, and another batch of kids, the Goldreichs, to keep them company, husband and wife were permitted long stretches of time alone.

On Winnie's first appearance at Liliesleaf, Nelson prepared her a meal: on the plate before her she found steak, mashed potatoes, green peas and a salad picked from Liliesleaf's garden. For dessert, he presented her with a carefully arranged basket of fruit.

As they began eating, it occurred to Nelson that his wife had not just gone quiet; she was positively furious. And it dawned on him that what he had just served her were signs of betrayal.

'He couldn't boil an egg,' Winnie said when recollecting this incident. 'He had never made me a cup of tea.'

Nelson spluttered out his protest: he had not been taught to cook by a lover, he said; in all this time without female companionship, he had been forced to learn for himself. Winnie grilled him: she pointed at each item on her plate and asked him how he had prepared it. And as he explained, she threw out the names of those she thought might be his lovers. 'I had people in mind,' she said later.[22]

She never did believe his protests. 'I had no illusions that I was the only one,' she told an interviewer shortly before her death. 'He was a playboy. I knew that.'[23]

In activist circles in 1961, while Nelson was underground, gossip about his love life was rife. There were women who for years after hinted heavily that they had slept with the Black Pimpernel. 'When he was underground he would take great risks,' a close friend of Nelson's, and a prominent activist in her own right, told an interviewer in the late 1990s. 'I mean, coming to me and me going to him, wherever he was. At one point, we stayed together for about eight to ten days.'[24]

One imagines Nelson and Winnie sitting alone together at Li-

liesleaf farm, Winnie smouldering, Nelson's discomfort growing. The
irony could not be greater. Three years later, on Robben Island, Nelson would discover that Brian Somana had been Winnie's lover while
tasked to watch out for her and the kids.

There is comedy in this scene at Liliesleaf, but it is deeply serious, too. Their courtship had been frenetic, dizzying; it had pressed the
boundaries of the acceptable. Each knew very well the other's sexualized relation to the world. Now, three years after marrying, they had
been more apart than together, and the question of infidelity was a constant disturbance.

Chapter 25

Having fought bitterly to launch an armed struggle, Nelson had to learn how to actually conduct it. He had trained as a lawyer, after all, and was an experienced political organizer, but about violence he knew nothing at all.

Now, at Wolfie Kodesh's apartment, then at Liliesleaf, he read: on the insurgency in Malaya, on the resistance to the French in Indochina, on the war in the Philippines. On Kodesh's bookshelf he saw Carl von Clausewitz's *On War*; he devoured it.[1] He found Menachem Begin's account of Haganah, the paramilitary organization founded in the last years of British Palestine. He read the account by Blas Roca, secretary of the Cuban Communist Party, of the Cuban Revolution.[2]

He read these books as a lawyer might: meticulously. When the police finally discovered Liliesleaf, they found sixty-five pages of notes, in Nelson's handwriting, on Mao's *Strategic Problems of China's Revolutionary War*, and also a thick précis of Che Guevara's *Guerrilla Warfare*.[3] Nelson was not so much reading as *studying*.

In truth, the strategic thinking of Nelson and his comrades was negligible. They knew that they were to embark upon 'armed propaganda', the bombing of government installations, avoiding the loss of human life. For what end? They hoped, vaguely, that it would instill hope among black South Africans, and they imagined that if the bombing demoralized whites, they might vote for change.

But what if whites were not demoralized? What if sabotage was ineffective? What next? 'There was a half-formed idea that somehow sabotage would prepare the ground for something more confrontational,' a close comrade of Nelson's at that time recalled. 'The process by which this evolution would come about was never very clear.'[4]

Most guerrilla movements begin amateurishly, and this one was no exception. Only two of the conspirators had any military expertise: one, Jack Hodgson, had been in a unit that operated behind German lines in North Africa in 1941, a distant memory now. Another, Arthur Goldreich, had served in the Jewish Palmach in its fight against the British in Palestine.[5]

Leaning heavily on these men's rusty knowledge, the would-be guerrillas did the best they could. At times they fumbled. On a week-day afternoon in mid-December, a car came to a standstill in Johannesburg's downtown traffic, black smoke belching from the windows. A crowd gathered and two traffic officers approached. One of the bystanders, a prominent journalist, recognized the driver as Ben Turok, a well-known activist. He sped off. It was a scorching summer day. On the floor of the car, a plastic jar filled with the acid to be used in a bomb had overheated.[6]

. .

And yet, for all the mishaps, on December 16, 1961, explosions went off in Johannesburg, Port Elizabeth and Durban. MK's work had begun.

If this was success, it was heavily qualified. One of the saboteurs, Petrus Molefe, was killed by the bomb he detonated. Another blew off his own arm. These were the first casualties in an armed struggle that would last for thirty years.[7]

In many ways, the armed struggle came to define the ANC, both for better and for worse. The notion of an armed popular insurrection became an article of religious faith for many of its leaders, constricting their tactics, narrowing their vision. And yet the idea of Umkhonto we Sizwe performed decisive symbolic work; when they revolted in the 1980s, South Africa's youth aligned en masse with the ANC, envisaging that its exiled army would come back to topple the regime.

. .

If Nelson and his comrades had been ill prepared for sabotage, this was nothing compared with the next phase they had planned: guerrilla war. Without an armoury, without trained personnel, they were beginning from scratch. Meeting secretly, the ANC's National Executive Committee decided to send Nelson abroad. African heads of state were due to meet in Ethiopia in February, and Nelson was tapped to lead the ANC's delegation. MK was quick to use the opportunity presented by its commander's presence abroad: Nelson was mandated to tour the continent seeking weaponry, matériel, and military training for large numbers of personnel and to talk to people who had actually fought a war.

Nelson was smuggled across the border into Bechuanaland on January 10, 1962. During the next six months, he travelled the length and breadth of Africa.

It was a journey of the heart. He was leaving South Africa for the first time, moving through states that had just acquired freedom; the spectacle of black people governing at times overwhelmed him.

In Addis Ababa, the Ethiopian capital, he watched a phalanx of troops march through the city before the gaze of their emperor, Haile Selassie. His head understood that Selassie was a dictator. But his gut was considerably more powerful. 'I was 44 years old,' he recalled, 'and this was the first time for me to see black armies commanded by black generals.'[8]

And in Rabat, Morocco, he watched a parade by the army of the National Liberation Front (FLN), which had been waging war in Algeria since 1954. In contrast to Selassie's gleaming soldiers, these were guerrillas; they wore turbans, tunics and sandals and carried a motley assortment of weapons: sabers, old flintlock rifles, battle-axes and assegais. The army he himself imagined forming, Nelson understood, would look more like this one.

At the tail end of the procession a military band was playing, and its leader caught Nelson's eye. Most of the marchers were pale-skinned Arabs. This one was built like a god and 'was as black as the night'.[9] Supremely confident in his magnificent body, he twirled a mace through his hands. As he marched past, a collective giddiness took hold of the small South African delegation: they rose from their seats and cheered. Feeling a little self-conscious, Nelson glanced around to discover that the people around the South Africans were laughing; they had become an audience to his and his comrades' exuberant racial pride.[10]

This moment sits awkwardly with Nelson's legacy. He is hardly associated with the celebration of black martial power. That violence might free the oppressed from psychological diminishment is an idea we connect to the likes of Frantz Fanon. Yet the force of this feeling burst spontaneously from Nelson's being. Watching a virile black soldier, he imagined the collapse of the apartheid regime. 'I felt sure', he wrote of this moment, 'that once our units, operating from friendly territory, put foot on our soil, they would grow in numbers and striking power so rapidly that Verwoerd would be plagued by all the problems that once tormented Chiang Kai Shek, Ngo Diem, De Gaulle, Batista and the British.'[11]

Within weeks, he was harshly disabused of this fantasy. In Rabat, he spent time at the headquarters of the Algerian revolutionary army, his guides veterans of the War of Independence. In the diary he kept at the time, and in the memoirs he would write later, he muted the shock of what he learned. But in conversations with comrades on Robben Island several years later he told bluntly of how his perspective had changed.[12]

Since 1956, two friendly neighbouring countries, Tunisia and Morocco, had harboured the Algerian revolutionary army. These territories in theory constituted crucial rear bases from which to support the war. Now, from his hosts, Nelson learned that the fortification the French had built, the Morice Line – an enormous barrier of minefields, electric fences, and artillery – had effectively sealed the Algerian border. Guerrilla units that did cross into Algeria sustained stunning casualties. The FLN was in fact largely cut off from its home country. The prospects of a military victory, Nelson was told, were zero.

Guerrilla warfare was useful, Nelson's hosts said, only insofar as it pressured the enemy to negotiate. As important, if not more so, was the political mobilization of people at home and the forging of alliances abroad. 'International public opinion', he was told, 'is sometimes worth more than a fleet of jet fighters.'[13]

Back home, Nelson's comrades at Liliesleaf were drawing up plans for guerrilla war. For the remainder of his life, he was impeccably polite about these plans. They were 'an honest attempt . . . to create an army', he said.[14] But he clearly understood, as he learned Algeria's lessons, the folly of what his comrades had planned.

And if international public opinion was indeed more valuable than war *matériel*, Nelson's first exposure to diplomacy was dispiriting, for he discovered that African opinion had turned against the ANC. Robert Sobukwe's performance at his 1960 trial was famous. Wherever Nelson went, Sobukwe was on people's lips. And the PAC, many of whose leaders had scattered across the African continent in Sharpeville's wake, had established effective diplomatic ties. They were poisoning the ANC's name. It was not a party of African nationalism, they had said; behind its commitment to what it called 'multiracialism' was its submission to white people, Indians and communists.

In Tanzania, the legendary Julius Nyerere told Nelson that the armed struggle must be postponed until Sobukwe was released from prison.[15] And when Nelson and Oliver Tambo met privately in Addis Ababa with Kenneth Kaunda, prospective president of Zambia, they discovered that he was alone in his party in supporting the ANC.[16] In Ghana and Egypt, Nelson and Tambo were unable to get audiences with Kwame Nkrumah and Gamal Abdel Nasser, the continent's two most influential statesmen.[17]

By the end of May, Nelson had visited Tanzania, Nigeria, Ghana, Liberia, Ethiopia, Morocco, Tunisia and Egypt. On June 7, his African tour finally over, he flew to London with Oliver Tambo. Having experienced, together, their organization's declining reputation in the circuits of African diplomacy, the two men had agreed between themselves that far-reaching action was necessary.

Quite how far-reaching would become apparent the following day when Nelson met with two senior exiled Communist Party leaders, Yusuf Dadoo and Vella Pillay. He told them bluntly that the ANC would from now on have to distance itself from its white and Indian allies and from the South African Communist Party. The two men were first shocked, then incensed. It was a tactical shift, Nelson protested, a question of image, not a change in substance. Their anger was not assuaged, and the meeting ended in acrimony. Pillay was spooked, not just by what Nelson had said, but by the way he said it; he was hard, unyielding, and cold. Within no time, rumours had reached South African shores that something was up with Nelson, that he was sounding like the PAC.[18]

After ten days in London, Nelson returned to Ethiopia, this time to undergo military training. The course was meant to last six months. Within two weeks the MK's high command recalled him urgently to South Africa. He had just had the opportunity, for the first and last time in his life, to pull the trigger of an automatic rifle.

Why he was recalled with such urgency remains uncertain, but Walter Sisulu, it appears, had grown gravely concerned about the rumours regarding his protégé; he wanted to hear from Nelson's own mouth what he had to say.[19]

On the night of July 23, 1962, Nelson crossed the border from Bechuanaland back into his native country. A white comrade, Cecil Williams, had come to fetch him. Throughout his African tour, Nelson had worn a khaki uniform, signalling that he was a soldier; now the same uniform placed him as Williams's chauffeur. It was a lacklustre cover; in Bechuanaland, the British magistrate had warned Nelson that the South African government was aware of his impending return.[20]

He went directly to Liliesleaf, where he told his organization's working committee of the PAC's escalating power abroad. He told of a Ghanaian official who had ripped a copy of the Freedom Charter from the wall and torn it to shreds. The ANC, Nelson said, should 'regard itself as the vanguard of the pan-African movement in South Africa', an idea until now associated exclusively with the PAC.[21]

The following day, he drove to Natal, once more playing chauffeur to Cecil Williams; he carried the same message about African primacy, first to comrades in Durban, then to the ANC's president, Albert Luthuli, in Stanger.

It is hard to exaggerate the degree of agitation he caused. Multiracialism was the Congress movement's existential core; it spoke not just to the manner in which the struggle should be fought but to the type of society to come. Nelson had opened a primal wound; responses to his message were raw. Dear old Indian friends like Ismail Meer and Monty Naicker were left feeling confused and betrayed. Among some, the sense of betrayal lingered for years.

The idea that Nelson was, at bottom, opaque – that one could spend years with him, share intimate experiences with him, talk through the night with him, and still know nothing of what he really thought – took root. There was especial puzzlement among his longtime Communist Party friends. They had spent almost two decades courting him. Now he could not have made it clearer that he was, before anything else, a black nationalist.

. .

On the evening of August 4, at a safe house in Durban, Nelson addressed a meeting of MK's regional command.[22] From there, astonishingly, he went to a party hosted by a photographer at *Drum* magazine. Many of the people there were unfamiliar. And he did nothing to conceal his identity; he was in fact still in his khaki uniform.[23]

When Nelson and Cecil Williams left Durban for Johannesburg the following day, the pretense of the chauffeur had been dropped; Nelson sat in the passenger seat while Williams drove. Some seventy miles into their journey, outside the town of Howick, they were flagged

down. The policeman who peered through the window looked hag-
gard; he had clearly not slept; he had been waiting on the side of the
road all night, Nelson surmised. When asked his name, Nelson said
he was David Motsamayi. The policeman nodded, asked a few routine
questions, and then suddenly lost patience. 'Ag, you're Nelson Mandela,
and this is Cecil Williams,' he said, 'and you're under arrest.'[24]

Sitting alone in a jail cell that night, Nelson was 'upset and agitated';
he had simply not thought through the prospect of getting caught.[25]
And yet, in London two months earlier, he had told several people that
upon returning to South Africa, he would probably be captured 'pretty
soon'.[26] His increasingly lax security, one imagines, was the expression
of a wish to flee the inevitability of arrest.

The morning after Nelson was caught, the news not yet public,
New Age newspaper got wind of what had happened. It was decided that
Wolfie Kodesh, who worked at New Age, should be the one to tell Winnie. He was serving a banning order and was not permitted to speak to
her, so he had to act with care. He took a colleague with him to a call
box in the street opposite Winnie's office; the colleague made the call,
telling Winnie to come down to the vestibule. Kodesh had not slept in
two nights; what with the news of the arrest, he must have appeared all
the more tired.

Winnie took one look at him. 'Is it Nelson?' she asked.[27]

A quarter of a century later, a retired CIA agent told The New York
Times that his agency had let the South African government know where
to find Nelson Mandela.[28] Nelson himself always remained sceptical of
this story. Indeed, he would come to blame his capture on his wife.

Chapter 26

On August 16, eleven days after Nelson's arrest, Wolfie Kodesh arrived early at the Johannesburg Magistrate's Court. His friend was appearing on remand that morning and Kodesh wished to give his support. He chose his seat carefully; he wanted to be the first person Nelson saw as he ascended from the cells below. A friendly face might give him 'a little upliftment', Kodesh thought.

The magistrate entered the court, the spectators in the gallery stood, and the orderly called for the prisoner.

'I can never forget,' Kodesh recalled. 'When he came up – and he's this tall, big, athletic man – he had . . . a kaross, like a skin, across [his shoulders], beads round his neck, beads round his arms, and he was half naked . . .

'[T]here was a complete hush. Even the policemen, I honestly think they went pale, to see this huge man standing there in his national costume.'[1]

Winnie had slipped him the outfit half an hour earlier. She had borrowed it from a Thembu family, the Festiles, who used it on ceremonial occasions and whom Nelson had known since his earliest days in Johannesburg.[2]

He did not so much as glance at the gallery; he fixed his stare upon the magistrate, who returned his gaze with palpable unease, 'like a mongoose staring at a snake', Kodesh thought.[3]

Winnie's costume was barely less dramatic than Nelson's. An outlandishly tall black wrap around her head, her body in raw white cotton, beadwork on her wrists, a bead tie around her neck: she was not just beautiful but towering. All about her in the black section of the gallery were dozens of women, also in ceremonial Thembu dress. The accused, his wife and their supporters in the gallery, together symbolizing black South Africa, were showing 'contempt for the court', as Nelson would put it.[4]

The remand hearing took just a few minutes. A crowd of more than a thousand had been waiting in the street outside; now, as the hearing adjourned, it moved in orderly rows down West Street, singing. So large an assembly of black people in the heart of white Johannesburg: for a moment it was as if time had leaped backward, over Sharpeville, the state of emergency, the bannings, the mass arrests.

In the front line of the marchers was Winnie Mandela. Those who had seen her in the courtroom must have raised an eyebrow for she had changed clothes; dressed in a tailored business suit and a fur toque, she headed toward the cordon of police officers blocking the street ahead.[5] This confrontation of the state's armed forces with beauty and style was perfectly choreographed. She would use it time and again, its force never fading.

.   .   .

Nelson's trial began two months later. He faced charges of leaving the country without a passport and inciting people to strike. At the last moment, the venue was moved to Pretoria in the hope that the crowds might be smaller. Two days before the trial, the government banned any gathering in the country connected to Nelson Mandela.[6]

He conducted his own defense and did not apply for bail. 'It would have had a bad effect,' he said later. 'I didn't want to do anything which suggested that I was not prepared for the consequences of the life I had chosen.'[7]

Granted permission to address the court, Nelson declared that 'the aspirations of the African people' were on trial. He turned to face the magistrate square on and spoke to him personally. 'I want to make it perfectly clear', he said, 'that the remarks I am about to make are not addressed to Your Worship in his personal capacity, nor are they intended to reflect upon the integrity of the court. I hold Your Worship in high esteem.'

Then he requested that the magistrate recuse himself. 'Why is it', Nelson asked, 'that in this courtroom I am facing a white magistrate, confronted by a white prosecutor, escorted by white orderlies? Can anyone honestly and seriously suggest that in this type of atmosphere the scales of justice are evenly balanced? Why is it that no African in the history of this country has ever had the honour of being tried by his kith and kin?'

He did not, Nelson said, consider himself 'legally or morally bound to obey laws made by a parliament in which I have no representation'.[8]

Over a period of two weeks, the prosecution called several dozen witnesses. Nelson, representing himself, cross-examined them all. He himself called none.

At the close of the trial, he pleaded in mitigation. He spoke for an hour, first about life before imperial conquest. 'The country was our own,' he said, 'in name and right . . . We set up and operated our own government. We controlled our own arms and we organised our own trade and commerce.'

He was, he said, a prisoner of conscience. 'I was made, by the law, a criminal not because of what I had done, but because of what I stood for, because of what I thought . . . [T]here comes a time,' he said, when a man 'can only live the life of an outlaw because the government has so decreed to use the law to impose a state of outlawry upon him.'

The magistrate called a recess, returned ten minutes later, and sentenced Nelson to five years in prison. As the court rose, Nelson turned to the gallery, raised a clenched fist, and shouted, '*Amandla!*' – 'Power!' – three times. The crowd returned his salute and began singing 'Nkosi Sikelel' iAfrika' as he was led away.[9]

. .

The strategy he adopted in the courtroom, Nelson wrote in his autobiography, occurred to him two months earlier, when he had appeared in the Johannesburg Magistrate's Court for remand. It struck him, he said, that although he was 'a handcuffed outlaw', the magistrate and attorneys all greeted him with deference. Once the proceedings began, their deference gave way to something even more striking: embarrassment.

'I had something of a revelation,' he would write. 'These men were not only uncomfortable because I was a colleague brought low, but because I was an ordinary man being punished for his beliefs. In a way I had never quite comprehended before, I realised the role I could play as a defendant . . . I was the symbol of justice in the court of the oppressor.'[10]

His account is bracingly unreliable. That his court strategy had come to him in a flash, that he worked it out all alone – none of this is true. He had in fact snatched Robert Sobukwe's court performance from two years earlier, all of it, and made it his own: the refusal to apply for bail or to be represented by a barrister; the declaration that he did not consider himself bound to obey the laws of a parliament in which he was not represented. He had hardly bothered to modify Sobukwe's words. 'Because I had no hand in making the law,' Sobukwe and his co-accused had said, 'I have no moral obligation to obey it.' 'We are not afraid of the consequences of our actions,' Sobukwe had declared, 'and it is not our intention to plead for mercy.' Even Nelson's gracious insistence that he had nothing personal against the magistrate was borrowed from the PAC man.

Just a year earlier, Nelson had publicly mocked Sobukwe for the path he had taken. He himself, he said, would forgo the 'cheap martyrdom' of jail; he had *proper* work to do.[11]

The irony was not lost on at least one newspaper reader. 'Nelson Mandela has to be congratulated for his growth,' a certain J. Marojane wrote sarcastically in early November 1962. 'He spoke in court the same language as Sobukwe did! It was a different Mandela this time from the one who said a few months back that he could not waste his time and sit in jail like Sobukwe did. He said he chose a much more difficult job, that of an underground leader. Now he was speaking as a leader who was not prepared to defend himself against an evil law but was prepared to lay down his life for his people and principles. Bravo! Now we have two great men in jail.'[12]

There is something more significant about his performance than that he took it from Sobukwe. A product of mission schools, Nelson had been steeped in Scripture in his teens. And he had been a believer; at Fort Hare, he spent many of his weekends in the villages around Alice teaching Bible study. As happened with so many aspiring young adults in the global mid-century, he abandoned belief when he settled in the city for a materialist conception of the world.

Now his Christian inheritance came back to him, not as a return to belief, but in his response to the culture around him. The reverence Sobukwe inspired, he knew very well, was for a martyr. The clergyman who opened the PAC's inaugural congress in 1959 had likened the gathering to the scene at Golgotha. And Nelson's own leader, the ANC's president, Albert Luthuli, had made redemption via suffering the cardinal theme of his leadership. 'The road to freedom is via the cross,' he wrote in his most famous pamphlet of the 1950s.[13] Later, he would declare that the path ahead 'was sanctified by the blood of martyrs'.[14]

Nelson had turned to violence because he believed it would inspire; without it, he feared, the ANC would lose the confidence of ordinary people. Now he had dropped one script and picked up another, the change so dexterous that most failed to notice. He would inspire not by violence but by facing his enemy's violence. He would inspire by suffering.

We come again to Winnie Mandela, her husband sentenced and jailed. The path to her has detoured through Nelson's adventure, for it was as a martyr's wife that she grew to fame.

Sitting in the archive, reading the daily papers, one watches an extraordinary myth form. Winnie had been an object of interest for some time, to be sure; now she was an object of *fascination*. When it reported Nelson's arrest, *Golden City Post* did not lead with the news that he had been caught; it led with Winnie's response to receiving the news. What did the beautiful wife feel? What did she think? What words did she choose? The newspaper was adamant that *its reporter* had informed Winnie of her husband's fate, although this was, of course, untrue.[1]

A month after Nelson's arrest, *Drum* ran a double feature on the most famous couple in the land. The story on Nelson was carried under the headline 'The Black Pimpernel'. Winnie's piece was headed 'My Man'. Her photograph ran down the length of the page. She is leaving her house, making her way along the concrete path between the front door and the gate. Little Zindzi is next to her, holding her hand. Winnie is a picture of mid-century style: a tightly knotted white tie hangs over her collarless black blouse; a fashionable winter coat is slung across her arm. 'Whatever she wears,' the caption reads, 'Winnie adds her own touch of elegance.'

The tone of the accompanying piece is one of wonder at the oddity of it all. Here is a woman, drop-dead gorgeous and the epitome of fashion. How did *she* end up in circumstances so strange?

She is insouciant, irony her favoured mode. 'The police are like members of my family now,' she says. 'They are in my house every day.' And yet she is not so frivolous as to diminish the tragedy. 'Every time the gate opens . . . , the children wait hopefully, believing that, one day, it will be papa and not a policeman.'[2]

Three months later, *Drum* ran another double feature, this one on

Winnie Mandela and Sobukwe's wife, Veronica. It is titled 'Drama of
the Two Leaders' Wives'.

'Two women sit in the townships, waiting,' the story begins. 'One
[Veronica] waits for the months to pass until she and her husband are
reunited. The other has to think in terms of years . . . Both know the
meaning of endurance.'[3]

Veronica would wait longer than anyone imagined then. Sobukwe
had been sentenced to three years' imprisonment and was due for
release in May 1963. As his release date approached, parliament passed a
law permitting the police to detain for a further twelve months, renewable indefinitely, anybody convicted of a political offense. Sobukwe
was detained under this law the moment his prison sentence ended; he
would spend the following six years in solitary confinement on Robben
Island.

As for Nelson, he had yet to be tried for a capital crime; neither
Winnie nor *Drum* knew that he would be imprisoned indefinitely.

But the kernel of the story is already in place in the closing months
of 1962. Winnie is to *wait*. She is to *endure*. And yet that is only half the
tale. For between the lines of each story, beneath the surface of each
photograph, it is understood that there are male readers who imagine
making love to her.

Sometimes it is almost explicit. In late 1963, for instance, when
Winnie was summoned before a judge for violating a banning order,
The World ran the story as its front-page lead. In the opening line, she
is described as 'the beautiful wife of the jailed ANC leader'. The story
then hurries through the details of the case before pausing to describe
her. 'Mrs. Mandela was dressed in a stunning red and white summer
dress matching the bag she carried,' the journalist wrote. 'She wore red
stiletto shoes . . . When she gracefully walked out of the court, a white
reporter from a daily newspaper remarked in appreciation, "she's a
pretty woman". And all eyes of the public were on her.'[4]

Winnie was to wait for Nelson's return before an admiring audience. Her story would be one of temptation: of men to cuckold their
country's most famous son; of Winnie to betray her heroic man. The
prospect of transgression formed the very frame of the tale.

And yet, if this is how Winnie's story was framed in the press, it
was hardly how she understood herself. Indeed, her conception of her
role at this time was remarkable, perhaps even shocking, and it would
go largely undetected for years.

'Most people do not realise', she wrote to Nelson in prison in December 1962, 'that your physical presence would have meant nothing to me if the ideals for which you have dedicated your life have not been realised ... In these hectic and violent years I have grown to love you more than I ever did before ... Nothing can be as valuable as being part & parcel of the formation of the history of a country.'[5]

What she expresses here is so liquid, so surprising: we need to cite her in another context to understand what she is saying.

Several years later, in a diary she kept in jail, she recounted a tense conversation with a brigadier Aucamp, the head of the prison in which she was being held.

'Why do you think I talk to you and not to any one of those [other detainees?],' she quoted him asking. '[I]t is because I acknowledge the fact that your people regard you as their leader in your husband's absence.'[6]

One finds oneself going back and reading the lines again; it is improbable that Brigadier Aucamp, or anyone else, for that matter, understood Winnie as *the* leader of black South Africa, certainly not in 1969. It was Winnie who understood herself thus.

The remarks she put in Aucamp's mouth shed the starkest light on what she told Nelson in that letter in December 1962. The marriage she conjured was a mythical, royal union: as Nelson's wife she was the leader of a nation.

Chapter 28

On the afternoon of July 11, 1963, the police raided Liliesleaf farm. The meeting they interrupted had been convened to discuss a document called 'Operation Mayibuye', a strategy for guerrilla war. One of the men around the table, Govan Mbeki, stuffed the document in an unlit stove and tried vainly to set it on fire.[1]

It was not the only document the police discovered that day. Liliesleaf had become a storehouse of incriminating information. In the treasure chest the police found was abundant evidence that Nelson Mandela headed MK's high command.

Nelson had by now been moved to Robben Island. A few days after the Liliesleaf raid he was driven back to Pretoria Central Prison, where he discovered much of the movement's underground leadership. Among them were Walter Sisulu, Govan Mbeki, Raymond Mhlaba, Elias Motsoaledi, Andrew Mlangeni and Rusty Bernstein, all of them central to the prosecution of the armed struggle.

It was about as devastating a blow as could be imagined. Joe Slovo, who was abroad at the time and who did not return for another twenty-seven years, remembered greeting the news with 'pessimism' and 'depression'.[2] The Charterist movement's organized presence in South Africa was close to destruction.

In October, Nelson and his comrades appeared in the Pretoria Supreme Court; they were charged with more than two hundred acts of sabotage aimed at promoting guerrilla warfare and armed invasion. The prosecution chose to try the men for sabotage instead of treason because the evidentiary threshold was considerably lower and the maximum sentence was the same: it was death.

It is doubtful that Nelson thought he'd hang. He certainly did not behave like a man who believed he might die. Before the Rivonia charges, he had enrolled for a law degree by correspondence at the University of London so that he might complete the course of study he had failed at Wits. Now, during the trial, he also began to study Afrikaans. That, perhaps, is the crispest reflection of his state of mind. Assuming that his enemy might lock him away indefinitely, he acquired fluency in its language, preparing, it seems, for a long engagement.

. .

A battery of distinguished lawyers lined up to defend the Rivonia defendants. To their discomfort, they discovered that their clients' primary aim was not to avoid execution but to explain their objectives. They were not going to contest evidence that was true, only that which slandered them. Nor did they plan to answer questions that might expose their comrades to arrest. In following this course, their lawyers explained, they might be signing their death warrants.[3]

Nelson and his comrades were brave, to be sure. But circumstances had not given them much choice. To be seen to be saving themselves now would shatter their credibility. Sobukwe's and Nelson's previous trials had conjured a spirit of principled sacrifice from which there was no retreat.

. .

For a long while, Winnie was prevented from attending the trial. Serving a banning order, she was permitted neither to travel to Pretoria nor to enter a courtroom. Finally, in April 1964, just as Nelson was to take the stand, it was decided that she could indeed go. Foolishly, the authorities imposed conditions: permission would be withdrawn 'if her presence in court, either by the manner of her dress or any other respect leads to an incident or incidents'. Winnie could sit in the gallery, but not in her Thembu costume.

The move backfired, as might have been foreseen. The newspapers plastered on their front pages pictures of Winnie in her traditional dress, announcing that this was what she *would have* worn to court. What she *did* wear became the subject of forensic attention: the hat, the skirt, the earrings, the necklace, the shoes. And everyone else in the black section of the gallery made sure to don traditional dress, Winnie's absent costume amplified a hundredfold.[4]

Her presence at the trial took the myth of her and Nelson's marriage to a dizzying pitch. The moment she stepped into the courtroom, the eyes of the journalists in attendance flicked between husband and wife. How did they respond to seeing each other? Did their emotions show in their faces? The answers were contained in the questions themselves. 'The attractive Mrs. Winnie Mandela looked long and lovingly at her husband,' the *Golden City Post*'s reporter wrote. 'And Mr. Mandela, who appeared to be restless, looked long and lovingly at her. They can only look at each other because both are banned and not allowed to speak to each other.'[5]

Love and beauty mingled with the prospect of death: Nelson's trial had made of his marriage a fairy tale.

. .

As Accused Number One, Nelson was the first to be called by the defense. It was decided that he should simply make a statement from the dock. His purpose was to deliver a message for the ages; the vagaries of question and answer would not do; he required the freedom to express himself with clarity.

He spoke for more than five hours. Among the most striking moments in his speech was his explanation of the turn to violence. He enumerated the myriad ways in which lawful protest had been closed down. 'We were placed in a position', he said, 'in which we had either to accept a permanent state of inferiority, or to defy the Government.'

It is what he said next that is most interesting. Ordinary people had already turned to violence of the most disturbing kind. Pointing to what had happened in Winnie's Mpondoland and the sites of other rural uprisings, he said that violence was 'taking the form, not of struggle against the Government – though this is what prompted it – but of civil strife between pro-government chiefs and those opposing them, conducted in such a way that it could not hope to achieve anything other than a loss of life, and bitterness'.[6]

In turning to sabotage, he and his comrades aimed to extract violence from everyday life. Ordinary people would be inspired by watching his disciplined acts of sabotage, rather than committing a far more destructive violence of their own. He would embody his people's will to fight, placing the burden on his own shoulders. And, with that, he would embrace on their behalf another burden: the prospect of death.

It was among the most compelling statements of leadership he ever made. It was also the first clear expression of the mature Mandela's abiding sense of the world. He had experimented a great deal: with insurrection, with revolution, with guerrilla warfare. Now he was clear that the struggle against apartheid should not tear to pieces the society that would survive it. This imperative informed much of what he did over the following three decades.

He had written his speech in his cell at night over a period of two weeks. Once he had completed a draft, he read it aloud to his co-accused. Then he gave it to his lawyers. They were greatly disturbed by its final sentence.

'I have fought against white domination,' Nelson had written, 'and I have fought against black domination. I have cherished the ideal of a democratic and free society in which all persons live together in harmony and with equal opportunities. It is an ideal which I hope to live for and to achieve. But it is an ideal for which I am prepared to die.'

Nelson was daring the judge to sentence him to death, two of his lawyers, Bram Fischer and George Bizos, complained. They begged him to take the last sentence out. He refused. Eventually, they reached a compromise and added three words.[7]

'But if needs be,' he said in court, 'it is an ideal for which I am prepared to die.'

It was late afternoon. He had been speaking since lunchtime. He sat down to a prolonged silence. The trial went on for another two months. During all of that time, Nelson recalled, the judge, a man named Quartus de Wet, did not once look him in the eye.[8]

.   .

As they awaited the verdict, the accused told their lawyers that they'd not appeal their sentence, even if it was death, for to do so would be understood by their followers as weakness. They discussed how they'd comport themselves if they learned that they were to die. Walter Sisulu was convinced that they would be executed. 'I thought I must go to the gallows singing,' he recalled, 'for the sake of the youth who follow us, so they will know that we fulfilled our task in life.'[9]

When the judge sat down to deliver the sentence, Sisulu believed that his fears were confirmed; de Wet was breathing so heavily that his judicial gown was heaving. 'If he was going to give us an ordinary sentence,' Sisulu thought to himself, 'he would not be so shaken.'[10]

Members of the defense team were in fact already aware that the lives of their clients would be spared. The evening before sentencing, George Bizos had met with the British consul general, Leslie Minford, who assured him that none of the accused would be sentenced to death and that one of them – Rusty Bernstein – would be acquitted. This is indeed what happened.[11]

It has been impossible to determine quite how much pressure the British and American governments exerted. But by the time the state began presenting its case, the United Nations General Assembly had passed a resolution by 106 to 1 calling on the authorities to abandon the trial.[12] The only vote against had been South Africa's. And two days before the verdict was handed down, the UN Security Council had urged that the defendants be granted amnesty.[13]

Nelson and his comrades had been put on trial for an amateurish plan of armed resistance. But their and their movement's conduct during the trial had been anything but amateurish. Organized mass protest all but crushed, armed propaganda all but stillborn, the international dimension of their struggle was gathering strength. In this arena, the ANC worked with sophistication. Just as Europe had abandoned its empires, South Africa was hunkering down on a version of colonial rule. On the southern tip of Africa, the case would increasingly be made, a late battle for human freedom still raged.

.   .

On the morning the sentence was passed, June 12, 1964, a large crowd gathered outside the court, eager to hear whether eight of the men inside were to die. They waited for hours, until 12:15 p.m., when a woman emerged from the building. It was Winnie Mandela.

She raised her fist and shouted, '*Amandla!*'

From mouth to mouth, a single word was whispered: 'life'; the men had been sentenced to life imprisonment, not to death. The crowd, most of whom were women, burst into song and began to move, as one, toward Church Square. White bystanders watched. Some sneered. A group of children ran sorties into the marching women, trying to trip them. From a window above, somebody threw a bucket of water. They marched on, making a circuit of the Palace of Justice.[14]

A few minutes later, the British broadcaster Robin Day interviewed Winnie Mandela. 'I am slightly relieved,' she told him. 'It could have been far worse than this. In fact, my people and I expected death sentences for all the accused.'

The interview was broadcast on the BBC that night. Her voice was clean and young; her huge eyes beamed an angelic clarity. The image was so incongruous with what she had said that most people probably missed it. 'My people and I expected . . .' She was speaking as the embodiment of a nation.

· ·

Two weekends after sentencing, a gathering assembled in a house opposite the Mandela residence in Orlando West. More than a hundred people came; they arrived on the Saturday night and partied into the following afternoon.

The occasion was Nelson and Winnie's sixth wedding anniversary, but neither husband nor wife was there. Nelson was on Robben Island serving the fifteenth and sixteenth days of a life sentence. Winnie, whose banning order did not permit her to attend social gatherings, was at home. The party, one of the guests declared, had been arranged to uphold a principle.[15]

The absence of the couple was somehow fitting, for the marriage was now a national institution quite apart from the two people who had wed. Nobody saw this more clearly than Winnie Mandela. A month earlier, while the Rivonia trial slouched toward its conclusion, she had invited her lover to live in the home she and Nelson had shared. The ensuing scandal spread like contagion through activist households in Johannesburg, jumped the ocean to exile circles in London, then found its way to the prison cells of Robben Island.

PRISON-DETENTION

. . .

Chapter 29

On May 2, 1963, the key turned in the ignition of a still-unnamed machine, pushing South Africa into a new era.

The only manifest sign was the coming into force that day of a new law, an addition to the General Law Amendment Act of 1963. It permitted the police to detain for ninety days without trial and without access to a lawyer anybody suspected of a politically motivated crime.

But that law was merely the one visible appendage of a treacherous new equipment, treacherous because its most powerful work would take place invisibly, in people's inner worlds.

Some months earlier, a handful of police detectives were approached to join a new unit dubbed the sabotage squad. It was so named because its members were to investigate those suspected of the just-minted crime of sabotage, defined broadly enough to include the casting of stones, or even blocking the free flow of traffic. They were given a crash course in political policing, itself cobbled together in haste.[1] With the ninety-day detention law in place on May 2, they had the tools to put into practice what they had learned.

Hundreds of people detained in the time that followed were confronted with something harrowing and unheralded, a focused and more or less standardized endeavour to extract from them what they knew. In addition to the torture of prolonged solitude, many were subjected to sleep deprivation for days on end, to standing on bricks or a sheet of paper for dozens of hours at a stretch, to episodes of extreme violence – the beating and shocking of genitals, suffocation – and to acts of cruelty and gestures of kindness offered in confusing relays.

It is hard to exaggerate the effects of this new campaign of torture on South Africa's activists and on their relations with one another. 'In a sense, up to about 1960/1,' Joe Slovo was to say, 'the underground struggle was fought on a gentlemanly terrain. There was still the rule of law.

You had a fair trial in their courts. Nobody was kept in isolation. Up to 1963, I know of no incident of any political prisoner being tortured.'[2]

The results of the new regime were immediate. Information, some of it reliable, some of it made up to get the torture to stop, spilled from the mouths of detainees. But the seepage of information was hardly the only consequence; the damage to people's moral lives was harder to measure. Torture trades in betrayal; no matter that one is hardly in control of one's perfidy, the moral legacy of what one has said lives on for years. Of the memoirs written by those who were tortured at this time, precious few do not conceal or simply avoid the matter of what one said that harmed others. Just now, as this author writes these lines, an accusation sits in his email in-box, levelled from one old man to another, concerning who betrayed whom more than half a century ago.

During the 1960s, the activists subjected to the new regime of detention without trial and bodily torture would tally in the hundreds. In the wake of mass uprisings in the 1970s and 1980s, the number would climb into the thousands, then into the tens of thousands. By the time apartheid ended, some seventy-eight thousand people would have been detained without trial. How many of them were beaten, electrocuted and sleep deprived, how many dunked in water until their lungs were flooded, how many broke and betrayed comrades, friends and loved ones, cannot be counted.[3]

.   .

The intrusion of the new regime of torture into Winnie Mandela's life was almost immediate.

In late June 1963, six weeks after the regime came into effect, the police detained three activists who had been regularly to Liliesleaf farm. They were Bartholomew Hlapane, Patrick Mthembu and Brian Somana.[4] These three men would all be tortured, and each would betray his comrades. The Liliesleaf raid, in which Nelson's colleagues were finally arrested, took place less than three weeks later.*

Somana was the young man Nelson had tapped to mind his family while he was on the run. It was he who had smuggled Winnie and

* There is evidence that the police had been monitoring Liliesleaf for some time. See Benneyworth, 'Trojan Horses'.

the children to see Nelson at Liliesleaf farm. When he was arrested, Somana had been visiting Liliesleaf for the better part of two years.

He was also, by this time, Winnie Mandela's lover.

The scandal of it had been reverberating through Johannesburg's activist ranks throughout the first half of 1963. It was not just that Winnie's husband was on trial for his life. It was the sheer visibility of the affair.

In addition to his work at *New Age*, Somana had a business that marketed a brand of sweets, the wrappers adorned with an image of Mickey Mouse. Now, as he and Winnie increasingly spent their time together, Winnie's car was adorned on its side by a picture of Mickey, for Somana was using her car to run his business.[5]

If Winnie Mandela alone were not distinctive enough, if an eccentrically painted car did not itself draw stares, the daily sight of the two of them encased in a Disney cartoon screamed for attention.

Their relationship might have remained no more than the subject of fierce gossip, but for an incident that occurred in the spring of 1963.

In early October, two Cape Town activists, Fikile Bam and Marcus Solomon, fled to Johannesburg.

They had been party to writing a document that had been reproduced too often and had passed through too many hands, discussing the feasibility of guerrilla warfare in South Africa.

Bam had left from the back door of his house just as the police opened his front gate; he had dashed to Cape Town's central train station and boarded a train. When it pulled in to Park Station, he had just the shirt on his back, his jacket left slung over his kitchen chair.[6]

Now, in Johannesburg, in hiding, Bam contacted his sister, Brigalia, and asked her to help him and Solomon escape South Africa. Brigalia got in touch with Winnie; they had studied together at the Hofmeyr School and had at one point shared a room. Winnie, in turn, enlisted Brian Somana's help.[7]

On a Friday morning in mid-October, Winnie's car came to get the two men from their place of hiding. Somana was driving; Winnie was in the passenger seat, both her daughters on her lap. Bam and Solomon got into the back. They were off to meet the people who would smuggle them to Botswana. Minutes into the journey, the car was stopped by police. The officers were purposeful; they made directly for Bam and Solomon, cuffed them and took them away.[8]

The police had clearly been lying in wait. They had taken no inter-est at all in Brian Somana or Winnie Mandela, not even acknowledging their presence in the car. Word soon swept through activist circles that Somana was working for the police.

A delegation from the Federation of South African Women (FED-SAW), of which Winnie was a founding member, went immediately to appeal to her to break off with Somana. So too did Soweto's most respected businesswoman, Constance Ntshona; she arrived unan-nounced at Winnie's house and demanded that Winnie never see Somana again.[9]

There is no direct record of Winnie's response. But something of its spirit is captured in a remark made more than two decades later by Hilda Bernstein, a prominent Johannesburg activist at that time. 'We tried to persuade her to break off this relationship,' Bernstein recalled. 'I mean that was a *terrible* time there. She had that same sort of obsti-nacy and arrogance that she later exposed, a refusal to listen to what people around her were saying.'[10]

Winnie's car kept appearing on Soweto's streets as it had before, Somana in the driver's seat, Winnie next to him, Mickey Mouse in his customary place on the door.

Soon, the couple grew bolder. Throughout 1963, Somana had lived a few blocks from the Mandelas with his wife and two small children. Now, in early May 1964 – a little over a month before Nelson was found guilty and sentenced – Somana moved in with Winnie. It would emerge at his divorce hearing two years later that his wife, Miriam, had presented him with an ultimatum: he should either end his romance with Winnie Mandela, or he should leave home. And so he left home and went to live at 8115 Orlando West.[11]

In early May 1964 it was widely believed that Nelson would be sen-tenced to death the following month. Winnie had invited into his bed a man increasingly believed to have betrayed the Rivonia defendants.

She was taking extraordinary risks. She was indeed on the cusp of personal catastrophe, for the fury she had provoked might have swept her into oblivion.

There is evidence that she knew this, that she felt disaster coming.

Some time before she left South Africa in late 1964, Barbara Harmel had lunch with Winnie in her office at the Johannesburg Child Welfare Society. They had gone downstairs together to buy their meal from a grocery store. Now, alone in the lift as they made their way back to the office, it dawned on Harmel that Winnie was in a state of extreme distress. 'They keep talking about me,' she recalled Winnie saying. 'They keep talking and talking and talking. One day Nelson will know the truth about me.' Harmel regretted that she did not take the opportunity to discover what was in Winnie's heart. Still hungry for her maternal love, she recoiled from the unwelcome vulnerability this formidable woman was displaying.[12]

In early September 1964, Winnie went to see Nelson on Robben Island for the first time. Ahead of her arrival in Cape Town, a letter had made its way from Johannesburg bringing forewarning of her misdeeds. In the wake of the Rivonia trial, FEDSAW had created support structures for the wives of those who had been jailed. The idea was to assist them getting to their husbands and to facilitate political work they might perform as their profiles grew. For Winnie's visit, an ambitious schedule had been planned; clandestine arrangements were made for her to meet with the underground structures that had formed street by street in the African townships of Cape Town.

Now, in the letter that preceded Winnie's arrival, FEDSAW members in Johannesburg warned Cape Town comrades 'that we must do nothing for Winnie, that Winnie was a sell-out', as one of the recipients of the letter recalled. The Cape Town women ignored the letter; indeed, they were incensed by it, considering it irresponsible gossip, and went ahead with Winnie's planned programme. And Winnie, of course, performed brilliantly in her clandestine encounters with township activists. 'She had wonderful meetings . . . in ten or fifteen streets in Langa, and the same thing in Nyanga.'[13]

That is how it would go with Winnie for years to come. She would scandalize some within her movement; others would rush to her defense. Their motives were varied: some shielded her because her marriage was a political asset that required protection, others because they saw in the wrath of her detractors a misogyny they knew all too well. When Barbara Harmel arrived in London in 1964, South African exile circles were dizzy with gossip about Winnie. And what she recalled above all was the outspoken voice of Rica Hodgson, a senior comrade in exile. 'Do you expect her to be celibate her whole life?' Harmel remembered Hodgson demanding. 'Rica was so angry,' she recalled. 'This was the swinging '60s, but I was struck to hear a left-wing adult talk this way.'[14]

Why did Winnie drive herself to the brink of excommunication?

It would be wrong to imagine that she was acting with coolness or calculation. We know from her subsequent career that she required to be frenetically present in the inner world of another. She required the boundarylessness, perhaps even the instability. Most likely she did not feel alive unless connected in this way. She probably felt the demands that she leave Somana an existential assault; she battened down and fought.

As speculative as these thoughts may be, they are crucial to understanding her trajectory not just in private life but, more especially, in politics. For she maintained this ceaseless agitation in both spheres: in her personal life, a succession of astonishingly unstable love triangles; in politics, something harder to pin down – a relationship to the masses of black South Africans demanding a state of constant activity and a vision of apartheid ending in insurrection.

. .

What finally ended Winnie's relationship with Brian Somana was not pressure exerted from the outside but the force of its inner turmoil.

In the closing months of 1964, a group of people took to meeting each evening at 8115 Orlando West. Aside from Winnie and Somana, they included Winnie's brother-in-law, Sefton Vuthela, the husband of her sister Nonalithi; the *Golden City Post* journalist Ronnie Manyosi; and Peter Magubane, a supremely talented documentary photographer whose star was rising.[15]

In years to come, Winnie and Magubane drew very close; the sacrifices Magubane made for Winnie and her children – he courted banning orders, imprisonment, torture, and much more – speak to extraordinary devotion. And it appears from the account of a man who attended those evening gatherings that Magubane and Winnie were already drawing close then, much to the ire of Brian Somana.[16] Precisely what happened on New Year's Eve is impossible to reconstruct, but Somana drew a gun, his intention apparently to threaten Magubane; the gun was discharged and Sefton Vuthela was shot in the finger. The following day, police took Somana into custody and charged him with attempted murder.[17]

This was not the first episode of high drama to take place at Winnie's house. A week earlier, in the early hours of December 24, Somana's wife, Miriam, had arrived with her brother-in-law and a police detective. They had pounded on Winnie's door, demanding that Somana come out. Sometime after 4:00 a.m., following three hours of door thumping and shouting, the lights came on and Winnie emerged from the house, followed a short while later by Somana.[18]

Matters escalated again three and a half weeks after the shooting incident at Winnie's house. In the early hours of January 24, Peter Magubane's car, which was in the garage at the Mandela house, was set alight. A neighbour later testified that he saw Somana's brother, Oscar, fleeing the scene. When the police went to the Somana residence shortly after the fire broke out, they found Oscar lying on the couch in the living room; under the blanket that covered him he was fully dressed: he had not even taken off his shoes.[19]

And so, the two Somana brothers stood trial in the opening months of 1965, one for attempted murder, the other for arson. Both were acquitted for lack of evidence. It was impossible to determine whether Somana had deliberately shot Vuthela or whether the gun went off in the course of a tussle, the magistrate in Brian's case ruled.[20] As for Oscar, the magistrate in that case could not hold back a racist slur. It was well known, he said, that Xhosas were fond of setting fire to one another's property, but in this instance the evidence was inconclusive.[21]

The two trials were not the only occasions in early 1965 when Winnie's love life was paraded in the news. Brian Somana was a minor Thembu aristocrat, while Miriam was descended from a well-known Gcaleka family. Now, in early March 1965, delegations of Thembu and Gcaleka luminaries descended on the Somana home, their intention to convene 'a little summit' to save the Somana marriage. The good and the great were there: prominent businessmen, senior bureaucrats in the Transkei administration, a member of the Diepkloof school board. 'I could not stand by and see this Thembu family being broken up,' one of those who convened the meeting told a journalist. 'The children are so young, the couple is so young.'[22]

The divorce was called off, for now, and the couple posed for the press with their two children, a picture of a happy family.

Weeks later, Miriam changed her mind and sued for divorce, naming Winnie as a co-respondent. For her part, Winnie made an urgent application to join the proceedings on the grounds that the Somanas were maligning her. The couple, she said in her affidavit, had 'simulated matrimonial differences'. Their motive was to erase the stigma attached to Brian because he was working for the police. 'He thought', Winnie wrote, 'that after it became generally known that he was associated with me, people would not believe that he was an informer.' And then she tore into Brian Somana. He was a violent man, she said, who threatened her with great harm if she did not dispel the rumours about him. He shot Winnie's brother-in-law and then attempted to blackmail her family into withdrawing charges by spreading the lie that she was his lover. The Somanas were hardly on the brink of divorce, she said. They were 'living under the same roof and enjoying one another's companionship', the current court proceedings a farce designed to hurt her and to embarrass Nelson Mandela.[23]

So much about Winnie's intervention prefigures her later trajectory. For the longest time, she had clung fiercely to Brian Somana in the face of a storm. Now she branded him a living embodiment of evil. This Manichaean view of human beings, indeed, of the same human being, at one time all good, at another diabolical, followed her in the decades ahead.

Another aspect of Winnie's conduct would echo into the future. She was discovering early something both she and Nelson learned well, along with many others who have exercised power: that even blatant lying might pay off, for time and circumstance have a formidable capacity to remake what passes for truth.

So it was in the case of Brian Somana. In the authorized biography of Nelson penned by Fatima Meer, a close friend of the family whose loyalty to Winnie was unwavering, the Somanas are cast as pawns in a 'sinister plan ... hatched ... to destroy the Mandelas by destroying Winnie's reputation ...

'Brian was a plant,' Meer writes, an 'instrument used by the police ... Mrs. Somana started divorce proceedings and cited Winnie as a co-respondent. But once this reached the press, the divorce proceedings were dropped ...

'A woman is vulnerable,' Meer concludes. 'A beautiful young woman, deprived of her husband, is a hundred-fold more vulnerable.'[24]

At the time, though, few believed what Winnie had said in her affidavit. In the press, the question increasingly arose whether Nelson knew, and, if he did, what he might do. In July 1965, the liberal *Rand Daily Mail* carried a story explicitly about this issue. 'Unnamed friends

(LEFT) Winnie's father, Columbus Madikizela.
(The World / Arena Holdings)

(RIGHT) Nelson's guardians: Jongintaba Dalindyebo and his wife Noengland in 1929.
(Wilhelm Blohm, Unity Archives Herrnhut)

Healdtown, 1938. Nelson is fifth from right in the back row.
(Courtesy of Luyolo Stengile)

Walter Sisulu, 1952.
(© Jürgen Schadeberg,
www.jurgenschadeberg.com)

Oliver Tambo, 1960.
(Drum Social Histories/BAHA/
Africa Media Online)

Walter Sisulu and Albertina Thethiwe's wedding, July 1944.
Evelyn and Nelson are immediately to the groom's right.
(Courtesy of the Sisulu family)

Nelson with his sons, Makgatho (on Nelson's lap) and Thembi.
(Alf Kumalo/Africa Media Online)

Evelyn with Thembi (*left*) and Makgatho.
(From the book Higher Than Hope *by Fatima Meer, photographer unknown)*

The first two photographs of Winnie Madikizela to be published.
The caption accompanying the first misspelled her name.
(left, Bantu World/Arena Holdings; right, Drum Social Histories/BAHA/Africa Media Online)

Lilian Ngoyi. *(Eli Weinberg, UWC-Robben
Island Museum Mayibuye Archives)*

Winnie's dress fitting at the Harmel's house, 1958. The woman next to Nelson is Ruth Mompati. Barbara Harmel is at the front right.

(Eli Weinberg, UWC-Robben Island Museum Mayibuye Archives)

Nelson and Winnie, 1958, probably shortly before their wedding.

(Eli Weinberg, UWC-Robben Island Museum Mayibuye Archives)

The government granted Winnie belated permission to attend the Rivonia Trial in 1964, as long as she did not wear traditional attire. Supporters did so in her stead.

(Bailey's African History Archive/ Africa Media Online)

Reading the first letter she received from Nelson on Robben Island.

(Alf Kumalo/Africa Media Online)

Nelson and Robert Resha (*far right*) meeting FLN leaders in Morocco, 1962.
(UWC-Robben Island Museum Mayibuye Archives)

Prisoners breaking stones in the courtyard outside the 'leadership section'
on Robben Island, 1964. Nelson's cell window is on the far right.
(Copyright of Cloete Breytenbach, courtesy of Leon Breytenbach)

of Nelson Mandela', the story went, 'say that he does not know about the Somana case and is still very much in love with his wife.'[25]

It made for an uncomfortable spectacle: a conversation taking place in a national newspaper behind the back of a cuckolded man.

The *Rand Daily Mail* was wrong, though; Nelson did know.

Chapter 30

Nelson Mandela arrived on Robben Island in a state of willed optimism. On the flight from Pretoria – a flight that had taken off in the dead of night – he imagined his life after his release. The international condemnation of the Rivonia trial had been so intense, he recalled thinking on that flight, that 'the government of Verwoerd could not last'.[1]

With him in the belly of the Dakota were six of his fellow Rivonia defendants: Walter Sisulu, Ahmed Kathrada, Govan Mbeki, Elias Motsoaledi, Raymond Mhlaba and Andrew Mlangeni. Nelson alone was not handcuffed, perhaps because he was a lawyer, perhaps because he was the leader. The only white man convicted in the Rivonia trial, Denis Goldberg, remained behind; he was kept in a section of Pretoria Central Prison reserved for whites.

The mood among the prisoners in the aircraft was surreally bright. Some had never flown before and were excited to see the world from these heights. Now, as dawn broke, their country revealed itself in the quickening light. The plane descended over a sprawling mountain range, the Matroosberg, and animated chatter broke out; it was ideal terrain, someone commented, for guerrillas to hide and to fight.[2]

Robben Island was not new to Nelson. He had been held there the previous May for three weeks. What remained in his mind most vividly was the journey out. At the Cape Town docks, he and three others were loaded into the hold of an old wooden ferry. Made to stand, still in shackles, they were thrown about in the swells. At sea, out of sight, the prison warders on deck unzipped their trousers and urinated through a porthole onto the heads of the prisoners below.[3]

It is hardly surprising that on his flight to Robben Island Nelson now flitted between thoughts of a soldier's life in the mountains and imminent release.

The Rivonia men were held together in one room for four days
while the block that would house them was being prepared, a row of
thirty single cells. Nelson's was seven by eight feet, long enough for him
to stretch out his body when he slept, but not by much. There was no
furniture at first, no bed on which to sleep, no desk at which to work,
just a sisal mat and three blankets. A single lightbulb burned all day and
all night.

The men were locked up alone from late afternoon for fifteen hours
each day. A warder staffed the section all night to ensure that they
neither talked nor read. Sometimes, he would take off his shoes and
stalk the section barefoot;[4] the inmates, in turn, would throw grains
of sand into the corridor so that they could hear him coming.[5] In the
mornings, the men would be let out to scrub the buckets in which they
had relieved themselves during the night. 'The smell hit me,' a warder
recalled of the first time he walked in the Rivonia defendants' section of
the prison. 'Disinfectant, mixed with the unmistakable smell of sweat-
ing bodies and urine.'[6]

Their weekdays were consumed by hard labour. At first, the prisoners were assembled cross-legged in lines in the courtyard where they
crushed large stones to gravel; warders walked between them enforcing a strict silence. After a few months, the work changed; they were
taken every day to a lime quarry, 'an enormous white crater cut into
a rocky hillside', Nelson wrote.[7] Handed picks and shovels, they were
instructed to dig out the lime. This they did day in and day out for the
following thirteen years.

Their cellblock was called B Section, or, informally, the leadership
section, for it had been decided to isolate the leaders of political organizations from the rest of Robben Island's inmates; the majority of prisoners were held in large communal cells some distance away. Whether
it had been a mistake to house the liberation movement's upper ranks
together, permitting them to talk, to learn and to plan, was a question
that reverberated through apartheid's security establishment for years.

The Rivonia seven were soon joined in B Section by several others.
Three were ANC men convicted in a separate trial: Wilton Mkwayi,
Mac Maharaj and Laloo Chiba. Then there was Zephania Mothopeng
of the PAC. All four of these men had been subjected to severe tor-

ture over prolonged periods. Maharaj had attempted suicide by cutting his wrists with broken eggshells.[8] As for Mothopeng, a prisoner kept in an adjacent cell for the duration of his torture had listened to him go insane. 'The noise is incoherent and frightening,' the prisoner had observed. 'He makes brief speeches, shouts slogans, sings and bangs on the door all night long, screaming, crying, kicking the wall.'[9]

There was no shortage of anguish in B Section; it housed men whose paths to Robben Island had nudged the far reaches of human experience. This battered crew would see out the years together. Newcomers would join, old-timers would leave; the same core would inhabit this place until close to apartheid's end.

What happened between these men as they worked and lived together? And what passed between them and their keepers? These are the hardest of questions, for there is no source one might trust. Nelson himself recorded his ethical duty to conceal the island's life. 'Frankness . . . is dangerous and must be avoided,' he wrote.[10]

Even those who are candid cannot be fully trusted; the most self-reflective among them know not to believe what they recall. 'I remember prison as a good experience,' Mac Maharaj told an interviewer many years after his release. 'I think I have unconsciously learned to [distill] from that experience all the good aspects.' In the course of the interview he recalled 'two years of ennui, of . . . a state of self-pity which I wouldn't want to reveal'.[11]

Nor were B Section's inmates good witnesses to one another's inner states. 'Our deepest personal pain was not something we shared with one another as a rule,' Kathrada wrote.[12] Indeed, 'living with the same faces day in and day out', he would confess in a letter to his lover, one loses interest in what others say and feel.[13]

The dominant feature of Nelson's life now was solitude. For fifteen hours a day every prisoner on B Section was alone with himself. What happened with Nelson during these hours?

The only reading material he was permitted at first were his law books; he had been given special dispensation to keep studying for his LLB by correspondence at University College London. From 4:00 p.m., when he was locked in his cell, until 8:00 p.m., when he was ordered to sleep, he busied himself with his studies. The remainder of the night was idle time; if he was caught studying after 8:00 p.m., he was punished. Nor was he permitted a darkened room; the overhead lightbulb burned all night. He was not allowed a clock; one imagines that he guessed from the birdsong when dawn was near.

At first, his connection to the outside world was shockingly restricted. Consultations with their lawyers aside, Nelson and the other B Section prisoners were allowed one visit every six months and only with close family. These visits were anything but private; a bevy of warders sat in, and if the conversation strayed beyond family matters, they intervened.

Initially, the B Section prisoners were permitted to write and receive just two letters a year, each no longer than five hundred words. Warders combed them for references to politics and censored them heavily; the first letter Nelson received from Winnie had literally been cut to shreds.

Aware that his correspondence was monitored, his early letters to Winnie were horribly stiff and confined to urgent, practical matters. 'I have passed Hoër Afrikaanse Taaleksamens and have now enrolled for Afrikaans-Nederlands Course 1 with the University of South Africa,' he wrote to her in February 1966. 'The fees and costs of text books have been prohibitive and my funds have run out. Tell G. Please do not pay from your account.'[14]

But by the late 1960s, as the restrictions on his communications eased, his letters became both more numerous and considerably more revealing. Notwithstanding that his enemy was reading them, he began truly to live through his correspondence: he ached for the beehives and the honeycombs of Qunu; he pined for Johannesburg's nightlife; more than anything else, he rekindled his romance with his wife.

His memories, we shall see, were so nostalgic, at times so utterly fantastical, we cannot but worry that he was drifting too far from the world as it was.

· ·

The first piece of news he received about Winnie, though, just months after his arrival at Robben Island, was anything but idyllic.

In late 1964, two activists from the Yu Chi Chan Club, a small, far-left organization based in Cape Town, were placed in B Section. They were Neville Alexander and Fikile Bam. Bam's fury with Winnie for her role in his capture was at its peak. The first moment he had with

Nelson, he spewed his anger. 'I didn't think she did the right thing by me,' he recalled shouting at Nelson. 'She exposed me to the police by associating with someone she ought to have known was an informer.' When the dressing-down was over, he turned his back and stormed off.[15]

That is how news of the Brian Somana scandal came to Nelson: through a confrontation with a man doused in rage.

Bam was not the last source of news about the affair. Nelson's warders went out of their way to ensure that he was informed. In a prison where newspapers were strictly prohibited, he would find in his cell press cuttings reporting the drama. He had a front-row seat to the whole affair: the trial of Brian Somana for attempted murder, the arson trial, the spectacular divorce proceedings.

Nelson's response was dramatic and brutal. He told Walter Sisulu and Ahmed Kathrada that he was to divorce his wife.[16]

Then he sought out the two Yu Chi Chan members and asked them for a meeting. With great formality he apologized to them on behalf of his organization.

'He thought, in the first place, of the political damage that such an incident might have caused,' Neville Alexander recalled, 'and we were quite taken aback. Because we would never even have dreamt of associating that kind of thing with the political movement from which the person came ... We said, "Look, we are fully behind you. We understand the situation, and if there is anything that we can do ..." '[17]

Why was Nelson's initial response so decisive, so apparently final?

His innermost feelings about Winnie's sex life were complicated, no doubt, but that he wished to divorce her for having a lover is implausible. He never expected her to be celibate, he always insisted; his place was not to know too much. 'One must not be inquisitive,' he said. 'It is sufficient that this is a woman who is loyal to me, who supports and who comes to visit me, who writes to me; that's sufficient.'[18]

Her offense, as Alexander's memory attests, was, in the first place, political. She had taken an informer to her bed, causing members of a rival organization to be jailed. She had shamed her movement.

In years to come, a strangeness pervaded Nelson's communication with Winnie; a letter suffused with romance suddenly turned to politics, and yet the same charged, erotic spirit remained. It is jarring to read, as if two circuits have crossed. In Nelson's mind, it appears, two commitments had mingled, political substituting for sexual fidelity. Winnie's violation of this pact was as intense and as personal as a lover's betrayal.

But it is not quite as simple as this – how could it be in matters so close to the heart?

Years later, Nelson read the sensational memoir of Canada's First Lady Margaret Trudeau in which she described, among other salacious episodes, her affair with Ted Kennedy. Nelson wrote to Winnie expressing his distaste. Its intimacy, he said, bordered on the improper. 'I am not in a position to judge to what extent the . . . book has damaged the political career of Premier Trudeau,' he wrote. 'A happy family life is an important pillar to any public man.'[19]

He appeared to forget, when he wrote these lines, the salaciousness of the Somana affair.

For all his flirting and preening, Nelson was a traditional bourgeois man. To command the public sphere, men must be patriarchs, their houses seen to be in order. He understood that Winnie might have lovers, but for her affairs to be reported in the newspapers was beyond the pale.

Perhaps this is what offended him most deeply: not her infidelity, not even her political betrayal, but his public humiliation.

. .

It is from Ahmed Kathrada that we know that Nelson resolved to divorce Winnie; he told several people a quarter of a century later when he was released from prison. What Kathrada does not say is why Nelson changed his mind. Probably he did not know. He was a decade Nelson's junior and was regarded as a nephew or a little brother. Walter Sisulu is the one who might have altered Nelson's course.

We cannot know what passed between them. We can only guess that it was from this man – who had taken young Nelson under his wing, had watched him twice fall in love, become a father, a lawyer, a famous leader, a prisoner – that Nelson learned to forgive.

. .

Winnie came to see Nelson in July 1965 while the scandal was on fire.[20] By the time he wrote his autobiography, he had erased the encounter from his mind. 'In July 1966 . . . I had my second visit from my wife,' he writes. 'It was almost exactly two years after the first visit.'[21]

It is hardly surprising. On the other side of the glass was the woman he had almost divorced. Behind her stood a phalanx of prying white men listening closely to every word they spoke. It could only have been the most horrible meeting for them both. Each wounded and angry, they were restricted to talking about the health of family and friends.

Chapter 31

The repercussions of the Somana debacle were lasting and deep. They shaped Winnie's life throughout the 1960s. And when she was jailed at the end of the decade, the legacy of the scandal guided her captors as they set about trying to tear her apart.

The road to her incarceration was a long one. The best place to start, perhaps, is in August 1968, with a woman named Mary Benson.

Benson – spirited anti-apartheid campaigner, future biographer of Nelson Mandela – had left South Africa two years earlier in the wake of a banning order restricting her to her home. Now, as her father lay dying in Pretoria, the government granted her leave to see him. The conditions of her visit were stringent. She could stay no longer than a month, was not permitted to leave the municipal district of Pretoria, and could under no circumstances meet with another banned person.

One morning, Benson answered the phone in her boardinghouse room to find the photojournalist Peter Magubane on the line. He said briefly how sorry he was about Mary's father and then announced that 'a great friend' would be visiting from Johannesburg.

'Because he sounded mysterious,' Benson recalled later, 'and because I knew she was a close friend of his, I assumed this was Winnie Mandela. Alas, I could not see her,' Benson explained to Magubane, for Winnie was banned and were Benson to violate the restrictions placed upon her she would jeopardize the future visits of other exiles. No, Magubane assured her; it was not Winnie.

That evening, a white woman, 'her head half veiled in [a] black beaded net', knocked on Benson's door. In an accent Benson could not place, her visitor introduced herself as Maud, put her finger to her lips, indicating that the room might be bugged, and ushered Benson into the street outside; in a car, parked discreetly under a tree, sat Winnie Mandela.

'I'm terribly sorry, I can't talk to you,' Benson told Winnie. She was, she recalled, 'furious with Peter and miserably embarrassed at having to rebuff her'. Winnie exonerated Benson with a generous smile. 'Maud will explain everything,' she said.

The mysterious Maud tucked her arm into Benson's and led her down the road to a Greek café. It was late winter and bitterly cold; the two women were the only patrons to brave the café's veranda.

Maud was effusive, solicitous, full of praise for Benson's courage. Her surname, she said, was Katzenellenbogen, and her father had been the first captain of the New Zealand All Blacks rugby team. Then she took out a pile of press cuttings reporting on the charitable work she did for black people. Winnie was now her employee, she said, assisting the families of political prisoners.

And then Maud came to the point. Winnie, she said, wanted her to go to England and for Benson to put her in touch 'with everyone there'. By 'everyone there' Benson understood the International Defence and Aid Fund (IDAF), the largest and most significant sponsor of anti-apartheid work, with which Benson was intimately involved. IDAF was banned in South Africa; the networks through which it funnelled money into the country were secret, the risks to those involved severe.

Benson returned to her boardinghouse suspicious, confused, and uncertain what to do. She was woken the following morning by a delivery; Maud had sent her an extravagant bouquet of flowers and an urgent request that they meet again. And so Benson saw Maud that evening; this time, a silent Indian man drove them to a local drive-in. When they arrived, he left the car to go to the bathroom; Maud explained, once he was gone, that his name was Moosa Dinath, and that she and he had lived together illegally for many years at massive risk to them both; sex across the colour line was a serious criminal offense and was assiduously policed. Maud described the relentless hostility of their white neighbours, year in and year out, hostility directed not just to them but to their young children.

'I thought of the couple's loneliness,' Benson recalled years later, 'of their danger in assisting Winnie Mandela and in flouting the Immorality Act. Moved and ashamed at having doubted, I found myself on an emotional seesaw.'

When Dinath returned to the car, the discussion came around to money once more. IDAF was secretly channeling funds into South Africa to assist the families of political prisoners through the office of the Anglican dean of Johannesburg. Winnie found this arrangement unsatisfactory, Maud said. Dinath was the director of a company with a bank account in London; the IDAF funds would be better funnelled into South Africa through that route. Benson, she repeated, should put her in touch immediately with 'the London people'.

When the couple dropped Benson at her boardinghouse, Maud placed a gift in her hands. 'Something to keep you warm,' she said. In her room, Benson unpacked the parcel to find 'frilly underwear in garish colours, pyjamas, a sweater and a scarf, Chanel Number 5 scent and chocolates'.

The following day, a dear friend of Benson's, the playwright Athol Fugard, flew from Port Elizabeth to see her. She told him the whole story. Hearing it out loud brought home its absurdity; she and Fugard found themselves giggling.[1]

.   .

Maud Katzenellenbogen, it turned out, was as sinister as Benson's experience would suggest, and the consequences of her presence in Winnie's life were dire.

It was Nelson, of all people, who led Winnie to Maud; he did so because he himself had been powerfully seduced.

At the very beginning of his imprisonment, in August 1962, Nelson was held in the hospital section of the Fort with four other prisoners. One of them was Moosa Dinath. Nelson had known him vaguely in the 1950s; he was a successful businessman, famous for being the first Indian to float a public company, and had been peripherally involved in anti-apartheid politics.[2] He was also a serial con artist and a crook; indeed, he was serving time not for political activity but for fraud.

That a prisoner convicted of a nonpolitical offense had been placed with Nelson ought to have aroused his suspicion. Instead, he was enchanted. 'He was a very intelligent fellow,' Nelson recalled. 'Very confident. Tall, light and handsome, you know ... very handsome ... Impressive.' And striking, too, for a man like Nelson, so attuned to matters of masculine honour, was the open contempt Dinath displayed to his captors; he even talked down to the head of the prison, a Colonel Minnaar, much to Nelson's delight. 'He just despised these fellows,' Nelson reflected with admiration.

Dinath regaled Nelson with tales from his world. 'He used to fascinate me the whole day about his dealings with the government . . . and with the Afrikaners, forming companies with them in partnership, with Cabinet Ministers, in those days already.'[3]

There is something astonishing in the sheer familiarity, indeed, in the timelessness, of the seduction. Here was Nelson, nationalist leader, son of the soil, locked in a cell with a true child of Mercury, cunning, tricky, ever so eloquent, able to deal with anyone, from any world.[4] There are echoes here of the reverence Nelson felt when he encountered Walter Sisulu, a man who had mastered Johannesburg with what seemed a mysterious power.

As his time with Dinath went on, extraordinary things began to happen. Late one night, the head of the prison walked into the hospital section with a famous barrister in tow. Dinath slipped out with them and did not reappear until morning.[5]

Some time later, when Winnie visited Nelson, she was called into Colonel Minnaar's office. Looking furtive and anxious, he peered out of the window and closed the door. Winnie feared for a moment that he wished to seduce her. Instead, Dinath walked in and Minnaar left the two of them alone. To her astonishment, Dinath told her that for a sum of 10,000 rand Minnaar could collude in Nelson's escape. She reported the plan to Nelson's comrades, who greeted the news with understandable suspicion. Before they could decide what to do, Dinath advised Winnie to walk away. It was a rotten deal, he said; Minnaar wanted the whole payment up front; there was nothing to bind him to his side of the agreement.[6]

Months later, Dinath was unexpectedly released from prison, years before he had served his sentence. In the meantime, he had encouraged Nelson to kindle a friendship between Winnie and his common-law wife, Maud Katzenellenbogen.

The two women saw each other constantly over the following seven years, their relationship heavily lubricated by material things. Winnie was a woman in need, and Maud provided a steady flow of money, groceries, and finally, when nobody else would employ her, a job.

More than that, the Somana affair had left Winnie isolated. The Sisulu home was just blocks away from 8115 Orlando West. And yet Albertina avoided Winnie like the plague. So did Lilian Ngoyi.[7] In 1965, Oliver Tambo himself set a trap to ascertain whether Winnie was a spy; he sent her a message that two senior ANC men had stolen into the country and wished to meet her at an address in Soweto. The venue was watched to see if the police would swoop; the results were inconclusive and Tambo's suspicions remained.[8]

In familiar circles, among people she ought to be able to trust, Winnie felt threatened, persecuted, ill at ease. A stranger who lavished her with attention was a safer bet.

· ·

Maud Katzenellenbogen and Moosa Dinath were of a criminal type one encounters in hard-boiled fiction: inveterate chancers, dishonest to the marrow of their bones, they were liable to sell the shirt off your back. In the late 1940s, Maud bought a quantity of gold for £5,000 from a mine worker who had smuggled it from his place of work. When the deal went wrong, she kidnapped his wife and daughter.[9] As for Moosa, he had been convicted over the course of his life for fraud and theft, for writing fake checks, for holding a false passport. Arcane connections with powerful people often got him off.[10]

The probable route to their collaboration with the security police was appropriately smutty. Maud's sister, Phyllis Peake, owned a high-end brothel in downtown Johannesburg. To weaken her competition, she periodically paid police detectives to sleep with and then arrest women employed by her rivals. One of these detectives was a certain detective sergeant Van Wyk. He testified in open court about his alliance with Peake, his cross-examiner none other than Joe Slovo. A few years later, he was promoted to the rank of major and recruited into the newly formed security police.[11]

If Moosa and Maud did indeed spy on the Mandelas, their relationship with Van Wyk is likely how it began. Moosa was placed in the hospital wing with Nelson not long after Van Wyk joined the security police. Soon after he had befriended Nelson, and Maud had befriended Winnie, the minister of justice personally ordered Moosa's release. He had two years of his sentence still to serve.[12]

It is strange to think of either Nelson or Winnie as quite this vulnerable. Both learned intuitively how to exercise power; both displayed astonishing self-confidence, even in the face of the fiercest odds. And yet, in the course of the 1960s, both were malevolently seduced. 'Fondest regards to our friends Moosa and Maud,' Nelson wrote to Winnie as

late as April 1969.[13] Nearly seven years had passed since he had listened
to Dinath's dazzling tales; the bewitchment, it seems, still held.

                                    .   .

    With Maud at her side, Winnie embarked upon a brave and per-
ilous course. The ANC banned, its leaders in prison and exile, she
attempted to build an underground network.
    Initially, Winnie and Albertina were to build an underground
together.[14] It was a powerfully romantic idea: the Sisulu-Mandela men
side by side in prison, their wives reviving the organization they had
forged.
    Albertina had refused point-blank to work with Winnie. 'She had
serious misgivings', her biographer wrote, 'about some of the people
with whom Winnie associated and the way she operated.'[15]
    Others put it more harshly. When a young woman confided in Li-
lian Ngoyi that she planned to join Winnie Mandela in clandestine
political work, Ngoyi did not mince her words. 'When the security police give you electric shocks to your genitals,' she asked, 'what will you
do?'[16]
    And so Winnie Mandela and Albertina Sisulu, who lived a stone's
throw from each other, built separate underground networks.
    As early as October 1964, Albertina was arranging for people from
Soweto to leave the country for military training and for those returning from abroad to train others.[17] And, in 1966, when the trade unionist
John Nkadimeng was released from prison, he and Albertina together
established an underground cell of five people. The work was terribly dangerous. Albertina and Nkadimeng were both banned and thus
forbidden to communicate with each other. They used Albertina's
seventeen-year-old son, Mlungisi, as a go-between; he retrieved notes
that Nkadimeng had left under a rock and handed them to his mother.[18]
    For all the risk the work entailed, its harvest was modest. Alber-
tina and Nkadimeng established sporadic communication with exiled
South Africans in Botswana and used this channel to smuggle a handful of people abroad. That was the high-water mark of their achievement. And, notwithstanding her caution, Albertina discovered in 1967
that one of the five people in her cell was a spy. She reported forlornly
to Walter in a thinly veiled code. 'Our gardens are not too good this

year,' she told him in 1966. 'The drought has been too much. The worms are so powerful that as soon as you put in plants they are destroyed instantly.'[19]

Winnie's underground network was considerably larger, its aims more ambitious. It consisted of several cells – quite how many is the subject of conflicting memories – of four people each. One member of every cell was also a member of another, and so the network was a series of interlocking circles. Winnie's cell was referred to as the 'nuclear', the 'leadership', or the 'adult' cell and had overall responsibility for the network.

Members were enterprising and creative. They inveigled themselves into Christian youth groups and church choirs, recruiting quietly but methodically among Soweto's youth.[20]

There was also some talk within the network of sabotage. Winnie's cell went so far as to plan setting fire to a commuter train at a station in the southwestern suburbs of Johannesburg. The project was aborted when suspicion grew that a member of the cell, a young man named Simon Sikosana, was a spy.[21] The suspicion was well founded; Sikosana, it emerged later, was briefing his handlers every day.[22]

Winnie understood full well that this work was quixotic. Despite the plans to burn a train, she looked dimly upon isolated acts of destruction. Indeed, she had come to view the sabotage campaign Nelson had led as hopelessly ineffectual. What was the use of blowing up the odd installation when it could be repaired in the blink of an eye? she recalled asking. It was a reasonable question. She had in mind a trained corps of saboteurs engaged in spectacular coordinated action. 'Something like setting fire to the Afrikaner farmers' mealie [corn] fields all over the country,' she suggested.[23] She knew full well that her underground network was light-years from accomplishing anything so grand.

. .

While running a clandestine network, Winnie was also a mother and a householder attempting to live from day to day. And the security police expended astonishing energy to render her life unlivable.

In early 1965, Winnie was served a new banning order: it restricted her to Orlando and barred her from entering an educational institution or a court. This effectively prevented her from doing her work at the

Johannesburg Child Welfare Society, which involved tracing people
across Johannesburg, placing clients in schools, and testifying in court.
Much to its embarrassment, her employer dismissed her.[24]

Deprived of income, Winnie scrambled for work. She found a job as
a clerk at a correspondence school for black journalists; within months,
the chief magistrate of Johannesburg had informed her employer that
since his college was an educational institution, Winnie could not enter
the premises.[25] The Anglican dean of Johannesburg then employed her
assisting the families of political prisoners; he, too, let her go because
of the police attention her presence courted.[26] Next, she worked as an
assistant to her attorney, but he asked her to leave when he took on a
politically sensitive case; her presence, he feared, would give the security police an excuse to raid his offices.[27] Finally, she found work with
Maud Katzenellenbogen, an arrangement the authorities mysteriously
let be.

The police also did what they could to hurt those close to her.
When Winnie's brother Msuthu came to live with her, he was charged
with vagrancy and thrown in jail. And when he successfully contested
the charge, he was rearrested, this time for being in Johannesburg without the requisite permit.[28]

As for Winnie's sister Nonyaniso, who had been living with her
since the early days of her marriage, the police hounded her relentlessly. Many years later, she recounted to this author how the police
beat her when they came around to find that Winnie was not at home.[29]
In 1969, she was thrown in prison, tortured and blackmailed into testifying against her sister.[30]

State agents were no less energetic in their quest to prevent Winnie's children from going to school. Shortly after she enrolled Zenani
in a Roman Catholic nursery school, the nuns sent Winnie a letter saying that her daughter had to go; the security police, Winnie surmised,
had paid them a threatening visit. Next, she placed her girls under
false names at a Coloured (mixed-race) school in central Johannesburg.
When the police got wind of that, the girls were forced to leave.[31]

Resigned to defeat, Winnie had her daughters shipped off to Swaziland to attend a private boarding school. This was in 1966; Zenani
was seven years old; Zindzi was not yet six. A wealthy British benefactor, Lady Elinor Birley, whom Winnie had befriended in Johannesburg, paid the girls' school fees.[32] She and her husband, Robert Birley,
were among several people who saw the Mandela family through these

straitened years. Another was David Astor, a wealthy heir and the editor of the London *Observer*. Nelson had met him on his London visit in
1962; Astor would extend his largesse to the Mandelas over the following thirty years.[33]

. .

It is probably fair to say that Winnie survived the 1960s because she
was unreservedly loved. Aside from Maud Katzenellenbogen's lavish
attention, there was Peter Magubane.

His first sight of Winnie was through the lens of his camera. It
was December 1955; she was nineteen, he twenty-three; he had been
assigned to photograph her graduation ceremony at the Jan Hofmeyr
School.[34] It took almost a decade for them to draw close, it seems, their
relationship baptized by gunfire and arson as Magubane replaced Brian
Somana in Winnie's affections.

From December 1964 until May 1969, they were inseparable. When
Magubane phoned Mary Benson at her Pretoria boardinghouse to say
that she should expect a surprise guest, she thought immediately that it
was Winnie, for the two were always together.

Magubane and Winnie both insisted that they were never lovers,
but their denials were surely for form's sake. 'Peter had a crush on Winnie,' Joyce Sikhakhane, a member of Winnie's underground network,
recalled. 'Were they lovers?' this author asked her. 'These were hushed
things,' she replied. 'You did not spread these things. It was a question
of solidarity.'[35]

As Sikhakhane spoke of Peter Magubane, an aura of gentleness
spread through the room. They were both employed at the *Rand Daily
Mail*, she as a journalist, he as a photographer, and they saw each other
every day. 'He was ebullient,' she recalls. 'He was jocular. He brought
the most wonderful spirit with him to work.'

When she began speaking of Magubane's relationship with Winnie, the feeling she exuded grew gentler still. 'Winnie's girls were so
fond of him, you know. They really liked him. He made provisions. He
brought groceries. He transported the girls to where they needed to go.
And he would bring his daughter, Fikile, who was Zeni's age, to stay
in Winnie's house. He was really like a dad or an uncle to those girls.'

Nelson knew early that Winnie and Magubane were lovers; that is
the recollection of Mac Maharaj, who remembers the warders telling

Nelson with glee that Winnie had aborted Magubane's child. Nelson never discussed matters this personal with anyone on Robben Island, except, perhaps, with Walter Sisulu. But it appears that he understood Magubane to be a ballast in Winnie's life; when Magubane came to visit him on Robben Island, Maharaj recalls, Nelson welcomed him warmly.[36]

Magubane's relationship with Winnie profoundly altered his fate. In 1969, he was thrown in prison, tortured, kept for hundreds of days in solitary confinement, and tried for terrorism. When he was released, he was banned for five years, stalling his career as a photographer. He suffered this fate as much for his personal devotion to Winnie as for his political commitment.

Many years later, in the 1990s, long after their lives had taken different paths, his loyalty to her remained resolute. 'Without Winnie,' he told Nelson's authorized biographer, 'Nelson wouldn't have been what he is. When newspapers could not write about him, she could have his problems publicised. Without her, the ANC would have been forgotten. She was the only person who stood by the ANC and said, "I dare you to stop me." She was prepared to die for it.'[37]

This is as powerful testimony to Winnie's career as anyone has offered. Over the course of his adult life, Peter Magubane gave Winnie Mandela more than his love; he bore witness to her spirit and her work.

. .

And then there was Maud. In security police memos there appear several references to a police informer described simply as 'a white friend of Winnie's'. We cannot know for certain that this is Maud, but it is likely. None of her full reports seem to have survived. What we have instead are brief distillations of what interested her handlers most.

It was Winnie's apparent paranoia that excited them. Her dear friend Helen Joseph 'is working against me'; the Rivonia trial barrister and leading communist Bram Fischer is trying to cajole her into exile because he is threatened by black nationalists; her lawyer, Joel Carlson, is out to make his fortune by taking money from IDAF to represent political prisoners.[38]

There is great sadness in reading these reports today. Whether the informer was embellishing to please her handlers we cannot know. Reliable or not, Winnie's enemy would use this information most cruelly.

Chapter 32

In September 1967, during his fourth year on Robben Island, Nelson's mother came to see him; they had laid eyes on each other just once since the end of the Rivonia trial in June 1964.

When time came for them to say goodbye, the warders watching on beheld a wrenching scene. Nelson offered his mother his cheek, pressing it against the glass barrier between them, his eyes shut tight. And Nosekeni, as one warder remembers it, put out 'her old, bony hand' and stroked her son's face through the glass.

On the path back from the visitors' block to the prison, Nelson's emotions were laid bare in his gait. 'It was the first time I had seen this tall, proud man, bowed,' the warder who accompanied him wrote.[1]

Nelson remembered his thoughts in this moment vividly. 'I was able to look at her as she walked away towards the boat that would take her to the mainland,' he told a correspondent. 'Somehow the idea crossed my mind that I would never again set eyes on her.'[2]

A year later, Nosekeni was dead.

'It was afternoon [when Nelson was informed],' Mac Maharaj remembered. 'When someone is called to the office, he comes back with news. But Nelson walks straight to his cell without saying a word. Walter follows him, sits with him, comes out after a long time, says, "Chaps, this is what happened: don't crowd him, go to him one by one, but give him space." We take turns to go to see him. He acknowledges our condolences briefly; we leave.

'The next morning, Nelson comes out fighting. He wants to see the commanding officer, he wants to go to the funeral. Now he is talking to us. But he has built a screen. We can't get behind it. And that's it. No more mention of his mother.'[3]

The letters he wrote at this time were in fact awash with his mother, and he told his correspondents that with the news of her death he lost his footing, at least for some time.

'For a few days I spent moments in my cell which I never want to remember,' he told one correspondent.[4] While losing his mother at any time would have been hard, 'behind bars this news can be a shattering disaster'. And in his case, he continues, it very nearly was.[5] One gets the sense that he looked down an abyss when Nosekeni died, that it took some wherewithal to steady himself and find safe ground.

What did her death mean to him? The answer perhaps lies in the identities of the people with whom he chose to bare his soul. He was refused permission to attend the funeral; instead, he was permitted to write thank-you notes to those who were there. And he used this dispensation to open himself to a sphere beyond his political world. The fragment just cited is to a man named Knowledge Guzana, not a comrade Nelson knew from politics, but a Transkei notable he met at university. In his letter he addresses Guzana not by his Christian name but by his clan name, Dambisa.

Among the first to receive a letter from Nelson after Nosekeni's death was Kaiser Daliwonga Matanzima, by now a resolute political enemy. It was with Matanzima that he shared the image of his mother walking toward the boat that would carry her away for the last time.

He thanked Matanzima for the many kindnesses he had shown in recent years: for travelling all the way to Qunu, twice, in 1962 and in 1964, to tell Nosekeni personally of Nelson's prison sentences; for visiting Winnie in Soweto when Nelson was jailed. 'This interest,' he wrote, 'stems not only from our close relationship, but also from the long and deep friendship that we have cultivated since our student days *kuwe la kwa Rarabe*.' Literally translated, these words mean 'to you from Rarabe', a subgroup of the Xhosa nation; they are an insider's reference to Nelson and Daliwonga's kinship ties.

He wrote other letters, less intimate, but no less revealing. In early 1969, for instance, he wrote to Daliwonga's son, Mthetho Matanzima, congratulating him on his installation as a chief and wishing him a happy reign. He ended the letter listing the chiefs to whom he 'would like to be remembered'. It was very long indeed, taking in a swathe of the senior Thembu aristocracy.[6]

These letters are considerably more than diplomatic. Years later, he wrote to Winnie in frustration, begging her to send him a visitor from the Transkei. He needed desperately to talk to *someone* from home, he complained, it didn't really matter who; he just wanted to spend an hour with a soul who *understood*.

To be thrown by the death of a parent is a widely shared experience. To take stock, in its wake, of whence one comes, is common too. When Nosekeni died, Nelson, it appears, took refuge in the world in which she had loved him, a world in which he was a Thembu royal.

How complex his mourning for his mother must have been and how tinged with regret. 'I had hoped to be able to look after her in her last days on earth and to bury her when she died,' he wrote to his oldest daughter.[7] Wrapped in his filial grief, it seems, was his mourning of the place from which he was severed and in which he was, profoundly and fundamentally, a black man and an African.

'Throughout my imprisonment my heart & soul have always been somewhere far beyond this place in the veld and the bushes,' Nelson told a correspondent two years after Nosekeni's death. 'I live across the waves with all the memories & experiences I have accumulated over the last half century – memories of the grounds in which I tended stock, hunted, played & in where I had the privilege of attending the traditional initiation school.' Although he had lived in a city for two decades before his arrest, 'I have never succeeded in shaking off my peasant background.'[8]

It is a striking remark for such an obviously cosmopolitan man. In years to come, the rural hinterland he nurtured in his thoughts grew more nourishing still, saving him, one might hazard to suggest, from his fame.

.   .

If his life as a son and as a Thembu grew sturdier when his mother died, his life as a father grew frailer. Thembi had by now rebuffed him, and it hurt a great deal. From Makaziwe and Makgatho he learned that his eldest had a two-year-old son. His requests for photographs of this, his first grandchild, and of his daughter-in-law were not forthcoming. He also learned from others that Thembi had abandoned school, not even acquiring a Junior Certificate, the minimum qualification for training in any profession, and had found work as a lowly driver.

His eldest child was lost to him, it seems, and he must have entertained the unwelcome thought that Thembi was lost to himself. We cannot know whether Thembi's failure as a student arose from the drama of his parents' divorce. But Nelson certainly convinced himself that his absence as a father was to blame. 'I sincerely believe', he wrote, 'that if I were home ... he would not have succumbed to abandoning school at a critical age in his life.'[9]

And when he discovered a little later that his younger son, Makgatho, had abandoned plans to study at university, he could not contain his rage. 'Have you neither pride nor conscience, strong will & independence?' he asked. 'Look out: take stock of your position before it is too late!'

Sitting in his prison cell, he imagined the downward trajectory of the Mandelas he had spawned. They would be 'condemned forever to the degrading status of being subservient to, & the object of exploitation by other human beings'.[10]

He took solace in the fact that his eldest daughter, Makaziwe, was doing well at school. But while he wrote with love, his expectations of her were uncomfortably naked, the fatherhood performed so stiffly the starch falls from the page. 'The language and style were good and the writing clear,' he said of the last letter he received from her. And he imagined aloud that she would 'become a doctor or scientist and use your knowledge, training and skill to help your people who are poor and miserable and who have no opportunity to develop'.[11]

It is hard to say how a thirteen-year-old might respond to these lines; it is unlikely that even the most remote of her schoolteachers would talk to her in this way.

. .

There was nothing stiff, though, in his letters to Winnie.

She had sent him a pile of family photographs, among them two portraits of herself, one 'big', he wrote, the other 'small'. The small one caused great excitement among his comrades. 'Is that not her younger sister?' they were asking. 'Madiba has been too long in jail, he does not know his sister-in-law.'

But it is the bigger picture, Nelson wrote, that had garnered his attention. It 'depicts all I know of you, the devastating beauty & charm which 10 stormy years of marriage have not chilled'. He displayed it for years to come on the makeshift bookshelf he was permitted to place in his cell. She sits in profile, her chin resting on her folded hands, her expression at once pensive and intense, as if her thoughts are far away.

He had clearly been staring at it for some time when he wrote to her. 'I suspect that you intended the picture to convey a special message that no words could ever express. Rest assured I have caught it.'[12]

What was it he believed Winnie had intended to impart? He did not say, directly, but declared that the portrait 'has sharpened my longing for you'. And then he recounted, in a code he hoped the eavesdroppers would not understand, her scandalous behaviour when they were courting: Nelson waiting in his Oldsmobile on Hans Street while Winnie declared her love to Barney Sampson in his blue van; Winnie going to Nelson's office to 'study' and receiving Barney when Nelson went to the gym.

He was flirting outrageously with her, armed just with his pen. How much freight these letters carried; how much work they had to perform. The woman who received them had not spent a night with him in seven years. She was out in the world, living a life about which he received occasional scraps of news. The times they were actually together were so sporadic and brief, the circumstances so reduced. Could he tell from these brief meetings whether his letters had done their work?

For a very private man, he betrayed a great deal to his comrades when Winnie came to see him. 'Just knowing that [she] was about to come brought such a change over Nelson,' Fikile Bam recalled, 'and it then flowed over to the rest of us.' By the morning of her visit, the whole of B Section was in a state of excitement.

'Nelson would literally come back glowing,' Bam continued, and all the news she had brought would pour from him. 'Of course, she always had something [to say] that was exciting.'

Bam was none too fond of either Nelson or Winnie. But telling so romantic a tale had clearly softened his heart. 'She was the centre of his life,' Bam concluded. 'He was absolutely in love with her.'[13]

Chapter 33

And then Winnie was arrested. They came for her at about 2:00 a.m. on May 12, 1969, storming through her front door in great numbers, turning her home inside out. They took her away in front of her daughters, who were left in the house alone. At the same hour, another two dozen people across Soweto and as far away as the city of East London were picked up from their homes. Another dozen would be arrested in the coming month.

Winnie's underground network, about which the police had always possessed intimate knowledge, was being brought to heel.

The arrests were made under the Terrorism Act that parliament had passed two years earlier. It empowered the police to detain anyone indefinitely, incommunicado, without access to a lawyer, without visits, whether from family, friends, or a clergyman, on suspicion of terrorism, defined so broadly as to include anyone who 'further[ed] and encourage[d] any political aim'. It expressly removed the power of any court to offer relief to those detained under its provisions. It also forbade the furnishing of any information about a detainee except with the consent of the minister of justice.[1]

Using the latitude the law gave them, the police cast a shroud of mystery over the raids. A full week after the arrests, they would still not say how many people had been detained; nor would they divulge their names, where they were being held, or for what crimes they would be charged. They said only that those in custody were suspected to have carried on the work of the ANC.

'One thinks of countries like Stalinist Russia when one hears of people disappearing,' complained the *Rand Daily Mail*, 'of police arriving in the middle of the night to take people away.'[2]

One person with an early inkling of what was happening was a lawyer named Joel Carlson. Having studied at Wits at the same time as Nelson, Carlson had embarked on an extraordinary career; off his own bat, he had become what would later be called a struggle lawyer, devoting his practice to defending people from the actions of the state. Over the past few years, he had exposed the torture to which detained activists had been subjected in one case after another. He had by now also acted for Nelson on several occasions and knew Winnie well. He had in fact briefly employed her in his practice.

Now the families of many of those who had been arrested on May 12 went to Carlson for help, among them Winnie's brother-in-law. Carlson took on their cases as a matter of course.

In the coming days, several of his new clients came to him with troubling news. A woman introducing herself as Mrs. Kay had appeared at their front doors; she must have thought Katzenellenbogen too much of a mouthful for her new friends. Flashing a newspaper picture of her and Winnie in an embrace, she spoke of their deep friendship. She talked, too, of her relationship with Moosa Dinath, a defiant act of interracial love. She advised that Joel Carlson was a rogue and should not be permitted to represent those in prison; besides, she added, the police were on the brink of detaining Carlson, and he would soon be quite useless to them. She knew a better lawyer, she said, a man named Mendel Levin. She persuaded some of Carlson's clients to accompany her to Levin's office and hand him power of attorney.[3]

And then, in London, from out of the blue, Mary Benson received a phone call from Peter Magubane, who would himself be jailed weeks later. 'Tanya will arrive in London on Thursday and will contact you,' he said mysteriously. Benson's phone rang again a little later: it was Maud; she was on her way.

Benson immediately contacted Oliver Tambo, who instructed her to see Maud and report back what she said. And what Maud said, of course, was that she had found Winnie a lawyer, 'a great fighter' named Mendel Levin. She had come, she said, to approach IDAF to raise money for his fee.[4]

In July, Moosa Dinath appeared on Robben Island to see his old friend Nelson Mandela. Nelson was beside himself with worry. Not only did he wonder what was happening to Winnie in jail, but her detention had cut him off from news of Zenani and Zindzi; he did not know who, if anybody, had taken responsibility for their care. And so, when the authorities told him that Dinath had requested permission to come 'for the express purpose of discussing family problems caused by Zami's detention'. he was very grateful indeed.[5]

What Dinath actually wanted to discuss, Nelson discovered, was Winnie's legal representation. He had lined up an excellent lawyer, he said: his name was Mendel Levin.

Whether Nelson had an inkling of his old friend's nefarious intentions is hard to say. But he was certainly puzzled by Dinath's counsel. For he knew Mendel Levin as a card-carrying member of the ruling National Party and as a disreputable man to boot; a decade earlier, he had stood trial for fraud, avoiding conviction by turning state witness. And among Nelson's Jewish friends, Levin was downright notorious; he was the first Jew to stand in an election as a candidate for the Nationalists, a party whose then leader, John Vorster, had spent World War II interned for his membership in a pro-Nazi paramilitary organization.

Nelson politely rejected Dinath's advice and requested that he instruct Joel Carlson to act for Winnie, a message Dinath failed to pass on.[6] And Nelson wrote urgently to Winnie, counseling her to spurn Levin and take Carlson as her lawyer.[7] But the police made that awfully difficult. They barred Carlson from seeing Winnie or any of his other clients. Levin, on the other hand, was permitted to see Winnie whenever he wished.[8]

The scene was set for the interrogation of Winnie Mandela.

· ·

Of the people detained in May and June 1969, two did not make it out alive. Caleb Mayekiso, arrested in the city of East London the night after Winnie was taken, lasted eighteen days in jail. The district surgeon determined that he had died of natural causes, but his wife said that he was healthy when the security police took him away.

The other was a prominent imam, Abdullah Haron. A postmortem reported twenty-six bruises on his body, a hematoma on his back and a fractured rib. The police gave evidence that he slipped on the stairs as he came out of interrogation.[9]

Those in Winnie's immediate circle were subjected to varying degrees of torture. All were interrogated continuously for at least five days, around the clock, not permitted to sleep, some not permitted to sit down. When Rita Ndzanga's interrogation began, she was struck in the face and fell to the floor, where she was repeatedly kicked. She was then picked up by her hair and placed on a pile of three bricks. Each time she fell off, she had a bucket of water thrown in her face, was dragged off the floor by her hair once more, and placed back on the bricks. Once, she watched a police officer wash clumps of her hair off his hands in the sink.[10]

Many were serially humiliated. Ndzanga's husband, Lawrence Ndzanga, was forced to stand on three bricks until he urinated down his leg. Another detainee was made to catch and kill with his bare hands the cockroaches that crawled across the floor. As for Peter Magubane, he was informed that Winnie was pregnant with his child; if he told them all he knew, she would be given a pill that would abort her pregnancy. If not, her tummy would swell and her name would be smeared.[11]

Especially painful, it seems, was how much the police knew. When Joyce Sikhakhane's interrogation began, the police informed her in shocking detail of all she had done over the previous year. Knowing that their purpose was to inflame her distrust of her fellow detainees, she could not help herself. She had been so loyal to Winnie; now she felt her fury at her mentor rising, a fury she could barely contain.[12]

.   .

What happened to Winnie during *her* interrogation?

Winnie wrote an affidavit recounting her interrogation five months later. It does not offer a transparent window onto what happened; nobody's account of their own torture ever can. But it does have an important virtue. Her aim in telling the story was not to mythologize it for a wider audience. Her lawyers asked her to tell the story as forensically as possible, focusing on every detail. And this she did.

The interrogation began on May 26, two weeks after she was detained, and went on continuously for five days. Whether because of her fame or for fear for her health, she was permitted to sit on a chair for the duration. Nor was she beaten. But she was not allowed to sleep. Whenever she drifted off, a police officer would clap his hands loudly next to her ear, jolting her awake. By the third day, she had grown ill; her hands and feet were swollen and blue, her heart was palpitating, and she suffered from dizzy spells.[13]

Her chief interrogator was a man named Theuns Swanepoel. Until early 1963 he had been a uniformed officer in the Flying Squad, the police's rapid response unit. Along with dozens of others, he had been recruited at immediate notice into the security police, given a three-week course in political policing, and set to work.[14] By May of that year he was one of the leading members of the 'sabotage squad', interrogating political detainees. He would most likely have partaken in torturing Brian Somana, along with the dozens more detained in May and June 1963.

By the time Winnie was jailed, Swanepoel had become a mythical figure in the ranks of the anti-apartheid movement. In his physical attributes, he was a torturer one might find in the pages of a nasty comic book. 'The most outstanding feature about him was his ugliness,' Joel Carlson wrote. 'His face was pockmarked, blotchy pink and purple. His nose was flabby with wide, flat nostrils. His ears stood out from his head beneath his close-cropped ginger hair and his head sat on his shoulders as if he had no neck.'[15] But if he was ugly, he was by no means stupid. In the memories of some – although certainly not all – he possessed a lethal combination of traits: on the one hand, a genuine curiosity about what lay in the depths of the human being he had captured; on the other, an unrestrained appetite for cruelty.

Mac Maharaj, for instance, was captured in 1964, in his head the names of every single member of the South African Communist Party active in the country. He was desperate to divulge nothing. Swanepoel made a grand entrance, Maharaj recalled. 'That was his style. He would walk into the room in the middle of an interrogation and the torture would stop. There would be a great sense of drama around his entry, and, usually, if you had not met him before, he would walk up to you, look you in your face, and ask: "Do you know who I am? I am Swanepoel. Do you know now who I am? Do you know what to expect from me?"'

Swanepoel had clearly given some thought to the encounter before he came into the room. Knowing that Maharaj had one good eye, he lit a match to it. Fearing that it would burn into its socket and that he would go blind, Maharaj panicked; he only just held back from talking, he recalled.

The following day, Swanepoel tried something else. Maharaj was taken to his office and told to strip naked and to put his penis on the desk. 'Then [Swanepoel] took a policeman's baton and started to stroke it, without ever taking his eyes off me, and then he raised the baton and brought it whacking down on my penis.' When Maharaj's agony began to subside, Swanepoel stood him up and ordered him to put his penis on the desk again. 'But this time, he did not hit it immediately. He picked up his baton, raised it, and waited for the expectation of pain to capture me before he hit.'

Day upon day, the ritual went on. Maharaj was taken to Swanepoel's office and ordered to put his penis on the desk. On some days, Swanepoel left Maharaj's body unscathed; he just stood there, the baton hovering in the air over the exposed penis all afternoon. Maharaj understood that were he to break, it was the expectation of pain, not the pain itself, that would do it.

And then, all of a sudden one day, Swanepoel did something new. He picked a badly beaten Maharaj off the floor, stood him against the wall, pressed the tip of a sword to his throat, and demanded that he talk. Trying desperately to conquer his fear, Maharaj had an epiphany: 'It suddenly dawned on me that he had handed me a gift. The gift was there in that sharp point on my throat. All I had to do was dive on it, and I would be dead.'

Swanepoel, who was staring Maharaj intently in the eye, read his thoughts in a flash. 'He panicked and withdrew the sword and walked out.'

As the meaning of this exchange began to settle, Maharaj understood that he had won. He and Swanepoel now both knew that it was Maharaj who held the trump in the bloody game they played: he could stop himself from talking by dying. Swanepoel stood back after that; he never again played a prominent role in Maharaj's torture. And Maharaj would have it confirmed that Swanepoel had taken in precisely what had happened. 'He told other detainees that he respected me.'[16]

That is Maharaj's recollection, at any rate. The story is worth telling in part because it is hard to know how reliable it may be. Nobody who has been tortured is a good witness to their ordeal. The experience as it happened is often untellable, for to a greater or lesser extent one has experienced a breakdown of self, a fragmented, disjointed experience hard to represent in narrative. To the extent that one places a coherent self in the story one tells, as Maharaj did, one is telling a heavily reconstructed story.

Maharaj depicts himself and Swanepoel as chess players, each at the top of his game. He goes so far as to imagine a perverse camaraderie between them; they walk away with a mutual respect for each other.

Maharaj wants a rematch; he would like to show Swanepoel that he can better him at his own job. 'My dream', he writes, 'was that one day I'd capture Swanepoel, and I believed I would be able to make him talk without physical torture.'[17]

. .

The Swanepoel Winnie remembered is unlike the one presented by Maharaj. She did not recall a tactical man aiming to outwit her. She remembered his raw hatred. And she described absorbing that hatred and making it her own. The significance of her memory of Swanepoel to her political career cannot be overstated. But it is only a partial guide to what happened between them.

Swanepoel was cruel to Winnie. When she fell ill as a result of her prolonged sleeplessness, her heart beating irregularly, her limbs swollen and blue, he not only persisted with the gruelling interrogation; he appeared to egg on her death. His aim, it seems, was to diminish her to the point of nothingness, to have her imagine herself as a corpse. The only useful thing she could leave behind, he and several of his colleagues suggested, was the information she might share before she expired.[18]

This is what Winnie recalled five months after her interrogation. It is most instructive and revealing.

Swanepoel surely calculated that Winnie's life was not actually in danger. Her death under interrogation would have been catastrophic for the government and a fate thus avoided. But her own fear that she was dying appears to have garnered his interest. His response was not just to pretend to egg on her death but to paint for her an image of her extinction.

This was a shrewd course of action. A lazier observer of Winnie would see a formidably strong person, full of confidence in her self-worth and brave in the face of death. A deeper intelligence sees in the theatrical aspects of her conduct a mortifying fear of nonbeing. Getting Maharaj to imagine his own corpse was precisely the wrong thing to do, for it showed him a path to victory. Getting Winnie to imagine herself dead was probably right.

Swanepoel spoke to her, too, about her marriage. It was not surprising, he said, that Nelson had hardly spent a night at home since marrying her. His life was testimony to the lengths a man might go to

escape a woman like her. Going underground, living for years like an
outlaw, then getting himself locked in prison forever. Had he been Nelson, Winnie would remember Swanepoel saying, he would have done
the same.[19]

But a cruel face is not all Swanepoel showed her. There was a period
during her interrogation, it seems, when he was beguiling. All she need
do, he said, was make a statement over the radio to the black people of
South Africa. There was every hope for improvement within the existing framework of law, she should tell them. They should abandon their
illegal struggles. Whites and blacks ought to cooperate, she should say.

Swanepoel described in exquisite detail the future she would
acquire in exchange. Nelson would be removed from B Section immediately and placed in a comfortable cottage. He would be allowed to
read and write all he wanted and to receive unrestricted visits from his
wife. Later, he would be released and settled in the Transkei, where
Winnie, Zenani and Zindzi could join him and live a serene country
life. Eventually, Nelson would be permitted to resume practicing as an
attorney.[20]

There is no evidence that Winnie even considered this offer. Swanepoel probably never imagined that she would take it. He had in fact
dangled a quite different bait, tailor-made to evade Winnie's detection.

When her interrogation was over, Mendel Levin, the lawyer Maud
had offered to Winnie's co-defendants, and whom Moosa Dinath had
come to Robben Island to persuade Nelson to hire, was permitted to
see Winnie. Conspicuously, Joel Carlson's requests to see her or any of
his other clients were denied.

Winnie told Levin that she was ill, perhaps even dying. And Levin
made a great show of demanding from the authorities that his client be
examined by a doctor. The authorities, of course, immediately obliged.[21]

Something else happened between Winnie and Mendel Levin.
From her prison cell she wrote a letter to IDAF in London saying that
Joel Carlson was not to be trusted and that money should be raised for
Levin to represent the defendants. When Carlson asked her some time
later why she had written the letter, she told him she had been sick and
that Levin had helped her.[22]

She had been caught in a trap. A familiar good-cop, bad-cop relay
had been assembled with the twist that the good cop was disguised as
her lawyer. It was an intelligent trap, for it was designed specifically for
its victim. Her interrogation had targeted her immense fear of death,

revealed by her hypochondria. As for Levin's role, it was shaped by the knowledge, helpfully imparted by Maud Katzenellenbogen, that Winnie was suspicious of Carlson.

Swanepoel had done to Winnie precisely what Maharaj had dreamed of doing to Swanepoel: she had done his bidding not because he held a gun to her head but because he had placed his desire in her heart.

As Mary Benson's testimony suggests, the security police had long wanted to use Moosa and Maud to get to IDAF. The reward would have been sweet. Not only would the funds of the Congress movement's greatest donor have been deposited into a bank account of an enemy agent, since dealing with IDAF was a crime in South Africa, controlling the funds might have brought a raft of internal activists down.

In this regard, Swanepoel's victory over Winnie was always going to be Pyrrhic. Mary Benson had long ago reported to Oliver Tambo what Moosa and Maud were up to. And Carlson had submitted a dossier to IDAF documenting their criminal history.[23] They were in fact so obviously suspect they might as well have had bells around their feet. Only Nelson and Winnie Mandela were deaf to the ringing, which is perhaps the most interesting aspect of the story.

Winnie did, in fact, in the nick of time, come to realize what was going on. In November 1969, just before the case finally came to trial, she wrote Levin an enigmatic letter which showed that the wool had been pulled from her eyes. 'You will agree with me as a legal man', she told him, 'that it is extremely difficult for a person behind bars in solitary confinement to understand people's motives.'[24]

When Levin asked her to persuade the other defendants to have him represent them, she agreed to see them in his presence one at a time. In English, she told them to accept Levin as their attorney. But she made sure to throw in a word of Xhosa beseeching them not to go near him.[25] Only she and Peter Magubane had given Levin power of attorney. They switched to Carlson on the day the trial began; all twenty-two were represented in court by a young but distinguished trio of barristers: David Soggot, George Bizos and Arthur Chaskalson.

As for Maud, she disappeared from Winnie's life as abruptly as she had arrived.

Chapter 34

When Winnie was detained, the authorities cut Nelson off from the world: they delivered his letters only sporadically and seldom gave him his mail. Wondering ceaselessly about the fate of his wife and children, he was driven near to distraction.

He wrote furiously to family, quite aware that they might never read what he said, beseeching them to mind his affairs. How was his son Makgatho's health? he asked a relative. Did he go for circumcision? Did he pass his examinations? He broached more practical matters, too. Did Winnie still possess the car when she was detained? Had arrangements been made to pay the telephone bill and the accounts?[1]

He believed that Winnie would be sentenced to life in prison. 'Perhaps never again will Mummy and Daddy join you in House no. 8115 Orlando West,' he counselled Zenani and Zindzi, aged ten and eight, respectively. 'For long you may live like orphans without your own home and parents, without the natural love, affection and protection Mummy used to give you.' He tried to allay the anger he anticipated that they would feel. Your mummy, he told them, was from a rich and respected family; she had specialist qualifications and held decent jobs; and even when Nelson went to prison, a good life beckoned, for she was offered a route abroad. She turned it all down, he said, to fight for her people.[2]

To Winnie he gave a quick-fire course in surviving jail. She should ask her sister to send leather picture frames as soon as possible, he advised. 'From experience I have found that a family photo is everything in prison, & you must have it right from the beginning.'[3]

These are, on the surface, the most practical of letters: a man is trying to arrange his affairs, to advise his loved ones, to bring a semblance of order to his upside-down world. And yet his knowledge that his letters will probably not reach their recipients complicates what they might mean. 'Even though [this letter] may only exist in form for me,' he wrote to Winnie, 'the records will bear witness to the fact that I tried hard & earnestly to reach you.'[4]

He was aware that he was rehearsing being a husband, a father, a householder, as much for his sanity as for his family, the outside world in actual fact beyond his grasp and his ken.

. .

In mid-July, two months after Winnie was jailed, Nelson received a telegram from the insidious Mendel Levin. He opened it to discover that his eldest son, Thembi, had died in a car accident, such an unwelcome message from so unwelcome a man, so keen to wheedle himself into the Mandelas' lives.

Months later, Nelson shared with a correspondent what had happened with him when he received the news. 'Suddenly my heart seemed to have stopped beating & the warm blood that had freely flowed through my veins for the last 52 years froze into ice. For some time I could neither think nor talk & my strength appeared to be draining out.'[5]

When he did not emerge from his cell for dinner, several of his comrades looked in. Unable to make human contact, he simply ignored them. And so Walter Sisulu was called to attend to his dear friend. In silence, Nelson handed him Levin's telegram. Once Sisulu had read it, he sat down next to Nelson and held his hand. They were together like that for some time, exchanging not a single word.[6]

That same evening Nelson wrote to Winnie, his heightened emotions bringing forth a series of crystalline images. He recalled a meeting with Thembi in July 1962, when he was in hiding and on the run.

'He was then a lusty lad of 17 that I could never associate with death,' Nelson wrote. 'He wore one of my trousers which was a shade too big & long for him ... As you know he had a lot of clothing, was particular about his dress & had no reason whatsoever for using my clothes. I was deeply touched for the emotional factors underlying his action were too obvious.

'[Thembi] had come to bid me farewell on his way to boarding school,' Nelson wrote. They had chatted for some time, an *enjoyable* chat, he recalled: 'I was indeed a bit sad when we ultimately parted. I could neither accompany him to a bus stop nor see him off at a station, for an outlaw, such as I was at the time, must be ready to give up even important parental duties. So it was that my son no! my friend, stepped out alone to fend for himself in a world where I could only meet him secretly and once in a while . . . I emptied my pockets and transferred to him all the copper and silver that a wretched fugitive could afford.'[7]

A young man going off alone into life, his useless father scrounging his empty pockets: it is almost self-pitying and it is intolerably sad.

His mother and son dead in quick succession, his wife in jail, the fate of his daughters unknown. 'If calamities had the weight of physical objects,' he wrote to Winnie a year later, 'we should long have been crushed down, or else . . . hunch-backed, unsteady on our feet.'[8]

But he was not crushed, and it is hard to resist the conclusion that he survived because of the Winnie he installed in his inner world. His letters to her now began to fill with an exquisite intensity, their meanings increasingly complex.

In November he heard that she was to stand trial, and he geared his letters to prepare her. 'The proceedings are likely to be the bitterest experience of your entire life to date . . . I write to warn you in time of what lies ahead.'

Until now, he had addressed her in his letters as 'My Darling'. This time, he chose another greeting. 'Dade Wethu', he called her. 'Sister' in Xhosa.

'The salutation to this letter will not surprise you,' he wrote. 'In the past I have addressed you in affectionate terms for then I was speaking to Nobandla, wife of Ama-Dlomo. But on this occasion I can claim no such prerogatives because in the freedom struggle we are all equals & your responsibility is as great as mine. We stand in the relationship, not of husband & wife, but of sister & brother. Until you return to 8115, or some other appointed place, this is how I will address you, OK?'

He added a line Winnie alone would understand. 'Perhaps,' he said, 'this arrangement will provide room for the legions of students, medical or otherwise, that have crossed the life of one or other of us.'[9] He was referring to a medical student, discussed in previous of their letters, who was courting Winnie at the same time as Nelson. Now that you and I are siblings, he was saying, you might sleep with others. He was flirting with her, notwithstanding that she was a 'sister' about to face the bitterest experience of her life.

And indeed, while he kept the salutation 'sister', the ferocity of his feelings for her grew. 'During the 8 lonely years I have spent behind bars,' he wrote a few months later, 'I sometimes wished we were born at the same hour, grown up together and spent every minute of our lives in each other's company.' He had heard news of how ill she had been in prison and described, as he imagined it, the diminished state of her body. 'But I know', he wrote, 'that every piece of your bone, ounce of your flesh & drop of your blood; your whole being is hewed in one piece out of granite, & that nothing whatever, including ailment, can blow out the fires that are burning in your heart.'[10]

A month later, he wrote again, this time describing how unbearable it was to imagine her suffering. 'I feel as if I have been soaked in gall,' he wrote, 'every part of me, my flesh, bloodstream, bone & soul, so bitter am I to be completely powerless to help you.'

In the next breath he shared his dream 'of you convulsing your entire body with a graceful Hawaiian dance... [whirling] towards me with the enchanting smile that I miss so desperately'. And then he recounted the first sparks of their romance. 'I am never certain whether I am free to remind you that [it was you who courted me],' he writes.[11]

These letters are all the more remarkable for his uncertainty that she will ever read them. In his solitude, he is resuscitating the great storm of their romance, writing her spirit into his prison cell, lest he navigate this catastrophe alone.

. .

In December, Winnie and her twenty-one co-accused finally stood trial for violating various provisions of the Suppression of Communism Act. Among them were her sister Nonyaniso, guilty primarily of living in Winnie's home, and Peter Magubane, who was arrested when he came to prison to bring Winnie food. The list of charges they faced was as threadbare as it was long. An exasperated IDAF pamphlet complained that 'the accused were not actually charged with selecting sabotage sites, or making or possessing the materials for explosives, or of establishing a means of making contact with guerrilla fighters ... but only with having discussed the possibilities of these things'.[12] As Winnie herself told the court when she was asked to plead, the trial was hardly the point of the exercise; the accused had already been punished by the police when they were held for months in solitary confinement and tortured.

Proceedings soon turned uncomfortable for the prosecution. The defense trained its attention on the torture to which many of the state witnesses had been subjected, and the judge, much to the surprise of all, allowed this line of inquiry to run. In February, from out of the blue, the state abandoned its case mid-trial; taken by surprise, the judge acquitted the accused at once and told them that they were free to go. But the moment he left the courtroom, the security police descended on the twenty-two and arrested them under the Terrorism Act all over again. The defense counsel scurried after the judge, told him what had happened, and appealed for him to intervene. Summoned to the judge's chambers, the prosecutor shrugged sadly and said that the matter was out of his hands; he could not control what the police did or did not do.[13]

. .

After she was returned to solitary confinement, the length of her incarceration unknowable, quite possibly interminable, Winnie fell into deep despair. We have an intimate record of her own fresh memories of this time, for when her lawyers were finally permitted to see her, they smuggled her a pen and paper.

Much to her alarm, she wrote, she discovered that she was talking aloud, conversing with her absent daughters. The thought of them triggered memories of their anguish on the night of her arrest, and she would begin crying hysterically. Once she had calmed down, a corrosive loneliness began to eat at her. 'The long and empty hours tore through the inner core of my soul,' she later wrote. 'There were moments when I got so fed up I banged my head against the cell wall. Physical pain was more tolerable.'[14]

In April, it came to her as an epiphany that she might kill herself. 'If I took my own life there would be no trial and my colleagues would be saved from the torturous mental agony of solitary confinement,' she reasoned. Her inner dialogue was scarcely coherent. She would starve herself slowly, she thought to herself, so that it seemed she had died of natural causes, thus sparing Nelson and the children the pain of knowing, but she would also write her family a secret farewell note that she would smuggle out of prison when the end neared.

She stopped eating. She no longer slept. And she began imagining the consequences of her suicide. 'My death would be a major contribution which would stir up world opinion,' she remembered thinking. The idea calmed her; indeed, she soon felt quite ecstatic. 'I enjoyed the bitter sweetness of unjust suffering and was quite excited when I thought how dramatic my death would be. I was so happy at times I fell asleep and hoped I would not get up the following day.'[15]

On May 1, two weeks after she had resolved to die, Winnie was taken from prison to security police headquarters in Pretoria to be interrogated again. The police, it appears, took alarm at her condition and arranged for a consultation with a doctor; shocked at the state of her health, he recommended that she be admitted to a hospital at once.

While in the ward, something of great consequence happened to lift her spirit and change her mind. A member of the hospital staff, a janitor, perhaps, or a nurse, was bringing her information from outside. And the news was very good indeed. At Wits University, students were planning a massive demonstration to commemorate the first anniversary of her and her comrades' arrest. The matter was all over the press. A lawyers' association had issued an expression of its discontent; prominent businessmen and clerics had spoken out. Under pressure, the justice minister had released a statement promising that the accused would soon be charged or released.

The news revived with a vengeance her desire to live. 'All my plans now changed,' Winnie wrote. 'I was thrilled at the prospect of facing a trial at last.' After seeing out the barrage of specialists sent to examine her – including two psychiatrists – she begged the matron to discharge her so that she could return to her comrades.[16]

On June 18, the accused were brought to court and charged all over again with furthering the aims of the ANC; Winnie, who had fallen ill once more, was back in the hospital and was charged in absentia. It was here, in her hospital bed, that the authorities finally gave her some of the letters Nelson had written. One is left to imagine her lying there, ill, exhilarated to be facing trial, Nelson's intensity washing over her. She wrote back to him at once.

'I still cannot believe that at last I've heard from you darling. You will notice the very difference in my handwriting, the hypnotising effect your lovely letters have on my scarred soul. All it needed was its natural drug after all.'

Their anniversary had just passed, and she told him that she had spent the day recollecting their wedding ceremony. As she lay on her back, 'gasping for breath with a temperature of 103', what came to her was an image of herself as a bride: 'A trembling little girl ... stood next to you in a shabby little back veld church in Pondoland and said, "I do." I often wonder', she added, 'if your memory of me isn't of that little girl.'

And then she ruminated on their time as husband and wife. 'We were hardly a year together when history deprived me of you,' she wrote. 'I was forced to mature on my own. Your formidable shadow which eclipsed me left me naked and exposed to the bitter world of a young "political widow". I knew this was a crown of thorns for me but I also knew I said "I do" for better or worse. In marrying you I was marrying the struggle of my people.'[17]

There is so much here. It's doubtful that Winnie thought herself 'a trembling little girl' when she married Nelson; despite her youth, she must have been aware of her considerable power. Already, she was no stranger to standing up to formidable middle-aged men. She had put Nelson himself through his paces, testing his desire for her by playing him off Barney Sampson, playing him off her father. He must have marvelled at the force of her presence in strong men's lives.

In this letter, a new arc has emerged, a rearrangement of the past so as to make sense of the present. How could it not be so, given all she has been through? An innocent little girl has experience now; she has gone to hell and back and is inducted into life. Does Nelson still know her? 'I often wonder if your memory of me isn't of that little girl.'

. .

On September 15, 1970, Winnie and her co-accused were finally acquitted. She had been in jail 491 days, some 400 of them in solitary confinement. Now she was to resume life at 8115 Orlando West.

'You are back,' Nelson wrote, '& in accordance with my promise I bid good-bye to "dadewethu" & return to "My darling" . . . the salutation I have used since August '62.'[18]

But if Winnie was home, she was in no substantial sense free. The authorities slapped a five-year banning order on her and on several of those with whom she had stood trial. Among them was Peter Magubane; it was now illegal for her to communicate with the man who had seen her through the darkness of the late 1960s at such considerable cost to himself. Those who came to visit her were harassed or even thrown in jail. Nelson's sister Leabie was detained after visiting Winnie; a relative of his, Tellie Mtirara, was picked up off the street and interrogated for hours before being released. Winnie's sister Niki was threatened with the loss of her job if she kept visiting Winnie; Nonyaniso was arrested after she was discovered in Winnie's house.

To maintain any contact at all with Winnie Mandela was to put oneself in harm's way.

Neither could Winnie travel freely, of course, nor speak publicly; her restrictions confined her to her home between 6:00 p.m. and 6:00 a.m. during the week, and from 2:00 p.m. to 6:00 a.m. on weekends. Political activity of any kind was strictly forbidden.

She cut a heroic figure in the wake of her trial. She and her house both became sacred. Walking home from school, Soweto students would take long detours to pass 8115 Orlando West, hoping, by chance, to see her in her garden, to greet her, to speak to her, this mythical, silenced woman.[19]

Her memory of prison haunted her, it seems, each hour of each day. When she was finally permitted to address an audience, five years after her release, the depth of her thinking and feeling about that time revealed itself.

'The frightful emptiness of those hours of solitude is unbearable,' she told a packed gathering at the Noordgesig Methodist Church in October 1975. 'Your company is your solitude, your blanket, your mat . . . All this is in preparation for the inevitable hell – your interrogation. It is meant to crush your individuality completely, to change you into a docile being from whom no resistance can arise . . .

'[Your] adaptation to prison [changes your] personality and out-look on life,' she continued. 'In some cases, it means severe moods from fervent hope to despair. What sustains you is the spontaneous defense mechanism, the granite desire to defend and protect at all cost [from] disintegration of personality. You ask yourself questions without answers day after day, week after week, month after month, and then you keep telling yourself: "I am sane." '[20]

She did not mention Theuns Swanepoel in her speech, but in time to come, she would reveal that he had lodged himself in her being, an intimate and unwelcome companion who simply refused to leave.

BRANDFORT-POLLSMOOR

. . .

Chapter 35

On the morning of June 16, 1976, students began gathering, at first in their hundreds, soon in their thousands, just a block from 8115 Orlando West. Those who opened their front doors to witness the river of teenagers washing past might have wondered whether they were in a waking dream: soccer matches aside, Sowetans had not congregated in such numbers in years. 'The girls ... in black-and-white check tunics ... looked particularly charming,' one of the young people in that crowd wrote later, 'and the boys wore grey pants, white shirts and black blazers, looking dignified in a boyish kind of a way.'[1]

Only a fifth of Soweto's teenagers attended school at that time,[2] and the uniforms on display signalled the pedigree of the crowd. But behind the earnestness of their attire lay a turbulence of spirit that had in recent months grown feverish.

The march that was to take place had been planned three days earlier by a just-minted action committee composed entirely of schoolboys. Its members were without experience in such matters; the last time Sowetans had marched in great numbers was before the banning of the ANC and the PAC in 1960; there was barely a memory to guide them, barely a set of rules to follow.

On the mornings of June 14 and 15, the members of that committee went from school to school informing students of the plan. After morning assembly, everyone would leave their respective school gates and make their way to Orlando West Junior Secondary School on Vilakazi Street. From there, the crowd would march to Orlando Stadium less than two miles away.

'We had read the Pied Piper of Hamelin,' one of the organizers of the march recalled, 'and we had a vision that it might work because as we were marching on the crowd became bigger and bigger and bigger.'[3]

It is true that the mood in four of Soweto's top schools had grown increasingly militant in the preceding months and that many who joined the march did so because they were furious. But as kids streamed out of their schools and joined the growing swell, their spirit was more steely than aggressive. They began singing 'Senzeni na?' (What have we done?), a doleful anthem, something of a South African equivalent to 'We Shall Overcome'. When sung in harmony by thousands of voices, its sadness courses through one's limbs.

At one point, a lone white woman drove by happenstance toward the crowd; it parted to allow her car through.[4]

. .

The students were protesting instructions issued the previous year that half the subjects in Standard Five and Form One – the equivalent of the seventh and eighth grades – be taught in Afrikaans. It was an astonishingly egregious thing to have done.

More than twenty years earlier, the apartheid government had written a blueprint for the education of black people. In line with its fiction that blacks would govern themselves in ethnic homelands, it envisaged that the education provided for black children in South Africa proper would be ethnically based – different schools for Tswana, Xhosa, Zulu, and so forth. For more than two decades, much of this plan had remained on paper. Then, in the early 1970s, as it belatedly scaled up mass high school education for blacks, the government began implementing many of the policies that had long lain dormant. Among its plans were that certain mainline academic subjects be taught in Afrikaans, a language belonging to no black people in particular and thus, in the hermetic logic of the planners, common to all.

In fact, it was common to nobody, not least to the teachers who would have to instruct in it. Indeed, many black teachers were barely able to converse in Afrikaans.[5] It was a spectacular display of indifference not just to young black human beings as such but to their education, and thus to their prospects, to their souls, to their very capacity to learn. The institution they cherished most had appeared to have been turned into a weapon against them.

In the months preceding June 16, anger had flared. Early in February, two board members of a Soweto school countermanded the instruction to teach in Afrikaans and were promptly dismissed. That was the last time anyone middle-aged raised a serious voice of protest. From then on, it was students who took the lead. At some Soweto schools, students tore up their books, suspended normal classes, and replaced them with student-led debates on current affairs. A month before the march, the entire student body of Orlando West Junior Secondary School, outside whose gates thousands of kids were now gathering, had begun boycotting classes. At Phefeni Junior Secondary School, students stoned their principal's office.[6]

The activity planned for June 16 was to be the first Soweto-wide coordinated action, a step into uncharted terrain.

. .

Something else was happening in South Africa at that time, something that had begun neither in Soweto nor among high school students but that nonetheless deeply informed the spirit of the teenagers who had planned the march. For the sake of convenience, its origin can be given a year, 1968, when a twenty-one-year-old medical student named Steve Biko led black students out of NUSAS – the National Union of South African Students – a putatively multiracial university-student body, and became president of the newly founded, blacks-only South African Student Organisation. In the years that followed, more organizations formed under the aegis of what would be known as the Black Consciousness Movement (BCM), most notably, the Black People's Convention, formed in 1972.

But to describe what was happening by reference to organizations is itself misleading, for the current that named itself Black Consciousness bore little intention, at least at first, to act in the world. Its most urgent work was introspective: a project to remake selves.

When the ANC and the PAC were banned and their activities crushed, much more than black organizations were destroyed, in the telling of Biko and his peers. Adulthood itself was erased among black South Africans, leaving fearful husks of human beings. Only white people acted in the world now.

'When I came to [university] . . . in 1966,' Biko commented, 'there was some kind of anomaly . . . where whites were in fact the main participants in our oppression and at the same time the main participants in the opposition to that oppression.'[7] To be black and join in anti-apartheid politics was to watch white people salve their consciences, Biko observed, all the more to enjoy their privilege when they got good jobs and settled down.

Biko has become the retrospective symbol of the movement in part because he was martyred; the police killed him while he was in their custody, his head smashed to a pulp, in September 1977. But he was also an astonishing human being, his voice larger and more powerful than the words that gave it form. If he had an animating idea during the last year of his life, it was that shedding the fear of death freed one to act. 'You are either alive and proud,' he told an interviewer shortly before he was killed, 'or you are dead, and when you are dead, you can't care anyway.'[8] All the introspective work Black Consciousness urged was preparation for going forth into a violent world.

It may be tempting to think of Black Consciousness as a new incarnation of the spirit of the PAC, which, similarly, refused to work with whites. But that would not be right. For one, the Black Consciousness Movement defined as black anyone whom the apartheid government did not classify as white, including Coloureds and Indians. Being black was a political condition brought on by white supremacy, not a biological inheritance. The PAC, in contrast, associated blackness with indigeneity and was hostile to working with Indians. In South Africa's fraught entanglement with questions of race, Black Consciousness was both an innovation and a breakthrough.

Besides, Black Consciousness activists claimed both the ANC and the PAC as part of their heritage and sought to replace neither. They believed that they were working in a parenthetic moment, their labour one of spiritual regrouping.[9]

Black Consciousness began in universities and in Christian seminaries, but as its adherents graduated, they acquired positions as schoolteachers, journalists and clergymen, taking with them their ideas. A lodestar of the Black Consciousness Movement, Abram Onkgopotse Tiro, taught in Soweto's Morris Isaacson High School in the early 1970s. He fled into exile in late 1973 and was assassinated in a parcel bomb explosion in Botswana the following year, bringing the taste of martyrdom to the students who had known him. Among the handful of teenagers who went from school to school on June 14, 1976, spreading word of the coming march, some had sat in Tiro's class and taken in his ideas.

.   .

Just before 11:00 a.m., a convoy of police trucks approached the crowd on Vilakazi Street, coming to a halt about a hundred yards away.

Several dozen police officers, their rifles loaded with live ammunition, poured from the vehicles and assembled in formation across the road. Thousands of students had amassed outside the school by then, and thousands more were winding their way there.

The students, loud with song until now, drew still; for a long moment, the two sides stared each other down. Then the students began singing again, and in response a police officer let loose a dog that went charging into the crowd. It was mobbed and killed, and with this first drawing of blood – not human but canine blood – the police opened fire and a slaughter began.[10]

The first to die was Hastings Ndlovu, a fifteen-year-old boy. The second was Zolile Hector Pieterson; a photograph of him in the arms of another boy, Mbuyisa Makhubu, while his sister, Antoinette, cried out in anguish, would become the most widely reproduced symbol of the brutality of apartheid.[11]

When news reached the thousands still making their way to Vilakazi Street that police had opened fire, they turned to rage; en masse it was decided 'to go and meet the police head-on', a student leader in that crowd recalled. The driver of a municipality van turned a corner just then to find himself facing the crowd. 'It was a white man', the same student leader recalled. 'Mostly the girls were in the forefront. I have never seen so many stones in my life raining on a target. In no time the [van] had no windows. And the student girls themselves actually fought among each other to get hold of the white man who was inside the car. They dragged him out. They pelted him with stones, with bottles, with their shoes as they were screaming. There was a young boy who was also looking for a way through to the white man. Finally, when they made space for him he produced a knife and stabbed a number of times in the chest of the white man.'[12]

A teenager in the crowd spotted the dead man's car keys on the ground next to his corpse. 'I picked them up,' he recalled later. 'The key ring was attached to a yellow tag. I will never forget that . . . He was a white man, but he had been crushed like he was nothing. The section of the crowd that had watched him die went mad. We went looking for vehicles to hijack. We wanted to use them as battering rams to smash down the storefronts of bottle stores.'[13]

In the hours that followed, the youth took possession of the township. They burned down administrative buildings, attacked beer halls and off-licences, and stoned delivery vehicles. Among the police officers sent to quell them was Theuns Swanepoel, the man who, seven years earlier, had led the interrogation of Winnie Mandela. Giving testimony the following year to a commission of inquiry into the violence, he would boast that he personally killed five people that afternoon.[14]

· ·

In the following weeks and months, the insurrection spread, first to other townships on the Witwatersrand, then to Pretoria, to East London, to Cape Town, and to more than a hundred smaller towns. It had no centralized leadership, which is in part why it was so hard to stop; it would simmer and explode in relays for more than a year before it was finally quelled. By then, many hundreds of youths had died, the exact number unknowable, for the authorities suppressed much information. Thousands were detained and tortured, a great many of them put on trial and sentenced to lengthy prison terms. Thousands more went into exile to look for Umkhonto we Sizwe, the army Nelson Mandela had founded fifteen years earlier; they wanted to train as soldiers and return to their townships armed.

South Africa would not be the same again. The exiled ANC, which in the early 1970s had grown weak and dispirited, was brought suddenly to life as thousands of youths came to join it. The armed struggle was finally yielding fruit, for the existence of an exiled army that might come back and defeat apartheid was the centrepiece in the story of the future taking shape.

Robben Island, too, would be utterly transformed by the uprisings as young veterans of these street battles poured into the prison. Nelson and his generation, who were growing old with one another for company, would be confronted with a surfeit of youth.

But the most profound change was on the streets of South Africa's townships. Biko was among those who understood that what had been spawned was a new attitude to death. '[The students] were not prepared to be calmed down even at the point of a gun,' he remarked in an interview in early 1977. 'And hence, what happened, happened. Some people were killed. These riots just continued and continued. Because at no stage were the young students . . . prepared to be scared.'[15]

The changes in fact went deeper than that. In July 1977, a distinguished anthropologist, Harriet Ngubane, visited Soweto for the first time since the uprisings. She immediately put pen to paper, for what she had witnessed was nothing less than a revolution in the meaning of death. The chief mourners at funerals had always been the family of the deceased. Now they stood silently in the background as young men conducted new funerary rites, their fists clenched, freedom songs, not hymns, issuing from their tongues. Indeed, mourning itself had been banished, for those who had lost loved ones were told not to suffer but to celebrate the courage of fallen soldiers.[16]

In years to come, nobody in South Africa would be more closely associated with these new rituals than Winnie Mandela, dubbed 'Mother', not of her children, but of 'the nation', her presence at funerals expected, the image of her fist raised over a coffin iconic.

Chapter 36

In the early winter of 1972, four years before the uprisings began, a photographer snatched a pic of Winnie as she was getting into her car. She had appeared in court moments earlier, charged with violating her banning order. The photograph is striking, though, not for what Winnie is doing but for what she is wearing: a checked winter dress ending an inch above her knee, large silver earrings dancing about the sides of her jaws and a large Afro placing the era to a T.[1] She could be off to UCLA to hear Angela Davis, or en route to Oakland to see Eldridge Cleaver. So thick with cultural traffic was the black Atlantic then that the photograph might have been taken on any of its shores.

On that particular shore at that particular time – Johannesburg, 1972 – a woman with an Afro and miniskirt signalled something quite specific. She was middle class; she either had been to university or aspired to do so; above all, she had taken in the spirit of the Black Consciousness Movement: were a white man to cross her path on the sidewalk, she would absolutely not get out of his way.[2]

Most remarkable about the picture, though, is the contrast between the worldliness of the style and the condition of the woman who wore it. Winnie was banned for the first half of the 1970s. Confined to her house for twelve hours each day, forbidden to be in the presence of more than one other adult at a time, permitted neither to speak publicly nor to be quoted, she was ostensibly cut off.

The spirit of the times enveloped her nonetheless, and in a manner that surely pleased her. Her sense of politics aristocratic – she had said that she became her people's leader when Nelson went to prison – the protagonists of that era came to pay her homage.

Soweto's schoolboy activists, for one, could barely keep away from her house.

'One had to negotiate one's way past her dog,' recalled Murphy Morobe, one of the students who organized the June 16 march. 'We were fascinated by the name she chose for him: Khrushchev. Folklore said that he was specially trained to detect members of the Security Branch. Once we had befriended him and made our way to the front door, Winnie would invite us in and offer us tea and cake. She was a point of reference, a leadership figure. Certain things you decide upon, you want to know that she is happy.'[3]

One young student, an emerging Black Consciousness leader called Tokyo Sexwale, moved into Winnie's house for the duration of his final year at high school. He felt that he was living among the sacred relics of a shrine. 'Here are [Nelson Mandela's] books, the original law books that he was using, full of dust,' Sexwale recalled. 'Here is his legal gown . . . Here is his chair, this is Mandela's bed, here is a doorknob which he used to open every morning as the father of the house.'

As for Winnie, Sexwale was struck by her swings between melancholy and exuberance. 'This was the Winnie who used to go to Robben Island from time to time', he remembered, 'to visit Nelson Mandela. This was the Winnie who brought back news of how he was. This was the Winnie who would come back very depressed sometimes . . . [B]ut in a few days' time, she is like a lark again, and there is excitement.'[4]

Beyond Soweto's schoolboys, the leading figures of the Black Consciousness Movement came regularly to pay their respects. Biko made a point of seeing Winnie whenever he was in Johannesburg. She, in turn, gushed about him. 'It was such a revitalizing experience to communicate with that man,' she told one of Nelson's biographers. 'There was a total vacuum, and if that man had not come into life then I shudder for the consequences to history.'[5] Indeed, on her visits to Nelson, she attempted to convey in a code the warders would not catch that a movement of great consequence was forming.[6]

Winnie also made contact with the ANC in exile. In March 1975, the thirty-two-year-old Thabo Mbeki, son of Nelson's fellow Robben Islander Govan Mbeki, was sent by the ANC to Swaziland. His tasks were to make contact with South Africa's student and labour movements, to establish a working underground, and to deliver a steady stream of recruits to MK.[7] In June of that year, Mbeki, together with his fellow operative Albert Dhlomo, wrote their first in situ report to the ANC's National Executive Committee. Among many other matters, they described their communications with Winnie.

'We are continuing to maintain contact with her on the most innocuous level,' they wrote. 'Her name keeps cropping up with couriers who want to know our attitude towards her. We are advising everybody to cut off all links with her for apart from anything else, she is so closely observed by the police that anybody who has contact with her stands a good chance of being seen by the police.'

They were stringing Winnie along. 'We have ... taken the view that through our own contact with her, we should continue to give her the impression that she is in fact not being cut off. But what we feared is beginning to happen, i.e. that she is now insistently asking us for directives. We are of course dilly-dallying in as much as, if we did, that would then serve as justification for her going around claiming to be directly in touch with the Executive.'[8]

That phrase, 'apart from anything else', hums with meaning, for clearly there was *much* else. The primary recipient of the report was Oliver Tambo, president of the ANC. Mbeki was by now Tambo's protégé and would have taken in the older man's views on Nelson's wife: the refusal to ditch Somana when it became apparent that he was an informer; Tambo's onetime suspicion that Winnie was herself a spy; Maud Katzenellenbogen and Moosa Dinath and their use of Winnie's friendship to attempt to infiltrate IDAF. Winnie, writer and recipient of the report would both have understood, was a booby trap liable to explode. She was to be isolated and diminished.

Two rival memories of the 1960s Winnie tussled: the wayward Winnie of the Somana affair versus the heroic Winnie of her trial. It is a sign of the ANC's dwindling influence at this time that Mbeki's attempts to isolate her meant little.

. .

As for Nelson, his serenading of his wife continued.

'I hope to ... be with you long after you have reached menopause,' he wrote in the last days of 1970, 'when all the gloss you now have will be gone & your body, your lovely face included, will be all wrinkles, skin as tough as that of a rhinoceros. I shall nurse and look after you in every way. Now & again we shall visit the farm, walk around with the fingers of my left hand dovetailing with those of your right, watching you dart off to pluck some beautiful wild flowers, just as you did on Sunday March 10 [their first date]. You were dazzling in that black white-spotted nylon dress. Every day will be March 10 for me. What does age or [a] little blood pressure matter to us. Nothing! Are you happy now? Say yes; that's what I like of you! I've always known you to be a good girl. Just keep there.'[9]

What did she make of such sweetness? Her letters to him from this time onward are locked up in her estate, and we cannot know how she replied. But we can imagine that she was struck, perhaps even troubled, by the unnerving doubleness her husband displayed. In the flesh-and-blood world they were revolutionaries, their lives twisted into unchosen forms: he in prison for who knew how long, she under an endless siege. And yet in Nelson's imagination, they were the homeliest of couples, walking together into a gentle old age. Did she find comfort in his vision? Or was she unsettled by its remoteness from their real lives?

In the year of the uprisings she turned forty, her adult life thus far turbulent beyond telling. And its tumult preceded her involvement in politics, its fever pitch congenital, it seems. There is something amusing in the fact that Nelson imagined *this* of all women bending her aging hips to pluck a flower as her doting husband looked on. Striking, too, that in his thoughts it was *he* who would nurse *her*, when his hips would creak long before hers.

. .

The measures the security police took to crush her spirit were extraordinary. Friends of hers from that time would be periodically woken in the middle of the night; it was Winnie on the phone, her voice filled with terror.[10] She heard footfalls on her roof, or the rattling of the lock in her front door. One night, her car was stolen, only to be mysteriously returned. On another, she woke to find a man pressing a cloth to her face, his evident intent to suffocate her. She fought and screamed, causing him and his accomplices to flee.[11]

Whenever family moved in to protect her, the authorities found reason to remove them. And when she built an eight-foot fence around her property, its northern facade was deemed to violate municipal laws.[12] Not even Khrushchev was spared; Winnie woke one morning in 1974 to find his poisoned corpse in the yard.

Raised to believe in her aristocracy, she became dirt poor; few were bold enough to employ her, for to have Winnie Mandela on one's premises invited attention from the police. Eventually, a white debt collector, a certain Frederick Squire, employed Winnie and Peter Magubane. The situation was awkward: since they were both banned, any con-

tact between Winnie and Peter was a criminal offense; it appears that
Squire was scrupulous in assigning them to separate shifts.[13]

In the early winter of 1972, Winnie and Peter fashioned a lovely, if
ill-advised, ritual. At noon each weekday, Peter would drive Winnie's
daughters into downtown Johannesburg together with a packed lunch.
He would find a parking spot close to Squire's premises and wait. When
her lunch hour came, Winnie would walk out into the street and look
for Peter's van; she would climb into the back and join her children to
eat. Peter remained in the driver's seat, staring ahead.

On the third day of this ritual, police swarmed the van and arrested
the two adults for breaking their banning orders. It was an especially
cynical maneuver, for what Winnie and Peter were contriving to share
was not a political conspiracy but the love and care of two girls.[14]

The trial proceedings dragged on for more than two years. Finally,
in October 1974, both were sentenced to six months in jail. A friend
of Winnie's in the gallery that day witnessed thirteen-year-old Zindzi
break down and weep. As an assortment of strangers looked on, Winnie
went to her daughter not to comfort her but to give her a dressing-down.
There are Security Branch operatives watching us, she admonished; do
not ever give them the satisfaction of seeing your pain.[15]

· ·

Winnie served much of her sentence in the Free State town of
Kroonstad. It was not the ordeal her detention in 1969 and 1970 had
been. As a sentenced prisoner, she was neither kept in solitary confinement nor interrogated by the police. Her children came to see her regularly, and her lawyer briefed her often on events in the world outside.

She and Peter were released on the same day in April 1975. Five
months later, something of great consequence happened. At the end of
September, Winnie's and Peter's five-year banning orders expired and
were not renewed. He was free to return to work as a photojournalist,
she to travel the country, to see whom she wanted, and, most important
of all, to speak.

Why was her banning order allowed to lapse? It would have taken
no more than the stroke of a pen to renew it.

The answer is to be found in a single paragraph of a document lying
in the South African National Archives. The police were running an
informer who managed to speak to Thabo Mbeki in Swaziland. Mbeki,

the informer reported, believed that Winnie was talking to the security police; indeed, he was feeding her false information to see how the police would respond. And Nelson, Mbeki appeared to suggest, was so besotted with Winnie that his judgment concerning her was impaired.

The security police sent this information to the justice minister's advisers, who counselled him not to renew Winnie's banning order. If she was causing this much trouble in her movement, why not let her loose?[16]

It is the sort of irony one expects to encounter in fiction. The decision to allow her banning order to lapse shaped the trajectory of the remainder of her life. Had she remained silenced, she would have played no public role in the uprisings. And had she played no public role, it is unlikely that she would have been banished from Soweto, a move that would make her world-famous.

Mbeki's attempt to diminish her had precisely the opposite effect. He had, unwittingly, launched her global career.

· ·

Twelve days after her banning order expired, Winnie took a flight to Durban. A crowd more than a thousand strong waited in a downtown hall to greet her.[17] Her host that day was the staunchly loyal Fatima Meer. She had orchestrated this event to celebrate the return of a queen and to toast an absent king.

The duty of introducing Winnie fell to a Lutheran minister named Manas Buthelezi. 'Nomzamo Mandela', he said, 'is more than just another black person ... Her experience serves as a magnifying glass through which we can see imprinted the details of the experiences of others. She is a window through which even the most uninitiated eye is introduced to the obscure, twilight existence of the banned and the detained. She was and is the incarnation of the black man's spirit.'[18]

It is hard to imagine words that might have rung sweeter in Winnie's ears.

Making up for the years of her sequestration, what Winnie did, above all, was *appear*. When an underground ANC operative, Raymond Suttner, was due to be sentenced in December 1975, she flew to Durban for the scene her presence would make at his trial. A young reporter in court that day knew Winnie's name, but not her face. 'I looked up at the balcony and saw this beauty,' she recalled. Winnie's head was in a towering cotton wrap that day, her chest and her arms draped in beads. 'Who *is* that?' the reporter asked, mouth agape. 'The court reporters around me could not believe I did not know who she was. But once I saw her, God Almighty.'[19]

These extravagant displays of her beauty exuded potent political meaning. 'She knew what her appearance meant to the people in the gallery,' a friend of hers from that time recalled. 'Not, "there walks Winnie"; no, "there walks a formidable black person".'[20] She was in her element, her taste for exhibition given unbridled license, its political intent more focused than ever before.

. .

On June 8, 1976, scarcely a week before the uprisings began, Winnie spoke at Naledi Hall in Soweto. The gathering had been convened by a group of Soweto parents concerned with the turmoil building in their children's schools. Attended by some three hundred people, the majority of them middle-aged, the meeting, according to a young journalist, was dragging; he was decidedly underwhelmed.[21]

Then Winnie was called to the stage. 'It is necessary from the outset to say that we are gathered here as fellow blacks,' she began, 'in a black atmosphere in a black community . . . This is why we are gathered here, not just to discuss common problems, but also to rediscover ourselves, our dignity and to instil in ourselves self-reliance and self-respect . . . [O]nly black people have a right to speak for blacks,' she continued, 'and white for white.'

It was as blunt an expression of the soul of Black Consciousness as ever was made, and quite provocative from the wife of a scion of the ANC. She would seldom speak like that again.

She took her audience back into history, pausing in the 1950s to claim, again, controversially for one associated with the ANC, that black people, to their shame, had never produced 'a single organisation that can claim to be truly national'. She condemned the black informers of the 1960s; they had betrayed their people because they 'felt acute guilt for their failure in contributing to their cause'.

This swipe at informers could only have unnerved her audience. Middle-aged, quiescent, afraid, they were uncertain how to act in these times. Now she was saying that those without clarity of purpose would end up working for the other side.

And in her next breath she did indeed turn directly on her audience. 'Events in our own locality have reduced us parents to shame,' she declared. 'It is an absolute disgrace that our children fight battles for us ... There couldn't be a worse insult to our nationhood ... How did each one of you feel when your child returned from school and said nothing to you while you saw his or her photograph in the press as having gone on strike without taking you into his confidence? You will agree with me that our young generation will spit over our graves, our generation of cowards.'[22]

A week later, the children revolted while their parents looked on. Their spirit had been captured to perfection by a woman twice their age. Her capacity to read, and then to exude, the feelings around her was unmatched.

. .

Once the uprisings began, Winnie spoke forthrightly, often provocatively, but she also tempered her actions. Shocked by the spiral of young deaths, she carved out a sober role. The Black Parents' Association was formed, its origin the town hall meeting at which Winnie had spoken so boldly, its role to give assistance to the students; Winnie was its only female member.

On August 4, as the revolt entered its seventh week, some twenty thousand people gathered outside a train station on the periphery of Soweto, their intention to march on Johannesburg. By now, the revolt's leaders understood that they could tear Soweto to pieces and the apartheid regime would remain largely unscathed; they had resolved to take the revolt to white South Africa.

That morning, a police commander pleaded with Winnie and her fellow Black Parents Association member Dr. Nthato Motlana to urge the students to turn back. She did. With a bullhorn borrowed from the police, she stood on the back of a pickup truck and told the thousands who had gathered to turn on their heels and save their own lives.[23]

A man who was a teenager in the crowd that day later remembered his mixed emotions. Seeing Winnie in the flesh had excited him. But his enthusiasm turned to dismay when she urged the students to disperse. 'To us this was giving in,' he recalled. 'We didn't want to accept what she was saying, but she was our leader, so we began to turn back, and as we did so, the police started opening fire.'[24] Three people were killed that day. Without Winnie's intervention, the death toll might have been in the hundreds.

That night, Winnie's house was firebombed. A few days later, an ominous meeting was held at the home of Soweto's mayor. It was proposed, according to some who were there, that Winnie's and Motlana's houses be burned to the ground and that any student who tried to force adults to observe a general strike be killed.[25]

What might have become of her had she remained in Soweto remains a moot point. On August 13, she was detained along with several other members of the crisis committee. She would be held at the Fort in Johannesburg until the end of the year.

· ·

With Winnie in jail again, Nelson had to manage the household's affairs from his cell. He would write to his family and hers, he told Winnie, to assist with the livelihoods of their daughters.

'Forget about . . . the house, rent, car, furniture and the telephone bills.' He has written to this one and that one to take care of these things. 'Chin up! . . . I do miss you and love you my dearest.'[26]

While Nelson was reassuring her, the security police were weaving a story.

By now, much of the original leadership of the revolt was either in prison or in exile. And those in prison were made to tell a tale. A meeting took place at Winnie's house on the evening of June 15, some of the students who had been detained were told by their interrogators. At that meeting, Winnie instructed student leaders to burn municipal buildings, to smash the storefronts of off-licences, to kill white people in their cars. When those under interrogation replied that they did not know of such a meeting, they were beaten. 'Eventually,' one of the detained students would tell a commission of inquiry the following year, 'I said I knew about the meeting, I was at the meeting. And then the beatings stopped.'[27]

Battering students to tell a story to the police's liking was blunt, to be sure, but it was not without reason. That a handful of adults had orchestrated the uprisings became a necessary illusion for white South Africans.

But something else was going on. By now, breathless stories of Winnie's time in jail in 1969-70 were swirling through Security Branch ranks. It was said that when the head of the Security Branch, Hendrik van den Bergh, interrogated her, she came up close to him and straightened his tie; he was so thrown, the story went, that the questioning broke down.[28] As for Swanepoel, it was said that she slowly unbuttoned her shirt in his presence, eventually exposing most of her breast; he had left the room in embarrassment.

There was clearly an erotic, perhaps sadistic, element to the Security Branch's relationship with her, the punishment they heaped upon her no doubt driven in part by desire. The role they conjured her playing in the uprising – an older woman coaxing boys into acts of violence – seems pretty heated, pretty charged. In retrospect, there is something spooky about the police's fabrications. A full decade later, a version of the Winnie they had invented took form in the real world. The football team of young men she'd establish in Soweto was horribly violent, and she was indeed their charismatic leader.

'I have lived with my generation all these years,' Nelson wrote to Fatima Meer in March 1971, 'a generation that is inclined to be conservative & to lean backwards most of the time. I'm keen to know a bit more about the new ideas stirring among the modern youth.'[1]

He did not know quite how lavishly his wish would come true.

News of the 1976 uprisings came to Robben Island months after they began when a single prisoner was transferred from an up-country jail. So unlikely was the tale he told that Nelson and his comrades did not believe him.[2] By early 1977, their world had been shaken to its core. Hundreds upon hundreds of the revolt's children came pouring in. Some were seasoned, university-educated Black Consciousness leaders. Most were younger, their ideas less formed; they had come straight from the fury of the insurrection.

What happened when they arrived has seldom been told as narrative; a sense of shame has forced the telling into fragments. The older prisoners seized upon the young and demanded their allegiance. It was as if scraps of meat had been cast into the cells of ravenous men.

One new prisoner would remember his first hours on the island as a harrowing dream. A warder led him down a corridor, the cells on each side packed with older men; they pressed themselves against the bars, 'crazy looking . . . excited'. 'Which organisation are you affiliated to?' they demanded, their hunger to claim him raw. Not just their urgency but the question itself unnerved him: he had never imagined that he might have to choose.[3]

When newcomers left their cells for breakfast in the mornings, older men brushed against them and stuffed notes in their pockets. 'The ANC's mother is Helen Suzman [a liberal member of parliament],' read one note, 'their father is Joe Slovo, their headquarters is in Moscow. Join the PAC.'[4] As for ANC notes, they beckoned youngsters to join in exchange for more food.

Testimony from this time is couched in language that deflects. But one can glimpse the shock nonetheless. Many newcomers 'collapsed', one of them recalled. 'They had to go to hospital' as a result of the 'mental pressure' of recruitment.⁵ 'You are new,' another commented. 'Coming into that environment . . . it shocks you . . . It tended to undermine your integrity as an individual.'⁶

En route to Robben Island, few, if any, of the youngsters imagined establishing a new organization. The Black Consciousness Movement was explicit in its intention to fracture black politics no further. Now, in the face of this aggression, the youngsters formed a new camp to defend themselves from the onslaught. And so, three organizations faced one another down: the ANC, the PAC, and the BCM.

Among the few Robben Island prisoners to speak frankly about what happened when the youngsters came was the psychologist Saths Cooper. Being jailed is 'horrific', 'dehumanising', he wrote. While it brings out the best in a few, 'narcissistic and exploitative behaviour' is more common. When all is said and done, he wrote, 'there is little difference between common law and political prisoners generally. Where the former are often organised into deadly rival gangs, the latter are organised into often warring political groupings.'⁷

By Robben Island's code of discretion, it was a scandalous thing to say; he had breached a taboo.

Things came to a head when a prominent Black Consciousness leader, Patrick 'Terror' Lekota, was recruited into the ANC. Scandalized, his comrades resolved to punish him. Somebody began playing a melodica to drown out the noise; another pushed Lekota to provoke him; when he fought back, he was rounded upon and struck on the head with a garden fork.⁸ 'I fell like a brick,' he later recalled. 'I nearly died.'⁹

· ·

Mandela, Sisulu, Kathrada, Mbeki: they and the other Rivonia defendants watched this violent competition at a remove. Housed in the leadership section, they did not witness firsthand the fracas in the communal cells.

Their isolation brought consequences of its own. Prisons are engines of rumour, of fantasy; they are places in which facts are hard to pin down. Throughout the late 1970s and early 1980s, stories about Nelson – that he had just last week made a secret deal with the apartheid regime, or that he was planning to make one tomorrow – often swept through the communal cells.

Over breakfast, a Robben Islander remembered, 'someone would tell you that a plane landed last night, and in it there were seven generals; they met with so and so and the revolution is being sold down the drain. And then it would be passed onto the next person through the grapevine, and by the time you come back from work in the afternoon, the whole area is abuzz analysing ... the information ... like it's very authentic.'[10]

Nelson recorded none of this in his autobiography. 'To be perceived as a moderate', is all he was prepared to say, 'was a novel and not altogether pleasant feeling.'[11]

. .

The recruitment battle raged for three years, ebbing at last in the spring of 1980. There is a story of how it ended, repeated so often and with such conviction that it has long become sacred.

Nelson gradually acquired 'a quiet authority over the younger inmates', the story goes.[12] Indeed, 'the body of prisoners ... united ... with Mandela as their leader'.[13] He won this influence, it is said, because he demonstrated the virtues of standing down. Once the island had calmed, prisoners could talk and exchange and make something new. Herein lies the magic of the place, so they say. The authorities had made a terrible mistake. They corralled together on one island every current in black politics. The Rivonia defendants; the Young Turks of 1976; the Africanists; the ideologues of Black Consciousness; the Trotskyists of the Non-European Unity Movement. Their enemy had built them a forum in which they could listen and talk to one another.

'The prisoners of Robben Island began to build a polity,' one historian wrote, 'and even a nascent parliament.'[14] Robben Islanders made the future itself, and as they were released, so they seeded it in the world at large.

It is important to tell a more plausible story lest Nelson himself disappear on the wings of this dream.

The recruitment battle ended because the ANC had won. By the final months of 1980, the PAC and the BCM had settled as stable minorities; everyone else was in the ANC. But the contest among older men to capture the young did not die. It became calmer, to be sure; it lost its cravenness. But in its more subdued form it was transferred into the ranks of the ANC.

There was no shortage of conflict among the older generation of ANC men. A distressed report smuggled from B Section to the exiled ANC spoke of discord 'at times reaching extreme tension and bitterness, at times abating in response to efforts to solve it'.[15] Even this was an understatement: from the late 1960s until deep into the following decade, Nelson and Govan Mbeki barely exchanged a word.

The roots of their conflict lay in the recent past. In late 1962, shortly after Nelson was captured, Mbeki and Joe Slovo had drafted a document on how the armed struggle should proceed. Titled 'Operation Mayibuye', it described a plan to topple the white regime.

It was a pastel-coloured romance, a pastiche of what had happened in Cuba. A hundred and twenty trained guerrillas would land in South Africa by ship or by air. They would spread across the country and incite ordinary people to rebel. Thousands upon thousands of civilians would be armed. They would rise up and destroy the regime.[16]

By the time this document was written, Nelson found its precepts incredible. The Algerians had convinced him that armed struggle had at best an auxiliary role to perform; apartheid would end via a negotiated settlement or not at all.

It is hard to exaggerate the contention 'Operation Mayibuye' spawned. To their dying day, Govan Mbeki and Joe Slovo insisted that the ANC and MK had adopted it. Nelson and his allies claimed that it was a draft proposal still under consultation when the Rivonia men were arrested.[17]

On Robben Island, 'Operation Mayibuye' was the foundation of all the trouble to come. The issues in contention would change: the role of the Communist Party in the national struggle; whether to contest Bantustan parliamentary elections; the landownership regime of the future. But whatever was on the surface, the substance of the dispute could not have run deeper: it concerned how apartheid would end and what sort of society would replace it.

Mbeki never for a moment accepted that Nelson was the leader of the ANC on the island. And in this he was not alone. The composition of the group that rallied around him varied as prisoners came and went.

As for Nelson's group, it was constant throughout the years: Walter Sisulu, Ahmed Kathrada, Laloo Chiba, and, until his departure in 1976, Mac Maharaj.

Nobody who lived on B Section could mistake the clannishness of Nelson's group. It was 'physically separate, secretive, highly organised', according to James April, who arrived on B Section in 1971.[18] The most ambitious of its projects was the writing of Nelson's autobiography. It kept them busy for several months in 1975 and then again the following year. Nelson wrote late at night and in the mornings gave his work to Maharaj; he transcribed Nelson's words into a tiny script and passed it on to Sisulu and Kathrada; they made notes and suggestions; Maharaj himself often altered the text in response.

When he was released in 1976, Maharaj smuggled a clean copy of the manuscript to London; Kathrada buried the original draft, in Nelson's hand, in several tins in the prison garden.[19]

Mbeki apparently knew of the project and gave it his nominal consent, but only because he judged that nothing would come of it.[20] The very idea must have offended him deeply. Not only did it elevate one comrade over others, violating a principle of collective leadership; not only did it elevate *Nelson*, a man whose leadership Mbeki did not accept. Exalting Nelson in this way revealed a vision of apartheid's end of which Mbeki deeply disapproved: a pact forged between famous men.

.   .

And so, when the youngsters were recruited into the ANC, they joined a divided group. While many respected and deferred to Nelson, they were in the main drawn to men hostile to his views. Chief among them was Harry Gwala, a 'veteran Stalinist', in Nelson's authorized biographer's view, who delighted the youth with his venom. 'We crammed daily into his tiny cell analysing all the conflicts in the world,' one of them later recalled. 'He didn't hesitate to take a swipe at anybody,' remembered another. 'He would go for Madiba.'[21] And when the ANC wrote a syllabus of instruction, compulsory for all its members on the island, it was Mbeki's influence that prevailed; for a course titled 'A History of Human Society', the only authors were Marx, Engels, and Lenin.[22]

.   .

The fractious world of Robben Island produced in Nelson Mandela a sense of embattlement. During his time in prison, it was his adversaries who described him to ANC activists on the outside. The first was Joe Gqabi, a close ally of Mbeki's, released in 1975; then Mbeki himself in 1987; then Harry Gwala in 1988. Each emerged from jail warning that Nelson was narrow, conservative and liable to sell out.

It is hard to exaggerate how deeply this upset Nelson or how threatened he felt. When Gqabi was released, Nelson wrote to Winnie advising her to have no contact with him, a letter that caused considerable distress in the ANC.[23] As for Mbeki and Gwala, they were freed while Nelson was in delicate talks with the apartheid regime; as they spread rumours of his perfidy, he would feel lonely and besieged.

In several of his letters in the 1970s, Nelson tells his correspondents that he does not live on Robben Island; his imagination has borne him elsewhere. Given the persistent acrimony, we should take him seriously when he says that he escaped.

Where did he go?

One place to which he persistently returned was the company of white statesmen. He read biographies of Lincoln, Washington, Disraeli; he read Churchill's war diaries and emerging works on John F. Kennedy.

By the time he was released in 1990, there was scarcely a head of state on the planet who did not wish to shake his hand. And yet, until his final years in prison, he had not met a single diplomat in the flesh;[24] it was in his head that he had conversed with them, over and over again.

Even the fiction he read was an extension of his taste for high politics. While he expressed dutiful admiration for Dostoevsky, this inward-turned moralist left him depressed. It was Tolstoy's *War and Peace* that fired him; he read it in three days flat.[25]

His strongest taste was for *Afrikaans* statesmen. He read biographies of Jan Smuts and of the Boer War leader Koos de la Rey. He wrote to South Africa's justice minister requesting a copy of Piet Meiring's *Ons eerste ses premiers: 'n persoonlike tergublik* (Our first six prime ministers: a personal recollection).[26]

He was especially consumed with those Afrikaans statesmen whose biographies mapped his own imagined career: men who were once outlaws and died national heroes. He devoured the first biography of John Vorster, South Africa's prime minister from 1966 to 1978, who had been interned during World War II for his membership in a fascist militia.

Christiaan de Wet was another favourite: leader of an armed rebellion during World War I, he was given a state funeral when he died and a place in the nationalist canon.

We must all imagine ourselves in the future: to cease doing so is to become a walking corpse. The point is the company Nelson was keeping. He was with his enemies, matching their souls against his.

It must have been a cold place. His companions were men who had humiliated him, men about whom he felt ambivalent at best; he summoned them into his inner world so that one day he might master them.

.   .

There are other places to which Nelson tried less successfully to flee. In a letter to an old comrade, Yusuf Dadoo, penned in 1975, he counted the friends who had died. 'Such losses make one feel alone,' he wrote, for it seemed that his own past was dying one person at a time. 'I've nothing to prod the memory,' he complained, just a few photos and the letters he receives from outside. There were 199 of them, he said, accumulated over thirteen years. Does Dadoo understand that he lives for Saturdays, when the mail arrives? If Oliver and Adelaide Tambo knew, they would surely have acknowledged his letters.

There is a hint of recrimination here. Do those who are free comprehend that memories alone cannot sustain life?

Another object helped him, he wrote: his tattered 1963 edition of *The Oxford Atlas*. 'It is one of my greatest companions. My thoughts are forever travelling up & down the country, remembering the places I've visited.'

It was the future that preoccupied him most, though, and it frightened him. 'I think much of . . . the problems of adjustment and of picking up old threads. It is mainly in this regard that I never really live on this island.'[27]

He was anxious. Some photographs, a pile of letters, a map: these were pitifully inadequate tools. There are limits to what imagination can achieve when the substance of one's life is gone.

Chapter 38

At dawn on May 16, 1977, a score of police officers descended on Winnie's house. They swarmed inside, stripped its innards, and loaded them onto the back of a truck: Nelson's law books, Winnie's linen, her clothes, the crockery in her kitchen, her dining table, her bed – everything that was not stuck down. They drove her and Zindzi southward, across the Vaal River and into the Free State, stopping after a five-hour journey in the hamlet of Brandfort. Outside a two-room house, a house without electricity, without water, without heat in this, the start of winter, they deposited mother and child. Winnie was handed her banishment order: she was to remain in this place, it stipulated, until December 31, 1981, more than four and a half years hence.

As she took in her new quarters, Winnie turned upon the man in charge. His name was Johan van der Merwe, head of the Security Branch in the province of the Free State. He would go on to become apartheid South Africa's last commissioner of police. Where did he expect her to put her furniture? she snapped at him. Most of it would not fit into this place. And where could she and Zindzi find a warm bath? Night had fallen, it was late; did he expect them to go to bed cold and dirty?

And so, the truck made its way into the white town centre, where van der Merwe emptied a garage to make space for Winnie's things. Then he found her and Zindzi a room in the town's hotel and told them they had an hour to bathe.¹ It was after 3:00 a.m. when they finally lay down for the night in their derelict new home, House 802 in Brandfort's nameless black township.

While they had done little to make it comfortable, the police had wired her new home with bugs. A retired policeman lived in the house next door, his job to change the tapes that ran day and night. Another officer was posted permanently across the road to police the terms of Winnie's banning order: nobody was permitted to enter her house save for its full-time residents, her doctor and her lawyer; out on the street, Winnie could be in the presence of no more than one adult at a time. There was no phone in the house, no means of communicating with the outside world. Nor, as she discovered the next morning, could she make herself understood to her neighbours. Their native tongue was Setswana, their lingua franca Afrikaans. Winnie spoke neither.

She would live here for eight years.

. .

Of all that her foes ever did to her, this was not just the cruellest; it was also the most ill-advised. In fact, just as he was about to sign the order banishing Winnie to Brandfort, a senior official beseeched the justice minister, Jimmy Kruger, to think again.

'Her banning to Brandfort might easily make her a martyr,' the official warned. 'We would be vulnerable for years to extremely distasteful and difficult-to-handle propaganda.' Might it not be wiser, the official continued, to confine her to her house in Soweto for twenty-four hours a day, save to shop for essentials and to visit the doctor? The state could even give her a monthly stipend equal to the salary she would have to forgo.[2]

The warning proved to be prescient. Not for the first time, an effort to destroy Winnie Mandela would escalate her fame.

. .

By 1977, banishment was not uncommon. Many political prisoners released during the 1960s were sent to hamlets far from their homes.[3] Robert Sobukwe himself, the PAC's leader, was confined to Kimberley after his release in 1969, where he lived out his days. The purpose of banishment was blunt and simple: it was to sever activists from the organizations they had built and to destroy their spirits.[4]

But Winnie's talent did not lie in establishing organizations, let alone in running them. Her talent lay in theatre, and she could not have been offered a more formidable stage.

Brandfort was a farming centre in the far reaches of the hinterland; it practiced apartheid in its most parodied form. The white town with its commercial high street and its comfortable homes, the run-down black township just out of sight; the siren that sounded at nine o'clock each evening chasing black people off the streets; convenience stores reserved for whites, while black customers were served through a hatch in the wall; the clothes shops where white women tried on various items while blacks pointed at what they wanted from the door.

There is a photograph of Winnie and Zindzi taken two weeks after they arrived. Winnie had been charged with violating her banning order already, and the two were leaving court. They were more than just beautiful, mother and daughter: their appearance was a declaration of war. Winnie in knee-high platform boots, her black leather coat swinging about her calves; Zindzi's tight pants tucked into cowboy boots, on her face the most triumphant of smiles.[5]

Soon after Winnie arrived, she and Zindzi walked into a fashion store instead of waiting at the door. When they were asked to leave, they refused and a sales attendant called the police. An hour later, the store filled with uniformed officers and Winnie still refused to go, insisting that Zindzi try on a dress. A crowd of more than a hundred people had gathered outside waiting to see who would win.

And so it went during her first weeks in Brandfort. When she went grocery shopping, she would not stand at the hatch in the wall; she would stride into the whites-only interior, taking her time, examining each row of groceries at leisure.[6] Before long, white residents of the town had written to the minister of justice demanding that she go.[7]

But the primary audience of these performances was not the white citizenry of Brandfort. The day Winnie was banished, the news coursed into the world. It was that rare story – so stark, so shocking, and with Winnie's beauty, so easy on the eye: the brave wife of the jailed leader dumped in this god-awful town. Once it was told, the telling went on and on.

Three days after Winnie's banishment, the U.S. vice president, Walter Mondale, was due to meet South Africa's prime minister, John Vorster, in Vienna. Now Mondale asked the U.S. embassy in Pretoria to brief him on Winnie Mandela; he wanted to raise her predicament with Vorster. It was acutely embarrassing, a moment of hard-won diplomacy tarnished from out of the blue.[8]

It was just a taste of what was to come. The tale of the banished beauty grew and grew. We can only guess at what might have happened had there been no story to tell. But we can take something of its measure by standing back and observing the international context at that time.

It may seem odd to think it now, but in the first half of the 1970s the Mandelas had become all but invisible. Between Winnie's release from prison in September 1970 and the start of the uprisings six years later, she and Nelson are mentioned just once in The *New York Times*. A scan of the London broadsheets tells a similar tale. Nelson and his fellow defendants, as his authorized biographer pointed out, had become 'largely forgotten men'.[9]

Nor was the ANC making great progress in rallying support to its cause. The Soviet Union funded its modest military activity. But among Western nations only Sweden gave substantial support. The politics of the Cold War were unfavourable to the ANC in the West. Its alliance with the South African Communist Party, its funding from Moscow: these did not play well, even among many who opposed apartheid fiercely.

And the South African government had eloquent allies. The country had boomed in the 1960s, along with so much of the rest of the world, bringing a raft of foreign investors. In finance, in mining, in manufacturing, in science and technology: South Africa had thick ties to significant interests abroad. With these interests came sophisticated voices. Many of the most influential thinkers of the time visited and commented on South Africa: the political scientists Samuel Huntington and Arend Lijphart, the rising star of neoclassical economics Milton Friedman. None of these men *supported* racial dictatorship. Their contention, rather, was that the force of capitalist development would itself destroy apartheid. The more the world invested, such men argued, the sooner apartheid would go.

The classiest of South Africa's diplomats parroted this line. In 1979, the South African cabinet minister Piet Koornhof told a puzzled National Press Club in Washington, D.C., that apartheid was dying. He would not rest, he said, until racial discrimination in his country was gone.[10]

The uprisings of 1976 were of course a terrible blow to the prestige of South Africa abroad. But they were hardly a victory for the ANC, marooned in exile, out of touch with the gathering spirit at home. The most significant event in the history of black politics had largely passed the ANC by. The British Anti-apartheid Movement, its loyalty to the ANC unconditional, did not quite know how to spin the story. In the end, it paid more attention to the ANC's reaction than to the revolt itself, an awkward effort to put its ally onstage.[11]

And then, in September 1977, just when the revolt was slipping from the international news, the security police killed Steve Biko. Few outside South Africa had heard of him before he died. Now the handsome face of a martyr was on front pages across the world.

But he too, of course, was unconnected to the ANC.

For all the news coming out of South Africa, none of it promoted the movement of Nelson Mandela. Historic events were attaching themselves to other names.

With one exception: Winnie in Brandfort.

Within a week of her banishment, foreign correspondents descended on her new home. It soon became a journey everyone *had* to make: the *Washington Post*, the *New York Times, Le Monde, Le Figaro, The Times* of London, the *Observer*. Less than a month had passed before an Associated Press reporter won a prestigious international award for her coverage of Winnie's life.[12] 'Winnie', the *Washington Post*'s Johannesburg correspondent would recall, 'was absolutely irresistible copy.'[13]

The pilgrimage itself was part of the tale: a long drive through the backlands of the Free State, the hamlet appearing from nowhere as one summited a hill. The wonderful props the Security Branch provided: cars with blackened windows on journalists' tails, figures with binoculars watching from the hills. The hostility of the white citizenry in the town centre, some going so far as to spit on visitors' shoes. And at the end of the journey the glorious Winnie Mandela, 'clad in purple robes and looking like an empress', as the filmmaker Richard Attenborough described her when he visited Brandfort,[14] striding from her 'hovel', her 'hut', her 'pitiful excuse for a home'.

Everyone reached for an angle. The *New York Times*'s Joseph Lelyveld described Winnie receiving Holy Communion in her minister's car: her banning order, Lelyveld explained, did not permit him inside.[15] Others wrote of the vegetable garden she planted for the hungry, or a clinic she was building for the sick. All described her visits to the white town centre and her flouting of its racist laws.

Barely known abroad before her banishment, Winnie was now famous. Ordinary people from across the planet wrote with outrage to Prime Minister Vorster. 'South Africa has more friends in the United States than you, perhaps, can imagine,' wrote a certain E. Warren Smith from Brooklyn. 'It is when we read accounts of the arbitrary treatment of people like Mrs. Nelson Mandela that friends of South Africa wonder if verbal support of your government is, after all, worth the trouble.'[16]

Winnie herself was deluged with mail. Her lawyer often arrived from Johannesburg with box loads in his trunk: letters of encouragement, words of advice, invitations to give lectures, to take up titular positions at charities and municipal councils, cash cheques. She hadn't the wherewithal to deal with them. They piled up alongside her furniture in the police garage in town.

She grasped in a flash the significance of what was happening. She could not be quoted in South Africa, her words all the more tantalizing when broadcast abroad. Over and over again, she said the same thing. There will be majority rule in South Africa. The president will be Mandela. 'We are fighting for a country which can only be led by him. He is the only hope for this country if the white man wants to save himself from the inevitable bloodbath.'[17]

She did not call him 'my husband' or 'Nelson' or 'Nelson Mandela'. Always, simply, Mandela, the repetition of the name so important.

All traces of Black Consciousness had vanished. 'Our founding document is the Freedom Charter,' she told a British television channel. 'It is our country's future constitution.'

What her tongue conjured was so simple, so entirely pared down.

South Africa's rightful government is in exile. Its leader is in jail.

That is all.

In banishing her, the government had accomplished what Oliver Tambo had struggled in vain to do: the names ANC and Mandela were, finally, all over the news.

Chapter 39

Something else of great import was happening at this time.

In August 1977, when Winnie's fame was three months old, Mac Maharaj arrived in exile with a copy of Nelson's autobiography, written so painstakingly and in such secrecy over a period of two years. The very idea of writing it had been hatched with a view to Maharaj's impending release. He would take the manuscript with him abroad, and it would be launched on Nelson's sixtieth birthday: July 18, 1978.

It was never published. Some in the ANC objected to Nelson's characterization of the turn to armed struggle, others to the very notion of celebrating one man. Most profound were doubts about Nelson himself. Nobody had spoken to him since 1962. Fragments of news about his feud with Govan Mbeki had reached the ANC in exile. There were 'insecurities', 'rumours about what people like Mandela were doing,' Maharaj recalled.[1]

Still, he persisted stubbornly. In Nigeria in late 1977, he was introduced to a man called Enuga Reddy, principal secretary to the United Nations Special Committee Against Apartheid. Mandela's sixtieth birthday was less than a year away, Maharaj told Reddy; why not use it to publicize his case?[2]

Many years later, when Maharaj met with this author, he had forgotten that he ever made the suggestion to Reddy. But he had, as Reddy's correspondence from that time attests, and the meeting of the two men in Nigeria was wonderfully fortuitous. For Reddy was perhaps the only person on earth who both understood the great potential of Maharaj's suggestion and had the wherewithal to execute it.

Reddy was an unusual protagonist in the struggle against apartheid. An Indian national, he had not set foot in South Africa on the day he met Mac Maharaj. He had spent much of the last quarter of a century in an office high up in the UN's headquarters in New York, at work on a project few of his colleagues quite understood.

Born in 1924 in a small village outside Madras, Reddy was the son of two devotees of Mohandas Gandhi. He was nine when the Mahatma visited his village to collect funds for the upliftment of the Harijans; his mother, to the dismay of her relatives, gave Gandhi all the jewels she had inherited from her mother. Eight years later, Reddy's father was jailed for three months for conducting satyagraha.[3]

Reddy did not inherit all of his parents' traits. While his father was a trader and a businessman, Enuga was bookish and hated handling money. What he did take from his parents was a passionate, lifelong commitment to Gandhi and his ideas.

In the mid-1940s, he went to New York to study politics. There he met W. E. B. Du Bois, Paul Robeson, Kwame Nkrumah, and others and was exposed to their international campaigning. He was already a committed advocate of the South African struggle, largely as a result of the legacy Gandhi had left there. In New York he absorbed the idea that decolonization was in its essence a global quest requiring a movement that spanned the world.[4]

Upon graduating, Reddy began an internship at the Union Nations. He remained there for the rest of his working life, his vision for what might be achieved through this gargantuan bureaucracy quite unique.

Formed in 1963, the Special Committee Against Apartheid was neglected almost entirely by the major powers, freeing Reddy, its founding principal secretary, to do with it as he wished. He set to work on two projects. One was to make the committee the nerve centre of anti-apartheid work across the globe. Through countless seminars, workshops, and conferences, he built a network of people spanning continents. His other project was to present the South African struggle in ways that bypassed the language of the Cold War. Anti-apartheid work, he understood, was stymied when sucked into a bipolar world. He wanted to reframe the whole question, to describe the struggle in South Africa in ways it had not been described before.[5]

When Maharaj suggested a celebration of Nelson's sixtieth birthday, Reddy took to it at once. As a devotee of Gandhi, he was no stranger to the extravagant use of celebrity in politics: Gandhi's spinning wheel; his scandalous near nakedness; his presidential-style tours of India; above all, his march against the salt tax, evoking the pilgrimage of a holy man. Reddy understood immediately the force of celebrating a jailed man's birthday, a man who had been silent and invisible for years.

He roused the global network he had so painstakingly built, writing to the head of the British Anti-apartheid Movement, to the equivalents in the United States, across Scandinavia, in Holland. His vision for the campaign was simple: ordinary people should be provided with birthday cards to send to Nelson Mandela on Robben Island. And the cards, Reddy stressed, should have a picture of Nelson Mandela.

The British Anti-apartheid Movement chose a photograph of Nelson in suit and tie in front of the famous Gothic arch on the northern side of Westminster Abbey; the Swedes, the Norwegians, the Dutch, the Germans, each chose their own photograph. For the first time, a series of images entered a circuit spanning the North Atlantic, images of a man nobody had seen in fourteen years.

Few who worked on the campaign foresaw its success. The 1970s had been such a difficult decade for anti-apartheid movements. Explaining the position of the ANC on economic sanctions, on cultural boycotts, and, above all, on violence: these conversations took place on difficult terrain. Mandela's birthday had a lightness, indeed, a vacuousness, some activists complained. The canvassing was so easy; everybody, it seemed, wanted to wish this mysterious man a happy birthday.

In early July 1978, birthday cards began arriving on Robben Island: hundreds at first, then thousands, then tens of thousands. Nelson's birthday came and went, and, still, the deluge did not cease. Most were from Britain and the Nordic countries, but countless more carried postmarks from across Western Europe and the United States. They came in giant batches: ten thousand from London alone; several thousand from Michigan State University, where much of the student body appears to have signed a card.

Undaunted by the volume, Robben Island staff followed the rules. Each card was opened, read, and then stapled back onto the outside of the envelope. The correspondence was then sorted by country. Since Nelson was not permitted to receive them, they were packed into boxes and stored. They remained there for several months until an exasperated official judged that they were taking up more space than they deserved. In early 1979, prison staff lugged the entire collection to the island's boiler room and threw it into the fire.[6]

On the day of his sixtieth birthday, Nelson was given just six cards: one from his wife, one apiece from his four children, and one from his lawyer.

. .

The most dramatic moment in the global campaign took place in London.

Days before Nelson's sixtieth, a giant birthday card found its way to a meeting of the Labour Party's National Executive, where it was passed around and signed. Labour was still in power at that time – it was unseated nine months later by Margaret Thatcher's Tories – and so when the card was returned to the Anti-apartheid Movement's offices, it sported the signatures of half the British cabinet. A canny member of the movement decided to make a fuss of what had happened; on July 18, Nelson's birthday, the card was taken with some ceremony to South Africa House on Trafalgar Square to be delivered to the country's high commissioner. Upon getting wind that it was on its way, the South African diplomatic staff panicked and locked the building.

The then twice-weekly ritual of Prime Minister's Question Time was under way in the House of Commons that day, and the country's leader, Jim Callaghan, was speaking from the dispatch box. A veteran Labour member of Parliament, Barbara Castle, rose to speak. Instead of asking the prime minister a question, she told of how she had just tried to deliver a birthday card to Nelson Mandela, only to have the door of South Africa House shut in her face. There was a great deal of tut-tutting on the Labour benches and shouts of 'Shame!' Callaghan stepped up to the dispatch box and with a broad and mischievous smile wished Nelson Mandela a happy sixtieth birthday.[7]

The idea of Nelson Mandela crossed a threshold at that moment. In the U.K. then, the Irish Republican Army's bombing campaign had triggered fear on the British mainland; the notion of an armed struggle bore unpleasant connotations. Equally, at that time, no Labour prime minister would want to associate himself with a movement perceived to be a client of Soviet power. And yet here was a man in jail for waging a bombing campaign, a man whose army was funded from top to bottom by the Soviet Union. And the prime minister was wishing him a happy birthday from the seat of legislative power. Something had begun, just faintly observable for now: the lifting of Nelson Mandela above his context, indeed, above *any* particular context, and into an orbit of his own.

. .

The excitement the story exuded might have ebbed and died. Stardom, after all, was so alien to the ANC. The organization's discomfort might have smothered the tale at birth.

That it did not was largely the doing of Nelson's former law partner, Oliver Tambo.

Mike Terry, leader of the British Anti-apartheid Movement, went to see Tambo around this time at his house in north London. The discussion, as he remembered it, was soon whittled down to its core. Why focus on Mandela? the two asked.

Bespectacled, soft-spoken, Tambo often remarked how much he delighted in his old friend's showmanship: the ridiculous car, the expensive suits, the exuberant courtroom style. He himself was so shy and contained, his biographer would remark; he took vicarious pleasure in his partner's flamboyance and, most especially, in his sexual prowess.[8]

Now, in the London suburb of Muswell Hill, a continent away from where Tambo's friendship with Nelson had begun, he and Terry answered their own question with precision. South Africa's political prisoners were ANC, PAC, Black Consciousness. These organizations were tussling for supremacy. To shine the stage light on Mandela was to shine it on the ANC.[9]

There is shrewd calculation here, to be sure, but there is also a certain loveliness. Tambo had been separated from Nelson nearly two decades. Now, all this time later, he was still taking pleasure in his friend's charisma; indeed, he had loaded it as one would a weapon and was using it to fight.

His campaign was masterful, not least for its discretion. He did not consult widely in the ANC; to do so would have risked losing the argument. He opened a channel of communication with the editor of the *Sunday Post* in Johannesburg, Percy Qoboza. The two men exchanged messages periodically for more than a year.

And then, in early 1980, South Africa's last white-ruled neighbour, Rhodesia, gave way to majority rule. In Zimbabwe's first democratic elections, held in late February, Robert Mugabe's ZANU-PF was swept into power. White South Africa was stunned; for the past two years it had been drip fed the idea that black Zimbabweans would support a compliant clergyman, Abel Muzorewa. In the end, 8 percent of Zimbabweans voted for Muzorewa's party, a combined 87 percent for the two movements that had waged guerrilla war. The parallels to South Africa were hard not to draw. Did the majority of black South Africans, too, support the armed movements abroad?

Two prominent Afrikaans newspapers made what was then a bold call. There must be a national convention, they opined, where the country's leaders, black and white, would meet.

Tambo and Qoboza used this moment to strike. On March 9, 1980, the *Sunday Post* ran a headline in massive font across its front page: 'Free Mandela'.

'Release Nelson Mandela,' the story began. 'This was the reply of South Africa's black leaders to a call this week for a national convention to bring about orderly change in South Africa ... Black leaders insist that before they can participate in such a convention, the Government must: release all political prisoners, including Nelson Mandela; allow all exiles to come home; lift bans on black organisations; and scrap apartheid.'

The story went on to quote black figures from across the political spectrum supporting the call to free Mandela: a homeland leader, two prominent clerics, a Black Consciousness Movement leader. Qoboza was hamming it up: the list of people he quoted was long and diverse but only moderately distinguished. It was a wonderful case of a newspaper orchestrating its own news.[10]

In his editorial that day, Qoboza announced a national petition to free Mandela. Over the following months, each edition of the newspaper would publish a barometer on its front page counting as the number of signatures grew. 'One of the realities we must face up to', he wrote, 'is that Nelson Mandela commands a following that is unheard of in this land. To embark on any solution or discussion without his wise input would only be following the blind politics of Ian Smith [Rhodesia's last prime minister] and Muzorewa in Zimbabwe and the outcome would be just as disastrous.'[11]

That Mandela commanded 'a following unheard of in this land' was, at that moment, untested, and almost certainly untrue. The point, of course, was to make it true.

Over the following weeks and months, the idea that no substantial change could begin in South Africa without Mandela became contagious. Primed by Tambo and Qoboza, Bishop Desmond Tutu, the charismatic general secretary of the South African Council of Churches, signed the petition in public and called on his fellow clergy to follow suit.[12] The following month, a guild of prominent Afrikaans writers

called for Mandela's release;[13] so did a council of some of the country's top medical researchers.[14] In parliament, the opposition politician
Frederik van Zyl Slabbert pointed out that South Africa had a long tradition of granting amnesty to those who had committed treason: Afrikaner nationalist dissidents in both world wars had been sentenced to
death and subsequently freed.[15]

And, of course, a global campaign to free Mandela followed on the
heels of the *Sunday Post*'s initiative. A year after Qoboza's editorial, the
petition he had launched made its way through Western Europe's and
North America's major cities. At the culmination of the British leg of
the campaign, Bishop Tutu told a crowd in London that black South
Africans had set a time limit for the inauguration of a prime minister
who looked like them. Five years, he said; a decade at the very most.
'And may that Prime Minister be Nelson Mandela,' he concluded.[16]

. .

Tambo, Reddy, Terry: together these men were creating the First
Couple of a future South Africa. Their success bore enormous risks.
They had strung this couple together with images and words. The
actual Nelson and Winnie Mandela remained backstage. Someday, the
myth and its shadow would meet. What might happen then?

Winnie was playing her banishment as well as anyone might hope.
But her performances were pro forma; she had not faced an exacting
test. And Tambo's misgivings about her ran deep; he must have wondered, if only in the privacy of his own thoughts, what it was he had
made.

As for Nelson, he was forty-one years old when Tambo last laid
eyes on him. Now he was on the cusp of old age. There was no saying
for certain what he had become.

In 1985, Nelson's future biographer Anthony Sampson, who had
known him fairly well in the 1950s, attended an exciting event in London. Oliver Tambo was unveiling a bust of Nelson in the heart of the
city, outside the Royal Festival Hall. There were speeches and toasts
and tributes, as was customary on ceremonial occasions. Finally, the
evening's denouement came, and Tambo lifted the covering from the
bust.

'There was this amazing figure,' Sampson recalled, 'more than
life-sized, which in my view bore absolutely no relationship to what

[Nelson] looked like at all. It was rather a caricature of the thick-set, muscular, thick-lipped black man, in a heroic posture, but with curiously insensitive features, it seemed to me.'

Making his way home that evening, Sampson entertained troubled thoughts. Heroic figures, he found himself thinking, were 'pretty uninteresting and not very attractive'. How might Nelson respond when confronted with this image of himself? He would not, he concluded, want to be in Nelson's shoes.[7]

Chapter 40

'At one time there was a certain farmer who... was married to a rich [man's] daughter,' Nelson wrote to Winnie in December 1977. The couple was prosperous and in love, he continued, and had a child they both cherished.

Then the man was called away to lead warriors to war and was captured by his enemy. Bitter that he had left her, his wife took up with a former lover. Provocatively, she wrote to tell her husband that her old flame wished to marry her. 'What she was doing was to make sure that the husband still loved her,' Nelson wrote. A proud man, he decided instead to call her bluff. 'Marry him,' he replied.

'It was hardly two years when news came that the husband was coming back and he was regarded as the true leader in the community,' Nelson wrote. The wife now wanted to reunite with him, but the milk had been spilled. To make matters worse, her child, angry that her mother had not waited, went to live with her returning father. The woman and her new husband descended into poverty and lived unhappily for the rest of their lives. 'Shame was on her,' Nelson concluded.[1]

What drove him to write this? It is one thing to be whipped into a frenzy of jealousy and doubt, quite another not to wait and ride it out. The fever lasted long enough to put pen to paper and then to post the letter. It is bracingly out of place; the rest of his letters to her are so relentlessly adoring, at times cloyingly sweet.

Winnie had been in Brandfort almost seven months now; she was not living with another man; she was alone with Zindzi trying to make a home in a living hell.

We do not have her side of the correspondence. Nelson's parable was most likely a reply to something she had written. What did she say? Had she been spiteful and cruel?

Since her banishment, Winnie had, despite her success in courting global sympathy, descended into the deepest depression. When she
visited Nelson, the sight of her spooked him: the blankness in her eyes,
the skin drawn over her cheeks. 'You looked a bit ill [when you last
came],' he wrote in January 1979, 'and the tiny pools of water in your
eyes drowned the love and tenderness they always radiate.' He was
shocked, too, by the weight she had lost. 'You frightened me,' he wrote.
'Frankly I don't want to see you again so starved & bony.'[2]

To Zindzi he was more forthright. 'You are the last straw to which
[Mum] clings,' he wrote to her, four months after the banishment, 'and
her happiness is very much in your hands.'[3]

Nelson was not the only one to sound alarm at Winnie's state. Her
lawyer, Ismail Ayob, who visited her regularly, reported on her condition to the head of IDAF in London. He had seldom seen a human
being quite so deep in despair. She was going to die in Brandfort, she
told him, and Nelson would die on Robben Island. The Mandelas
would perish and apartheid would go on.[4]

Those of her letters from this time that are accessible are relentlessly bleak. 'The empty long days drag on and on,' she wrote to a friend
in May 1979, 'one like the other, no matter how hard I try to study. The
solitude is deadly, the grey matchbox shacks so desolate simply stare at
you as lifeless as the occupants, who form a human chain of frustration
as they pass next to my window.'[5]

The banishment she suffered would have been cruel on anybody.
But on Winnie, a person who needed such intense attachment to others, it must have been especially hard. During the only other period
when she had been so cut off – her solitary confinement in 1969 and 1970
– she had almost taken her life.

A little less than a year into her banishment, the intensity for which
she hungered finally came. It did so in the form of a young white doctor. From out of the blue he wrote her a letter, hand delivered to avoid
prying eyes. He ran a general practice in the nearby town of Welkom,
he told her, a practice dedicated entirely to the town's black settlement.
He was in sympathy with her. Might he help her in any way? The letter
was signed Chris Hattingh.

Four decades later, those of a certain age who grew up in Thabong, Welkom's black township, remember Hattingh well. Most black
people were not even aware of his Afrikaans name. He was known by
his Sesotho nickname, Dr. Molapo. Everyone was welcome in his medi-

cal practice, it was recalled, whether or not they could pay. He worked ceaselessly, opening soon after dawn, so that people could visit before work, closing after 10:00 p.m., when the last of his patients went home.[6] He was one of those unusual white South Africans, their stories barely recorded, who responded to apartheid in this way.

Hattingh's sister, Suzanne, who was studying medicine in Bloemfontein at the time, later recalled her brother's excitement at his burgeoning friendship with Winnie: the sixty-mile trip he made to Brandfort almost every day, despite his busy practice; the financial help he gave her – for several months, he heavily subsidized Winnie's and Zindzi's lives; the exhilaration he felt when sneaking her out of Brandfort in the early hours of the morning. His relationship with Winnie was dangerous, he told Suzanne; the security police were tailing him; he was feeling unsafe. At times she thought that he was making it all up; there was a breathlessness in his tales that smacked of fantasy.[7]

She was never certain, but Suzanne Hattingh suspected that her brother and Winnie were lovers. The security police, who bugged Winnie's phone conversations with him and listened in when he visited, were in no doubt. 'Dr. Hattingh,' a police officer wrote in an internal memo, 'on the pretext that he was giving medical services to her, paid regular visits to Mrs. Mandela who did not exactly hide the relationship.' Indeed, the memo continued, they displayed their amorous feelings for each other on the streets of the white town, scandalizing 'a shocked Brandfort public'.[8]

In October 1978, several months after meeting her, Hattingh offered Winnie a job. She would commute to Welkom each morning, run his surgery, and practice social work among his patients. It was the most exciting prospect; she would be out of the house from dawn until late, busy, working, absorbed in the lives of other human beings. She would also earn a salary. Until now, IDAF – the London-based fund Maud Katzenellenbogen and Moosa Dinath had used their friendship with Winnie to try to infiltrate – had secretly been funnelling a small stipend to her to keep her afloat.

She began the soul-destroying task of applying to the minister of law and order, who was responsible for her banning order, to take the job; it took months and a hefty pile of correspondence.

Finally, on the afternoon of March 5, 1979, the last of the paperwork permitting the arrangement was signed. At about eight that night, Hattingh closed his practice and set off from Welkom to see Winnie.

In the early hours of the following morning, Suzanne was woken by a phone call; her brother, she was told, had died in a car accident; she should come immediately to the mortuary to identify the body. The whole business took an age – waiting to see the corpse, filling in the paperwork – it was dawn by the time she arrived at the scene of her brother's death. The police said that he had hit a cow in the darkness, but there was no bovine corpse at the roadside, nor a trace of blood on the asphalt.

Suzanne knew the professor of forensic pathology who conducted the autopsy; she had just recently sat in his classes. Over the coming months, she asked him repeatedly for the report; there was always another reason why he could not share it just yet. In the decades to come, the suspicion never left her that the police had forced her brother off the road; finding him still alive in his car, they had smashed in his head.

After Chris Hattingh's funeral, which was attended by hundreds of Thabong's black residents, Suzanne was called outside to find Winnie Mandela waiting for her. They had never met before. By way of greeting, Winnie embraced her and wept. Then she asked Suzanne for her phone number and hurried off.

The two women met often. Winnie, Suzanne sensed, needed to see her, needed her proximity, needed the presence of a person who had been close to Chris Hattingh. She spoke of him ceaselessly, of how much he had meant to her, of how much he had done for her family. It struck Suzanne that Winnie was mourning him fiercely.[9]

Nearly three months after she was due to begin working for him, Winnie wrote to Mary Benson about the death of Chris Hattingh. 'They killed him and have got away with it,' she wrote, 'like the Steve Bikos, but this one is worse as the world will never know. I haven't got over the shock yet and I never knew I could grieve so much for someone other than my own kind. In a way it's taught me a deeper depth of love which might have been superficial or ideological, now it's real and honest for those who identify with us so completely.'[10]

· ·

Nobody felt the depths of Winnie's despair during her time in Brandfort as acutely as her husband.

In a dream Nelson had in April 1981, he and Winnie were in a hill-top cottage. Below them was a deep valley, bisected by a river. Winnie got up and walked down the hill, 'not as erect in your bearing as you usually are', he recounted to her in a letter, '& with your footsteps less confident. All the time your head was down, apparently searching for something a few paces from your feet. You crossed the river & carried away all my love, leaving me rather empty and uneasy.'

He waited. At the first sign of her return, he bounded down the hill to meet her.

'The prospect of joining you in the open air & in such beautiful surroundings evoked fond memories & I looked forward to holding your hand & to a passionate kiss.'

But he lost sight of her in the ravines and returned to the cottage alone to find that it was filled with his colleagues. Amid the crowd, he came upon Winnie 'stretched out on the floor in a corner, sleeping out depression, boredom and fatigue. I knelt down to cover the exposed parts of you with a blanket.'[11]

. .

Not long after Hattingh's death, Zindzi confided in the family doctor in Johannesburg that Winnie was drinking heavily. It was not just that she drank every night, Zindzi reported, it was that she did not stop until she was drunk. The doctor, who was considerably younger than Winnie, having met her in Black Consciousness circles in the early 1970s, raised the matter with her cautiously. Decades later, he vividly recalled her cold reply. 'Zindzi must be hallucinating,' she snapped. 'I do not drink.'[12]

. .

The most remarkable fact about the suffering of Winnie Mandela is this: she might have left Brandfort at any moment; she chose not to.

In July 1980, she was visited in her house by the national head of the Security Branch, Johann Coetzee.[13] Neither of them appears to have left a record of the encounter. Did she invite him to sit at her cramped kitchen table? One imagines that she forced him to conduct his business standing.

He had come to resolve an escalating problem. The most esteemed of Brandfort's white citizens were lobbying fiercely to have Winnie removed. They had in fact sent the justice minister, Alwyn Schlebusch, an ultimatum: if he failed to send her elsewhere, the municipal government would act unilaterally and simply throw her out.

Schlebusch was in a veritable panic. 'I am not prepared for Brandfort to carry the burden any longer,' he wrote to Coetzee in June 1980. 'They have made their contribution.' He instructed Coetzee to come up with an alternative by the end of August.[14]

Now Coetzee told Winnie that she could reside anywhere in South Africa she wished except for Greater Johannesburg, which, of course, included Soweto, just ten miles from the centre of Johannesburg. She would still be banned from participating in political life. But she could live in a city surrounded by other people and she could work.

She was tempted. Influential friends put out feelers in the corporate world. First, she was offered employment at the Sigma motor vehicle assembly plant in Pretoria. She turned it down because the proposed salary was too low. Two other motor companies, Datsun and BMW, also offered her work. Then a subsidiary of the South African conglomerate Anglo American offered to employ her, also in Pretoria, but for a much better wage.

One can only guess the turmoil she suffered deciding what to do. She applied for permission to live in Pretoria; permission was swiftly granted. At the last moment, she changed her mind. She would not leave Brandfort, her lawyer informed the Justice Ministry, unless her banning order was rescinded and she could return to Soweto.[15]

Schlebusch was incensed. 'She is fighting a psychological war in an effort not to lose her status as a martyr,' he complained to Coetzee.[16]

Of everything her enemies said of her, this was among the most insightful. Brandfort was destroying her. And yet the theatre she performed there was priceless. 'I am a living symbol of whatever is happening in the country,' she wrote during her banishment.[17] It was too precious to give up.

Only the churlish cannot admire her deeply. Her enemy had presented her with the starkest choice: her well-being or her political power. She would be damned if she played their game, she told her lawyer.[18] Defiantly, she stayed put.

.   .

There was another, more insidious dimension to the game the security police played.

From the moment she got to Brandfort, a stream of young people made contact with her, saying that they wanted to leave the country and join MK. It was natural that they should do so; she was among the most militant of her generation and the wife of MK's founder, to boot.

She soon found a route into exile for her young charges and a senior ANC leader to receive them. It happened through old Transkei connections. A cousin, Prince Madikizela, was a lawyer who worked in the magistrate's office in Umtata, the Transkei's capital. He had also, since the early 1960s, kept up ties with the handful of ANC personnel stranded in Lesotho and Swaziland. Both countries were landlocked, Lesotho surrounded entirely by South Africa, Swaziland by South Africa and the Portuguese colony of Mozambique: it was extremely difficult for ANC operatives to leave. Then, in 1975, when Portugal relinquished Mozambique and Frente de Libertação de Moçambique, which was sympathetic to the ANC, took power, a route suddenly opened from Lesotho and Swaziland to the outside world.

At precisely this time, in early 1975, a rising star in the ANC and MK, the thirty-two-year-old Chris Hani, established himself in Lesotho.[19] At some point after his arrival, probably sometime in 1977, he began receiving recruits from Winnie. She sent them to Prince Madikizela in Umtata; he used his position in the magistrate's court to provide them with legitimate travel documents; they crossed the border with a simple cover story and never returned.[20]

And so, the ANC in exile presented two quite different faces to Winnie Mandela. In Swaziland, Thabo Mbeki had tried to isolate her. In Lesotho, Chris Hani now received recruits from her. This duality – some wanting to neutralize her as wayward and dangerous, others profoundly moved by her audacity and her courage – had followed her all her days.

But there is a twist in this story's tail, and it changes the meaning of everything.

In early 1979, the ubiquitous Mac Maharaj – his time on Robben Island more than two years behind him, his new role to head the ANC's Political and Reconstruction Department – visited Chris Hani in Lesotho. Reporting on the operation he had established, Hani told Maharaj that he had received twelve recruits from Winnie Mandela.

Upon arrival, recruits were given pen and paper and instructed to sketch their life histories – where they grew up and went to school, through whom they became involved in politics, through whom they were recruited into MK. This simple exercise was extremely valuable; for those recruits who had been planted by the apartheid authorities, it took an unusual degree of skill to tell a credible tale.

By this measure, Hani told Maharaj, of the twelve people Winnie had sent to him, ten were plants.[21]

It was not just Chris Hani who detected the problem. In 1982, a prominent young activist, Wantu Zenzile, president of the recently formed Congress of South African Students, arrived in exile in Swaziland bearing messages from Winnie; it was she who had sent him, he said, and she who had arranged his safe passage. Within weeks, he confessed that in detention he had been tortured and turned and that the security police had expressly directed him to go to Winnie in Brandfort.[22]

The Zenzile debacle shocked the ANC's operatives in Swaziland and Mozambique, setting off a cycle of paranoia. In Maputo, one of them would recall, Jacob Zuma, at that time the ANC's deputy chief representative in Mozambique, opened a map of South Africa on a table. Ceremoniously, he took out a ruler and began to calculate the country's central point. 'What is the nearest town to this point?' she recalled him asking. 'Brandfort!' he exclaimed in answer to his own question. 'That is why they put her there. Everyone passes through the central point, no matter where they are going. They put her on a highway so that everyone would come to her and she would send them to us!'[23]

It was a wildly paranoid account of Winnie's situation. In banishing her to Brandfort, the South African government had made a terrible mistake, gifting the ANC a story too good to make up. What they were doing now is perhaps best understood as revenge. She might use her presence in Brandfort to broadcast a powerful tale to the world; *they* would use it to drip poison into the ANC, one plant at a time.

· ·

In Brandfort, Winnie was a famous icon, she was a recruiter of guerrilla soldiers, and she was the mother of two daughters.

Several months before her banishment, her older child, Zenani, who boarded at a private high school in Swaziland, fell pregnant. The family doctor, Joe Veriava, broke the news to Winnie. She was beside herself, he recalled, and went on at length about her failings as a mother. 'What is Nelson going to say?' she kept asking. 'He is going to be absolutely furious.'[24]

But not only had the child's father proposed marriage; he was, quite literally, a prince, the son of King Sobhuza of Swaziland. What Winnie thought might unfold as a scandalous schoolgirl pregnancy gave way to a royal wedding. Kaiser Daliwonga Matanzima came from the Transkei to Johannesburg to begin bridewealth negotiations with the king's people.[25] Then a delegation of Thembu notables travelled to Swaziland to break bread with their prospective in-laws.[26] Nelson, by all accounts, was thrilled. 'My father is a very traditional man,' Zenani told a journalist, 'and the fact that I, a member of the Thembu royal family, am marrying into a royal family, gives him great joy.'[27]

When Winnie was banished, Zenani was just beginning her new life in Swaziland. She watched her mother's Brandfort existence from afar.

It was another matter with Zindzi. Home for the holidays when the police came to take Winnie away, she went along to Brandfort.

For a long while now, people had remarked ad nauseam on her likeness to her mother. It was not just that she was beautiful, nor just her taste for fashion. It was her capacity, congenital, it seems, to command attention. 'My small daughter', Winnie wrote when Zindzi was nine years old, 'is an embarrassing extrovert', a child one had to 'pinch in time' before she mouthed off something inappropriate.[28] For as long as anyone could remember, she had, it seems, been irrepressibly charismatic.

And yet her charisma was deceptive if it suggested an independent spirit. Despite her evident willfulness, despite all the tales that have gathered on the way she could command a room, she did not, until deep into adulthood, forge an existence separate from her mother. There were always plans for her to start a life of her own. Friends in Britain arranged for her to study there, but she failed her A-levels and could not go. She tried to enroll at Wits University but did not have the qualifications. She began studying at the University of Cape Town (UCT) but abandoned her studies in order to return to her mother. She finally got into Wits, but failed her exams. She was forever returning not just to her mother but to an adjunctive role in her mother's dramatic life.

From the earliest times, Winnie appears to have possessed her daughters with furious jealousy.

'I once wrote to [Winnie] during the early seventies what I considered to be a romantic letter from a man who adored and worshipped his beloved wife,' Nelson recalled in correspondence with a friend. 'In the course of that letter I remarked that Zeni and Zindzi had grown beautifully and that I found it a real pleasure to chat with them. My beloved wife was furious and, when I reached the last line of her letter, I felt . . . very fortunate to be so far from her physically. Otherwise I would have lost my jugular vein. It was as if I had committed treason. She reminded me: "I, not you, brought up these children whom you now prefer to me!" I was simply stunned.'[29]

By the time of her banishment, the jealousy Winnie felt toward her daughters appears to have shifted exclusively to Zindzi. The traces are scant, but no less powerful for that.

Sixteen years old when she went to Brandfort with her mother, Zindzi had fallen in love some time earlier with a twenty-year-old man called Oupa Seakamela. Their relationship was very serious indeed. As early as July 1977, Nelson was writing to Zindzi and Oupa jointly. He was hungry to know more about Oupa, he wrote, but it seems Winnie had refused to speak of him. 'Zindzi once promised that Mum would tell me all about Oupa,' he wrote, 'but as you both know, she has always been hard pressed by pressure of work & other problems & up to now she has not been able to give me a full sketch. Perhaps,' he hinted heavily, 'Zindzi will now have to do it.'[30]

When Winnie was banished, Zindzi's initial intention was to stay for a while in Brandfort, then return to Swaziland to complete high school, and then marry Oupa Seakamela. She would not abandon her mother: she would visit on weekends and during holidays; she would be there when she could.

It was surely a reasonable proposition for a young woman beginning adulthood. Winnie was in the most difficult circumstances and Zindzi would provide support. But she would also prepare the foundations of her own life.

Winnie demurred; she wanted her daughter to stay with her in Brandfort. It is not hard to understand why. Coping with her banishment under any circumstances would have been hard enough; the prospect of enduring alone must have been terrifying.

It is the arguments Winnie deployed that command attention.

Zindzi was seeing a psychiatrist at the time of her mother's banishment. Now, in a letter to a friend, Winnie told of how shocked Zindzi was to hear her doctor's advice that she stay with her mother in Brand-fort; indeed, stay *all of the time* in Brandfort: the psychiatrist, Winnie claimed, had strongly advised Zindzi not to return to Swaziland for school.[31]

It is hard to imagine a psychiatrist advising a sixteen-year-old girl to leave her school to share in her mother's banishment. More plausible is that this is what *Winnie* made of the situation. If you separate from me, your health is in danger, Winnie appeared to be telling Zindzi. You must abandon *everything* to be with me, even school in Swaziland. The doctor himself says so.

It would appear that the doctor said no such thing. In an affida-vit he filed in a case to determine whether Zindzi was a member of her mother's household, he in fact wrote precisely the opposite. 'I am particularly concerned that Zinzi's [*sic*] inter-personal relationships at Brandfort have been rendered virtually non-existent,' he wrote. 'Part and parcel of the process towards the resolution of her problems depends on meaningful interaction with her friends.'[32]

In August 1978, Seakamela moved into the house in Brandfort. If Zindzi could not lead a life away from Winnie, she would bring it to her mother's house. The three were to become a fixture in Brandfort. Everyone who met Winnie met Zindzi and Oupa, too. They were, by all accounts, a charming and companionable couple.

Two years passed before Zindzi finally spent an extended time away from Brandfort; plans were afoot for her to attend university in the U.K., and she went to Helen Joseph's house in Johannesburg to study for her A-levels.

She did not get her A-levels, of course, and she did not go to the U.K.; she returned to Brandfort.

Chapter 41

'Sometimes I feel like one who is on the sidelines, who has missed life itself,' Nelson wrote to Winnie in January 1979. 'Touching your hand or hugging you as you moved up & down the house, enjoying your delicious dishes, the unforgettable hrs in the bedroom, make life taste like honey.'

As so often in his letters, he suddenly turned to an uncomfortable subject:

> On 2/12 Zindzi hinted that she & you planned to be here on her birthday. I looked forward to that day as I would be seeing both of you [together] for the first time. But on the morning of that dy I prayed that you might not come. Unconsciously, during the previous dy & night I worked a little harder than I realised. I thought the eyes might betray me again, much to your concern as when Zindzi visited me on 21/10. I was, therefore, much relieved when you did not turn up.[1]

He writes obscurely, in part to shelter from prying eyes, and, perhaps, too, because he is embarrassed. Subsequent gossip among prison warders who witnessed the incident makes its nature clearer: the previous October, Zindzi had come to see him, and he had mistaken her for his wife.

Zindzi, one assumes, reported what had happened to her mother. Winnie's reaction, probably in a letter, is inaccessible. But it must have been severe. For Nelson now woke to discover that he was dreading seeing her.

One wonders whether it was a moment of revelation for Winnie. She had long understood that Nelson's view of her was frozen in time. 'I often wonder', she had written to him back in 1970, 'if your memory of me isn't . . . of a trembling little girl [standing] next to you in a shabby little back veld church.'

Every subsequent letter he wrote to her must have deepened her unease. Here was a man replaying, over and over, a romance from 1958. Those encounters on Robben Island, he on one side of the glass, she on the other: she must have known that they carried into that room increasingly discrepant views of each other, of their marriage, of whatever future they might have together.

She had not actually *seen* him, she wrote in the early 1980s, since before he went to jail. 'The lighting [in the visiting room on Robben Island] was very bad and the glass partition so thick—I could never see a clear picture of him, just a silhouette really.'²

Did she wonder how on earth they would make a marriage were he to be freed? It was probably unfathomable, a question to be put off.

Chapter 42

Cape Town winters are notoriously inclement. Drizzle falls monotonously for days on end. Out at sea, squalls bring sudden bursts of rain and sleet.

On the *Susan Kruger*, the ferry bearing visitors to Robben Island, inmates' loved ones were confined to the top deck, no matter the season, by virtue of the colour of their skins. They disembarked in duffle coats, thick jackets and blankets, brought from home to fend off the wind and the wet.

On an August morning in 1980, Winnie Mandela arrived on Robben Island with an infant in the folds of her blanket. The child was Zindzi's firstborn, Zoleka, brought from the mainland to meet her grandfather. She was four months old. Such an encounter was strictly forbidden; nobody under the age of sixteen was permitted to visit a prisoner; Nelson had been denied meetings with his own children until they came of age.

The first member of staff to catch sight of the child was a twenty-year-old warder named Christo Brand. When the time came to usher her to Nelson, he instructed Winnie to leave the infant in the waiting room in the care of others. She protested briefly, then quickly obeyed.

Tasked with monitoring Nelson's visits, Brand sat behind his prisoner, a receiver clasped to his ear. He could see only the back of Nelson's head when Winnie told him that his grandchild was not a hundred paces away. Decades later, he recalled Nelson's face when he turned around: it bore a wistfulness so intense that he had to look away.

'Please, Mr. Brand,' Nelson asked. 'Is it possible to see the baby? Please let me see this little child.'

He would lose his job if he relented, Brand explained. There was nothing he could do.

As the visit went on, his prisoner's agitation seemed only to grow. Twice more, Nelson turned around in his chair to ask his warder to

make an exception. Twice more, Brand refused. Once Winnie had left
the room, Nelson shot the final arrow in his quiver: could Brand at least
arrange that he watch his wife as she left the island carrying the child?
Again, Brand said no.

. .

Christo Brand had known Nelson Mandela a little less than a year.
He was nineteen years old on the day they met; Nelson was almost
sixty-one. Why this teenage warder came to see Nelson the way he did
is hard to say, but he did not see the monstrous terrorist of whom his
superiors had spoken; he saw a man in a state of sorrow.[1]

It was in part the things Brand noticed about Nelson's relationship
with his wife. He had been on Robben Island just a few weeks the first
time Winnie came to visit. As he walked with Brand from B Section,
Nelson had dropped to a crouch and picked a Namaqualand daisy from
the side of the path. In the visiting room, he had put it in Winnie's line
of sight on his side of the glass.[2]

There were other moments. Once, Brand looked on as a warder
told Nelson not to bother waiting for letters from Winnie; the authorities, the warder said, had discovered that she had yet another new boyfriend, this one a member of the Security Branch.

'Sir,' Brand recalled Nelson answering quietly. 'I am inside here,
powerless. She is a flesh-and-blood human being living in the outside
world. I can't be jealous about what she is doing, or tell her what she can
and cannot do.'[3]

Brand admired Nelson for his self-control. But behind it, he sensed
deep anguish. His senior colleagues were torturing Nelson, he understood, even if his poise concealed his pain.[4]

But what struck Brand most forcefully was a spectacle that recurred
on B Section like clockwork for half an hour each morning and again at
dusk: the figure of Nelson, alone, tending his garden.

The plot ran against the southern boundary of B Section's courtyard, fifty feet long by eight feet wide. While Nelson had planted
wildflowers along the border, Brand noticed, his real interest was in
growing food: tomatoes, carrots, onions, spinach, and even a peach
sapling.[5]

Robben Island is a cruel host for a gardener. Flat and almost treeless,
the Cape's southeaster whips across it with fury. Nelson had learned to

grow vegetables in the fecund hills of the Transkei, where everyone's fingers are green. Here, Brand noticed at once, he was struggling.

And it happened that the youngster had some wisdom to impart. Having grown up on a farm outside the coastal hamlet of Stanford, he knew a thing or two about gardening in a southeaster. On one of his biweekly visits to the mainland, Brand bought some netting. The following Monday morning, he stood respectfully at the edge of Nelson's garden and offered help. That evening, the two were crouched together, discussing how best to protect the most tender of Nelson's plants from the weather.

By the time Winnie stole her granddaughter onto the island, Nelson and Brand had become something of a fixture: the elderly African and the young Afrikaner, standing in the twilight before a narrow strip of land, conferring in the politest tones about pigeon droppings and rainwater.

· ·

Now, as Brand walked back into the visitors' centre, where Winnie was waiting for the ferry, she took 200 rand from her handbag, £315 in today's values, and tried to place it in his hand. 'Please, sir,' he remembered her asking, 'let my husband see the baby for a few seconds.'

He declined once more. Instead, he asked Winnie if he could hold the child. He had never held an African baby in his arms, he told her awkwardly in explanation. Then he asked her to follow him back to the interview room, for she and Nelson had forgotten to confer about seeking a permit for her to visit at Christmas. He locked her in the booth, went around to Nelson's side, where the microphones were now turned off and the window looking onto his visitor was closed. He handed Nelson the child.

To his astonishment, Nelson's eyes were soon wet with tears. He dropped his head, kissed the baby on the cheek, and then handed her back to Brand. Winnie was not two feet away from this scene and had no idea what had transpired.[6]

Two decades passed before Nelson talked of the incident to Brand; during the remainder of his time as a prisoner, neither man mentioned it.[7] What had passed between them was very complex indeed. A distinguished man in late middle age had to beg a fresh-faced boy to hold and kiss his own flesh and blood: the scene arose from the deep centuries of racial humiliation.

And yet, that is hardly the end of what the encounter might mean. They were enclosed in a room, the door locked, the microphones off, the hatch to the window shut. In this secrecy, Brand had made an offering upon which he wagered his career. In that resides an ancient kernel of friendship – making oneself vulnerable to another, offering him one's trust.

Chapter 43

Late one afternoon in April 1982, a phalanx of senior prison warders walked unannounced into Nelson's cell. He was to pack his belongings at once, he was told, for he was being transferred to a mainland prison. The warders moved on to the cells of Walter Sisulu, Raymond Mhlaba and Andrew Mlangeni: they were going, too.

Nelson had been on Robben Island more than seventeen years. It took him less than half an hour to pack. The four were marched summarily down the corridor, their comrades left to guess from the boxes they carried that they were not coming back.*[1]

Of all the cruelties Robben Islanders suffered, this violent uprooting offended most. However cramped and unchosen, the space one inhabits has become one's own. The photograph of one's wife at eye level next to one's desk; the line of law books on the shelf to one's left; the old *Oxford Atlas,* always in reach so that the mind can wander at will: to the extent that one has acquired some mastery over one's world, it is a mastery ingrained in that space. More than that, one has been thrown into a life with companions one did not choose; learning to tolerate them, learning to be tolerated by them, has been hard, hard work. 'You have lived with these people so many years,' Nelson's fellow B Section inmate Laloo Chiba commented about his own abrupt departure, 'and you are not given the courtesy of saying farewell.'[2]

They were ferried to the mainland, bundled into a truck, and driven for forty minutes through the darkness. At journey's end, their guards led them up three flights of stairs and into a large cell: it was fifty by thirty feet, in each corner, a bed with sheets, blankets, pillows and towels.[3]

---

* Walter Sisulu remembers things differently. In his recollection, Nelson was in the hospital when he, Mlangeni and Mhlaba were transferred.

They were in Pollsmoor Prison, just fifteen miles from the centre of Cape Town.

The men had been moved on the orders of South Africa's justice minister, Kobie Coetsee. He was troubled by the hegemony the ANC had come to command on Robben Island. The prison had become a place, he believed, where young activists learned at the feet of ANC leaders and then returned to seed its influence in the world.

It was thus not enough to take key ANC leaders off the island; they were to be sealed off entirely from other prisoners. At Pollsmoor, the presence of the four men – soon to be five, when Kathrada joined them six months later – was kept secret from the rest of the prison; nobody but a handful of select warders could enter the floor of the building they occupied; they were sequestered in their own world.

It was quite different from Robben Island. They had flushing toilets and hot-water showers; there was linen on the beds: these were comforts Nelson had not known in twenty years. There were also freedoms unheard of before: the prisoners had an FM radio and could listen to stations that broadcast from South Africa; they could read uncensored copies of local newspapers as well as *Time* and the *Guardian Weekly* from abroad. They had never before in their careers as prisoners been quite this close to the outside world.[4]

But this life brought new difficulties, too. Nelson had spent most of each day on Robben Island alone. Now, from the moment he woke to the moment he slept, there were the voices of others, the eyes of others, the tics and the habits of aging men.

He began immediately to look for refuge.

The cell opened onto the building's rooftop, a walled area fifteen feet wide and seventy feet long. Taking in the space and the sunlight, Nelson wrote to the head of the prison requesting material for a garden. Fifteen forty-four-gallon drums were duly delivered; they were cut in half lengthways to produce thirty giant pots. Soil, vegetable seeds and a set of basic implements were brought from prison grounds.

Within months of his arrival, Nelson was working on his plants for several hours each day.[5] His gardening was scrupulous, systematic. He read as widely as he could about technique, made a careful record of his own evolving practice, and was fastidious about recording his yield. It was soon extensive. He grew onions, eggplants, cabbage, cauliflower, beans, spinach, carrots, cucumbers, broccoli, beetroot, lettuce, tomatoes, peppers and strawberries. At its height, his garden boasted almost nine hundred individual plants. On Sundays, he harvested, offering some of his yield to warders and sending the rest to the prison kitchen.[6]

He had come to cultivate a vast world, one that lay within the prison walls but lived by rhythms of its own.

Although he worked largely in solitude, he occasionally invited Walter Sisulu to join him. Their friendship now forty-one years old, they'd labour together in wide-brimmed straw hats and gardening gloves, mainly in silence.

Once, Nelson looked up from his work and pointed his trowel at Sisulu.

'Do you see this man here?' he asked, addressing himself to a warder who was gardening with them. 'He is why I am here. He took me into politics when I was a mere boy. Then he found me a wife. Then he took me deeper into politics. My punishment is that I am forced to grow old with him here.'

Sisulu, the warder recalled, chortled quietly without looking up from his work.[7]

. .

The rest of Nelson's life was communal. Who thought of it is lost now, but his garden left sufficient space on the rooftop for a tennis court. The prisoners applied for white paint and string to draw the court's lines. From the Red Cross came tennis rackets, poles and a net, footwear, balls and clothes. It was a truncated court, too short and far too narrow, which was perhaps just as well, for none of the players were getting younger.[8]

Nelson was nearly sixty-four when he was moved to Pollsmoor; Sisulu turned seventy less than six weeks after they arrived; Raymond Mhlaba was sixty-one. Andrew Mlangeni and Ahmed Kathrada were a sprightly fifty-six and fifty-two, respectively.

There was a doubleness to the existence of these men. They had been sealed up in this place because their influence had been deemed too great, and during his time in this prison Nelson would indeed become among the most influential people in the world. But they were also men growing grey together, the conditions of their lives rendering them prematurely old.

Their aging was nowhere clearer than in their relation to Christo

Brand. He had been transferred to Pollsmoor shortly before they arrived; now he was one among the select warders assigned to their cell.

It was something of a refuge for him. Pollsmoor was a wild prison, the relationship between warders and the infamous 'Number' gangs one of heart-stopping violence.[9] To be locked up all day with a group of placid, genteel men was something of a blessing. Soon, Brand was playing table tennis with them, his torso naked, his warder's jacket and shirt draped over a chair.

As time wore on, his connection with them grew increasingly complex. He was, on the one hand, an agent of their enemy: he spied on them through the one-way glass that looked into their cell; on occasion he was instructed to wear a bug.

But he became, too, a dedicated factotum to increasingly fussy men.

Each of the prisoners could spend up to 25 rand a month at the prison tuckshop. Since they were not permitted to enter the prison at large, Brand did their buying for them. Soon, he offered them much more: he would leave the prison grounds on his motorbike and head for a large supermarket; combing the aisles, he would record the prices of dozens of items. His prisoners pored over the lists he had made, each with pencil in hand, calculating what he could afford to buy. Brand then returned to the supermarket with each man's order in his pocket: Sisulu and Kathrada usually asked for coffee, Nelson for muesli rusks, Sensodyne toothpaste and an Oral-B toothbrush. Brand walked the aisles clutching five baskets, one for each prisoner; he paid for their purchases separately, making sure that nobody spent over his monthly limit.

His services soon grew more elaborate. Once, he offered Nelson half of a sandwich he had brought from home. Nelson murmured with pleasure as he chewed and asked Brand what sort of bread he had just eaten. It was whole wheat, which Nelson had never tasted before. Now he wanted five loaves a month, enough for his breakfast every day. But bread, of course, goes stale when bought only monthly. And so Brand put it in his freezer at home and brought a quarter of a loaf at a time, already sliced to the thickness Nelson preferred.

The secret life the two men had begun in the visiting room on Robben Island grew more intricate. Once, when they were alone together, Brand put his finger to his lips, showed Nelson a tiny microphone attached to the button of his prison jacket, and then touched his ear. Their conversation, he wanted Nelson to understand, was being monitored live. Then he delivered the question he had been told to ask:

'Mandela, how would you feel if you heard that Winnie was sleeping with other men?'

Brand became increasingly attuned to Nelson's moods. Sometimes his prisoner could not bear the company of his cellmates any longer, Brand noticed; so he offered to lock Nelson in a warder's office, a place strictly barred to inmates. Once, when he returned to let Nelson out, Brand found him boiling with rage. His bladder full, his pounding on the door unheard, he had urinated out of the window. Now, his voice curt, his anger unmasked, he demanded a bucket of water to clean up the mess he had made.

Nelson was forty years Brand's senior and a man of enormous pride. The line between caring for his charge and humiliating him, Brand understood, was awfully fine.[10]

· ·

As if to remind them that they were getting no younger, Nelson and Sisulu between them underwent four bouts of surgery while they were together at Pollsmoor, Sisulu for a prostate procedure, Nelson twice for his prostate, once for a growth on the back of his head.

Brand was there when the growth was removed, scrubbed up, in a surgical gown, mask and hat. He watched Nelson lose consciousness, watched the skin being pulled from his skull and the growth being cut away. In the recovery room, he stood attentively over his charge, waiting for him to open his eyes.[11]

He was there again for Nelson's first bout of prostate surgery. This time, he was joined in the recovery room by a second warder who succumbed to the temptation to play a nasty game. 'We have had to hide you away because people are threatening to kill you,' the warder had whispered into the unconscious Nelson's ear. 'People calling you a kaffir have said that they want you dead.'

Nelson had woken later in a state of alarm, his memory of the threat vivid. 'You were just dreaming,' Brand reassured him. 'You are safe.' Groggy, confused, Nelson told Brand that he needed urgently to relieve himself. Finding that his prisoner was too disoriented to use his hands, Brand put a urine bottle to Nelson's penis.[12]

· ·

One morning in the winter of 1984, Nelson and Brand made their way to the reception area for a regular visit from Winnie. When they got to the visiting booths, they were shooed on and led to a small room. Minutes later, Winnie walked in and threw her arms around Nelson. He had been given no notice, no time to compose himself: for the first time in twenty-two years, he was touching his wife.

The way Brand recalled it, Nelson briefly lost his bearings. He was nervous, jittery, hugging her, kissing her, hugging her again. They sat down, holding hands, looked at each other, and giggled. Nelson customarily brought a notebook and pencil to his encounters with Winnie. He was forever asking her to send messages, to see to family matters, and made lists of his requests. Now he did not know what to do with his hands. He put the notebook down so that he was free to touch his wife. Then he picked it up again awkwardly and paged through it.

He was like a fumbling teenage boy finally alone with his girl.[13]

HEADLONG

. . .

Chapter 44

In September 1978, while Nelson was serving his seventeenth year in prison, Winnie her second year of banishment, a storm erupted at the summit of South African power. In the midst of a funding scandal and a brewing palace coup, Prime Minister John Vorster, who had ruled since 1966, resigned. His place was taken by a man who had served in his cabinet throughout his long term of office: P. W. Botha.

What had happened was much more than the substitution of one leader for another. A quite different sensibility, a different canon of concepts and ideas – one that had been evolving out of sight, behind the doors of training academies, offices, and boardrooms – now came out into the world.

South Africa's new prime minister had contempt for the man he replaced. Vorster was inert and visionless, in Botha's view, and the civil service he had built was chaotic and amateurish. He wished to regear the organs of state to do something new.

Botha had been minister of defense for the past twelve years and came to office saturated in this experience. The military, he believed, was among a handful of public institutions in South Africa capable of executing complex tasks. He set about centralizing power and placed the military at the heart of his regime. A previously moribund committee, the State Security Council, consisting largely of cabinet ministers in security portfolios, was revived. It was given its own extensive implementing apparatus, the National Security Management System, with line functions extending into regions throughout the country.[1]

What Botha built was a shadow executive branch attached to a shadow bureaucracy. So armed, he set to work.

Botha's strategic thinking had also grown from his exposure to the South African Defence Force. For some while now, the country's military academies had been preoccupied with the lessons of France's war in Algeria. The writings of the French general André Beaufre had acquired something of a biblical status among the strategists in apartheid's army. To be conversant with his work was a benchmark of intellectual competence. To read him in the original French was to be a high priest.[2]

At the core of Beaufre's doctrine of counterinsurgency was the idea that the war was won or lost not militarily but psychologically. One's real enemy, the doctrine proposed, was in fact quite small in number; one's primary task was to isolate him by winning the allegiance of the general population. And since one controlled the state apparatus, the balance of forces was tilted heavily in the government's favour; one had both the hard power to crush the enemy's spirit and the soft power to give his potential constituency a measure of well-being.

Following Beaufre, the thinkers around Botha spoke of a 'total strategy', total because the operational theatre now spilled over from the battlefield into *all* spheres of life: the media, the classroom, the workplace, the built environment, the structures of political representation.[3]

It is striking how large Algeria loomed in imaginations on either side of South Africa's great political divide. From Algerian freedom fighters in Morocco, Nelson Mandela had learned back in 1962 the most significant lesson of his political career: that the apartheid government could not be defeated outright and would have to be negotiated out of power. From Algeria, Botha believed he had learned the opposite lesson: that through an adroit combination of warfare and reform, the ANC could be slayed.

Acting with urgency, Botha implemented wide-ranging reforms. And in keeping with the central tenets of apartheid thinking, he envisaged different fates for white, black, Coloured, and Indian South Africans.

The reforms concerning black people were far-reaching indeed. Legislation was passed giving black trade unions legal recognition. Black people who had lived and worked in 'white' South Africa longer than a decade were now considered permanent residents. The leases on homes like that of Nelson and Winnie Mandela were extended from thirty to ninety-nine years, and there was talk of transferring those leases into title deeds. Legislation was drafted to create a new system of black local government with the power to tax residents and to change the built environment.

To Coloureds and Indians, Botha offered something grander. Indeed, the diva at the centre of his great opera, adorned in gown and jewels, her very entrance to the stage subjected to a referendum among the white members of the audience, was a brand-new national legislature. South Africa's parliament would no longer be exclusively white. A new 'tricameral' parliament, with separate chambers for whites, Coloureds and Indians, was presented to the world.

Everyone save the country's black majority would vote in national elections.

It was a beguiling concoction. On the one hand, the reforms were substantial. Black workers at the heart of the industrial economy now had the right to strike. Swathes of people long considered visitors in white South Africa were now permanent residents. Botha had, without question, given black people tangible power.

And yet the script of the drama had been written alone; there was not a single black co-author. And the all-white authorship showed: the highest elected position open to a black politician in Botha's new order was that of mayor in a racially segregated local government.

Indeed, Botha's intense need to dominate shaped his project. Never mind sharing power with unfamiliar faces: he did not even trust his own cabinet to make executive decisions nor his own civil service to implement them. To centralize power so tightly while dispersing it: paradoxes like these do not lend credibility to the story one tells. 'We Afrikaners are trying to find the secret to sharing power without losing control,' a business leader close to Botha said, his bluffness exposing the anxiety at the heart of the project.[4]

With hindsight we know that Botha failed. A decade after he came to power, his successor unbanned the ANC and released Nelson Mandela, beginning a nation's short journey to majority rule. But exactly *how* Botha failed is not obvious, not even in hindsight. Accurately describing the character of the forces he unwittingly unleashed is so important, for these forces shaped the subsequent careers of Winnie and Nelson Mandela.

. .

Botha would have done well to heed the words of another Frenchman, one whose thinking was both deeper and more expansive than that of a military strategist like Beaufre. 'The social order destroyed by a revolution is almost always better than that which immediately preceded it,' Alexis de Tocqueville famously wrote in his account of the French Revolution, 'and experience shows that the most dangerous time for a bad government is when it sets about reform.'[5]

It is not just that reform raises expectations. Something more interesting than that is at play. When a ruler institutes reforms, he by that very act provides his enemy with a platform to contest them, a *legal* platform. To reform is to give your enemy a legitimate place in your own order and to risk him destroying it from within.

In the case of which Tocqueville wrote, Louis XVI called an ancient forum, the Estates General, which had not sat in centuries, to ratify dramatic changes to the tax regime. It was a forum *he* called, unearthed from the depths of his own constitutional order, and its activities set in train what became the French Revolution.

What happened to Botha was not dissimilar. Every one of his major reforms created a sphere in which his enemy bettered him. In 1979, he legalized black trade unions, his aim to split workers between urban insiders and migrant outsiders. By 1985, much of the black working class was organized; its leaders called wave upon wave of general strikes, periodically bringing the economy to a standstill.[6]

Botha's flagship reform, the new Tricameral Parliament, opened another new front that he had to defend. In August 1983, three months before whites were to decide whether to accept the new arrangement, a great coalition rose to oppose it. It comprised churches, civic associations, youth, women's and student groups, even sports clubs. Its work among prospective Coloured and Indian voters was devastatingly effective. When elections for the new parliament were held in 1984, voter turnout among those who were not white was negligible. Those elected to office were pilloried as stooges.

More than that, the coalition itself took an organizational form. Launched with bunting, flags and song at a mass rally in Cape Town, it was called the United Democratic Front (UDF). Without apology, it revived the Charterist tradition of the banned ANC: describing itself as 'non-racial', celebrating anniversaries like the writing of the Freedom Charter, it wrote its own story as a chapter in the quest for freedom led by Oliver Tambo and Nelson Mandela.[7]

And so here was a legal entity, its books audited, its taxes paid, its support for a banned movement barely concealed. Botha had resurrected a version of his enemy inside his country's borders, with a licence to organize and to speak. The commanders of his security apparatus were acutely aware of the irony. Years later, Johan van der Merwe, apartheid South Africa's last commissioner of police, still expressed his frustration: the intention of the UDF's leaders, he recalled, was quite clearly to destroy the existing order, and yet they were breaking no law.[8]

. .

Something else happened in response to Botha's reforms, something more dramatic, more frightening, and, quite literally, more incendiary than the launch of an organization.

The new version of black local government Botha introduced was self-funding; to raise revenue, it had to hike rents and service charges among the residents who fell within its jurisdictions. The early 1980s was a time of economic recession in South Africa, as it was through much of the world. The unemployment rate was higher than ever before in the country's history.[9] It was not a good time to tell people to pay for a new form of government whose legitimacy was dubious already.[10]

On September 3, 1984, in Sharpeville, site of the famous 1960 massacre, residents rose in revolt against rent increases. 'All day long,' one commentator wrote, 'angry mobs roamed the streets, burning businesses, government buildings, and cars; throwing stones; battling with police.'[11]

In the early afternoon, when the last of the township's public buildings was on fire, the mob turned its anger on the houses of municipal councillors. Those unlucky enough to be at home were dragged into the street and slaughtered.[12] They were not the only ones to die that day. Several of the rioters, some of them children, were shot dead by police. By the end of the week, the fallen numbered forty, among them the deputy mayors of Sharpeville and neighbouring Evaton.[13]

Within days, the revolt had spread to neighbouring townships; within months, to the coastal cities of East London and Port Elizabeth, and to several towns in the interior of the eastern Cape. Other parts of the country, including Winnie and Nelson Mandela's Soweto, were slower to join. But by the end of 1985, much of black South Africa was in a state of revolt.

The outstanding feature of the uprising was its spontaneity. Nobody had organized it. The organizations that had arisen in response to Botha's reforms were to all intents and purposes spectators. 'We were trailing behind the masses,' one of the UDF's early leaders reflected some time later.[14]

A second striking feature of the revolt was its youthfulness; high school students across the country boycotted classes and poured onto the streets, where they were joined by older youths from the ranks of the unemployed. And they were not just young: they were overwhelmingly male. The teenagers who took to the streets on June 16, 1976, in their blazers and school shoes were equally divided between the sexes. Now those on the front lines were largely boys and young men.[15]

The spirit of the revolt was starkly Manichaean; the world was divided between the uprising and its enemy, and everybody was told to choose sides. This found expression not just in the killing of municipal councillors and the destruction of government property but in other forms, too. Early in the troubles calls went out for the residents of black townships to boycott white-owned businesses. Youths surrounded train stations and taxi terminuses and searched middle-aged commuters returning from work. If they were found to have bought groceries in town, they were punished. The spectacle of teenage boys forcing elderly women to drink the cooking oil they had purchased became a feature of these early days.

Another remarkable feature of the revolt was the homage it paid to the ANC.

It was a rebellion conducted in song and dance. No crowd formed without singing, whatever the context – melody was the signature of the rebellion – and the crowds sang of Oliver Tambo and Nelson Mandela. These two elderly men, the days of their law practice now nearly three decades old, were rendered mythical, almost godlike, their return promising a rebirth of the world.

It was not just that the revolt worshipped Mandela and Tambo. It worshipped them as soldiers. 'Umkhonto we Sizwe is everywhere,' went the lyrics of the most popular freedom song of the time. And the signature dance of the revolt – the *toyi-toyi* – was an improvised military drill, the dancers holding imaginary Kalashnikov rifles, their voices imitating the sound of gunfire.

On the face of it, the ANC's abiding dream had come true. Way back, in late 1962, when Govan Mbeki and Joe Slovo had written 'Operation Mayibuye', they conjured a phalanx of guerrillas inspiring South Africa's masses to rise. Now the masses had indeed risen, the name of the ANC's army on their tongues.

From exile, the organization lent the uprising its support. 'In every locality and in all parts of the country,' Thabo Mbeki urged in mid-September on Radio Freedom, an ANC propaganda arm, 'we must destroy the enemy organs of government.'[16] And in his annual message delivered four months later, Tambo called upon the masses to render South Africa ungovernable.[17]

And yet, while the talk sounded bold, the voice was that of a spectator 'shouting from the sidelines', as an astute commentator put it.[18] The ANC was quite incapable of leading an insurrection. In the midst of losing its capacity to work from Mozambique and Lesotho – the result of an accord signed that same year between South Africa and Mozambique – its operational lines into South Africa were severely damaged.

The situation throughout 1985 was awfully mercurial; it took hard and rigorous minds to think clearly.

A genuine insurrection was under way. Should the flames of the uprising be fanned in the hope that the apartheid regime itself catches fire and explodes?

On the other hand, an ensemble of formidable organizations had recently evolved: the trade union movement, the UDF. Their power lay in their legality. Should the lines between insurrection and legal campaigning vanish, it is these precious organizations that might go up in flames.

How to name the struggle against apartheid: Was it a revolution? Or was its mainstay a peaceful movement for fundamental change?

These questions divided people in the UDF at home and in the ANC abroad. They agitated old wounds on Robben Island and in Pollsmoor. And they also, for the first time in their long union, revealed to Winnie and Nelson Mandela whom, exactly, each had married.

Chapter 45

That Winnie Mandela might watch a revolution at a distance was always unlikely. Never mind that she was banished to a corner of the Free State: from its earliest stirrings, in 1980, a full three years before the formation of the UDF, she had done her utmost not just to get involved but to lead. And she had done so, as had now long been her way, through a consuming relationship with a lover.

'[You will find a] rather strange-looking fellow called Matthews Malefane who lives with Winnie as a general factotum – bodyguard guard (what have you?),' the liberal parliamentarian Helen Suzman wrote to a colleague as she coached him in preparation for visiting Brandfort. 'Don't be put off by his appearance – he's a Rastafarian.'[1]

That parenthetical 'what have you?' is the loveliest addition; it is both a primly raised eyebrow and a tribute from one powerful older woman to another. For the 'strange-looking' M.K. Malefane was a strikingly beautiful twenty-one-year-old man when he moved in with the middle-aged Winnie. Suzman could scarcely hold back her curiosity.

The very sight of Malefane wagged tongues. 'I don't think anyone in our little rural town had seen a man with dreadlocks before,' the son of Winnie's Brandfort lawyer recalled. 'And here was this incredibly handsome man with his hair dancing around his shoulders. People stared.'[2]

It was Zindzi who introduced Malefane to Winnie on one of her permitted visits to Soweto. He was just embarking upon adult life, an aspiring fine artist. But now – as with Zindzi and her education, as with Peter Magubane and his career as a photographer, as with Brian Somana and his young family – Malefane took position as a satellite in a planet's orbit, his own life project on hold.

Soon after he moved in with Winnie, he began to paint her. On the wall of her tiny living room, throughout her last years in Brandfort, his portrait of her hung. Composed in the grandiose style of socialist realism, not uncommon in the artwork of the anti-apartheid struggle, it has Winnie gazing fiercely into the future.[3]

He was painting her as the leader of a revolution, and – as improbable as it may seem in the context of her banishment – in his day-to-day life he set about trying to make her so.

.   .

The earliest beginnings of the UDF were a series of study groups formed by veterans of the 1976 uprisings; the most consequential were in Soweto, Durban and Cape Town; their key members all became leading figures in the UDF.[4] Watching from a distance, chafing against her exclusion, Winnie asked Malefane to form a study group of his own, the Youth African Study Association, in the early summer of 1980.[5] She also sent him out to roam the Free State's towns in search of young men.

Years later, one of those recruited, Gregory Nthatisi, remembered Malefane approaching him on the streets of Mangaung, the black township adjoined to Free State's provincial capital, Bloemfontein.

'So one day . . . a Rastafarian was just walking around Bloemfontein asking to see comrades,' Nthatisi said. 'He met some other people who . . . brought him to me. And this man told me that Winnie Mandela would like to see me in Brandfort. I didn't trust this man . . . I didn't understand. I didn't know Mrs. Mandela.'[6]

Intrigued, Nthatisi made inquiries with his grandmother and discovered that he had distant relatives in Brandfort. Armed with their address, and thus with an excuse to be a young black man on the streets of a strange town, he took the train from Bloemfontein. After two nervous days with his relatives, he plucked up the courage to walk past Winnie's house. Finding the front door open, he simply went inside.

She welcomed him with enthusiasm, and he returned the next week and the week after that. Over the following months, she sent him to Cape Town and Port Elizabeth with travel money in his pocket and instructions to recruit more young men. Once he had assembled a dozen or so willing youths, she told him to bring them to Brandfort. They were arrested at the entrance to the township, the police clearly aware that they were coming. Just Nthatisi himself got away. Winnie arranged to have him smuggled into Swaziland, where he stayed with Zenani for a while before joining MK.[7]

There was a daftness to what Winnie was doing – trawling strange youths from the streets of dusty towns to sit at her feet and learn. But there was, too, extraordinary self-belief: the idea that a two-person show, Malefane and she, could assemble a national network of young men, *any* young men; that the sheer force of her presence might instill in them the deepest loyalty. This was not crazy at all; it presaged what was famously to come.

Soon, she embarked upon an even more audacious plan. During the course of 1981, Malefane travelled the country and met with leading anti-apartheid figures. He briefed them on a plan to begin a nationwide front, dubbed Maluti, which would finally reunite the ANC and the PAC. When asked where the idea came from, he said enigmatically that it had Winnie's backing, implying that it had been sanctioned by the ANC.

The idea was mysterious and caused a flurry of concern among activists across the country. 'We were worried,' recalled an ANC underground operative, Popo Molefe, who later became the national secretary of the UDF. 'We thought that it was an attempt to set up a movement to rival the African National Congress.'

Eventually, Molefe went to see Winnie in Brandfort. 'I explained to her', he said, 'that there was no way in which such an organisation could get off the ground if people who mattered were not consulted on the issue, and that there was no clarity as to what this organisation was all about, what was its objective.' Winnie, he recalled, looked back at him incredulously. But it was sanctioned by the ANC, she said. 'Our representatives in Swaziland, Lesotho, Botswana and Lusaka have given it the go-ahead,' Malefane chipped in.[8]

None of this was true. ANC operatives in Swaziland and Mozambique were in fact as alarmed about Winnie's idea as Molefe and certainly had not given it their blessings.[9]

One senses that for Winnie the question of who did or did not sanction the idea was beside the point. 'In my husband's absence I am the leader of my people,' she had written from prison back in 1970. In the intervening years the idea that she, personally, embodied the revolution had only grown stronger.

. .

For a brief period in the early 1990s, M.K. Malefane spoke with candour about his relationship with Winnie.

'We talked and talked,' he recalled to a journalist about the day he met her. 'She wanted to find out about my political commitment – I wasn't interested. I wanted to talk about philosophy or poetry.'

The mismatch of interests did nothing to dissipate the sexual chemistry.

'She had a string of appointments – people waiting outside her house to see her. We locked ourselves in the lounge and talked while the others waited outside. Then she saw me out and kissed me through the bars of the gate.'

He described her with unblushing reverence. 'She was a tormented soul and so physically beautiful that she appeared as a kind of goddess. I was overwhelmed. I didn't see a political figure . . . politics were nothing, they were mundane; in my mind she was on a higher plane.'[10]

To those who witnessed it from the outside, Winnie and Malefane's relationship appeared unstable, tumultuous, liable at any moment to explode.

Once, driving through the western Free State, a clergyman who knew Winnie well spotted Malefane walking along the verge of a provincial road. He was far from Brandfort, a good ten miles out, and so the minister pulled over and offered him a ride. Malefane was in a dreadful state; he muttered over and over again that he must leave Winnie at once, without delay, that he could not stand being with her in that house another moment. He had nothing with him, no bag, not even a toothbrush. The clergyman took him for a long drive and, once his passenger had calmed down, drove into Brandfort's black township and dropped him off at Winnie's home.[11]

There can be little question about the depths of her anguish at this time, witnessed, above all, in the amount of alcohol she had begun to consume. Brandfort was a small town, Winnie a famous figure; the town's mayor, Jurie Erwee, was also the owner of its off-licence, and he dined out on the sheer quantity of spirits Winnie's household acquired.[12]

But small-town gossip is the least of the evidence we have. Once, one of Winnie's lawyers, Priscilla Jana, received a panicked call from Zindzi. Her mother, she said, was so horribly, so chronically drunk that she was not sure what to do. Jana rushed to Brandfort with a medical doctor. 'It was very tragic to see Ma Winnie in that condition,' she recounted later.[13]

In her sobriety, too, Winnie revealed her despair. So many who spent an afternoon or an evening with her commented not just on the intensity of her sadness but on how she *shared* it, projecting it with great force to those in her company.

Among them was a senior Methodist cleric, John Scholtz, who ministered to Winnie for several years. On Christmas Day in 1982, he recalled, Winnie travelled to Cape Town to see Nelson in Pollsmoor Prison. She was not permitted to stay in Cape Town the night and was required to be back in Brandfort by 8:00 p.m. And so she flew to Cape Town in the morning, saw Nelson, and then boarded a late afternoon flight to Bloemfontein.

Scholtz and his wife met her at the airport and drove her to Brandfort. As they made their way into the night, he recalled, a feeling of utter wretchedness pervaded the car; Winnie barely spoke the entire journey, but he could *feel* her sorrow, as if it were inside him too. By the time they reached Brandfort, her melancholy had infected him.

He and his wife could not leave her in such a state, not on Christmas Day, and so they decided, the three of them, to defy the terms of Winnie's banning order and to break bread together in her tiny home.[14]

.   .

In January 1985, after a long period of turmoil, Malefane left Winnie and took up with a woman in Soweto. On an evening a few days after his arrival in town, he and his new love were having dinner with friends when Winnie made an astonishing entrance.

'She just flew across the room and shouted, "You're coming back with me or you know what will happen,"' he recalled seven years later. The others in the room had not yet taken in her fury; the famous Winnie Mandela had arrived from out of the blue, and people rose to greet and hug her. She brushed them aside. Malefane, who knew all too well what was happening, made for a telephone to call an uncle who lived nearby. 'She tore the phone off the wall,' he recalled, 'threw it to the ground and began hitting me.'

Malefane managed to usher Winnie outside and found to his horror two young men waiting there, young men he had known well in Brandfort, one carrying a crowbar, the other an ax. 'Kill the dog!' he remembered Winnie shouting to them. They moved toward him, half-heartedly, an apologetic look in their eyes.

One of them took a dutiful swing at Malefane with his crowbar; he ducked and ran into the night.[15]

A week later, Malefane and Winnie had reconciled. He was off to Cape Town to attend film school; Winnie paid the first installment of his fees. Over the following year, when Winnie and Zindzi visited Nelson, it was, on some occasions, Malefane who collected them from Cape Town's airport, took them to Pollsmoor, waited outside the gates and took them home.[16]

This was not the first act of violence Malefane had witnessed in Winnie. In the winter of 1983, two nine-year-old Brandfort boys had been playing outside her house. Her grandchild, who was staying with her at the time, accused the two boys of stealing her tricycle. Winnie stormed out of her house, took the leather belt off her waist, wrapped it around her fist, and struck one of the two boys, Andrew Pogisho, her belt buckle opening a deep gash in his forehead. To Malefane's shock, she kept hitting the boy with her buckle, despite the sight of a great deal of blood. He threw himself on her, and the two of them fought each other with their fists in the dust.[17]

Pogisho's mother laid a charge of assault with the police, and Winnie stood trial later that year. The boy himself gave testimony in a closed hearing. Winnie contested his evidence, and neither Malefane nor the half a dozen or so neighbours who had witnessed the incident were called. She was acquitted. In her own testimony, she said that the people of Brandfort's forlorn township had been so defeated by apartheid that they had lost the capacity to parent. 'It was in sympathy with the mother's inability to bring up children in a normal situation that I acted,' she said.[18]

.   .

It is difficult to write about a woman in this way, for one risks tramping worn and familiar paths: the woman crazed by jealousy; the woman driven murderous by her proximity to power. From Jezebel to the life-ruining femmes fatales of film noir, the stories into which violent women fall are old and deep and hard to avoid. It behooves us to strain against these tales and to hold close what an unfamiliar figure Winnie was.

Most arresting is the sheer number of norms she transgressed through the years. When her husband was on trial for his life, she took a married man who had a young family into her bed. When her public image was at its most sexualized, an object of shameless male desire, she imagined herself the leader of her people. When she was forty-four, she seduced a boy her daughters' age and shared her life with him. When he left her, she ordered men with crowbars to break his bones. She flouted every rule of comportment expected of a woman in her position. And she did so with an aristocratic absence of reserve, rendering her the most singular, the most astonishing woman.

Her most remarkable feature of all was her relation to her country.

A couple of months after the national uprisings began in 1984, a documentary filmmaker, Peter Davis, conducted a long interview with Winnie. Without prompting, she began speaking of Theuns Swanepoel, the man who had tortured her. She had clearly been living with him, close to the surface of her consciousness, all this time.

What she said about him was bracing and unexpected.

She had been made by Swanepoel, she told Davis. For she had, in the most troubling way, grown very close to him, close enough to feel his hatred for her and for black people in general; she had, indeed, *learned* that hatred and turned it back upon him. The war between them was to the death.

'It was [through Swanepoel] that I discovered the type of hate I had never encountered before in my life,' she said. 'He taught me how to hate him [back] . . . By the end of my interrogation, I knew that if my own father or brother walked in . . . and was on the other side . . . if I had a gun, I would fire.'

Her relationship with Swanepoel, she continued, had shown her how apartheid would end.

'I realized then that the Afrikaner had closed the chapter of negotiation . . . [O]ur patience had been tested and had endured for too long. I knew then that somehow, there had to be a political crisis in this country, for us to reach the ultimate goal."[9]

As she spoke these words, an insurrection had erupted in her country. She had, to all intents and purposes, said that apartheid could not end peacefully, that it was a war to the death. She had done so not by talking of what was happening out in the world but by virtue of what was going on between her and Swanepoel in her head. Her interior landscape and the landscape of her nation appear to have been indistinguishable to her.

. .

The uprisings began in the Vaal Triangle in early September 1984. They were slow to reach Soweto; it was not until mid-1985 that any sustained action began there. The moment it did, Winnie defied her banishment order and went home to 8115 Orlando West.

The precise circumstances are not entirely clear. In August 1985 she was in Johannesburg for medical treatment when her house in Brandfort was burned to the ground. During a visit to Nelson she told him that she suspected the security police.[20] But in the police's internal communications an informer's report circulated, one they were not sure whether to believe, claiming that Winnie had paid a group of youths to destroy her house.[21] The truth is probably lost by now. In any event, after her Brandfort house was burned, she refused to return.

During her first three months back in Soweto, she and the authorities held a precarious truce. They dared not arrest her for defying the terms of her banishment. For her part, she kept her head low, seldom appearing in public.

On December 3, the truce broke. A massive funeral was held that day in Mamelodi, a township outside Pretoria, where twelve youths had been killed by police. An estimated fifty thousand people converged; it was among the largest gatherings to form during the insurrectionary period. A host of luminaries, many of them senior UDF officials, spoke. Shortly after the funeral ended and the gathering had begun to disperse, a Mercedes-Benz drove into the cemetery and Winnie Mandela emerged from the backseat.

An electric charge surged through the remaining crowd. Several hundred youths drew around her, singing, toyi-toyiing, leading her to the graveside. Most of those gathered had never seen her in the flesh, and many could not believe their eyes. 'It is not her,' a woman shouted. 'It is only her daughter.' If Winnie could bring the world to a standstill, another was heard to remark, imagine what would happen if Nelson were released. 'He would not get halfway down the street before he was mobbed,' someone answered.[22]

The public address system had been dismantled and packed away, but the crowd demanded that Winnie speak. A makeshift podium was brought to her, and as she stepped up, a hush came over the two thousand or so people who remained.

'I bring you a message of love from those you sent outside to help fight for this liberation that has led to our burying our children,' she said. 'I bring you a message of love from your leaders inside prison. Pretoria has failed to rule this country. The solution of this country's problems lies in black hands. We promise that the mandate you gave us shall be carried through to the hilt. We shall lead you to freedom.'

One needs to grasp the millenarian spirit of those times to understand the force of what she had said. She was speaking not on behalf of one of the innumerable legal organizations that had arisen in recent years but as the embodiment of the banned ANC. Nobody else inside the country's borders had done that; nobody else had the license or the courage.

Then she turned to the twelve fresh graves before which she stood. 'This is our country,' she said. 'The blood of these heroes we buried today shall be avenged.'[23]

. .

Two weeks later, a contingent of police arrived at her house with an order compelling her to leave the Greater Johannesburg area at once. She need not return to Brandfort in terms of this new order; she could indeed live anywhere in South Africa she liked, save for the only city in which she had a home.

What followed might have come from a farce. The commanding officer ordered Winnie to leave Soweto. She protested that she had nowhere else to go. They argued at the tops of their voices for some time. Eventually, Winnie was lifted off her feet and dragged to a waiting car. She was driven to the Holiday Inn at Johannesburg's international airport and ordered to remain there indefinitely. The moment the police left, she went home.

The following morning, a different group of police officers came for her. This time, she was arrested for contravening her banning order and held overnight in a police cell. She appeared in court the following morning and again went home to be confronted by the police. And so it went.[24]

The next arrest was spectacular. On December 28, a small army of plainclothes police forced Winnie's car off a Johannesburg freeway. On the verge of the road, a white middle-aged policewoman put her hand on Winnie's shoulder and ordered her into a police car. It was as if the devil himself had touched her. Her body lurched with scarcely suppressed violence; her face right up against the white woman's, she let loose a deluge of rage, her ferocity extraordinary to behold.

The exchange was filmed; the footage re-emerged periodically in the decades to come, its symbolism stark, the black woman's anger so impressive, so utterly unashamed; her foe seems literally to shrink.

The following day, Winnie appeared in court for the fourth time in less than two weeks. When the proceedings were over, she was taken by car to a friend's house in Kagiso, a black township on Johannesburg's western periphery. While she was inside, drinking tea, word spread that she was there; within half an hour, a crowd of more than a thousand youths had gathered outside, singing, toyi-toyiing, demanding to see her. A squadron of riot police arrived, and the crowd was ordered to disperse. For a few tense moments, the two sides faced each other down. A local leader, a nun named Sister Bernard Ncube, put down what she was doing and raced to the scene. Standing on the back of a pickup truck, she persuaded the youths to go home.[25]

The very idea of Winnie had become combustible, the mere rumour of her presence liable to conjure large crowds.

·   ·

For the following four months, she holed up in a suburban hotel. She spoke often to the foreign press – she could still not be quoted in South Africa – giving a running commentary on events. But she scarcely left her room.

And then, from out of the blue, in early April 1986, a judge ruled that a banning order similar to Winnie's was illegal. The decision was narrow and technical, but it was definitive. Her own banning order was for all practical purposes null and void. While the state security services decided what to do next, Winnie was free.

She began immediately to travel and to speak. In Brandfort, at a large funeral, she spoke as the leader of an imminent insurrection. 'You will be told when the time has come to take action,' she told the mourners. 'You will march to that lily-white part of Brandfort and take the wealth that is rightfully yours and the land that is your birthright.'[26]

Back in Johannesburg the following week, she gave three speeches on one day – April 13, 1986 – and what she said in those three speeches transported her and her image into an uncharted world.

A little over a year earlier, on March 21, 1985, in the car-manufacturing town of Uitenhage, police had opened fire on a gathering en route to a funeral. Nineteen people had died. In the wake of these killings, a crowd had assembled seeking vengeance. It converged on a mortuary owned by a town councillor and hacked to death three members of his family as they tried to escape. And then, while the councillor and his son were trapped inside, certain that death awaited them should they leave, the mortuary was set alight. Once it was clear that father and son had been consumed by the flames, the crowd moved on.

Two men, recognized as employees of a businessman with an unsavory reputation, crossed the crowd's path. They were rounded upon, kicked and beaten. Tires were thrown around their necks; they were then doused in petrol and set alight.[27]

As this grim new spectacle was reported, it was given a name – 'necklacing' – and with its christening, the practice spread. Over the next five years, 406 people died this way.[28] South Africa's public broadcaster, tightly controlled by the government, went out of its way to film such killings and show them to the nation. The most spectacular of these broadcasts ran on the evening of July 20, 1985. A government agent, posing as a member of MK, had given a group of youths a batch of hand grenades rigged to detonate in their hands. Eight young men had blown themselves up. At their funeral, a young woman was picked out by the crowd and accused of being the traitor's girlfriend. She was kicked and stoned for some time before a tire was thrown around her neck and set alight. As she burned to death, the crowd circled her and sang.[29]

Now, nine months later, in three successive speeches delivered at gatherings around Johannesburg, Winnie spoke for the first time of necklacing. Our enemy, she said, is far more heavily armed than we are. 'We have no guns. We only have stones, boxes of matches and petrol.' 'Together, hand in hand,' she said a few hours later, 'with our boxes of matches and our necklaces, we shall liberate this country.'[30]

The ANC had yet to condemn necklacing when Winnie uttered

these words. The reasons for its hesitation were complex. One was a certain brittleness, a fear. When the insurrections began, the ANC had lent rhetorical support, but the practical assistance it was able to offer was negligible. By its own lights, those rising against apartheid ought to be armed; that they were facing automatic weapons bare-handed was, in a sense, the ANC's fault. To condemn those in the trenches for using the weapons of the weak – their own bodies, stones, and, indeed, fire – seemed only to draw attention to the ANC's failures.

The necklace, the MK commander Chris Hani said in an interview in December 1985, is not a weapon of the ANC. 'But I refuse to condemn our people when they mete out their own traditional forms of justice to those who collaborate. I understand their anger. Why should they be as cool as icebergs when they are being killed every day?'[31]

What Winnie had said, though, was of a different order. She was not speaking to the narrow audience that read the ANC's journal or listened to Radio Freedom; she was addressing large crowds in front of the international media. Nor was she defending necklacing from a distance, as a weapon of the weak. She was *owning* the practice, celebrating it. 'Together, hand in hand,' she had said, 'we will liberate our country' with necklaces.

And she was a middle-aged woman of stature; this, perhaps more than anything, shaped what her words meant.

'When we heard [what she had said] we were very excited, excited to have the endorsement of a senior leader,' recalled Mondli Makhanya, now one of South Africa's most respected newspaper editors, then a youth on the barricades.[32] It was not just that she was a senior leader: the encouragement had issued from the lips of a mother – a mother of her own biological children, to be sure, but also of all the black children of a nation. She was identifying with the violence of her offspring, and the sheer uncanniness of this carried immense power. It shot a frisson of excitement into the world.

And yet her words were also met with revulsion, both in South Africa and across the world. And its depth stemmed, too, from her age and her gender. For a middle-aged woman to appear to celebrate the burning of live human flesh drew from the depths of myth a figure long hated, she herself rounded upon and burned: the figure of an unnatural woman.

At its bimonthly meeting held in mid-May, the State Security

Council, by now the highest decision-making body on matters of security in the country, discussed what to do. It would be simple to issue Winnie a new banning order, the council resolved, but 'at present and especially because of her indiscriminate remarks, it is tactically not desirable'.[33]

Her enemy was happy for her to keep talking.

Chapter 46

Something else was happening at this time, something unprecedented and as yet unnamed.

One way to tell the story is to begin in July 1983, at Alexandra Palace in north London, where a modestly attended concert was held. The very clumsiness of its title – 'African Sounds Festival in Celebration of Nelson Mandela's Birthday' – speaks to its awkward provenance.

Buoyed by the success of the sixtieth-birthday campaign, the British Anti-apartheid Movement had resolved to celebrate Nelson's sixty-fifth birthday, too. Its key personnel had for more than two decades kept strong personal ties to exiled South African musicians, and in one of countless conversations the idea of a concert had emerged. The movement was vastly inexperienced in the field of popular culture; this first venture was uncertain, the crowd the concert drew small.

One of the people in the audience that day was a shy young man from Coventry called Jerry Dammers. He was also the leader of a band called the Special AKA. Founded six years earlier as the Specials, it was, by 1983, enormously successful, with several U.K. Top Ten singles under its belt.

Dammers had not heard of Nelson Mandela; he only attended the concert because he ran into an old friend who was going. While listening to the music, he picked up a pamphlet and read that in prison Mandela was given shoes too small for his feet.[1]

Winnie was the source of the story. Earlier that year, during a visit from his wife and daughter, Nelson had complained that a new pair of shoes was pinching his toe. To his astonishment, he read in a newspaper the next day that his toe was to be amputated.[2]

The image of the prisoner's feet stuck in Dammers's mind. He was working at that moment on an instrumental tune, and when he got home he began putting lyrics about Mandela to it.[3]

The song that ensued, 'Free Nelson Mandela', reached the U.K. Top Ten Singles list in late 1984.

It became the best-selling song Dammers would write, and it brought Mandela's name 'from the political world into people's living rooms', as the British parliamentarian and anti-apartheid activist Peter Hain observed.[4]

. .

By the mid-1980s, Nelson Mandela was already enormously famous. In a document compiled by South Africa's Department of Foreign Affairs in 1983 – the apartheid bureaucracy's hunger to quantify *all* information on proud display – the honours thus far bestowed upon him across the world were named. A block of flats in the East End of London had been christened Mandela Heights; a room in an art gallery in Glasgow was named the Mandela Room; he had been given the freedom of the city of Rome, and of the town of Olympia in Greece; a high school in the village of Ilmenau, West Germany, had been named after him; an avenue in Harlow in the U.K. bore his name; 12,443 people in Bulgaria had signed a petition calling for his release; 20,000 well-wishers in the German Democratic Republic had sent him postcards, as had several thousand people in Sri Lanka. The document went on like this for twenty-three pages, the accolades categorized by country in chronological order.[5]

But his entry into popular culture was of a different order.

It was not just the sheer numbers of young people who now heard his name. It was what that name came to mean.

There might have been any number of ways to tell this story other than through Jerry Dammers. One might have told of Peter Gabriel's 1980 hit celebrating Steve Biko, or the 1985 song 'Sun City', in which forty-nine artists – among them Bruce Springsteen, Bob Dylan, Miles Davis, and Lou Reed – sang of never performing in apartheid South Africa.[6] The meaning of the tale resonates beyond any of its particular episodes. It concerns what was then a just-emerging relationship between music and politics, of which Nelson Mandela was to be the greatest beneficiary.

The 1960s, rather than the 1980s, is of course remembered today as the decade par excellence of politically aligned music. But its politics were quite different from what emerged twenty years hence. The alle-

Soweto school children march on the morning of June 16, 1976, before the first shots were fired. The excitement etched on their faces tallies with testimony that the spirit of the marchers was benign before the police arrived.

(Drum Social Histories/BAHA/Africa Media Online)

(ABOVE LEFT) Winnie and Zindzi leaving court in Bloemfontein, 1977. Winnie was charged with breaking the conditions of the order banning her to Brandfort. *(Rand Daily Mail/Arena Holdings)* (ABOVE RIGHT) Winnie outside 8115 Orlando West after a stint in prison, 1974. With her is the Alsatian Krushchev, whom she would later find poisoned in her yard. *(Alf Kumalo/Africa Media Online)*

(LEFT) Winnie and Zindzi in Brandfort, May 1977.
(Peter Magubane)

Winnie in Brandfort with Fatima Meer, whose own banning order had recently expired, 1983. Winnie visited the Brandfort post office at a scheduled time every morning and afternoon to receive calls on the public phone, a party line.
(Steven Linde)

An artist's impression of Nelson featured in a Congress of South African Trade Unions (COSATU) poster, 1989. The portrait was based on descriptions by people who had visited him in jail; publishing his image was illegal and only jailers, prisoners, and a few visitors had seen him since 1964.
(COSATU Media Collective / The South African History Archive)

The Nelson Mandela Seventieth Birthday Tribute concert,
Wembley, London, 1988.
(Dale Cherry/Daily Mirror/Mirrorpix/Getty Images)

(LEFT) Winnie at the funeral of a Brandfort youth, 1985.
(*Alf Kumalo/African Pictures*)

(RIGHT) Stompie Seipei's mother, Joyce Seipei, with Jerry Richardson, who confessed to killing her son, outside the TRC hearings, 1997. Richardson arrived at the shoot unexpectedly and asked to be photographed alongside Seipei.
(*Jillian Edelstein, from the book* Truth and Lies: Stories from the Truth and Reconciliation Commission)

Winnie, 1985.
(*David Turnley/ Corbis/VCG via Getty Images*)

Winnie and Nelson at the rally held to celebrate Nelson's release at FNB Stadium near their Soweto home on February 13, 1990. Nelson spent the previous night, his first back in Johannesburg, alone in a suburban house near Lanseria Airport.
(Udo Weitz/Associated Press/Shutterstock)

Nelson gives an impromptu speech on his return to 8115 Orlando West, February 13, 1990. *(Graeme Williams/African Pictures)*

(ABOVE) 8115 Orlando West, shortly after Nelson's release, February 1990.
(Alf Kumalo/African Pictures)

(RIGHT) At a press conference in the United Kingdom, 1990.
(Fiona Hanson/PA Images/Alamy)

(BELOW) Nelson speaks to boys at the historically white King Edward VII School, Johannesburg, 1993.
(Louise Gubb/CORBIS SABA/Corbis via Getty Images)

(TOP) Nelson flanked by Winnie and Graca Machel, 2010.

(Yunus Mohammed/Foto24/Gallo Images)

(CENTER) Nelson's funeral procession, Qunu, 2013.

(Felix Dlangamandla/Foto24/Gallo Images)

(LEFT) Winnie, December 2016, fifteen months before her death.

(Karina Turok, karinaturok@gmail.com)

giances between musicians and the social movements they championed
back in the 1960s were more or less direct. And with political commitment came fidelity to a counterculture, and thus to the idea that one's
music was pitted against the mainstream, an awkward proposition for
those whose records began selling in the millions. Hence, the famous
incident at the Newport Folk Festival in 1965 when some of Bob Dylan's
fans booed him for singing with electric accompaniment, thus betraying folk for commercial rock.[7]

Political pop of the 1980s was not in any way against the commercial mainstream; on the contrary, political commitment became a question of branding. An assortment of causes – famine, the environment,
repression of dissent behind the Iron Curtain, the war in Lebanon,
apartheid in South Africa – were chiselled into sound bites by the producers of major televised events and pitched to the managers of pop
artists; they then haggled over words and images to the finest degree.[8]

This branding was itself an expression of something now ambi-
ent: style as an emblem of political attachment – the display of one's
political identity in the clothes one wears, in the establishments one
frequents, in the books one reads, and, indeed, in the music to which
one listens.[9]

In retrospect, it may seem inevitable that Nelson Mandela would
come to occupy so grand a place in the lifestyle politics of the 1980s.
His was perhaps the most tellable story about the death throes of the
colonial epoch, itself one of the great stories of the age. And it did often
seem that powerful currents beyond the comprehension of those calling for his release bore their campaign along. The Jerry Dammers hit,
for instance, was more akin to manna from heaven than the product of
hard work.

Skill and shrewdness nonetheless had their place in what was to
come.

The Jerry Dammers hit gave the British Anti-apartheid Movement an inkling of riches it could scarcely have imagined. And it went
chasing these riches, as it might. When Nelson's seventieth birthday
approached in 1988, the movement literally threw all it had at music. It
wagered everything in its coffers, and thus its very posterity, on a concert to be held at Wembley Stadium in London and broadcast around
the world.[10]

The movement was in unfamiliar territory now; it brought in
events producers who knew little of its politics but much about popu-

lar culture. And as these outsiders got to work, so the nature of the event changed. At first, it was to demand freedom for Nelson Mandela and for all political prisoners in South Africa and South-West Africa; it was also to express solidarity with the ANC and the South West African People's Organisation (SWAPO). Soon, the other political prisoners, SWAPO and the ANC were dropped. And then, as several bands wavered over whether to perform at a concert demanding freedom for a man who advocated violence, even the call to free Mandela was abandoned. The event simply became 'The Nelson Mandela 70th Birthday Tribute.'

The concert's political message, as its producer, Tony Hollingsworth, remarked, was now within the grasp of a five-year-old child: a man is in prison because he is black, and it is wrong. That is all.[11]

There was also a great deal of luck. Behind the scenes, Margaret Thatcher's government was leaning heavily on the national broadcaster, the BBC, not to carry the event. 'It began to appear as if the BBC might pull out,' the Anti-apartheid Movement leader Alan Brooks recalled, 'and if the BBC had pulled out, that was an end to international coverage. One band and then another . . . would have pulled out, and we'd be left with a half-empty Wembley Stadium and a bill of bills that high, and we were staring bankruptcy and the end of the Anti-apartheid Movement in the face. It was terrible. Going into the office each day . . . felt like walking on glass.'

And then, of all people, South Africa's blundering foreign minister, Pik Botha, came to the rescue, launching a public attack on the BBC for broadcasting the event. 'From the moment that happened we knew we were safe,' Brooks recalled, 'because there was no way that the BBC could back down under the onslaught of the South African regime.'[12]

In the end, sixty-seven broadcasters screened the concert. It went out across the Soviet Union and India, to the viewers of Rupert Murdoch's new Fox channel in the United States, to countries throughout Latin America and Europe. Among the most widely broadcast live television events in history at that time – some 600 million are estimated to have watched it – it was bettered that year only by the opening ceremony of the Olympic Games. As for the musicians who performed, 'it seemed', wrote one commentator, 'that all the key living figures in the history of political pop had been assembled on one stage at last', all framed by a giant, quarter-century-old photograph of Nelson Mandela.[13]

In the wake of the concert, the British Anti-apartheid Movement commissioned Gallup to determine Mandela's name recognition among the country's population. Almost everybody knew who he was – 92 percent of Britons – and 70 percent supported his release. Sympathy for him crossed party lines: 97 percent of Labour supporters wanted him freed, which was perhaps not surprising, but so did a healthy majority of Conservative Party supporters at 59 percent. The same poll asked whether people knew the name of the member of Parliament in their district: just one in two did.[14]

. .

As popular culture seized Nelson Mandela, rendering him a household name, something else was happening to strengthen his cause; two of the South African government's greatest strengths were turning to weaknesses.

One was the presence of friendly governments in the citadels of world power. Margaret Thatcher's administration in the U.K. and Ronald Reagan's in the United States offered as benign a face as the South African government could reasonably expect. Motivated by racial solidarity and by Cold War fears, they were hostile to sanctions against South Africa, and they were implacably hostile to the ANC. As Mandela's cachet grew, they reminded the world that he was a proponent of violence and that the Soviet Union was his organization's greatest friend.

Another strength was the sheer density of South Africa's commercial connections to the world. Many of the West's leading banks bought South Africa's sovereign debt. Many of its largest motor manufacturers assembled vehicles there. South African gold was held as a store of value by the world's largest central banks. Its platinum was used in petroleum and plastic products across the world. South Africa's global integration placed the country's elites in partnerships with powerful actors with great influence.

In the 1980s, this combination of friendly governments and deep connections turned against apartheid South Africa. As Thatcher and Reagan drove market reforms through their own societies, fierce resistance grew. And as opposition escalated, so Thatcher's and Reagan's friendship with South Africa became a target of their domestic foes. This connection found a voice in trade unions, in church movements,

in the British Labour Party, in the Congressional Black Caucus in the
United States. Most especially, it found a voice on university campuses.
Across British and American society, the question of apartheid was
becoming a proxy for battles closer to home.

And precisely because of the ubiquity of South Africa's business
connections, every campus, every town, every workplace, was a potential theatre of conflict. There was scarcely a major university in America whose endowment was not in some way invested in South Africa;
scarcely a worker whose wage did not pass through a bank that had
bought South African debt; scarcely a city or a state whose legislature
could not be lobbied to impose meaningful sanctions.

Campaigns to divest from South Africa and to boycott its exports
had begun in Britain in the late 1950s and in the United States in 1965.
For decades, the fortunes of these campaigns had ebbed and flowed, but
they had never been supported by more than small minorities, not even
in the wake of June 1976.

In the 1980s, the success of these campaigns soared. There are so
many stories that might be told. One is the passing of the Comprehen-
sive Anti-apartheid Act in the U.S. Congress in 1986, imposing sanctions on South Africa. The act overrode a veto Reagan had placed on
a previous incarnation of the law; the fight between the president and
Congress was one of the great dramas of mid-1980s American politics.[15]

For all of this theatre, a single event shook South Africa's government more violently than any other. On July 31, 1985, Chase Manhattan
Bank resolved to call in its loans to the South African government and
to terminate its borrowing facilities going forward. The panic in South
Africa's cabinet was voluble. The minister of finance, Barend du Ples-
sis, phoned the foreign minister, Pik Botha, late that night, imploring
him to intervene. 'The country is facing inevitable bankruptcy,' Botha
recalled his colleague saying. 'Can you help? Is there not somebody in
the United States who could talk to the bank?' Botha contacted that
inimitable fixer, Henry Kissinger, who told him that there was nothing
he could do and that other banks would soon follow suit.[16]

South Africa did not go bankrupt, nor was there a prospect that it
might. The country did indeed default on $13 billion of debt but within
six months negotiated a rescheduling. The lion's share of its debt was in
any case domestically held, and there was never a possibility that this
would dry up.[17]

It was not the threat to its coffers but the wound to its spirit that damaged South Africa's government most. In sheer practical terms, it had the capacity to go on governing for years. By mid-1986, its armed forces had contained the insurrection and proven their ability to keep doing so indefinitely. The economy was stagnant but hardly near collapse. What had weakened substantially was the nerve to go on governing in this way. 'The majority of whites continued to desire acceptance in the Western world,' Afrikanerdom's premier historian has written of these times. 'If apartheid satisfied their material desires, it increasingly left unrequited the yearning of people for recognition of their own worth.'[18] In the face of global scorn, Afrikanerdom's elite was morally exhausted.

. .

The young Nelson Mandela who came to Johannesburg in 1941 was touched by grace. Tall and beautiful, his aristocracy showing in his very gait, he turned heads. People stopped what they were doing and helped him. Within weeks of his arrival, Walter Sisulu and Gaur Radebe, two of the most well-connected black men in the city, had resolved to run a few steps ahead of him, pushing obstacles out of his path.

His confidence in the world was lodged deep in his being.

Did the things that came to him when he was in his sixties surprise him? World fame was really the least of it. Far uncannier was this: while he sat in prison, the history of his country bent itself around him; he became its dead centre, its eye. After more than three hundred years of white rule, the country's governors were looking for a way out. And the only way was through him.

He knew this. He knew it absolutely. In January 1985, P. W. Botha announced in South Africa's parliament that he would free Mandela on condition that he renounce violence. Nelson replied publicly via his daughter Zindzi. 'My father says', she told a packed stadium in Soweto, 'I cannot sell my birthright, nor am I prepared to sell the birthright of the people to be free . . . Only free men can negotiate. Prisoners cannot enter into contracts . . . I cannot and will not give any undertaking at a time when I and you, the people, are not free.'[19]

These were the first words heard from him in twenty-one years. I know you need me, he was telling the South African government. And you're going to have to work much, much harder than that.

Chapter 47

In September 1985, news leaked that Nelson Mandela was in the hospital. The diagnosis was vague at first – the rumour simply that he was undergoing urological tests – and as the uncertainty lingered, concern grew. Stocks dipped on Johannesburg's bourse. Newspaper editorials asked whether South Africa could survive his death. As for Winnie, she threatened court action to take his care out of his enemy's hands; she rushed to Cape Town bearing the names of trustworthy black doctors: the family physician, the head of urology at Baragwanath Hospital.

But the Nelson she found upon her arrival in Cape Town was sanguine and at ease; indeed, he was positively buoyant. It was not just that he was receiving the finest medical treatment, he assured her, as she and her daughters gathered around his hospital bed: it was the *attitude* of his doctors.

'Both the physician, Dr. Le Roux, and the urologist, Dr. Laubscher, are very sophisticated and mature people,' he reassured his family. 'Dr. Laubscher has actually been to Umtata . . . He was trained in England. And he has an Irish wife. You do forget about his name and his colour when you discuss medical terms with him.'

And if these assurances were not enough, he lavishly praised the nurse in charge of his care, a Sister Ferreira. 'The name can make you a bit concerned,' he conceded, 'but . . . she is just a person who is interested in the particular problem you have, and she made me feel extremely comfortable.'

Nelson's relationship with his doctors and nurses was in fact more than a year old, he now revealed. He apologized for not telling Winnie earlier; he had quite deliberately asked the prison authorities *not* to inform her whenever he was taken to see a specialist; he did not want to upset her.

Paging through his diary, he described in astonishing detail the history of his care: Dr. Laubscher's diagnosis of a cyst on his right kidney on September 6, 1984; the investigative surgery performed on September 13; the discovery that his prostate was enlarged.

He went on like this for some time: a string of dates, the definite diagnoses, the indeterminacies; his cholesterol levels the last six times they were tested and the precise dates of these tests; the debate over whether to take out his prostate 'from the front' or 'through the stomach'; how the procedure was usually performed in Europe; how Dr. Laubscher had not *told* him to have the prostate removed, but had *recommended* it; the name of the anesthetist who would be putting him under.[1]

In the face of Winnie's insistence that the Baragwanath urologist get involved, he relented, but only to be sporting.

'How old is he?' Nelson asked cautiously. 'Where did he train?'

Here was a conversation between a prisoner and his family. At stake was whether to trust the hands of white doctors on his black body. In reassuring them, he revealed a hinterland, intensely experienced and secret until now, littered with dates and medical procedures and kind people.

Nelson had now been in prison for twenty-three years. He was growing old without a wife, without children, his relation to the men around him limited. It is little wonder that he spoke with such warmth of the people who took such scrupulous care of his health.

That his enemy had provided this care mattered greatly. Four years later, when South Africa's National Intelligence Service (NIS) compiled a summative document on the relationship the government had built with Mandela, its authors singled out his medical treatment. 'His handling during his illness', they wrote, 'brought to the fore a generosity in his approach and thinking.'[2]

.   .

In early November, Nelson had his prostate removed under general anesthetic. Some ten days later, South Africa's justice minister, Kobie Coetsee, walked unannounced into his hospital room. 'Though I acted as though this was the most normal thing in the world,' Nelson later recounted, 'I was amazed. The government, in its slow and tentative way, was reckoning that they had to come to some accommodation with the ANC.'[3]

Dressed in a blue-checked gown, Nelson rose from his chair and greeted his guest warmly, chiding him for not coming earlier. 'He acted as though we had known each other for years,' Coetsee later recalled, 'and this was the umpteenth time we had met.'[4]

It *was,* in a sense, the umpteenth time they had met, for Nelson had been rehearsing variations of this moment in his head for years.

He offered his guest tea. They made small talk, not discussing politics at all. The only contentious matter Nelson raised was his wife. He asked that she be permitted to live in her house in Orlando West in peace. Coetsee acknowledged what Nelson had said but committed to nothing.

Both men were impressed.

'He came across as a man of Old World values,' Coetsee recalled, 'an old Roman citizen with *dignitas, gravitas, honestas, simplicitas.*'[5]

In truth, if two people had ever *wanted* to like what they saw, it was they.

. .

On his return to Pollsmoor, Nelson was taken not back to his rooftop cell, his garden, and his comrades but to the basement of another building. There he found all his possessions – his books, his photographs, his study materials. He had not been consulted or forewarned; he had simply been moved.

His new accommodation was 'palatial' by prison standards: three separate rooms, one for sleeping, another for studying, and a third for exercising. But they were dingy and damp with little natural light, and his garden, he knew, would go to ruin in his absence.

There is a discrepancy between Nelson's memory of this moment and his captors' contemporaneous records. As Nelson recalled it, the head of the prison, Fred Munro, did not know why his prisoner had been moved; he was simply following instructions from the head office. Alone, Nelson gathered his thoughts and 'came to a realisation' that his solitude presented 'a certain liberty': he could begin talking secretly to his enemy.[6]

But, in fact, the secrecy was mutually contrived. When Nelson asked to see his comrades, Munro forbade him to meet them together. He could have forty minutes with each alone, and only if he undertook to conceal Coetsee's visit.

Nelson readily agreed. 'He considers the matter to be extremely confidential and does not want to damage mutual trust at all,' Munro writes.

Indeed, Munro reported in his prisoner a barely constrained excitement. Nelson declared that he had an important role to play in his country's future, and in the next breath he was talking of his life after prison: he'd live in Orlando West again; no other place was acceptable to him.

In describing Nelson's mood, Munro used the most affecting phrase. '*Hy is baie in sy noppies*,' he wrote. The colloquial spirit is so hard to translate; it means, in essence, that Nelson is absolutely ebullient.[7]

The following day, he was permitted to meet with his comrades one by one. The moment he laid eyes on his old friend Walter Sisulu, the warder on duty reported, Nelson wept.[8]

Chapter 48

Ore than most human beings ever do, Nelson Mandela had
changed.

Throughout his last decade of freedom, he had lived – headily,
inexhaustibly – in the present: the intensity of a life in politics, the
adrenaline induced by the danger, the whole business eroticized by a
series of sexual liaisons.

He had tended so little to things that might last, leaving behind
a wrecked marriage, an estranged son, a mother without means; even
his second marriage was a fragile thing, assembled with the thrill of
transgression.

In prison, the present wasted away. Only the past and the future
remained, both largely foreign to him until now. Once he found them,
he worked on them ceaselessly, year upon year, threading who he had
been to who he'd become once his endless confinement was over. And
as his imaginings changed him, he became a strikingly ordinary man:
the nourishment he found in kinship, the prospect of growing old with
his wife, his craving for accomplishment in his children. His longings
became so commonplace, so familiar.

And if one steps back, beyond Pollsmoor, beyond his native South
Africa, if one takes in the four and a half billion people on earth during
his twentieth year in jail, the way Nelson Mandela was most typical –
joining the greatest, the most widely shared aspiration of humanity at
that time – was in how he imagined the education of his children.

'You are mistaken to think that talking about [your grandchildren]
may bore me,' he wrote to Frieda Matthews, the widow of his onetime
teacher and comrade Z. K. Matthews, in 1987. She had written to him
waxing lyrical about the great universities her kin were attending, and
it struck her, as the pages piled up, that she was the parody of a proud
grandmother.

'Having regard to your family background,' Nelson continued, 'there is nothing particularly astonishing in your grandchildren reaching out for the stars . . . But even when making allowance for that, what they have achieved gives a person in prison a fairly clear picture of the far-reaching changes which are taking place in Southern Africa today . . . It would seem that some kind of diaspora is in full swing and children . . . are scattered all over the world and, in the process, horizons are widened beyond recognition . . . With this background, they come home to an environment not yet ready to accommodate them.'[1]

This idea – that one sends children off to learn and that they come back unrecognizable, their very beings not just new but strange – this was perhaps the most narcotic, the most inspiring idea to seize ordinary people in the twentieth century. Sociologists of education have called it 'psychic mobility', the capacity to imagine, through the transformations one hopes to witness in one's children, dramatic change.[2]

Nelson Mandela inhabited this vision. He scarcely had time to get to know his children when he was free. Now, in his head, and in the notes of his diary, was a sprawling map; it traced the trajectories of children and grandchildren, nieces and nephews, great-nieces and great-nephews. Each was a project; each had to be watched with care.

There is a dark underside to this idea, of course; it is the thought of what might happen to one's children were they *not* to be educated. This prospect haunted Nelson Mandela. That he would leave descendants 'condemned forever to the degrading status of being subservient to . . . other human beings' was the stuff of his nightmares.[3]

Most frightening of all was that the fault would be *his,* a consequence of how he had lived when he was free.

During his time in prison, Nelson Mandela enlisted his fame into the service of his descendants' education. He did this without reserve or shame. The sheer consistency, the sheer *tenacity* with which he hit on his influential visitors to raise scholarship funds is astonishing to behold.

The American lawyer Samuel Dash, the British politician Nicholas Bethell, the South African parliamentarian Helen Suzman, the leading South African Quaker H. W. van der Merwe, the businessman Tony Bloom: anyone with means, with influence, with access to people who might open doors, was enlisted in the project to educate the Mandelas.

When his granddaughter Nandi was admitted as a student to the University of Cape Town but hadn't the money to pay the fees, he coached her on what to do.

'Go to Prof. Van der Merwe', he advised when she came to see him, 'and ask him to make an appointment for you at the German Embassy ... When you see the Ambassador, insist on a private audience. Tell him that your father was my son and that he died in an accident. Tell him you were brought up by your mother ... and she can't afford University fees. Tell him your grandfather is Nelson Mandela ... Tell him I want not only the scholarship, but also money for your board and lodging, money for books and pocket money.'[4]

One can hear the machinery at work in his mind. When he was younger, he had chosen politics over family. As a result, he had become a man without income, without assets, a man who could not provide. That his choices might leave the Mandelas who survived him non-people was intolerable. He was righting a wrong before it was too late, playing his proper part, at the last opportunity, in the cycle of life.

.   .

Assessing the state of his progeny during his last years in prison, Nelson found that the audit was mixed. Makaziwe, Evelyn's daughter, was in the United States and pursuing a graduate education. He had never managed to build a connection of substance with her and her relationship with Winnie had long soured. As for Zenani, she and her husband were both studying for degrees at Boston College; their fees and expenses were paid for by a man named Robert Brown.

Nelson's son, Makgatho, was cause for much anguish. He had to all intents and purposes cut ties with Nelson; he last visited his father in 1983. And what Nelson knew of his life was very painful indeed. He was an alcoholic, his life ruinously unstable. Through a series of proxies and benefactors, Nelson had taken over the care of Makgatho's child, Mandla. He was in fact taking nothing less than an obsessive interest in the boy's welfare, forever asking after him, forever demanding to see him, watching vigilantly over his education. It is hard to resist the thought that in Mandla's dislocations, his fate decided by the benevolence of others, Nelson saw his own childhood.[5]

But nobody preoccupied him more than his youngest child, Zindzi. She had still been at high school when she was swept up with her mother and dumped in Brandfort. And in the maelstrom that followed, she had abandoned school and struggled to return. Efforts to begin her university education had floundered: attempts to register her at Wits had failed; benefactors in the U.K. had spoken of getting her into a university there, but it had come to nothing.

Zindzi was the most famous of his children. When she was sixteen, she published an anthology of political poetry that had caused something of a stir in the United States.[6] And while her mother was banned, she spoke regularly on public platforms as her proxy. Strikingly beautiful, commanding a stark, simple eloquence, she turned heads when she spoke.

But Nelson understood that her political profile was no substitute for an education. And he seemed troubled, too, by the instability of her romantic attachments. By the age of twenty-four, she had left the fathers of both of her children. And her relationship with the second man had ended very badly.

In the style of a patriarch who decides what is best for his children, Nelson resolved that Zindzi should study in Cape Town. 'He believed that if she was close to him, in the same city,' recalled Christo Brand, the young warder who had secretly allowed Nelson to hold his grandchild, 'he could control her in some way.'[7] Throwing the heft of his fame behind the endeavour, he cajoled the university, cajoled funders. He let it be known that Nelson Mandela *required* his daughter to attend university, and not just any university: he required her to attend UCT.

Christo Brand was by now something of an executive secretary to his prisoner—buying his food, posting his mail, going on endless errands throughout the city on his behalf—and found himself deeply embroiled in the quest to educate Zindzi Mandela. After she arrived in early 1985, Brand was sent, sometimes weekly, at times daily, to see that she was settled in her accommodation, that her studies were going well, that she was getting her meals. Many years later, Zindzi joked that Brand was an honourary Mandela, so ensconced in family matters had he become.[8]

And if this were not enough, Nelson received dispensation for his friend H. W. van der Merwe to pay him special visits, over and above his regular allotment, for the express purpose of reporting on Zindzi's academic progress.[9]

There was something overbearing in Nelson's relation to Zindzi. One evening, Brand recalled, he was sent to her student residence to give her a message from her father. When he returned with the news that he could not find her, Nelson descended into a state of agitation that took Brand aback.[10]

Zindzi was a twenty-four-year-old woman when she began studying at UCT. One can only imagine how she bristled. Her very presence
in Cape Town was her father's will, not hers. Now she found that he had
fashioned an elaborate apparatus to watch her, notwithstanding that he
was locked up in jail.

. .

It takes a hard heart not to feel for Nelson. The life his daughter
was secretly living, in concert with his wife, was beyond his ken.

The first inkling came in late February 1987 with news that Zindzi
had been arrested at 8115 Orlando West. The police, Nelson was told,
had found a machine-gun pistol in a suitcase under her bed.

Chapter 49

When Winnie moved back to 8115 Orlando West in the spring of 1985, defying the order that had banished her to Brandfort, the Soweto to which she returned was in a state of insurrection.

It is a feature of insurrections that the closer one gets to them, the more opaque they become.

On the tongues of those who fight, the terrain is simple: there is the regime on one side, the people on the other. But that is not how it plays out at the level of the neighbourhood or even the street. Violence is available during insurrections to a degree it is not in calmer times, and it comes to fill the slightest fractures: between neighbours, between districts, between rival businesses, between families, between the old and the young.[1]

It is hard to count the number of such fractures in Soweto at that time; they were by their nature forming and re-forming from day to day. There was the conflict between youths aligned with the UDF and those who supported the Black Consciousness–aligned Azanian People's Organisation (AZAPO). At times it spouted episodes of extravagant violence. In April 1986, for instance, the funeral of an AZAPO activist killed on the streets was attacked by a group of youths; they burned down the tent that sheltered the mourners and then set the coffin alight. Two weeks later, the mob returned to set fire to the dead man's house.[2]

That same year, a middle-aged woman was ordered by a street committee to deliver her two grandsons for punishment; their crime was to belong to the Azanian Students' Movement. She refused and went home, only to watch a crowd several dozen strong surround her house. When she came out to reason with them, she was shot in the stomach and the neck and bled to death outside her front gate.[3]

There were also outbursts of territorial violence between the youths of different neighbourhoods. On a Saturday night in March

1986, for instance, a young man from Orlando East ran over and injured a youth in Diepkloof. Anticipating vengeance from Diepkloof youths, the mother of the young man hired one of Soweto's most feared gangs, the Kabasa, to protect her house. A few hours later, a petrol bomb was lobbed through her window to flush the Kabasa out, and as they ran into the street, they were gunned down.[4]

Countless young men used the veneer of politics to rob and steal. In 1986, Soweto business operators complained of youths approaching them for money to sponsor the funeral of a fallen comrade, a thinly veiled demand to empty the cash register or face the consequences.[5] Car drivers returning to Soweto were stopped at the edge of the township to have their vehicles requisitioned, ostensibly for the struggle.[6] Youths invaded classrooms on the guise that they were enforcing a school boycott, their intent to molest the schoolgirls they chased into the street.[7]

A world this violent soon grows mercurial, the line between real and imaginary danger hard to pin down. In early 1988, rumours coursed through Soweto that children were being abducted en masse. At the height of the panic, parents began arriving at schools in the middle of the morning to fetch their sons and daughters. It was said that the culprits were prowling Soweto with the letter *H* painted on the sides of their cars. Word began to spread that they were undertakers using the corpses of children for some ill-defined purpose. On a Friday night in February, five Soweto undertakers were assassinated in their homes.[8]

. .

The leaders of the UDF at home and of the ANC in exile were acutely aware of this wildness. But the question of how to discipline the revolution produced an array of conflicting answers.

It is hard to lay out this terrain without oversimplifying; there was no single view in the UDF, no single view in the ANC. In the broadest terms, the secretariat of the UDF, the people who ran it from day to day, understood the grassroots associations that had formed during the uprisings of 1984 to 1986, street committees, block committees – so-called organs of people's power – as tools to bring order and civility to the struggle. And there were powerful attempts to do so. One such was the Soweto Parents' Crisis Committee, formed at the instigation of UDF leaders to address the crisis in the schools. Its attempts to impose

the authority of procedure upon political action, to conduct the struggle by a mutually agreed set of rules, was striking. Those who initiated
it did so for fear of the revolution destroying itself. 'The zeal of the
youth had [already] alienated many older residents,' a historian of the
insurrection wrote, paraphrasing a deep concern held by UDF leaders
that what had begun as a revolt against apartheid would become an
internecine war among black people.[9]

Nelson Mandela was very much of this view. Criminal elements
were now involved, he counselled Winnie shortly after her return to
Soweto, and innocent people were getting hurt. He spoke about Germans being shot dead by their own during World War II and about the
violence that had erupted during the Defiance Campaign. 'We must
be careful what we instruct our people because we are in a delicate
situation.'[10]

But there was another view – one especially current in exile – that
the violence of the insurrection should be not diminished but properly
directed. There were simplistic and sophisticated versions of this view.
Some of them were extraordinarily naive, sprouting from the heads of
people who had not seen South Africa in two decades, people who had
spent a lifetime conjuring and reconjuring what had happened in Russia in 1917, in Cuba in 1959. The masses of South Africans had fashioned
their own organs of insurrection, a senior MK figure eulogized, armed
only with their innate creativity. All that remained for the ANC was
gently 'to tell them: this is what to do; this is the way forward'.[11]

.   .

At first, it appeared to some that Winnie's intent was to tame the
wildness, for the body she formed a year after her return to Soweto –
the Mandela United Football Club – was a response to a dreadful event:
the murder of a twenty-nine-year-old woman called Masabata Loate.
A veteran of the 1976 uprisings, Loate was completing a five-year prison
sentence for treason when the uprisings began. Shocked by the violence
to which she returned after her release, she spoke out against some
of the more brutal practices of her neighborhood's youths, counselling
them against stoning the cars of innocents and against beating shoppers
returning from town. On a Friday night in October 1986, a group of
twenty or so Orlando West youths turned on her and chased her to her
grandmother's house. They caught her just before she reached safety

and killed her in the most gruesome fashion, stabbing her all over her torso and head and breaking her limbs with an ax.[12]

In the wake of her killing, the youths turned on one another, for among the politically active young men in the neighbourhood was her brother, and he wanted vengeance for his sister's death. This is when Winnie intervened. She took both factions back to her house. She clothed them, fed them, gave them a place to sleep.[13] Once they had settled, she established house rules, kept a register to monitor comings and goings, forbade boys to leave after dark. The way she explained it to Nelson – although she gave him different explanations at other times – an exchange evolved between her and these youths. She sheltered them from life on the streets; for their part, they protected her, for being Winnie Mandela in Soweto in 1986 was deeply unsafe.[14]

And she did something else. She approached one of Soweto's most famous residents, the legendary goalkeeper Patson Banda, and offered him the job of turning these street kids into a reputable football team. A set of yellow and black tracksuits was made with the words Mandela United FC emblazoned on the back; boots and kit were bought.

'Initially, the team did play,' a longtime resident later recalled, 'and they had some talented youth; some of them were on their way to becoming good footballers.'[15]

Banda lasted just a few months, pleading that he did not have the time. He approached a distant relative of his, Jerry Richardson, the coach of an amateur neighbourhood team called Lucky Brothers.[16] In March 1987, Richardson assumed the job.[17]

It is implausible that Winnie ever intended to form just a football team. She was, after all, the most outspoken proponent of revolution in her country. Over the previous decade, she had spirited many a young man across the border to join the ANC's army; in Brandfort, she had attempted to fashion a national network of militant young men. Every time she spoke in public, she readied her audience for an imminent call to battle. That she might choose to divert youths at the heart of an insurrection into football would constitute a renunciation of all that she was.

Within a month of the football team's formation, something of Winnie's intent began to show. Among her neighbours was a respected women's activist and UDF leader named Dudu Chili. On an afternoon in November 1986, Chili's teenage son, Sibusiso, told his mother that members of the football team wished to kill him because he had refused to join. Chili, who knew Winnie fairly well, went immediately to her house to ask what was going on.

The scene that confronted her was unusual and a little ominous. Unlike almost any other Soweto home, one could not simply walk through Winnie's front gate; a group of youths stood in the street, blocking one's way. Winnie was summoned and came outside; Chili asked her why members of the team wanted to kill her son.

'Dudu,' she later recalled Winnie saying, 'if he's not in the football club, obviously the other boys will think he's a sell-out.'

Chili went home in something of a daze, not quite sure whether she had properly absorbed the meaning of Winnie's words. 'That really scared me,' she remembered years later, 'because in those times when somebody is labelled a sell-out it means he must die.'[18]

Quite how much was at stake for those young men who refused the football team's approach soon became apparent. On May 26, 1987, two brothers, Peter and Phillip Makhanda, were taken forcibly from their home, driven to Winnie's place, and put in an outhouse on the property. They were severely beaten. One of them, Peter, was hung by the neck from the roof until the rafters broke and he fell to the ground. A plastic bag was pulled over his face and his head dunked in a bucket of water, an imitation of one of the apartheid security police's most familiar methods of torture.

Then the carving began. The boys were placed on chairs and their hands tied behind their backs. Using a penknife, a member of the football team cut the letter M – for Mandela – into their chests and 'Viva ANC' down the lengths of their thighs. The wounds were then doused with battery acid. Nowhere in the boys' statements do they describe the pain; suffice it to say that they were made to watch their flesh burn.

A police car was heard cruising outside in the middle of the night, and the Makhanda brothers were bundled away and taken to the house of Winnie's driver, John Morgan. They were locked in a garage, from which they escaped and ran immediately to Meadowlands police station, where they wrote lengthy statements about what had happened.

Three men stood trial for the assault – John Morgan, Absolom Madonsela, and Isaac Mokgoro. Winnie was neither questioned by the police nor called as a witness. The accused were acquitted on the grounds that the Makhanda brothers had offered conflicting evidence. That their testimony was poor is hardly surprising. The football team had been paraded before them, with no one-way mirror to protect them, while they were asked to point out their would-be killers, men still very much at large. Astonishingly, the magistrate appeared to concede that they had been kidnapped and tortured by residents of Winnie's house in the very same breath as saying that nobody could be held responsible. 'The experience must have been so frightening that their powers of observation were affected and their minds were more on how to get through the ordeal alive,' he wrote in his judgment.[19]

A small group of politically active parents quietly rebelled. Dudu Chili, along with several other concerned mothers and fathers, confided in Albertina Sisulu, who immediately smuggled a report to the ANC in Lusaka. Much to her consternation, the recipients of her report – Oliver Tambo most likely among them – simply did not believe what she was saying about Winnie Mandela. She wondered later whether what she had described was so extreme as to appear to have been invented by an enemy propagandist.[20]

In truth, aside from reporting to her exiled organization, out of touch and far away, there was little Sisulu and the activists around her might do. They could hardly give Winnie up to the apartheid government's police. Nor could they expose her actions to a general audience, for to accuse her in public of grave crimes was as good as going to the authorities. A conspiracy of silence evolved. The township's newspaper of record, the *Sowetan*, reported faithfully day after day on innumerable acts of violence, but about the actions of Winnie's football club the newspaper wrote nothing at all until much later.

As for the police, their role in the football club's destiny was, we shall see, very complex indeed. Suffice it to say for now that it was decided at the highest level that Winnie Mandela could not be prosecuted while her husband was secretly talking to the government.

The world in which the football club formed was thus one in which violence carried significantly more power than it does in quieter times. All the countervailing forces – law, public exposure, moral beseechment – were curtailed. When Winnie insinuated to Chili that her son might die if he did not join, Chili understood that there was little to stop the team from killing him.

And so Sisulu, Chili, and others did what they could. Sisulu made contact with those boys in the club over whom she held some authority, including three of her own nephews, implored them to leave, and offered to arrange safe refuge.[21] Some time later, her house was burned down; she strongly suspected that it was an act of revenge for daring to steal the club's boys.[22]

.   .

Years later, when Winnie was a parliamentarian in a democratic South Africa, she spoke with unusual candour about those times to her private secretary, a man she had come to like and trust.

'Black people', he recalled her telling him, 'had made lives for themselves within the constraints of apartheid'; most were resigned to going on that way forever. 'They had to be more scared of me than of the apartheid regime if they were going to rise up,' he remembered her saying.[23]

These are important words. She understood fear as a political technology, indeed, as *the* political technology par excellence, capable of fashioning the most important divide in her country, that between the apartheid state and black people.

But that is very abstract. What did she actually want to do, in the most concrete terms, in Soweto, in 1987? How was her football team to contribute to the fall of apartheid?

Stated baldly, she wanted to receive MK soldiers coming from abroad; she wanted also to receive weapons from them; she wanted them to train and arm the members of her football team, to have them attack government installations and town councillors and police. She envisaged such actions spreading countrywide, always under the influence of returning MK soldiers, such that no functionary or ally of the apartheid government would find safe ground on which to walk.

She did not conjure this idea from nothing. It is a version, after all, of the idea embodied in 'Operation Mayibuye', the document Govan Mbeki and Joe Slovo penned in 1962, in which a few hundred returning guerrillas inspire a nation to rise.

It might have been stripped of the romanticism with which it was conceived, it might indeed have been the most brutal incarnation of this vision imaginable, but what she imagined was familiar to South Africa's revolutionary tradition.

Strange beyond reason, though, was the notion that Winnie herself – the most famous, the most visible, the most watched woman in the country – could possibly play a leading role in executing this vision.

And stranger yet was the idea that she could assume this position by fiat, without consultation, as if the fact that she was Winnie Mandela were authority enough.

It was not long before returning MK soldiers did indeed seek her out, looking for refuge, for a place to store arms, and for support.[24] Nor was it long before they began carrying out missions with members of her household.

In none of this was Winnie alone. From mid-1985, MK combatants began returning in large numbers with minimal support. Typically, they were given a small amount of cash, a few grenades, and an assault rifle and told to fend for themselves.[25] All sorts of people helped them. All sorts of people received impromptu training from them. The line between armed action initiated by MK and that taken by groups in the name of MK, their actual connection to the exiled army remote, quickly blurred.[26]

Winnie was thus one among untold numbers of people who took MK soldiers in and helped them with their work. In 1986 alone, 263 people were arrested for giving guerrillas succour.[27]

But that is hardly the end of the story. For one, it should be asked what sorts of returning MK soldiers came to Winnie.

'To knock on the door of a well-known activist was against all instructions,' an MK combatant recalled years later. 'Those who came to her and said that they had received training from the outside would either have been extremely ill-disciplined or agents provocateurs.'[28]

One gets a sense of the sort of returning MK soldier who approached Winnie Mandela in the story of a guerrilla fighter named Oupa Seheri.

On the evening of January 24, 1987, Seheri went to Winnie's house with an AK-47 concealed in his bag. He was ushered to Zindzi's bedroom, where he conferred with a young man named S'thembiso Buthelezi, a founding member of the Mandela United Football Club and Zindzi's lover.

Buthelezi gave Seheri a Škorpion machine pistol. It had been smuggled into the country by another returning MK soldier, Vuyisile Tshabalala, who had, by now, come to know Winnie well. Seheri left Winnie's house with the machine pistol; his AK-47 remained behind for safekeeping. He intended to sleep with the Škorpion in his bed that night and to use it the following day to train a clandestine group of Soweto youths.

Seheri did not, however, go directly home. He went to a Soweto bar with his machine pistol concealed in his jacket.

Within a couple of hours he was drunk, and when a stranger brushed past him, he took umbrage and threw a punch. The stranger's name was Xola Mokhaula. He overpowered Seheri without much effort, disarmed him of his machine pistol and took it home.

Hours later, Mokhaula's mother's house was raked with automatic gunfire while several people stormed through the kitchen door; two of them were Seheri and his girlfriend, the remainder members of the Mandela United Football Club. S'thembiso Buthelezi was in the thick of the drama; he had driven members of the club to Mokhaula's house in Winnie's car.

In his search for the Škorpion, Seheri terrorized the members of the Mokhaula household. To show the seriousness of his intent, he shot a young man called Mlando Ngubeni in the hip; Ngubeni crawled away into an adjoining bedroom, where he bled to death.

Seheri eventually found his gun and executed Mokhaula on his way out, a grim punishment for having won a fistfight started by another man.[29]

Seheri was arrested the following day. Under torture, he began to speak. On January 27, Winnie's house was raided; Buthelezi and several other members of the football club were arrested and taken away.

. .

The shooting spree at Xola Mokhaula's house, the subsequent police raid on Winnie's place, the arrest of S'thembiso Buthelezi and other members of the household – this series of incidents slowly unravelled the world Winnie had made.

Each member of the club detained in the raids was interrogated, tortured, made to speak. What did they say? And what deals had they made? Many of them returned to Winnie's house in the following months, and the question of who might be spying ate that house up from the inside.

Chapter 50

A month after they arrested S'thembiso Buthelezi and other members of the household, the police raided again. This time they found a Škorpion machine gun pistol in a suitcase under Zindzi's bed. They promptly arrested her.

It was now that a tale finally had to be told to Nelson Mandela, for his daughter's arrest was all over the news. He had thought that she was living in Cape Town, a diligent student at UCT.

Winnie hastily assembled a story for her husband's consumption, only one part of which was true: S'thembiso Buthelezi, she told Nelson, correctly, was Zindzi's lover. But she hid from Nelson that Buthelezi was a founding member of the football club. In the story she told, he was a student at UCT; Zindzi had met him in class; they had fallen in love; she had brought him up to Johannesburg to visit. It so happened that the police raided while they were there; they planted a weapon under Zindzi's bed. 'It was a Škorpion,' she added. 'Some weird machine gun.'[1]

Nelson must have smelled a rat. For when Zindzi and Winnie next came to see him, the first words to issue from his mouth were not about the gun or the arrest or what had happened at the Soweto house. Instead, he asked Zindzi whether she was back at university after the year-end vacation.

'Not yet,' she replied.

'When do they open?'

'They opened last week.'

In response to the dismay that must have shown on Nelson's face, Winnie intervened. 'She's not back at university because she's upset about Buthelezi's arrest.'

'How does that stop you from going to school?' Nelson snapped.

'Tata [Dad],' Zindzi replied. 'I have problems with my conscience.'

'Well how does it help at all not to continue with your studies?' Nelson asked. 'This is the type of life your family undergoes. You must go back immediately. I cannot understand the reason for your not attending. You support S'thembiso. You love him. That is enough. You must go back immediately unless you can show me that there is something absolutely essential which requires you to stay away.'

'She has a guilty feeling because of the attitude of his brothers and sisters,' Winnie explained. 'They felt that his relationship [with Zindzi] would lead to this sort of trouble . . . Now they are saying I told you so.'

'They will not stop saying so even if Zindzi does not go [back to university],' Nelson replied incredulously.

He did not understand, and it took many conversations with his wife and daughter until he finally *did* understand, that their point was not to reason but to obscure.

'I will never sleep in my grave if she has no qualifications!' he implored Winnie.

'Go back!' he commanded Zindzi. 'Get your things and go back to university!'[2]

. .

Less than a month later, Winnie told Nelson flatly that Zindzi was no longer a student at UCT; their daughter was living with her in Soweto and had registered to study at Wits. The way she told the story, neither she nor Zindzi had had much say in the matter. The decision had been made by George Bizos, Nelson's old friend and lawyer.

'It is because the police keep saying they are awaiting word from the attorney-general as to whether to charge her or not,' Winnie explained. 'And so George thought it was better to transfer her to Wits and let her study there so they don't disrupt her studies in Cape Town.'

As she must have anticipated, Nelson exploded.

'Why was I not consulted?' he shouted. 'Why did she lie to me?'

But she didn't lie, Winnie replied. When she last visited Nelson, George had yet to make the decision.

The conversation became knotted in a dispute about precise dates, precise facts, when exactly Zindzi knew she was leaving for Johannesburg, whether this was before she last saw Nelson. It was a pointless conversation, and Nelson's exasperation finally got the better of him.

'I know how to deal with you people!' he threatened.

'You keep saying I can't deal with family matters,' Winnie replied. 'So I went to George.'[3]

. .

How much about his wife and daughter's life did Nelson Mandela surmise?

Each letter he wrote or received was read by his enemy, each conversation with a visitor recorded and transcribed. He knew this. And he ensured that everyone who visited or corresponded with him knew it, too.

And so even for those who might *want* to tell him what was happening in his home, there was little opportunity.

And if he himself had entertained dark thoughts, or had just fleetingly wondered, or had woken in the night with the sense that something was terribly wrong, he would have neither given voice to these feelings nor committed them to paper.

There was only one forum in which he might talk and listen privately: in privileged consultations with his lawyers. And he had, for now, given these up. For by 1987 he was talking secretly, if fitfully, to senior government officials, and as proof of his *bona fides*, proof that these talks really were secret, he had resolved that his enemy would hear every word he said.[4]

'It is a matter of national interest that I not have an unsupervised visit,' he told Winnie enigmatically.[5]

. .

In August 1987, Winnie and Zindzi came to see him together. Zindzi's studies at Wits were, predictably, not going well, and Nelson picked a fight with her. Winnie, as had become her wont, intervened to protect Zindzi from her father's anger.

'We cannot discuss these difficulties here,' Winnie said, interrupting Nelson's interrogation of his daughter.

'They have to be discussed!' Nelson snapped. 'There should be no reason whatsoever.'

'I don't think you have an idea of the problems,' Winnie interjected. 'We can't discuss them here. I think it is best for [Zindzi] to see you with an attorney . . . so that they can explain to you in a privileged visit.'

'No, no, no. I don't even want to listen to that,' Nelson shot back. 'Zindzi must explain to me why she has persistently refused to stay at varsity [university] because I insisted that she stay . . . Whatever the problem is, it has been complicated by her refusal to carry out my recommendation.'

He turned to Zindzi now. 'You must explain to me why you are not at varsity.'

Zindzi was mute.

'What is your problem!' Nelson demanded.

'I do not know how to put it to you', Zindzi finally replied, 'without being very careless in things I have to disclose here, now.'

'No, no, don't,' Winnie said, intervening.

'Let me explain to Tata', Zindzi continued, 'that I took up the cause of our people, something which I feel very strongly about, because of my background. You have seen in the papers that we have a shortage of manpower and I am needed because of certain skills I have.'

'No, no, no. I take strong exception to that,' Nelson shot back. 'You should have come to discuss the matter with me because I have told you that your education is first.'

'I could not foresee the various crises we would be in now,' Zindzi replied, 'our manpower reduced drastically.'

'No, no, no! Don't tell me about that! Don't tell me about that! I am in the struggle here. Your mother is in the struggle. There is no reason for that at all. I have told you that your first priority is education.'

'I wish sometimes that people who bring instructions to us had access to you,' Winnie said. 'I had problems when this sort of thing happened and when I had direct difficulties with those people they had angry comments to me . . . These people made statements no parent can take . . . I foresaw what was going to happen as a mother.'

'No, no, no! I asked you that Zindzi should go back to varsity and I told you to send me a telegram to confirm this!'

He turned to Zindzi. 'What are you going to do now!'

There was a long silence. Then Zindzi began to weep.

'No, Zindzi,' Winnie said. 'That should not be your reaction.'

'I asked you what you are going to do!' Nelson shouted.

In response to which she wept some more.

'Zindzi, you are not going to break down here,' Winnie said. 'Please don't do that here. I told you at home that you are not going to do that here.'

Now she turned to Nelson. 'I wish', she said, 'that there was a way to make children look forward to visits here with you.'

It was the most vicious blow.

'This is so unfortunate,' she continued, getting up to go. 'Come, Zindzi.'

Mother and daughter left the interview room, and the thirteen-year-old Mandla, who had been waiting outside, came in. Nelson chatted with the boy for a few minutes and as he was saying goodbye asked the warder to call Zindzi back in, even though the visit had now run overtime.

'She cannot go like that,' Nelson explained. 'Can I please see her for just a few minutes?'

The warder agreed without argument and called Zindzi back in.

'You know, darling,' he said, once she was settled, 'for you to leave like this is going to make my whole life miserable. I love you. You must appreciate as a parent I would like to see you equipped for life. My interest in the family is foremost. The question of you being in varsity has been an obsession with me. It would have been better if you had indicated to me why you left but I had to find out this way. I was given drips of information which are not coherent to your staying away. What do you expect me to do?'

His question prompted her to begin to weep again.

'Darling, why won't you talk to me?'

'I am hurt,' she replied.

'Come sit here. Come sit on my lap. You are a strong person. You must talk to me. What use can I be to the nation if I cannot take interest in my own child? You must talk to me.'

She was still weeping and the warder transcribing the conversation could not make out everything she said in reply. 'I am going to be charged and I am going to jail,' is all he managed to hear.

'You can still go back to varsity. If you can, go and tell people that I insist. If they object, tell them to send a suitable person to be accompanied by an attorney to come and see and discuss this with me. If they want to charge you, let them charge you while you are at varsity. This is why I wanted you in Cape Town. I knew this was going to happen.

'I love you and you are close to my heart. This is the one thing that can kill me more than anything else. I faced the last 25 years and nothing could break me. This could. If anyone can send me to the grave early, it is you. I want you to go back otherwise I will be very hurt indeed. Please go back. Be strong. Don't break down when you come here and this should not be the last time. Next time come alone and see me. Please, wipe your tears and know that I am here. The friendship between us must be maintained. So next time come alone. Okay, darling. Goodbye.'

She did not return his farewell; she got up and left.[6]

.   .

Of the three figures in these encounters, it is Zindzi who stands out. She has told her father that she has given up her studies to become a guerrilla fighter, an act of strength and resolve if ever there was one. But in the face of his wrath, she is a frightened child. The dissonance draws attention.

The appearance Zindzi offers the world is deceptive. She is beautiful and charismatic; she writes lucid poetry and speaks to large audiences with poise. But behind this facade she appears to be a person without force of her own. Eight years have passed since she accompanied her mother to Brandfort. Since then, every attempt to strike out and live her own life has failed. Plans to study in the U.K. and in Johannesburg fell apart. Plans to marry her lover and live with him in Johannesburg were aborted; her lover had to come and live in her mother's house instead. She abandoned her studies at UCT to become absorbed once more into her mother's world, her mother's politics, her mother's vision of how apartheid should end.

And now, in the face of her father's will – which he expresses with the tyranny of a biblical patriarch – she breaks down and weeps. She is twenty-six, but her formidable parents have kept her a child. They are at war over her; she is both the subject of this war and its impotent witness.

And in the battle between the older Mandelas it is Winnie who wins; it is hard to miss how decisively she has shaped the outcome of the encounter. 'I wish', she has said, 'that there was a way to make children look forward to visits here with you.' She has made of Nelson a brute, an ogre, a man who breaks children and makes them cry.

'This should not be the last time,' he pleaded with Zindzi. He understood that his relationship with her hung by a thread. And he understood, too, that this was his wife's will. 'Next time come alone and see me,' he pleaded. 'The friendship between us must be maintained. So next time come alone.'

. .

The political dimensions of what had happened in that room were no less intricate. Despite the presence of recording devices, and in the face of her mother's attempts to stop her, Zindzi had told Nelson that she had been recruited into MK. Once the news was out, Winnie played the helpless mother, unable to stand up to those who had enlisted her daughter to fight. 'I wish sometimes that people who bring instructions to us had access to you,' she had said. 'These people made statements no parent can take.'

What did Nelson make of this?

'What is actually happening,' he told one of his lawyers, Priscilla Jana, when she came to see him in December 1987, three months after Zindzi and Winnie's visit, '[is that Zindzi is] engaged in activities which I am sure are not authorised by our organisation ... We have got one leadership in this country ... and if there is one thing that is extremely dangerous, it is for anybody, especially for a member of a family of a person who is held in high esteem by his opponents, to do anything which suggests that instructions come from anywhere but the leadership that is directing the struggle.'

And so he understood full well that his daughter had been enlisted by a wayward, maverick force in his own ranks.

He told Jana to relay a message to Zindzi.

'I have had enough. You are going to have a lot of things destroyed for which we have fought all our lives ... I am not requesting Zindzi, I am instructing her, to come down to UCT and to stay at campus. If she doesn't do so it is her own decision, but then she must leave the house. I will have nothing to do with her again if she doesn't do that.'

He has warned that he will wash his hands of his daughter. But what of his wife? Did he believe her when she said that she could only stand by helplessly while these wayward forces recruited Zindzi into their ranks?

'I think that Zindzi cannot [bear] entire responsibility,' Jana says at one point.

'No, no. I understand,' Nelson interrupts. 'It is because we are discussing her. There are other people involved. You can rest assured that in almost all my visits I have been trying to correct that, but somehow I am helpless. I get promises, and then the same thing continues.'

He omits Winnie's name because the conversation is being recorded, but he is of course referring to her; he thus understands that despite her protestations she has encouraged her daughter to join a renegade armed band.

'I can assure you that other people have tried as well,' Jana says.[7]

They both know that she is referring to Oliver Tambo's futile attempts to rein in Winnie Mandela.

And so Nelson understands that Winnie was complicit in Zindzi's abandonment of her studies at UCT and that she encouraged Zindzi to join a wayward force in MK.

But did he understand that Winnie herself *was* the wayward force? It is hard to say.

. .

In February 1988, Winnie came to see him alone. The visit began civilly enough, but the moment the conversation turned to Zindzi, husband and wife began to feud. And as the spirit of the encounter darkened, the bitterness that had been welling up inside Nelson spewed.

The warder on duty paraphrased this part of the conversation, and we cannot know the precise words Nelson used. They appear to have been desperately furious. 'I've been here 25 years now,' the warder has him shout. '[I have experienced] humiliation after humiliation. You cannot know what [is going on in your house]. You cannot know. What you started will not be tolerated by any man!'

Winnie appeared to change the subject.

'Before visiting time is over, I must tell you this,' she said, the direct transcript of their conversation now back in place. Nelson's sister Leabie has spoken of a child, a girl, who claims to be Nelson's daughter. 'I have forgotten her name.' An argument has erupted over who should pay for her education.

'They say she is your child,' Winnie repeated. 'Leabie says so.'

'What is the surname?' Nelson asked.

'I have forgotten the girl's name. And the mother's name also. But they said you would know her.'

'How old is she?'

'Apparently Zindzi's age,' Winnie replied, no doubt pointedly.

'You can tell Leabie I know nothing of the sort,' Nelson snapped.

'I suggest that she comes here.'

'I don't want any of your suggestions.'

'How do I convey your message to her?'

'That is your problem,' Nelson replied.

'Is that your message about the child?'

'Yes.'

'She has done nothing wrong.'

'I know,' he conceded.

'Your attitude is wrong.'

'I don't want to hear more about it. If you're going to talk, talk about something else, not that subject.'[8]

Winnie was so much better than Nelson at this, her timing exquisite. Not a couple of minutes earlier, he was accusing her of terrible things. At the click of her fingers, he had become a callous man, leaving in want the child his philandering had spawned.

Chapter 51

I t is hard to resist comparing Nelson Mandela's relationship with his wife and daughter to the bond he built with his enemy. If one strips away the politics and the history, if one looks simply at the human fabric, the comparison is stark. Between Nelson and Winnie there is concealment and deceit; between him and his enemy there is a will to be clear. With his daughter he is obtuse and unwise; with his enemy he is unfailingly acute.

A long hiatus followed Nelson's initial encounter with Kobie Coetsee in his hospital room in November 1985. The two men met just once in 1986 and only sporadically during the course of the following year. For all of this time, Nelson kept these meetings secret.

'I chose to tell nobody,' he writes in his autobiography. 'Not my colleagues upstairs or those in Lusaka . . . I knew that my colleagues upstairs would condemn my proposal, and that would kill the initiative before it was even born.'[1]

Only in May 1988 did the talks take on a more formal character. At this time, P. W. Botha appointed a team of several officials to meet with Mandela at regular intervals.[2]

It was now that Nelson resolved to tell his closest comrades what he was doing. They were deeply wary, not least his dearest and most trusted friend, Walter Sisulu. 'I could see he was uncomfortable,' Nelson recalled, 'and at best, lukewarm.'[3] As for Oliver Tambo, he smuggled a letter to Nelson to raise his concern. 'What, he wanted to know, was I discussing with the government,' Nelson remembered. 'Oliver could not have believed that I was selling out, but he might have thought that I was making an error of judgment. In fact, the tenor of his note suggested that.'[4]

Tambo's and Sisulu's suspicions soon dimmed. But the suspicions of many others did not. Once news that he and his enemy were speaking was abroad, rumours that Nelson had cracked and was being used periodically swirled. At moments, these fears reached hysterical pitch, like in April 1989, when Nelson's old foe Govan Mbeki, now free, sent a call to activists across South Africa to cut ties with Nelson.[5] And in July of the same year, when news reached the ANC in exile that Nelson had met with P. W. Botha, the fever rose again; among the stories going around senior ANC circles was that Nelson had been drugged and taken to see Botha by force.[6]

Nelson could not have heard all these rumours, but he felt their pressures acutely. In the early months of 1988, Christo Brand noted the signs of stress in his charge. 'He was so very on edge at that time,' Brand recalled. 'He had no sense of humour at all.' At times, his behaviour was so out of character, Brand felt he was in the presence of a stranger. Once, when Nelson woke to discover that the morning newspaper was nowhere to be found, he summoned the night-duty warder and spewed rage. 'I thought for a moment that Mandela was going to hit him,' Brand wrote.[7]

The pressure under which Nelson was putting himself was deliberate. 'Both sides regarded discussions as a sign of weakness and betrayal,' he wrote. 'Neither would come to the table unless the other made significant concessions . . . Someone from our side needed to take the first step.'[8]

Nelson understood he had given his enemy the wherewithal to destroy him. For he knew, as two shrewd commentators have put it, that the government might 'accept his invitation, but with the ulterior motive of trapping him, discrediting him among his people and decapitating the ANC leadership at a crucial moment.'[9]

And his enemy knew that he knew this. 'He was prepared to place his political life in the hands of the dominant Afrikaner "establishment" that controlled his life,' a National Intelligence Service memo from the time observes. 'If the Government and the team had wanted to maliciously exploit the talks with [him], this could have led to his destruction.'[10]

This was the most creative act of his political career. The ANC and the South African government were facing a classic prisoner's dilemma. Both wanted a negotiated end to apartheid. But neither trusted the other. Nelson offered his enemy the means to destroy him as a way of showing his bona fides; in so doing, he had offered them a chance to show theirs. It was a brilliant move.[11]

He did not lose clarity of purpose. From the start, he let it be known to his interlocutors that talking to him was no substitute for talking to the ANC. He told them, too, that his organization would not begin to negotiate a settlement before it was unbanned, political prisoners set free and security legislation rescinded. Nor could the ANC contemplate suspending violence until these conditions were met.

Two months before his release, the government's National Intelligence Service wrote a secret assessment of Nelson Mandela. It is among the most trenchant analyses of his character and his politics there is. That it was his enemy who saw him so clearly is of the greatest irony.

The document – almost certainly penned by the NIS head, Niël Barnard, and his deputy, Mike Louw – describes Nelson Mandela as a man of some vanity. In prison, he became 'one of the world's most famous martyrs and he has an urgent need to live up to this fame by sacrificing his freedom to a role of great statesmanship in the few years that may still be bestowed upon him'. He needs 'to perpetuate his name'.

But he will not compromise on his principles in this quest. He can be trusted to keep his word, they write, 'but that he could be "bought" to betray his loyalty to his organization and his deep-rooted political philosophy is not possible'.

Indeed, they argue, he thinks that history is on his organization's side, that it will triumph by virtue of its principles. 'He believes . . . that if the government can first be provoked to "engagement", the moral power and logic of the ANC's cause will win the day.'

That the authors of the report have come to admire Nelson shines through. 'One is struck by his spiritual power,' they write, 'the lack of bitterness, his natural courtesy, as well as his personal integrity. He will conceal truths and even present skewed ones to substantiate his argument, but lies and dishonesty are not in his nature.'

Above all, they believe that a peaceful way out of apartheid is unlikely without him. They urge their principal to make haste. 'His health is good, but his ankles are visibly swollen due to moderate heart failure which is not unexpected at his age. Furthermore, he realizes that his own camp as well as the Government is entering a period of political acceleration and that, if he cannot play his card soon, his personal political role could be severely damaged.'[12]

Hurry, they implore. There is not much time.

Chapter 52

In reaching out to his enemy, Nelson Mandela believed that he might save his country.

He would save it from further bloodshed, from the further hardening of hearts, from wounds that do not heal long after the war has been won.

Whether he knew quite how much damage had already been done is unclear. He certainly had little inkling of how thoroughly the brutality of his country had invaded his home at 8115 Orlando West.

. .

Winnie built her household in a world full of young men's violence, and she harnessed that violence; hers was, in an obvious sense, a household of its time. And yet her home was also singular, for she scrambled what was expected of mothers, of lovers, of daughters, of sons, breaking a string of taboos.

It is hard to exaggerate the machismo that characterized youth culture in Soweto at that time. To an astonishing degree, sexual violence against young women and girls was an anodyne fact of life. 'The community seemed to treat rape as if it were just some minor inconvenience,' recalled the radio personality Redi Tlhabi in her memoir of growing up in Orlando East in the 1980s and 1990s. 'It was not uncommon for a young woman to be walking down the street and for someone, even another woman, to point to her and snigger, "*Phela*, this one was raped by so-and-so." So-and-so would be a well-known thug still roaming the streets without a care in the world.'

Tlhabi herself lived 'with the suffocating fear that one day it would be my turn. I was big for my age, and while my classmates were still sitting with their legs apart, I couldn't afford to be so childlike and carefree ... I often attracted the attention of much older boys and young men. When I ignored them, the word rape fell from their lips with ease while their friends and onlookers just laughed."[1]

The rawest recruits to this culture of machismo resided under Winnie's roof. And while they lived in her house, some committed acts of violence as cruel as any they had witnessed on the streets. But in the house itself, the relationship between the sexes was like nothing they would have seen elsewhere. Both Winnie and Zindzi took lovers from the young men who lived on their property. But these men did not exercise power over the women with whom they slept, not on the surface at any rate. On the contrary, to be chosen by them was to have a portion of *their* power bestowed upon one.

S'thembiso Buthelezi, members of the household later testified, and, after he was jailed, Zindzi's new lover, Sizwe Sithole, acquired superior status in the house by virtue of sleeping in Zindzi's bed.[2] And both fell on their swords to keep mother and daughter out of jail, their status as loyal lieutenants and lovers conjoined.

As for Winnie, her choosing a lover among the members of her household speaks so illuminatingly to the state of her being at this strange, difficult time.

Nearly a decade later, a woman who shared a lover with Winnie in the late 1980s gave testimony at South Africa's Truth and Reconciliation Commission (TRC). Her name is Evodia Nkadimeng. Hers is a most complex tale, and it is well to tell it one step at a time.

A UDF activist, Nkadimeng was detained by police in the provincial town of Potgietersrus, 170 miles north of Johannesburg, in January 1988. She soon learned that three male activists were being kept in the same jail, for they began smuggling letters to her via common-law prisoners. Among them was a man named Johannes Mabotha. The letters from him soon ceased, for he was released.

When Nkadimeng was let free in July, Mabotha began coming unannounced to her home and flirting with her. They became lovers. He told her in confidence that he was an MK operative and wished to recruit her into the armed struggle.

It so happened that Nkadimeng was going regularly at that time to see an old friend in jail. His name was Martin Sehlapelo, an MK soldier who had been captured and was about to receive a lengthy prison sentence.

On her visits to Sehlapelo, Nkadimeng confided about her new lover, Johannes Mabotha. The more she described him, the more uneasy Sehlapelo became. He recognized him as a man who, months earlier, had been placed in a cell adjacent to his own, his obvious intent to extract information. Sehlapelo surmised that Mabotha was what later become known in South Africa as an askari, an MK guerrilla who had been captured, turned and set to work for the other side.[3]

His suspicion was precisely correct. It was revealed in time that Mabotha was indeed an askari; his police commander was Eugene de Kock, a man who would become notorious as the head of a secret assassination squad housed at a farm called Vlakplaas.[4] Among other activities, members of the squad scoured railway stations, taxi ranks and shebeens for the faces of MK soldiers they had known in exile; when they found a person they recognized, they hunted him down and slayed him.

Sehlapelo told Nkadimeng that her life was in danger. He advised her to keep seeing Mabotha until the opportunity arose to kill him. It was her life versus his, Sehlapelo advised.[5]

· ·

In early January 1989, when he had been coming sporadically to see Nkadimeng for several months, Mabotha told her something startling and unexpected; for the last few weeks, he said, he had been living in Winnie Mandela's house in Soweto.

She did not believe him. It was only when he brought other people who lived with Winnie to Evodia's house – the football coach, Jerry Richardson, and two others, Xoliswa Falati and Katiza Cebekhulu – that she understood that he truly did live in the home of the struggle's most famous woman. This troubled her deeply. For if Sehlapelo's suspicions were right – and she was increasingly certain that they were – Winnie Mandela had a spy in her home.

'You know, Evodia,' she recalled Mabotha telling her, 'in Mrs. Mandela's house, I am a trusted person.'

'How did they come to trust you?' Nkadimeng asked.

'You cannot believe it, I know that Mrs. Mandela has got white hair.'

'How did you come to know that?'

'No, Mrs. Mandela allows me to touch her here,' he replied, placing his hand behind his ear.

'You know,' he continued, 'there's nobody allowed to use her bathroom except myself.'[6]

There is wide-eyed wonder here: a grown man is ventriloquizing a small boy, a boy who has been permitted to sleep with his mother.

Cautiously, Nkadimeng raised her suspicions about Mabotha with the other three members of the Mandela household. She found them surprisingly receptive to what she was saying. Indeed, they seemed positively excited. Mrs. Mandela had drawn much too close to Mabotha, they told her; she was in love with him and he had, as a result, grown far too powerful. They urged her to come back with them to Soweto to tell Winnie personally of what she knew.

Nkadimeng must have surmised in this moment the state Winnie's household was in. The envy, the rivalry, the mutual suspicion, the will to stab others in the back. She arrived at a perilous situation; she had no idea how Winnie might respond to what she was about to say. To her relief, Mabotha was not there. She told Winnie as carefully as she could all she knew.

'I could see from her face that she was shocked,' Nkadimeng told the TRC. 'She even excused herself for a few minutes from that meeting after I explained the whole thing.' But when Winnie returned, her discomposure had vanished; she was expressionless and hard.

Nkadimeng remained in Soweto for about two weeks. Winnie found her a place to stay and sent a car each morning to fetch her; she spent her days at Winnie's house before being returned to her lodgings in the evening. It was a treacherous time. Mabotha was back now and was not at all pleased to discover what Nkadimeng had told Winnie. 'I could feel that I was in real danger and I could be killed at any time,' she told the TRC.[7]

To this author, Nkadimeng told a more detailed and complex story. The football team, she soon realized, had been forbidden to talk to her, and so although people were all about her, none so much as returned her greeting.

Something stranger still was happening. Mabotha came and went. For every moment he was there, he did not leave Winnie's side. 'They moved through the house hand in hand,' Nkadimeng recalled. 'When she goes to the kitchen, he goes. When she is watching TV, he is sitting next to her, still holding her hand. Wherever she moved, he moved with her.'

Soon, members of the household began making meaningful eye contact with Nkadimeng. 'It was clear that Mama's relationship with Mabotha was upsetting everybody,' she recalled. 'We just used our eyes to communicate our dissatisfaction.'

Eventually, Zindzi began confiding in Nkadimeng. 'Evodia,' she remembered Zindzi saying, 'something strange is happening in this house. That man is confusing my mother. He does not even allow me to have privacy with her. I feel I no longer belong in this house. I in fact tried to attack him with an empty bottle the other day; my mother stopped me.'

A few days after that conversation, Nkadimeng was arrested. 'Do you know why Mrs. Mandela hates you so?' she recalled her interrogator, Warrant Officer Jan Augustyn, asking her during an interminable interrogation. 'Not because you said Mabotha was a spy, but because you said you slept with him.'[8]

.   .

Another, somewhat quirky, piece of evidence was presented to the TRC. The Soweto security police, who were bugging Winnie's bedroom, listened in while she and Mabotha made love. Once, Mabotha fell from the bed and crashed to the floor. Winnie, fearing that he was injured, became enormously gentle. 'She told him how sorry she was that he may have hurt himself,' the policeman who read the transcript of the conversation testified.[9] He giggled as he gave his testimony and was upbraided by the lawyer cross-examining him.

Beyond the prurience and the titillation, his nervous laughter was perhaps a response to the incongruity: this famously hard woman was also very tender and apparently in love.

.   .

These wisps of testimony are ethereal and strange. One nonetheless recognizes in them something familiar. A certain lack of boundaries accompanied Winnie's relations with others. It is there in her affair with Brian Somana in the early 1960s when she clung to him in the face of personal destruction; it is there, too, in the way Theuns Swanepoel, her torturer, invaded her spirit, his will to destroy her lodged forever in her head.

In late 1988, shortly before she met Johannes Mabotha, Winnie was quietly asked to hide two members of MK. She placed them in Jerry Richardson's house. Someone tipped off the police that they were there, for on the afternoon of November 9 the house was raided by a heavily armed squad. In the shoot-out that ensued, both guerrillas and a police officer died.

Richardson was taken into custody and then released two weeks later without being charged. With the clarity of distance, one looks upon this moment in amazement. Richardson, we now know, had been recruited as a police informer about a year after he began working with Winnie; the policeman who died that day was in fact his handler. It was Richardson, a Security Branch officer would testify to the TRC, who told the police that two guerrillas were hiding in his house.[10] Could the police not have done more to conceal this? To release him without charge after the men he'd been hiding were betrayed was to put a sign announcing his perfidy around his neck.

Astonishingly, Winnie appears not to have suspected Richardson at all, neither during the two weeks of his detention nor after his release. While he was still being held, her suspicions alighted elsewhere, on two youths – aged nineteen and twenty one, respectively – who had visited the guerrillas while they were in hiding. One of them was Lolo Sono. The other, his friend Siboniso Tshabalala.

On a Sunday evening in mid-November, Lolo's father, Nicodemus Sono, who had known Winnie since the uprisings of 1976, returned home to find a member of Winnie's household waiting at his front gate. He led Sono down the road to where Winnie's van was parked and invited him to step inside. Winnie was there, as were several members of the football team. And so was his son, Lolo, who had been so disfigured that his father barely recognized him. 'His face . . . was actually pulped,' Sono testified, 'as if someone had . . . crushed him against the wall.'

When he saw his father, Lolo tried to speak, but Winnie shut him up. She told Sono that she had come to show him his son the spy.

Sono tried to reason with her. Lolo could not have betrayed the guerrillas, he said. He had in fact done so much to assist them over the months, at great risk. One of them was a beloved relative, a man Lolo deeply admired.

As he spoke, he detected in Winnie a hardening – 'she suddenly changed and ... looked at me the other way' is how he put it – and he immediately stopped reasoning and instead begged for his son's life. 'Leave Lolo with me because he has already been beaten,' he recalled pleading. 'If it's for punishment, I understand that he's been punished; can't you please leave him with me.'

Sono had known Winnie for twelve years now. When she answered him, her tone was like nothing he had heard from her before. 'She was really not speaking to me as I always knew her; ... she raised up her voice; she was speaking very loud. "I cannot leave him with you! He is a spy!"' She told him she would send his son into exile where the ANC would decide what to do with him.

The van took off, circled the block and stopped outside Sono's house. He glanced again at his son as he was preparing to leave.

'He was in a terrible state,' Sono remembered. 'He was shaking.' And he noticed for the first time that his son was wet. He must have passed out during his torture, Sono thought, and had a bucket of water thrown over his head. 'I asked her may I please get a jersey for Lolo because by then I thought he's feeling cold.'

To this, Winnie agreed. Father and son were permitted to get out of the van and walk as far as the front gate, accompanied by 'a hefty man with a gun on his hip'. Sono called for his wife to bring a jumper. She brought one and went immediately back into the house. Sono helped Lolo into the jumper and watched him climb back into the van. It drove off.

For a long time, he believed that Winnie had done what she had said and that his son was somewhere in exile. The alternative was too ghastly to contemplate.[11]

Lolo Sono's corpse, riddled with stab wounds, was found and delivered to a government mortuary days after his father's encounter with Winnie. Unable to identify the body, the authorities had given him a pauper's burial. A quarter of a century passed before the remains were exhumed and identified as belonging to Lolo Sono.[12]

On that same Sunday when Nicodemus Sono encountered his badly beaten son, men from Winnie's household came to the home of Lolo Sono's friend Siboniso Tshabalala to find that he was not there. When he finally came home late that night, his mother advised him to flee. He chose not to. He would rather just go to Winnie's house the following morning, he told his mother, and find out what these men wanted.

When his mother left for work the next day, Siboniso was sleeping. She returned in the evening to find that he was gone. In his bedroom cupboard, all his shoes, save one pair, were in their usual place. He must be planning to return this evening, she reasoned.[13]

His remains were exhumed with Sono's all those years later. He, too, had been stabbed to death.

Chapter 53

During the final years of his incarceration, Nelson Mandela's captors began preparing him for life as a free man. It began with periodic car journeys into the world outside.

The first was to a vineyard opposite Pollsmoor Prison where he was offered the opportunity to walk alone among the vines and help himself to their fruit. 'Surely the farmer will shoot me if he sees me picking his grapes?' Nelson asked. He was told that the farmer was a friend, and the warders accompanying him watched as his figure slowly receded and was lost among the vines.[1]

Months later, after a visit to the doctor, the convoy taking Nelson back to Pollsmoor Prison turned onto Beach Road in Sea Point. Alongside it is one of Cape Town's loveliest public spaces, a pedestrian promenade stretching along the oceanfront for two or more miles.

It was about 8:00 p.m. and the world had grown dark. Christo Brand was driving Nelson that evening. He pulled into a parking place next to the ocean and offered to walk with Nelson to a small beach below. Nelson looked out to Robben Island, a scattering of lights on the surface of the ocean.

'What is that place out there?' he asked.

Brand told him that it was his old prison.

Nelson did not believe him. 'He was certain that the water he could see was a river,' Brand recollected, 'but I told him to listen to the waves. I then took him across a few rocks . . . and told him to dip his hand in the water. "You see, it's salty," I said to him.'

The two men stood there for some time, Nelson's moment of confusion causing some awkwardness between them. 'I've never been out this late before,' he said finally. They walked back to the car in silence.[2]

.   .

In July 1988, Winnie informed Nelson that their home at 8115 Orlando West had been burned to the ground.

'It was a reaction to the concert,' she told him, referring to the seventieth birthday tribute that had just been broadcast across the world.

'No doubt,' Nelson replied.

'It was because we were front page news,' she continued. 'It was clear that it was going to happen.'[3]

For a man whose connection to his past had long felt tenuous, the news that his home had been destroyed was disorienting in the extreme. 'We had lost invaluable family records, photographs, and keepsakes – even the slice of wedding cake Winnie had been saving for my release,' he wrote. 'I had always thought that some day when I left prison I would be able to recapture the past when looking over those pictures and letters, and now they were gone.'[4]

His house had in fact been burned by schoolboys. Members of Winnie's football team had raped a girl from their school and this was their vengeance. As the flames engulfed the house, neighbours stood and watched, their ambivalence about the destruction of Winnie's home expressed in their inaction.[5]

. .

Two years earlier, Winnie had begun construction on a spacious new house in a plush section of Soweto known colloquially as Beverley Hills. Its grandeur had courted controversy. The money to fund the construction was gathered in a trust administered by the lawyer Raymond Tucker, the donors all anonymous.[6] One of those who had raised funds for the house was an American named Robert Brown; he had struck up a friendship with Winnie shortly after she returned to Soweto. He had already, by now, raised money for Zenani and her husband to study at Boston College.

Brown's association with the Mandela family caused trouble. By 1988, he had persuaded Winnie to sign over power of attorney to conduct business on behalf of the Mandelas abroad. Among the deals in the offing was the sale of the rights to a film on Winnie's life to Bill Cosby, a development that caused consternation in ANC ranks abroad and among activists at home.

Now, in the wake of the destruction of the house at 8115 Orlando West, a Soweto crisis committee was formed. Consisting of several senior UDF leaders, it was tasked to manage the debacle that was the Mandela United Football Club and to sever the Mandela family from Robert Brown.

The question of money was always going to be difficult. Nelson was a prisoner who had not earned a cent since his days as a lawyer. The government's decades-long harassment of Winnie had stolen from her the wherewithal to earn a living. The couple's global status and their poverty sat awkwardly together. That they required benefactors went without saying. As Nelson told Robert Brown on the one occasion they met, in the visiting room at Pollsmoor, 'One thing that has given us a great deal of inspiration is the support of friends ... There is nothing to worry a parent [more than that] the children should not have the opportunity which you as a parent would have provided if you were in a position to do so.'[7]

How to accumulate family assets with dignity was among the delicate tasks ahead.

.   .

Two weeks after he learned that his house had burned down, Nelson woke gasping for breath. He was taken immediately to the hospital and into surgery, where he was diagnosed with tuberculosis. He put it down to the dampness of the quarters in which he had been living over the last two and a half years.[8] Christo Brand saw its roots in the stress of the secret talks and in the crisis in his family. 'A strong, fit man for the whole time I had known him, he now seemed to be growing older and weaker in front of my eyes,' Brand was to write.[9]

He spent six weeks in a private clinic. One evening in early December, a senior warder came into his room and told him to prepare to leave. He was driven, later that night, not back to Pollsmoor but into the hinterland, through the wine-farming town of Paarl, onto the grounds of Victor Verster Prison, through a wooded area, and finally to the entrance of a whitewashed cottage. He was told that the cottage was his – that he would live here until the day he was freed.[10]

The aging patriarch finally commanded a home, after a fashion. It had a spacious lounge, a well-equipped kitchen, and three bedrooms. On the grounds was a swimming pool and several shady trees.

It was a halfway house befitting a statesman where he could receive people from the outside, not as a prisoner in the visiting room of a jail, but as a *host;* he had a full-time chef with whom he carefully prepared menus and an assortment of wines. But what a strange and perverse home it was, the chairs fitted with recording devices, even the trees and flower beds littered with bugs.[11]

Among his first guests was Walter Sisulu; they had spent no more than forty minutes together since Nelson left their communal cell three years earlier.

The two men embraced while Christo Brand looked on. He believed that he detected in both of them not just happiness but relief. Nelson wanted immediately to give Sisulu a tour of his home. They admired the en suite bathroom, something neither had seen before. In the kitchen, Nelson put a beaker of water in the microwave oven and turned it on; the two men watched through the oven window until the water boiled, then regaled each other with what humanity had invented since they were last free.

Toward the end of Sisulu's visit, they locked themselves in the toilet, the one place in the house, they reasoned, where they could talk without being heard.[12] '[Nelson is] well though obviously lonely,' Sisulu wrote to a friend the following day. 'How can it be otherwise when he only talks to prison warders?'[13]

Within a week of Nelson's move, the commissioner of prisons, Willie Willemse, had what he thought was a brain wave. Winnie should be invited to live with her husband in the cottage at Victor Verster Prison. What better way to prepare him for life as a free man? And what an opportunity for the couple: to have the time to rediscover each other before they stepped into the whirlwind outside.[14]

Nelson warmed to the idea at once. But when he reported it to Winnie, she was incredulous.

'Well, that did it for me,' she said many years later. 'That's when I realised I had lost him. I didn't believe that he would actually expect me to go and live with him in prison . . . that I had been tortured to the extent that I would give in and go and surrender.'[15]

Chapter 54

In December 1987, a young Methodist minister named Paul Verryn moved into a church mission house a few blocks from Winnie's place.

Verryn was not a 'struggle priest', in the language of those times; he was neither a fiery polemicist nor an underground member of the ANC. But he was deeply sympathetic. When the insurrections began, he threw himself at tending people who had been tortured in detention. And when activists were on the run from the police, they understood that he would hide them.

That is how he built the household he did. During his previous appointment, in the white suburbs of the town of Roodepoort, his manse filled with an assortment of refugees: activists in danger, people torn from their homes by the troubles, youngsters just out of prison. At times, some thirty or forty souls sheltered there. Verryn barely had space for them. Four or five people slept to a bed; the floors of the sitting room and the passage to the bedrooms were strewn with sleeping bodies.[1]

When he moved to Soweto, he took his crew of stowaways with him. And once he had settled, more people came still.

It takes a kind of total commitment, a surrendering of oneself to one's work, to build the sort of household Verryn did. It is not just that he had yielded his privacy – even his bedroom had given way to the deluge of refugees. He had opened his mental life to a torrent of disfiguring experiences, for everyone who came to him came straight from the cauldrons of those extreme times.

The only other person in Orlando West who had surrendered herself so completely, allowing the world outside to refigure the household within, was Winnie Mandela. She, too, had flooded her home with people who had witnessed and taken part in the worst of those times.

And so here were two households bookending Orlando West, the household of Winnie Mandela and the household of Paul Verryn.

There is a sense in which Verryn's home *was* Winnie's, or a version of it at any rate; it was a precise facsimile of the veneer she had offered the world: a place of refuge for those hiding from the police, for those torn from their homes.

Winnie did not go over to the manse to meet Paul Verryn. And although a practicing Methodist, she did not worship in his church; she went each Sunday instead to the next closest Methodist congregation about half a mile away.

But from what was to follow, it is apparent that she took much interest in the minister and in what happened in his manse. Indeed, she must have wondered what sort of man would choose to make a home that so closely resembled hers.

The precise facts of what happened are probably lost forever. But what is clear is this: Two of the people who sheltered in the manse in the latter months of 1988 – a woman in her thirties called Xoliswa Falati, and a nineteen-year-old man called Katiza Cebekhulu – had previously lived with Winnie. They both claimed in years to come that she had sent them to Verryn in order to bring back stories of sexual abuse. Falati did precisely that. In late December 1988, she informed Winnie that Verryn had invited Cebekhulu into his bed and sodomized him. She said that two or three other young men living in the manse had also had sex with Verryn. She also mentioned a fourth person, not a young man, but a fourteen-year-old boy, James 'Stompie' Seipei, who she said she had discovered was a spy.

On the evening of December 29, 1988, a van carrying Falati, Jerry Richardson, and several members of the Mandela United Football Club arrived at the manse. Verryn was not there. Falati pointed out three of the house's residents: Pelo Mekgwe, Thabiso Mono and Stompie Seipei. And then, at the last moment, she pointed to a fourth: Kenny Kgase. 'Kenny is too clever,' one of the young men remembered her saying, 'and he can't just be left behind.'[2] The four were escorted out of the house. Katiza Cebekhulu joined them, but of his own volition; later that night, he joined in the beating of the captives.

As they filed into the van, members of the football club began singing freedom songs, and their prisoners were told to join in. One of them, Kenny Kgase, asked where they were going.

'Mommy wants to see you,' he was told.

'Do you mean Mrs. Winnie Mandela?' he asked.

'Yes, that is who I mean.'

'Well, then, fine,' he replied. 'Things are okay.'

'No,' he was told. 'Mommy is angry and things are not okay.'

The youths were taken to the garage at the back of Winnie's house. Seipei was repeatedly accused of being a spy; the other three were accused of having sex with the white man.

Everyone was sitting on his own chair. Jerry Richardson looked around and ordered another to be brought for 'Mommy'. Winnie came in and sat, and the captives were formally introduced to her. She asked Seipei why he had spied, asked the other three several times why they had allowed the white priest to fuck them up the ass. When Seipei protested that he was no spy, when the other three denied that they had had sex with Verryn, she stood up and slapped and punched them one by one.[3]

'*Umholi* [the leader] has been in jail 26 years for your benefit, yet you are continuing your nonsense,' Kgase later recollected Winnie saying. 'You are not fit to be alive.'[4]

She appeared to be telling them that for a black man to have sex with a white man constituted political and racial betrayal. Indeed, they had betrayed Nelson Mandela personally.

When she punched her captives, she was wearing on one of her fingers an ornate ring with a heavy stone. A woman who cared for the young men in the months to come remarked on the damage it had done to Kenny Kgase's eye; it took six months to heal, she recalled.[5]

The others in the room joined in the beating. Soon after they did, Winnie left the room. In her absence, the captives were slapped and punched and whipped. Several times, each was thrown high in the air and allowed to fall to the floor. All the while, Seipei was told that he had spied; the others that they had permitted Verryn to sodomize them.

The three older captives began to understand that the beatings might stop if they told the story their torturers demanded; it was not long before they agreed that they had slept with Verryn. The assaults on them soon ceased. Each was badly injured. The following morning, they were ordered to mop their own blood and there was a lot to mop, they recalled. But none sustained permanent physical injuries.[6]

It was a different story with Seipei. They continued to beat him that night and then resumed the next day. By the evening of December 30 his face was disfigured, his head misshapen. 'There were a lot of things we did to [him],' Richardson recalled. 'We kicked him like he was a ball. He was so badly tortured that at some stage I could see that he would ultimately die.'[7]

It does not appear that the intent was to kill him. More likely is that he died because of dynamics that evolved between him and his captors in the hours after he was kidnapped. When the uprisings began in his hometown, Parys, in late 1984, he was ten years old. Along with several other boys, he formed a group called the Fourteens that joined the action heartily, breaking windows, throwing petrol bombs, attacking town councillors' homes. They were doing the destructive things children do, but in a time when such delinquency was given license and reward. And if that aspect of his childhood was bracing, another was much more so: all of those boys in the Fourteens were captured several times by the police, held briefly and tortured.[8]

Some of those who got to know Seipei – Johannesburg activists who gave him shelter, a lawyer at whose offices he chose for a time to spend his days – recalled him as a child without boundaries, a child who responded with hostility to the most reasonable requests. One can imagine that he hadn't the wherewithal to offer his submission to his torturers, as the three older captives had had the savvy to do. He might very well have died because he was so quintessentially a child of his times.[9]

. .

Several accounts of Seipei's death have been told, all of them suspect. Katiza Cebekhulu has claimed on several occasions that he saw Winnie stab Seipei in the neck.[10] But of all the characters in this drama, Cebekhulu is perhaps the most unreliable; his accounts of every aspect of the story veered wildly over the years.

At the TRC, Jerry Richardson testified that Winnie ordered him to take Seipei from the property, kill him and dispose of his body. But much of what Richardson said at the TRC proved untrue. He claimed, for instance, that he killed Lolo Sono and Siboniso Tshabalala, the two young men whose remains were exhumed nearly a quarter century after they were murdered. It is strange to hear a man confess to a murder he could not have committed; he was still in jail on the day their bodies were found.

Johannes Mabotha gave his own account of Seipei's death to a police detective once he had been captured and tortured. Richardson, he said, reported to Winnie after the fact that he and another had taken Seipei to a field and killed him. Winnie, Mabotha said in his affidavit, was 'upset' and reprimanded him.[11]

Richardson described in graphic detail his version of the killing of Stompie Seipei, a version consistent with the forensic evidence subsequently gathered. Although it does not illuminate Winnie's role, it is the most credible testimony we have of the last moments of Seipei's life.

Two days after the beatings began, on New Year's Eve, Richardson testified, he went out to look for an appropriate place to bury a corpse. By evening, he had found a deserted spot near New Canada railway station, the same station outside which Winnie, twelve years earlier, had implored several thousand marching youths to turn around and save their own lives.

The following morning, Richardson left the property with Seipei and a member of the football team. 'I had to help Stompie along because he was very ill, very weak,' Richardson told the TRC. 'We dragged Stompie along.'

They took him to the spot opposite the railway line Richardson had chosen the previous evening.

'This is the most painful part,' Richardson continued. 'I don't know whether I should proceed. I slaughtered him. I slaughtered him like a goat. We made him lay on his back and I put garden shears through his neck and they penetrated to the back of his neck and I made some cutting motion.'[12]

. .

It is not entirely certain that Winnie sent Falati and Cebekhulu to Verryn's manse with the explicit instruction to bring back tales of abuse. What is certain is that when Falati did so report, Winnie took up the campaign with alacrity, assembling her team to punish the youths.

Her own voice does not help us understand why she did that. She was not even in Soweto on the night the four were taken to her house, she said eighteen months later, an incredible claim. Thabiso Mono, Kenny Kgase, Pelo Mekgwe, Jerry Richardson, Katiza Cebekhulu, Xoliswa Falati, her driver, John Morgan: all testified to her role. It would have taken a conspiracy of improbable scale to assemble such a fiction.

There is little question that she wished to destroy Paul Verryn.

'It was as if there was a quite specific plan to eliminate me,' he told an interviewer several years later, 'if not my physical person, certainly to eliminate any cause for me to carry on being. It was like killing somebody and then forcing them to carry on living their life.'[13]

It is hard to reconjure now the sense Verryn's presence in Orlando West must have conveyed. This quiet, uncharismatic man, white, bearded, dog collared, a cross around his neck, opening his home to those in flight and in need.

It was too conspicuous – too attention stealing – a performance to take place on Winnie's terrain. The story she told – of a white man perverting black children – is a story of evil conjured by the vast energy of rage.

In October 1988, two months before the kidnappings, Verryn reported to his bishop rumours that he was abusing young men in his care.[14] The whispering must have reached Winnie's ears. It must have set her imagination afire.

Her abhorrence for the sex she alleged took place in Verryn's home was situational. She was not, in less charged circumstances, a homophobic woman. Among those who drew close to her over the years were gay men who wore their sexual identities proudly on their sleeves. She not only enjoyed their company but took delight in their pride.[15]

Her weaving of the story as one of pedophilia and abuse is even more starkly circumstantial. Verryn was thirty-six years old in December 1988; Kenny Kgase was twenty-nine; Pelo Mekgwe and Thabiso Mono were both twenty-one. Had they chosen to have sex with Verryn – and it has been established that he had sex with nobody in his care[16] – everyone involved would have been a consenting adult.

If her fury was situational, it was no less real for that. For years now, she had cast her interior world over her nation, and it had been projected right back into her mind. Her war to the death with Theuns Swanepoel had become a war between all South Africans. Now, as she raged at Paul Verryn, he became a vector of perversity among the children of her country.

.   .

Something else about the torturing of those youths draws attention.

Verryn's house, in Winnie's view, was a place of illicit sex and spying; that is why the youths were kidnapped and beaten. It is surely no coincidence that at this precise moment the entanglement of sex and spying was eating Winnie's own house from within.

Just a month earlier, Lolo Sono and Siboniso Tshabalala had been executed for allegedly giving away the hiding place of two guerrillas. Shortly after they died, Jerry Richardson was released from custody and went straight to Winnie's place; upon his arrival, senior members of the household immediately accused him of informing. And well they should. For the police to release him without charge two weeks after he had been found to be hiding guerrillas is among the more extraordinary strands of the tale. He survived, by his own telling, because Winnie favoured him and nobody she favoured could possibly be a spy.[17]

The Sono-Tshabalala-Richardson debacle was only one among many. Johannes Mabotha was also in the house at this time. Cebekhulu and Falati had information that he was a spy; they watched Winnie shelter him because he shared her bed. Cebekhulu himself allegedly confessed weeks later to a senior member of the liberation movement that he had been recruited as a police informer in the city of Pietermaritzburg some time before he met Winnie.[18]

What a perilous situation. The line between who was and was not a spy in that house had been entirely lost by now.

There are other stories about that household – all of them involving betrayal and murder – that this narrative has not explored. On October 16, a little more than a month before the executions of Sono and Tshabalala, Sizwe Sithole, Zindzi's lover, had shot dead a fellow member of the football club, Thole Dlamini. That murder had triggered consequences of its own. A member of the household, Lerothodi Ikaneng, had protested against Sizwe Sithole's power to decide who should live and die. As a result, he himself was ordered killed and had fled Soweto.[19]

Another murder associated with the club took place at this time. On December 18, eleven days before the kidnappings from the Methodist manse, a young woman called Kuki Zwane was killed. She was the lover of a member of the football team, and suspicion had arisen in the preceding weeks that she was a spy.[20]

These spiralling tales of informing and killing may well account, in part, for why Winnie had the four youths taken from the manse and brought to her home. To have her household turn its attention on the place down the road was simply to deflect attention from itself. The beating of those young men and the killing of that boy were perhaps a matter of survival, the survival of the collective organism Winnie's household had become.

. .

And yet the attack on the manse and on four of its residents was also the undoing of the club. Lolo Sono, Siboniso Tshabalala, Thole Dlamini, Kuki Zwane: these were ordinary people without voice; their deaths brought no consequences.

On December 29, Winnie attacked, for the first time, an institution with heft and with independence, an institution not bound to silence by the struggle's code. She had attacked the body she had known longer than any other, the one that had stolen her mother's attention when she was a small child.

She had attacked the Methodist Church.

Chapter 55

During the first week of January 1989, the three surviving young men who had been kidnapped from the manse – Kenny Kgase, Thabiso Mono, and Pelo Mekgwe – were integrated into Winnie's household. Each was given a Mandela United tracksuit. Each was assigned quotidian duties: guarding, cleaning, and the like. A few days into January, they accompanied Winnie and the team to a large and conspicuous funeral; the father of one of Soweto's most famous musicians, Sipho 'Hotstix' Mabuse, had died.

As part of their initiation, they were to participate in a killing. Lerothodi Ikaneng, the football team member who had taken umbrage at the assassination of Thole Dlamini, had returned to Soweto after three months in hiding. He was duly caught. In a remote field, Mekgwe, Kgase and Mono were forced to hold down his limbs while Jerry Richardson slit his neck with a pair of garden shears. He was left for dead.[1]

On January 7, Kenny Kgase escaped from Winnie's house. He made his way to the Central Methodist Church in downtown Johannesburg, where he raised the alarm. The church contacted the Soweto crisis committee – the group of senior UDF leaders that had formed the previous July after the burning of Winnie and Nelson's house.

Nine days of negotiations ensued. The crisis committee and the church demanded the release of the young men. Winnie refused. Nelson Mandela and Oliver Tambo were briefed. Tambo spoke to Winnie directly on the phone and ordered her to release the young men. She still refused.

Finally, on January 16, Thabiso Mono and Pelo Mekgwe were released from Winnie's lawyer's office into the care of the Methodist district bishop.

That night, they and Kenny Kgase were brought to a church hall in Dobsonville, Soweto, where a group of 150 Sowetans had assembled.

They told the meeting that they had been taken against their will to Winnie's house, where she and the football team had beaten and whipped them. They took off their shirts and displayed their scars. They said that they had confessed to sex with Verryn under duress, but now that they were free they could testify that it was not true at all.

Verryn himself was there, as were all the remaining members of his household. One after the other, they said that the minister had never made sexual advances on them nor, to their knowledge, on anyone else in his care.

While they were speaking, Katiza Cebekhulu made a dramatic appearance. He described his own participation in the beatings and said he feared that Stompie Seipei was dead.

Then Lerothodi Ikaneng rose to speak. For Kgase, Mekgwe and Mono, it was as if a ghost had risen from the dead; they thought that Richardson had killed him. He unbandaged his throat to reveal the ear-to-ear wound the shears had made. It was still raw; the black stitches binding it protruded.

Some in the audience called for those assembled to march on Winnie's house and 'deal with her'. They were talked down. It was decided instead that a delegation would visit her the following day. A motion was passed that the football team be forbidden to use the name Mandela.

Eleven days later, the left-wing *Weekly Mail* ran a story on the Dobsonville meeting, breaking a long and painful silence. More than two years after its formation, the football club's violence was reported in print.[2]

. .

On the day this news was published, January 27, 1989, the story took the most dramatic and unexpected twist.

That afternoon, a prominent activist and doctor was shot dead in his Soweto surgery. His name was Abu Baker Asvat. A founding member of the Azanian People's Organisation, he was a significant figure in Black Consciousness circles. He had also grown famous and much loved in Soweto for his work as a doctor, and his ties to the township's political elite were intimate. Albertina Sisulu was employed as a nurse in his surgery, and the two had grown very close; in the wake of his death, Sisulu described him as her son.[3]

Asvat in fact died in Sisulu's arms. After admitting two young men for their appointment with the doctor, she heard gunshots, rushed into the surgery and found her friend wounded and dying.

Asvat was also Winnie Mandela's personal physician. He had been among her most regular visitors in Brandfort, helping her establish a modest clinic and a feeding scheme; at times he made the trip to the Free State as often as once a week.[4] He and Winnie had remained close after her return to Johannesburg; every Friday night, Winnie joined Asvat and his family for dinner.[5]

Now, in the wake of Asvat's murder, Winnie gave the strangest interview to the South African *Sunday Times*. Asvat, she suggested, was killed because he had examined the boys she had taken from the manse and had medical evidence that they had been abused.[6] Before this moment, there had been no hint in the public media that Asvat's death was connected to Winnie Mandela. Two young men had been apprehended for the murder, and the police had said that their motive appeared to be robbery.

Winnie's comments were surely a sign of her escalating panic. For they drew attention to another possibility, rumours of which had begun circulating among activists in the wake of the doctor's death: that Asvat had been called to Winnie's house to attend to the mortally injured Seipei, had seen that he was dying, and was thus the bearer of the most dangerous knowledge.

In the time immediately before his death, family and close friends of Asvat's later attested, he had not been himself. For years, he had driven back and forth at night between Soweto and his home in nearby Lenasia. Now, in January 1989, he began all of a sudden to ask friends to follow him home. On the night before he was killed, he had a flat tyre while he was on his way home. He drove on, too afraid to stop and change it; he feared that 'they', he told his wife mysteriously when he got home, had set him up to be attacked.

On the morning of his death he made two failed attempts to see his lawyers and then arrived late for Friday prayers. He was so distracted, fellow worshippers attested, that he did not lay his right hand over his left, as Muslim men do when praying, but held them flat together, a conspicuous error that drew frowns of concern.[7]

The two men convicted of murdering Asvat initially described the killing as the result of a botched robbery. But on the eve of their trial, one of them changed his story; his co-accused, he told the police, had been contracted by Winnie to kill Asvat. The investigating officers in the case chose to suppress this tale and to run instead with the accused men's initial story, much to the discomfort of the prosecutor. 'My gut feeling all along', he told *The Christian Science Monitor* more than two years after the trial's conclusion, 'was that there was something very strange . . . [T]his was not an armed robbery or murder, but an assassination.'

The police, he added, 'had simply not explored this avenue'.[8]

. .

By early February, Seipei's face was appearing every day in the pages of the nation's newspapers. In the midst of this frenzy, on February 9, a state pathologist, working on a hunch, examined the corpse of an unidentified boy picked up more than five weeks earlier. In addition to performing an autopsy, she took his fingerprints for identification; a few days later, they were found to match the prints on the identity card records of James 'Stompie' Seipei.[9]

. .

When news broke that the body was Seipei's, several protagonists in South Africa's political drama made a series of decisions. Each had enormous consequences.

Winnie Mandela sent Johannes Mabotha to Botswana. His instruction was to contact South African media from the other side of the border. The body lying in the state mortuary, he was to tell them, could not possibly be Stompie Seipei's; he had personally *seen* Seipei in a refugee camp in Botswana. It was not Winnie Mandela Seipei was fleeing, he was to add, but the security police.[10]

Mabotha left Soweto, but he did not go to Botswana. How could he have? He was an MK soldier who had turned; going anywhere near his former comrades in exile would place him in grave danger.

He phoned Winnie from a call box the day after he left.

'I am so glad you phoned,' she said.

'I phone from far.'

'I did not sleep,' she said. 'I rolled around and [then] walked around to [look for you].'

'Where did you check?' he asked.

'In the garage, [to see if] you are not there.

'You are not far,' she continued. 'It seems you are near. How is it going?'

'I just wanted to phone.'

'Please,' she said, 'if you arrive at school [that is, to ANC personnel in Botswana], let them not ask so many questions. Register and come back.'

'I will register and come back early,' he replied.[11]

It appears that she privately doubted that he would ever go to Botswana. 'I phone from far,' he said. 'You are not far,' she replied. 'You sound near.'

She was, perhaps, in that strange but common state of knowing, but at the same time not knowing, that he had indeed betrayed the ANC, as Evodia Nkadimeng had been telling her, and would never go to Botswana.

He called again four days later from the town of Groblersdal, less than two hundred miles north of Johannesburg. He had run out of money, he said. He needed more. She told him she would arrange to wire funds to the nearest post office. When he arrived to collect the transfer, he was ambushed by police; the Soweto Security Branch had been listening in on his and Winnie's calls.[12]

It may never be determined for certain why Mabotha came into Winnie's life. He might have done so on the instructions of the police. More likely, though, is that he absconded from his police post and went to Winnie off his own bat, his motives and his reasoning now forever lost. For what happened to him after his capture suggests that he was guilty of a great betrayal.

Within an hour of his arrest, Eugene de Kock, head of the assassination squad at Vlakplaas and Mabotha's commander, was called. He put down what he was doing and drove to Groblersdal, where he met several Soweto Security Branch detectives.

In an outhouse on an isolated farm, Mabotha was assaulted without pause for a period of seven hours, the police officers working on him in alternating groups of two. They had information, De Kock testified, that while living with Winnie, Mabotha had been involved in the shooting of two police officers and in the burying of a cache of arms and ammunition. They wanted, above all, to know where the arms were hidden.

'He was in a blanket,' De Kock recalled. 'His clothing had been taken off so that he would not get urine on [it] . . . He was strangled, he was hit and kicked. Care was taken that no bones were broken and . . . that his face was not harmed, although his nose and mouth did bleed . . . That afternoon he was a tired, broken, hurt man.'[13]

But he still had not talked. Throughout those seven hours, according to De Kock, he had scarcely uttered a word.

Mabotha was detained for eight months. He was then handed back to De Kock, who took him to an isolated place in the countryside and shot him dead at point-blank range. Then his corpse was destroyed.

'When he was handcuffed . . . and you were leading him to your guillotine,' De Kock was asked under cross-examination at the TRC, 'did he ever ask for mercy from you?'

'He didn't say a word,' De Kock replied. 'He refused to speak . . . He took what he received perhaps in the way the ideal soldier would take it.'[14]

. .

Resolutely, the world had ceased yielding to Winnie Mandela's will. The manse was still standing. The minister's reputation was intact. The men she had seized were talking, and she could not control what they said. A corpse had been found, and it, too, was beginning to speak.

Verryn later said that there had been a plan to kill him and then force him to carry on living his life. This is precisely the prospect Winnie herself now faced. She was on the verge of excommunication, of nonbeing. For a woman who had for the longest time lived to be seen, this was calamitous on an unmeasurable scale.

Her lover was in the hands of brutal men. She must have known that they would not spare him.

What did this mean to her?

Two years after her ordeal in Soweto, Evodia Nkadimeng returned to the Mandela house. Winnie came to the gate to meet her, threw her arms around her, welcomed her.

'She asked me where Mabotha was,' Nkadimeng recalled. 'I said I didn't know. "You must look for him,' Winnie said.'[15]

. .

When Seipei's corpse was identified, two other decisions were made, both by senior figures in South Africa's liberation movement. They could not have been more different.

On the evening of February 15, three members of the UDF's national secretariat, Mohammed Valli Moosa, Murphy Morobe and Azhar Cachalia, sat at Cachalia's dining room table drafting a statement; Morobe read it at a press conference the following afternoon. On the table in front of them were the affidavits Kgase, Mono and Mekgwe had written upon reaching safety. The three UDF leaders were fully informed.

'We are outraged by the reign of terror [Mrs. Mandela's football club] has been associated with,' part of the statement read. 'The Democratic Movement has uncompromisingly fought against violations of human rights from whatever quarters. We are not prepared to remain silent when those who are violating human rights claim to be doing so in the name of the struggle against apartheid.

'We are outraged', the statement continues, 'at Mrs. Mandela's complicity in the recent abductions and assault on Stompie. Had Stompie and his three colleagues not been abducted by Mrs. Mandela's "Football Team" he would still be alive today.

'The Mass Democratic Movement hereby distances itself from Mrs. Mandela and her actions. We call upon our people, in particular, the Soweto community, to exercise this distancing in a dignified manner.'[16]

Years later, Cachalia remembered the discussions he and his colleagues had that evening around his dining room table. 'At some point, I became won over to the law,' he said, 'not just in its instrumental sense. There was intrinsic value in the law itself. You don't just fight for political power. You have values. You want a different society. What Winnie was accused of doing was completely antithetical to that vision. Regardless of whether she was manipulated by the police – and maybe she was, and it would certainly be a mitigating factor – she is still morally and legally accountable for what she did.'[17]

· ·

Six days later, a very different response came from the highest ranks of the exiled ANC.

'In the course of time,' the ANC said in a public statement, 'the [football club] became involved in unbecoming activities which have angered the community . . . We have every reason to believe that the club was infiltrated by the enemy and that most of its activities were guided by the hands of the enemy for the purpose of causing disunity in the community and discrediting the name of Nelson Mandela . . .

'[I]t is necessary that Comrade Winnie Mandela be helped to find her way into the structures and discipline of the mass democratic movement. It will be of paramount importance that she co-operates with all those involved in the resolution of the problem.'

The statement ended with a scarcely veiled instruction to the internal activists to reverse their decision. 'We are confident', it read, 'that the mass democratic movement will open its doors to her in the interests of the struggle of our people.'[18]

On February 26, Murphy Morobe and his colleague Sydney Mufamadi met with fifteen members of the ANC's national working committee in Lusaka, Zambia. Oliver Tambo chaired the meeting. The only record of what transpired are the notes taken surreptitiously by a South African government informer.

Tambo and Morobe upbraided each other gently, with the greatest decorum. The ANC's statement contradicted the mass democratic movement's, the informer has Morobe complain. The media was now reporting a rift between the ANC and the internal movement.

In response, Tambo introduced a new matter: the feelings of Nelson Mandela. 'We were governed by a desire to protect Nelson and his role,' the informer's notes have Tambo saying. Nelson prefers the ANC's statement to the MDM's because the latter 'is very sharp and could have left Winnie Mandela exposed to action by hostile forces.

'He feels she has supported him for twenty-six years and he has a moral obligation to support her.'[19]

One of the struggle's two great patriarchs had spoken on behalf of the other: Nelson Mandela wished to protect his wife.

Chapter 56

From the letters he wrote, and from his conversations that his captors recorded, it appears that Nelson Mandela reached two conclusions in February 1989.

The first is that his wife had buckled, in spirit and in mind, in the face of what she had lived through.

The second is that she had been framed.

Winnie came to see him on January 18, two days after the release of Mono and Mekgwe and the community meeting at the Dobsonville hall, the one that had almost resolved to march to her house to do violence to her. There is no transcript of their conversation, just a schematic summary, and not a very adequate one at that. We get little notion of the spirit evolving in the room.

Boys in her care went to the Methodist church for training, the eavesdropper has Winnie tell Nelson, where they learned sodomy from the white clergyman and were now doing it to each other. We are not given Nelson's response to Winnie's apparent admission that she had the boys taken from the manse. But we know from conversations he subsequently had with others that he believed in this moment to have been in the presence of a person who had lost her mind.

Winnie went on to complain that demands were being made upon her to have the boys living on the property removed. She did not like this at all and accused Nelson of being behind the demands.[1]

She appeared to believe that the situation was still in hand. Three men had written affidavits implicating her in grave crimes; activist circles were swirling with talk about the whereabouts of Stompie Seipei; less than two days had passed since an assembly of 150 people debated whether to storm her house and attack her. She appeared still to think that she could keep the football team and that life could go on.

A month later, on the day the UDF statement condemning Winnie was released, Nelson wrote to her, addressing her as 'darling mum'. It is not clear whether he was aware yet of the statement, but from the urgency of his letter it appears that he was.

Seipei should be returned to his mother, he pleaded. He believed, despite official confirmation that the body in the morgue was Seipei's, that the boy was in Winnie's care. He must have imagined a vast and intricate conspiracy against his wife – doctored postmortems, false medical reports.

Serious errors might have been made by several parties, he wrote, referring, of course, to Winnie's errors, among others. But that was nothing compared with the distortions in the statements of 'well-known' interests, distortions being parroted in the media. The real purpose was 'to destroy images, to sow divisions, to bring the violence currently raging in Natal to the Witwatersrand. We must be absolutely vigilant and do everything in our power to destroy this wicked plan.'

'Remember that I love you and that you are constantly in my thoughts,' he concluded. 'Affectionately, Madiba.'[2]

.   .

He received a visit the following day from the Reverend Anton Simons, the Methodist Church's chaplain to Pollsmoor Prison. He recounted to Simons in full what he thought had happened.

A child staying at the Methodist manse came to Winnie to say that sodomy was being committed there, he told Simons. She sent a car to fetch four more boys. They all said that they were sexually assaulted.

That she took the kids was a very bad mistake, he continued. She should instead have gone to Bishop Peter Storey of the Methodist Church to report; he might have dealt with the matter internally.

'The church must not think that I support Winnie in this conduct,' he said. 'It was a grave mistake, and you must tell the leaders of the church that I ask for forgiveness.'

Winnie was a woman who has been alone for twenty-six years, he said. She broke. She broke under the pressure of the apartheid regime.

But he did not believe that the football team murdered the boy. Seipei was due to appear in a court case on February 27, he explained, and his co-accused killed him so that he would not speak. The police were exploiting Winnie's mistake to divide people, he said.[3]

A little over a week later, on February 26, Winnie and Zindzi came to see him. Jerry Richardson and another had just been charged for Seipei's murder, and the national dailies had made it their front-page leads. He was certain, he assured his wife and daughter, that the body was not Seipei's. The boy was clearly alive. And if he was dead, it was the police who killed him. They would not dare bring the matter to court.[4]

· ·

How spectral and sinister the world must have seemed to Nelson Mandela. He believed that his enemy was stoking war among black South Africans and that its primary tool was his wife. For decades, they had tormented her without respite; the moment she broke, they were waiting to pounce.

Did he believe that the men with whom he was talking, men he had grown to trust, were in the know? Did he think that they had given personal approval to the framing of Winnie Mandela as the murderer of a child? It is hard to imagine that he did not entertain the thought.

· ·

Whether Nelson's view of the Seipei killing changed over the following months is impossible to say. Between April and July 1989, his enemy's record of his conversations falls more or less silent. And during this time, he and Winnie grew estranged.

In April, she refused to come and see him.[5] When she finally came in May, he refused to see her.[6]

And then, in late August, Zindzi's older sister, Zenani, and her husband, Muzi, paid a call to Nelson in his cottage at Victor Verster during a trip home from the United States. The content of their conversation, as recorded by Nelson's jailers, is dramatic and startling, but what to make of it is not entirely clear.

Nelson warned his daughter and son-in-law, as he did many of those who came to see him, that their conversation was being monitored. And it appears that for at least some of their visit he took them to a place the bugs could not reach. What we thus have is part of a conversation, conducted by people acutely aware that it is being overheard.

Even then, the record is inadequate. Remember, it is not a verbatim transcript, but a warder's notes, written in Afrikaans; he has been listening to a conversation in one language and has summarized it in another. When one translates his notes back into English, the language that emerges is not Nelson's at all. And so, we do not know the words a very careful man chose to use; nor do we witness the cadences of the conversation as it evolved.

What we have instead is an apparent character assassination delivered in bullet notes. Nelson tells his guests that Winnie sleeps with one man today and another tomorrow, and that she has been doing so since he went underground. He was captured outside Howick in August 1962, he says, because Winnie had told her lover that he was going to Durban, and Fikile Bam was arrested because Winnie was sleeping with an informer. He lists a string of men she has slept with from the 1960s until the present. He says he has done his best to save the marriage, but that an embarrassing situation is approaching. She is living like a rich woman, but she is bankrupt; the ambassadors have been warned not to give her more money. As for Zindzi, he says that she should be taken away from Winnie because he cannot stand it any longer.[7]

The manner in which the conversation was recorded shrouds its form and its spirit. Was it an outburst of fury? Or was it delivered like a lawyer constructing an argument? It would appear that in the wake of the Seipei crisis Nelson received a deluge of very grim information about the conduct of his wife; whoever whispered in his ear did not spare him.

Like so many men before him on the brink of divorcing their wives, he lays the case out to the children, and he lays it on thick. The righteousness, the woundedness, the self-justification: this is a set piece performed in countless homes across the second half of the twentieth century. Shorn of its flesh, the marriage he describes is a skeleton of accusation. The eccentricity of the setting – a South African prison, the furniture stuffed with bugs, the most powerful men in the land hungrily listening in – should not distract from the formulaic character of the scene.

Was Winnie responsible for his capture outside Howick? Was she already sleeping with Brian Somana in August 1962, and did she tell Somana that Nelson was going to Durban? Nelson's captors might well have told him that, but why should he have believed them? Nelson himself later remarked that he had been awfully careless in Durban, that far too many people knew where he was.[8]

That the thought had seeded long ago in his mind, and that it had never died, tells an interesting story. He had almost divorced Winnie in the early months of 1965 over Brian Somana. It appears that only the intervention of Walter Sisulu persuaded him to reverse course. In the interim, he had forgiven her in spades. With his pen, he had, over the following twenty years, crafted an exquisite portrait of his love, writing her over and over again into the very core of his being. All the while, the grievance lay buried, unnoticed, probably unthought.

· ·

By December 1989, though, three months after Zenani and Muzi's visit, Winnie and Nelson had yet again changed course. Winnie was coming regularly to see him. The discussions between them were calm and wide-ranging. They talked politics and family. They talked about friends. It appears that Winnie had mollified him as he reached the brink of divorcing her. She had written a letter of surrender, or at least of pacification; she was obeying his instructions, she wrote; she was cooperating with the UDF, with the crisis committee; she was ceding to his will.[9]

Nelson had veered from feeling the duty to protect a broken woman to the desire to divorce a loathsome woman. Now he had again made peace with her.

As for Winnie, she had swung from refusing to see him to mollifying him.

Their marriage now vastly unstable, they knew that sometime soon, perhaps in a matter of months, they would live together again for the first time in twenty-seven years.

Chapter 57

A year earlier, on January 18, 1989, in the midst of the Seipei debacle, P. W. Botha had a stroke. The Big Crocodile, as he was known, was wounded, but not quite fallen; he clung to power in unseemly fashion. A long period of uncertainty followed. Only in mid-August was he finally replaced as president of South Africa by F. W. de Klerk.

A week before De Klerk took office, Oliver Tambo, too, was struck down by a stroke in his office in Lusaka, effectively ending his active life in politics. He lived another four years, a shadow of his former self.

As these aging men were felled, Nelson Mandela envisaged the most dramatic, the most indispensable, role for himself.

By late August, the ANC had publicly laid out its preconditions for negotiating with the South African government. They included the unbanning of proscribed organizations, the release of all political prisoners, the lifting of the state of emergency, and the withdrawal of troops from South Africa's townships.[1] There were other preconditions, too, but the organization made it understood that these were sacrosanct.[2]

For its part, the South African government had said that it would not begin to negotiate a settlement with the ANC until the organization suspended its armed struggle and cut ties with the South African Communist Party.

One of the two sides would have to give ground if negotiations were ever to begin.

In his secret talks with justice minister Kobie Coetsee and with the head of the National Intelligence Service, Niël Barnard, Nelson had emphatically insisted that ending the alliance with the SACP was an intolerable condition; the government could not deign to choose the ANC's allies, he said. He was much more forbearing on the question of suspending the armed struggle.

Now he pondered the delicate mechanics of the whole business:

How would the two sides garner sufficient mutual trust to cross the threshold together?

What settled in his mind was the idea of a synchronous announcement. On the same day, perhaps even at the same hour, the government would unban the ANC and the ANC would suspend the armed struggle. The next morning, the country would wake up to find that it had crossed the threshold together.

Only he could make this possible, Nelson believed. Only he could vouch to the ANC that the men to whom he had been talking were genuine in seeking a settlement; only he could vouch to the government that the ANC would play ball.

The time he had spent in clandestine conversation, he believed, made him a unique broker.

But selling the idea to the ANC was too intricate a matter to resolve by written messages or over the phone. He would secretly go to Lusaka, he imagined, and address the ANC's national executive in person. Alternatively, arrangements would be made for the national executive to arrive quietly in South Africa to meet with him.[3]

None of it was to be. In February 1990, in a move of great shrewdness, De Klerk simply unbanned the ANC and announced that he would release Mandela, no conditions attached. Nelson was taken by surprise. So was everyone, in fact.[4]

What might have happened had De Klerk taken Nelson up on his eccentric scheme? Most likely, it would not have gone well. Nelson Mandela had been away for a long time; he was no longer a known entity among his comrades. Had he swooped into Lusaka with his dramatic plan, he would almost certainly have been greeted with unease, if not with alarm.

In the months before his release, a great wariness about Nelson was abroad in the highest ranks of his movement. In November 1989, in a comment he understood would be conveyed to the South African government, Thabo Mbeki said that Mandela was only sixth in the ANC's hierarchy and his position after his release would have to be assessed.[5] In the same week, Cyril Ramaphosa, general secretary of the National Union of Mineworkers and one of the most influential internal leaders, described Nelson as 'one of those people who may have to be considered for a leadership position in the ANC'.[6]

His comrades were cautious. They were waiting to discover who Nelson Mandela was.

How important were the secret discussions he had with the South African government? How historic a role did he play?

In the time before his release, other channels opened between the government and the ANC. In February 1988, South Africa's intelligence services began communicating indirectly with Thabo Mbeki, via an intermediary, the political philosopher Willie Esterhuyse.[7] Nineteen months later, in September 1989, the two sides encountered each other face-to-face for the first time: two senior South African intelligence officials travelled to Lucerne, Switzerland, where they met with Mbeki and Jacob Zuma. They returned with the message that the ANC was ready to talk.[8]

Nelson was informed beforehand that the intelligence services would meet with Mbeki; in Niël Barnard's recollection, he was furious. South Africa is reputed to have the best intelligence service in the world, Barnard has Nelson snap. Why can't it arrange to bring Mbeki to Victor Verster and join the discussions here? His concern, in Barnard's telling, was that unless talks were directly with him or with Tambo, they would split the ANC.[9]

He imagined himself in the most thespian role, swooping into Lusaka from out of the blue, the key to the future in his bag. Negotiations were 'my baby', he told Margaret Thatcher four months after his release.[10] It is a telling turn of phrase, a claim to nativity, to personal creation.

History did not quite offer him the role he had envisaged. But that is hardly to say that he was dispensable. He had become the personal embodiment of his people's quest for freedom. So much hinged on the flesh-and-blood person he was. His enemy had learned three vital things about him: he had a strange regality, an otherworldly aura of personal power; he would be a tough adversary in the time to come; and he believed the only alternative to a settlement was a ghastly war.

In the absence of such a figure, would the South African government have had the stomach to leap into so uncertain a future? It is impossible to say.

Chapter 58

In late January 1990, two weeks before Nelson Mandela's release from prison, the police raided a house in White City, Soweto, where they found an AK-47, a handgun and a stash of ammunition. Also at the house that morning was Sizwe Sithole, a senior member of the Mandela household, Zindzi's lover and the father of her infant child. He admitted at once that the weapons and ammunition were his and left the property in the company of police.

That afternoon, Sithole confessed to the murder of Thole Dlamini, a fellow member of the Mandela United Football Club. He also told the police of his involvement in a hand grenade attack on a meeting of the Sofasonke Party and an armed invasion of a policeman's home. In a statement he made before a magistrate that evening, he said that the police had been after him ever since he killed Dlamini and that today they had finally arrested him.[1]

Three days later, on January 30, Sithole was interrogated all morning by Jan Augustyn, a Soweto Security Branch detective. Late that afternoon, a little more than two hours after his interrogation ended, Sithole's corpse was found in the shower hanging by a belt and a pair of shoelaces.[2]

Why Sithole had a belt and shoelaces would remain a mystery. At various points during his days in detention, he was reported to have had neither.

The following week, a senior judge, Richard Goldstone, held an inquest into Sithole's death. Among many others, he interviewed the police officers who had arrested and interrogated Sithole, and the fellow detainees who had spoken to him in the cells.

There was no doubt that Sithole had committed suicide, Goldstone found. Two autopsies were performed within thirty-six hours after his death, one on behalf of the state, the other on behalf of Sithole's family;

both concluded that he had died by hanging and had sustained no other recent injuries.

The judge went on to offer three reasons why Sithole might have taken his life.

The first was simply the prospect of remaining in prison a long time.

The second and third, though, appeared to involve Winnie and Zindzi Mandela.

His cellmates, the judge reports, testified that Sithole expressed a great deal of anger and hurt during the last days of his life. 'People in Orlando West', he had said, had either framed him or falsely accused him; which is not quite clear. That is the second possible reason Goldstone gives for the suicide: those close to Sithole had betrayed him.

The third reason concerns something Sithole said to Jan Augustyn during his final interrogation. 'The deceased', Goldstone writes, 'made serious allegations of criminal conduct on the part of Winnie Mandela and her daughter, Zinzi [sic].' This, the judge offered, was the third possible reason Sithole had taken his own life: he had betrayed his lover and her mother.[3]

What Sithole said about Winnie and Zindzi was recorded in Augustyn's interrogation notes. Goldstone ruled that they not be made public, and they have lain unread in a restricted section of a government archive ever since. But the lawyers and judicial staff involved in the hearing all read Augustyn's notes at the time. Two of those people, approached by this author thirty years later, independently remembered the notes the same way.[4]

The wife of a prominent Soweto businessman, they both say, was a friend of Winnie Mandela's. Sometime in 1989, she came to Winnie and Zindzi complaining that her husband was a serial adulterer. Mother and daughter promptly sent Sithole and others to raze one of his business premises to the ground.

If Sithole did indeed die for that, the pathos is overwhelming. The incident had little to do with the liberation of black South Africans; it was one of those innumerable acts of private vengeance, most of them lost to history, born of the contagion of violence that besets unstable times. And if he took his life for fear of betraying Winnie and Zindzi, he undoubtedly died in vain. A case of treason against Winnie Mandela had just then been discarded lest talks with her husband derail. The authorities would not have troubled her for burning a man's business to the ground.

· ·

And yet the story is nonetheless meaningful.

The arson to which Sithole confessed was not an isolated incident. In June 1988, another Soweto businessman, Joseph Laballo, successfully sought an urgent interdict against Winnie and his wife. Following matrimonial trouble, Laballo said in his affidavit, his wife had complained to Winnie, who in turn ordered her football team to remove him from his home. When he tried to return, Winnie, his wife, and members of the team had threatened to kill him. Among other things, the interdict prevented Winnie or his wife from entering his business premises or removing stock.[5]

· ·

In early 1989, at around the time Winnie acquired a taste for destroying the property of unfaithful men, she took a guest on a tour of her garden. The guest in question, a university lecturer named Teresa Oakley-Smith, soon became Winnie's love rival, and then, years later, her dear friend.

Winnie pointed to a bird's nest in a solitary tree. 'That's a weaver's nest,' Oakley-Smith remembered Winnie saying. 'Do you know how things work with them?'

Oakley-Smith confessed to knowing little about birds.

'Oh, then you don't know,' Winnie went on. 'Among weavers, the men build the nest. And if the women don't like it, they tear it down.'[6]

Winnie took such delight in this, Oakley-Smith recalled. Little did she know how literally her host had taken the weavers' lesson.

As for her own marriage, Winnie had not exactly set fire to a building Nelson owned, but she had shown the greatest contempt for his assumption of patriarchal power. When he instructed his daughter to study in Cape Town, Winnie had surreptitiously helped Zindzi escape his wishes. When he had commanded Winnie to assist him in his quest for a peaceful end to apartheid, she had, behind his back, packed his home with weapons and done her utmost to make war.

. .

Four days after the death of Sizwe Sithole, on February 2, 1990, F. W. de Klerk announced the unbanning of the ANC and the impending release of Nelson Mandela. The world was taken by surprise. De Klerk had set no conditions: the ANC's alliance with the South African Communist Party remained, as did its armed struggle. Nobody had expected it to come this soon or this decisively, not least Nelson Mandela; the role he had envisaged in orchestrating this moment had been summarily swept aside.

On February 4, two days after De Klerk's announcement, Winnie came to see Nelson at Victor Verster for the second to last time.

'How is Zindzi?' Nelson asked.

'Not good. She won't eat. She won't sleep. I can't communicate [with her]. It is such a heartbreaking story.'

'Tell Zindzi that what happened, happened,' Nelson advised. 'She must go on with her life.'

They talked of other matters for some time, the spirit between them apparently calm, the conversation wide-ranging. He called her darling and told her how good it was to see her.

A change of mood seemed to come over him, and he brought the discussion back to Zindzi.

It was odd, he said, that she was falling in love with a man who was twenty years old.

Winnie sighed.

'She is 29,' Nelson continued. 'That she is with a 20-year-old man is not right.'

'She does not talk to me about her love life,' Winnie replied.

'Zindzi must be handled in a completely different way,' he persisted. He began to whisper so that his jailers would not hear him.

When the eavesdroppers picked up their voices again, they were talking of De Klerk's decisiveness and Nelson's impending release.

After some time, Nelson returned once more to Zindzi. The warder listening in now began paraphrasing, and so the words are his, not Nelson's. The tone of the conversation had shifted, the warder commented; Nelson had grown agitated.

He was very worried about Zindzi's ways with random men. She had left Buthelezi for a marijuana smoker (Sithole). Winnie was failing to discipline her daughter. Things were not right with her; she must start seeing a psychologist. Buthelezi went to prison to protect the family, he went on; Buthelezi was loyal to us. She thinks she can just make kids and it ends there. She has to use her own money to care for them. Winnie spoils her.

We cannot hear the tone he chose; nor can we be certain of the precise words. But it sounds very much like acute distress. He was not long from walking into the world, and things were not right out there; they were not right at all.

Winnie said nothing, it appears; she simply waited for the monologue to end.

'How is your health?' he asked.

'Fine.'

'When is the child's funeral?'

'On Saturday.'

'Are you going?'

'I have not decided.'

He gave Winnie a letter he had written to Zindzi. 'Darling,' he wrote, 'what has happened has happened and no useful purpose can be served by torturing yourself over it. Pull yourself up, darling, and remember that we love you very dearly. Let's forget what we cannot be changed [*sic*] & love you. Tata.'[7]

· ·

Five days later, Nelson was taken to the Cape Town residence of the president of South Africa. There, F. W. de Klerk told him that he would be released in less than forty-eight hours. Nelson was taken aback; he had expected to have longer to prepare.

He would be flown in a private jet to Pretoria, De Klerk explained, from where he would quietly be freed.

Nelson took umbrage. His people needed another week to prepare for his release, he said. And he would *not* be flown to Pretoria; he would be freed from Victor Verster.

De Klerk appears not to have expected this at all. The two men bargained. The president twice left the room to make calls. By midnight they had come to an agreement: Nelson would be released in two days, as the government had planned, but from Victor Verster, as Nelson demanded.

How dare the government make decisions without consulting him, Nelson complained to the warders on duty at his cottage the following morning. 'They are scared of the crowds,' he told members of his reception committee later that day.[8]

This most pragmatic and patient of prisoners was concluding his confinement in a state of rebellion.

. .

Among the flurry of last-minute tasks now at hand was to bring Winnie to Cape Town. At lunchtime on February 10, Nelson was informed that she would be on a chartered flight leaving Johannesburg at 7:30 a.m. the following morning, arriving in time to be at his side as he left the prison gates. Their convoy was to make its way through the Winelands toward the city; at 4:30 p.m., Nelson would make a speech from a balcony on Cape Town's Grand Parade. [9]

Nelson appears to have had been informed that trouble was brewing, and that Winnie might not be on that flight, for early on the morning of his release he inquired whether anyone had made contact with his wife. He paced the cottage until 9:00 a.m., still in his pajamas, asking periodically if somebody had spoken with Winnie. He had a bath, changed into his suit, took a nap. Lunchtime came and went and there was still no word.

Finally, at 2:00 p.m., news reached Nelson that Winnie had landed at Cape Town's international airport. A little over an hour later, she finally arrived. The couple had a few moments alone before the cottage filled with people. Helicopters clattered overhead, and in the din the bugs did not pick up a word of this final conversation between the prisoner and his wife.[10]

Winnie was late because she had taken offense; in Johannesburg, she had discovered that Murphy Morobe, the man who had spoken at the press conference a year earlier distancing the internal movement from her actions, was on the same chartered flight. She had refused point-blank to travel with him on board. She finally took off from Johannesburg four hours later than planned.[11]

Morobe's presence might have been the proximate trigger for her decision to be late. But it takes little digging to come to a deeper reason. Today was Nelson's day on the grandest scale. Hundreds of millions of

people the world over wanted to see what he looked like and to hear
what he would say. Winnie could scarcely have found a bolder statement of her ambivalence about this day: about its politics, about the
resumption of married life, about living in the shadow Nelson cast.

· ·

Nelson walked out of the gates of Victor Verster Prison holding
Winnie's hand. He had been twenty-seven years and six months in jail.

Both wore dark business suits. Both looked a little bewildered. In
response to the crowds that had gathered at the prison gate, Winnie
raised her fist. Nelson hesitated, looked around him, and then raised his
fist, too. By the time they crossed the threshold between the prison and
the world, they had settled into this pose: one hand clutching the hand
of their spouse, the other hoisted in triumph.

The following morning, this image adorned the front pages of
newspapers across the world.

Chapter 59

It is always a shock to see what three decades have done to a person. The strapping, rambunctious man in the photographs – a man about to throw an arm around you and grin in your face – had long vanished when Nelson Mandela stepped back into the world. 'The hair has gone grey and the boxer's shoulders are shells under the awkward jacket now,' the *New York Times*'s Robert McFadden wrote on the day of Nelson's release. 'The face [is] like parchment and the voice [is] strained.'[1]

Within days, that face had donned an extraordinary assortment of masks: the wooden patriarch, the charming host, the delighted old man. That mouth would grimace as if it had not smiled in seventy years before opening into a Buddha-like glow.

The more recognizable the face became, the deeper the spirit beneath it seemed to hide.

This opacity was perhaps inevitable in a man who had ascended into myth. On his first full day out of prison he arrived in Johannesburg, which had long ago been his home, and what he brought came more from the realm of magic than from the mundane world.

Much of Soweto simply did not turn up for work. Nor did people stay at home. They converged on the streets in their hundreds of thousands to celebrate on an epic scale. This author, nineteen years old, was in that endless crowd, unconcerned that he had lost his bearings and knew not where he was, for everywhere on this unworldly day was home.

Hours before Mandela's plane touched down, and a full day before he was scheduled to speak, rumours swirled that he had arrived at Orlando Stadium and was about to address the crowds. Around the township, people dropped what they were doing and ran. By mid-afternoon, some fifty thousand had gathered outside the stadium gates, Mandela still a thousand miles away.[2]

He spoke at Soccer City the following afternoon, just six miles from his home. In an arena designed to seat eighty thousand, almost double that number filled the stands: people jammed the aisles, squeezed two to a seat; people climbed the stadium walls. Not a single uniformed official of the state was there, the vast crowd's only shepherd a group of marshals assembled in haste. It did not seem remotely unsafe. That lives may be lost on a day like this, even by accident, seemed incongruous.

You could barely make him out as he walked into the stadium, a flash of silver hair way down on the pitch below; a few beats passed before the crowd clocked that it was him. And then a whistling arose. Within moments it had quickened into a deafening, alien, scarcely human sound, both shrill and unfathomably deep. It chopped up human movement, as if we were under a strobe. So electrically intense, so eerily out of body, it seemed to radiate from that single man below.

I had been to a hundred rallies over the previous couple of years, had absorbed the spirit of a hundred crowds. Nothing had come close to what happened in that moment – the suspension of time, the sheer density of energy, the sense that we were someplace outside our lives.

As the whistling died, the spirit left, quickly, unexpectedly, and everyone seemed suddenly alone. So much blood had spilled in the vicinity of this very stadium, month upon month, year upon year. The moment that collective feeling ebbed, one wondered whether it had existed at all.[3]

. .

In the late afternoon, he returned to 8115 Orlando West, which had been rebuilt in the wake of its destruction by fire, after an absence of nearly twenty-nine years. Thousands converged outside. He addressed the crowd for just a few moments before disappearing into the house.

By the following morning, a rumour was going around Vilakazi Street.

It was not him.

He had spoken so briefly, it was said, and entirely in English. Why had he not uttered a single word in his native Xhosa? Was it to mask a foreign accent? And why did he choose to appear in the late-afternoon light, when faces are cast in shadow?[4]

It was a strangely appropriate response to a man who had become myth: a flicker of doubt, a question as to whether the eyes had deceived.

Shortly after he was released, the South African novelist and future Nobel laureate Nadine Gordimer received a message that Nelson Mandela wished to see her. She was flattered. They had known each other slightly before he was jailed and had been in touch sporadically since; he had written generously to her about one of her novels, *Burger's Daughter,* which he had read in prison.

'We were alone in Johannesburg some few days later,' Gordimer recalled. 'It was not about my book that he spoke, but about his discovering, on the first day of his freedom, that Winnie Mandela had a lover.'[5]

Nelson had in fact been told of Winnie's lover during his final months in prison; he had written to her demanding that she get 'that boy' out of the house.[6] His name was Dali Mpofu, a prominent student activist and a trainee lawyer. He was also two generations younger than Nelson; his time on this earth coincided, almost exactly, with Nelson's time in prison.

Mpofu and Winnie had apparently drawn close in the early months of 1989, precisely when Johannes Mabotha had vanished into the clutches of the police. The timing is no surprise. All her adult life Winnie had skirted solitude, her relation to another at a necessary fever pitch. And, as in so many of her previous relationships, this one involved another; Mpofu's lover, the Wits University academic Teresa Oakley-Smith, was pregnant with Mpofu's child. The upset that followed was another recurring feature of Winnie's life.

Nelson knew that Winnie and Mpofu were still together shortly after he was released. When she arrived at Victor Verster those many hours late, her lover was in tow; he was among the group standing behind Nelson that evening on Cape Town's Grand Parade.

Winnie had sent her husband the starkest message: she was no Penelope waiting for Odysseus to return.[7]

.   .

Upon arriving in Johannesburg, Nelson and Winnie had planned to go directly to Soweto, a grand homecoming for the township's most famous son. But by late morning, the crowd at their house had swelled to thousands and concerns were raised about whether it was safe.

An alternative was hastily arranged: a family near the private airport where their flight would land was asked to vacate their house. Nelson, Winnie, Zindzi and two grandchildren would sleep there the night.

By evening, the house was teeming with people: Nelson, Winnie, Zindzi, and her children; Walter and Albertina Sisulu; various members of the reception committee that had been assembled to manage Nelson's release.

The mood in the modest living room was tense. Among the members of the reception committee present that evening were Azhar Cachalia, Murphy Morobe, Sydney Mufamadi – men Winnie now regarded as mortal enemies. Nelson, some of those in that room recalled, was grimly silent.

Walter came to sit next to Nelson, and the two old men held hands. The spectacle of their intimacy imprinted itself in the memory of one of those present that evening: here was a deep, old friendship, of unabashed brotherly love, in a room filling with ill will.

Winnie kept demanding to go home. She did not want to sleep in the suburbs, she said; she wanted, at very least, to change her clothes. But from Soweto the messages kept coming that the crowd was still swelling, their homecoming unsafe.

Eventually, Winnie upped and left, and Zindzi and her children followed her. Nelson now worked with members of the reception committee on the speech he would give the following day. And then, one by one, they left, and the Sisulus, too, returned to Soweto, leaving Nelson to spend the night alone.[8]

. .

That he summoned Nadine Gordimer, a woman he scarcely knew, to share what was in his heart suggests distress and befuddlement, a sense of not knowing what to do. He had by now spent decades making a self through family: alone, in a cell, in one letter after another, he had conjured a wife with whom he was in love, children preparing to soar.

He understood that he was weaving a myth, and the knowledge caused great anxiety. 'I think much of . . . the problems of adjustment and of picking up old threads,' he had written as long ago as 1975. An old map, a handful of photographs, a collection of letters: this was a dangerously spare assortment of aids with which to imagine a life.

But imagine it he did, and what he had conjured was the only life he had.

.   .

A week after Nelson was freed, Azhar Cachalia was asked to chair a press conference at which Nelson was to speak. He obliged, and when the event was over, he returned to his office to work.

Late that night, after the press conference had been broadcast on television news, the phone on Cachalia's desk rang. 'I am warning you to stay away from Mandela,' Winnie's distinctive voice said. She hung up. Cachalia sat there, stunned, alone in his law firm's empty offices, wondering whether she had just threatened to kill him.[9]

It was not just Nelson she was fighting to possess. Months earlier, Teresa Oakley-Smith, heavily pregnant with Dali Mpofu's child, had spotted Winnie in a minivan outside her house. She had stepped unin- vited into the van and given Winnie a piece of her mind. 'I received an extremely unpleasant telephone call from Mrs. Mandela at about 9 o'clock that night,' Oakley-Smith later testified in an affidavit. 'She made a number of vitriolic remarks about my whiteness and the custom of white women to steal black men. The general tone was very threat- ening and I felt anxious. I received two strange calls during the night with women laughing, but nobody spoke.'[10]

When Oakley-Smith's son was born in December 1989, Winnie told friends that she was planning to adopt a baby for her and Dali: a child to match her rival's child.

.   .

Winnie and Nelson were astonishingly scarred human beings. The nightmare Winnie inhabited can scarcely be held in one's head. That everything one possesses — one's husband, one's lover, one's public standing — is forever on the brink of theft. That one must constantly threaten others to keep oneself from drowning — the life Winnie lived at this time was ghastly beyond telling. The many stories of her epi- sodes of narcotic escape are hardly surprising.

Nelson's scars were of such a different ilk. His pain was — for now at least — still and contained. At four o'clock on the morning after Nel- son was freed, Trevor Manuel, one of the UDF leaders managing his

release, was woken by his phone. It was Nelson. 'Where are my weights?'
he asked. 'I need to exercise.'[11]

The personal discipline that had held him together these many
years would not pause, not even on this day.

One cannot live just off discipline. It does not, alone, produce the
meaning, the people, the narrative arc, that make for a human life.

Chapter 60

Two weeks after Nelson's release, he and Winnie began to travel, their first stop Lusaka, headquarters of the ANC.

The scene on the tarmac was 'epic, existential', one of those there remembered.[1] Cleaved asunder in the 1960s, Nelson's generation was finally reunited. 'It feels real now! I touched him!' Joe Slovo shouted after throwing his arms around Nelson.[2] From Ruth Mompati he received a more contained greeting. 'Hello, comrade', a friend heard her say in a quiet voice.[3]

Dispersed among his old friends and fellow travellers on the tarmac were more than a dozen African heads of state, the prime minister of Malaysia, and diplomats from farther afield. Also there was the PLO's Yasser Arafat. They had come to stand in his halo's glow, the excitement the decolonized world had once kindled relit on this day.

The most urgent task on Nelson's trip to Lusaka took place behind closed doors. In an all-day meeting of the ANC's national executive, he was given the floor for several hours. Painstakingly, he told the story of his secret talks with the government: he had never negotiated on the ANC's behalf, he explained; he had only facilitated contact. He reiterated his commitment to economic sanctions, to the armed struggle, and, most of all, to majority rule.[4]

He had not been long on the road before he was humbled by his wife. Addressing students at the University of Zambia, he horribly misread the crowd. Kenneth Kaunda, Zambian president since 1964, would be swept from power in an election the following year, and many of the students in the audience that day would rally behind his ouster. Nelson thanked Kaunda profusely for his support for the ANC before exhorting the students to be disciplined and to respect authority. His audience, which had until now listened politely, audibly groaned.

He had hardly taken his seat when shouts for Winnie to speak arose. She did not agree with everything the previous speaker had said, she remarked in her impromptu speech. Students should indeed obey authority, but only if the university administration listened to their views.

She had taken the temperature masterfully and received rapturous applause; the discomfort on the faces of her husband and his hosts was barely concealed.[5]

A few days later, the couple now in the Tanzanian capital of Dar es Salaam, senior members of the travelling party were woken in the night to be told that a crisis had arisen. They arrived at State House, the official residence of the country's president, where Winnie and Nelson were staying, to find Winnie packing; she wished to cut short the visit and take Nelson home. 'Our people need us,' a member of the party remembered her pleading. 'We cannot be apart from them for so long.' Nelson demurred; it was unthinkable not to honour commitments, he was saying; the schedule must be obeyed. Walter Sisulu stepped in to mediate, and by dawn Winnie had agreed that the tour could proceed.

The party left the capital city and headed west, spending a night at an MK training camp in the city of Iringa. They were dressed in MK uniforms, met with rank-and-file soldiers, toured the grounds. 'Winnie was calm there,' a member of the delegation recalled. The time with the combatants 'gave her the fuel to see through the rest of the tour'.[6]

The politics of the marriage now gave off a whiff of comedy. For Nelson, the revolution had entered Thermidor. The fervour of the last quarter century was to be doused, the young reeled in. Such thoughts were horrifying to Winnie Mandela. The starched obedience, the deference to stale authority: she rebelled against these from the depths of her being.

. .

For months, their travels scarcely ceased. They went to Zimbabwe, to Namibia, to Algeria, to Egypt. They went to Stockholm to visit the ailing Oliver Tambo. In April they were in London for another globally televised concert, this one to celebrate Nelson's release.

In June, they visited Paris, Bonn and Rome, where they had an audience with the pope. In an early morning phone call, Margaret Thatcher lectured Nelson on the pace of his schedule. He had a historic task ahead of him, she counselled with unmasked condescension: he must remain fresh and preserve his strength![7]

On June 20, they arrived in New York.

From JFK International Airport, their cavalcade made its way through Queens and Brooklyn en route to a ticker-tape parade in Manhattan. In East New York, in Bedford-Stuyvesant, in Fort Greene, much of Brooklyn's black population came out to greet them. And as they approached midtown, tens of thousands of people disgorged from Harlem across 110th Street, heading south. Three-quarters of a million New Yorkers came out to bear witness to the Mandelas that day.[8]

At city hall, they were met by New York's first black mayor, David Dinkins, its black police commissioner, Lee Brown, and a phalanx of black clergy, administrators and city politicians. 'The visit of the freedom fighter has positioned [black New York], for a minute, in the centre of world politics,' wrote the Harlem correspondent of *The Village Voice*. 'It made us the first family. And it has given us, again, an accessible past.'[9]

The past to which speech after speech referred was biblical. Dinkins spoke of Mandela as a twentieth-century Moses, 'leading the people of South Africa out of enslavement at the hands of the pharaoh'.[10] At an event Nelson addressed the next day in Bedford-Stuyvesant, his 'silver Afro hair' was described by a journalist as 'a halo'.

'This is truly a religious experience,' the journalist continued, 'a man back from the dead to lead the living, and an authentic African queen.'[11]

When he was not swept into the Old Testament, it was into an African American renaissance. Mandela had 'filled a void . . . left by the deaths of Dr. Martin Luther King and Malcolm X', a veteran of the civil rights movement told a journalist. 'Thank God Mandela has lit a fire that was extinguished in the 1960s,' another declared. 'When he gets back on that plane, we have to keep that fire alive.'[12]

Nelson understood his audience well. Addressing tens of thousands of people at Yankee Stadium, he spoke of 'that unbreakable umbilical cord' connecting black South Africans and black Americans. He named Du Bois, Garvey, and Martin Luther King as among the men who had inspired him. He paid tribute to Harlem, symbol of 'the strength of resistance and the beauty of black pride'.[13]

As the rally was drawing to a close, a call broke out somewhere in the crowd for Winnie to speak. Within moments, it had spread across the stadium. 'We want Winnie!' fifty thousand people chanted. When she obliged, throwing a clenched fist into the air as she reached the podium, the crowd thundered in reply.[14]

Two days earlier, Winnie had addressed the congregation of the House of the Lord Pentecostal Church in Harlem. 'This sister's presence in our midst is enough,' Betty Shabazz, Malcolm X's widow, had said as she introduced Winnie to the audience. 'She shouldn't have to speak. To have gone through what she has gone through, and to see her looking so pleasant, so composed! There must be a God. Got to be a God.'[15]

Winnie certainly did speak. When she appeared on *The Phil Donahue Show,* her host remarked that her husband seemed more trusting and less angry than she did.

'I must confess, I do battle with myself about believing the sincerity [of the South African government],' she replied. 'As far as I'm concerned, we will watch that negotiation table: if anything goes wrong, I will be the first to . . . take up arms and fight.'[16]

. .

At the end of the New York leg of the trip, the broadcaster Ted Koppel hosted Nelson at a town hall meeting in Harlem.

Koppel went at Nelson hard. How did he explain his friendships with Libya's dictator Muammar Gaddafi and Cuba's Fidel Castro? Did Nelson have nothing to say about the way these men governed their countries?

These were fair questions. Koppel was the first to confront Nelson with the discomfort of being universally loved. Does everyone get to stand in his halo's light?

Nelson was clearly briefed that Koppel intended to be tough, for the pose he struck from the start warned of the unfriendliness to come. He sat as still as a statue, ramrod straight, the muscles in his face cast in stone. And this rigid, unmoving body pointed *away* from Koppel; he did not once in over an hour make eye contact with his host or even so much as look at him. Koppel was made to converse with the side of Nelson's face.

'I think I know better about this matter, Mr. Koppel, than you,' Nelson said in reply to the first probing question, much to the Harlem audience's delight.

When Koppel paused before replying to one of Nelson's retorts, the trace of a smile finally crossed his face. 'Have I paralyzed you?' he asked.

Confronted with questions he did not like, he threw the heft of his grandeur in his interviewer's face. He appeared to delight in the role.[17]

. .

As the tour proceeded, its underbelly was kept discreetly concealed.

Several months earlier, the day after Nelson's release, in fact, Jerry Richardson was scheduled to stand trial for the murder of James 'Stompie' Seipei. In deference to the great man, the presiding judge had agreed to postpone the trial. It finally began in May, just a month before Nelson and Winnie's triumphant march through Western Europe and the United States.

It did not go well for Winnie.

Kenny Kgase, Thabiso Mono and Pelo Mekgwe all took the stand: Winnie had beat them with her fists and with whips, each said, before letting her football team loose. She had condemned them for betraying their race and the struggle for freedom, had told them that they were not fit to live. Their testimonies were so graphic, so plausibly detailed, and largely consistent with one another. Each described, with ominous precision, the violence meted out to Stompie Seipei.

For his part, Richardson denied killing Seipei; he swore, too, that Winnie herself was not even in Johannesburg on the day the young men were taken from the manse. But in his summing up, Richardson's defense counsel told the court, much to the astonishment of the gallery, that his client had lied. 'He is protecting himself from others because if he mentions their names his life won't be worth much,' the counsel had said.[18]

In the last week of May, the presiding judge found Richardson guilty of murdering Stompie Seipei. He also ruled on the question of Winnie Mandela's involvement: she was present when the young men and Seipei were beaten, he wrote in his judgment, 'for at least a part of the time'.

For several years now, and for conflicting reasons, powerful men in the South African state had kept Winnie from standing trial. Lolo Sono, Siboniso Tshabalala, Abu Baker Asvat, Thole Dlamini, Kuki Zwane, Xola Mokhaula: Winnie was not so much as questioned in connection with these and other crimes associated with the workings of her home.

In fact, tension had arisen in the late 1980s at the summit of the South African state about how the criminal justice system ought to approach Winnie Mandela. The minister responsible for policing, Adriaan Vlok, wanted very much to go after her, but only for high treason and only once the police had made an airtight case. He instructed that Winnie not be charged with any crime while the case was being assembled.[19]

But when, in 1988, the police handed the attorney general of the Witwatersrand a 650-page docket describing a case against Winnie of high treason, he promptly put it aside. Although he would never admit to succumbing to pressure, those secretly talking to Nelson had decided that prosecuting his wife would interfere with their work.[20]

Now, in May 1990, just three months after Nelson's release, a finding of criminal culpability against Winnie had finally leaked from the courts. The calculus had changed. The conspicuousness of not charging her had risen to a din. The attorney general nonetheless waited a full four months before announcing that she would face trial. And it was during this four-month period that the Mandelas embarked upon their European and American tour.

As the couple made their way through the capital cities of Europe, no one dared raise the matter. One does not interrogate the Messiah about the murder of a fourteen-year-old child, not with his wife at his side.

There was an exception. In Bonn, in mid-June, at a crowded press club, just days before the Mandelas' triumphant arrival in New York, a German journalist asked Nelson to comment on the allegations against his wife.

A great hush came over the room as the great man readied his reply.

'A press club is not a place to discuss rumours,' Nelson had snapped. 'Let's deal with matters of public interest.'

The chair invited the journalist to formulate a more well-defined question. But before he could do so, Thabo Mbeki, who was flanking Mandela, intervened.

'It is not clear why the question has been posed,' he said. 'To assist you, there is a trial going on in South Africa, but Mrs. Mandela has not been charged.'[21]

It was a taste, a forewarning, of how Nelson Mandela was to exercise his newfound power.

Chapter 61

They had been back home mere weeks when Nelson began to reveal how far he was prepared to go.

By then, the ANC was starting to re-establish itself in South Africa. Across the country, it was founding local branches after an absence of thirty years.

In July, in Orlando West, a newly constituted ANC branch held a ballot for its executive committee, and when the votes were counted, it was discovered that Winnie Mandela was not going to hold office. Her neighbourhood had turned on her in the wake of the football club's deeds. She was, in the clearest terms, being sidelined.

On the Sunday after the ballot, several senior ANC members received an early morning phone call from Nelson Mandela summoning them to his house. Among them were Amos Masondo, a future Johannesburg mayor, and Barbara Hogan, who would serve in successive national cabinets. At that time, they were members of an interim leadership collective responsible for re-establishing the ANC.

Once they had assembled at his house, Nelson informed his comrades that their task was to establish a new ANC branch. There and then, they were to go door to door, signing up members: it was a Sunday; people were at home; it would not be hard.

An awkward feeling descended upon the group. Nelson had not so much as mentioned Winnie's name. But that they had been summoned to conjure from nothing a branch for her to claim as her own was as clear as a pane of glass. Dutifully, the group piled into a car; under Nelson's command, they went door to door.

From his place in the backseat of the car, Amos Masondo began to protest. 'What you have asked us to do is not right, Madiba,' he said.

Nelson was in the passenger seat, his back to Masondo. 'He turned around,' Hogan recalled, 'and he began tearing shreds out of Amos. It was nasty. It was vitriolic. And it went on for some time. The rest of us said nothing. But the feeling in that car was uncomfortable; we knew that what we were doing was very wrong.'[1]

. .

It did not end there. Soon after, the ANC's Pretoria-Witwatersrand-Vereeniging region held its first elective conference in a large hall in Alexandra township. Winnie was standing for election that day to the region's executive. Not long before the voting was scheduled to commence, Nelson arrived unannounced amid a phalanx of bodyguards and walked onto the stage.

Within minutes, whispering had spread through the hall: he was there to ensure that Winnie was elected, it was said.

All of a sudden, the delegates felt awfully exposed. No provision had been made for a secret ballot; candidates were to be elected by a raising of hands. And Nelson, so plainly visible on the stage, made a great show of *watching*, his mouth turned down, his face grave.

As the voting commenced, his bodyguards, a delegate in that hall recalled, 'were all over the place, muscling in, taking command. They went so far as to get involved in the counting of votes. What was happening really was not subtle at all.'[2]

The votes were counted, and Winnie was duly elected onto the executive. Mandela remained another perfunctory ten minutes and then promptly left, taking his bodyguards with him.

. .

He had now ensconced his wife into two of his organization's tiers. She held executive office in her branch and in her region. What remained was a place for her in the national tier.

In August, Winnie was duly appointed to head the ANC's Welfare Department. Her primary task would be sensitive and logistically difficult: to tend to the thousands of exiles returning from abroad, many of them poorly educated and ill-equipped to readjust to home. Her appointment caused consternation. From more than a hundred ANC branches, letters of complaint poured in.[3] None of these letters received so much as a reply.

. .

And then, on September 17, the attorney general of the Witwa-tersrand, Klaus von Lieres, finally announced that Winnie Mandela would face trial. She was charged with four counts of kidnapping and four of assault with intent to cause grievous bodily harm. Seven oth-ers would join her in the dock: Xoliswa Falati and her teenage daugh-ter; Winnie's driver, John Morgan; and four members of the football team, Katiza Cebekhulu, Gift Mabelane, Sibusiso Mabuza and a minor whose name was not disclosed.

A week later, the Mandelas' lawyer, Ismail Ayob, contacted IDAF in London to request that it fund Winnie's legal defense. IDAF – the fund the security police had attempted to infiltrate many years earlier through Winnie's relationship with Maud Katzenellenbogen and the lawyer Mendel Levin – was by now one of the largest registered chari-ties in the U.K., receiving substantial annual contributions from gov-ernments across Europe. In the thirty-four years of its existence, it had secretly funnelled more than £100 million into South Africa, funding the legal fees of thousands of detainees and defendants, paying for their education by correspondence, for the welfare of their families, and for the schooling of their children.

And IDAF, of course, had a special relationship with Nelson Man-dela and his generation of activists. It was founded back in 1956 to fund the defense in the Treason Trial and had gone on to bankroll the defense at Rivonia. And when the Rivonia defendants found themselves on Robben Island, it had paid for their wives to visit them. In the case of Winnie Mandela, it had gone further, providing her with regular income while she was stranded in Brandfort.[4]

IDAF's trustees deliberated painfully over Nelson's request before turning it down. This was a criminal, not a political case, they resolved; it did not fall within their ambit.[5]

At six o'clock on a Sunday morning in mid-October, IDAF's direc-tor, Horst Kleinschmidt, was woken by a phone call at his home in Lon-don. It was Nelson Mandela.

Kleinschmidt's association with the Mandela family went back nearly two decades. In the treacherous years of the early 1970s, he and his then wife, Ilona, had offered Winnie steady support. Kleinschmidt had been in the gallery when Winnie was sentenced to six months in prison in 1975, and had, on the spot, taken on the legal guardianship of her daughters. As for Ilona, she was jailed in 1977 for refusing to testify against Winnie; Winnie had violated her banning order by meeting with Ilona and another person, and Ilona had been subpoenaed to give evidence at her trial.[6]

Nelson was polite to Kleinschmidt that early Sunday morning. But he was also firm. IDAF, he said, should reconsider its decision not to pay his wife's legal fees.[7]

The fund consulted with its donors. While the Nordic countries agreed to pay for Winnie's trial, the European Community, which donated a hefty £800,000 a year, gave an emphatic no. If IDAF so much as touched the case, it warned, its grant would be savagely cut.[8]

It was Nelson Mandela's wish against the future contribution of a major donor.

One did not say no to Nelson Mandela, it was agreed. The best one could do was to make him aware of the costs the fund would incur.

No sooner was this awkward episode over than another arose. When the Mandelas' lawyer, Ismail Ayob, lodged his first invoice with IDAF for his work on Winnie's trial, the hourly rate was vastly above the premium the organization's policy permitted it to pay. Once more, the trustees wrung their hands before deciding to refuse to pay Ayob's bill.

Kleinschmidt now received another early morning phone call from Nelson Mandela. This one was not nearly as polite. He had thought that the family had a friend in Kleinschmidt, Nelson said. Now he was not so sure. Did Kleinschmidt hold a grudge against the Mandelas?[9]

Some time later, from out of the blue, two men representing the Coca-Cola Company visited Kleinschmidt at his office in London. They wished to pay for Winnie Mandela's trial, they informed him.[10]

It was to be a complicated business. The money would pass through a web of intermediaries to conceal its origin. Kleinschmidt was unhappy. So were the trustees. IDAF had never before received money from a private company. Nor had a donor ever attached specific conditions on how its money should be spent. Reluctantly, the organization agreed.

Still, the saga did not end. Another phone call came from Nelson Mandela. IDAF, he said, must transfer the money it had received from Coca-Cola directly to the Mandela Family Trust. Once more, the phone call was unpleasant. Once more, IDAF's trustees wrung their hands. In the end, they did as Nelson wished.[11]

What Coca-Cola expected in return is hard to say. It was not a great deal of money – £53,000, in the end[12] – a cheap investment in the personal attention of a future head of state.

Nelson Mandela was a year out of prison. He had corrupted the democratic processes of his organization; he had wounded a fund to which he, personally, owed an enormous debt; he had received covert money from a private corporation.

He did not do any of this to augment his political power, nor to grow wealthy, nor, still, to line the pockets of his friends. His motivations were far more personal and harder to fathom than that.

· ·

Among those closest to Nelson at this time was Barbara Masekela, his chief of staff. A well-known figure in the ANC in exile, she went on to serve as South Africa's ambassador to France and the United States. But now, from 1990 to 1995, she was Nelson's adviser and political confidante.

They first worked together when Masekela co-managed that glorious visit to New York. On the last day of the trip, Nelson had asked her to join the group that ate with Winnie and him every night.

'Why don't you like me?' he had asked when she arrived. He was not five months out of prison and was flirting with great delight.

'What do you mean?' she replied. 'I like you.'

'Every night,' he said, 'everyone comes here to eat and talk. But not you.'

'I am writing your speeches,' she replied. 'I am preparing your day.'

'I want you to work with me,' he said. 'I want you to be my chief of staff.'

The bond between them grew strong in the time to come. It was not long before some of Nelson's closest friends gossiped that they were lovers. But it seems unlikely that this was so.

'Naturally people thought we had a love affair,' Masekela told this author, 'but that is not right. Our connection was very deep, close, trusting, professional, but also familial. He would arrive unannounced at my house with his bodyguard. He would want simply to talk.'[13]

'Madiba was an actor,' Masekela said, the moment we sat down to our first interview. 'He was completely honest about it. We would catch him primping just before some delegation or person came to talk to him. You could actually see him becoming this Nelson Mandela, the great forgiver, the Thembu princeling. We would catch him doing it and he would laugh. He would not hide it. We were all women, you see. He would not do it in front of men.'

All the senior figures in Nelson's office at that time – Masekela, Jessie Duarte and Frene Ginwala – were women. 'It was not preconceived that it would be that way,' Masekela remarked. 'It is just who I ended up hiring. Here we were, three women running the office of the president in this most patriarchal organization. It was an unusual situation. It worked well. He was so very comfortable around women, not as a patriarch, but as someone who had been loved by women since he was a boy.'

If Masekela had watched him become Nelson Mandela, seen him primp and fuss and rehearse his role, who was he before he primped? Who was he offstage?

'He was a deeply wounded man,' she said bluntly. 'He was one of the saddest human beings I have known. From time to time, you felt it come out of him. It was sadness and anger mixed together: *fierce* anger. It must have taken masterful discipline not to show it. It would come without words, most often when we were in a crowd. He would stop waving. There was just a stillness, a grim, frightening stillness, and an almost unbearable sadness.'

I asked her to recall a specific instance.

'We were in Tanzania,' she said, 'in a village near the great Ngorongoro Crater. It was one of the most beautiful things I have ever seen. It was vast and it was full of animals: hyenas, zebra, buck, moving through in great numbers. In a village nearby, the people had lined the street to greet him. They were simple, rural people. They just shouted, "Mandela! Mandela!" It was really quite moving. He was fine, cheerful, his usual self. But as the convoy got to the village and we found ourselves among these people shouting, it came over him. This terrible sadness. It was palpable. You could see it in his face.

'It is no coincidence that it happened to him among poor people,' she added. 'People from the hinterland. He was sad for them and sad for himself.'

From time to time, Masekela decided unilaterally to take him out of circulation. 'I would hide him,' she recalled. 'I would say, "Madiba, you need to take three days." I would find very unlikely places. Only his security would know. I would make the arrangements, fix the place up, drop him off in the middle of the night, let him be for a while. It was always somewhere rural, somewhere he could walk.'

She wondered aloud whether twenty-seven years in prison would have damaged a quieter, less rambunctious soul as severely as it had damaged Nelson Mandela. 'The thing about Madiba', she said, 'is that he loved life so much. Nobody will ever be able to measure the loss of that freedom, the loss of that love of laughter, of life itself.

'And that', she continued, 'that is what his love of Winnie was all about. You see, he really felt, in his deepest heart, that he had something in kind with her. He thought that human beings had to have that sort of fire because he had it.

'Even during the darkest days, when what was happening between him and Winnie was truly terrible, the *delight* he would take in her was so striking. Once, Alfred Nzo and Thomas Nkobi, the secretary-general and treasurer of the ANC, came to him. Madiba, they said, she has gone too far; we must go as a delegation to see her: you, the sec-gen, the treasurer, to challenge her formally. Madiba said, "You go. I am not going." The moment they left his office, he started grinning from ear to ear. He was anticipating her response. He knew that they would come back with their tails between their legs. He could barely contain himself.'

It was not just Winnie who delighted him so. In the countless hours he and Masekela spent together, he gave voice to whatever came into his mind, and so often this attention turned, in a stream of consciousness, to Lilian Ngoyi, the leading activist with whom Nelson's first wife, Evelyn, had accused him of having an affair.

'He was in awe of her,' Masekela recalled. 'That gumption. When she got up to speak, he would say, she was stronger than any man.

'Everyone knew that they had had a relationship,' she added, 'but he would not go that far [as to say that to me].'

He talked, too, about Ruth Mompati. But when Masekela asked about their relationship, he flatly denied that they had ever been lovers. 'He had that lawyer's stubbornness,' Masekela said. 'They choose a line of defense, and once they have chosen it, they never retreat. Because to retreat would be to admit total failure.'

Nelson's friendship with Masekela must have provided great solace: that he felt sufficiently safe in her presence to offer that bottomless sadness; that he would stray far enough from his guard to allow the 1950s to come rushing back in. What he shared with her is indeed irretrievably sad. Here was a man reaching for the core of what made him human, and what he found was the ghost of a mid-century gentleman, flirting and playing and making love with the women who made him truly alive.

'To spend twenty-seven years in the prime of one's life [in prison] is a tragedy,' he said in an unguarded moment shortly after his release. 'I regret those years that I have wasted.'[14] There is no self-deceit here; he absolutely knew what had happened to him.

What did he think he was doing when he bulldozed a path for Winnie back into the ANC? What was he imagining when he ruined those who would not pay for her trial? It is unlikely that he was deluded in any straightforward way. He surely knew, at least to some degree, the extent of the damage – to him, to his wife, to the relation between them. It is improbable that he imagined that they would be happily married again. He was, perhaps, straining to retrieve something of value from the ruins of those awful years: battered, storm swept, unable any longer to provide shelter, those ruins had once been home.

.   .

The glimpses we have of their domestic life at this time are grim. They were both so busy; apart from anything else, there was scarcely time for the rhythms of a life together to form. Several years later, Zindzi described to a friend the scene on a rare occasion when the family ate together. From the room next door, the phone rang. 'You should answer,' Nelson said coolly to Winnie. 'It will be Dali.' The family laboured on at their meal in silence.[15]

As had always been the case with her lovers, Winnie was living much of her life with Dali by her side. She had appointed him her deputy in the Welfare Department of the ANC; they spent their days and their evenings together. He had, for now, suspended his law career, dedicating his working life exclusively to her.

What Nelson offered Winnie now was a patriarch's protection on the grandest scale: chiselling her a place into each tier of their organization, moving the earth to fund her trial. What she offered in return was a patriarch's humiliation; she was cuckolding him in the open, without the slightest attempt at disguise.

The sympathy Winnie elicited in this came, at times, from places that at first blush seem unlikely.

Barbara Masekela, for instance, witnessed Nelson's pain with empathy and from close quarters. Nor was she by any measure Winnie's friend. And yet about Winnie's love life she was full of great fellow feeling.

'She loses her husband young,' Masekela told this author. 'She is at the height of her sexual powers. She is free. She can do what she wants. And then he comes back. She is a person in her own right now. But she still calls him Tata – father.' Masekela opened her arms, in her face a trace of distaste. 'All these years later, I still struggle with that.'[16]

'You know,' she remarked on another occasion, 'something that irritated us [women in the office] about Madiba. There was a greengrocer's across the road. We would pool our money and one of us would go to buy fruit. He would take so long to get out his money. He would count the cents. We'd say, "We don't have time, we will pay." "No, no," he'd protest. "This is good money!" And he'd go on counting those coins.

'That is the image that comes to my mind when I think of what Winnie faced in her marriage. Those jail years kept him away from social developments. He may have been briefed about social changes, but he could not keep track. He was in many ways an old gentleman from the past. So I see poor Winnie. She is meant to return to being the woman in love. She has had other experiences, has met other people. Now there has to be dinner on the table. Can you imagine?'[17]

Chapter 62

On the eve of Winnie's trial, in early February 1991, four of her co-accused disappeared.[1] Their attorneys were instructed to find them. Warrants were issued for their arrest. When the trial began, they were still nowhere to be found; they had simply vanished.

Three of them, it emerged later, Jabu Sithole, Sibusiso Mabuza and Gift Mabelane, were at a transit camp in Botswana in the care of members of the ANC. High-ranking officials of the organization had had them spirited away.[2]

The fourth missing man, Katiza Cebekhulu, had a more troubling story to tell.

With his consent, it appears, ANC personnel took him on a strange and circuitous trip, first, by car, to the Mozambican capital, Maputo, then, a week later, by plane, to the Angolan capital, Luanda, and finally to Lusaka. There, he was received by Zambian officials and put up in the city's Victoria Hotel.[3] He remained there for three months until he violated the unwritten conditions of his stay. In an interview with a Zambian newspaper, he claimed that the ANC had kidnapped him; he wished to return home, he said; his testimony would bring down Winnie Mandela.

His Zambian hosts promptly removed him from his hotel room and threw him in jail. Straining for a serviceable reason, they claimed that he had broken immigration law and was being held pending deportation. It took a horribly long time. When Kenneth Kaunda was swept from power in November 1991, Cebekhulu was still in prison. Kaunda's successor, Frederick Chiluba, learned of the South African in his custody days after he assumed office. But he too, although no friend of the ANC, would not let Cebekhulu go. With the assistance of an outraged British member of Parliament, Cebekhulu applied to a succession of countries for asylum. But the story he told, that he was on the run from

Nelson Mandela's ANC, was too eccentric, its tenor too jarring with the spirit of the times. Nobody, it appeared, wanted to take him. He finally left Zambia for an undisclosed country of asylum more than two years after he arrived.[4]

. .

The four co-accused were not the only ones to disappear. On the night of February 10, a week after the trial began, three ANC men came to Paul Verryn's manse in Soweto and left with Pelo Mekgwe.[5] He, Kenny Kgase and Thabiso Mono, the three surviving men kidnapped by Winnie's football team, were all to testify for the prosecution. It emerged later that Mekgwe, too, had been spirited across the border.

The moment he disappeared, Kgase and Mono told the court that they were too afraid to testify. 'I feel strongly about the obligation,' Kgase said from the witness stand, 'but life is such a precious thing to me, and I really want my life.'[6]

One week in, the trial was on the brink of collapse. Four co-accused had vanished. A key state witness had been whisked away. The remaining two were too petrified to speak. The prosecutor complained that without their testimony the medical and forensic evidence he had gathered was useless.

. .

How involved was Nelson Mandela in the assault on his wife's trial?

In 1997, in a horribly careless moment, the former Zambian president Kenneth Kaunda said on camera that Oliver Tambo had asked him on behalf of Nelson Mandela to receive Katiza Cebekhulu.[7] In the ensuing scandal he backtracked a little. 'I must clarify that I did not receive direct communication from Mr. Oliver Tambo on this matter,' he said. 'It was [Zambian] government officials who informed me that they had received such a request from officials of Mr. Tambo.' He simply took it on faith, he said, that Mandela supported the action.[8]

It is unlikely that Nelson was personally involved. He had, by now, delegated what a close colleague of his called 'the political management of his wife' to Tokyo Sexwale and Chris Hani, a shrewd move on Nelson's part, because Winnie admired both men very much. Sexwale conceded that members of the ANC's Special Projects Department, which he himself ran, had used ANC resources to smuggle Mekgwe to Botswana. But he claimed that this had happened behind his back.[9]

If Nelson did not know the details, if he was not personally involved, what happened clearly carried his implicit approval. He never once expressed a qualm about the disappearance of witnesses and accused. And when a condemnation of these disappearances was placed in a speech he was to deliver, he simply skipped over it and turned the page.[10]

As revealing as these silences was the show of force he assembled as the trial began.

Flanked by Joe Slovo and Chris Hani, and by the ANC's secretary-general, Alfred Nzo, he swept into the courtroom grim-faced and severe. A posse of ANC marshals had preceded him, their bearing swaggering, a little threatening. They had wrested command of the gallery from court officials, clearing the first two rows to make way for 'the leadership'.[11]

They did more than that. They demanded that members of the press show them their credentials; they interrogated members of the public sitting in the pews about who they were and why they had come to see Winnie's trial. Outside, still more ANC marshals commandeered the area around the court. The left-wing *Weekly Mail* expressed horror. 'Arrogant ANC marshals . . . took control of the streets,' the newspaper complained, 'strutting around in makeshift military fatigues and abusing journalists and others.'[12]

As the trial proceeded, the aura of thuggishness grew darker. On a morning in April, deep into the trial, Winnie Mandela made her way to the courthouse as usual amid a bevy of young men. Without warning, she stopped and turned and pointed a finger at a man she had spotted in the crowd. Employed as a reporting assistant by the London *Independent*, he had researched a damning piece the newspaper published seven months earlier on the Mandela United Football Club.

'Here's an SB [Security Branch],' she said loudly, before gesturing to him to come nearer. 'You're here as what?' she snapped. 'As a journalist?' Now she turned to the spectators who had assembled to watch the scene. 'You remember that famous story in the *Independent* where a group of people were gathered together to say that I was a criminal? Well, this is the man who did it. He is an SB.' The journalist turned and walked slowly away, half expecting to have to flee the crowd.[13]

In the courtroom itself, a group of highly credentialed litigators, all of them deeply associated with the struggle against apartheid, assembled to defend Winnie Mandela. There was Pius Langa, who went on to become South Africa's chief justice; Dikgang Moseneke, a former Robben Islander, who became his country's deputy chief justice; and George Bizos, Nelson's dear friend of almost fifty years.

Winnie denied that she had been in Soweto when the young men were taken from the manse; her co-accused, whose legal fees the Mandelas paid, swore that she was not there; a woman from Brandfort testified that Winnie had come to see her the very day the young men were kidnapped; a young man from her neighbourhood claimed to have driven her to the Free State.

But what Winnie could not deny, for she had said as much over and over again in the press, was that she knew that the youths had been taken from Paul Verryn's manse to her home. Bizos was left to launch a vicious assault on the minister. The goings-on in the manse, he said, were brought to Winnie's attention from a sense of 'concern and disgust'.[14] As Winnie had done from the beginning, he conflated the grooming of children with consensual sex among adults, his argument buoyed by an unpleasant racial motif. Homosexuality, he told the court, was 'especially repugnant to black people'.[15]

Winnie continued the onslaught. 'What kind of beast is this,' she asked in a media interview during her trial, 'who wears a collar on Sundays and goes to preach to parents of these children? . . . At night, he becomes something else.'[16]

. .

Alarm was growing in influential quarters of the ANC. The disappearance of the accused and of a witness; the goonish behaviour around the court; the distasteful line of defense. These reflected poorly on the mental state of Nelson Mandela. What would he do, it was increasingly asked, if Winnie were thrown in prison?

The commentary of the London *Independent*'s South Africa correspondent, John Carlin, indicated the changing concern in certain quarters of the ANC. In the year since his release, Carlin wrote in the midst of the trial, Mandela had become singularly indispensable to South

Africa's peaceful transition. He had also thus become uniquely powerful. 'He listens, but, in the end, he rules.'[17]

What his wife's trial had done to his mind was thus of cardinal
importance. 'His own mental and physical health are tied to the health
of the ANC.'[18]

Those whispering in Carlin's ear were growing increasingly desperate. 'We wondered whether we had created a monster,' an ANC
leader recalled years later. 'Inventing the figure of Nelson Mandela was
among the most effective political strategies in modern history. Now it
was on the brink of bringing the house down on our heads.'[19]

What was going on with Nelson Mandela? Was his mental health
indeed precarious, as some close to him increasingly believed?

There is a broader landscape to consider as one answers these
questions. Beyond the courtroom, beyond Winnie and Nelson's house,
South Africa's transition had triggered terrible bloodletting. The violence out in the world and the fierce feelings in their marriage had
entangled in unexpected ways.

Chapter 63

When F. W. de Klerk unbanned the ANC, he did not intend giving up power. A long, grinding transition would wipe the sheen from Nelson and his movement, De Klerk calculated, rendering them fallible, ordinary, disappointing. If he could build an alliance with the right black allies, he might just defeat the ANC at the polls.[1]

Nor did he envisage majority rule. The constitutional proposals the National Party released in 1990 sketched a bicameral parliament. While the lower chamber would be elected on a common roll, the Senate would be much more intricate; it would have 130 members, 10 each from ten newly constituted regions, and another 10 each representing Afrikaners, English speakers, and Asians, respectively. Legislation would require a two-thirds majority in this chamber to pass. As for the executive, South Africa would have not a new president but a rotating chairmanship shared by the major parties.[2]

De Klerk got none of what he set out to achieve. A little over four years after he unbanned the ANC, it won a landslide victory in a system of proportional representation. South Africa's new constitution made no reference to ethnic groups, just to individuals. Its greatest concession to the privileged was to enshrine the right to private property, but not unconditionally.

It is often forgotten how decisively Mandela won. It is equally forgotten at what cost his victory came. Between the beginning of the insurrections in 1984 and his release six years later, some five thousand people died in political violence. During the four years that followed, three times that number died.[3] That the transition was heralded as miraculously peaceful is a misnomer. It was a time of bloodshed unparallelled in the history of modern South Africa.

There is no uncontentious way to describe what the violence was about. In the mid-1980s, in the thick of the insurrectionary period, several black residential areas in the province of Natal were slated for incorporation into the self-governing territory of KwaZulu. Resistance to the move soon descended into internecine warfare, on one side supporters of KwaZulu's chief minister, Mangosuthu Buthelezi, his Zulu cultural movement, Inkatha, and the institution of the Zulu monarchy; on the other, supporters of the UDF.[4] The conflict assumed the character of warfare in part because the authorities took sides; in 1985, the South African Defence Force secretly trained and armed Inkatha militias; and, in one instance at least, the police took part in the slaughter of civilians. But the millenarian strain in the ANC also contributed to the bloodiness of the conflict. Chief instigator on the ANC's side was Nelson's old Robben Island comrade Harry Gwala, who had once kindled fire in the hearts of young inmates within the prison walls.[5]

In mid-1990, just months after the unbanning of the ANC, the violence spread from Natal to Greater Johannesburg. The proximate cause was the remaking of Buthelezi's Inkatha movement into a nationwide political party to rival the ANC. But the roots of the troubles lay deeper than political-party rivalry.

Scattered throughout Johannesburg were dozens of gargantuan single-sex hostels. Vast slabs of concrete, arranged in closed blocks to seal their inhabitants inside, they were veritable monuments of white South Africa's hostility to black people. They were the residues of an abandoned vision in which black men worked, but never lived, in the city, labouring in factories by day, bedding down in walled compounds by night.

By the time Nelson was released, these monstrous structures had long strayed from their original purpose. Apartheid's greatest ambition, to control human movement absolutely, had been washed away in an uncorralled influx to the cities. Several million people had descended upon metropolitan South Africa during the course of the 1980s, forming shack settlements on the urban fringes, erecting structures in backyards and cramming into municipal hostels. Bed space in some of these hostels was by now rented in twelve-hour shifts; in others, rooms were commandeered by religious denominations, by members of a trade union, etc. Adjacent shack settlements, too, were ruled by an assortment of hastily assembled groups.

A wildness was encroaching on South Africa's cities; vast zones were outside law or regulation, zones where strangers were forced to cohabit and where everything – from shelter, to work, to clean water, to safety – was in short supply.

The violence that descended upon Greater Johannesburg traced the geography of the old migrant worker hostels. On the eve of the violence, hostels on the East Rand, in the inner city, in Alexandra and Soweto, some of them profoundly cosmopolitan until then, emptied of non-Zulu residents. And, in some areas, the Zulu-speaking residents of adjacent shacklands were chased into hostels: a silent, ominous ethnic separation was presaging what was to come.

The war that ensued never engulfed the whole city. Soweto's hostels remained quiet most of the time. In Alexandra, in Kagiso, in the inner-city district of Jeppe, the fighting was sporadic. The initiatives that contained the troubles in these areas make for an extraordinary story that is largely untold. But in two townships to the east of the city, Thokoza and Katlehong, the war was bitter and endless and shockingly bloody. Trains carrying ordinary people to work were raked with gunfire. Hostels were raided and looted of anything portable: pots, pans, gas stoves, the carcasses of just-slaughtered animals. Pieces of hostel building were torn down and carried away: window frames, door frames, the bricks from once-solid walls.[6]

In Thokoza, in a zone between the hostels and the township, rows of houses were cleared, the streets left ominously empty. Every so often, one of the two sides dumped the corpse of a victim into this no-man's-land. It would lie there for days, a grim beacon of the culture of death now abroad.[7]

. .

For Nelson Mandela, the eruption of violence must have come as déjà vu, for it had already happened in his mind. Eighteen months earlier, when news reached him that Stompie Seipei was dead, he thought that Winnie had been framed. The real motive, he told her, was 'to bring the violence currently raging in Natal to the Witwatersrand'.[8] His enemy, he surmised, was using his wife to ignite a war among black people in the heart of urban South Africa.

That his mind had conjured this, in a flash, the moment he heard of Seipei's death, speaks volumes. He was talking in secret to his enemy at this time, and the talks were going well. Ties of trust had grown.

But to enter these talks in good faith, he surely had to put down his rage: at his persecution, at his wife's persecution, at the destruction of his personal world. Now, in response to the most harrowing, the most undigestible news about Winnie, his suspicion and his fury frothed up from his depths.

Eighteen months later, as the violence he had imagined came to pass, a version of his original suspicion returned. He grew very angry with F. W. de Klerk. South Africa's president, he believed, either was allowing his security forces to inflame the conflict or was too afraid to stop them.

His suspicions were not without foundation. Eugene de Kock, the man who had assassinated Johannes Mabotha, confessed later that he supplied machine guns, automatic weapons, grenades and cash to Inkatha on Johannesburg's East Rand.[9] And when local Inkatha leaders were arrested, De Kock's operatives at times doctored forensic evidence, paid the accused's bail and worked with local police to have charges dropped.[10]

Nelson's anger at De Klerk soon curdled into loathing. A famously controlled man, he would, on occasion, set upon De Klerk savagely. 'Even the head of an illegitimate, discredited minority regime, as his is,' Nelson told a stunned audience at the beginning of formal negotiations in December 1991, De Klerk sitting just a few feet away, 'has certain moral standards to uphold ... [V]ery few people would want to deal with such a man.'[11] He was responding, in the heat of the moment, to an accusation De Klerk had just made, but his vitriol had clearly been brewing.

Two years later, he attacked De Klerk viciously again, this time at a dinner in Stockholm following their joint award of the Nobel Peace Prize. The prime minister of Sweden hosted the event; it was attended by about 150 people, including several Nobel laureates. De Klerk spoke first that night, his speech, as befitting the occasion, brief and pro forma. As he was closing, he said something innocuous on the face of it: both sides had made mistakes, he remarked; there was plenty of blame to go around.

When Nelson got up to speak, his face was grey with rage. 'Everyone, including me, was actually shocked by what Mandela said quite unexpectedly,' George Bizos recollected. 'He gave the most horrible detail of what had happened to prisoners on Robben Island, including the burying of a man with his head sticking out and [warders] urinating on him.' He did not so much as mention De Klerk, but his obvious intent was to throw scorn on his Nobel Prize.

'This had a terrible effect on De Klerk,' Bizos recalled. He sent an emissary, his foreign minister, Pik Botha, to tell Bizos that if Nelson ever did anything like that again, he would respond in kind. 'To my knowledge,' Bizos said, 'that was the end of the personal relationship between the two of them.'[12]

. .

The bloodshed that beset Johannesburg was linked, in Nelson's mind, to a vicious assault on his wife. There is a hint of paranoia here, an aroma of persecution.

Here was a man whose vocation was to suppress his bitterness, to offer, always, a reconciliatory face. And yet his grievance with the men who had jailed him was so raw, so deep.

He defended his wife with cruelty, with corruption, with a taste to humiliate others. Here, and perhaps only here, was the wounded, the aggrieved, the blindly furious Nelson Mandela.

. .

Shortly after the violence erupted, Nelson did something dramatic. Secretly, he authorized the purchase of large stocks of AK-47 assault rifles, Makarov pistols and grenades to be distributed to the members of self-defense units across Greater Johannesburg.[13]

The self-defense units had arisen spontaneously at the onset of the violence. While they nominally aligned themselves with the ANC, they were chaotic, disorganized, and ridden with conflict. Nelson was made to understand that the ANC could not just arm them but order them; trained MK soldiers would bring discipline and purpose to their work.

Among those at the heart of the operation was Ronnie Kasrils, a senior figure in MK. He was a fugitive when the violence erupted, the police on his tail, and he began his work with self-defense units while on the run. Years later, he recalled a secret meeting with Nelson and the ANC's treasurer, Thomas Nkobi, who quite literally handed Kasrils bags of cash to buy weapons, while Nelson grimly looked on.[14]

Not long after he began this work, Kasrils received a message that

Winnie Mandela wished to see him. A rendezvous point was arranged outside Baragwanath Hospital on a busy thoroughfare where cars and pedestrians streamed into Soweto. He was among the most wanted people in the country at this time, his photograph plastered across the front pages of the newspapers; he was more than a little nervous. He got into her car and they drove into the Soweto traffic. 'Let us go somewhere we can talk properly,' he later remembered Winnie saying.

To his horror, she took him to the back of her house. 'Jesus! What is she doing?' he thought to himself. 'It was a nervy little meeting, to put it mildly.'

What Winnie wanted was weapons, as many as Kasrils could deliver.

Over the following months, he obliged. 'She is a doer, she is brave, she gets things done,' Kasrils reasoned. He imagined her as the best possible conduit for the arming of self-defense units across Soweto and the West Rand.

It was not long before he discovered the paltriness of her knowledge. 'She had such an amateurish understanding,' he recalled. 'I had to explain to her how these weapons would be used, how protection units function. She knew absolutely nothing. I sent somebody who was above ground and in touch with me who could give the members of the units proper lessons.'

Winnie was a demanding customer. She made contact as often as once a week, each time scaring the life out of Kasrils. When he resolved that it was simply too dangerous to keep meeting her, she began sending Dali Mpofu in her place.

'We hit it off,' Kasrils recalled. 'He was energetic, his spirit was good, he was optimistic. I gave him weapons by the sackful.'

But even after she had handed Kasrils over to Mpofu, Winnie struggled to remain uninvolved. 'I would meet Dali at least once a month,' Kasrils said. 'Winnie says, "Can you do something? We need something tomorrow." But Winnie would already have been in touch with me the night before. "What do you have for us this time? We need more of those hand grenades." She was filled with such excitement, the excitement of arming people, of getting things done.'

Kasrils can no longer precisely date the incident, but he recalls it vividly. He was no longer a fugitive by this time and had arranged to meet Winnie at her Soweto home. It was evening, about nine o'clock. Several women from Kagiso township were with her. They wanted

Kasrils to extend the training he was offering self-defense units in Soweto to them.

'Mandela came home while we were meeting,' Kasrils recalled. 'He is a guy who wears a mask. You don't see what he is thinking. But just fleetingly, I saw him get a jolt, a look of absolute shock. I thought, Jesus, what is going on with him.

'He spoke briefly to us and went to bed.

'It was a seminal moment for me. I really started thinking: things are not right. We knew about Dali. But we thought, now that Nelson is out, maybe they are sorting out their lives. They were husband and wife in the struggle together. Surely he knows that she is distributing weapons? It dawned on me that he did not. He came home and saw Ronnie Kasrils in his living room and thought, Jesus, he is giving weapons to my wife.'

One can only speculate what exactly spooked Nelson in that moment. No doubt, he understood in a flash that flooding an anarchic city with weapons might not be a good idea.

But perhaps he also understood something deeper, something about himself.

He was, in many ways, a blunt and simple man. Zindzi was not educated: he would use his influence to place her in university. Winnie had been put on trial: he would use his muscle to get her off. Defenseless people were being attacked: he would arm them.

He was like a man with a pile of nails hammering together a box.[15]

Perhaps he grasped in that moment just how helpless he was: in rescuing his wife and daughter from what had already befallen them; in saving his people from a horror already wrought.

Chapter 64

On May 13, 1991, Justice Michael Stegmann found Winnie guilty of kidnapping and accessory after the fact to assault. Her alibi, he ruled, was 'reasonably, possibly true'; he was thus not certain that she was present during the beatings and found her not guilty of assault. But he rejected her testimony that she was not involved in the abductions.

'To imagine that all of this took place without Mrs. Mandela as one of the moving spirits is like trying to imagine "Hamlet" without the Prince,' Stegmann wrote.

Her aim in kidnapping the youths, he ruled, was to force them to confess that Verryn had molested them. Her intent was to destroy Verryn.

He proceeded to tear her character apart. 'She showed herself on a number of occasions', he wrote, 'to be a calm, composed, deliberate and unblushing liar.'[1]

When the court adjourned, Nelson made his way from the gallery to the dock, threw his arms around Winnie, and kissed her on the mouth.[2]

'I did not beat up any child,' she told the reporters who had gathered around the couple. Asked for his thoughts, Nelson turned away. 'My wife has made a statement,' he said.[3]

They left the court hand in hand, a simulacrum of the image they had cast fifteen months earlier when Nelson was freed.

There was no phalanx of grandees this time, no Joe Slovo or Chris Hani in tow. The crowd of supporters outside, more than a thousand strong on the day the trial began, had shrunk to just over a hundred.

They made for a disconcerting pair. Winnie, a reporter on the scene wrote, broke into 'a broad smile of triumph, her fist raised'. Nelson, for his part, 'looked as if his mother had died'.[4]

The following morning, Stegmann sentenced Winnie to six years in jail. The harshness was unexpected. Winnie, who had worn a mask of composure throughout the trial, audibly gasped.[5] Expressions of shock came from further afield. Archbishop Desmond Tutu, who later chaired the Truth and Reconciliation Commission, becoming the face of South Africa's brand of healing, expressed horror. Her life has been tragic, he said. She had brought up two children alone in the most gruelling circumstances. She had suffered beyond measure. 'Who are we to say how we would have reacted' to what she had endured? The sentence, he declared, was 'shockingly severe'; he was left feeling deeply sad.[6]

More than a year later, an appeals court replaced the punishment Stegmann had imposed with a noncustodial sentence; Winnie would not go to prison. But nobody knew this at the time.

Nelson was no longer in Johannesburg when the sentence was passed. He was in the university town of Stellenbosch, a thousand miles away, to address a group of students. When news of the sentence broke, a posse of journalists raced from Cape Town to see him. They made the journey with 'a feeling of excitement and dread', one of them wrote. 'It [was] quite possible that they were about to witness the collapse of the negotiation process, if Mr. Mandela decided not to accept Mr. Justice Stegmann's verdict.'

They found Nelson sitting on a sofa 'in a charming Cape Dutch' room, the window behind him framing the mountains beyond the boundary of the town.

'As you know, my wife was sentenced to six years this morning', he read from a prepared statement. 'I have never believed that she was guilty of assaulting anyone. My faith in her has been vindicated. The witnesses who accused her of assault and other terrible crimes have been thoroughly discredited. The judge found her guilty of not reporting assaults committed by others. I believe she did not know about them.' The matter was going on appeal, he continued. 'We trust that soon her name will be cleared completely. The last word on this issue has not yet been spoken.'

He put the statement aside and took questions.

Had he lost confidence in South Africa's judicial system? he was asked.

'It is premature to deal with that point now,' he replied quietly. 'It is proper to leave the matter in the hands of the appeal court.'

How did he feel when he heard news of the sentence?

'Well,' he said, 'in light of the judgment delivered yesterday, the sentence was not unexpected.'

His aides stepped in to hurry him to his next appointment, but he was not quite ready to go. He lingered to banter with the journalists, joshing, grinning, as if he were among old friends. He had promised to do an interview with the national broadcaster in Afrikaans, he said, and he was nervous. *'My kennis van Afrikaans is swak.'* My knowledge of Afrikaans is weak.

He was airing one of his more familiar personae: bluff, self-mocking, a little surprised at being so famous. It sat forever on his dressing table alongside several others, always ready to wear.

As he was leaving, he stopped abruptly; he had one more thing to say. Negotiations between the ANC and the government would go on, he said, the expression on his face now dead serious. What was happening with his wife was another matter. Then he turned and left.[7]

. .

Did he know from the start that he would draw back from the brink? When he bullied his organization into giving his wife senior positions, when he cracked heads to fund her trial, when co-accused and witnesses began to disappear – did he know that he would stop?

One imagines that there were times when he did not, times when he envisaged the world in flames as he sheltered his wife.

Chapter 65

In the wake of her trial, Nelson Mandela banished his wife from her place in his heart. It is impossible to say how it happened: whether via a slow churning or a sudden epiphany; whether in a decisive moment or after a period of lingering doubt. We have only a series of outward signs.

Shortly after the trial, when Trevor Manuel was in Johannesburg for a meeting of the ANC's national executive, Nelson insisted that he cancel his hotel accommodation and spend the night. They arrived at the house in the evening; Winnie was not there.

'You know,' Manuel recalled Nelson saying to him, apropos of nothing, 'Mum does not behave like a wife.'

Nelson then told Manuel a story that made him feel enormously uncomfortable.

'And as for that young boy ...,' Nelson went on.[1]

Mac Maharaj had a similar experience. Winnie was caught up in drinking, in drugs, Nelson told him one day from out of the blue; she was having sexual relationships with others, not just with Dali, but with several others.

'He told me in a confiding tone,' Maharaj recalled, 'as if he were telling me alone.'

Only in hindsight did it dawn on Maharaj that Nelson was relating the same story, probably in the same words, to a selection of senior ANC figures.[2]

If these orchestrated conversations suggest a coolness on Nelson's part, they are deeply misleading. Those to whom he showed his heart – so often women, it seems – witnessed his pain and confusion.

'He would phone in the middle of the night in a terrible state,' a confidante of Nelson's, a woman Winnie's age, told this author. '"I need somebody to talk to," he would say. "Nomzamo cannot do this to me."'

The confidante looked back on that time with regret. 'There was so much talk about Madiba and Winnie,' she reflected. 'We would talk of them as leaders, as powerful people. But in fact they were not coping; neither of them was. We should have thought of them less as leaders than as people in need of professional help.'[3]

The separation came abruptly. One night in mid-November 1991, members of Nelson's staff received an urgent call from their boss. He had to leave his home at once, he said; he could not wait until morning. Arrangements were hastily made. An hour later, he was gone.

It appears, from the testimony of one who was on the Mandela property that night, that, in a drunken state, Winnie had done something to shock and upset Nelson.[4]

That this led him to flee, rather than to seek help for his wife, speaks a great deal. His heart had of course hardened over the preceding months; this was a catalyst for his departure, not a cause. But what he fled, in the heat of the moment, was a loss of control. In prison, he had come to prize, above all, an ironclad discipline over self.

One wonders whether what he witnessed that night invoked all the times he himself had lost control, as when he allowed for young men to be whisked to strange lands to alter the outcome of a trial.

· ·

After Nelson left, a long interregnum followed. He stayed for several months on the estate of a prominent Afrikaans businessman in the northern suburbs of Johannesburg before acquiring a home of his own in the plush suburb of Houghton. Winnie lived in the Soweto house. Officially, the separation was a secret, although increasingly poorly kept. The state of suspension lingered until the end of March 1992, when something happened to bring things to a head.

For the duration of Winnie's trial, the Mandelas had seen to the legal fees of her co-accused. More than that, Xoliswa Falati and her daughter lived in a room in the Mandelas' yard. Their lawyer's bills were paid, their stomachs filled, their lodging free; the Mandelas had done what they could to score the tune Falati sang.

Now, during the long passage between their conviction and their appeal, a dispute erupted between Falati and Winnie, apparently over whether the Mandelas would continue to pay Falati's legal fees. On an evening in late March, Winnie walked into Falati's room waving a pis-

tol. She took fistfuls of her tenant's clothes, threw them into the yard
and ordered her to leave.

Barefoot, clad just in her nightgown, Falati fled.

Once she had reached a place of safety, she called two people: a
journalist at the *Sowetan,* Ruth Bhengu, and Nelson Mandela. Bhengu
and Nelson arrived on the scene at about the same time, Bhengu to
write a story, Nelson to arrange for a locksmith to let Falati into her
room. Nelson asked Bhengu that she not write about what she had
seen. He began by pleading that the story would sink Winnie's appeal;
when that seemed not to convince Bhengu, he appeared to imply that
he might find her a job in the state-run media when the ANC came to
power.

By the time she returned to the *Sowetan*'s offices, Nelson had spoken to her editor. As nettled by Nelson's bullying as his reporter had
been earlier, he let the story run.[5]

Its publication set off an extraordinary chain reaction. International media tracked down Falati, from whom breathless stories spilled.
John Morgan, Winnie's driver, told a newspaper that he had lied on the
witness stand; Winnie, he now claimed, had been at home when the
youngsters from the manse were brought to her property and had led
the subsequent assault. He promptly scurried into hiding, fearing for
his life.

From his place in exile, Katiza Cebekhulu told a reporter that he
had been involved in the killing of Abu Baker Asvat on Winnie's orders.
And just days after Bhengu's *Sowetan* story, *The Christian Science Monitor*
published the findings of a painstaking investigation: one of the men
convicted of Asvat's murder had written an affidavit on the eve of the
trial saying that Winnie had contracted his accomplice to carry out the
killing.[6]

In the second week of April, Nelson's dear friend and soul mate,
Walter Sisulu, went to see him, at the request, it appears, of senior figures in the party.

There were no bugs hidden in the furniture this time, no unwelcome ears; it is likely that both men took the discussion to their graves.

The events of the past two years might well have put a strain on
their friendship. Abu Baker Asvat had been a son to Sisulu's wife,
Albertina; the bluntness of Nelson's campaign to defend Winnie would
have pained the Sisulus deeply.

Sitting with Nelson in prison in the autumn of 1965, Sisulu had talked his friend out of divorcing his wife. Now, twenty-seven years later, he nudged him the other way.

On April 13, at ANC headquarters in Johannesburg, an austere Nelson Mandela, Sisulu at his left flank, Oliver Tambo at his right, announced his separation from his wife.

He read stiffly, his spectacles perched halfway down his nose.

'Comrade Nomzamo and myself contracted our marriage at a critical time in the struggle for the liberation of our country,' he read. 'Owing to the pressures of our shared commitment to the ANC and to the struggle against apartheid, we were unable to enjoy a normal family life.'

He praised her courage, her singular contribution to the struggle; he spoke of her persecution, of the burden of raising children on her own.

'Her tenacity reinforced my personal respect, love and growing affection,' he continued. 'It also attracted the admiration of the world at large. My love for her remains undiminished.'[7]

He took off his glasses, tucked them into his jacket pocket, and stood. 'Ladies and gentlemen,' he said. 'I hope you'll appreciate the pain I have gone through and I now end this interview.'

The trio of old men filed out in silence. Nobody in that crowded room uttered a word.[8]

. .

A few days later, the most extraordinary scene took place in Nelson's office. Fatima Meer – friend to both Mandelas since the 1950s, Nelson's biographer, Winnie's great defender – requested an audience with Nelson. For moral support, she took with her a trusted old friend.

'When she approached me,' the friend recalled, 'she said, "Winnie does not believe that he will divorce her. Let's go to Madiba and apologize on Winnie's behalf. Let's beg him not to leave her."

'Does Winnie really not believe it?' the friend recalled asking. 'He has announced it. It is done.'

'I think that we can still stop him,' she remembered Meer replying.

When they were ushered into Nelson's office, he rose from behind his desk and came out to greet them.

'Fatima did not warn me what she was going to do,' her friend recalled. 'In front of Madiba, she dropped first to her knees, then lay flat on her belly, quite literally sprawling on the floor at his feet. She began speaking in a loud, clear voice: "I am pleading for forgiveness for Winnie."

'That man went down like lightning to pick Fatima off the ground. "You cannot do that to me!" he yelled. "Fatima, you cannot do that!"'[9]

All these years later, the friend confessed, the memory still left her feeling hollow inside. One thinks of the weaver's nest in Winnie's garden. What a terrible irony that she, of all women, felt so beholden to her marriage to a man.

.   .

Two days after Nelson's announcement, Winnie held a press conference of her own. She was resigning as the head of the ANC's Welfare Department, she said. She raged against her enemies, but her heart was not in it. She looked shell-shocked, bewildered.[10]

In the days that followed, the buffers around her appeared to fall. In the past, when journalists had visited the town of Parys in the Free State to talk to Stompie Seipei's mother, Joyce Seipei, local ANC activists had answered questions on her behalf. As she sat in silence, they had peddled the astonishing fiction that Stompie was still alive. Now the henchmen had vanished and she was free to talk. 'At last,' she said, 'it seems that the truth about my son is emerging.'[11]

On the same day, a journalist interviewed the woman who had given Winnie an alibi, vouching that she had been in Brandfort when the youngsters were kidnapped from the manse. Now she said that she could not remember the precise date Winnie was there.[12]

Most human beings would no doubt have surrendered now. Heavily wounded, Winnie Mandela picked herself up and went out to fight.

On April 20, exactly a week after Nelson had announced the separation, she toured the most violence-torn areas in Johannesburg. Astonishingly, she spoke on behalf of the ANC, saying that if the violence continued, her organization would pull out of talks with the government.[13]

Wherever there was bloodshed over the following week, she was there. Two hours after a shoot-out between a group of Sowetans and police, she arrived on the scene. 'We will do everything in our power to save ourselves,' she declared, holding up a bag of spent shells she had picked up off the ground. 'All these', she continued, 'were to kill you in your sleep.'

The next day she was in Sharpeville, where eight ANC members had been shot dead. The day after, she spoke on a platform in the heart of ongoing violence in the Natal Midlands, where she launched a scathing attack on F. W. de Klerk and Mangosuthu Buthelezi.[14]

A month later, several dozen women staged a sit-in at the ANC's headquarters in downtown Johannesburg, bringing its operations to a halt. They were there to demand that Winnie be reinstated as the head of the ANC's Welfare Department. All were residents of a shack settlement at the heart of the war on the East Rand; they had been bussed into town, it emerged, by the executive of the ANC Women's League region Winnie controlled.[15]

. .

In early September, somebody in the senior ranks of the ANC detonated a bomb under Winnie Mandela.

A letter was sent anonymously to a journalist.[16] Dated March 17, 1992, and written in Winnie's hand, it had been found in Dali Mpofu's desk drawer at ANC headquarters in April after he and Winnie cleared out.

> Dali, I suggest you read the contents of the two letters I referred to last night at 12:30 a.m. and remind yourself that I am not another Terreza you used when it suited you and dumped when it suited you. I will never be used by you for *ukufeba kwakho* [your sleeping around] and you use our things we acquired together for running around fucking at the slightest emotional excuse . . .
>
> Thinking back, I am horrified at your dishonesty, dali, you were prepared to go along with Terreza's *City Press* report to the effect that you separated with her because of me when it is quite clear that she had given you up in February of 1991 when she found you sleeping with Nonxolisi that Saturday morning. Do you remember how in love we were then? You were able to come to me my love with a straight face as if nothing had happened & in fact on most occasions I was responsible for your quarrels with Terreza, even when she telephoned Pumla to tell her all that rubbish about how you didn't marry her because of me . . .
>
> *Ndoze ndibe sisibanxwa sakho mina* dali [I won't be your bloody

fool, Dali], before I'm through with you you are going to learn
a bit of honesty and sincerely know what betrayal of one's
trust means to a woman!

You lie to me and suggest that in order to preserve our
relationship you have to have a relationship as a cover to
defuse our problem? I understand and know how difficult it
was for me to accept that reality but it eventually dawned on
me that because I love you so much I had to agree with you
even though I was shattered at the thought of you lying and
pretending to love this other woman and as you said 'you were
just involved with Imogen' and you never said you loved her.

Your shabby treatment of me last night has compelled me
once more to show you I can do exactly the same dali, I beg
nothing from you and you are not going to make me another
Terreza . . .

You think you can wish away certain things dali, not with
me. I tell you I am in trouble with the Simmonds Street a/c
[ANC Welfare Department bank account] which reflects over
R160,000 drawn over a period for you you don't even bother
to check how we can overcome this. I tell you Ayob has been
sent by tata [Nelson] to get an accountant to investigate my
a/c! I tell you Ntombi is gossiping about the cheques we used
to ask her to cash for us in the name of the Dept & how I gave
you all that money & you and I are now being investigated.
Instead you chose not to talk to Ntombi's sister because she is
talking about the friend of the woman you were sleeping with
on the 21st floor.

The only time you have time to talk to me is about women
ofeba nabo [you are sleeping with] as you are doing right now.
You are supposed to care so much for me that the fact that I
haven't been speaking to tata for five months now over you is
not your concern. I keep telling you the situation is deteriorat-
ing at home, you are not bothered because you are satisfying
yourself every night with a woman you are 'involved' with and
you are not in love with her.

How long do you think I will buy this? I've written this
letter because clearly it has become impossible for us to have
any healthy discussion in the current atmosphere. There are
certain things I am finding difficult to resist doing for you to

remember always how much you have hurt and humiliated me
as a woman . . .

I am going to university for the tut[orial] I was preparing
and I'll go and deliver the copy of those letters. I have discovered what you got used to from your white hag since we seem
unable to communicate.

It's me.[17]

· ·

We all go through so many states each day. Had Winnie written to
Dali a few hours later, something different might well have spilled from
her pen. A biographer ought to be wary of the idea that any document
reveals his subject's essence.

But, in its rawness, this letter exudes something transcendent. It is
not just the content; it is the very form. The collision of thoughts and
feelings, bashing each other around the page; the interruption of one
thought by another in the course of a single sentence. It takes a form
like this to give expression to what Winnie was feeling.

When the letter begins, its author is a jilted lover. But many other
anxieties soon crowd in. An investigation into embezzlement is under
way; Winnie and Nelson's relationship has broken down; and then
there is the recurring figure of Teresa Oakley-Smith: 'Terreza', the
very mangling of her name a proxy for the violence Winnie feels.

This frenzy, barely manageable, liable at any minute to break its
seams, followed Winnie Mandela through the decades.

It is most obvious in the cauldron of the late 1980s: the blind hatred
of Paul Verryn; the clinging to Johannes Mabotha; the force of feeling
that caused her to torture Nicodemus Sono, torture him by making
him watch helplessly as his battered son was driven away.

But it goes further back than that. Setting men with crowbars on
M.K. Malefane, another lover who has jilted her. And years before that,
the gunfight at her home between Brian Somana and Peter Magubane.
And, before that, Winnie's refusal to chase Somana from her bed,
much to the horror of her comrades, after it was revealed that he was
a spy.

And, before that, the drama of Winnie's dual courtship of Nelson
Mandela and Barney Sampson, Nelson rushing Winnie to Barney's

hospital bed when he attempted to take his life. And the pitching of Nelson against her father, Columbus thundering at her wedding that his daughter was a witch.

That letter to Dali was written at a moment in time, but one senses so strongly in it the relentlessness, the turmoil, of being Winnie Mandela.

When she returned to Soweto from Brandfort, she had long borne a state of insurrection in her soul. What followed was uncanny; for the first time in her fifty years, the violence of the world without mirrored the violence of the world within. The household she formed by the power of her charisma, a household only conceivable in insurgent times, was made by her, an expression of her, its instability, its ceaseless need to act, long familiar to her.

.   .

Three days before the letter was splashed across the weekend papers, Barbara Masekela was informed of its existence. She phoned Nelson in the evening, told him she had something to tell him in person, and got into her car.

'Do you have the letter?' he asked, once she had explained why she had come.

'I do.'

'Read it to me,' he said.

'I can't.'

'I insist,' she recalled him saying. 'Read it to me.'

She read it from start to finish, then looked up and studied his face. He was impassive, inscrutable; it struck her for the hundredth time, his capacity to hide what he felt.[18]

.   .

After Barbara Masekela left his house that evening, Nelson called his old friend and foot soldier George Bizos. Would he please go to Winnie, Nelson requested, and ask whether the letter was hers?

Bizos paid Winnie a call at Zindzi's house in Johannesburg's eastern suburbs. They sat down together at the kitchen table; he said nothing, simply passed her the letter in silence.

She glanced at it, burst into tears, and said that she had been betrayed.[19]

Four days after the letter was published, Winnie resigned from all of her positions in the ANC. She was gutted, this most eloquent of public speakers rendered barely coherent. 'Battle lines are easy where battle lines are clearly drawn,' she said. 'Yet it is my belief that this is not the time to expend our energies on deciphering battle lines and becoming deliberately confused in a struggle for self-preservation.'[20]

A friend of hers from that time — who wishes to remain unnamed and who witnessed the state she was in — recalls her heaped up in a ball, weeping, bereft, her skin grey, her state of shock in her wide eyes. The sight sent a chill down her friend's spine. It was not just the sheer intensity of her grief and her suffering. It was that the spectacle offended against nature. A woman so big, so grand; to see her punctured was violent; it left a nauseating feeling.

She must have thought she was extinguished, that she was watching the world from a state of nonbeing.

She was not close to extinguished. She had, in fact, yet to reach her zenith.

ENDS

. . .

Nelson Mandela had been free for two months and two days. I am no longer sure how many of us were in the hall – a thousand, two thousand – we were packed in like pickled fish.

The first sign of his coming was the clatter of the blades; his presence directly above brought proceedings to a halt; our whistling and our hooting chased the speaker off the stage. Nothing ordinary could carry on now that he was near.

And then he was before us, in the flesh, on the stage. As had happened in the Soweto stadium two months earlier, a brittle magic seized the hall. He moved within the currents of the electricity we made, blisteringly charged. And yet also so eerily serene, that beaming, beatific face hardly of this world.

Knowing now what was happening in his life, and, to a small degree, in his heart, I understand that the serenity was a mirage. It did not emanate from him at all, but from the space between us, a space of fantasy and longing. He was, I know now, torn up inside, full of sorrow and a kind of desperation.

We were in the Bantustan of KaNgwane at the final national conference of the South African Youth Congress, an organization with more than a million members born during the insurrection. If the children of the uprisings ever gathered in one place at one time, it was here and now. Delegates had come from the killing fields of Natal, from the barricades of Soweto and the East Rand, from dozens of provincial towns that had caught fire. How many in that hall would die in the violence to come is unknowable now. The children making revolution in Mandela's name hushed to hear him speak.

As he sat on the stage, waiting to give his keynote address, his eye roamed the hall. He was studying us intently, looking for what I did not know. We found out at the close of his speech.

He spoke as he always did, reading monotonously from a pile of papers. We listened politely. Some fifteen minutes in, his prepared speech completed, he put his pages aside and began speaking off the cuff. Scanning the hall, he told us, he saw, in the sea of black faces, several whites. Now, he said, he wanted these white people to come onto the stage to shake his hand.

I do not recall his exact words, and they appear not to have been recorded, but the sense of what he said was this: Everyone in this hall has sacrificed, but the black people among us fought in support of our communities. The whites did something different: they turned against their kind. Excommunication, he said, is a bitter fate. These five people deserve our thanks.

Sheepishly, we picked a path through the bodies and filed onto the stage.

So many people who met Mandela in those early years reported a feeling of transcendence. They sensed the presence of an elevated being, of one who had suffered and forgiven. I did not share in that experience. He looked right through me when he shook my hand, so clearly just going through the motions. Had we met again the following day, I was certain he'd have no idea who I was.

It isn't hard to fathom why he chose to do what he did. Your enemy, he was telling his audience, is not a white nation but a political system. He feared more than anything a racial war. Gathered here were the frontline warriors. He wished to place thoughts in their heads and feelings in their hearts.

I was there as an invited observer from a fraternal organization, the National Union of South African Students, whose membership had been exclusively white since Steve Biko walked out twenty-two years earlier. My comrades and I had hardly been excommunicated from our communities. Our positions in student politics were credentials, not stains, and the friends we made in the struggle positioned us supremely well in our careers. A number soon made a lot of money, or exercised a lot of influence, or both.

Many of the delegates in the hall, whom Nelson instructed to applaud us, had seen death in the recent past and would see more soon. We shared the same hall for three days before departing for our separate futures.

·   ·

A long time passed before gestures like the one Nelson made that day began to offend. For the following two decades he basked in saintly glory.

What happened to South Africa during that time was an act of grace. An ocean apart, something extraordinary was under way. The industrialization of China, unprecedented in speed and scale, brought a commodity boom that lasted for more than a decade. Although few South Africans would see it this way, it delivered a gift of plenty. When the country conducted a census in 2011, it found that life had improved for everybody. The income of the poorest fifth had increased by more than 30 percent in the last decade. The ANC government had built three million houses and given them away to the poor. It had grown the welfare system dramatically and now made monthly cash payments to a quarter of the population. Although the country was at the centre of an AIDS pandemic, two million people were on antiretroviral treatment. And through all of this, the national debt shrank.

The wounds of a wretched past had hardly healed. South Africa remained among the most violent countries in the world, its unemployment staggeringly high; even at the height of the commodities boom, it dropped only to 22 percent. And although things improved for everyone, the country grew ever more unequal.

But a great transition is a beguiling time, and much is not as it seems. Even the meaning of growing inequality is slippery. Prosperity was sufficiently widespread for everyone to see someone they knew get ahead. A black person who moves from a segregated township to a suburb, buys a fancy car, puts their children in a good school: the spectacle tells a story of overwhelming power. Those left behind cannot but help go along on the journey, in their heads, imagining that they will be next.

Everything new was a sign of revolution, even growing concentrations of wealth.

. .

Throughout this time, Nelson's persona grew increasingly benign, his presence in public life ever more ethereal. Even his five years as president of South Africa, from 1994 to 1999, were largely ceremonial. He handed the running of the country to his deputy, Thabo Mbeki.

His own job, as he saw it, was to see off the two greatest threats to his country's new order.

The first of these dangers was the curdling of white fear into counter-revolution. He had tea with the widow of apartheid's most infamous leader, Hendrik Verwoerd, in the separatist white enclave where she was seeing out her days. She was a tiny woman, no taller than Nelson's shoulder. The images of him beaming down at her, radiant, his face crinkled with laughter, are priceless. They are the work of a master of spectacle.

Famously, he donned the Springboks rugby jersey, the captain's number 6 on his back, and threw his fists in the air. Alongside him, the strapping white lad who had led the team to victory lifted the Rugby World Cup.

He beguiled white South Africans into the new order, throwing at them all the munificence it was in his power to perform.

The second great threat to democracy, in Nelson's eyes, was majoritarian excess. He dealt with this, too, via spectacle: that of a humble man exercising power. In his inaugural address as South Africa's leader, he spoke of the end of his presidency five years hence. On this of all days, a day of utter exuberance, he drew attention to the limits of his own authority: it was rule-bound, he said; and it was borrowed for the shortest time.

Here was an elderly man – almost seventy-six when he assumed office – aware that his heyday was behind him. His fantastic fame appeared to leave him sober; it was a pallid substitute, he understood, for the personal happiness beyond his grasp. What was left to him was his innate talent to perform. That he chose to play an ebullient man who exercised power with modesty speaks of wisdom. That this character had little to do with the actor who played him speaks of great discipline and vocational pride.

· · ·

While Nelson was president, Winnie appeared to fade.

When the ANC's general membership chose two hundred parliamentary candidates to stand for election in 1994, she came thirty-first, a name lost in a crowd.[1] The stain of the football team, of the kidnappings from the manse, of Stompie Seipei, had not destroyed her, but it had robbed her of her claim to lead.

Upon becoming president, Nelson appointed Winnie deputy minister of arts, culture, science, and technology, among the most junior positions in his executive. It was at once a signal of recognition and a slight. Within a year he had fired her for going abroad on business without authorization. The day after her dismissal, a broad front of the ANC's allies – trade unions, civic associations, the Communist Party – hosted a press conference endorsing his decision.[2]

Two years later, amid its wrenching public inquiries into the crimes of the past, the TRC convened a special hearing to receive testimony on the Mandela United Football Club. Winnie herself had demanded it. Her name had by now issued from the mouths of so many who had testified; in place of this endless innuendo, she said, she wanted a formal hearing to clear her name.

Her move appeared to backfire. One witness after another testified to the terrible deeds committed in her home, their tales gruesome and unrelenting; she sat listening stone-faced in the gallery, the remnants of her team at her flanks looking awfully menacing.

'I have never been this depressed at a Truth Commission hearing,' Antjie Krog wrote in her celebrated chronicle of the TRC. 'It's like reporting on a third-rate movie – this miasma of scandal, arrogance, ambition, lies, and unbridled gangsterism.'[3]

It seemed that Winnie had been handed an unenviable place in history: she would stand as a monument to the revolution's underbelly, a reminder of lives lost for nothing.

But Krog said something else in her chronicle, and a quarter of a century later it reads as prescient and fresh.

'I . . . have a distinct feeling', she wrote, 'that . . . this hearing has nothing to do with me, with whites. Blacks are deciding among themselves what they regard as right and wrong. They are making that decision here, today. Either a black person may kill because of apartheid – or none of us may kill, no matter the reason. This hearing has little to do with the past. It has everything to do with the future.'[4]

What she detected was subterranean back then, its rumbling audible only to the sharpest ear.

. .

When did Nelson's reputation begin to turn among young black South Africans?

In 2017, the South African–born economist Ian Goldin, who had worked with Nelson in the 1990s, returned to his native country to promote a book. Alongside a host of other interviews, he appeared on breakfast television. Whenever he mentioned Nelson Mandela, his interviewer, a young black man named Katlego Maboe, changed the subject. Once the interview was over and the camera had stopped rolling, Goldin asked Maboe why he would not discuss Mandela. Because young people feel he sold them out, he remembered Maboe replying.[5]

By the time it was relayed to Goldin, the news that something was wrong with Nelson was de rigueur among young, educated black South Africans. It is hard to pin down precisely when the murmuring began; when Nelson died in 2013, it was growing pretty loud.

Democracy was nineteen years old by then. The tide of epochal change – so churning, so beguiling, so prone to whip up fever – had receded. What remained on the shore looked horribly familiar. The form of the cities chiselled into the world over the course of the twentieth century – plush business districts and well-appointed suburbs, still overwhelmingly white; ringing them out of sight, forlorn acres of houses and shacks, still overwhelmingly black. That the basic shape of the past remained, so resolutely baked into the world, spoke dimly of what had happened in the time after Nelson's release.

In the same year Goldin's interviewer gently steered him from Nelson's memory, a young poet, Koleka Putuma, wrote a poem, '1994: A Love Poem', that coursed through social media for years:

> I want someone who is going to look at me
> and love me
> the way that white people look at
> and love
> Mandela.
> Someone who is going to hold onto my memory
> the way that white people hold onto Mandela's legacy.
> A lover who will build Robben Island in my backyard
> and convince me that I have a garden
> and fresh air, a rainbow and freedom.
>
> A TRC kind of lover.

You don't know love
until you have been loved like Mandela.
You don't know betrayal
until you have been loved like Mandela.
You don't know fuckery
until you have been loved like Mandela.
You don't know msunery
until you have been loved like Mandela.

And this is one of the many residues of slavery:
being loved like Mandela.[6]

The poem says nothing about Nelson's intentions. Its anger is trained upon the white people for whom he is a talisman. And what a powerful talisman: a small minority had dictated the terms of a momentous transition, leaving their privilege unscathed, the rest of the country betrayed.

The idea that Nelson was duped – too old to have his faculties about him, captured for too long to retain clarity of thought – began to swirl about his native land. And the notion that the root of his confusion lay in his separation from Winnie – that, too, began to take hold.

'When Nelson Mandela returned from prison,' Julius Malema, president of the Economic Freedom Fighters (EFF), a populist break-away from the ANC, told an audience at the Oxford Union in 2016, 'he got separated from Winnie Mandela, and went to stay in the house of a rich, white man ... They had access to him twenty-four hours. And they told him that what he represents will not be achieved. That's when he turned against himself. Because the Nelson we are celebrating now is not the Nelson we celebrated before prison and during prison. It is a stage-managed Nelson Mandela who compromised the fundamental principles of the revolution ...

'We do not say that Nelson sold out. That is too harsh. He was too old. He was tired.'[7]

One should not exaggerate what was happening. When he spoke those words, Malema's EFF had garnered the votes of 1.1 million people compared with 11.4 million for the ANC. The country's leaders still invoked Nelson's name as a matter of course. A great love for him remained in much of the black population, especially among the middle-aged.

But a churning had begun. The standard story of what had happened when apartheid ended was under scrutiny. Most profoundly, when young black people looked for a usable past, they increasingly turned their gaze from Nelson, searching for figures who had been suppressed, figures like Steve Biko, Robert Sobukwe, and, indeed, Winnie Madikizela-Mandela.

.   .

Winnie, too, was old by now, and repeatedly battered, to be sure. But she was by no means tired. She sensed the growing doubts about Nelson, and her actions suggest that she grasped very early what this might mean for her.

If she and Nelson shared anything, it was their talent to tell their stories as myth: an intuitive talent, lightning fast, faster than conscious thought. The myth Winnie now began to make from both of their lives, hers and his, was her most powerful creation yet.

'They wonder', she wrote, shortly before Nelson's death, in an afterword to her prison diary, 'why I am like I am ... [T]hey have a nerve to say, "Oh, Madiba is such a peaceful person, you know. We wonder how he had a wife who is so violent?"

'The leadership on Robben Island was never touched; the leadership on Robben Island had no idea what it was like to engage the enemy physically. The leadership was removed and cushioned behind prison walls ...

'They did not know what we were talking about and when we were reported to be so violent, engaged in the physical struggle, fighting the Boers underground, they did not understand that because none of them had ever been subjected to that, not even Madiba himself. They never touched him, they would not have dared.'[8]

She does not say it as starkly as this; it is just below the surface: what her husband was locked away from all those years was the experience of being black; so thoroughly and, indeed, for so long that it had become puzzling to him. 'They did not know what we were talking about,' she wrote, when she tried to explain what she was going through.

Hers, in contrast, was a distillation of black experience, the pure essence of it. 'We were part of an experiment,' she wrote of her detention in 1969. 'They were using me as a barometer ... [to] measure the

heat of the country.'9 She had become the very index of what black
people could take.

Again, she does not say it out loud, but it is the more effective for its
silence. What the powerful had done those twenty-seven years was create a dummy adversary; it *looked* like the representative of black South
Africa, but it had long become something else.

In this story, what happened in Soweto in the late 1980s – Stompie
Seipei and the young men taken from the manse; the disappearance of
Lolo Sono, Siboniso Tshabalala – is cast in a very different light. It is
evidence that she was framed, that a scandal was conjured to destroy
her, for she was too radical, too resolute, to be allowed to succeed.

In the mid-1990s, a former security policeman called Paul Erasmus
received a message that Winnie wished to see him. Some of what he
had been saying of late had come to interest her intensely.

Erasmus had suffered a breakdown during apartheid's final years.
In pain and in search of absolution for what he and his colleagues had
done, he broke ranks and began to speak. He spent much of the transition to democracy in a witness protection programme, testifying to a
commission of inquiry to gunrunning, sabotage, and torture.

What interested Winnie was his position in a structure called
Stratcom, short for Strategic Communications, a propaganda arm of
the State Security Council tasked, among other things, with spreading
misinformation about the anti-apartheid movement. Winnie tried to
get Erasmus to testify in her divorce hearing against Nelson.10 She did
get him to give evidence at her TRC hearing. It is not hard to understand why his words had garnered her interest.

Stratcom, Erasmus told the world, was mandated by its masters to
neutralize the radical wing of the ANC by spreading disinformation
about its leaders. 'Number one, of course, was Winnie,' he said. 'I set
out to destroy her and pretty much almost did.'11 He told of placing stories in the international press about her relationship with Dali Mpofu;
of her drinking and her drug taking; and, of course, about the kidnapping and murder of Stompie Seipei.

The tale he told was simplistic and misleading: compliant ANC
leaders are left alone, their reputations unsullied; the real radicals
brought down in a hail of scandal and lies. As the TRC's officers pointed
out to Erasmus when he took the stand, two of its own commissioners
were victims of Stratcom's propaganda, including Desmond Tutu, its
chair.

But, for Winnie, Stratcom was a usable story, and as she told it, its reach and its power grew. The members of her football team who informed for the police were its agents. The murders they committed were intended to destroy her reputation. And the killing of Stompie Seipei: that, too, was Stratcom.

'Stompie was killed by [the state's] own men,' Winnie said in an interview in 1999. 'The system planted this Jerry Richardson. [Stompie] was killed by their agents so that I should be blamed for his death.'[12]

And those who broadcast the news of her football team's misdeeds – they, too, did Stratcom's bidding, whether they knew it or not. Thus, the journalists at the left-wing *Weekly Mail* who broke the story of the kidnappings from the manse – they, she said in an interview toward the end of her life, were doing the work of Stratcom. And the UDF leaders who distanced their organization from her – that was Stratcom's work.

She was brought down low because she would never compromise, would never forgo revolution. For South Africa's fake transition to proceed, she had to be made a witch.

Whether this sounds like paranoia, or whether, instead, it has the feel of a long-suppressed truth, depends on where you stand. By the time Nelson died, the alienation of the young from the order his name branded was profound. The idea that the transition had been stitched up, those who resisted it silenced or killed, was hardly incredible. That a fearless, uncompromising woman turned out to be a killer of children was a suspect tale that smacked of untruth.

In the story Winnie told near the end of her life – a story now acquiring escalating power – her own performance at the TRC became a potent symbol. She sat there in the witness box, defiant, implacable. Each allegation she simply dismissed as 'preposterous', 'nonsense', 'rubbish'. Having demanded the hearing, she washed her hands of the entire business.

What she was dismissing, an astute commentator has observed, were the foundations of her country's new order. 'She was attuned to the ways in which the TRC was already being seen by radicals as a mode of whitewashing, a process that required confession and forgiveness of black people but little in the way of accountability for white people,' the South African scholar Shireen Hassim has written. 'By refusing to tell her story in the scripted form ... she stands as the sentinel for the radicals who see the transition to democracy as a defeat for the revolution, not its victory.'[13]

. .

Winnie Madikizela-Mandela was a person who lived to be seen. There is thus some irony in the fact that her most powerful performance was posthumous, the stage assembled by her death.

She died after a long illness on April 2, 2018, at the age of eighty-one. At her funeral – held at Orlando Stadium, less than two miles from the house she and Nelson once shared – the battle lines of a bitter dispute were drawn in the contrasting colours in the stands. Half the stadium paraded the black, green and gold of the ANC, the organization to which she had belonged her entire adult life; the other half, the bright red of the populist breakaway, the EFF, which claimed her as its inspiration.

Winnie's daughters, Zindzi and Zenani, pinned their own colours to the mast; controversially, they invited the EFF's leader, Julius Malema, to give a keynote speech.

Before the thousands who had come to mourn her, Malema addressed Winnie herself.

'Mama,' he said, 'some of those who sold you out to the regime are here. What is funny, Mama, is that they are crying the loudest, more than all of us who loved you.

'Mama, the UDF cabal is here. The cabal that rejected you, that disowned you, and sent you to the brutal apartheid regime, is here.

'When they called a press conference during the dark days of apartheid, when the regime was prepared to kill, and said in that press conference, you are not part of them, they are here today.'

He switched addressees and began talking to the ones who had turned on her.

'We see you in your beautiful suits: betrayers, sellouts. We see you.'

Then he spoke to Winnie again, beseeching her to answer a question.

'Mama, you never told us how we must treat them when they come here. I am waiting for a signal, Mama.'[14]

Murphy Morobe, the leader who had read out the UDF's statement that day in February 1989 condemning Winnie's actions, was not in the stadium when Malema uttered these words.

'I would usually attend a funeral like that,' he recalled. 'A sixth sense told me that it would be an unpleasant experience.'[15]

Not long after the funeral, in the spring of 2018, a feature-length documentary on Winnie's life was broadcast on national television. Made by the French filmmaker Pascale Lamche, it told Winnie's version of what had happened in the late 1980s and early 1990s in its bluntest and most conspiratorial form. For many young South Africans, it was the most authoritative version of their country's transition to democracy that they had seen.

A national storm erupted in its wake. On social media, terrible accusations were made against Nelson, against the ANC and the UDF, against Desmond Tutu.

The storm subsided after a time, but while it lasted, Winnie's power was greater than any she had exercised in life. Facts long nailed down had come unstuck. Basic truths about what had occurred in the recent past were thrown into doubt.

She had broken the back of her former husband's story, and it is doubtful that it will ever be mended.

. .

Between life as myth and life as day-to-day practice there is always, of course, a gap, and what happens in that gap is sometimes astounding.

Winnie summoned Paul Erasmus because she had use for the story he told. But once they met face-to-face something more interesting than simple utility began to grow.

When he met Winnie, Erasmus was in hiding from his former colleagues and in great fear, his attempts at contrition endangering his life.

'I got a call from a journalist to say that Winnie wished to see me,' he recalled. 'He took me to her lawyer's office in Pretoria. I was terrified. I thought she would devour me.'

Full of shame and remorse, he stood before her and began to speak.

He went on for two hours without pause, telling of his attempts to smear her name, of raking her house with gunfire late at night, and of other things too, like torturing a woman to within an inch of her life, of making her speak, finally, by pointing a gun at her son's head.

'I did not take my eyes off her for all the time I was speaking,' he recalled. 'Some way into my story, I noticed that her eyes had grown wet with tears. Then she began openly to weep. I just carried on.

'When I finally finished, there was a long silence. I wanted to run.

'She had been sitting all the time I was speaking. Now she got up, walked across the room, and put her arms around me. In this embrace, we both wept.'

.   .

In the years following their first encounter, Erasmus's life grew more torrid still. His wife left him, and he fought a bitter battle for the custody of his children; members of his family denounced him for his perfidy and washed their hands of him; he spent years unemployed, living at times in a shelter for the homeless.

Throughout this dreadful time, Winnie nursed his wounded soul via his children.

'When I got custody of my son, Dylan,' he recalled, 'she reached out to me like you wouldn't believe. Our friendship really developed around him. The tenderness she showed him: my eyes still well with tears when I think about it. When she heard that he had been assaulted, she rushed to him, took him to a private psychiatrist, paid the bills. The psychiatrist's report went to Winnie, not to me. The doctor advised to take Dylan to live where he was last happy. His happiest time had been in George, before things started falling apart. So we relocated.'

Winnie and Erasmus embarked upon crackpot schemes together. Once, Erasmus met a man who told him he could cure AIDS by oxygenating the blood. 'He showed me how it worked,' Erasmus recalled. 'To this day, I believe that oxytherapy works. The one person I knew who had the strength to take this up was Winnie. I phoned her. She came immediately to see for herself. We went off to Kenya to inspect the equipment that made this medicine. We were there for ten days. Each morning, she gathered everyone around to pray for this medicine that could save the lives of thousands.'[16]

.   .

During the last year of his life, Erasmus spent several hours talking to this author. For most of that time, he insisted that Winnie had nothing to do with the death of Stompie Seipei.

'Stompie and Jerry Richardson were both working for the security police,' he said. 'Stompie was going to spill the beans on Jerry; Jerry was going to spill the beans on Stompie. Jerry killed Stompie before he could talk.'[17]

In the last conversation we had, Erasmus, apropos of nothing, suddenly threw this baseline truth into doubt. 'Maybe she did order Stompie's killing,' Erasmus offered. 'But that is how things were in those days.

'Mind you, when I think of how she was with Dylan, I can't imagine her ordering the death of a child. I think what happened is that she ordered them to really *moer* him. I can see her doing that.'[18]

'That is how things were in those days.'

Things in those days were horrible beyond belief. A license to do great harm was abroad, a license that had been distributed liberally across South African society. It is perhaps not surprising that two people who exercised that license – one a white man, the other a black woman – found each other. What he sought from her was the absolution he doubted he deserved. What she sought from him was the terrible guilt, experienced at a safe distance, in another human soul.

· ·

If this seems too pat, it should be said that Erasmus was just the first in a line. Winnie appeared to crave the presence in her life of white men who had been violent under apartheid, men now in pain and filled with an unrequitable need to be cleansed.

Another was Jan 'Doc' Pretorius, also a former security policeman, also wrenched by the things he had done, also in some trouble when they met. He wrote a book about his relationship with her called *The Last Wish of Winnie Mandela*. A strange cocktail of spiritual renewal, moralizing, and exposés of arms dealing, it is awash with awe. A chance encounter with Winnie, he declared, changed his life. 'Winnie would become a closer member of my family than any of my siblings or my parents,' he wrote. 'I became her white son.'[19]

Another who drew close to Winnie during the last years of her life was her minister, Gary Rivas. A senior Methodist cleric, he was not a former security policeman at all. But as a conscript in the apartheid military, he had trained as a paratrooper and was thrown into counter-insurgency operations, which were notoriously violent.

'It was hectic stuff,' he told this author. 'It was horrific.'[20]

He was yet another white man ill at ease with his past who felt Winnie staring into his soul.

'To be honest with you,' he said, 'I would go to the hospital [when she was ill] or to her home to take sacraments and . . . nine times out of ten . . . it was actually she who had pastored me.

'She would turn the focus completely. She had a sensitivity. She could read between the lines.'

He believed that she was seeing the horror of his soldiering days and the damage it had left inside him. 'I have a sense that she knew,' he said. 'She must have known.'

There is a particular moment, etched forever in his mind.

A number of people had gathered around Winnie's hospital bed. Among them was a group of American visitors: they were veterans of Bloody Sunday, the day in 1965 when a civil rights march from Selma to Montgomery, Alabama, was attacked by state troopers.

Several stalwarts from the South African struggle were also among the people gathered around Winnie's bed.

They were recalling the old days, as veterans do: the Americans, the march to Montgomery; the South Africans, historic moments at which they were present.

As the chatter went on, Rivas felt his unease growing.

'They were all talking about what they did,' he recalled. 'And here I am, with the military service I had done in the apartheid army. And I am thinking, hey, man, if the conversation turns to me, and they ask, "What did you do?"'

As his anxiety quickened, he felt a hand gently take hold of his. It was Winnie's.

They did not exchange a word. But he knew from his depths that she understood what was happening inside him. He felt his anxiety subside. She would protect him; he knew absolutely that she would protect him; she would not allow for him to be exposed.[21]

It is an exquisite moment, and perhaps the closest we will come to glimpsing the dying Winnie's connection to her own past. This tuning in to the suffering of one who has committed violence; the fascination with it; the constant absolving, again and again.

·   ·

On his eightieth birthday, two and a half years after his divorce, Nelson Mandela remarried.

He and his bride, Graça Machel, had much in common. She was also the product of Methodist mission schools, hers six hundred miles north of his, in southern Mozambique. Her education and her pedigree placed her in the upper echelons of her country's black elite. She, too, had been a black student at an overwhelmingly white institution; she left Mozambique in her twenties to study at the University of Lisbon.

Machel had even more in common with Winnie, for she had also married the leader of her country's struggle for freedom. She met Samora Machel as the movement he led, Frente de Libertação de Moçambique, or FRELIMO, was coming to power and served in his cabinet as minister of education. He was twelve years her senior and the father of five children when they wed; as Winnie had, she chose a man who brought with him a cluttered past.

When Machel married Nelson, he had eleven months to serve as president of South Africa. She thus became First Lady of a southern African state for the second time. But what a different First Couple and what a different state. FRELIMO was unique in southern Africa for the severity of its ideas. After coming to power in 1975, Machel periodically ordered that the streets of the capital, Maputo, be swept of vagrants, prostitutes, drunks and the idle, who were placed in reeducation camps to 'decolonize their minds'.[22] By 1980, ten thousand Mozambicans were held in such camps, including two of Samora Machel's nieces.

That was hardly the end of the extremity of those times. Liberated Mozambique was born into civil war, FRELIMO's foe, Resistência Nacional Moçambicana, sponsored by the governments of Rhodesia and South Africa. Hundreds of thousands were displaced by the conflict and an untold number died.[23] Whether Samora Machel himself should be counted among the casualties is disputed. In October 1986, his Maputo-bound plane crashed in South African territory, killing him and thirty-three others. A South African commission of inquiry found the cause to have been pilot error, but the suspicion that the plane was lured off course by a South African decoy beacon has never died.

By the time she met Nelson, Machel had long transmogrified from revolutionary to global ambassador. She was an outspoken advocate on women's rights and the rights of children; she had done prominent work on the welfare of refugees. August institutions had showered her with awards, honorary degrees and exalted positions. She was, like Nelson, a full-fledged member of the great and the good.

The couple's celebrity qualities concealed something obvious. When they wed, Nelson Mandela and Graça Machel had *lived;* behind him lay twenty-seven long years in prison; behind her, involvement in a doctrinaire social experiment, civil war, the sudden death of a spouse. They both understood something about frailty and pain, and something, too, about imperfection.

In the testimony of some who observed the marriage at close quarters, Machel began to bring a semblance of order to Nelson's relationship with his family. The sprawling, fractious, bickering clan was gathered at regular intervals. Members of the family who had drifted were invited back in. In this spirit, Machel urged Nelson to enter a truce with Winnie, and she, too, began to appear regularly at family gatherings at Nelson's house in Johannesburg's northern suburbs.

There was sadness in this attention to form and to ritual, for it stood in for something beyond Nelson's reach. Some of those close to him and his affairs expressed horror at the lust with which members of his family chased fortunes on the back of his name. 'Those family gatherings were dreadful,' an associate of Nelson's commented. 'The mercenary behaviour was naked and shameless.'

In late 2008, several months after Nelson's ninetieth birthday, a member of his medical team was assigned to spend time with him to assess his physical and emotional state. Doctor and patient bonded, it seems, and Nelson confessed to being sad and depressed. His years in prison had deprived him of his family, he said, and relationships had never mended.[24]

. .

During his time with Machel, Nelson lived in three places: in the house in Johannesburg he acquired when he left Winnie; in his beloved childhood village, Qunu, where he built a home precisely resembling his cottage at Victor Verster Prison; and, for a while, in Maputo, where he built a house for Machel.

A friend who visited Nelson in Maputo reported walking through the front door to find herself face-to-face with an outsized painting of Samora Machel. 'It dominated the house,' she recalled. 'I would look at Nelson, who was old and frail, and then look up at the towering man in the picture.' After a few days, she plucked up the courage to ask Graça about it. 'I want people to know who the real man of the house is!' Machel had joked. Behind her joshing was something quite serious. Hers and Nelson's was an autumnal relationship; his great love was Winnie, hers, Samora. He was eighty when they wed; almost everything lay in the past.

. .

During the last days of January 1996, nearly eighteen years before his death, while he was the president of South Africa, Nelson wrote a set of detailed instructions for his funeral, instructions that in the end were not carried out.

That he gave such sustained thought to his death at this time, while running a country and in perfect health, tells a story in itself. From the tone of the instructions, it appears that being dead was a familiar feeling to him, long rehearsed. He was not a man likely to have contemplated suicide, not even remotely. But he did appear to have thought of death as a relief.

Above all, his instructions are an act of defiance. For a lifetime, he has surrendered himself to service, to fame, to myth. He is spent. The corpse he imagines is that of a man from a small village in the Transkei.

'To all whom it concerns,' Nelson wrote.

> I set out hereunder for the direction of my family members and for all those who are close to me, the wishes for my funeral.
>
> I would like to have a simple funeral not merely from the point of just words but also [i]n the way it is carried out.
>
> I would like my coffin to be a simple one made of planks from the village of Qunu.
>
> I would like my coffin to be carried from my house in Qunu and only if it is necessary to be transported, by a horse drawn wagon, to the gravesite.
>
> I would like my grave to be a simple one and to be covered by stones to be found in the village. The tombstone should be a large rock from the village or from the area of Qunu which should have the name "MANDELA" inscribed on it.
>
> I specifically direct that nothing should be added which detracts from the simplicity of the funeral or of the grave.
>
> The community in Qunu has given me some land. I have

paid consideration for this land. It is on this land that I would
like to be buried.

With regard to the funeral services, I would like the Priest
who serves the majority of the community in Qunu to attend
to this aspect but I ask that all of our major religious faiths –
Christianity, Hinduism, Islam and Judaism – be represented
at the funeral.

I know that my family members and those who are close to
me believe that it should be different but I know that they will
respect my deepfelt wishes in this regard. I believe that this is
the way, the only way that I can sleep in peace.[25]

. .

Four years after he died, one of Nelson's doctors published a memoir describing his medical treatment during his last years. Machel was
enraged; she took legal action, and the book was swiftly removed from
the shelves.

Among its revelations was that Winnie was alone with Nelson
when he died.

She in fact appears to have spent a good deal of time with him
toward the end of his life. As his dementia grew worse, he refused to
eat. And, in his addled state, he would call for his former wife.

And so Winnie came to feed him.

Once, a little more than a year before Nelson's death, a friend
bumped into Winnie on the streets of Mthatha, a short drive from Nelson's home in Qunu, and asked what she was doing so far from home.

'It's this chief!' she reported Winnie exclaiming. 'He has been going
on about me. First he decided to leave me; now he won't eat without me.
I am supposed to fly all this way to feed somebody!'

She appeared to delight in the whole business.

It was apparently at Machel's insistence that Winnie was there
while Nelson was dying. 'It was obvious to Graça that Winnie must be
a chief mourner,' a friend of the family told this author. 'A good death
must be the summation of a life. And Winnie had been Nelson's great
love.'

Fifty-six years and ten months after their first date, Winnie and
Nelson were alone together for the very last time. One of them was

near death and unconscious. The other was as lucid as ever, her own mortality closer than she might have thought.

Within five years they were both gone.

Their myths will remain, ever evolving, over decades, perhaps over centuries, into what it would be too bold to say.

The Coetsee Collection

From chapter 47 of *Winnie and Nelson,* I begin to quote verbatim conversations between Nelson Mandela and people who came to see him in prison: among others, his wife, his children and grandchildren, his niece, his chaplain. I also cite some of what Mandela said during the secret talks he had with senior members of the South African government while he was a prisoner.

On turning to the notes section of this book, readers will find that each of these citations is from the H. J. 'Kobie' Coetsee private collection housed at the Archive for Contemporary Affairs at the University of the Free State.

There is a story to tell about the Coetsee collection: why it is housed where it is, why its contents became public and why I have used it.

When he left office in 1994, apartheid South Africa's last minister of justice and prisons, Kobie Coetsee, took with him a file he had been assembling for a decade. The subject of the file was Nelson Mandela. Among a host of other documents, it contained the voluminous record generated by the eavesdropping Coetsee had instructed his staff to perform on his most famous prisoner. These included transcripts of conversations Mandela had with his visitors and notes warders took while listening in. It also contained a partial record of Mandela's secret talks with Coetsee and other senior government officials. The file is some fifteen thousand pages long.

To say that Coetsee took the file with him is a polite way of saying that he stole it. It belongs to the South African state and ought to have been lodged in due course in the South African National Archives. Coetsee's theft of the file is best situated in a much wider history of misappropriation and destruction; apartheid officials across the vast apparatus of the state destroyed, stole and hid untold thousands of state documents during South Africa's transition to democracy.[1]

The Mandela file remained in Coetsee's home for almost two decades; upon the death of his widow, it was transferred, along with the rest of his papers, to the Archive for Contemporary Affairs at the University of the Free State in Bloemfontein. The head of that archive duly catalogued the Mandela file and assembled a meticulous finding aid. But she told neither the Nelson Mandela Foundation nor the South African National Archives of its existence.

Instead, she appears to have informed a very select circle of scholars, for in 2018 and 2020, respectively, two books based on its contents were published: *Die tronkgesprekke: Nelson Mandela en Kobie Coetsee se voorpuntdiploma-sie* (The prison talks: Nelson Mandela and Kobie Coetsee's leading-edge diplomacy), by Willie Esterhuyse and Gerhard van Niekerk; and *Prisoner 913: The Release of Nelson Mandela,* by Riaan de Villiers and Jan-Ad Stemmet.

It was as a result of the publication of these books that I became aware of Coetsee's Mandela file. I contacted the archive sometime in 2020 to discover that access to the collection was open. The COVID pandemic had barred visitors, but the archivists offered to scan all fifteen thousand or so pages of the Mandela file for a fee and to deliver them to me electronically.

On receiving the file, I sent one electronic copy to the chief archivist at the Nelson Mandela Foundation and another to Mandela's old comrade Mac Maharaj, who was at work on a book about the talks that led to the unbanning of the ANC and the release of Mandela. Then I set about reading them.

They are tricky documents to work with. Nelson and Winnie were both aware that their conversations were being recorded. Nothing they said can be taken as a transparent window onto their thoughts. Nelson often whispered or made signs or found other ways to communicate undetected. 'We are not alone,' he informed his visitors, almost without fail. The documents thus contain what Nelson *chose,* albeit it in a highly attenuated sense, his captors to hear.

They are nonetheless enormously revealing, at times painfully so. Nelson's relationship with his youngest daughter breaks down before the eavesdropping audience; his conversations with Winnie carry all the duplicity, deceit and cruelties that spouses inflict on each other. There is very intimate material here.

Had Coetsee not stolen the file, I am unlikely to have had access to it, certainly not in its raw unredacted form. Although I myself played by the book and broke no law, I am a beneficiary of its theft.

Any defense I offer must ring hollow, for what I say is necessarily self-serving. I used the material because luck brought it to me and I wanted to write the best book I could.

In lieu of a defense, I want to say two other things instead.

The Nelson Mandela who emerged from prison chose to conceal his suffering, his bitterness and his anger. He molded a mask of avuncular good cheer and took it wherever he went. He did so because he felt that this was the mask his country's future required him to wear.

Now, a decade after his death, he is paying a price for wearing that mask. When young black people turn to past figures for inspiration, many increasingly look past Nelson to men and women who would not forgive and who showed their anger without shame.

Frantz Fanon, Steve Biko, Winnie Madikizela-Mandela.

Winnie, so gifted at reading her times, picked this up at once. Nelson Mandela, she said toward the end of her life, was not angry like her because he did not suffer like her.

One thing I hope this book has achieved is to restore the image of both Winnie and Nelson Mandela as people who suffered and grew furiously angry — suffered so much that words barely begin to describe it — because they were black people who dared to defy a racist regime.

That is one of the reasons I chose for this book's epigraph words written by the great playwright August Wilson, whose life's project was to place each of his many black characters in a four-hundred-year history of exploitation. Nelson and Winnie Mandela come from that history. The Coetsee collection exposes the pain inflicted upon them in a way only very intimate material can.

In using the Coetsee collection, I can show this pain, but I cannot claim to stand aloof from it. I have been able to come up so close precisely because Nelson Mandela was the captive of a racist regime, his privacy serially invaded.

Here is the other thing I want to say about the material in the Coetsee collection.

To read the transcripts of Winnie and Nelson's conversations is to intrude on a marriage. But it is also, I discovered, an intrusion of another kind. As one reads, one finds that Nelson is the odd one out. There are things that both the reader and Winnie know but that Nelson does not. And they go to the heart of what matters to him. Such as that Zindzi has abandoned university and is getting deeply involved with the football club. And that Winnie, however incompetently, is trying to spark an armed insurrection while Nelson strives for a peaceful settlement.

The sharpness of this dramatic irony — where one character and the reader know something another character does not — is usually reserved for fiction; it is rare that material in the real world orchestrates such a moment.

The structure of the situation throws stunning light on Winnie, on Nelson, on their marriage.

We see Winnie in all her effectiveness; her mastery over these encounters with her husband is nothing less than extraordinary.

And yet.

The clock is ticking.

The day of Nelson's freedom will soon come.

On that day Winnie will take her place as his wife, no matter that she has grown to despise his politics, for everything is now about him.

Within two years, she will have a dear friend place herself at Nelson's feet, begging him to preserve the marriage.

Winnie is at once the most commanding figure and a figure of terrible subjection.

As for Nelson, he is his enemy's captive. And yet, in quick time, he has also become a very powerful man indeed. What a dizzying, dangerous combination.

Upon his release, he will learn, on the hoof, how much of his immense influence is hollow and how much is real. He will learn by abusing his position in public life to try to save his marriage.

Without the content of the Coetsee collection, we cannot grasp what was at stake for him; without the Coetsee collection, we cannot gather the sympathy we need to understand him.

Power is frighteningly ephemeral; it can turn without warning into its opposite. This is among the many lessons offered by the lives of Winnie and Nelson Mandela. The myth of their tale is necessary. So, too, is the illumination of their human frailty. I feel fortunate to have had the material at hand to tell so delicate a story.

Acknowledgments

I accrued many debts writing this book.

To all who had personal experience of the two protagonists and agreed to speak on the record: your names are scattered throughout the endnotes; here I wish to express my gratitude to you collectively.

I am deeply grateful to those who facilitated access to vital documentary sources and to key interviewees. Thank you to Fran Buntman, Luli Callinicos, Donald Cragg, Barbara Hogan, Bart Luirink, Prince Madikizela, Mac Maharaj, Philani Mkhanywa, Neil Morrison, Piers Pigou, Eleanor Sisulu, John Scholtz, Redi Tlhabi, Hannes van Zyl, and Tim and Ilse Wilson.

Like all historical researchers, I owe a debt to those who preserve and manage the archives from which I draw. Thank you to Gabriele Mohale at Wits Historical Papers, an extraordinary repository of South Africa's archival history; the Archive for Contemporary Affairs at the University of the Free State; Lebohang Sekholomi at the University of the Western Cape Robben Island Museum Mayibuye Archives; the staff at the Weston Library at Oxford University; the South African National Archives in Pretoria; the High Court archive in Johannesburg; the Beinecke Rare Book and Manuscript Library at Yale University; Meg Hartzenberg, who looks after the Methodist Archive at the Cory Library, Rhodes University; and Cathy Robling at the Marston Memorial Historical Center in Indianapolis.

Thank you to those who lent me access to their private archives: Eric Abraham, William Beinart, Horst Kleinschmidt and Hugh Macmillan. I am grateful to Mandy Jacobson and Liza Key, who went out of their way to give me access to the archive forming as they worked on the life of Winnie Madikizela-Mandela. They also allowed me to watch early cuts of the documentary on Winnie's life Mandy was directing, *The Trials of Winnie Mandela,* and to read the film transcripts.

Serendipitous encounters led me down new avenues. Bumping into Lynn M. Thomas in Gainesville, Florida, reset my thinking on the young Winnie Madikizela; a beer with David Lan led to Herald Loomis and Martha Pentecost; a visit to Jacob Dlamini's office to a record of the UDF leaders' meeting with Oliver Tambo in Lusaka; a last-minute coffee arrangement with Hannes van Zyl to the Kobie Coetsee Papers. Many thanks to all of you.

The Nelson Mandela Foundation has been generous to a T. Thank you to Sahm Venter for her assistance during the early stages of this project, to Razia Saleh for helping me navigate the foundation's archives, to Zandile Myeka for her help sourcing photographs, and to Verne Harris, who lent me his vast expertise.

I profited a great deal by presenting parts of this book to critical audiences. So many crucial ideas germinated in the to-and-fro of these seminars. Many thanks to Dan Magaziner and Louisa Lombard for arranging for me to present at the African Studies Seminar at Yale; to Jean and John Comaroff, who invited me to present at the African Studies Workshop at Harvard; to Jacob Dlamini, who hosted a seminar at the Princeton History Department; to the organizers of the symposium held in honour of Professor Luise White at the University of Florida at Gainesville in the spring of 2019; and to William Beinart, Max Bolt, Thomas Cousins and Rebekah Lee, co-facilitators of the South Africa Discussion Group at Oxford University.

St. John Haw gave me hours of his time and lent me his perspicacity and his wisdom. My understanding of the two protagonists is profoundly indebted to our discussions.

My research assistant, Daniel Sher, worked with rigour, enterprise and deep intelligence. I could not have asked for more.

My agent, David Godwin, helped me immeasurably in conceptualizing this project. 'I want to write two books,' I told him on the phone one morning in March 2018, 'one on Nelson Mandela, the other on Winnie Madikizela-Mandela.'

'Better to write one book on both,' he replied.

David aside, Oliver Aiken and Colin Bundy were generous enough to read complete drafts of this book. So was my sister, Carol Steinberg, a cherished first reader for more than two decades now, alongside the many other roles she plays in my life.

Winnie and Nelson has been blessed with wonderful editors. Many thanks to Annie Olivier and Jeremy Boraine at Jonathan Ball Publishers, Arabella Pike and Jo Thompson at HarperCollins, and Marcella van der Kruk at Atlas Contact. I owe special thanks to *Winnie and Nelson*'s lead editor, John Freeman at Knopf, and assistant editor Sarah Perrin, for the delicate labour that made this a better book.

To the formidable Russell Martin, whose knowledge of South African history is jaw-dropping, many thanks for your fact-checking.

This book was acquired on behalf of Knopf by Dan Frank, who died shortly before I completed a draft. He was in my head as an imagined first reader as I wrote. What a shock it was to learn that the wise, gentle man I was conjuring each day at my desk was dead.

Jonathan Ball also died while I was writing *Winnie and Nelson*. He published my first book, and all my subsequent books, too, and championed them with his vast and eccentric energy. No author could have dreamed up a more beneficent publisher.

For their love, I thank Oliver Aiken, Lael Bethlehem, David Jammy, and, always, Lomin Saayman.

Notes

ABBREVIATIONS

ASP   Anthony Sampson Papers, Bodleian Library, Oxford

CC   H. J. 'Kobie' Coetsee, private collection, Archive for Contemporary
      Affairs, University of the Free State

CRS   Nelson Mandela, conversations with Richard Stengel, Nelson
      Mandela Centre of Memory

HTH   Fatima Meer, *Higher Than Hope*

LWF   Nelson Mandela, *Long Walk to Freedom*

PBS *Frontline* 'The Long Walk of Nelson Mandela' interview archive

PLNM *The Prison Letters of Nelson Mandela*

UPM   Nelson Mandela, unpublished memoir (1976), Nelson Mandela Centre
      of Memory

INTRODUCTION

1. *LWF*, 199.
2. For the bespoke suits, see Bizos, *Odyssey to Freedom*, 338.
3. Sampson, *Mandela*, 107.
4. Adelaide Tambo, interview by John Carlin, circa 1999, PBS *Frontline*.
5. Winnie Mandela, *Part of My Soul Went with Him*, 58.
6. Ibid., 58–59.
7. *HTH*, 121–26.
8. Rusty Bernstein, interview by Anthony Sampson, Aug. 18, 1996, ASP, Dep. 168.
9. Cited in *HTH*, 119.
10. Sampson, *Mandela*, 113.
11. Nelson Mandela to Winnie Mandela, Aug. 1, 1970, in Madikizela-Mandela, *491
    Days*, 190.
12. Nelson Mandela to Winnie Mandela, April 2, 1969, in *PLNM*, 80.
13. Ibid.
14. *HTH*, 120.
15. Gilbey, *Lady*, 38.
16. Peterson, *Ethnic Patriotism*.
17. Kenyatta, *Facing Mount Kenya*, 175.
18. Cited in Guha, *Gandhi: The Years That Changed the World*, 247.
19. Gandhi, *Autobiography*, 9.
20. Nehru, *Discovery of India*, 40–41.
21. Vaillant, *Black, French, and African*, 280–82.

CHAPTER 1

1. Nelson Mandela, interview, in *Mandela: Son of Africa, Father of a Nation*.
2. UPM, 1.

3. Mostert, *Frontiers.*
4. Etherington, *Preachers, Peasants, and Politics.*
5. See, for instance, Guy, *Heretic.*
6. *LWF,* 15–16.
7. *HTH,* 7.
8. Chief Ndaba Mtirara, Chief Anderson Joyi, and Chief Jonginyaniso Mtirara, interview by John Carlin, circa 1999, PBS *Frontline.*
9. Nelson Mandela to Winnie Mandela, Dec. 28, 1970, in *PLNM,* 206.
10. *HTH,* 7.
11. UPM, 3.
12. CRS, CD 23/64, March 9 and 10, 1993.
13. *LWF,* 18.

CHAPTER 2
1. Chief Ndaba Mtirara, Chief Anderson Joyi, and Chief Jonginyaniso Mtirara, interview by John Carlin, circa 1999, PBS *Frontline.*
2. UPM, 20; *LWF,* 27–28.
3. Wagenaar, 'History of the Thembu and Their Relation to the Cape'.
4. Bonner, 'The Headman, the Regent, and the "Long Walk to Freedom"', 61.
5. Hyslop, *Classroom Struggle,* 2–8.
6. Wilson, *Reaction to Conquest,* 135–77.
7. UPM, 27.
8. Ibid., 26.
9. Boehmer, *Nelson Mandela,* 28.
10. *LWF,* 35.
11. Ntantala, *Life's Mosaic,* 71.
12. Ibid., 71–72.
13. Hofmeyr, *Portable Bunyan,* 120.
14. Nadine Gordimer, 'Nelson Mandela', unpublished manuscript (1964), Microfilm Reel 12A:2:XM33, Karis and Carter Collection, Historical Papers Collection, Wits University, Johannesburg.
15. Macaulay, *History of England,* 12.
16. Ibid., 13.

CHAPTER 3
1. UPM, 40.
2. Kenya's first president, Jomo Kenyatta, was also trained by Malinowski, and Senegal's founding president, Léopold Senghor, was steeped in the study of French ethnography. See Kenyatta, *Facing Mount Kenya;* Vaillant, *Black, French, and African.*
3. Bunche, *African American in South Africa,* 136.
4. UPM, 38.
5. CRS, CD 25/64, March 10–11, 1993.
6. Cited in Sampson, *Mandela,* 24.
7. Ntantala, *Life's Mosaic,* 81–82.
8. *LWF,* 47.
9. Ntantala, *Life's Mosaic,* 73.
10. Thomas, 'Modern Girl and Racial Respectability in 1930s South Africa', 463–64.
11. Bunche, *African American in South Africa,* 128.
12. Gordimer, 'Nelson Mandela', unpublished manuscript (1964), Karis and Carter Collection.
13. CRS, CD 26/64, Tape 6, March 11, 1993.

14. Ntantala, *Life's Mosaic*, 16–17.
15. *LWF*, 54–55.
16. CRS, CD 25/64, March 10–11, 1993.

CHAPTER 4

1. Hogue, *History of the Free Methodist Church in North America*, 274–75.
2. Anna C. Brodhead, 'From Foreign Fields', *Missionary Tidings*, May 1910, 7, Marston Memorial Historical Center, Indianapolis.
3. Ibid.
4. General Mission Board, Free Methodist Church, minutes, 1909, 348, Marston Memorial Historical Center.
5. Stapleton, *Faku*, 1–10; Hunter, *Reaction to Conquest*, 349.
6. Batts, *History of the Baptist Church in South Africa*, 143.
7. J. P. Brodhead, 'Fields Ready for Harvest', *Missionary Tidings*, May 1910, 2–3, Marston Memorial Historical Center.
8. See Comaroff and Comaroff, *Of Revelation and Revolution*, vol. 1, chap. 5; Mokoena, *Magema Fuze*.
9. Walter Madikizela, interview by William Beinart, June 4, 1982, audiocassette, Beinart personal collection, Oxford.
10. Ibid.
11. Prince Madikizela, interview by author, Oct. 21, 2018.
12. Walter Madikizela, interview by Beinart.
13. Prince Madikizela, interview by author, June 1, 2018.
14. Prince Madikizela, interview by author, Oct. 21, 2018.
15. See Gibbs, *Mandela's Clansmen*, 33.
16. Walter Madikizela, interview by Beinart.

CHAPTER 5

1. Prince Madikizela, interview by author, July 5, 2018.
2. *HTH*, 97.
3. Ismail Ayob, interview by author, March 13, 2019.
4. *HTH*, 97–112.
5. Nobantu Mniki, interview by author, July 11, 2018; Nonyaniso Madikizela, interview by author, Oct. 15, 2018.
6. *HTH*, 97.
7. Winnie Mandela, *Part of My Soul Went with Him*, 47.
8. Ibid.
9. *HTH*, 106.
10. Cited in ibid.
11. Nonyaniso Madikizela, interview by author, Oct. 15, 2018; Nobantu Mniki, interview by author, July 11, 2018.
12. Prince Madikizela, interview by author, June 1, 2018.
13. *HTH*, 103.

CHAPTER 6

1. Prince Madikizela, interview by author, July 5, 2018; Nobantu Mniki, interview by author, July 11, 2018.
2. Isabella Somtseu, interview by author, June 2, 2018.
3. The list is compiled from material at the Methodist archives at the Cory Library, Rhodes University, Grahamstown. Many thanks to Meg Hartzenberg and Donald Cragg.
4. Isabella Somtseu, interview by author, June 2, 2018.
5. Ibid.

6.   *HTH*, 112.
7.   Zola Dabula, interview by author, Oct. 20, 2018.
8.   Ibid.
9.   Bezdrob, *Winnie Mandela*, 38.
10.   Hyslop, *Classroom Struggle*, 10–11.
11.   Gilbey, *Lady*, 27.
12.   Brigalia Bam, interview by author, June 22, 2020.
13.   Ibid.
14.   *HTH*, 111–12.
15.   Ibid., 111.
16.   Manoim, 'Black Press', 220.
17.   Thomas, *Beneath the Surface*, chap. 4.
18.   *Zonk!*, Aug. 1949, Beinecke Library, Yale University.
19.   Glaser, *Bo-Tsotsi*, 50–51.
20.   *Sunday Independent*, Sept. 8, 1996, cited in Sampson, *Mandela*, 111.
21.   Her name was Mary Malahlela. She graduated first from Fort Hare, then from Wits Medical School in Johannesburg. Winnie came to know her well. Rehman, 'Against the Odds'.
22.   Her name was Desiree Finca. See Manyathi-Jele, 'Gender Transformation', 16–18.
23.   Brandel-Syrier, *Reeftown Elite*, 165.
24.   Jan H. Hofmeyr School of Social Work, 'Announcements' 1951, South African Institute for Race Relations, Rheinallt Jones Papers, AD843RJ, Nb9, Wits University Historical Papers.
25.   For a brilliant potted biography of Maxeke, see Campbell, *Songs of Zion*.
26.   Phillips to the Secretary of the Union of South Africa Department of Education, Nov. 23, 1949, South African Institute for Race Relations, Rheinallt Jones Papers, AD843RJ, Nb9, Wits University Historical Papers.
27.   Bezdrob, *Winnie Mandela*, 45.
28.   Prince Madikizela, interview by author, July 5, 2018.
29.   Madikizela-Mandela, *491 Days*, 33.
30.   Nobantu Mniki, interview by author, July 11, 2018.
31.   Madikizela-Mandela, *491 Days*, 237.

CHAPTER 7

1.   UPM, 47.
2.   Walter Sisulu, interview by John Carlin, circa 1999, PBS *Frontline*.
3.   Walter Sisulu, *I Will Go Singing*, 45.
4.   Richard Stengel, interview by John Carlin, circa 1999, PBS *Frontline*.
5.   Elinor Sisulu, *Walter and Albertina Sisulu*, 1–18.
6.   Walter Sisulu, *I Will Go Singing*, 14.
7.   Sampson, *Treason Cage*, 156.
8.   Elinor Sisulu, *Walter and Albertina Sisulu*, 36; Walter Sisulu, *I Will Go Singing*, 31.
9.   Elinor Sisulu, *Walter and Albertina Sisulu*, 44.
10.   Ibid., 66.
11.   *LWF*, 69.
12.   UPM, 68.

CHAPTER 8

1.   Beinart, *Twentieth-Century South Africa*, 187.
2.   *LWF*, 70.
3.   Glaser, *Bo-Tsotsi*, 48–70.

4.	Kuper, *African Bourgeoisie*, 425.
5.	CRS, CD 25/64, March 10–11, 1993.
6.	UPM, 49–50.
7.	CRS, CD 25/64, March 10–11, 1993.
8.	Anthony Sampson, interview by John Carlin, circa 1999, PBS *Frontline*.

CHAPTER 9
1.	*LWF*, 72.
2.	Gerhart and Karis, *From Protest to Challenge*, 4:130; Moodie, 'Moral Economy of the Black Miners' Strike of 1946', 1–35; Kruger, 'Drama of Country and City', 565–84.
3.	CRS, CD 29/64, March 16, 1993.
4.	Ibid.
5.	Ibid.

CHAPTER 10
1.	Howard, *Garden City to Come*. For an intellectual history of the idea of the garden city in South Africa's modernist planning circles, see Pinnock, 'Ideology and Urban Planning', 150–68.
2.	Sampson, *Drum*, 30–31.
3.	Elinor Sisulu, *Walter and Albertina Sisulu*, 46.
4.	Walter Sisulu, *I Will Go Singing*, 57.
5.	Evelyn Mase, interview by Angus Gibson and Jo Menell, circa 1993, ASP, Dep. 169.
6.	Ibid.
7.	CRS, CD 29/64, March 16, 1993.
8.	*HTH*, 39.
9.	Much later, Nelson began paying bridewealth to Evelyn's family, but this was to retrofit tradition onto what, in the first instance, was a story of young urban love.
10.	Evelyn Mase, interview by Gibson and Menell, ASP, Dep. 169.
11.	Ibid.
12.	*LWF*.
13.	Joe Matthews, interview by Anthony Sampson, n.d., ASP, Dep. 168.
14.	Evelyn Mase, interview by Gibson and Menell, ASP, Dep. 169.
15.	Nelson Mandela to Irene Buthelezi, Aug. 3, 1969, in *PLNM*, 121.
16.	Matthews, interview by Sampson, ASP, Dep. 168.
17.	*HTH*, 41.
18.	Evelyn Mase, interview by Gibson and Menell, ASP, Dep. 169.
19.	*HTH*, 41.
20.	Matthews, interview by Sampson, ASP, Dep. 168.
21.	*HTH*, 41.
22.	Ibid., 57.

CHAPTER 11
1.	UPM, 66.
2.	Sisulu, interview by Anthony Sampson, Nov. 1995, ASP, Dep. 168.
3.	UPM, 64.
4.	Murray, 'Nelson Mandela and Wits University', 274.
5.	*LWF*, 84.
6.	Murray, 'Nelson Mandela and Wits University', 273.

7.   Cited in ibid., 276.
8.   Cited in Smith, *Young Mandela*, 88.
9.   Jules Browde, cited in Sampson, *Mandela*, 35.
10.   CRS, CD 36, March 23 and 25, 1993.
11.   Cited in Sampson, *Mandela*, 34.
12.   Browde, *Relatively Public Life of Jules Browde*, 40–44. Nelson recounts the episode in the classroom in his autobiography, but he confuses De Klerk with another man. See *LWF*, 90.
13.   Nussbaum, *Anger and Forgiveness*, chap. 3.
14.   Cited in Murray, 'Nelson Mandela and Wits University', 278.

CHAPTER 12
1.   Glaser, *ANC Youth League*, 20–27.
2.   Mda, interview by Gail M. Gerhart, Jan. 1, 1970, Mafeteng, Lesotho, ASP, Dep. 107.
3.   This rendering belies much complexity. The questions of what form postcolonial states would take, who would belong to them, and the form their relations to European states would assume were fiercely contested. Among a large literature, see Cooper, *Citizenship Between Empire and Nation;* Getachew, *Worldmaking After Empire*.
4.   Campbell, *Songs of Zion*, 277.
5.   Ibid., 276. On Madie Hall's public career in South Africa, see Berger, 'African American "Mother of the Nation"'.
6.   Mda, interview by Gerhart, ASP, Dep. 107.
7.   Walshe, *Rise of African Nationalism in South Africa*, 379–411; Gish, *Alfred B. Xuma*.
8.   Guha, *Gandhi Before India*.
9.   Lodge, *Black Politics in South Africa Since 1945*, 35–36.
10.   Dubow, *Apartheid*, 1–31.
11.   'Basic Policy of Congress Youth League', www.sahistory.org.za.
12.   Bernstein in conversation at the Mandela Campaign Workshop, Anti-apartheid Movement Oral History Project, Witness Workshop, Oxford, 1999. Transcript in author's possession.
13.   CRS, CD 30, March 17 and 18, 1993.
14.   Ibid.
15.   *HTH*, 34.
16.   UPM, 101.
17.   Phillips, *Crux of the Race Problem*, 31.
18.   CRS, CD 36, March 23 and 25, 1993.

CHAPTER 13
1.   Bonner, 'Antinomies of Nelson Mandela', 39.
2.   Ibid., 40.
3.   Matthews, interview by Anthony Sampson, ASP, Dep. 168.
4.   Sampson, *Mandela*, 68.
5.   CRS, CD 32/64, March 18–19, 1993.
6.   Kuper, *Passive Resistance in South Africa*, 135–36.
7.   Breier, 'Death That Dare(d) Not Speak Its Name'.
8.   Sampson, *Mandela*, 73.
9.   Walter Sisulu, *I Will Go Singing*, 81; CRS, CD 32/64, March 18–19, 1993.
10.   Bank and Carton, 'Forgetting Apartheid'.
11.   On the importance of the local to understanding the Defiance Campaign, see Lodge, *Black Politics in South Africa Since 1945*.
12.   Walter Sisulu, *I Will Go Singing*, 91.

CHAPTER 14

1. Statement by Nelson Mandela, Treason Trial Exhibits, case 725-1958, NRM 48, South African National Archives.
2. Joe Matthews, interview by Anthony Sampson, ASP, Dep. 168.
3. Bizos, *Odyssey to Freedom*, 338.
4. For the brown suit, see Matthews, interview by Sampson, ASP, Dep. 168; for the silk scarf, see Kuzwayo, *Call Me Woman*, 139.
5. Godfrey Pitje, interview by Angus Gibson and Jo Menell, April 11, 1994, ASP, Dep. 168.
6. Ibid.
7. '21 Women in Court', *Golden City Post*, May 1, 1955.
8. See, for instance, 'Mandela Was Fined for Contempt', *World*, Sept. 19, 1956.
9. Many have written on Nelson Mandela and the law but few as trenchantly as Jacques Derrida. Derrida, 'Laws of Reflection'. On the character of law in apartheid South Africa, see Dyzenhaus, *Hard Cases in Wicked Legal Systems*.
10. 'Three Important Visitors', *Bantu World*, Sept. 10, 1955, 5.
11. Pitje, interview by Gibson and Menell, April 11, 1994, ASP, Dep. 168.
12. Fleming, 'Now the African Reigns Supreme'.
13. *LWF*, 193.
14. Matthews, interview by Sampson, ASP, Dep. 168.
15. Angus Gibson, interview by author, May 25, 2018.

CHAPTER 15

1. The quotations above are all drawn from Mda, interview by Gail M. Gerhart, Jan. 1, 1970, ASP, Dep. 107.
2. CRS, CD 32/64, March 18–19, 1993.
3. Pitje, interview by Angus Gibson and Jo Menell, ASP, Dep. 168.
4. Mda, *Sometimes There Is a Void*, 20.
5. Gerhart, *Black Power in South Africa*, 109, 143.
6. Albert Luthuli, Nobel lecture, Dec. 11, 1961, www.nobelprize.org. For the originality of Luthuli's political thought, see Soske, *Internal Frontiers*, 165–96.
7. Can Themba, 'Treason Arrests!', *Drum*, Jan. 1957, 18.

CHAPTER 16

1. Joyce Sikhakhane, interview by author, July 9, 2018.
2. CRS, CD 35/64, March 19, 1993.
3. Mda, *Sometimes There Is a Void*, 41.
4. Joe Matthews, interview by Anthony Sampson, ASP, Dep. 168; 'ANC Storm Ends in Unity', *Bantu World*, Oct. 17, 1953.
5. Statement by Nelson Mandela, Treason Trial Exhibits, case 725-1958, NRM 48, South African National Archives.
6. Ibid.
7. *Evelyn Mandela v. Nelson Mandela*, Particulars of Claim, Central Native Divorce Court, case NDC 342, 1956, South African National Archives.
8. Statement by Nelson Mandela, Treason Trial Exhibits, case 725-1958, NRM 48, South African National Archives.
9. Landau, 'Gendered Silences'.
10. *HTH*, 79.
11. Ibid., 93.
12. Prince Madikizela, interview by author, June 1, 2018.
13. CRS, CD 37, March 23 and 25, 1993.
14. *HTH*, 78.
15. Sampson, *Mandela*, 110.

16.   Joseph, *If This Be Treason,* 209.
17.   Leon and Lorna Levy, interview by author, July 7, 2018.
18.   Amina Cachalia, interview by Anna Trapido, Oct. 5, 2007, Nelson Mandela Centre of Memory.
19.   See, for instance, 'The Treason Trial Defendants: How They Manage to Survive', *Drum,* Aug. 1958, 29.
20.   Cited in Evans, 'Lilian Ngoyi: Fighting with Clipped Wings', 124.
21.   Ngoyi, cited in *Voice,* circa March 1980.
22.   *HTH,* 125.
23.   Ngoyi to Ray Alexander, Sept. 11, 1973, Lilian Masediba Ngoyi Collection, Wits Historical Papers.
24.   Ngoyi, cited in *Voice,* circa March 1980.
25.   Ngoyi to Belinda Allan, Nov. 28, 1975, in Daymond, *Everyday Matters,* 303.
26.   Barbara Masekela, interview by author, Dec. 12, 2018.
27.   CRS, CD 36, March 23 and 25, 1993.
28.   'Treason Trial Defendants: How They Manage to Survive', 29.
29.   Leon Levy, interview by author, Oct. 16, 2018.
30.   Evans, 'Lilian Ngoyi', 121.
31.   Leon Levy, interview by author, Oct. 16, 2018.
32.   Ruth Mompati, 'The Most Powerful Woman in the African National Congress', in Russell, *Lives of Courage,* 113.
33.   Sophia de Bruyn, interview by author, March 20, 2019.
34.   Ruth Mompati's memories of Nelson are drawn from several conversations she had shortly before her death with a friend and confidante who wished to remain anonymous and whose integrity I have no reason to doubt.

CHAPTER 17

1.   *HTH,* 113–14.
2.   Monthly general committee meeting minutes, 1953, Helping Hand Club for Native Girls Papers, A2052 Ba, Wits Historical Papers.
3.   *HTH,* 114.
4.   Weinbaum et al., *Modern Girl Around the World.*
5.   Shula Marks, *Divided Sisterhood.*
6.   Kuzwayo, *Call Me Woman,* 159.
7.   Glaser, 'Mark of Zorro'; Themba, *Will to Die;* Modisane, *Blame Me on History.*
8.   Monthly general committee meeting minutes, Dec. 1952, Helping Hand Club for Native Girls Papers, A2052 Ba, Wits Historical Papers.
9.   Phillips, *Crux of the Race Problem,* 13–14.
10.   See especially Phillips, *Bantu in the City.*
11.   Ibid., 91, 90.
12.   Phillips, *Bantu Are Coming,* 107.
13.   Phillips, *Bantu in the City,* 97–98.
14.   Minutes of monthly general meetings of Helping Hand Club for Native Girls, Aug. 4 and Sept. 22, 1953, Helping Hand Club for Native Girls Papers, A2052 Ba, Wits Historical Papers.

CHAPTER 18

1.   Jan Hofmeyr School of Social Work, Annual Report, Dec. 12, 140, Rev. Ray Phillips Papers, Wits Historical Papers, A1444.
2.   Nkomo, *Story of My Life,* 34.
3.   Kuzwayo, *Call Me Woman,* 158–59.
4.   Berger, 'From Ethnography to Social Welfare'; Cobley, *Rules of the Game,* chap. 5.

5. Bam, interview by author, June 22, 2020.
6. Cited in *HTH*, 115.
7. Cited in ibid., 116.
8. Thornberry, *Colonizing Consent*, 71–73.
9. Bam, interview by author, June 22, 2020.
10. *HTH*, 117.
11. *Sunday Independent*, Sept. 8, 1996, cited in Sampson, *Mandela*, 111.
12. Can Themba, 'Dolly in Films!', *Drum*, Feb. 1957, 48.
13. Can Themba, 'Dolly and Her Men!', *Drum*, Jan. 1957, 39, 41.
14. Driver, '*Drum* Magazine (1951–59) and the Spatial Configuration of Gender', 238.
15. I am grateful to Oliver Aiken for this observation.
16. *HTH*, 117.
17. *Bantu World*, Jan. 8, 1955, 9.
18. *Bantu World*, Dec. 18, 1954, 3.
19. *Bantu World*, Dec. 25, 1954, 10.
20. Minutes of monthly general meetings of Helping Hand Club for Native Girls, Jan. 23, 1954, Helping Hand Club for Native Girls Papers, A2052 Ba, Wits Historical Papers.
21. 'After the Ball Was Over', *Golden City Post*, Dec. 11, 1955, 8.
22. 'Social Students Graduate from Jan Hofmeyr School', *Bantu World*, Dec. 17, 1955, 3.
23. This is an estimate based on annual admission rates recorded shortly before Winnie arrived. Jan Hofmeyr School General Committee minutes, Feb. 9, 1949, Rev. Ray Phillips Papers, A1444, Wits Historical Papers Collection.
24. Horwitz, *Baragwanath Hospital Soweto*.
25. June Gill (née Dwolatzky), interviews by author, July 15 and 22, 2019; 'Appointed Social Worker at Baragwanath Hospital', *Bantu World*, Jan. 7, 1956, 6.
26. June Gill (née Dwolatzky), interview by author, July 15, 2019.
27. 'Show Me the Way to Get Home', *Golden City Post*, Jan. 26, 1958, 9.
28. Julian Riekert, email to author, Feb. 17, 2019.
29. June Gill (née Dwolatzky), interview by author, July 15, 2019.

CHAPTER 19

1. Barbara Masekela, interview by author, Oct. 18, 2018.
2. Nonyaniso Madikizela, interview by author, Oct. 18, 2018.
3. Prince Madikizela, interview by author, June 1, 2018.
4. Winnie Madikizela-Mandela, interviewed in *Mandela: Son of Africa, Father of a Nation*.
5. Winnie Mandela, interview by Peter Davis, 1984, Villon Film Archives, www .villonfilms.ca.
6. Barbara Harmel, email to author, June 14, 2018; Ahmed Kathrada, interview by Anna Trapido, Oct. 8, 2007, NMAP 2009/15, Nelson Mandela Centre of Memory.
7. Winnie Mandela, interview by Davis, 1984.
8. *LWF*, 216.
9. Much of this account of the wedding is drawn from Fatima Meer's detailed description of it in *HTH*, 119–26.

CHAPTER 20

1. Nelson Mandela to Zindzi Mandela, Dec. 9, 1979, in *PLNM*, 391.
2. Winnie Madikizela-Mandela, interview by Anna Trapido, Dec. 6, 2007, NMAP 2009/15, Nelson Mandela Centre of Memory.

3.   Winnie Madikizela-Mandela, interview by Anthony Sampson, Oct. 22, 1996, ASP, Dep. 169.
4.   *HTH*, 127.
5.   Madikizela-Mandela, interview by Trapido, Dec. 6, 2007.
6.   *LWF*, 221.
7.   *HTH*, 129.
8.   Madikizela-Mandela, interview by Trapido, Dec. 6, 2007.
9.   Barbara Harmel, interview by author, May 25, 2018.
10.   Ben and Mary Turok, interview by author, July 8, 2018.
11.   Leon and Lorna Levy, interview by author, July 7, 2018.
12.   Among those on the Joint Committee of the then Children's Aid Society when it was founded in 1932 were Mr. and Mrs. J. D. Rheinallt Jones, A. B. Xuma, and the legendary Charlotte Maxeke. 'Founding Documents', Johannesburg Child Welfare Society Archive, Johannesburg.
13.   Nobantu Mniki, interview by author, July 11, 2018.

CHAPTER 21
1.   'Transvaal Africanist Cut Loose', *Drum*, Dec. 1958, 26–31.
2.   Albert Luthuli, 'If I Were Prime Minister', *Drum*, Dec. 1961, 31–37.
3.   Robert Sobukwe, Opening address to the PAC Inaugural Convention, in Karis and Carter, *From Protest to Challenge*, 3:542–48.
4.   Glaser, *Bo-Tsotsi*, 84–86; Gerhart, *Black Power in South Africa*, 223–24.
5.   Cited in Lodge, *Black Politics in South Africa Since 1945*, 201.
6.   Michael Harmel, 'Revolutions Are Not Abnormal', *Africa South*, Jan.–March 1959.
7.   Gerhart, *Black Power in South Africa*, 234; Lodge, *Black Politics in South Africa Since 1945*, 203.
8.   Frankel, *Ordinary Atrocity*; Lodge, *Sharpeville*.
9.   See, for example, Coetzee, *Youth*.
10.   Adelaide Tambo, interview by John Carlin, circa 1999.
11.   Giliomee, *Afrikaners*, 523–24; Kenney, *Verwoerd*, 195.
12.   Pogrund, *War of Words*, 84.
13.   Pogrund, *How Can Man Die Better*, 153.
14.   Lewis Nkosi, 'Robert Sobukwe: An Assessment', *Africa Report* 7, no. 4 (April 1962): 7–9.
15.   UPM, 365.
16.   Pogrund, *How Can Man Die Better*, 164–76.
17.   Leon Levy, interview by author, July 7, 2018.

CHAPTER 22
1.   *HTH*, 150.
2.   Winnie Madikizela-Mandela, interview by Anna Trapido, Dec. 6, 2007.
3.   Pogrund, *War of Words*, 76.
4.   Winnie Mandela, *Part of My Soul Went with Him*, 60.
5.   *HTH*, 150.
6.   *LWF*, 255.

CHAPTER 23
1.   Sampson, *Mandela*, 140.
2.   Walter Sisulu, *I Will Go Singing*, 117.
3.   Lodge, *Black Politics in South Africa Since 1945*, 233.
4.   Hyslop, 'Mandela on War', 162–81.

5.   Sampson, *Mandela*, 141.
6.   *LWF*, 256.
7.   'A New and Powerful Call for Unity', *Drum*, May 1961, 56.
8.   'Banned Political Parties Unite in New South Africa Coalition', *New York Times*, March 27, 1961, 4.
9.   'New and Powerful Call for Unity', 57.
10.   *LWF*, 232.
11.   Winnie Mandela, interview by Peter Davis, 1984, Villon Film Archives, www .villonfilms.ca.
12.   Pogrund, *War of Words*, 96.
13.   'End-of-May Plans Speed Up', *Golden City Post*, May 21, 1961, 2.
14.   Soske, *Internal Frontiers*, 169.
15.   'African "Action Council" Wants Talks', *World*, May 13, 1961, 1.

CHAPTER 24
1.   Walter Sisulu, *I Will Go Singing*, 119.
2.   Nelson Mandela, interview by Brian Widlake, *Roving Report*, ITN, 1961, www .youtube.com.
3.   For a debate on Luthuli's position on nonviolence, see Couper, *Albert Luthuli*; Suttner, 'Road to Freedom Is via the Cross'; Couper, 'Emasculating Agency'; Vinson and Carton, 'Albert Luthuli's Private Struggle'.
4.   *LWF*, 322.
5.   Principally, Stephen Ellis. See his 'Genesis of Armed Struggle in South Africa, 1948–61'.
6.   Hepple, *Young Man with a Red Tie*, 106.
7.   For firsthand accounts of those who attended at least one of these two meetings, see Meer, *Fortunate Man*; Bernstein, *Memory Against Forgetting*, 271–74.
8.   For a measured and interesting counterfactual, see Dubow, 'Were There Political Alternatives in the Wake of the Sharpeville-Langa Violence in South Africa, 1960?'
9.   For an opposing view, see Suttner, *ANC Underground in South Africa*.
10.   Kodesh, interview by John Carlin, circa 1999, www.pbs.org.
11.   Lorna Levy, interview by author, July 7, 2018.
12.   CRS, CD 45/64, April 9, 1993.
13.   Kodesh, interview by Carlin, circa 1999.
14.   CRS, CD 45/64, April 9, 1993.
15.   Ibid.
16.   The man's name was Vivian Ezra. Glenn Frankel, *Rivonia's Children*, 70–71.
17.   UPM, 418–19.
18.   Mac Maharaj, interview by author, March 12, 2019.
19.   Kodesh, interview by Carlin, circa 1999.
20.   'Victory for African Builders' Union', *New Age*, Oct. 24, 1957, 3.
21.   Meredith, *Mandela*, 127.
22.   Winnie Madikizela-Mandela, interview by Anna Trapido, Dec. 6, 2007, NMAP 2009/15, Nelson Mandela Centre of Memory.
23.   Winnie Madikizela-Mandela, interview in *The Trials of Winnie Mandela*, forthcoming, African Oral History Archive.
24.   Amina Cachalia, interview by John Carlin, circa 1999, PBS *Frontline*.

CHAPTER 25
1.   Kodesh, interview by John Carlin, circa 1999, PBS *Frontline*.
2.   Sampson, *Mandela*, 153–54.

3.   Lodge, *Mandela*, 93.
4.   Bernstein, *Memory Against Forgetting*, 211.
5.   Ibid., 209.
6.   Pogrund, *War of Words*, 100–101.
7.   Bernstein, *Memory Against Forgetting*, 212–13.
8.   UPM, 428.
9.   *LWF*, 299.
10.   CRS, Tape 17, April 13 and 15, 1993.
11.   UPM, 429.
12.   Neville Alexander, interview by John Carlin, circa 1999, PBS *Frontline*; Mac Maharaj, interview by author, March 12, 2019.
13.   *LWF*, 298.
14.   CRS, CD 45/64, April 9, 1993.
15.   *LWF*, 290.
16.   CRS, Tape 17, April 13 and 15, 1993.
17.   Ibid.
18.   Sampson, *Mandela*, 169.
19.   Maharaj, interview by author, Dec. 18, 2018.
20.   Sampson, *Mandela*, 170.
21.   Rivonia Trial, file 1641, South African National Archives, Pretoria.
22.   Kasrils, *Armed and Dangerous*, 62.
23.   Sampson, *Mandela*, 171.
24.   *LWF*, 314.
25.   Ibid., 315.
26.   Antony Sampson in conversation with Dennis Goldberg, Dec. 13, 1996, ASP, Dep. 168.
27.   Kodesh, interview by Carlin, circa 1999, PBS *Frontline*.
28.   'A Loophole in U.S. Sanctions Against Pretoria', *New York Times*, Oct. 13, 1986, A18.

CHAPTER 26
1.   Kodesh, interview by John Carlin, circa 1999, PBS *Frontline*.
2.   CRS, Tape 18, April 16, 1993.
3.   Kodesh, interview by Carlin, circa 1999.
4.   CRS, Tape 18, April 16, 1993.
5.   'Police Check Rand Protest Marchers in Tribal Dress', *Rand Daily Mail*, Aug. 18, 1962.
6.   'Vorster Bans All Mandela Meetings for Two Days', *Star*, Oct. 13, 1962.
7.   CRS, Tape 18, April 16, 1993.
8.   'Nelson Mandela's First Court Statement – 1962', O'Malley: The Heart of Hope, Nelson Mandela Foundation, omalley.nelsonmandela.org.
9.   *LWF*, 333.
10.   Ibid., 317.
11.   'No Surrender, Mandela Says', *World*, July 1, 1961.
12.   'Readers' Letters', *Golden City Post*, Nov. 5, 1962, 5.
13.   Luthuli, 'Road to Freedom Is via the Cross', 141.
14.   Albert Luthuli, 'What June 26th Means to African People', *New Age*, June 27, 1957.

CHAPTER 27
1.   'The Two-Year Shock!', *Golden City Post*, Aug. 12, 1962, 1.
2.   Nathaniel Nakasa, 'My Man', *Drum*, Sept. 1962, 69.

3.   'Drama of Two Leaders' Wives', *Drum*, Dec. 1962, 35–37.
4.   'Winnie Mandela Trial', *World*, Sept. 30, 1963, 1.
5.   Cited in Nelson Mandela to Winnie Mandela, June 23, 1969, in *PLNM*, 98.
6.   Madikizela-Mandela, *491 Days*, 60.

CHAPTER 28
1.   Bernstein, *Memory Against Forgetting*, 231.
2.   Slovo, interview by Anthony Sampson, April 20, 1994, ASP, Dep. 168.
3.   Broun, *Saving Nelson Mandela*.
4.   'This Is Banned', *Golden City Post*, April 19, 1964.
5.   'The Long, Long Looks', *Golden City Post*, April 26, 1964.
6.   Nelson Mandela, Statement from the dock, April 20, 1964, *State v. Nelson Mandela and Others*, db.nelsonmandela.org.
7.   Bizos, interview by John Carlin, circa 1999, PBS *Frontline*.
8.   *LWF*, 368.
9.   Walter Sisulu, *I Will Go Singing*, 5.
10.   Ibid., 127.
11.   Clingman, *Bram Fischer*, 320.
12.   E. S. Reddy, 'Resolution of the United Nations General Assembly on the Rivonia Trial, 11 October 1963', www.sahistory.org.za.
13.   'Text of the UN Council's Resolution on South Africa', *New York Times*, June 10, 1964.
14.   Aggrey Klaaste, 'I'll Never Forget Rivonia', *Drum*, July 1964, 54.
15.   'Absent – but Guests Drink to Mandela', *World*, June 29, 1964, 12.

CHAPTER 29
1.   Hennie Heymans, interview by author, May 2, 2020.
2.   Slovo, 'The sabotage campaign', 24.
3.   Coleman, *Crime Against Humanity*, 47, 53, 56.
4.   Glenn Frankel, *Rivonia's Children*, 102.
5.   Roseinnes Phahle, 'Reminiscences of the Arrest of Fikile Bam and Marcus Solomon', South African History Online, Aug. 2019, www.sahistory.org.za.
6.   Ibid.
7.   Brigalia Bam, interview by author, June 22, 2020.
8.   Solomon, interview by author, July 8, 2020.
9.   Phahle, 'Reminiscences of the Arrest of Fikile Bam and Marcus Solomon'.
10.   Bernstein made this remark while interviewing Ray Alexander. Alexander, interview by Bernstein, n.d., Oral History of Exiles, MCA7, Transcripts, vol. 15, Robben Island Mayibuye Archives, University of the Western Cape.
11.   'Mrs. Winnie Mandela Accused of Adultery', *Rand Daily Mail*, March 10, 1965, 12.
12.   Barbara Harmel, interview by author, May 15, 2018.
13.   Alexander, interview by Bernstein, n.d., Oral History of Exiles, MCA7, Transcripts, vol. 15, Robben Island Mayibuye Archives.
14.   Barbara Harmel, interview by author, May 15, 2018.
15.   Phahle, 'Reminiscences of the Arrest of Fikile Bam and Marcus Solomon'.
16.   Ibid.
17.   See 'Shot at Mandela Home – Trial Starts', *World*, Jan. 5, 1965.
18.   'Mrs. Winnie Mandela Accused of Adultery', 12.
19.   'Witness Says He Loved Winnie Mandela', *Rand Daily Mail*, May 26, 1965.
20.   'Ex-detainee Is Cleared in Shooting Charge', *Rand Daily Mail*, May 6, 1965.
21.   'Oscar Somana Not Guilty', *Rand Daily Mail*, May 9, 1965.
22.   'Somanas Make Up, Drop Divorce', *World*, March 10, 1965.

23.   'Somana S.B. Spy, Winnie Says', *Post*, April 11, 1965.
24.   *HTH*, 286.
25.   'Mandela Not Told of Wife's Case', *Rand Daily Mail*, July 14, 1965.

CHAPTER 30

1.   CRS, CD 1/64, Dec. 3–4, 1992.
2.   Ibid.
3.   Sampson, *Mandela*, 181.
4.   Kathrada, *Memoirs*, 201.
5.   CRS, CD 1/64, Dec. 3–4, 1992.
6.   Gregory, *Goodbye Bafana*, 92.
7.   *LWF*, 403.
8.   O'Malley, *Shades of Difference*, 131–32.
9.   Kathrada, *Memoirs*, 12–13.
10.   UPM, 605.
11.   Cited in Buntman, *Robben Island and Prisoner Resistance to Apartheid*, 78–79.
12.   Kathrada, *Memoirs*, 206.
13.   Ibid., 237.
14.   Nelson Mandela to Winnie Mandela, Feb. 17, 1966, in *PLNM*, 31.
15.   Fikile Bam, interview by John Carlin, circa 1999, PBS *Frontline*.
16.   Angus Gibson, interview by author, May 25, 2018; Barbara Hogan, interview by author, Oct. 15, 2018.
17.   Alexander, interview by John Carlin, circa 1999, PBS *Frontline*.
18.   CRS, CD 22/64, March 8–9, 1993.
19.   Nelson Mandela to Winnie Mandela, May 6, 1979, in Winnie Mandela, *Part of My Soul Went with Him*, 137.
20.   'Nelson and Winnie Meet: It's Still Love', *Post*, July 11, 1965.
21.   *LWF*, 424.

CHAPTER 31

1.   'MB's "Experience" of Winnie, Leading to the 1969 Trial', ASP, Dep. 168.
2.   *HTH*, 205.
3.   CRS, April 17, 1993.
4.   I am drawing on Yuri Slezkine's distinction between Apollonian and Mercurian. See his *Jewish Century*.
5.   *LWF*, 322.
6.   *HTH*, 207.
7.   Elinor Sisulu, *Walter and Albertina Sisulu*, 285.
8.   'MB's "Experience" of Winnie, Leading to the 1969 Trial'.
9.   'Memorandum: Conspiracy: Levin/Katzenellenbogen et al., July 1, 1969', Joel Carlson South African Legal Files, box 6, folder 22, New York Public Library.
10.   'Court Told of "Dark-Skinned Frenchman"', *Sunday Times*, Nov. 29, 1963.
11.   'Memorandum: Conspiracy: Levin/Katzenellenbogen et al., July 1, 1969'.
12.   'Indian Jailed for Fraud Is Released by Vorster', *Sunday Times*, Feb. 10, 1963.
13.   Nelson Mandela to Winnie Mandela, April 2, 1969, in *PLNM*, 80.
14.   Mac Maharaj, interview by author, Dec. 18, 2018.
15.   Elinor Sisulu, *Walter and Albertina Sisulu*, 284.
16.   Ibid., 285.
17.   Houston, 'Post-Rivonia ANC/SACP Underground', 605–6.
18.   Elinor Sisulu, *Walter and Albertina Sisulu*, 273.
19.   Ibid., 268.
20.   Houston, 'Post-Rivonia ANC/SACP Underground', 647–48.

21.   Ibid., 652.
22.   Carlson, *No Neutral Ground*, 297–98.
23.   Madikizela-Mandela, *491 Days*, 49.
24.   'Job for Mrs. Mandela if Ban Is Eased', *Rand Daily Mail*, Feb. 23, 1965.
25.   'Winnie Told to Quit Her New Job', *Rand Daily Mail*, March 1, 1966.
26.   Ffrench-Beytagh, *Encountering Darkness*, 151–67.
27.   Carlson, *No Neutral Ground*, 265.
28.   'Son of Kei Minister in Court', *Rand Daily Mail*, Aug. 10, 1967.
29.   Nonyaniso Madikizela, interview by author, Oct. 15, 2018.
30.   Carlson, *No Neutral Ground*, 313.
31.   Shanti Naidoo, interview by author, March 8, 2020.
32.   Winnie Mandela, *Part of My Soul Went with Him*, 89.
33.   See, for instance, Nelson Mandela to Adelaide Tambo, Jan. 31, 1970, in *PLNM*, 155.
34.   *HTH*, 117.
35.   Sikhakhane, interview by author, July 9, 2018.
36.   Mac Maharaj, interview by author, Dec. 18, 2018.
37.   Sampson, *Mandela*, 256.
38.   Memorandum, n.d., Directorate of Security Legislation, Department of Justice, South African National Archives.

CHAPTER 32

1.   Gregory, *Goodbye Bafana*, 138–39.
2.   Nelson Mandela to Chief K. D. Matanzima, Oct. 14, 1968, in *PLNM*, 58.
3.   Maharaj, interview by author, Dec. 18, 2018.
4.   Nelson Mandela to Irene Buthelezi, Aug. 3, 1969, in *PLNM*, 121.
5.   Nelson Mandela to Knowledge Guzana, Oct. 14, 1968, in *PLNM*, 60.
6.   Nelson Mandela to Chief Mthetho Matanzima, March 17, 1969, in *PLNM*, 75–77.
7.   Nelson Mandela to Makaziwe Mandela, Feb. 16, 1969, in *PLNM*, 65–67.
8.   Nelson Mandela to Douglas Lukhele, Aug. 1, 1970, in *PLNM*, 185.
9.   Nelson Mandela to Makgatho Mandela, March 31, 1970, in *PLNM*, 162.
10.   Ibid., 162, 163.
11.   Nelson Mandela to Makaziwe Mandela, Feb. 16, 1969, in *PLNM*, 65–67.
12.   Nelson Mandela to Winnie Mandela, April 2, 1969, in *PLNM*, 80.
13.   Bam, interview by John Carlin, circa 1999, PBS *Frontline*.

CHAPTER 33

1.   For the full text of the Terrorism Act, see en.wikisource.org/wiki/Terrorism _Act,_1967.
2.   'Silent Arrests', *Rand Daily Mail*, May 20, 1969.
3.   Affidavits of Amelia Sikakane, Rosemary Arnold, and Christiane Duval, Joel Carlson South African Legal Files, box 6, folder 22, New York Public Library.
4.   'MB's "Experience" of Winnie, Leading to the 1969 Trial', ASP, Dep. 168.
5.   Nelson Mandela to Niki Xaba, July 15, 1969, in *PLNM*, 102.
6.   CRS, April 17, 1993; Carlson, *No Neutral Ground*, 267.
7.   Nelson Mandela to Winnie Mandela, Aug. 5, 1969, in Madikizela-Mandela, *491 Days*, 125–26.
8.   'Winnie Mandela Well, Say Police', *Rand Daily Mail*, June 17, 1969.
9.   International Defence and Aid Fund, *South Africa: Trial by Torture – the Case of the 22* (London: IDAF, 1970), 34.
10.   Ibid., 24.
11.   Ibid., 24, 25, 33.
12.   Sikhakhane, interview by author, July 9, 2018.

13. International Defence and Aid Fund, *South Africa: Trial by Torture*, 26.
14. Hennie Heymans, interview by author, May 2, 2020.
15. Carlson, *No Neutral Ground*, 186.
16. O'Malley, *Shades of Difference*, 122–26.
17. Ibid., 126.
18. International Defence and Aid Fund, *South Africa: Trial by Torture*, 26.
19. Winnie Mandela, interview by Peter Davis, 1984, Villon Film Archives, www .villonfilms.ca.
20. Carlson, *No Neutral Ground*, 292.
21. 'Winnie Mandela Well, Say Police'.
22. Carlson, *No Neutral Ground*, 294.
23. 'Memorandum: Conspiracy: Levin/Katzenellenbogen et al., July 1, 1969', Joel Carlson South African Legal Files, box 6, folder 22; 'MB's "Experience" of Winnie, Leading to the 1969 Trial'.
24. Winnie Mandela to Levin, Nov. 11, 1969, in Madikizela-Mandela, *491 Days*, 133.
25. Carlson, *No Neutral Ground*, 295.

CHAPTER 34

1. Nelson Mandela to Tellie Mtirara, July 15, 1969, in *PLNM*, 104.
2. Nelson Mandela to Zenani and Zindzi Mandela, June 23, 1969, in *PLNM*, 95.
3. Nelson Mandela to Winnie Mandela, June 26, 1969, in *PLNM*, 99.
4. Nelson Mandela to Winnie Mandela, Aug. 1, 1970, in *PLNM*, 182.
5. Nelson Mandela to Irene Buthelezi, Aug. 3, 1969, in *PLNM*, 121.
6. *LWF*, 447.
7. Nelson Mandela to Winnie Mandela, July 16, 1969, in *PLNM*, 107.
8. Nelson Mandela to Winnie Mandela, July 1, 1970, in *PLNM*, 179.
9. Nelson Mandela to Winnie Mandela, Nov. 16, 1969, in *PLNM*, 134–41.
10. Nelson Mandela to Winnie Mandela, June 20, 1970, in *PLNM*, 175–76.
11. Nelson Mandela to Winnie Mandela, Aug. 1, 1970, in *PLNM*, 181–83.
12. International Defence and Aid Fund, *South Africa: Trial by Torture*, 9.
13. Carlson, *No Neutral Ground*, 324–25.
14. Madikizela-Mandela, *491 Days*, 23, 25.
15. Ibid., 25–26.
16. Ibid., 28.
17. Ibid., 181–82.
18. Nelson Mandela to Winnie Mandela, Oct. 1, 1970, in *PLNM*, 197.
19. Murphy Morobe, interview by author, Nov. 7, 2019.
20. Southern African News Agency, Information Service Document Number 2, Jan. 1976, Eric Abraham private archive.

CHAPTER 35

1. Mkhabela, *Open Earth and Black Roses*, 52.
2. Dubow, *Apartheid*, 326n84.
3. Murphy Morobe, testimony to the Truth and Reconciliation Commission, July 23, 1996, www.justice.gov.za.
4. Ibid.
5. Hirson, *Year of Fire, Year of Ash*, 176.
6. Ibid., 177–78.
7. Biko, *I Write What I Like*, 144.
8. Ibid., 152.
9. Biko, interview by Gail Gerhart, Oct. 24, 1972, Karis-Gerhart Collection, www .aluka.org. For an intellectual history of Black Consciousness, see Magaziner, *The Law and the Prophets*.

10.   Morobe, testimony to the Truth and Reconciliation Commission, July 23, 1996.
11.   The photograph was taken by the journalist Sam Nzima.
12.   Dan Montsitsi, testimony to the Truth and Reconciliation Commission, July 22, 1997, www.justice.gov.za.
13.   'Bra X', interview by author, March 27, 2007.
14.   Brooks and Brickhill, *Whirlwind Before the Storm*, 11.
15.   Biko, *I Write What I Like*, 145.
16.   Ngubane, 'Politics of Death in Soweto'.

CHAPTER 36
1.   *Rand Daily Mail*, May 11, 1972.
2.   Alexander and Mngxitama, 'Interview with Deborah Matshoba', 275.
3.   Morobe, interview by author, Nov. 7, 2019.
4.   Sexwale, interview by John Carlin, circa 1999, PBS *Frontline*.
5.   Winnie Madikizela-Mandela, interview by Anthony Sampson, ASP, Dep. 169.
6.   Sampson, *Mandela*, 269.
7.   Gevisser, *Thabo Mbeki*, 343.
8.   ANCL 2/36/28, Mbeki and Dhlomo to NEC, June 14, 1975, ANC Archive, Fort Hare University.
9.   Nelson Mandela to Winnie Mandela, Dec. 28, 1970, in *PLNM*, 207.
10.   Ilona Tipp, interview by author, June 8, 2018.
11.   'Bid to Strangle Winnie', *Rand Daily Mail*, Nov. 20, 1972.
12.   Horst Kleinschmidt, 'Newsletter 21: A Foot Soldier Remembers the Mandela Family', Dec. 2013, www.horstkleinschmidt.co.za.
13.   'Jobs Wait for Winnie and Peter', *Rand Daily Mail*, Oct. 2, 1974.
14.   'Banned Couple Met in City, State Alleges', *Rand Daily Mail*, Nov. 15, 1972.
15.   Kleinschmidt, 'Foot Soldier Remembers the Mandela Family'.
16.   Inperking: Winnie Mandela, file 10/3/2/1-1501, Aug. 21, 1975, Directorate of Security Legislation, South African National Archives, Pretoria.
17.   'Big Durban Welcome for Winnie Mandela', *Rand Daily Mail*, Oct. 13, 1975.
18.   Manas Buthelezi, speech, Durban, Oct. 12, 1975, Horst Kleinschmidt private archive.
19.   Peta Thornycroft, interview by author, May 12, 2020.
20.   Tipp, interview by author, June 8, 2018.
21.   Mashabela, *People on the Boil*, 21.
22.   Winnie Mandela, 'Speech Delivered at the Launch of the Black Parents' Association', Kleinschmidt private archive.
23.   '"I Failed", BPA Man Told Police', *Rand Daily Mail*, Sept. 15, 1976.
24.   Douglas Ramaphosa, interview by Hilda Bernstein, circa 1989, Oral History of Exiles, MCA7, Transcripts, vol. 13, Robben Island Mayibuye Archives, University of the Western Cape.
25.   'Winnie Fears for Home and Family', *Rand Daily Mail*, Aug. 16, 1976.
26.   Nelson Mandela to Winnie Mandela, Sept. 1, 1976, in *PLNM*, 324–25.
27.   'We Lied Under Pressure, Say Two', *Rand Daily Mail*, March 16, 1977. See also Pohlandt-McCormick, 'Controlling Women'.
28.   Hennie Heymans, interview by author, May 2, 2020.

CHAPTER 37
1.   Nelson Mandela to Meer, March 1, 1971, in *PLNM*, 229.
2.   Sampson, *Mandela*, 276.
3.   Vumile Gladstone Matthews, interview by Fran Buntman, May 14, 1996, Barbara and John Buntman Robben Island Interview Archive.

4.   Ahmed Kathrada, interviews by Fran Buntman, July 18 and Oct. 31, 1994, Buntman Robben Island Interview Archive.

5.   Eric Molobi, interview by Fran Buntman, May 30, 1996, Buntman Robben Island Interview Archive.

6.   Murphy Morobe, interview by Fran Buntman, Nov. 17 and Dec. 1, 1994, Buntman Robben Island Interview Archive.

7.   Cooper, 'Psychological Impact of Political Imprisonment and the Role of the Psychologist', 141.

8.   Kathrada, interviews by Buntman, July 18 and Oct. 31, 1994, Buntman Robben Island Interview Archive.

9.   Sampson, *Mandela*, 280.

10.   Kgalema Motlanthe, interview by Fran Buntman, Dec. 5 and 7, 1994, Buntman Robben Island Interview Archive.

11.   *LWF*, 577.

12.   Sampson, *Mandela*, 283.

13.   Ibid., 203–4.

14.   Buntman, *Robben Island and Prisoner Resistance to Apartheid*, 5.

15.   Bundy, *Govan Mbeki*, 127.

16.   'Operation Mayibuye', *State v. Nelson Mandela and Nine Others*, Wits Historical Papers, AD 1844, www.historicalpapers.wits.ac.za.

17.   Bundy, *Govan Mbeki*, 116.

18.   Ibid., 129.

19.   O'Malley, *Shades of Difference*, 177–79.

20.   Kathrada, interview by Fran Buntman, July 18, 1994; Mac Maharaj, interview by author, Sept. 1, 2020.

21.   Sampson, *Mandela*, 288–89.

22.   Colin Bundy, introduction to *Learning from Robben Island*, by Mbeki.

23.   Mac Maharaj, interview by author, Dec. 18, 2018.

24.   Anti-apartheid Movement Workshop, Oxford, 1999, William Beinart private archive.

25.   Sampson, *Mandela*, 286.

26.   Nelson Mandela to Jimmy Kruger, Feb. 12, 1975, in *PLNM*, 282.

27.   Nelson Mandela to Dadoo, Nov. 1, 1975, in *PLNM*, 282–85.

CHAPTER 38

1.   Van der Merwe, interview, June 21, 2017, African Oral History Archive, Johannesburg.

2.   Inperking, Winnie Mandela, April 13, 1977, Directorate of Security Legislation, South African National Archives, Pretoria.

3.   Joseph, *Tomorrow's Sun*.

4.   Badat, *Forgotten People*.

5.   'Winnie – No Details of the Charge', *Rand Daily Mail*, June 4, 1977.

6.   Winnie Mandela, *Part of My Soul Went with Him*, 27–29.

7.   'New Twist on Winnie', *Sunday Post*, Oct. 18, 1980.

8.   'U.S. Top Brass Pose Removal of Winnie', *Rand Daily Mail*, May 19, 1977.

9.   Sampson, *Mandela*, 223.

10.   Dubow, 'New Approaches to High Apartheid and Anti-apartheid', 319.

11.   Gurney, '1970s', 480.

12.   'Mandela Story Wins Award', *Rand Daily Mail*, June 15, 1977.

13.   Allister Sparks, interviewed in *The Long Walk of Nelson Mandela*, www.pbs.org.

14.   Attenborough and Hawkins, *Entirely Up to You, Darling*, 41.

15.   '"Banished" in South Africa, She Vows to Overcome', *New York Times*, March 17, 1981.

16.   Smith to the Prime Minister of South Africa, June 4, 1977, Directorate of Security Legislation, South African National Archives.
17.   *Panorama*, BBC, June 15, 1981.

CHAPTER 39

1.   O'Malley, *Shades of Difference*, 217.
2.   Mike Terry, Anti-apartheid Movement Workshop, Oxford, 1999.
3.   Enuga S. Reddy, South African History Online, www.sahistory.org.za.
4.   Reddy, interview by Lisa Brock, July 20, 2004, www.noeasyvictories.org.
5.   Thorn, 'Meaning(s) of Solidarity'.
6.   Brand, *Doing Life with Mandela*, 74.
7.   'Mandela Gets Formal Greeting from Callaghan', *Daily Dispatch,* July 19, 1978.
8.   Callinicos, *Oliver Tambo*, 197.
9.   Terry, Anti-apartheid Movement Workshop, Oxford, 1999.
10.   'Free Mandela', *Sunday Post,* March 9, 1980.
11.   '"Free Mandela" Petition Launched', *Sunday Post,* March 9, 1980.
12.   '"Free Mandela" Campaign Begins', *Rand Daily Mail,* March 11, 1980.
13.   'Skywersgilde Backs Call to Free Mandela', *Star,* April 19, 1980.
14.   'Free Mandela – Doctors', *Rand Daily Mail,* April 20, 1980.
15.   Allister Sparks, 'Why the Mandela Debate Is So Important', *Rand Daily Mail,* April 19, 1980.
16.   '"Free Mandela" Campaign Reaches UK Climax', *Rand Daily Mail,* April 2, 1981.
17.   Anthony Sampson, Anti-apartheid Movement Workshop, Oxford, 1999.

CHAPTER 40

1.   Nelson Mandela to Winnie Mandela, Dec. 4, 1977, in *PLNM,* 351–52.
2.   Nelson Mandela to Winnie Mandela, Jan. 21, 1979, in *PLNM,* 370.
3.   Nelson Mandela to Zindzi Mandela, Sept. 4, 1977, in Winnie Mandela, *Part of My Soul Went with Him,* 96.
4.   Horst Kleinschmidt to Aziz Pahad, Sept. 15, 1980, Horst Kleinschmidt private archive.
5.   Winnie Mandela to Mary Benson, May 24, 1979, in Winnie Mandela, *Part of My Soul Went with Him,* 44.
6.   Bizana Ngezi, interview by author, Feb. 11, 2019.
7.   Suzanne Hattingh, interview by author, Feb. 21, 2019.
8.   Inperking: Winnie Mandela, MP.5/1 PLEG. 9/15, Feb. 18, 1980, Directorate of Security Legislation, South African National Archives, Pretoria.
9.   Hattingh, interview by author, Feb. 21, 2019.
10.   Winnie Mandela to Benson, May 25, 1979, in Winnie Mandela, *Part of My Soul Went with Him,* 45.
11.   Nelson Mandela to Winnie Mandela, April 26, 1981, in *PLNM,* 415–16.
12.   Joe Veriava, interview by author, July 12, 2018.
13.   Horst Kleinschmidt to Aziz Pahad, Sept. 15, 1980, Kleinschmidt private archive.
14.   'Wysiging van inperkingsbevele: Nomzamo Winnie Mandela', n.d., Directorate of Security Legislation, South African National Archives.
15.   Secretary of Justice to Ismail Ayob and Associates, Aug. 26, 1980; Ismail Ayob to Secretary of Justice, Sept. 15, 1980, Directorate of Security Legislation, South African National Archives.
16.   'Wysiging van inperkingsbevele: Nomzamo Winnie Mandela'.
17.   Winnie Mandela, *Part of My Soul Went with Him,* 27.
18.   Horst Kleinschmidt to Aziz Pahad, Sept. 15, 1980, Kleinschmidt private archive.
19.   For an account of Hani's time in Lesotho, see Macmillan, *Chris Hani,* 73–82.
20.   Prince Madikizela, interview by author, June 1, 2018.

21. Mac Maharaj, interview by author, Dec. 22, 2018.
22. Ivan Pillay, interview by author, April 19, 2021.
23. Sue Rabkin, interview by author, Nov. 6, 2019.
24. Veriava, interview by author, July 12, 2018.
25. 'Winnie's Daughter's Royal Wedding', *Rand Daily Mail*, April 14, 1977.
26. 'Zeni Mandela Gets the Nod', *Rand Daily Mail*, May 12, 1977.
27. 'Zeni's Dad Is Glad', *Rand Daily Mail*, April 22, 1977.
28. Madikizela-Mandela, *491 Days*, 43.
29. Nelson Mandela to Zamila Ayob, June 30, 1987, in Nelson Mandela, *Conversations with Myself*, 212.
30. Nelson Mandela to Zindzi Mandela and Oupa Seakamela, July 24, 1977, in *PLNM*, 347.
31. Winnie Mandela to Horst Kleinschmidt, Dec. 9, 1977, Kleinschmidt private archive.
32. Affidavit of Ronald Garb, *Nomzamo Winnie Mandela v. G. Prinsloo and M. R. Ramolahloane*, Supreme Court of South Africa, Orange Free State Division, Aug. 1977.

CHAPTER 41
1. Nelson Mandela to Winnie Mandela, Jan. 21, 1979, in *PLNM*, 370.
2. Winnie Mandela, *Part of My Soul Went with Him*, 133.

CHAPTER 42
1. Brand, interview by author, Aug. 20, 2020.
2. Brand, *Doing Life with Mandela*, 82.
3. Ibid., 78.
4. Brand, interview by author, Aug. 20, 2020.
5. Brand, *Doing Life with Mandela*, 49.
6. Ibid., 34.
7. Brand, interview by author, Aug. 20, 2020.

CHAPTER 43
1. *LWF*, 509.
2. Chiba, interview by Wolfie Kodesh, April 3, 1995, Oral History of Exiles, MCA 6-258, Robben Island Mayibuye Archives, University of the Western Cape.
3. *LWF*, 513.
4. Sampson, *Mandela*, 324.
5. Kathrada, *Memoirs*, 312.
6. *LWF*, 516.
7. Christo Brand, interview by author, Aug. 20, 2020.
8. Brand, *Doing Life with Mandela*, 114–15.
9. Steinberg, *Number*.
10. Brand, *Doing Life with Mandela*, 126.
11. Ibid., 141.
12. Ibid., 142.
13. Ibid., 133–34.

CHAPTER 44
1. Seegers, *Military in the Making of Modern South Africa*, 163.
2. Frankel, *Pretoria's Praetorians*, 52–53, 64; Henri Boshoff, interview by author, April 4, 2004.
3. Beaufre, *Introduction to Strategy*.
4. Giliomee, *Last Afrikaner Leaders*, 147.
5. Tocqueville, *The Ancient Regime and the Revolution*, 159.

6.   Friedman, *Building Tomorrow Today*; Baskin, *Striking Back.*
7.   Seekings, *UDF*; Van Kessel, *Beyond Our Wildest Dreams.*
8.   Johan van der Merwe, June 21, 2017, African Oral History Archive, Johannesburg.
9.   Feinstein, *Economic History of South Africa*, 200–223.
10. Dubow, *Apartheid*, 210.
11. Tom Lodge, 'Rebellion: The Turning of the Tide', in Lodge and Nasson, *All, Here, and Now*, 65.
12. Rantete, *Third Day of September.*
13. Simpson, 'Umkhonto we Sizwe We Are Waiting for You', 162.
14. Seekings, 'Trailing Behind the Masses'.
15. Marks, *Young Warriors*; Bridger, *Young Women Against Apartheid.*
16. Barrell, 'Conscripts to Their Age', 347.
17. Oliver Tambo, 'Render South Africa Ungovernable!', Jan. 8, 1985, www.sahistory .org.za.
18. Barrell, 'Conscripts to Their Age', 384.

CHAPTER 45
1.   Suzman to Zac de Beer, Sept. 17, 1984, Helen Suzman Papers, Gb3.2.6, Wits Historical Papers.
2.   Meyer and Werner de Waal, interview by author, March 19, 2019.
3.   John Scholtz, interview by author, June 5, 2018.
4.   Seekings, *UDF*, 31.
5.   'Aanvullende memorandum ten opsigte van Winnie Mandela', n.d., Director-ate of Security Legislation, Department of Justice, South African National Archives, Pretoria.
6.   Twala and Seekings, 'Activist Networks and Political Protest in the Free State, 1983–1990,' 769.
7.   Nthatisi, interview by author, Nov. 9, 2020.
8.   Seekings, *UDF*, 41–42.
9.   Ivan Pillay, interview by author, April 19, 2021; Sue Rabkin, interview by author, Nov. 6, 2019; Terence Tryon, interview by author, Nov. 5, 2019.
10. Graham Boynton, 'Winnie Mandela', unpublished essay commissioned by *Vanity Fair*, Nov. 1992.
11. Interview by author, June 19, 2018.
12. Gilbey, *Lady*, 134.
13. Jana, interviewed in *The Trials of Winnie Mandela*, documentary series, African Oral History Archive, Johannesburg.
14. Scholtz, interview by author, June 5, 2018.
15. Boynton, 'Winnie Mandela'.
16. Winnie and Zindzi Mandela, visit to Nelson Mandela, Dec. 10, 1985, CC, PV 357, 1/M1/1-51.
17. Gilbey, *Lady*, 135–36; Boynton, 'Winnie Mandela'.
18. 'Winnie Mandela Defends Her Chastisement of Child', *Rand Daily Mail*, Nov. 17, 1983.
19. Winnie Mandela, interview by Peter Davis, 1984, Villon Film Archives, www .villonfilms.ca.
20. Kol. Coetzee na Pretoria, berignommer 49, Aug. 14, 1985, Directorate of Security Legislation, Department of Justice, South African National Archives.
21. Welkom No 6, 1985/08/29, Brandstigting huis van Winnie Mandela, Director-ate of Security Legislation, Department of Justice, South African National Archives.

22.   Sefako Nyaka, 'The Day Pretoria's Buses Stopped: Thousands Stay Away for Massive Mamelodi Funeral', *Weekly Mail*, Dec. 23, 1985.

23.   'Winnie Mandela, Defying Pretoria, Vows Vengeance', *New York Times*, Dec. 4, 1985.

24.   Winnie Mandela, founding affidavit, *Nomzamo Winnie Mandela v. Minister of Law and Order*, Dec. 26, 1985, Supreme Court of South Africa, Witwatersrand Local Division.

25.   'Kagiso Youths Clash with Police as Winnie Visits', *Star*, Jan. 2, 1986.

26.   'Winnie Mandela Assails Pretoria', *New York Times*, April 6, 1986.

27.   James Myburgh, 'How the Necklace Was Hung Around Winnie's Neck', Politicsweb, April 17, 2018, www.politicsweb.co.za.

28.   Truth and Reconciliation Commission of South Africa Report, vol. 3, 1998, 23, www.justice.gov.za.

29.   Truth and Reconciliation Commission of South Africa, Human Rights Violations hearing, Feb. 4, 1997, Duduza, www.justice.gov.za.

30.   'Winnie Mandela Asserts Black Liberation Is Near', *Washington Post*, April 14, 1986.

31.   '25 Years of Armed Struggle: Army Commissar Chris Hani Speaks', *Sechaba*, Dec. 1986, 18, disa.ukzn.ac.za.

32.   Makhanya, interviewed in *The Trials of Winnie Mandela*.

33.   'Vergadering van die Staatsveiligheidraad in Tuynhuys', May 12, 1986, Directorate of Security Legislation, Department of Justice, South African National Archives.

CHAPTER 46

1.   Rachel, *Walls Come Tumbling Down*, 519.

2.   *LWF*, 516–17.

3.   Rachel, *Walls Come Tumbling Down*, 519.

4.   Ibid., 521.

5.   'Aksies Rakende Mandela', n.d., Directorate of Security Legislation, Department of Justice, South African National Archives, Pretoria.

6.   Denselow, *When the Music's Over*, 188–90.

7.   Shelton, *No Direction Home*, 301–4.

8.   Tony Hollingsworth, Anti-apartheid Movement Workshop, Oxford, 1999.

9.   Giddens, *Modernity and Self-Identity*; Beck, *Reinvention of Politics*.

10.   Alan Brooks, Anti-apartheid Movement Workshop, Oxford, 1999.

11.   Hollingsworth, Anti-apartheid Movement Workshop, Oxford, 1999.

12.   Brooks, Anti-apartheid Movement Workshop, Oxford, 1999.

13.   Denselow, *When the Music's Over*, 276.

14.   Klein, 'Strategies of Struggle', 108.

15.   Minter and Hill, 'Anti-apartheid Solidarity in United States–South Africa Relations'.

16.   Giliomee, *Last Afrikaner Leaders*, 191.

17.   Feinstein, *Economic History of South Africa*, 229.

18.   Giliomee, 'Democratization in South Africa', 90.

19.   'Statement by Nelson Mandela Read on His Behalf by His Daughter Zindzi at a UDF Rally to Celebrate Archbishop Tutu Receiving the Nobel Peace Prize, Jabulani Stadium, Soweto', Feb. 10, 1985, www.mandela.gov.za.

CHAPTER 47

1.   Winnie, Zindzi, and Zenani Mandela, visit to 913, Sept. 11, 1985, CC, 1/M1/1-51.

2.   National Intelligence Service memo, Dec. 9, 1989, CC, 1/M1/1-33.

3.   *LWF*, 524.

4. Sparks, *Tomorrow Is Another Country*, 24.
5. Ibid.
6. *LWF*, 525.
7. Report on 913, Dec. 4, 1985, CC, PV 357, 1/M1/1-51.
8. Gesprek 913 met vier sekerheidsgevangenes, Pollsmoor Prison, Dec. 3, 1985, CC, PV 357, 1/M1/1-51.

CHAPTER 48
1. Nelson Mandela to Matthews, Feb. 25, 1987, in *PLNM*, 492.
2. Gambetta, *Were They Pushed or Did They Jump?*; Mandler, *Crisis of the Meritocracy*.
3. Nelson Mandela to Makgatho Mandela, March 31, 1970, in *PLNM*, 162, 163.
4. Nandi Mandela, visit to 913, April 16, 1988, CC, PV 357, 1-M1-1-28.
5. The material on Makaziwe, Zenani, Makgatho and Mandla Mandela is all drawn from recordings of family visits to Mandela in prison. See, for instance, Zindzi Mandela visit, April 1, 1984, CC, PV 357, 1/M1/1-51; Winnie visit, Feb. 9, 1986, CC, PV 357, 1/M1/1-51.
6. Zindzi Mandela, *Black As I Am*.
7. Brand, interview by author, Aug. 20, 2020.
8. Brand, interview by author, Sept. 22, 2020.
9. Brand, interview by author, Aug. 20, 2020.
10. Ibid.

CHAPTER 49
1. For a classic statement, see Kalyvas, *Logic of Violence in Civil War*.
2. 'War at the Weekend', *Sowetan*, May 26, 1986.
3. 'Grandma Killed After Home Is Bombed', *Sowetan*, Dec. 1, 1986.
4. '5 Killed as Pupils Fight Soweto Gang', *Star*, March 20, 1986.
5. 'Why Fund Was Launched', *Sowetan*, Feb. 21, 1986.
6. 'Attack Them', *Sowetan*, April 29, 1986.
7. 'Gangs Disrupted Classes, SPCC', *Sowetan*, Jan. 30, 1986.
8. 'Shock and Anger', *Sowetan*, March 7, 1988.
9. Seekings, *UDF*, 176.
10. Winnie Mandela and Ismail Ayob, visit to 913, Dec. 27, 1985, CC, 1/M1/1-51.
11. Barrell, 'Conscripts to Their Age', 429.
12. 'Woman Activist Slashed to Death on Soweto Street', Associated Press, Oct. 19, 1986, apnews.com.
13. Lerothodi Ikaneng, testimony to TRC special hearing; John Carlin, 'Terrorised by "Winnie's Boys"', *Independent*, Sept. 21, 1990.
14. Winnie and Zindzi Mandela, visit to 913, March 8, 1987, CC, PV 357, 1-M1-1-24.
15. Mtutuzeli Matshoba, interview by author, March 13, 2019.
16. Ibid.
17. Winnie and Zindzi Mandela, visit to 913, March 8, 1987, CC, PV 357, 1-M1-1-24.
18. Myburgh, 'How the Necklace Was Hung Around Winnie's Neck'.
19. South Africa, *Truth and Reconciliation Commission of South Africa Report*, 2:560; Gilbey, *Lady*, 164–66; Gift Nthombeni, testimony to the Truth and Reconciliation Commission special hearing on the Mandela United Football Club (hereafter cited as TRC special hearing on Mandela United FC), Dec. 2, 1997, www.justice.gov.za.
20. Elinor Sisulu, *Walter and Albertina Sisulu*, 504.
21. Nicholas Claxton, Winnie Mandela and the Missing Witness, BBC Television, 1997, nicholasclaxton.com.
22. Albertina Sisulu, testimony to TRC special hearing on Mandela United FC, Dec. 1, 1997, www.justice.gov.za.

23. Alan Reynolds, interview by author, March 18, 2019.
24. Gregory Nthatisi, interview by author, Nov. 9, 2020.
25. Barrell, 'Conscripts to Their Age', 440.
26. Rueedi, 'Our Bushes Are Houses'.
27. Barrell, 'Conscripts to Their Age', 440.
28. Martin Sehlapelo, interview by author, Feb. 26, 2021.
29. This account of what happened that evening is drawn from the following
    sources: Lerothodi Ikaneng, testimony to TRC special hearing on Mandela
    United FC, Dec. 2, 1997, www.justice.gov.za; and the respective testimonies
    of Collin Dlamini, Aaron Makhunga, and Faith Mokhaula in *State v. Oupa
    Alex Seheri and Others,* Rand Supreme Court, Johannesburg, Nov. 1988, South
    Gauteng High Court Archives. Seheri and his girlfriend were convicted of
    murder. Buthelezi was found guilty of illegal possession of a firearm and jailed.

CHAPTER 50

1. Winnie and Zindzi Mandela, visit to 913, March 8, 1987, CC, PV 357, 1-M1-1-24.
2. Ibid.
3. Winnie and Nandi Mandela, visit to 913, April 4, 1987, CC, PV 357, 1-M1-1-24.
4. Christo Brand, interview by author, Sept. 22, 2020.
5. Winnie and Zindzi Mandela, visit to 913, March 8, 1987, CC, PV 357, 1-M1-1-24.
6. Winnie, Zindzi, Mandla, and Gaddafi Mandela, visit to 913, Aug. 30, 1987, CC, 1/
   M1/1-24.
7. Jana, visit to 913, Dec. 15, 1987, CC, PV 357, 1/M1/1-54.
8. Winnie Mandela, visit to 913, Feb. 16, 1988, CC, PV 357, 1/M1/1-28.

CHAPTER 51

1. *LWF,* 526.
2. Barnard and Wiese, *Secret Revolution,* 255; *LWF,* 533.
3. *LWF,* 535.
4. Ibid., 535–36.
5. O'Malley, *Shades of Difference,* 300–309.
6. Barnard and Wiese, *Secret Revolution,* 243.
7. Brand, *Doing Life with Mandela,* 170–71.
8. *LWF,* 525–26.
9. Read and Shapiro, 'Transforming Power Relationships'.
10. National Intelligence Service memo, Dec. 9, 1989, CC, 1/M1/1-33.
11. Read and Shapiro, 'Transforming Power Relationships'.
12. National Intelligence Service memo, Dec. 9, 1989, CC, 1/M1/1-33.

CHAPTER 52

1. Tlhabi, *Endings & Beginnings,* 39–40.
2. Gift Nthombeni, testimony to TRC special hearing on Mandela United FC,
   Dec. 2, 1997, sabctrc.saha.org.za; Lerothodi Ikaneng, testimony to TRC special
   hearing on Mandela United FC.
3. Sehlapelo, interview by author, Feb. 26, 2021.
4. On askaris, see Dlamini, *Askari;* on Eugene de Kock, see Gobodo-Madikizela,
   Human Being Died That Night.
5. Sehlapelo, interview by author, Feb. 26, 2021.
6. Nkadimeng, testimony to TRC special hearing on Mandela United FC, Nov.
   28, 1997, sabctrc.saha.org.za.
7. Ibid.
8. Nkadimeng, interview by author, Feb. 19, 2021.

9.   Daniel Bosman, testimony to TRC special hearing on Mandela United FC, Jan. 28, 1998, www.justice.gov.za.
10. Jan Potgieter, testimony to TRC special hearing on Mandela United FC, Jan. 29, 1998, www.justice.gov.za.
11. Nicodemus Sono, testimony to TRC special hearing on Mandela United FC, Nov. 24, 1997, sabctrc.saha.org.za.
12. 'Bodies Exhumed in Killings Tied to Winnie Mandela', Grio, March 12, 2013, thegrio.com.
13. Nomsa Tshabalala, testimony to TRC special hearing on Mandela United FC, Nov. 24, 1997, sabctrc.saha.org.za.

CHAPTER 53

1.   Brand, Doing Life with Mandela, 158.
2.   Ibid., 176.
3.   Winnie Mandela, Zindzi Mandela, and Zindzi's child, visit to 913, Aug. 3, 1988, CC, 1/M1/1-28.
4.   LWF, 540.
5.   Mathiane, Beyond the Headlines, 58.
6.   Winnie Mandela, Zindzi Mandela, and Zindzi's child, visit to 913, Aug. 3, 1988, CC, 1/M1/1-28.
7.   Zenani and Muzi Dlamini and Robert Brown, visit to 913, May 8, 1987, CC, 1/M1/1-24.
8.   LWF, 541.
9.   Brand, Doing Life with Mandela, 184.
10. Barnard and Wiese, Secret Revolution, 175.
11. Ibid., 196.
12. Ibid., 198.
13. Elinor Sisulu, Walter and Albertina Sisulu, 487.
14. Barnard and Wiese, Secret Revolution, 221.
15. Winnie Madikizela-Mandela, in The Trials of Winnie Mandela, African Oral History Archive, Johannesburg.

CHAPTER 54

1.   Verryn, interview by author, Nov. 8, 2019.
2.   Mono, testimony to TRC special hearing on Mandela United FC, Nov. 26, 1997, www.justice.gov.za.
3.   Ibid.; Richardson, testimony to TRC, Mekgwe, testimony to TRC, Falati, testimony to TRC, www.justice.gov.za; testimonies of Mekgwe and Mono, State v. JVM Richardson and Others, Rand Supreme Court, case 184/89, Gauteng High Court Archive.
4.   Testimony of Kgase in State v. John Morgan and Three Others, case 167/90, Rand Supreme Court, Gauteng High Court Archive.
5.   Ruth Rice, interview by author, March 17, 2019.
6.   Mono, testimony to TRC; Richardson, testimony to TRC, Mekgwe, testimony to TRC, Falati, testimony to TRC, www.justice.gov.za; testimonies of Mekgwe and Mono, State v. JVM Richardson and Others, Rand Supreme Court, case 184/89, Gauteng High Court Archive.
7.   Richardson, testimony to TRC special hearing on Mandela United FC, Nov. 26, 1997, www.justice.gov.za.
8.   Mofolo Mohapi, interviews by author, March 15 and 29, 2021.
9.   I am indebted to Matthew Chaskalson for this thought.
10. Interviewed in Winnie Mandela and the Missing Witness, BBC Television, 1997, nicholasclaxton.com.

11.   Johannes Kgobodi Mabotha @Temba, MK name Tladi Tlaubatla, statement, 1989-05-09, Staat teen W. Mandela, docket.

12.   Richardson, testimony to TRC special hearing on Mandela United FC, Nov. 26, 1997, www.justice.gov.za.

13.   Interviewed in 'Winnie Mandela and the Missing Witness'.

14.   Storey, *I Beg to Differ*, 353.

15.   Alan Reynolds, interview by author, March 18, 2019; Jean-Yves Ollivier, interview by author, April 29, 2021.

16.   His bishop, Peter Storey, conducted a close investigation, as did the judges in the trials of Jerry Richardson and Winnie Mandela. See Storey, *I Beg to Differ*, 361–63.

17.   Richardson, testimony to TRC special hearing on Mandela United FC, Nov. 26, 1997.

18.   'Gesamentlike Vergadering: National Working Committee van die African National Congress en lede van die United Democratic Front', South African Police, March 25, 1989.

19.   South Africa, *Truth and Reconciliation Commission of South Africa Report*, 2:566, www.justice.gov.za; Ikaneng, testimony to TRC special hearing on Mandela United FC, Dec. 2, 1997, www.justice.gov.za; Phumlile Dlamini, testimony to TRC special hearing on Mandela United FC, Dec. 1, 1997, sabctrc.saha.org.za.

20.   South Africa, *Truth and Reconciliation Commission of South Africa Report*, 2:568; Richardson, testimony to TRC special hearing on Mandela United FC, Nov. 26, 1997.

CHAPTER 55

1.   Ikaneng, testimony to TRC special hearing on Mandela United FC, Dec. 2, 1997, www.justice.gov.za.

2.   'Soweto Anger at Winnie Team', *Weekly Mail*, Jan. 27, 1989; Storey, *I Beg to Differ*, 358–63.

3.   Soske, 'Life and Death of Abu Baker "Hurley" Asvat'.

4.   Joe Veriava, interview by author, July 12, 2018.

5.   Ibrahim Asvat, testimony to TRC special hearing on Mandela United FC, Dec. 1, 1997, www.justice.gov.za.

6.   'Winnie Claims Sinister Link in Doctor's Killing', *Sunday Times*, Jan. 29, 1989.

7.   Soske, 'Life and Death of Abu Baker "Hurley" Asvat', 353.

8.   John Battersby, 'Winnie Mandela: Focus of Controversy', *Christian Science Monitor*, April 6, 1992.

9.   Patricia Klepp, testimony to TRC special hearing on Mandela United FC, Dec. 2, 1997, www.justice.gov.za.

10.   Joseph du Toit, testimony to TRC special hearing on Mandela United FC, Jan. 28, 1998, www.justice.gov.za.

11.   Gesprek, 89-02-17, Temba—W. Mandela, Staat teen W. Mandela, docket.

12.   Hanif Vally, leading the evidence of Evodia Nkadimeng, TRC special hearing on Mandela United FC, Nov. 28, 1997, www.justice.gov.za.

13.   De Kock, testimony to TRC special hearing on Mandela United FC, Jan. 29, 1998, www.justice.gov.za.

14.   Ibid.

15.   Nkadimeng, interview by author, Feb. 19, 2021.

16.   'Statement by Mass Democratic Movement on Winnie Mandela', Feb. 16, 1989.

17.   Cachalia, interview by author, Nov. 5, 2019.

18.   'ANC Statement on Winnie Mandela and "Mandela Football Club"', Feb. 21, 1989, www.politicsweb.co.za.

19.   'Gesamentlike Vergadering: National Working Committee van die African National Congress en lede van die United Democratic Front', South African Police, March 25, 1989.

CHAPTER 56

1.   Winnie Mandela, visit to 913, Jan. 18, 1989, CC, PV 357, 1/M1/1-38.
2.   Nelson Mandela to Winnie Mandela, Feb. 16, 1989, CC, PV 357, 1/M1/1-39.
3.   Simons, visit to 913, CC, PV 357, 1/M1/1-60.
4.   Winnie and Zindzi Mandela, visit to 913, CC, PV 357, 1/M1/1-38.
5.   Ismail Ayob, visit to 913, April 1, 1989, CC, PV 357 1/M1/1-54.
6.   Priscilla Jana, visit to 913, June 1, 1989, CC, PV 357 1/M1/1-34.
7.   Zenani and Muzi, visit to 913, Aug. 27, 1989, CC, PV 357 1/M1/1-38.
8.   CRS, Tape 18, April 16, 1993.
9.   Barnard and Wiese, *Secret Revolution*, 223.

CHAPTER 57

1.   These preconditions were enshrined in the Harare Declaration, adopted by the Organisation of African Unity on Aug. 21, 1989, omalley.nelsonmandela.org.
2.   Salmon, *Unwinding of Apartheid*, 335.
3.   These passages on Nelson's plans for a simultaneous announcement are drawn from several conversations and phone calls he had during his last six months at Victor Verster, all archived in the Coetsee Collection. Kobie Coetsee, visit to 913, Oct. 6, 1989, 1/M1/1-35; Gerrit Viljoen and Kobie Coetsee, visit to 913, Oct. 10, 1989, 1/M1/1-35; S. S. van der Merwe and Mike Louw, visit to 913, Dec. 5, 1989, 1/M1/1-35; Frank Chikane, visit to 913, Dec. 18, 1989, 1/M1/1-59; 913's telephone conversation with Alfred Nzo and Thabo Mbeki, Dec. 19, 1989, 1/M1/1-36; 913's telephone conversation with Thabo Mbeki, Jan. 17, 1990, 1/M1/1-65; 913's telephone conversation with Thabo Mbeki, Jan. 22, 1990, 1/M1/1-65.
4.   For a record of the British government's surprise, see Salmon, *Unwinding of Apartheid*.
5.   Ibid., 335.
6.   John Carlin, 'Grandmaster or Pawn?', *Independent* (London), Dec. 13, 1989.
7.   Esterhuyse, *Eindstryd*.
8.   Gevisser, *Thabo Mbeki*, 545–47; Spaarwater, *Spook's Progress*.
9.   Barnard and Wiese, *Secret Revolution*, 214–18.
10.   Salmon, *Unwinding of Apartheid*, 386.

CHAPTER 58

1.   Police docket, Orlando WR443-10-88.
2.   Report of the Commission of Inquiry into the Death of Clayton Sizwe Sithole, Feb. 20, 1990, 11.
3.   Ibid., 13.
4.   Both asked to remain anonymous. Author interviews, Nov. 2020.
5.   'Threats, Abuse: Mandela's Wife Interdicted', *Pretoria News,* June 15, 1988.
6.   Oakley-Smith, interview by author, Feb. 25, 2021.
7.   Winnie Mandela, visit to 913, Feb. 4, 1990, CC, 1/M1/1-28, 1/M1/1-38.
8.   'Chronology of Events Around Mandela After His Release Is Made Known to Him', n.d., CC, 1/M1/2-10.
9.   Gregory, *Goodbye Bafana*, 360–61.
10.   'Chronology of Events Around Mandela After His Release Is Made Known to Him'.
11.   Barnard and Wiese, *Secret Revolution*, 298; Trevor Manuel, interview by author, March 14, 2019.

CHAPTER 59

1. Robert D. McFadden, 'Man in the News: An Unwavering Opponent and an Unpredictable Leader of South Africa; Nelson Mandela', *New York Times*, Feb. 12, 1990.
2. '3 Rallies Today for Mandela', *Star*, Feb. 13, 1990.
3. The description of Mandela's arrival in the stadium is drawn from my own memory and from 'Stadium Packed for "Welcome Home" Rally', *Star*, Feb. 14, 1990.
4. Niq Mhlongo, interview by author, Nov. 4, 2019.
5. Nadine Gordimer, 'Nelson Mandela', *New Yorker*, Dec. 16, 2013.
6. Meredith, *Mandela*, 453.
7. I am borrowing from Njabulo Ndebele, who likens Winnie to Penelope in his novel, *The Cry of Winnie Mandela*.
8. The description of the evening draws from several sources: Sally Rowney, interview by Anna Trapido, Nov. 9, 2007, Nelson Mandela Centre of Memory; Jean de la Harpe, interview by author, March 17, 2021; Cachalia, interview by author, June 1, 2021.
9. Cachalia, interview by author, Nov. 5, 2019.
10. Testimony of Teresa Oakley-Smith, June 13, 1991.
11. Manuel, interview by author, March 14, 2019.

CHAPTER 60

1. Albie Sachs, interview by author, Oct. 18, 2018.
2. 'Old Allies Greet Mandela in Zambia', *New York Times*, Feb. 28, 1990.
3. Author interview, Oct. 23, 2018.
4. *LWF*, 571–72.
5. Hugh Macmillan, unpublished memoir.
6. Trevor Manuel, interview by author, March 14, 2019.
7. Salmon, *Unwinding of Apartheid*, 385–86.
8. 'Mandela Gets an Emotional New York City Welcome', *New York Times*, June 21, 1990.
9. Cited in Lodge, *Mandela*, 196.
10. 'Mandela Gets an Emotional New York City Welcome'.
11. Cited in Lodge, *Mandela*, 198.
12. Cited in ibid., 197.
13. *LWF*, 583.
14. 'Wowed by Winnie', *Los Angeles Times*, June 26, 1990.
15. 'Nelson and Winnie Mandela in the Metropolis', *The Village Voice*, July 3, 1990.
16. Archived at the African Oral History Archive, Johannesburg.
17. 'A Town Meeting with Nelson Mandela', *The Koppel Report*, ABC, June 21, 1990, www.youtube.com.
18. Meredith, *Mandela*, 430.
19. Moontlike Inperking/Aanhouding ingevolge die veiligheidsnoodregulasies: Nomzamo Winnie Mandela, Oct. 11, 1988, Directorate for Security Legislation, Department of Justice.
20. Niël Barnard, interview by John Carlin, circa 1999, PBS *Frontline*.
21. 'Hectic Anniversary for Mandelas', *Star*, June 13, 1990.

CHAPTER 61

1. Hogan, interview by author, Oct. 18, 2018.
2. Interview by author, Nov. 2018; 'Is "Caesar's Wife" Hungry for Power?', *Star*, Feb. 21, 1991.

3. Meredith, *Mandela,* 432.
4. Herbstein, *White Lies.*
5. Ibid., 320.
6. Horst Kleinschmidt, interview by author, July 7, 2018; Ilona Tipp, interview by author, June 8, 2018.
7. Kleinschmidt, 'Foot Soldier Remembers the Mandela Family'.
8. Herbstein, *White Lies,* 321.
9. Kleinschmidt, 'Foot Soldier Remembers the Mandela Family'.
10. Herbstein, *White Lies,* 321.
11. Kleinschmidt, 'Foot Soldier Remembers the Mandela Family'.
12. Herbstein, *White Lies,* 321.
13. Masekela, interview by author, Oct. 18, 2018.
14. 'A Town Meeting with Nelson Mandela', *The Koppel Report,* ABC, June 21, 1990, www.youtube.com.
15. Terry Oakley-Smith, interview by author, March 2, 2021.
16. Masekela, interview by author, Oct. 18, 2018.
17. Masekela, interview by author, Dec. 12, 2018.

CHAPTER 62

1. 'Winnie Trial: Warrants for Bail Jumpers', *Star,* Feb. 2, 1991.
2. 'Trio Fled "Using Infiltration Routes"', *Star,* Feb. 23, 1991.
3. 'Winnie Trial: One of the Missing Accused Found', *Star,* May 17, 1991; Hugh MacMillan, email to author, June 4, 2020.
4. Winnie Mandela and the Missing Witness, BBC Television, 1997, nicholas claxton.com.
5. 'ANC Link as Witness Vanishes', *Star,* Feb. 13, 1991.
6. 'Winnie: State Stumped', *Star,* Feb. 14, 1991.
7. 'Winnie Mandela and the Missing Witness'.
8. 'Kaunda Clarifies Statement on Cebekhulu Abduction', SAPA, Sept. 12, 1997.
9. 'ANC Smuggled Out Key Winnie Witness', *Star,* April 12, 1992.
10. Patrick Lawrence, 'Winnie May Be Forced in the Cold', *Star,* April 13, 1992.
11. 'Supporters, Top ANC Leaders, Pack the Courtroom', *Star,* Feb. 5, 1991.
12. *Weekly Mail,* Feb. 8, 1991.
13. John Carlin, 'Winnie Threatens Independent Man', *Independent,* April 13, 1991.
14. 'Winnie's Fan Club Quietly Disappears', *Star,* March 10, 1991.
15. 'Bishop Tells of Soweto Leaders Rescuing Youths', *Daily Telegraph,* March 16, 1991.
16. Gilbey, *Lady,* 270.
17. John Carlin, 'Winnie Mandela's Hold on the Soul of the ANC', *Independent,* Feb. 17, 1991.
18. John Carlin, 'Can Samson Survive Delilah?', *Independent,* May 14, 1991.
19. Interview by author, Oct. 27, 2018.

CHAPTER 63

1. Waldmeir, *Anatomy of a Miracle,* 150; Giliomee, *Last Afrikaner Leaders,* 313.
2. Sparks, *Tomorrow Is Another Country,* 125–26.
3. Dubow, *Apartheid,* 268.
4. Kentridge, *Unofficial War.*
5. For the security forces' relationship with Inkatha in Natal at this time, see De Haas, 'Violence in Natal and Zululand'. For the culture of political intolerance in the ANC in Natal at this time, see the memoir of the trade unionist Johnny Copelyn, *Maverick Insider,* 153–81.

6.   On the violence in Greater Johannesburg in the early 1990s, see Sitas, 'New Tribalism'; Segal, 'Human Face of Violence'; Bonner and Nieftagodien, *Kathorus*; Kynoch, *Township Violence and the End of Apartheid*.
7.   Robert McBride, interview by author, July 17, 2014.
8.   Nelson Mandela to Winnie Mandela, Feb. 16, 1989, CC, PV 357, 1/M1/1-39.
9.   De Kock, *Long Night's Damage*, 235.
10. Kynoch, *Township Violence and the End of Apartheid*, 108.
11. Sparks, *Tomorrow Is Another Country*, 132.
12. Bizos, interview by John Carlin, circa 1999, PBS *Frontline*.
13. Ronnie Kasrils, interviews by author, Dec. 11, 2018, and May 14, 2019.
14. Kasrils, interview by author, May 14, 2019.
15. I am grateful to St. John Haw for this formulation.

CHAPTER 64

1.   Judgment, *State v. Winnie Mandela and Others*, 167/90, Rand Supreme Court, South Gauteng High Court Archives.
2.   Carlin, 'Can Samson Survive Delilah?'
3.   'I Didn't Beat Up Any Child', *Star*, May 14, 1991.
4.   Carlin, 'Can Samson Survive Delilah?'
5.   'Complete Absence of Compassion', *Star*, May 15, 1991.
6.   'Dismay, Glee Greet Winnie's Sentence', *Star*, Feb. 15, 1991.
7.   Shaun Johnson, 'Stoicism in the Mountains', *Star*, May 16, 1991.

CHAPTER 65

1.   Manuel, interview by author, March 14, 2019.
2.   Maharaj, interview by author, Dec. 22, 2018.
3.   Interview by author, June 2020.
4.   Interview by author, Oct. 2018.
5.   Ruth Bhengu, 'Falati Kicked Out of Mandela Home', *Sowetan*, March 30, 1992; Gilbey, *Lady*, 273–75.
6.   John Battersby, 'Winnie Mandela: Focus of Controversy', *Christian Science Monitor*, April 6, 1992.
7.   'Husband's Tribute to "Comrade Nomzamo"', *Star*, April 14, 1992.
8.   Carlin, *Knowing Mandela*, 41.
9.   Interview by author, June 2020.
10. 'I Did It for My People', *Star*, April 16, 1992.
11. 'First Ray of Joy Shines on a Mother', *Star*, April 19, 1992.
12. 'New Shadow over Winnie', *Star*, April 19, 1992.
13. 'Unbowed, Winnie Launches Sharp Attack on Government', *Star*, April 21, 1992.
14. 'Fiery Winnie Fighting Back', *Star*, April 25, 1992.
15. 'Winnie Now "Jockeying for Power"', *Star*, May 23, 1992.
16. Peta Thornycroft, interview by author, May 12, 2020.
17. Copy of original letter in author's possession.
18. Masekela, interview by author, Oct. 18, 2018.
19. Bizos, *65 Years of Friendship*, 209.
20. 'Winnie Resigns from All ANC Positions', *Star*, Sept. 11, 1992.

ENDS

1.   John Battersby, 'The ANC's List of Candidates Contains Some Surprises,' *Christian Science Monitor*, Jan. 24, 1994.
2.   'Mandela Fires Wife from South Africa Cabinet Post', *Los Angeles Times*, March 28, 1995.
3.   Krog, *Country of My Skull*, 258.

4.   Ibid.
5.   Goldin, email correspondence with author, July 22, 2021.
6.   Putuma, *Collective Amnesia*, 103.
7.   Julius Malema, speech delivered at the Oxford Union, Sept. 18, 2016, www
      .youtube.com.
8.   Madikizela-Mandela, *491 Days*, 234–35.
9.   Ibid., 235.
10.   Erasmus, interview by author, May 13, 2020.
11.   Mpo Lakaje, 'Stratcom: What It Actually Was and Means', *Eyewitness News*,
      April 27, 2020, ewn.co.za.
12.   Madikizela-Mandela, interview by Malou von Sivers, Nov. 4, 1999, cited in
      Hassim, 'Life of Refusal'.
13.   Hassim, 'Not Just Nelson's Wife', 909.
14.   'Angry Julius Malema at Winnie Mandela Funeral', April 17, 2018, YouTube,
      www.youtube.com.
15.   Morobe, interview by author, Nov. 7, 2019.
16.   Erasmus, interview by author, May 13, 2020.
17.   Ibid.
18.   Erasmus, interview by author, Jan. 5, 2021.
19.   Pretorius, *Last Wish of Winnie Mandela*, 3.
20.   Rivas, interview by author, May 30, 2018.
21.   Ibid.
22.   Machava, 'Reeducation Camps, Austerity, and the Carceral Regime in Socialist
      Mozambique'.
23.   Newitt, *Short History of Mozambique*, 164.
24.   Ramlakan, *Mandela's Last Years*, 29.
25.   A copy of the document, signed by Mandela and dated Jan. 29, 1996, is in the
      author's possession.

THE COETSEE COLLECTION

1.   Harris, 'They Should Have Destroyed More'.

Bibliography

ARCHIVAL SOURCES

Abraham, Eric. Private collection.

African National Congress Archive. Fort Hare University, Alice.

African Oral History Archive. Ichikowitz Family Foundation, Johannesburg.

Barbara and John Buntman Robben Island Interview Archive. Robben Island Museum.

Beinart, William. Private collection.

Carlson, Joel. South African Legal Files, New York Public Library.

Child Welfare Society Archive, Johannesburg.

Coetsee, H. J. 'Kobie'. Private collection. Archive for Contemporary Affairs, University of the Free State, Bloemfontein.

Directorate for Security Legislation Archive. South African National Archives, Pretoria.

Free Methodist Archive. Marston Memorial Historical Center, Indianapolis.

Helping Hand Club for Native Girls Papers. Wits Historical Papers, Johannesburg.

Karis-Gerhart Collection. www.aluka.org.

Kleinschmidt, Horst. Private collection.

Lilian Masediba Ngoyi Collection. Wits Historical Papers, Johannesburg.

The Long Walk of Nelson Mandela interview archive. PBS *Frontline*, www.pbs.org.

Macmillan, Hugh. Private collection.

Mandela, Nelson. Conversations with Richard Stengel. Nelson Mandela Centre of Memory.

———. Unpublished memoir (1976). Nelson Mandela Centre of Memory.

Methodist Church Archives. Cory Library, Rhodes University, Grahamstown.

Newspapers: *Bantu World, Drum, Gold City Post, New Age, Rand Daily Mail, Sowetan, Star, Sunday Times*. Wits Historical Papers, Johannesburg.

O'Malley Archive. Nelson Mandela Centre of Memory. omalley.nelsonmandela.org.

Oral History of Exiles. Robben Island Mayibuye Archives, University of the Western Cape, Cape Town.

Phillips, Ray. Papers. Wits Historical Papers, Johannesburg.

Sampson, Anthony. Papers. Bodleian Library, Oxford.

Suzman, Helen. Papers. Wits Historical Papers, Johannesburg.

Trapido, Anna. Papers for *Hunger for Freedom*. Nelson Mandela Centre of Memory.

Treason Trial Exhibits. South African National Archives, Pretoria.

Truth and Reconciliation Commission of South Africa Archive.

Villon Film Archives. www.villonfilms.ca.

Xuma, A. B. Papers. Wits Historical Papers, Johannesburg.

DOCUMENTARY FILMS

The Long Walk of Nelson Mandela. Directed by John Carlin. *Frontline*. PBS, 1999. www.pbs.org.

Mandela: Son of Africa, Father of a Nation. Directed by Angus Gibson and Jo Menell. 1996.

Winnie. Directed by Pascale Lamche. 2017.

Winnie Mandela and the Missing Witness. Directed by Nicholas Claxton. BBC Television, 1997. nicholasclaxton.com.

BOOKS AND ARTICLES

Alexander, Jocelyn, and JoAnn McGregor. 'The Travelling Toyi-Toyi: Soldiers and the Politics of the Drill'. *Journal of Southern African Studies* 46, no. 5 (2020): 923–40.

Attenborough, Richard, and Diana Hawkins. *Entirely Up to You, Darling.* London: Arrow, 2008.

Badat, Saleem. *The Forgotten People: Political Banishment Under Apartheid.* Johannesburg: Jacana, 2012.

Bank, Leslie J., and Benedict Carton. 'Forgetting Apartheid: History, Culture, and the Body of a Nun'. *Africa* 86, no. 3 (2016): 472–503.

Barnard, Niël, and Tobie Wiese. *Secret Revolution: Memoirs of a Spy Boss.* Cape Town: Tafelberg, 2015.

Barrell, Howard. 'Conscripts to Their Age: African National Congress Operational Strategy, 1976–1986'. PhD diss., University of Oxford, 1993.

Baskin, Jeremy. *Striking Back: A History of Cosatu.* Johannesburg: Ravan Press, 1991.

Batts, H. J. *History of the Baptist Church in South Africa: The Story of 100 Years, 1820–1920.* Cape Town: T. Maskew Miller, 1922.

Beaufre, André. *An Introduction to Strategy.* London: Faber, 1965.

Beck, Ulrich. *The Reinvention of Politics: Rethinking Modernity in the Global Social Order.* Translated by Mark Ritter. Cambridge, U.K.: Polity Press, 1996.

Beinart, William. *Twentieth-Century South Africa.* 2nd ed. Oxford: Oxford University Press, 2001.

Benneyworth, Garth Conan. 'Trojan Horses: Liliesleaf, Rivonia (August 1962–11 July 1963)'. *Historia* 62, no. 2 (2017): 68–86.

Benson, Mary. *Nelson Mandela: The Man and the Movement.* 1986. New York: Norton, 1994.

Berger, Iris. 'An African American "Mother of the Nation": Madie Hall Xuma in South Africa, 1940–1963'. *Journal of Southern African Studies* 27, no. 3 (2001): 547–66.

———. 'From Ethnography to Social Welfare: Ray Phillips and the Representations of Urban Women in South Africa.' *LFM Social Sciences and Missions* 19 (Dec. 2006): 91–116.

Bernstein, Rusty. *Memory Against Forgetting: Memoirs of a Life in South African Politics.* Johannesburg: Penguin, 1999.

Bezdrob, Annè Marié du Preez. *Winnie Mandela: A Life.* Johannesburg: Penguin, 2003.

Biko, Steve. *I Write What I Like.* London: Heinemann, 1978.

Bizos, George. *Odyssey to Freedom.* Johannesburg: Random House, 2007.

———. *65 Years of Friendship: A Memoir of My Friendship with Nelson Mandela.* Johannesburg: Umuzi, 2017.

Boehmer, Elleke. *Nelson Mandela: A Very Short Introduction.* Oxford: Oxford University Press, 2008.

Bonner, Philip. 'The Antinomies of Nelson Mandela'. In *The Cambridge Companion to Nelson Mandela,* edited by Rita Barnard. Cambridge, U.K.: Cambridge University Press, 2014.

———. 'The Headman, the Regent, and the "Long Walk to Freedom"'. In *Reassessing Mandela,* edited by Colin Bundy and William Beinart, 35–66. Johannesburg: Jacana, 2020.

Bonner, Philip, and Noor Nieftagodien. *Kathorus: A History.* Cape Town: Maskew Miller Longman, 2001.

Bozzoli, Belinda. 'Why Were the 1980s "Millenarian"? Style, Repertoire, Space, and

Authority in South Africa's Black Cities'. *Journal of Historical Sociology* 13, no. 1 (2000): 78–110.

Brand, Christo. *Doing Life with Mandela: My Prisoner, My Friend*. With Barbara Jones. Johannesburg: Jonathan Ball, 2014.

Brandel-Syrier, Mia. *Reeftown Elite: A Study of Social Mobility in a Modern African Community on the Reef.* London: Routledge & Kegan Paul, 1971.

Breier, Mignonne. 'The Death That Dare(d) Not Speak Its Name: The Killing of Sister Aidan Quinlan in the East London Riots of 1952'. *Journal of Southern African Studies* 46, no. 6 (2015): 1151–65.

Bridger, Emily. *Young Women Against Apartheid: Gender, Youth, and South Africa's Liberation Struggle.* Oxford: James Currey, 2021.

Brooks, Alan, and Jeremy Brickhill. *Whirlwind Before the Storm: Origins and Development of the Uprising in Soweto and the Rest of South Africa from June to December 1976.* London: IDAF, 1981.

Broun, Kenneth S. *Saving Nelson Mandela: The Rivonia Trial and the Fate of South Africa.* Oxford: Oxford University Press, 2012.

Browde, Daniel. *The Relatively Public Life of Jules Browde.* Johannesburg: Jonathan Ball, 2016.

Bunche, Ralph J. *An African American in South Africa: The Travel Notes of Ralph J. Bunche, 28 September 1937–1 January 1938.* Edited by Robert R. Edgar. Athens: Ohio University Press, 1992.

Bundy, Colin. *Govan Mbeki.* Athens: Ohio University Press, 2012.

———. *Nelson Mandela.* Stroud: History Press, 2015.

Buntman, Fran. *Robben Island and Prisoner Resistance to Apartheid.* Cambridge, U.K.: Cambridge University Press, 2003.

Callinicos, Luli. *Oliver Tambo: Beyond the Ngele Mountains.* Johannesburg: David Philip, 2011.

Campbell, James C. *Songs of Zion: The African Methodist Episcopal Church in the United States and South Africa.* Oxford: Oxford University Press, 1995.

Carlin, John. *Knowing Mandela.* London: Atlantic, 2013.

Carlson, Joel. *No Neutral Ground.* London: Davis-Poynter, 1973.

Clingman, Stephen. *Bram Fischer: Afrikaner Revolutionary.* 2nd ed. Johannesburg: Jacana, 2013.

Cobley, Alan. *The Rules of the Game: Struggles in Black Recreation and Social Policy in South Africa.* Santa Barbara, Calif.: Greenwood Press, 1997.

Coetzee, J. M. *Youth.* London: Secker & Warburg, 2002.

Coleman, Max, ed. *A Crime Against Humanity: Analysing the Repression of the Apartheid State.* Johannesburg: Human Rights Committee of South Africa, 1998.

Comaroff, Jean, and John L. Comaroff. *Of Revelation and Revolution.* Vol. 1. Chicago: University of Chicago Press, 1991.

Cooper, Frederick. *Citizenship Between Empire and Nation: Remaking France and French Africa, 1945–1960.* Princeton, N.J.: Princeton University Press, 2016.

Cooper, Saths. 'The Psychological Impact of Political Imprisonment and the Role of the Psychologist'. In *Psychology and Apartheid,* edited by Lionel Nicholas and Saths Cooper. Johannesburg: Vision/Madiba, 1990.

Copelyn, Johnny. *Maverick Insider: A Struggle for Union Independence in a Time of National Liberation.* Johannesburg: Macmillan, 2016.

Couper, Scott. *Albert Luthuli: Bound by Faith.* Pietermaritzburg: University of KwaZulu-Natal Press, 2010.

———. 'Emasculating Agency: An Unambiguous Assessment of Albert Luthuli's Stance on Violence'. *South African Historical Journal* 64, no. 3 (2012): 564–86.

Daymond, M. J., ed. *Everyday Matters: Selected Letters of Dora Taylor, Bessie Head, and Lilian Ngoyi.* Johannesburg: Jacana, 2015.

De Haas, Mary. 'Violence in Natal and Zululand: The 1990s'. In South African Democracy Education Trust, *The Road to Democracy in South Africa, vol. 6, Part 2,* 876–957. Pretoria: Unisa Press, 2013.

De Kock, Eugene. *A Long Night's Damage: Working for the Apartheid State.* Johannesburg: Contra Press, 1998.

Denselow, Robin. *When the Music's Over: The Story of Political Pop.* London: Faber, 1989.

Derrida, Jacques. 'The Laws of Reflection: To Nelson Mandela in Admiration'. In *For Nelson Mandela,* edited by Jacques Derrida and Mustapha Tlili, 13–42. New York: Seaver Books, 1987.

Dingake, Michael. *My Fight Against Apartheid.* London: Kliptown Books, 1987.

Dlamini, Jacob. *Askari: A Story of Collaboration and Betrayal in the Anti-apartheid Struggle.* New York: Oxford University Press, 2015.

Dominguez, Jorge I. *To Make a World Safe for Revolution: Cuba's Foreign Policy.* Cambridge, Mass.: Harvard University Press, 1989.

Driver, Dorothy. '*Drum* Magazine (1951–59) and the Spatial Configuration of Gender'. In *Text, Theory, Space: Land, Literature, and History in South Africa and Australia,* edited by Kate Darian-Smith, Liz Gunner, and Sarah Nuttall. London: Routledge, 1996.

Dubow, Saul. *Apartheid, 1948–94.* Oxford: Oxford University Press, 2014.

———. 'New Approaches to High Apartheid and Anti-apartheid'. *South African Historical Journal* 69, no. 2 (2017): 304–29.

———. 'Were There Political Alternatives in the Wake of the Sharpeville-Langa Violence in South Africa, 1960?' *Journal of African History* 56 (2015): 119–42.

Dyzenhaus, David. *Hard Cases in Wicked Legal Systems: Pathologies of Legality.* 2nd ed. New York: Oxford University Press, 2010.

Ellis, Stephen. 'The Genesis of Armed Struggle in South Africa, 1948–61'. *Journal of Southern African Studies* 37, no. 4 (2011): 657–76.

Esterhuyse, Willie. *Eindstryd.* Cape Town: Tafelberg, 2012.

Evans, Martha. 'Lilian Ngoyi: Fighting with Clipped Wings'. In *Illuminating Lives,* edited by Vivian Bickford-Smith and Bill Nasson. Johannesburg: Penguin, 2018.

Feinstein, Charles. *An Economic History of South Africa: Conquest, Discrimination, and Development.* Cambridge, U.K.: Cambridge University Press, 2005.

Ffrench-Beytagh, Gonville. *Encountering Darkness.* London: Collins, 1973.

Fleming, Tyler. '"Now the African Reigns Supreme": The Rise of African Boxing on the Witwatersrand, 1924–1959'. *International Journal of the History of Sport* 28, no. 1 (2011): 47–62.

Frankel, Glenn. *Rivonia's Children: Three Families and the Cost of Conscience in White South Africa.* New York: Farrar, Straus & Giroux, 1999.

Frankel, Philip. *An Ordinary Atrocity: Sharpeville and Its Massacre.* New Haven, Conn.: Yale University Press, 2001.

———. *Pretoria's Praetorians: Civil-Military Relations in South Africa.* Cambridge, U.K.: Cambridge University Press, 1984.

Friedman, Steven. *Building Tomorrow Today: African Workers in Trade Unions, 1970–1984.* Johannesburg: Ravan Press, 1986.

Gambetta, Diego. *Were They Pushed or Did They Jump? Individual Decision Mechanisms in Education.* Cambridge, U.K.: Cambridge University Press, 1987.

Gandhi, Mohandas. *Autobiography: The Story of My Experiments with Truth.* New York: Dover, 1983.

Gerhart, Gail M. *Black Power in South Africa: The Evolution of an Ideology.* Berkeley: University of California Press, 1978.

Gerhart, Gail M., and Thomas Karis, eds. *From Protest to Challenge: A Documentary History of African Politics in South Africa, 1882–1964.* Vol. 4, *Political Profiles, 1882–1964.* Stanford, Calif.: Hoover Institution Press, 1977.

Getachew, Adom. *Worldmaking After Empire: The Rise and Fall of Self-Determination*. Princeton, N.J.: Princeton University Press, 2019.

Gevisser, Mark. *Thabo Mbeki: The Dream Deferred*. Johannesburg: Jonathan Ball, 2007.

Gibbs, Timothy. *Mandela's Clansmen: Nationalist Elites and Apartheid's First Bantustan*. London: James Currey, 2014.

Giddens, Anthony. *Modernity and Self-Identity: Self and Society in the Late Modern Age*. Cambridge, U.K.: Polity Press, 1991.

Gilbey, Emma. *The Lady: The Life and Times of Winnie Mandela*. London: Jonathan Cape, 1993.

Giliomee, Hermann. *The Afrikaners: Biography of a People*. London: Hurst, 2003.

———. 'Democratization in South Africa'. *Political Science Quarterly* 110, no. 1 (1995): 83–104.

———. *The Last Afrikaner Leaders: A Supreme Test of Power*. Charlottesville: University of Virginia Press, 2012.

Gish, Steven. *Alfred B. Xuma: African, American, South African*. New York: New York University Press, 2000.

Glaser, Clive. *The ANC Youth League*. Athens: Ohio University Press, 2013.

———. *Bo-Tsotsi: The Youth Gangs of Soweto, 1935–1976*. Oxford: James Currey, 2000.

———. 'The Mark of Zorro: Sexuality and Gender Relations in the Tsotsi Subculture on the Witwatersrand'. *African Studies* 51, no. 1 (1992): 47–68.

Gobodo-Madikizela, Pumla. *A Human Being Died That Night: Confronting Apartheid's Chief Killer*. London: Granta, 2006.

Gregory, James. *Goodbye Bafana: Nelson Mandela, My Prisoner, My Friend*. London: BCA, 1995.

Guha, Ramachandra. *Gandhi Before India*. New York: Knopf, 2013.

———. *Gandhi: The Years That Changed the World*. New York: Knopf, 2018.

Gurney, Christabel. 'The 1970s: The Anti-apartheid Movement's Difficult Decade.' *Journal of Southern African Studies* 35, no. 2 (2009): 471–87.

Guy, Jeff. *The Heretic: A Study of the Life of John William Colenso, 1814–1883*. Pietermaritzburg: University of Natal Press, 1983.

Harris, Verne. '"They Should Have Destroyed More": The Destruction of Public Records by the South African State in the Final Years of Apartheid'. *Transformation* 42 (2000): 29–56.

Hassim, Shireen. 'A Life of Refusal: Winnie Mandela and Violence in South Africa'. *Storia delle Donne* 10 (2014).

———. 'Not Just Nelson's Wife: Winnie Madikizela-Mandela, Violence, and Radicalism in South Africa'. *Journal of Southern African Studies* 44, no. 5 (2018): 895–912.

Hepple, Bob. *Young Man with a Red Tie: A Memoir of Mandela and the Failed Revolution, 1960–1963*. Johannesburg: Jacana, 2013.

Herbstein, Denis. *White Lies: Canon Collins and the Secret War Against Apartheid*. Oxford: James Currey, 2004.

Hirson, Baruch. *Year of Fire, Year of Ash: The Soweto Schoolchildren's Revolt That Shook Apartheid*. 2nd ed. London: Zed, 2016.

Hofmeyr, Isabel. *The Portable Bunyan: A Transnational History of 'The Pilgrim's Progress'*. Princeton, N.J.: Princeton University Press, 2004.

Hogue, Wilson T. *History of the Free Methodist Church in North America*. Vol. 1. 2nd ed. Chicago: Free Methodist Publishing House, 1918.

Horwitz, Simone. *Baragwanath Hospital Soweto: A History of Medical Care, 1941–1990*. Johannesburg: Wits University Press, 2018.

Houston, Gregory. 'The Post-Rivonia ANC/SACP Underground'. In South African Democracy Education Trust, *The Road to Democracy in South Africa*. Vol. 1, *1960–1970*. Cape Town: Zebra, 2004.

Howard, Ebenezer. *The Garden City to Come*. Cambridge, Mass.: MIT Press, 1965.

Hyslop, Jonathan. *The Classroom Struggle: Policy and Resistance in South Africa, 1940–1990*. Pietermaritzburg: University of Natal Press, 1999.

———. 'Mandela on War'. In *The Cambridge Companion to Nelson Mandela*, edited by Rita Barnard, 162–81. Cambridge, U.K.: Cambridge University Press, 2014.

Jana, Priscilla. *Fighting for Mandela*. London: Metro, 2016.

Joseph, Helen. *If This Be Treason*. London: André Deutsch, 1963.

———. *Side by Side*. London: William Morrow, 1987.

———. *Tomorrow's Sun: A Smuggled Journal from South Africa*. London: Hutchinson, 1966.

Kalyvas, Stathis. *The Logic of Violence in Civil War*. Cambridge, U.K.: Cambridge University Press, 2006.

Karis, Thomas G., and Gwendolen M. Carter, eds. *From Protest to Challenge*. Vol. 3, *Challenge and Violence*. Stanford, Calif.: Hoover Institution Press, 1977.

Karis, Thomas G., and Gail M. Gerhart. *From Protest to Challenge*. Vol. 5, *Nadir and Resurgence, 1964–1979*. Bloomington: Indiana University Press, 1997.

Kasrils, Ronnie. *Armed and Dangerous: From Undercover Struggle to Freedom*. Johannesburg: Jacana, 2014.

Kathrada, Ahmed. *Memoirs*. Cape Town: Zebra, 2004.

Kenney, Henry. *Verwoerd: Architect of Apartheid*. 1980. Johannesburg: Jonathan Ball, 2016.

Kentridge, Matthew. *The Unofficial War: Inside the Conflict in Pietermaritzburg*. Cape Town: David Philip, 1990.

Kenyatta, Jomo. *Facing Mount Kenya*. New York: Vintage, 1962.

Kepe, Thembela, and Lungisile Ntsebeza, eds. *South Africa's Mpondo Revolts After 50 Years: Meanings and Significance*. Leiden: Brill Academic Publishers, 2011.

Klein, Genevieve. 'Strategies of Struggle: The Nelson Mandela Campaign'. In *Popular Politics and Resistance Movements in South Africa*, edited by William Beinart and Marcelle Dawson, 94–116. Johannesburg: Wits University Press, 2010.

Krog, Antjie. *Country of My Skull*. Johannesburg: Random House, 1998.

Kruger, Loren. 'The Drama of Country and City: Tribalization, Urbanization, and Theatre Under Apartheid'. *Journal of Southern African Studies* 23, no. 4 (2007): 565–84.

Kuper, Leo. *An African Bourgeoisie: Race, Class, and the Politics of South Africa*. New Haven, Conn.: Yale University Press, 1965.

———. *Passive Resistance in South Africa*. London: Jonathan Cape, 1956.

Kuzwayo, Ellen. *Call Me Woman*. London: Women's Press, 1985.

Kynoch, Gary. *Township Violence and the End of Apartheid: War on the Reef*. Oxford: James Currey, 2018.

Landau, Paul. 'Gendered Silences in Nelson Mandela's and Ruth First's Struggle Auto/Biographies'. *African Studies* 78, no. 2 (2019): 290–306.

Lodge, Tom. *Black Politics in South Africa Since 1945*. Johannesburg: Ravan, 1983.

———. 'Insurrectionism in South Africa: The Pan-Africanist Congress and the Poqo Movement, 1959–1965'. PhD diss., University of York, 1984.

———. *Mandela: A Critical Life*. Oxford: Oxford University Press, 2006.

———. *The Red Road to Freedom: A History of the South African Communist Party, 1921–2021*. Johannesburg: Jacana, 2021.

———. *Sharpeville: An Apartheid Massacre and Its Consequences*. Oxford: Oxford University Press, 2011.

Lodge, Tom, and Bill Nasson. *All, Here, and Now: Black Politics in South Africa in the 1980s*. London: Hurst, 1991.

Luthuli, Albert. 'The Road to Freedom Is via the Cross'. In Gerald Pillay, *Albert Luthuli: Voices of Liberation*. 2nd ed. Cape Town: HSRC Press, 2012.

Macaulay, Thomas Babington. *The History of England from the Accession of James the Second*. Vol. 1. New York: Frederick A. Stokes & Brother, 1888.

Machava, Benedito. 'Reeducation Camps, Austerity, and the Carceral Regime in Socialist Mozambique (1974–1979)'. *Journal of African History* 60, no. 3 (2019): 429–55.

Macmillan, Hugh. *Chris Hani*. Johannesburg: Jacana, 2014.

Madikizela-Mandela, Winnie. *491 Days: Prisoner Number 1323/69*. Athens: Ohio University Press, 2013.

Magaziner, Daniel. *The Law and the Prophets: Black Consciousness in South Africa, 1968–1977*. Athens: Ohio University Press, 2010.

Maharaj, Mac, ed. *Reflections in Prison*. Amherst: University of Massachusetts Press, 2001.

Mandela, Nelson. *Conversations with Myself*. London: Macmillan, 2010.

———. *Long Walk to Freedom*. London: Little, Brown, 1994.

———. *The Prison Letters of Nelson Mandela*. Edited by Sahm Venter. New York: Norton, 2018.

Mandela, Winnie. *Part of My Soul Went with Him*. New York: Norton, 1985.

Mandler, Peter. *The Crisis of the Meritocracy*. Oxford: Oxford University Press, 2020.

Mangcu, Xolela. 'Mandela: The Untold Heritage'. In *Reassessing Mandela,* edited by Colin Bundy and William Beinart, 35–66. Johannesburg: Jacana, 2020.

Manoim, Irwin Stanley. 'The Black Press, 1945–1963: The Growth of the Black Mass Media and Their Role as Ideological Disseminators'. Master's thesis, University of the Witwatersrand, 1983.

Manyathi-Jele, Nomfundo. 'Gender Transformation: Is Enough Being Done?' *De Rebus,* Jan./Feb. 2015, 16–18.

Marks, Monique. *Young Warriors: Youth Politics, Identity, and Crisis in South Africa*. Johannesburg: Wits University Press, 2000.

Marks, Shula. *Divided Sisterhood: Race, Class, and Gender in the South African Nursing Profession*. London: Palgrave, 1994.

Mashabela, Harry. *A People on the Boil: Reflections on June 16 and Beyond*. 2nd ed. 1987. Johannesburg: Jacana, 2006.

Mathiane, Nomavenda. *Beyond the Headlines: Truths of Soweto Life*. Johannesburg: Southern Books, 1990.

Mbeki, Govan. *Learning from Robben Island: The Prison Writings of Govan Mbeki*. Cape Town: David Philip, 1991.

———. *South Africa: The Peasants' Revolt*. London: Penguin, 1964.

Mda, Zakes. *Sometimes There Is a Void*. New York: Farrar, Straus and Giroux, 2011.

Meer, Fatima. *Higher Than Hope: The Authorized Biography of Nelson Mandela*. London: Penguin, 1988.

Meer, Ismail. *A Fortunate Man*. Cape Town: Zebra, 2002.

Meredith, Martin. *Mandela: A Biography*. 1997. New York: PublicAffairs, 2010.

Minter, William, and Sylvia Hill. 'Anti-apartheid Solidarity in United States–South Africa Relations: From the Margins to the Mainstream'. In South African Democracy Education Trust, *The Road to Democracy in South Africa*. Vol. 3, *International Solidarity*, 745–822. Pretoria: Unisa Press, 2008.

Mkhabela, Sibongile. *Open Earth and Black Roses: Remembering 16 June 1976*. Johannesburg: Skotaville, 2001.

Mngxitama, Andile, Amanda Alexander, and Nigel C. Gibson, eds. *Biko Lives! Contesting the Legacies of Steve Biko*. New York: Palgrave, 2008.

Modisane, Bloke. *Blame Me on History*. 1963. New York: Touchstone Books, 1990.

Mogashoa, Moroka Humphry. 'South African Baptists and Finance Matters (1820–1948)'. PhD diss., University of KwaZulu-Natal, 2004.

Mokoena, Hlonipha. *Magema Fuze: The Making of a Kholwa Intellectual*. Pietermaritzburg: University of KwaZulu-Natal Press, 2011.

Moodie, Dunbar. 'The Moral Economy of the Black Miners' Strike of 1946'. *Journal of Southern African Studies* 13, no. 1 (1986): 1–35.

Mostert, Noël. *Frontiers: The Epic of South Africa's Creation and the Tragedy of the Xhosa People*. New York: Knopf, 1992.

Msimang, Sisonke. *The Resurrection of Winnie Mandela*. Johannesburg: Jonathan Ball, 2018.

Murray, Bruce. 'Nelson Mandela and Wits University'. *Journal of African History* 57, no. 2 (2016): 274.

Ndebele, Njabulo. *The Cry of Winnie Mandela*. Rev. ed. Johannesburg: Picador Africa, 2013.

Nehru, Jawaharlal. *The Discovery of India*. 1946. Delhi: Oxford University Press, 1994.

Newitt, Malyn. *A Short History of Mozambique*. London: Hurst, 2017.

Ngubane, Harriet. 'The Politics of Death in Soweto'. Paper presented to the Southern African Social History Seminar, SOAS, 1978.

Nicol, Mike, et al. *Mandela: The Authorised Portrait*. London: Bloomsbury, 2006.

Nkomo, Joshua. *The Story of My Life*. London: Methuen, 1984.

Ntantala, Phyllis. *A Life's Mosaic*. Johannesburg: Jacana, 2009.

Nussbaum, Martha. *Anger and Forgiveness*. New York: Oxford University Press, 2016.

O'Malley, Padraig. *Shades of Difference: Mac Maharaj and the Struggle for South Africa*. London: Penguin, 2007.

Peterson, Derek. *Ethnic Patriotism and the East African Revival: A History of Dissent*. New York: Cambridge University Press, 2012.

Phillips, Ray E. *The Bantu Are Coming*. New York: Richard R. Smith, 1930.

——. *The Bantu in the City: A Study of Cultural Adjustment on the Witwatersrand*. Alice: Lovedale Press, 1937.

——. *The Crux of the Race Problem: Are Black People Human Beings?* Stellenbosch: Student Christian Association of South Africa, 1947.

Pinnock, Don. 'Ideology and Urban Planning: Blueprints for a Garrison City'. in *The Angry Divide: Social and Economic History of the Western Cape*, edited by Wilmot G. James and Mary Simons, 150–68. Cape Town: David Philip, 1989.

Pogrund, Benjamin. *How Can Man Die Better: Sobukwe and Apartheid*. London: Peter Halban, 1990.

——. *War of Words: Memoir of a South African Journalist*. London: Seven Stories Press, 2000.

Pohlandt-McCormick, Helena. 'Controlling Women: Winnie Mandela and the 1976 Soweto Uprising'. *International Journal of African Historical Studies* 33, no. 3 (2000): 585–614.

Posel, Deborah. 'Car Troubles: Race on the Road'. Presentation to the South Africa Discussion Group, Oxford University, May 21, 2019.

Pretorius, Jan G. *The Last Wish of Winnie Mandela: Transnational Organised Crime in Sport, the Economy, and Politics*. Pretoria: Malan Media, 2020.

Putuma, Koleka. *Collective Amnesia*. Johannesburg: uHlanga, 2017.

Rachel, Daniel. *Walls Come Tumbling Down: The Music and Politics of Rock Against Racism, 2 Tone, and Red Wedge*. London: Picador, 2016.

Ramlakan, Vejay. *Mandela's Last Years*. Johannesburg: Penguin, 2017.

Rantete, Johannes. *The Third Day of September*. Johannesburg: Ravan Press, 1984.

Read, James, and Ian Shapiro. 'Transforming Power Relationships: Leadership, Risk, and Hope'. *American Political Science Review* 8, no. 1 (2014): 40–53.

Rehman, Amanda-Bea. 'Against the Odds: A Social History of African Female Doctors in South Africa, 1940s–2000s'. Master's thesis, University of KwaZulu-Natal, 2017.

Rueedi, Franziska. '"Our Bushes Are Houses": People's War and the Underground During the Insurrectionary Period in the Vaal Triangle, South Africa'. *Journal of Southern African Studies* 46, no. 4 (2020): 615–33.

Russell, Diana E. H., ed. *Lives of Courage: Women for a New South Africa*. London: Basic Books, 1989.

Salmon, Patrick, ed. *The Unwinding of Apartheid: Documents on British Policy Overseas, Series III, Volume XI*. London: Routledge, 2019.

Sampson, Anthony. *Drum: An African Adventure*. 2nd ed. London: Hodder and Stoughton, 1983.

———. *Mandela: The Authorised Biography*. London: Harper Press, 1999.

———. *The Treason Cage: The Opposition on Trial in South Africa*. London: Heinemann, 1958.

Sartre, Jean-Paul. 'What Is a Collaborator?' In *The Aftermath of War*, translated by Chris Turner. New York: Seagull Books, 2008.

Seegers, Annette. *The Military in the Making of Modern South Africa*. London: I. B. Tauris, 1996.

Seekings, Jeremy. '"Trailing Behind the Masses": The United Democratic Front and Township Politics in the Pretoria-Witwatersrand-Vaal Region, 1983–84'. *Journal of Southern African Studies* 18, no. 1 (1992): 93–114.

———. *The UDF: A History of the United Democratic Front in South Africa*. Athens: Ohio University Press, 2000.

Segal, Lauren. 'The Human Face of Violence: Hostel Dwellers Speak'. *Journal of Southern African Studies* 18, no. 1 (1992): 190–236.

Shelton, Robert. *No Direction Home: The Life and Music of Bob Dylan*. London: Omnibus Press, 1986.

Simpson, Thula. '"Umkhonto we Sizwe We Are Waiting for You": The ANC and the Township Uprising, September 1984–September 1985'. *South African Historical Journal* 61, no. 1 (2009): 158–77.

Sisulu, Elinor. *Walter and Albertina Sisulu: In Our Lifetime*. London: Abacus, 2003.

Sisulu, Walter. *I Will Go Singing: Walter Sisulu Speaks of His Life and Struggle for Freedom*. With George M. Houser and Herbert Shore. Cape Town: Robben Island Museum, 2008.

Sitas, Ari. 'The New Tribalism: Hostels and Violence'. *Journal of Southern African Studies* 22, no. 2 (1996): 235–48.

Slezkine, Yuri. *The Jewish Century*. Princeton, N.J.: Princeton University Press, 2004.

Slovo, Joe. 'The Sabotage Campaign'. *Dawn: Journal of Umkhonto we Sizwe*, Souvenir Issue, 1986, 24–25.

Soske, Jon. *Internal Frontiers: African Nationalism and the Indian Diaspora in Twentieth-Century South Africa*. Athens: Ohio University Press, 2017.

———. 'The Life and Death of Abu Baker "Hurley" Asvat, 23 February 1943–27 January 1989'. *African Studies* 70, no. 3 (2011): 337–58.

South Africa. *Truth and Reconciliation Commission of South Africa Report*. Vol. 2. Cape Town: TRC, 1998. www.justice.gov.za.

Spaarwater, Maritz. *A Spook's Progress: From Making War to Making Peace*. Cape Town: Zebra, 2012.

Sparks, Allister. *Tomorrow Is Another Country: The Inside Story of South Africa's Negotiated Revolution*. Johannesburg: Struik, 1994.

Stapleton, Timothy J. *Faku: Rulership and Colonialism in the Mpondo Kingdom (1780–1867)*. Waterloo: Wilfrid Laurier University Press, 2001.

Steinberg, Jonny. *The Number*. Johannesburg: Jonathan Ball, 2004.

Storey, Peter. *I Beg to Differ: Ministry amid the Teargas*. Cape Town: Tafelberg, 2018.

Suttner, Raymond. *The ANC Underground in South Africa*. Johannesburg: Jacana, 2008.

———. '"The Road to Freedom Is via the Cross": "Just Means" in Chief Albert Luthuli's Life'. *South African Historical Journal* 62, no. 4 (2010): 693–715.

Themba, Can. *The Will to Die*. London: Heinemann, 1972.

Thomas, Lynn M. *Beneath the Surface: A Transnational History of Skin Lighteners*. Durham, N.C.: Duke University Press, 2020.

———. 'The Modern Girl and Racial Respectability in 1930s South Africa'. *Journal of African History* 47 (2006): 461–90.

Thorn, Hakan. 'Meaning(s) of Solidarity: Narratives of Anti-apartheid Activism'. *Journal of Southern African Studies* 35, no. 2 (2009): 417–36.

Thornberry, Elizabeth. *Colonizing Consent: Rape and Governance in South Africa's Eastern Cape*. Cambridge, U.K.: Cambridge University Press, 2018.

Tlhabi, Redi. *Endings & Beginnings: A Story of Healing*. Johannesburg: Jacana, 2012.

Tocqueville, Alexis de. *The Ancient Regime and the Revolution*. Translated by Gerald Bevan. 1856. London: Penguin, 2008.

Twala, Chitja, and Jeremy Seekings. 'Activist Networks and Political Protest in the Free State, 1983–1990'. In South African Democracy Education Trust, *The Road to Democracy in South Africa*. Vol. 4, *1980–1990*, 765–813. Pretoria: Unisa Press, 2010.

Vaillant, Jean. *Black, French, and African: A Life of Leopold Sédar Senghor*. Cambridge, Mass.: Harvard University Press, 1990.

van Kessel, Ineke. *Beyond Our Wildest Dreams: The United Democratic Front and the Transformation of South Africa*. Charlottesville: University of Virginia Press, 1999.

Vinson, Robert, and Benedict Carton. 'Albert Luthuli's Private Struggle: How an Icon of Peace Came to Accept Sabotage in South Africa'. *Journal of African History* 59, no. 1 (2018): 69–96.

Wagenaar, Elsie J. C. 'A History of the Thembu and Their Relation to the Cape, 1950–1900'. PhD diss., Rhodes University, Grahamstown, 1988.

Waldmeir, Patti. *Anatomy of a Miracle*. London: Penguin, 1997.

Walshe, Peter. *The Rise of African Nationalism in South Africa: The African National Congress, 1912–1952*. London: Hurst, 1970.

Weinbaum, Alys Eve, et al., eds. *The Modern Girl Around the World: Consumption, Modernity, and Globalization*. Durham, N.C.: Duke University Press, 2008.

Wilson, Monica. *Reaction to Conquest: Effects of Contact with Europeans on the Pondo of South Africa*. 1936. Berlin: Lit, 2009.

Index

Permissions Acknowledgments

Grateful acknowledgment is made to the following for permission to reprint previously published materials:

Little, Brown, an imprint of Hachette Book Group, Inc.: Excerpt from *Long Walk to Freedom* by Nelson Mandela. Copyright © 1994 by Nelson Mandela. Reprinted by permission of Little, Brown, an imprint of Hachette Book Group, Inc.

Liveright Publishing Corporation: From *The Prison Letters of Nelson Mandela* by Nelson Mandela, edited by Sahm Venter. Copyright © 2018 by the Estate of Nelson Rolihlahla Mandela. Copyright © 2018 by the Nelson Mandela Foundation. Concept and design copyright © 2018 by Blackwell and Ruth Limited. Reprinted by permission of Liveright Publishing Corporation.

Manyano Media: "1994: A Love Poem" by Koleka Putuma, from the anthology *Collective Amnesia*, originally published in South Africa by Manyano Media, Cape Town, in 2017. Copyright © 2017 by Koleka Putuma. Reprinted by permission of Manyano Media.

Pan Macmillan South Africa: Excerpts from *491 Days: Prisoner Number 1323/69* by Winnie Madikizela-Mandela, originally published in South Africa by Picador Africa, an imprint of Pan Macmillan South Africa, Johannesburg, in 2013. Copyright © 2013 by Winnie Madikizela-Mandela. Reprinted by permission of Pan Macmillan South Africa.